Mastering Active Directory

Automate tasks by leveraging PowerShell for Active Directory
Domain Services 2016

Dishan Francis

BIRMINGHAM - MUMBAI

Mastering Active Directory

First published: June 2017

Production reference: 1280617

Published by Packt Publishing Ltd.
Livery Place
35 Livery Street
Birmingham
B3 2PB, UK.

ISBN 978-1-78728-935-2

www.packtpub.com

Credits

Author
Dishan Francis

Copy Editors
Yesha Gangani
Alpha Singh
Stuti Srivastava
Madhusudan Uchil

Reviewers
Daniel Dieterle
David Green
Florian Klaffenbach
Paul Silva

Project Coordinator
Virginia Dias

Acquisition Editor
Heramb Bhavsar

Proofreader
Safis Editing

Content Development Editor
Sweeny Dias

Indexer
Rekha Nair

Technical Editors
Komal Karne
Vishal Kamal Mewada
Khushbu Sutar

Graphics
Kirk D'Penha

Production Coordinator
Aparna Bhagat

About the Author

Dishan Francis is a technology consultant with 12 plus years of experience in the planning, design, and implementation of network technologies. His background includes hands-on experience with multiplatform and LAN/WAN environments. He has a demonstrated record of success in troubleshooting servers, increasing efficiency, and optimizing the access to and utilization of shared information. He is a specialist in extending technology services from corporate headquarters to field operations.

Dishan is a dedicated and enthusiastic information technology expert who enjoys professional recognition and accreditation from several respected institutions. When it comes to managing innovative identity infrastructure solutions to improve system stability, functionality, and efficiency, his level of knowledge and experience place him among the very best in the field.

He is a three-time Microsoft Most Valuable Professional Awardee in Enterprise Mobility. He is also a Microsoft Imagine Cup judge. He has maintained a technology blog called `www.rebeladmin.com` over the years, with useful articles that focus on Active Directory services. Also, he spends his free time mentoring students and professionals. He currently works with Frontier Technology Limited.

Acknowledgement

It was a dream to write a book one day, but I didn't expect it to happen this soon. I was writing to my blog and for Microsoft blogs for years but it is not the same when it comes to a book. Although I wrote this book, there were many behind me thoughout this journey. Without their support, it would have been an impossible task to complete.

First of all, my thanks go to the great editorial team at Packt Publishing Limited, for giving me opportunity to write and publish this book—especially Heramb Bhavsar, Sweeny Dias, and Khushbu Sutar who made this whole experience smooth and fun. Also, I'd like to express my gratitude to all the reviewers and editors. Their comments made this book more valued.

I would like to express my sincere appreciation to my friends in Microsoft Canada, especially Simran Chaudhry, MVP Community Program Manager, and Anthony Bartolo. They are the people who bring me to you via lots of community events, public speaking, and blogs.

I would like to express my deepest gratitude to my current employer, Edwin Wong, MD of Frontier Technology Ltd, and my former employer, Dominic Macchione, CEO of Rebelnetworks Inc, for giving me opportunity to enhance my knowledge and apply it to practice.

As always, I'd like to thank my lovely wife Kanchana Dilrukshi and my little girl Selena Rosemary for the support and courage they give. For months, I was only able to spend hour or less per day with them. I missed many play sessions, and swimming sessions with my daughter. I missed many family functions. But still they understood my commitment to the book and helped me to stay focused.

Also, I'd like to thanks my parents for everything they did to make me who I am today. My extended gratitude goes to my parents-in-law and all other relations. Although most of them do not know about Active Directory, they were checking from time to time to see how I was doing with the book and encouraged me to stay focused and finish it.

About the Reviewers

Daniel Dieterle has over 20 years of IT experience. A former Microsoft MCSE and HP-certified Network Integration Specialist, he performed server installs, administration, and services for companies throughout Upstate New York and across Northern Pennsylvania. Currently, he is an internationally published IT author who focuses on testing the security of Microsoft-based systems.

David Green is an IT professional from the South of England, with a wealth of experience from both the public and private sectors. He currently works as a senior systems consultant at the Coretek Group, who provide IT support, consultancy, and infrastructure services to businesses and education, covering on-premises, hybrid, and cloud services.

Previously, David has worked in Formula One™; food manufacturing; and the education sector, where he always looked to provide robust and scalable IT solutions that contributed to business objectives.

David also writes a blog where he posts solutions he finds to problems, and a fair amount of PowerShell-related content. He always tries to help where he can and generally tries to learn something useful every day.

This is another opportunity David has had to contribute to a book. Previous opportunities include *Getting Started with PowerShell* by Michael Shepard and *Active Directory with PowerShell* by Uma Yellapragada.

More information, including contact details, can be found on his website at http://www.tookitaway.co.uk.

> *I'd like to thank my family, my friends, and my colleagues, who are always there for me when I need them and have helped make me the person I am today. Work, learn, play, and have fun! It's your intentions, attitude, and what you do with your opportunities that set you apart.*

Florian Klaffenbach started his IT career in 2004 as a 1st and 2nd level IT support technician and IT salesman trainee for a B2B online shop. After that, he moved to a small company, working as an IT project manager planning, implementing, and integrating from industrial plants and laundries to enterprise IT. After spending a few years there, he moved to Dell Germany. There, he started from scratch as an enterprise technical support analyst, and later worked on a project to start Dell technical communities and support over social media in Europe and outside of the U.S. Currently, he is working as a solutions architect and consultant for Microsoft Infrastructure and Cloud, specializing in Microsoft Hyper-V, File Services, System Center Virtual Machine Manager, and Microsoft Azure IaaS.

As well as his job, he is active as a Microsoft blogger and lecturer. He blogs, for example, on his own page, `Datacenter-Flo.de`, or the Brocade Germany Community. Together with a very good friend, he founded the Windows Server User Group Berlin to create network of Microsoft IT pros in Berlin. Florian maintains a very tight network with many vendors such as Cisco, Dell, and Microsoft and their communities. This has helped him to gain experience and get the best out of a solution for his customers. Since 2016, he has also been Co-Chairman of the Azure Community Germany. In April 2016, Microsoft made him a Microsoft Most Valuable Professional for Cloud and Datacenter Management.

Florian has worked for several companies, such as Dell Germany, CGI Germany, and his first employer, TACK GmbH. Currently, he works at msg service ag as a senior consultant Microsoft Cloud infrastructure. The following are the books he has worked on:

- *Taking Control with System Center App Controller*
- *Microsoft Azure Storage Essentials*
- *Mastering Microsoft Azure Development*
- *Mastering Microsoft Deployment Toolkit 2013*
- *Windows Server 2016 Cookbook*
- *Implementing Azure Solutions*

I want to thank Packt Publishing for giving me the chance to review this book.

Paul Silva is a Microsoft technical architect, consultant, and educator from Long Island, New York.

As CEO of iLyncU, Inc., Paul consults on Active Directory and Skype for Business projects worldwide, on behalf of iLyncU, Microsoft Corporation, and others.

As a Microsoft Certified Trainer, Paul also delivers technical speeches and has participated in the creation of Hands-on Labs for Microsoft's yearly training events, and for the Microsoft Official Courseware.

Since 1999, Paul has participated in Microsoft-sponsored speaking tours, Learning Solution events, and has launched a public service project, *Learning for Loutraki*, to bring technology and learning to the elementary and middle school students of Loutraki, Greece.

www.PacktPub.com

For support files and downloads related to your book, please visit www.PacktPub.com. Did you know that Packt offers eBook versions of every book published, with PDF and ePub files available? You can upgrade to the eBook version at www.PacktPub.com and as a print book customer, you are entitled to a discount on the eBook copy. Get in touch with us at service@packtpub.com for more details. At www.PacktPub.com, you can also read a collection of free technical articles, sign up for a range of free newsletters and receive exclusive discounts and offers on Packt books and eBooks.

https://www.packtpub.com/mapt

Get the most in-demand software skills with Mapt. Mapt gives you full access to all Packt books and video courses, as well as industry-leading tools to help you plan your personal development and advance your career.

Why subscribe?

- Fully searchable across every book published by Packt
- Copy and paste, print, and bookmark content
- On demand and accessible via a web browser

Customer Feedback

Thanks for purchasing this Packt book. At Packt, quality is at the heart of our editorial process. To help us improve, please leave us an honest review on this book's Amazon page at `https://www.amazon.com/dp/1787289354`.

If you'd like to join our team of regular reviewers, you can e-mail us at `customerreviews@packtpub.com`. We award our regular reviewers with free eBooks and videos in exchange for their valuable feedback. Help us be relentless in improving our products!

Table of Contents

Preface

Microsoft Active Directory is the most widely used identity management solution. It can centrally manage identities across the infrastructure. It is equipped with different role services, features, and components that helps us handle identities securely and effectively according to business requirements. For the last 20 years, Microsoft kept improving Active Directory, and the recent release of Active Directory 2016 further emperies its approach to rectify industry requirements and protect identity infrastructures with emerging security threats. However, a technology-rich product is not simply going to make a productive, reliable, scaleable, secure identity infrastructure. It needs the knowledge about Active Directory roles services, components, and features. It also needs knowledge about how to use those effectively to match different operation requirements. Then only we can plan, design, manage, and maintain robust identity infrastructure. That's what is exactly covered in this book. Throughout, this book talks about Active Directory roles service, technologies, and features and then, how to implement those according to best practices.

What this book covers

Chapter 1, *Active Directory Fundamentals*, explains what is Active Directory and its characteristic. It also explains the main components (physical and logical structure), objects types, and role services of the products. It also covers the new features available in AD DS 2016 in a nutshell.

Chapter 2, *Active Directory Domain Services 2016*, explains what's new in AD DS 2016 and how it will help improve your organization's identity infrastructure.

Chapter 3, *Designing Active Directory Infrastructure*, talks about what needs to be considered for Active Directory infrastructure design. It also describes how to place the AD DS logical and physical components in the AD DS environment.

Chapter 4, *Active Directory Domain Name System*, explains how DNS works in the AD DS infrastructure. It also includes information about the DNS server component, different types of DNS records, zones, and DNS delegation.

Chapter 5, *Placing Operations Master Roles*, talks about the FSMO roles and its responsibilities. It also describes the best way to place those in different AD deployment topologies.

Chapter 6, *Migrating to Active Directory 2016*, covers the AD DS installation with different deployment topologies. It also provides step-by-step guide to migrate from an older version of AD DS to new AD DS 2016.

Chapter 7, *Managing Active Directory Objects*, explains how to manage Active Directory objects using different snaps-in, MMC, and PowerShell commands. It will also demonstrate how to create objects (small scale and large scale) using different methods. It also explains how to query about objects in AD.

Chapter 8, *Managing Users, Groups, and Devices*, explains in detail the different types of objects and how to use those with different infrastructure requirements.

Chapter 9, *Designing OU structure*, teaches you how to design the OU structure properly using different models. It will also describe how to manage the OU structure and delegate control.

Chapter 10, *Managing Group Policies*, explains Group Policy objects and its capabilities. It also talks about how to use those appropriately in an infrastructure.

Chapter 11, *Active Directory Services*, walks us through the more advanced Active Directory topics, such as AD LDS, Active Directory replication, Active Directory sites, Active Directory database maintenance, RODC, AD DS backup, and recovery.

Chapter 12, *Active Directory Certificate Services*, explains planning, deployment, and maintenance of Active Directory Certificate Services.

Chapter 13, *Active Directory Federation Services*, focuses on AD Federation Services planning, designing, deployment, and maintenance. It also explains the new features of AD FS 2016.

Chapter 14: *Active Directory Rights Management Services*, explains the AD role, Active Directory Rights Management Service, and how to use it to protect organization data.

Chapter 15, *Active Directory Security Best Practices*, covers the Active Directory security best practices and new concepts that you can use to secure your identity infrastructure and protect your workloads from emerging threats.

Chapter 16, *Advanced AD Management with PowerShell*, is full of PowerShell scripts that can be used to manage, secure, audit, and monitor Active Directory environment.

Chapter 17, *Azure Active Directory for Hybrid Setup*, explains how you can extend your on-premises AD DS infrastructure into Azure Active Directory.

Chapter 18, *Active Directory Audit and Monitoring*, teaches you how to monitor your AD DS infrastructure using different tools and method. It also demonstrates how to audit Active Directory environment.

Chapter 19, *Active Directory Troubleshooting*, explains how to troubleshoot the most common Active Directory infrastructure issue using different tools and methods.

What you need for this book

This book is written to demonstrate the management of Active Directory in the Windows Server 2016 environment. While all code samples provided here work in the Windows Server 2016 environment, some will work in the Windows Server 2012 R2 and Windows Server 2012 environments as well:

- Readers of this book need a basic knowledge about Microsoft Active Directory Domain Service and related terms.
- PowerShell commands and scripts have been used heavily in this book. Readers should have basic knowledge and experience on PowerShell and relevant tools.
- All the PowerShell commands and scripts were tested on PowerShell Version 5; these may not be compatible with the older PowerShell versions.
- PowerShell scripts have been represented in the way readers can easily understand. Therefore when using those in the environment, pay attention to the extra spaces and line breaks. It is recommended to use PowerShell ISE to run the scripts.
- All the configuration examples are tested on systems which run Windows Server 2016. Some of these may not be applicable for older version of AD DS and role services.

Who this book is for

This book is ideal for IT professionals, system engineers, and administrators who have a basic knowledge about Active Directory Domain Services. A basic knowledge of PowerShell is also required, as most of the role deployment, configuration, and maintenance is explained using PowerShell commands and scripts.

Conventions

In this book, you will find a number of text styles that distinguish between different kinds of information. Here are some examples of these styles and an explanation of their meaning.

Code words in text, database table names, folder names, filenames, file extensions, pathnames, dummy URLs, user input, and Twitter handles are shown as follows: "For my application, I have created metadata file under `https://myapp.rebeladmin.com/myapp/federationmetadata/2007-06/federationmetadata.xml`."

A block of code is set as follows:

```
xJeaEndPoint Demo3EP
{
  Name = 'Demo3EP'
  ToolKit = 'FileSystem'
  Ensure = 'Present'
  DependsOn = '[xJeaToolKit]FileSystem'
}
```

When we wish to draw your attention to a particular part of a code block, the relevant lines or items are set in bold:

```
xJeaEndPoint Demo3EP
{
  Name = 'Demo3EP'
  ToolKit = 'FileSystem'
  Ensure = 'Present'
  DependsOn = '[xJeaToolKit]FileSystem'
}
```

Any command-line input or output is written as follows:

```
Enter-PSSession -ComputerName localhost -ConfigurationName demo2ep
```

New terms and important words are shown in bold. Words that you see on the screen, for example, in menus or dialog boxes, appear in the text like this: "Afterwards, in the **Security** tab, select **First Line Engineers** and click on **Advanced**."

Warnings or important notes appear in a box like this.

Tips and tricks appear like this.

Reader feedback

Feedback from our readers is always welcome. Let us know what you think about this book-what you liked or disliked. Reader feedback is important for us as it helps us develop titles that you will really get the most out of. To send us general feedback, simply e-mail feedback@packtpub.com, and mention the book's title in the subject of your message. If there is a topic that you have expertise in and you are interested in either writing or contributing to a book, see our author guide at www.packtpub.com/authors.

Customer support

Now that you are the proud owner of a Packt book, we have a number of things to help you to get the most from your purchase.

Downloading the example code

You can download the example code files for this book from your account at http://www.packtpub.com. If you purchased this book elsewhere, you can visit http://www.packtpub.com/support and register to have the files e-mailed directly to you. You can download the code files by following these steps:

1. Log in or register to our website using your e-mail address and password.
2. Hover the mouse pointer on the **SUPPORT** tab at the top.
3. Click on **Code Downloads & Errata**.
4. Enter the name of the book in the **Search** box.
5. Select the book for which you're looking to download the code files.
6. Choose from the drop-down menu where you purchased this book from.
7. Click on **Code Download**.

Once the file is downloaded, please make sure that you unzip or extract the folder using the latest version of:

- WinRAR / 7-Zip for Windows
- Zipeg / iZip / UnRarX for Mac
- 7-Zip / PeaZip for Linux

The code bundle for the book is also hosted on GitHub at https://github.com/PacktPubl ishing/Mastering-Active-Directory. We also have other code bundles from our rich catalog of books and videos available at https://github.com/PacktPublishing/. Check them out!

Downloading the color images of this book

We also provide you with a PDF file that has color images of the screenshots/diagrams used in this book. The color images will help you better understand the changes in the output. You can download this file from https://www.packtpub.com/sites/default/files/down loads/MasteringActiveDirectory_ColorImages.pdf.

Errata

Although we have taken every care to ensure the accuracy of our content, mistakes do happen. If you find a mistake in one of our books-maybe a mistake in the text or the code-we would be grateful if you could report this to us. By doing so, you can save other readers from frustration and help us improve subsequent versions of this book. If you find any errata, please report them by visiting http://www.packtpub.com/submit-errata, selecting your book, clicking on the **Errata Submission Form** link, and entering the details of your errata. Once your errata are verified, your submission will be accepted and the errata will be uploaded to our website or added to any list of existing errata under the Errata section of that title. To view the previously submitted errata, go to https://www.packtpub.com/book s/content/support and enter the name of the book in the search field. The required information will appear under the **Errata** section.

Piracy

Piracy of copyrighted material on the Internet is an ongoing problem across all media. At Packt, we take the protection of our copyright and licenses very seriously. If you come across any illegal copies of our works in any form on the Internet, please provide us with the location address or website name immediately so that we can pursue a remedy. Please contact us at copyright@packtpub.com with a link to the suspected pirated material. We appreciate your help in protecting our authors and our ability to bring you valuable content.

Questions

If you have a problem with any aspect of this book, you can contact us at questions@packtpub.com, and we will do our best to address the problem.

1

Active Directory Fundamentals

Welcome to the world of managing identities! Doesn't it sound fun? As system administrators, system engineers, and infrastructure engineers, we spend a significant amount of time every day managing identities in organizations. These identities can be user accounts, applications, or other resources. Over 15 years, Microsoft Active Directory has maintained its premier position in the market by helping organizations build their identity infrastructures. As a directory service, it stores an organization's identity data in a central repository and allows us to arrange it in a hierarchical organizational structure to satisfy the business' needs.

Over the years, Microsoft has been releasing a new version of Active Directory with new features and enhancements. For the last 12 years, I have worked on thousands of different Active Directory-related projects and answered lots of questions through my blog. For me, it's straightforward: providing a feature-rich product is not enough to maintain a secure, efficient, and reliable identity infrastructure. Just two Christmases ago, I gave a pack of watercolors to my little girl, Selena, as her present. I still remember the excitement in her eyes and how much fun it was trying different colors on a canvas and her Christmas dress. In the end, it was just a bunch of lines and color patches. This Christmas too, I (Santa) gave her a new drawing pad and watercolor pack. Now she knows how to draw different objects and place them nicely on the canvas and make something meaningful. It is practice, creativity, and guidance that have helped her do it. This book is meant to equip you with knowledge using in-depth analysis and best practices in order to use the Microsoft Active Directory service and its components in a secure, efficient way to address modern identity infrastructure requirements.

Even though this book is more for administrators and engineers who have basic knowledge of Active Directory, it is not a bad idea to re-read and refresh your memory about the building blocks of the Microsoft Active Directory service before we dive into advanced topics. In this chapter, you will learn the following:

- Benefits of using Active Directory
- Understanding Active Directory components
- Understanding Active Directory objects
- Active Directory server roles

Benefits of using Active Directory

A few years ago, I was working on an Active Directory restructuring project for a world-famous pharmaceutical company. According to the company policy, I had to travel to their headquarters to perform the project tasks. So, on a rare sunny English morning, I walked into the company's reception area. After I explained who I am and why I was there, the nice lady at the reception, Linda, handed me a set of forms to fill in. They asked for my personal details, such as name, phone number, how long I will be there, and in which department. Once I filled out the forms, I handed them over to Linda, and she had to make a few calls to verify whether my visit was expected and confirm my access to different buildings with the respective department managers. Then she made a card with my details and handed it over to me. She instructed me on how to use it and which buildings I was allowed into.

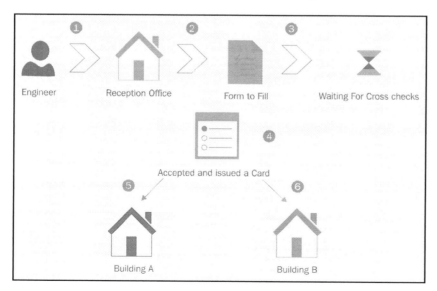

When you think about this process, you'll find that it contains the functions of a directory service:

- The forms that Linda handed over to me contained certain questions to help her understand who the person was. They were predefined questions and I had to answer them in order to register my information in their system.
- Once I submitted the forms, she didn't hand over the electronic card right away. She made calls to verify my identity and also confirm which buildings I would have access to. Then, my details were registered with the system, and it generated an electronic card that had my photo and a bar code. With that, I became a part of their system, and that particular card was my unique identity within their organization. There would be no other visitor with the same bar code and identification number at the same time.
- If I needed to get access to buildings, I needed to tap the card at the entrance. Could I use my name or any other cards to get through? No! The locking system of the building doors only recognized me if I presented the correct card. So, having a unique identity in their system was not enough; I needed to present it in the correct way to get the required access.
- I went to another building and tried to tap the card. Even when I used it correctly, the doors wouldn't open. The guard in the building asked for my card. Once I handed it over, he scanned it with a bar code reader and checked some information on his computer screen. Then he informed me that I was not allowed into that building and guided me to the correct building. This means that my information can be accessed from any building through their system to verify my identity and access permissions.
- When I used the card in the correct buildings, it allowed me to step in. In the system, it first verified my identity and then checked whether I was *authorized* to work in that facility. If I was authorized, the system allowed access; if not, it rejected my request to enter.
- When I entered and left the building, I did not have to record my time. But the managers in that department knew how many hours I had worked as my check-in and check-out times had been recorded in the system and they could review the information anytime.

This system acts as an *authentication* and *authorization* system. It uses different protocols and standards to manage and protect identities saved in a central database. This is the primary need of a directory service.

Every organization has its own organizational structure. The most common way is to group roles, assets, and responsibilities into different departments, such as sales, IT, production, and quality assurance. Apart from skills and knowledge, employers use company resources such as applications and hardware devices to achieve company goals. In order to use these resources efficiency, it's important to have some kind of access control in place. The resources should be available for the required users at the required time. This is very easy if all this data about users, applications, and resources is recorded in a central repository and uses authentication and authorization to manage resources. This is how the directory service was born. Different service providers have different directory services, for example, the Novell directory services, Oracle directory service, and Red Hat directory service. The Microsoft Active Directory service is the most commonly used directory service in modern enterprises.

In 1988, the **ITU Telecommunication Standardization Sector (ITU-T)** developed industry standards for directory services, called **X.500**. This was the foundation for Microsoft Active Directory services. In X.500, the **Directory Access Protocol (DAP)** was defined, and many alternatives were made available to enable use with the TCP/IP networking stack. The most popular alternative was **Lightweight Directory Access Protocol (LDAP)**. The first version of it was released in 1993 with limited features. The University of Michigan released the first **stand-alone LDAP daemon (slapd)** server in 1995. The matured version of LDAP, LDAPv3, was released in 1997, and most vendors, including Microsoft, started developing directory services based on LDAP. Microsoft released it first Active Directory version with Windows 2000.

Centralized data repository

Active Directory stores the identity information of users, applications, and resources in a **multi-master** database. This database is a file called `ntds.dit`. This database is based on **Joint Engine Technology (JET)** database engine. The data in this database can be modified using any alternative domain controller. The Active Directory database can store some 2 billion objects. Users can use the identity data stored in Active Directory from anywhere in the network in order to access resources. Administrators can manage authentication and authorization of the organizational identities from a centralized location. Without directory services, identities would be duplicated across different systems and add administrative overhead to manage.

Replication of data

There are organizations that use a single domain controller. But when it comes to complex business requirements such as branch offices, redundancy, it is required that they have multiple domain controllers (we are going to look at domain controller placement later in a different chapter). If the identities are managed from a centralized system, it's important that each domain controller be aware of the changes that have been made to the Active Directory database. Say, user Jane in the sales department forgets her password and requests the IT department to reset it. In 30 minutes' time, she's going to be working from a branch office located in a different city. The IT administrator resets her password from the headquarter's domain controller, DC01. In order to have a successful login from the branch office, this change to the directory needs to be replicated over to the domain controller in the branch office, DC05. Microsoft Active Directory has two types of replications. If a domain controller advertises the changes made on that particular domain controller to neighboring domain controllers, it is called **outbound replication**. If a domain controller accepts changes advertised by neighboring domain controllers, it called **inbound replication**. The replication connections (from who and to whom) and replication schedule can be modified based on the business requirements.

High availability

High availability is important for any business-critical system in an organization. This is applicable to domain controllers too. On other systems, in order to implement high availability, we need to make software or hardware changes. With built-in fault-tolerance capabilities, Active Directory domain controllers do not need additional changes. A multi-master database and replication of domain controllers allow users to continue with authentication and authorization from any available domain controller at any time.

Security

Data and identity security are very important in modern businesses. We are living in a world where identity is the new perimeter. A significant portion of this book is focused on how to use Active Directory features to secure your identity infrastructures from emerging threats. Active Directory allows you to use different authentication types, group policies, and workflows to protect the resources in your network. Even applications benefit from these technologies and methodologies to secure the identities used within applications. This helps administrators build different security rules based on departments and groups in order to protect data and workloads. It also forces individuals to follow organizational data- and network-security standards.

Auditing capabilities

Setting up advanced security policies will not be enough to protect your identity infrastructure. Periodic audits will help you understand new security threats. Active Directory allows you to capture and audit events occurring in your identity infrastructure. They can be related to user authentication, directory service modifications, or access violation. It also helps you collect data from a centralized location, which will help you troubleshoot authentication and authorization issues users may have.

Single sign-on

In an organization, there are different applications in use. Each of these applications has a different authentication mechanism. It will be difficult to maintain different user credentials to authenticate on different applications. Most application vendors now support integration with Active Directory for authentication. This means that with Active Directory credentials, you can authenticate on different systems and applications used by your organization. You will not need to keep typing your credentials to get access. Once you authenticate on a computer, the same session will be used to authenticate other Active Directory *integrated* applications.

Schema modification

Any kind of database has its own structure, called **schema**. This is also applicable to an Active Directory database. This schema describes all objects in Active Directory. By knowing the schema, you can modify or extend it. This is important for the development of Active Directory integrated applications. Microsoft publishes **Active Directory Service Interfaces** (**ADSI**) with a set of COM interfaces, and it can be used to access Active Directory service features from different network providers. Application developers can use it to develop their application to be Active Directory-integrated and publish it to the directory. Users can search for the service through Active Directory, and applications can access Active Directory objects as required.

Querying and indexing

By maintaining a central data repository, Active Directory also allows users and applications to query objects and retrieve accurate data. If I need to find user John's account, I do not need to know which branch he is in or what department he belongs to. With a simple Active Directory query, I will be provided with information about the user account. In a manner similar to when we add a new object to the directory, objects will publish its attributes and make it available for users and applications for queries.

These are some of the main capabilities of the Active Directory service, and these features will be explained in detail in later chapters, including how to plan, implement, and maintain them within your identity infrastructure.

Active Directory components

Active Directory components can be divided into two main categories:

- Logical components
- Physical components

When you design your identity infrastructure, you need to consider both components. Logical components of the Active Directory structure can change at any given time according to business requirements. But you won't be able to easily modify the physical components compared to logical components. The placement of these components will define the efficiency, security, reliability, and manageability of your identity infrastructure. So, it's crucial that we get it right in the beginning before we move on to advanced identity infrastructure planning.

Logical components

Each business has its own hierarchical organization layout. It may contain multiple branch offices, multiple groups of companies, and many different departments. Each of these components in the business carries out different operations. Operations in the sales department are completely different from the IT department. Everyone is bound to the company by following different operational guidelines and targets. When we design the identity infrastructure, we need to match it with the company hierarchical layout in order to manage resource and security effectively. Logical components of the Active Directory help you structure the identity infrastructure by considering design, administration, extensibility, security, and scalability.

The Active Directory logical structure contains two types of objects. Objects can be either **container objects** or **leaf objects**. Container objects can be associated with other objects in the logical structure. Leaf objects are the smallest components in the logical structure. They will not have any other child objects associated.

Forests

Amazon is the world's largest rain forest. There are different animal species, and more than 400 tribes live in there. Each of these animal species is different from each other. Reptiles, mammals, snakes, fish all have different characteristics and we can group each of them by considering their characteristics. Tribes living in the forest also have their own language, culture, and boundaries. But all these animals and tribes share one forest. They use food, water, and other resources from the Amazon forest to survive. Amazon forests have well-defined boundaries. Another forest in 100 miles from an Amazon forest is not called an Amazon forest. Its name and boundaries are unique.

The Active Directory forest also can be explained in a similar way. The Active Directory forest represents a complete Active Directory instance. It is made of one or more domain and domain trees. I will be explaining what domain and domain trees are in detail later in this chapter. Each domain has its own characteristics, boundaries, and resources allocated. But at the same time, it shares a common logical structure, schema, and directory configuration within the forest. Similarly, tribes have a relationship with the forest and different tribes, and domains in the Active Directory forest will have a two-way trust relationship. Different tribes in the Amazon forest aren't named after *Amazon*. Each tribe have its own name. Similarly, domains in a forest can contain any domain name:

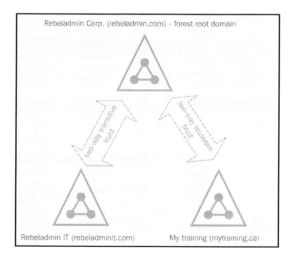

The first domain controller in the Active Directory service deployment is important. When you create the first domain, it will create the forest as well. Then, the first domain will become the forest root domain. A domain tree contains its own root domain. But forests can contain multiple root domains.

In the previous diagram, **Rebeladmin Corp.** is an IT solution provider. The `rebeladmin.com` is the forest root domain. It does have another two companies: one is **Rebeladmin IT** with the domain name `rebeladminit.com`, and it provides managed IT services. The other company is **My training**, with the domain name `mytraining.ca`, and it provides IT training to professionals. The `rebeladminit.com` and `mytraining.ca` both are root domains in their own domain trees. Both domains in the forest will trust each other with **two-way transitive trust**.

Two-way transitive trust is a logical link between domains where the trusting domain honors the logon authentication of the trusted domain. When considering the previous example, users in `rebeladminit.com` can authenticate into `mytraining.ca` domain and vice versa. Any object located in domain inherently trusts other objects in other domains in the same forest. This is not the same as when considering authentication between forests. For that, it may (depending on the trust method) require additional login credentials. An organization can have a single forest or multiple forests based on the company's business requirements.

When Microsoft releases a new Active Directory service version, new features are bound to the forest and domain functional levels. If you want to use Active Directory Domain Services 2016 forest level features, your directory's Active Directory forest should use the Windows Server 2016 forest functional level. Before Windows Server 2012 R2, forest functional level upgrades were one-way. Now it is possible to roll back to the lower forest functional level if required. This is if the forest function level is lower it allowed to add the latest domain controller version. For example, if the forest function level is Windows Server 2008, it is allowed to install the domain controller inside the forest with the operating system Windows Server 2016. But this doesn't mean it can use features provided by Windows Directory Services 2016 until it upgrades its domain and forest functional levels. If you upgrade the forest function level to Windows Server 2016, you can have only domain controllers running a minimum of Windows Server 2016.

Domains

Referring back to my example about the Amazon forest, we can say there are more than 400 tribes living in the Amazon forest. Each of these tribes is unique in certain ways. Each tribe has a different language and culture. Each tribe has its own territory to do their hunting, farming, and fishing. Each tribe know its boundaries and does not cross others' boundaries as that can lead to a war between tribes. Each tribe has its own tools and methods for hunting and farming. Also, each tribe has different groups assigned for different tasks. Some are good at hunting, some are good at farming, and some are good at cooking. All their contribution help them survive and grow as a tribe.

The Active Directory domain too can be explained in a similar way. The domain contains the logical components to achieve administrative goals in the organization. By default, the domain become the security boundary for the objects inside it. Each object has its own administrative goals. Individuals in tribes have different identities and responsibilities, but all of them are part of the tribe and the forest. In the same way, all the objects in the domain are part of a common database. Also, everyone in the tribe still needs to follow some of the common rules. Objects in the domain are also controlled by the security rules defined. These security rules are only applicable within that particular domain and are not valid for any object outside the domain boundaries. A domain also allows you to set smaller administrative boundaries within the organization. In the previous section, I explained that a forest can contain multiple domains. Managing a forest is difficult as its administrative boundary is large, but the domain allows you to set smaller administrative targets. Active Directory is divided into multiple partitions to improve efficiency. The domain is also a partition of Active Directory. When I described the Active Directory forest, I had mentioned that every domain inside the forest shared the same schema. Each of the domain controllers also has a copy of the domain partition, and it is shared only by the domain controllers within the same domain tree. All the information about objects in that particular domain is saved in that domain partition. This ensures that only the required data is replicated across the domain trees and forests:

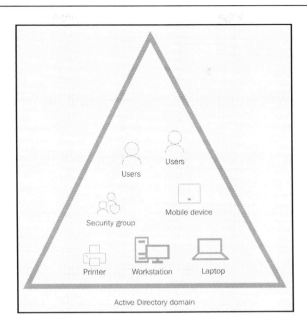

The Active Directory domain's functional levels define the Active Directory capabilities. With every new version of the directory services, new features are added to the domain's functional level. In order to use the features within the domain, the domain functional level need to be upgraded. The version of domain function level you can run on the domain depends on the forest functional level. You cannot have a domain functional level higher than the forest functional level.

Domain trees

I am 33 years old and am living in the UK with my daughter and wife. My parents are still living in Sri Lanka, where you can find sunshine all year and white beaches. After our wedding, I moved into new a house, but that didn't mean I was not a part of the family anymore. I am still the son of my parents. I carry my father's surname. I also inherit traditions and characteristics from my parents. My children will have their own families one day, but in the end, we all are part of the same family tree. A **domain tree** is a collection of domains that reflects the organization's structure. My parents and I are bound by a parent-child relationship. It is obviously different from other kinds of relationships. Similarly, domains inside the domain tree have a parent-child relationship. The first domain in the domain tree is called the **parent** domain. This is the root domain as well. All other domains in the domain tree are called the **child** domain. There will be only one parent domain in a domain tree.

In some documentations, the child domain is also called a **subdomain**. When dealing with internet domains, sometimes, it is required to create additional place holder, a sub URL. For example, `rebeladmin.com` is the domain name used for the website and organization needed to host another website in order to maintain support requests. But it needs to use the same contiguous namespace. To do that, we can create another folder in the domain root and create a DNS record for the `support.rebeladmin.com` subdomain:

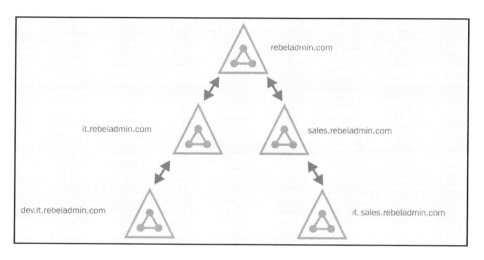

An Active Directory forest, can contain non-contiguous domain names. But within the domain tree, it will share the same contiguous namespace. In the previous example, **rebeladmin.com** is the parent domain for the domain tree. It has two child domains, **it.rebeladmin.com** and **sales.rebeladmin.com**. As you can see, it shares the same **rebeladmin.com** namespace. Similarly, when it goes down in the next level in the domain tree, it shares the namespace from the preceding level. Each of the child domain maintains its own domain partition. This configuration data will be replicated only to the domain controllers in the same child domain. When the child domain is introduced to the domain tree, it will automatically create a trust relationship with the parent domain. If two child domains on different domain trees want to authenticate, authenticated traffic must pass through the forest root domains.

All domain trusts within the Active Directory forest are two-way transitive trusts. Two-way trust means the authentication requests can be processed between two domains in both ways. Transitive means it goes beyond the initial two-way trust between domains and trusts its child domains too even though there is no direct connection.

Organizational units

In the preceding section I explained, how we can group the objects using domains and forests. But within the organization, objects can be categorized into different groups considering the operations, organizational structure, geographical locations, or roles and responsibilities. As an example, organizations have multiple departments. We can convert each of these departments into child domains and group each of the department objects. But the child domain needs a separate domain controller as it will have a separate domain partition. Isn't there a better way to group these objects within the domain? That's where organizational units come in. Organizational units help group objects on a smaller scale within the domain. The most common way is to group objects that have similar security and administrative requirements together. For example, there are more than 50 users in the sales department. The sales department uses common shared folders and printers. Their security requirements for data and network are similar. We can create an **organizational unit (OU)** called **sales** and **group** and put all the sales department users into it. We can apply security policies to the OU level now instead of the user level.

When deploying a domain controller, it creates a default OU structure to segment the most common object types, such as users, computers, and domain controllers. The administrator can add, remove, and delete OU as required.

 Sometimes, I have seen engineers removing/modifying the default OU structure. All these default OUs have different security policies attached. If it really needs to be changed, it is important to compare the security policies applied and reattached to the new OU if required. I highly recommend that you do not modify/remove domain controllers' default OU at least. That said, you are still allowed to add or change security policies applied to default OUs.

Once an object is assigned to an OU, it inherits security settings and permissions applied on the OU level. If the same object is moved to a different OU, then it will apply the settings from the new OU and discard the settings that were applied from the previous OU. Organization units also help delegate administrative control to individuals for specific tasks. Domain administrators have privileges to manage any objects within the domain. But it's possible to create administrators and assign them to manage objects and resources on an organization level. For these administrators, the OU will be the security boundary. They will not be able to modify any other objects outside that particular OU. I will be explaining delegated administration later in this book. Organizational units are container objects. They can be associated with similar or other objects. Similar to the domain parent-child relationship, OUs also can contain child OUs. These are also called **nested organization units**.

OUs also can contain object types such as users, groups, contacts, computers, organizational units, and printers:

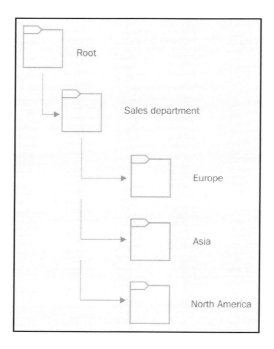

In the previous example, Rebeladmin Corp. has a **Sales department**. In the OU hierarchy, the first thing you need to do is create an OU called **Sales department**. All the regional offices too have their own sales department. Most of the security and administrative requirements for objects in the sales department are the same. But creating OUs based on geographical areas will allow domain administrators to delegate control over those objects to individuals or groups in the regional office. Also, if a specific security policy needs to be applied to a regional office sales department, it can be applied on a relevant OU level rather than applying it to the entire **Sales departments** across the branch offices. All the child OUs inherit the permissions applied from its parent OU by default. In the previous example, individuals or groups who have permission to control **Sales department** objects have control over the objects in **Europe**, **Asia**, and **North America** OUs by default. The OU hierarchy is independent. It is not going to affect any other domain OU hierarchy. The OU also can contain objects from the same domain only.

Physical components

In the previous section, I explained the logical components of the Active Directory. Now it's time to look into the physical components. Even though logical and physical components are equally important in the Active Directory Domain Service design, they are independent. Replication is the core feature of the Active Directory Domain Services. If a system has multiple domain controllers, changes made in one domain controller should be replicated to others. Physical component placement can affect Active Directory replications in certain ways. Logically, components can be easily rearranged compared to physical components.

Domain controllers

The domain controller is a computer that runs a Windows Server operating system and holds the Active Directory Domain Services role. It can be either a physical server or a virtual server.

Virtualized domain controllers are not always suited for the infrastructures. I have seen some engineers host domain controllers in virtualized environments while the same virtualized environment (cluster) build uses the same domain. If virtualized domain controllers go down with the cluster, authentication will not work either. In such an environment, physical domain controllers are important for a reliable identity infrastructure.

The domain controller holds the directory partition that will be replicated to the other domain controllers in the same domain. The domain can have any number of domain controllers. The number of domain controllers is dependent on the enterprise's size, geographical placement, and network segmentation. In Windows NT, it uses multiple domain controllers but it maintains a single-master schema.. This means that directory changes can be made from a specific domain controller only. After Windows 2000, there has been support for the multi-master mode. Any object-level changes made in one domain controller will be replicated to all other domain controllers (directory service-related). That said, some of the Active Directory-related operations role changes can be modified by the designated operation master role owner (FSMO roles) only.

Before Windows 2000 domain services, one of the domain controllers acted as the **primary domain controller** (PDC) and all other additional domain controllers were called **backup domain controller** (BDC). Some people still use this terminology to describe the operations of the domain controllers in the infrastructure. But after Windows Server 2000, the only difference between domain controllers was either their **Flexible Single Master Operation** (FSMO) role holder or the global catalog server. Some documentation listing read-only domain controllers and read/write domain controllers are two different categories, but for me it's rather an operation change than category. Read-only domain controllers are used with specific administrative requirements when you do not trust the security of the domain controller.

Global catalog server

The global catalog server holds the full writable copy of objects in its host domain and the partial copy of the objects in other domains in the same forest. The partial replica contains a copy of every object in the forest and the most commonly used attributes used by queries. Applications and users in one domain can query for the objects in another domain (same forest) via the global catalog server. All domain controllers in the domain will not be a global catalog server by default. When installing the first domain controller, it will become the global catalog server, and other domain controllers can promote them as global catalog servers according to business requirements. Every domain controller in the domain does not need to be a global catalog server.

Active Directory sites

The AD DS site defines a physical topology of the network. Sites can be separate buildings in a campus network and branch office in a separate city or even in a separate country. As an example, Rebeladmin Corp. has its head office located in **London office, UK**. It is running a few domain controllers (**DC01** and **DC02**) within its physical network. It uses IP address allocation for the network with subnets 192.168.148.0/24, 10.10.10.0/24 and 172.25.16.0/24. Due to the business requirements, the company opened a branch office in **Toronto, Canada**. It got its own domain controllers (**DC03** and **DC04**) running, but logically, it is in the same Active Directory forest and domain. Both networks are interconnected with a leased line. The Canada network uses IP subnets 10.11.11.0/24 and 172.0.2.0/24:

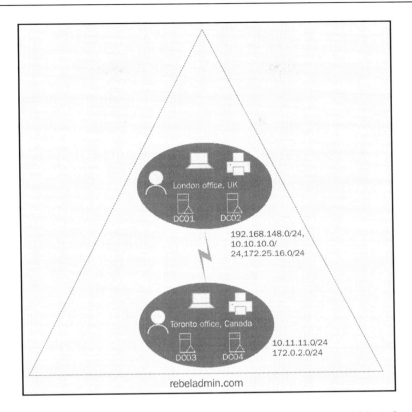

In the preceding diagram, the two offices can be called the two sites. This is because it is clearly two network segments. The Active Directory logical design does not really consider physical network segmentation. Since they are in the same domain and forest, **DC01** to **DC04** should replicate changes to each other in order to maintain a healthy identity infrastructure.

Mainly, there are three benefits we can identify:

- **Replication**: In a typical AD DS setup, all domain controllers are set to replicate changes between each other assuming all are connected via fast network links. But in the real world, they're not. Sometimes, connections between two sites are 256 kbps or 512 kbps. The same links will be used for other enterprise operations as well. Using AD DS sites, it's possible to perform bandwidth optimization and replication schedule changes for reliable replication across domain controllers.

- **Service location**: In the Active Directory setup, there are other services integrated that help in company operations, for example, Active Directory certificate services and exchange services. Using sites and the subnet setup, we can point users to the nearest server for the services. So, users in the Toronto site are severed by the Microsoft Exchange Server (mail server) in Toronto site when they try to access an email instead of passing the request to the site in London.
- **Authentication**: When a user logs in to the domain, they need to communicate with the domain controller for authentication. In the preceding example, a user on the Toronto site does not need to connect to a domain controller in the London site for authentication. AD DS sites will allow you to ensure that users in the Toronto site will use the nearest domain controller for authentication. This will reduce latency and bandwidth through the site links.

Since AD DS sites represent a physical network topology, when changes are made to the physical topology, they needs to be updated on the AD DS site configuration as well. A great example is when the IP address subnet is added to the network. If a new subnet is added, this information needs to be updated in the AD DS site subnet section too. Sometimes, engineers forget to do that, and this will prevent infrastructures from having full benefits of AD DS sites.

Active Directory objects

If we need to describe a person or thing, we use different adjectives. This can include personality, ethical background, physical appearance, or characteristics. Most of these are not unique. For example, when you talk about a 6-feet boy, there can be lots of 6-feet boys in the city. But it still explains the *person* that we're trying to describe is definitely not a girl. If we need to uniquely identify a person or thing, we need some unique attributes associated with them. If it's a person, the passport number, telephone number, or national insurance number will make the person unique from others. If it's a thing, the serial number or bar code associated with it makes it unique.

Within an organization, there are many physical entities. These can be either employees or resources. In order to manage those using Active Directory Domain Services, each of these physical entities needs to be presented to Active Directory. Active Directory will understand these entities as objects.

In Active Directory, there are two types of objects. *Container objects* can store other objects in the Active Directory. The domain itself is an example of a container object. The organizational unit is also a container object. *Leaf objects* cannot store other objects in Active Directory. A service account is an example of a leaf object.

As we use adjectives to describe a person or a thing, Active Directory objects needs attributes to describe their nature. For example, the following screenshot shows the wizard you will get when you create a new user account. In the wizard, in the following screenshot (left-hand side), **First name**, **Last name**, **Full name**, and **User logon name** are attributes. In the same way, when you create a computer account, it needs a **Computer name** attribute to describe it (right-hand side):

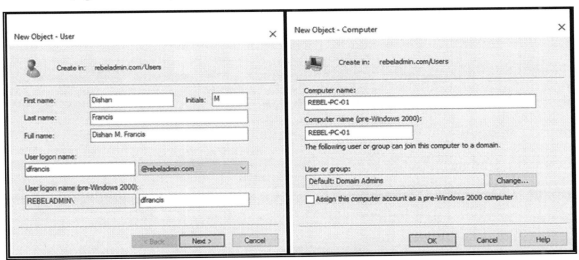

According to the preceding screenshot, depending on the object type, the associated attributes are changed as well. Also, it doesn't matter if you create one user object or hundreds of user objects in Active Directory; you still need to use the exact same attributes to describe the object you are creating. This is because each of the objects is attached to an object class. Within the Active Directory schema, it is defined which attributes are attached to each *object class*. When you sign up for the online service, the first time, it will provide you an online form to fill. At the backend, it is attached to a database. The information you provided will be recorded in the database for future use. If you need to sign up for the service, you must provide the answers to the questions that are asked. You cannot change the questions you need to answer because the database will not be able to understand it. The database got a table designed with columns, rows, and data types to store the data that will be captured from the form. Similarly, object class attributes are defined by a schema. Active Directory does have different types of object classes. Users, groups, computers, printers, and domain controllers are examples of object classes.

Some of these attributes are mandatory for object classes. For example, in user account creation, **User logon name** must be provided to continue. But if we do not provide the **Last name**, we can still proceed with user account creation. Attribute values also need to be provided with an acceptable data format that is defined by the schema. Sometimes, due to the operational requirements, organizations may require custom attributes. By modifying the Active Directory schema, it is possible to add additional attributes to the object classes. This will be demonstrated further in Chapter 7, *Managing Active Directory Objects*.

Globally unique identifier and security identifier

In a city or organization, there can be multiple people with the same name. But their passport number or national insurance number will be unique to them. So, in order to identify a person or thing accurately from a similar group, we need to consider the unique value associated.

In the Active Directory database, nearly 2 billion objects can be stored. How will it uniquely identify each and every object? Every time we create an object in Active Directory, it will be assigned with one or two unique values. If it is a user or group object, it will receive a **globally unique identifier (GUID)** and **security identifier (SID)**. The GUID value will be saved in the objectGUID attribute in each object and the SID value will be saved in the objectSid attribute in each object.

In order to view the GUID and SID values for the user account, the following PowerShell command can be run from the domain controller:

```
Get-ADUser username
```

The username can be replaced by the actual username of the user.

In the following figure, ObjectGUID lists the GUID value and SID lists the SID value associated with the user account:

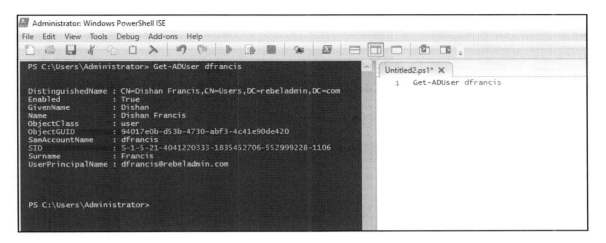

`ObjectGUID` is a 128-bit value and is applied to each and every object in Active Directory. This value is not just for the particular Active Directory domain. It is valid globally as well. Once a GUID is assigned to an object, it will be there until the object is deleted from the directory. Modifying or moving objects will not change the value of the GUID. The `ObjectGUID` attribute value will be published to global catalog servers. If an application in a domain needs to search for a user object, the best method will be to query using `ObjectGUID` as it will give an accurate result.

There is a misunderstanding that the GUID value is a *unique value*. None of the documentation say that this value is unique. They only say it is quite unlikely to have a duplicated GUID as method it used to generate is complex.

The `SID` value for an object is unique within its domain. The `SID` values associated with the user will be changed if the user object is migrated to another domain. An `SID` value assigned by one domain will not be accepted by another domain. As soon as a user object is migrated to another domain, a new `SID` value will be generated. Then, the old `SID` value will be saved in the `sIDHistory` attribute. This attribute can contain multiple values. When the system creates a Kerberos ticket for user authentication, it will consider a new `SID` value and all other `SID` values listed in the `sIDHistory` attribute. `sIDHistory` is important, especially in Active Directory restructuring. The resources in the domain decide access or deny permissions to a user account based on their **access control list (ACL)**. This ACL uses the `SID` values. So, if an object moves to a different domain without `sIDHistory`, it will lose its access to resources until ACL is modified. But if the system considers `sIDHistory` when granting access token and if the old `SID` value is moved over to the new domain, the user is still allowed to access the resources he/she was assigned.

Distinguished names

Distinguished names in Active Directory can also be used to identify an object uniquely. This is very similar to the way your postal address works. A postal address uses a hierarchical path to uniquely identify you. Starting from the country, it goes to province then to the city, street, and house number. The same way, using the full path to the object within the directory will help you uniquely identify an object.

There are three types of Active Directory naming attributes that have been used to generate distinguished names:

- `organizationName` (O) or `organizationalUnitName` (OU): Organization represents the root-level domain. The organization unit refers to the OU in which the object is located.
- `domainComponent` (DC): This is the naming attribute for the domain and the DNS. If the DNS name for the domain is `rebeladmin.com`, the domain component for it will be `DC=rebeladmin,DC=com`.
- `commonName` (CN): This refers to the objects and containers within the directory.

In the previous screenshot, when the query for the domain user is returned, the distinguished name for the user is as follows:

```
CN=Dishan Francis,CN=Users,DC=rebeladmin,DC=com
```

There, `DC=rebeladmin,DC=com` represents the domain name, `CN=Users` represents the user container, and at the end, `CN=Dishan Francis` represents the actual object name.

The **relative distinguished name** (**RDN**) is a unique value within its parent container. For the preceding example, the RDN for the object is `CN=Dishan Francis`. Active Directory allows you to have the same RDN for multiple objects within the directory, but all of them need to be in separate containers. It is not allowed to have the same RDN for the object within the same container.

In the previous section, you learned that the `SID` values for the object will not be changed unless it's migrated to a different domain controller. Changing values in the object will not modify the `SID` value. But if the hierarchical path got changed for an object, DN will be changed. For example, if you move a user object from one OU to another, the DN value for the user object will be changed.

Active Directory server roles

There are five main Active Directory server roles. These roles are grouped together as the required Active Directory environment in order to set up and configure Active Directory server roles:

- **Active Directory Domain Services (AD DS)**
- **Active Directory Federation Services (AD FS)**
- **Active Directory Lightweight Directory Services (AD LDS)**
- **Active Directory Rights Management Services (AD RMS)**
- **Active Directory Certificate Services (AD CS)**

After Windows Server 2008, these roles can be installed and configured using Windows Server Manager. It is the same in Windows Server 2016:

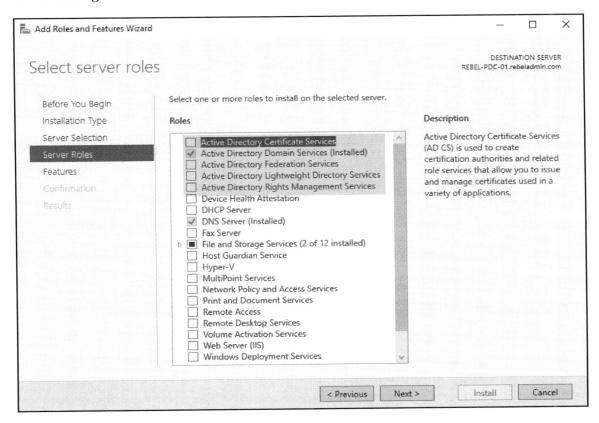

Each of these server roles can also be installed and configured using PowerShell. The following PowerShell cmdlets can be used to install Active Directory server roles:

PowerShell cmdlets	Description
`Install-WindowsFeature AD-Domain-Services`	This cmdlet will install the AD DS role.
`Install-WindowsFeature AD FS-Federation`	This cmdlet will install the AD FS role.
`Install-WindowsFeature ADLDS`	This cmdlet will install AD LDS.
`Install-WindowsFeature ADRMS`	This cmdlet will install AD RMS. This role has two subfeatures, which are AD Rights Management Server and identity federation support. If required, these individual roles can be installed using `Install-WindowsFeature ADRMS, ADRMS-Server, ADRMS-Identity` or `Install-WindowsFeature ADRMS – IncludeAllSubFeature`. It will install all the subfeatures.
`Install-WindowsFeature AD-Certificate`	This cmdlet will install AD CS. This role has six subroles, which are certification authority (`ADCS-Cert-Authority`), **Certificate Enrollment Policy Web Service** (`ADCS-Enroll-Web-Pol`), **Certificate Enrollment Web Service** (`ADCS-Enroll-Web-Svc`), **Certification Authority Web Enrollment** (`ADCS-Web-Enrollment`), **Network Device Enrollment Service** (`ADCS-Device-Enrollment`), and **Online Responder** (`ADCS-Online-Cert`). These subfeatures can be added individually or together.

The `Get-WindowsFeature` command will list all the roles and subfeatures available along with the name that can be used with PowerShell to install the role. When you install the roles, it is important to add `-IncludeManagementTools` as management tools for the role will not be installed by default.

Active Directory Domain Service

In the previous sections in this chapter, I explained what Active Directory and its components are. As a recap, I would like to list down some key points about AD DS:

- AD DS can manage an organization's resources in a secure, efficient manner, and it helps organize objects in a hierarchical structure.
- The Active Directory forest is an identity infrastructure security boundary and the forest can contain multiple domains with their own directory partitions.
- The Active Directory domain maintains a multi-master database to store data about objects and replicate it with other domain controllers in the domain. Any writable domain controller in the domain can add, modify, or delete objects from the Active Directory database, and other domain controllers will be aware of these changes.
- The organizational unit will be used to arrange objects in Active Directory in a hierarchical structure. It is also used to delegate permissions for administrative tasks.

Read-only domain controllers

With Windows Server 2008, Microsoft introduced a new type of domain controller called **read-only domain controller (RODC)**. It allows organizations to have domain controllers in locations where data security and network security cannot be guaranteed.

Domain controllers contain a writable copy of the AD DS database. It is replicated among all the domain controllers in the same domain, but the read-only domain controller will have a read-only AD DS database.

This feature is useful in a *branch* network. Not every branch office of an organization can afford a fully blown network with a high-speed leased line, protected data center facility, and IT staff. If it's an Active Directory environment and if the branch office needs to be connected to the corporate environment, engineers will need to deploy the domain controller in the branch office network too. But if the branch office has limited connection to a corporate network, less IT resources, and poor physical data and network security, it can be a greater security threat to corporate networks by deploying a domain controller in that network. But deploying RODC will guarantee that the identity infrastructure security from such threats and users in the branch office will still be able to use the fast and reliable authentication and authorization capabilities of AD DS.

RODC holds a copy of Active Directory objects and attributes from writable domain controllers, except the account passwords. If any changes need to be done in objects, they need to be done in a writable domain controller. Sometimes, the branch office may host applications that need write capabilities to the directory services. These requests will be pointed to the writable domain controller instead of RODC.

Active Directory Federation Services

AD FS allows you to share identities between trusted identity infrastructures based on a **claim-based authorization (CBA)** mechanism. Modern day organization workloads are complicated. Application service providers have shifted most of their applications to the cloud (SaaS). Also, organizations share web-based systems and applications between them for the operations. Almost all these systems need some kind of authentication and authorization process to allow users to access the applications or systems. This makes the identity infrastructure requirements complicated.

Rebeladmin Corp. is a manufacturing company. Northwood industrial is a partner company of Rebeladmin Corp. Rebeladmin Corp. has a web-based content management system to track sales leads, orders, and projects. As a partner company, sales users from Northwood industrial like to access this system. Both companies use their own identity infrastructures. An easy way to do this is to set up an Active Directory forest trust between two organizations. But that is an administration and security nightmare. If Rebeladmin Corp. has many partners, will it be practical to have a forest trust each and every organization? It also adds additional operational cost to facilitate secure communications links between organizations. It is only one application the partner company wants to access, but providing trust will open up additional security threats to the Rebeladmin Corp infrastructure. AD FS allows you to provide access to protected applications without any of these hazels. It will trust identities from completely different identity infrastructures and pass identity information as *claims* to the organization that hosts the applications. Then, the company that hosts the application will map these claims to claims that the application understands and make the authorization decisions. The important point here is that this process will be done with minimum changes to the infrastructure. Both organizations will keep maintaining their own identity infrastructures. Communication will happen only via an HTTPS protocol, and there will be no need to open up additional firewall ports between the organization's networks.

In normal scenarios, if you share a web-based system or application between two identity infrastructures, the partner organizations need to provides the two credentials. One credential is to authenticate it to their own infrastructure, and the second one is to authenticate it to the remote infrastructure. AD FS will allow users to have a single sign-on experience to the application.

Organizations today use more and more web-based applications. Some are for their own operations, and some are client-focused. If these are Active Directory-integrated applications, opening them to public internet can create security threats. AD FS can also be used to provide multi-factor authentication to web-based applications. AD FS can be hosted in **demilitarized zone (DMZ)** in the network, and it will be the only public-facing interface for the applications. Once users successfully have .

There are four AD FS role services:

- **Federation service**: The federation servers' hosted federation service will route authentication requests from identities in another identity infrastructure using a federated web single sign-on or from clients through the internet using the web single sign-on design method. These design options will be explained in detail in `Chapter 13`, *Active Directory Federation Services*.
- **Federation Service Proxy**: Federation proxy servers can be places in DMZ (the perimeter network segment) and forward claims to the federation service located in a secure network. This adds an additional layer of security for web-based applications.
- **Claims-aware agent**: AD FS uses claim to create trust between two identity infrastructures. The claims-aware agent can be used in the application web server to allow queries for AD FS claims. Then, the application will use claims in the AD FS security token to make the authorization decision.
- **Windows Token-based Agent**: This agent is to be installed on a web server that hosts Windows token-based application. It will convert the AD FS security token into the Windows access token, and the application will make an authorization decision based on that.

These federation roles can be installed on separate servers based on the organization's federation requirements.

Active Directory Lightweight Directory Services

My little girl Selena went to McDonald's more than average last month as she wanted to collect all kinds of different furby connect toys included in kids' meals. But when we go to McDonald's, we can't buy just the toy. Whether you're hungry or not, you still need to buy the kids' meal to get the toy.

Some applications require a directory-enabled environment to operate. But there is no need to be in a fully blown Active Directory environment. Microsoft developed AD LDS to enable data storage and retrieval for directory-enabled applications without the dependencies required for AD DS. When we deploy AD DS, it keeps its own directory partition and the schema inherited from the forest. If we need an additional directory partition, it is required that you deploy another domain or child domain, but AD LDS allows you to maintain an independent schema with each AD LDS instance. You can also host multiple AD LDS instances on one computer.

AD DS and AD LDS both are builds based on the same core directory service technologies. AD LDS does not need to depend on the Active Directory domain or forest setup. But in an AD DS environment, AD LDS can use AD DS for authentication.

Active Directory Rights Management Services

AD RMS help organizations protect sensitive data getting unauthorized access.

Let's say Peter received a document that contains some sensitive data about company stock prices. Peter sends it to Liam. We know this should be a confidential conversation between Peter and Liam. How can we verify that this data has not been passed on to another user? What if someone gets a printed copy of this document? What if Liam edits this and adds some false information? Using AD RMS, you can prevent this kind of misuse of confidential corporate data. AD RMS can be used to encrypt managed identities and apply authorization policies to your files, emails, and presentations. This will prevent files from being copied, forwarded, or printed from unauthorized people. This also allows file expiration, and it will prevent users from viewing the data of a document over a period of time.

AD RMS contain two roles services:

- **Active Directory Rights Management Server**: This installs the AD RMS server service that requires you to protect the content in organization.
- **Identity Federation Support**: AD RMS service also supports integration with AD FS services. It will allow you to protect content between two organizations without setting up AD RMS in both infrastructures. This role service helps integrate AD RMS with AD FS.

Active Directory Certification Services

AD CS helps organizations build **public key infrastructure (PKI)** in an easy, cost-effective way. Digital certificates issued by the certification authority can be used to authenticate users, computers, and devices. The certification authority is responsible for receiving certificate requests, verifying certificate requests, and issuing, renewing, and revoking certificates.

There are six role services for AD CS:

- **Certification authority (CA)**: Mainly, there are two types of CAs. Microsoft named them root and subordinate CA. The placement of these on a network will be dependent on the PKI design. CA is responsible for issuing certificates to users, computers, and devices. It will also manage the validity of certificates.
- **Certification Authority Web Enrollment**: This is a web interface that connects to CA in order to allow users to submit certificate requests, retrieve issued certificates, and download the certificate chain.
- **Online Responder**: This will receive and respond to individual user requests to verify the status of digital certificates.
- **Network Device Enrollment Service**: This service allows non-domain joined network devices to obtain certificates.
- **Certificate Enrollment Web Service**: This role service works with Certificate Enrollment Policy Web Service and allows users and computers to perform certificate enrollment using HTTPS. It also allows certificate enrollment for domain computers or devices that are not connected to the domain and computers or devices that are not part of the domain.
- **Certificate Enrollment Policy Web Service**: This publishes the certificate enrollment policy information to users and computers.

Summary

This is the end of the introductory chapter on Active Directory fundamentals. I am sure most of you are already aware about most of the functions of AD DS. But refreshing your knowledge about Active Directory components and their operations before we deep dive into the advanced topics wasn't in vain. In this chapter, we also covered Active Directory objects, GUID and SID values, and DN. Later, I explained the Active Directory server roles and their core values.

In the next chapter, you will learn about new features and enhancements to AD DS 2016, specifically about the new approach to protect identities from modern security threats.

2
Active Directory Domain Services 2016

Microsoft **Active Directory Domain Services (AD DS)** have been in the industry for more than 15 years now. The first Microsoft AD version was released with Windows Server 2000. After that, with each and every Microsoft Server release, a new AD DS version was released too. Those changes improved the functions, security, manageability, and reliability of identity infrastructures.

Each and every time Microsoft releases a new version of their software, IT engineers, IT professionals, and administrators rush to figure out what is *new* in it. It's good practice to be on top of industrial trends. At the time I started writing this book, there weren't many resources available to explain the new features of AD DS 2016.

Microsoft released AD DS 2016 at a very interesting time technologically. As I stated in the previous chapter, today's identity infrastructure requirements for the enterprise are challenging. Most companies use cloud services for their operations (**Software as a Service (SaaS)**) and lots of them have moved their infrastructure workloads to the public cloud. Identity infrastructure services need to support these new challenges in industries as these cloud services and workloads are also attached to enterprise identities. Microsoft has already released Azure Active Directory which can be used to integrate on-premise AD DS instances with cloud. So, workloads and applications hosted in Azure can use the same identity for different authentications. These new requirements are also extending the security boundaries of an enterprise's identity infrastructure. The legacy protections used for identity infrastructures no longer fall in line with these new changes. One of the key questions for IT professionals is how to protect their identity infrastructure with these new extended security boundaries. Considering these industry trends and requirements, the primary investment in AD DS 2016 was *identity infrastructure security*.

In this chapter, the following AD DS 2016 features will be explained in detail:

- Privileged Access Management
- Time-based group memberships
- Microsoft Passport
- Active Directory Federation Services improvements
- Time sync improvements

AD DS 2016 features

AD DS improvements apply to its forest and domain functional levels. Upgrading the operating system or adding domain controllers that run Windows Server 2016 to an existing AD infrastructure isn't going to upgrade the forest and domain functional levels. In order to use or test these new AD DS 2016 features, you need to have the forest and domain function levels set to Windows Server 2016. The minimum forest and domain functional levels you can run on your identity infrastructure depend on the lowest domain controller version running.

For example, if you have a Windows Server 2008 domain controller in your infrastructure, even if you add a Windows Server 2016 domain controller, the domain and forest functional levels need to be maintained as Windows Server 2008 until the last Windows Server 2008 domain controller is removed from the infrastructure.

Deprecation of Windows Server 2003 domain and forest functional levels

Windows Server 2003 is no longer supported by Microsoft. When I talk to customers, I still see organizations (even banks, retailers, and pharmaceuticals) using Server 2003 on their production networks. There are enough reasons to upgrade from Server 2003 and I am not going to explain them here. The same holds true even for AD DS. Sometimes, it is not easy to upgrade from one version to another, especially under a limited budget. But it's always important to evaluate the risks an enterprise will have without an upgrade. We need to be mindful of protecting the right stuff and investing in the correct areas of operation.

 If you haven't yet upgraded from AD DS 2003 either, this is the right time to make that decision.

Windows Server 2003's forest and domain functional levels have been deprecated in AD DS 2016. The same happened in Windows Server 2012 R2: if you create a new domain, you cannot use a Server 2003 domain or forest functional levels. As shown in the following diagrams, you cannot deploy an AD DS 2016 domain with a Server 2003 domain and forest functional levels:

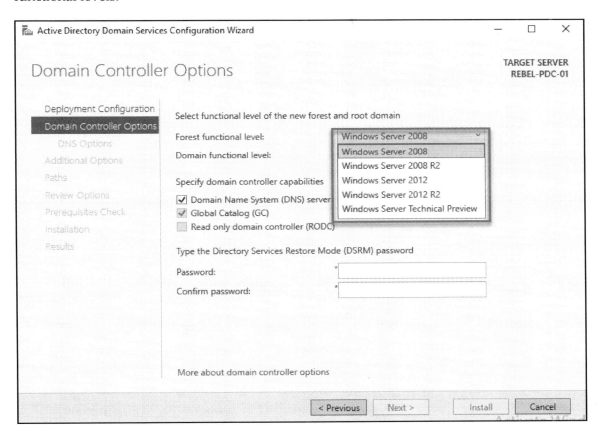

Forest functional level

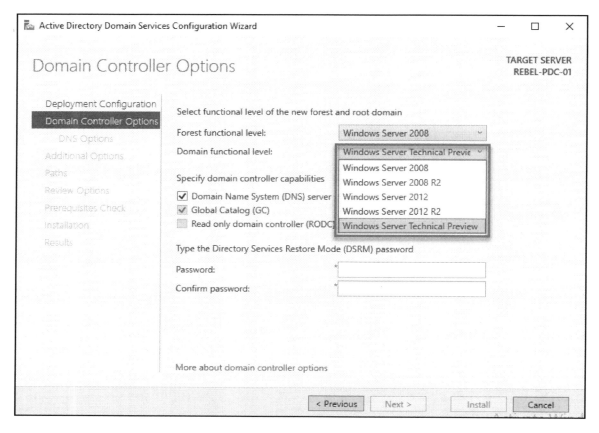

Domain functional level

If your domain was originally created using Windows Server 2003 and you need to migrate to Server 2016, you can still do it. You can add a domain controller with Server 2016 and migrate FSMO roles over. In some documentation, I have seen people stating it's not possible to migrate from Server 2003 to 2016 directly, but that's not true.

Deprecation of File Replication Services

In Windows Server 2000, Microsoft introduced **File Replication Service (FRS)**; it is used to replicate the AD SYSVOL folder.

SYSVOL is a folder that contains public files from the domain that needs to be replicated to other domain controllers in the domain. It contains files required for group policies and user logon scripts.

FRS has had lots of issues when it comes to replications, especially performance wise. FRS always replicates the entire file, no matter what kind of changes you've made. This is an issue for AD sites connected by slow WAN links. FRS does not have API or WMI support, which can be used to monitor performance. It also doesn't support any health-reporting mechanisms. FRS was replaced by **Distributed File System Replication (DFSR)** in Windows Server 2003 R2, and since Server 2008, DFSR has been used to replicate the SYSVOL folders.

DFSR supports partial file-change (block-level) replications instead of entire files. This aids in faster replication and optimized bandwidth usage between AD sites connected by WAN links. It also supports file compression and can control on a per-file-type basis. The number of files that can be transferred (inbound/outbound) has been increased compared to FRS. DFSR also has a self-healing system for filesystem problems.

With Windows Server 2008 R2, FRS has been deprecated, and if you deploy a new domain with a Windows Server 2008 domain and forest functional level at minimum, it will use DFSR by default to replicate SYSVOL. If you're migrating from a Windows 2003 domain environment, FRS-to-DFSR migration will be manual. This is one of the steps most engineers forget when they do domain migrations from older versions. FRS deprecation remains the same in AD DS 2016. The migration steps from FRS to DFSR work in the same way and will be explained in a later chapter.

Privileged Access Management

Privileged Access Management (PAM) is one of the most-discussed topics in presentations, tech shows, IT forums, IT groups, blogs, and meetings in the past few years (since 2014) when it comes to identity management. It has become a trending topic, especially after the Windows Server 2016 preview releases. In 2016, I traveled to several cities in several countries and found myself involved in many presentations and discussions about PAM.

First of all, this is not a feature you can enable with a few clicks. It is a combination of many technologies and methodologies that come together and make a workflow or, in other words, *way of living* for administrators. AD DS 2016 includes features and capabilities supporting PAM in the infrastructure, but it is not the only thing it has. This is one of the greatest challenges I see about this new way of thinking and new way of working: replacing a product is easy, but changing a process is more complicated and challenging.

I started my career with one of the largest North American hosting companies around 2003. I was a systems administrator at that time, and one of my tasks was to identify *hacking* attempts and prevent workloads becoming compromised. In order to do that, I had to review lots of logs on different systems. But around that time, most attacks from individuals or groups comprised of putting their names on the hacked websites to prove that they could hack them. The average daily number of hacking attempts per server was around 20 to 50. Some colocation customers were even running their websites and workloads without any protection (even when advised against it). But as time went by, year by year, the number of attempts dramatically increased, and we were beginning to talk about hundreds or thousands of attempts per day. The following graph is from the latest *Symantec Internet Security Threat Report (2016)*, and it confirms that the number of web-based attacks have increased by more than 117% since 2014:

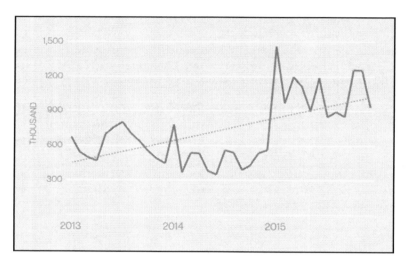

Web attacks blocked per month: Symantec Internet Security Threat Report (2016)

Not only have the numbers changed but so has the motive behind the attacks. As I said, in the earlier days, it was script kiddies who were after fame. Later, as users started to use more and more online services, the purpose of attacks changed to financial gain. Attackers started to focus on websites that stored credit card information. In the past 10 years, I had to change my credit card four times as my credit card information was exposed due to hacks on the websites I had used them with. This type of attack still happens in the industry.

When considering the types of threats, after the year 2012, most things changed. Instead of fame or financial gain, attackers started to target *identities*. In the earlier days, the data about a person was in different formats. For example, when I walked into my medical center 15 years ago, before I saw the doctor, the administrative staff had to go and find the file that had my name. They had a number of racks filled with files and papers, which included patient records, treatment history, test reports, and so on. But now, things have changed: when I walk in, no one in administration needs to worry about my file. The doctor can see all my records from his computer screen with a few clicks. In this way, data has been transformed into digital format. More and more data about people is getting transformed into digital format. In such a healthcare system, I become an **identity**, and my identity is attached to data and also to certain **privileges**. Think about your bank—an online banking system. You've got your own username and password to type in when you log in to the portal. So, you have your own identity in the bank system. Once you log in, you can access all your accounts, transfer money, make payments, and so on. The bank has granted some *privileges* to your identity. With your privileges, you cannot look into your neighbor's bank account. But your bank manager can view your account and your neighbor's account too. This means that the privileges attached to the bank manager's identity are different. The amount of data that can be retrieved from the system depends on identity and privileges.

Not only that, some of these identities are integrated with different systems. Industries use different systems related to their operations. These can be an email system, CMS, or billing system. Each of these systems holds data. To make operations smooth, these systems are integrated with one identity infrastructure, and it provides a single sign-on experience instead of using different identities for each and every application. It's making identities more and more powerful within any system. For an attacker, what is of more worth—focusing on one system or targeting the identity attached to data and privileges on many different systems? Which one would cause more damage? If the target is an identity having highly privileged access to the systems, it's a total disaster, isn't it?

Is it all just about usernames, passwords, and admin accounts? No it's not; identities can cause more damage than that. Usernames and passwords just make it easy. Just think about recent well-known cyber-attacks.

 Back in July 2015, a group called **The Impact Team** threatened to expose user account information of the *Ashley Madison* dating site if its parent company, *Avid Life Media*, did not shut down the *Ashley Madison* and *Established Men* websites completely.

For example, in the Ashley Madison website hack, was it financial value that made it dangerous? No, it was the identities that caused damage to people's lives. The identities were enough to expose names and humiliate people. It ruined families, and children lost parents to divorce. This proves that it's not only about permissions attached to an identity; individual identities themselves are more important in the modern *big data* phenomenon.

It's only been a few months since the USA presidential elections, and by now, we can see how much news can be generated with a single tweet. It isn't necessary to have special privileges to post a tweet; it is the identity that makes that tweet important. On the other hand, if that Twitter account got hacked and someone posted a fake tweet on behalf of the actual person who owns it, what kind of damage could it cause to the whole world? In order to do so, would one need to hack Jack Dorsey's account? The value of an individual identity is more powerful than Twitter's CEO.

According to the following latest reports, the majority of the information exposed by identity attacks are names, addresses, medical reports, and government identity numbers:

Top 10 Types of Information Exposed

▶ Financial information includes stolen credit card details and other financial credentials.

	2015 Type	2015 %	2014 Type	2014 %
1	Real Names	78%	Real Names	69%
2	Home Addresses	44%	Gov. ID Numbers (e.g., SSN)	45%
3	Birth Dates	41%	Home Addresses	43%
4	Gov. ID Numbers (e.g., SSN)	38%	Financial Information	36%
5	Medical Records	36%	Birth Dates	35%
6	Financial Information	33%	Medical Records	34%
7	Email Addresses	21%	Phone Numbers	21%
8	Phone Numbers	19%	Email Addresses	20%
9	Insurance	13%	User Names & Passwords	13%
10	User Names & Passwords	11%	Insurance	11%

Source: Symantec Internet Security Threat Report (2016)

Attacks targeting identities are rising everyday. The following graph shows the number of identities that have been exposed as compared to the total number of incidents:

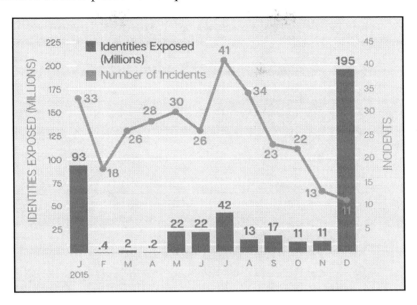

Source: Symantec Internet Security Threat Report (2016)

In December 2015, there were only 11 incidents, and 195 million identities were exposed. This shows how much damage these types of attacks can make.

Each and every time this kind of attack happened, the most common response from engineers were "Those attacks were so sophisticated!", "It was too complex to identify!", "They were so clever!", "It was zero-day attack," and so on. Is that really true?

 Zero-day attacks are based on system bugs and errors unknown to vendors. The latest report shows the average explore time to be less than 7 days, and 1 day to release a patch (*Symantec Internet Security Threat Report (2016)*).

The *Microsoft Security Intelligence Report Volume 21 (January through June 2016)* contains the following graph, which explains the complexity of the vulnerabilities. It clearly shows that a majority of vulnerabilities are still less complex to exploit. High-complexity vulnerabilities still comprise less than 5% of the total vulnerability disclosures. This proves that attackers are still after low-hanging fruit.

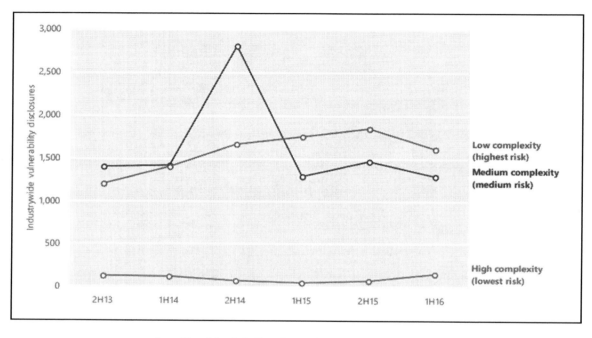

Source: Microsoft Security Intelligence Report Volume 21 (January through June 2016)

Microsoft AD is the leader in identity infrastructure solution providers. In all this constant news about identity breaches, the Microsoft AD name also appears. And people start to question why Microsoft can't fix it. But if you analyze these problems, it's obvious that just providing a technology-rich product is not enough to solve these issues. With each and every new server OS version, Microsoft releases a new AD version. With every release, there are new features to improve identity infrastructure-security. But when I go to work on an AD project, I see the majority of engineers not even following security best practices defined by AD versions released 10 years ago!

Think about a car race: race categories are usually based on engine displacement—3.2 L, 5 L, and so on. In a race, most of the time, it's the same models or the same manufacturer's cars. If it's the same manufacturer, and if they have the same engine capacity, how does one win and the other lose? It's in fact the car's tuning and the driver's skills that decide the winner and loser. If AD DS 2016 can fix all identity threats, that's really good, but simply providing a product or technology hasn't seemed to have worked so far. That's why we need to change the way we think about identity infrastructure-security. We should not forget that we are fighting against human adversaries. The tactics, methods, and approaches they use are changing every day. The products we use do not have such frequent updates, but we can change their ability to execute an attack on the infrastructure by understanding fundamentals and using products, technologies, and workflows to prevent it.

Before we move on to identity-theft prevention mechanisms, let's look into a typical identity infrastructure attack:

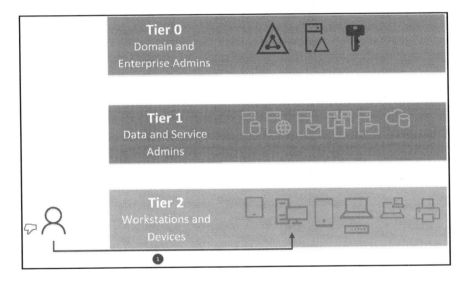

The Microsoft tiered administration model is based on three tiers. All these identity attacks start by gaining some kind of access to the identity infrastructure and then move laterally until they have the keys to the kingdom: the Domain or Enterprise Admin credentials. Then, they have full ownership of the entire identity infrastructure.

As the preceding diagram shows, the first step of identity attacks is to get some kind of access to the system. They do not target the Domain Admin or Enterprise Admin account first. Getting access to a typical user account is much easier than a Domain Admin account. All they need is some kind of beachhead. For that, even now, the most common attack technique is to send out a phishing email. It's typical that someone will still fall for that and click on it. Now, they have some sort of access to your identity infrastructure, and the next step is to start moving laterally to gain more privileges. How many of you have completely eliminated local administrator accounts in your infrastructure? I'm sure the answer will be almost none. Users keep asking for software installations and system-level modifications to their systems frequently, and most of the time, engineers end up assigning local administrator privileges. If the compromised account is a local administrator, it becomes extremely easy to move to the next level.

If not, the attacker will make the compromised system misbehave. Who will come to the rescue? It's the super-powered IT help desk people, of course. In lots of organizations, IT help desk engineers are Domain Admins. If not that, they're at least local administrators to systems. So, once they receive the call about a misbehaving computer, they RDP or log in locally using a privileged account. RDP always sends your credentials in plaintext. If the attacker is running a password-harvesting tool, it's extremely easy to capture the credentials. You may wonder how a compromised *typical user* account can execute such programs. It so happens that Windows OSes do not prevent a user from running any application in their user context. They will not allow a user to change any system-level settings, but they will still allow the user to run scripts or user-level executables:

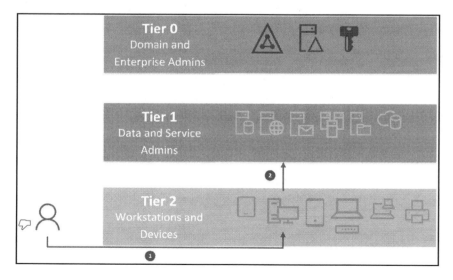

Once an attacker has gained access to some identity in an organization, the next level of privileges to own will be **Tier 1**. This is where the application administrator, data administrator, and SaaS application administrator accounts live. In a typical modern-day infrastructure, we have too many administrators. Primarily, we have domain administrators and enterprise administrators, and then we have local administrators. Different applications running on the infrastructure have their own administrators, such as Exchange administrators, SQL administrators, and SharePoint administrators. Other third-party applications, such as CMS and billing portal, may have their own administrators. If you are using cloud services, SaaS applications have another set of administrators. Are we really aware of the activities happening in these accounts? Mostly, engineers only worry about protecting Domain Admin accounts but, at the same time, forget about the other kinds of administrators in the infrastructure. Some of these administrator roles can cause more damage to a business than a Domain Admin. These applications and services decentralize management in the organization. In order to move laterally with privileges, these attackers only need to log in to a machine or server where the administrators log in. **Local Security Authority Subsystem Service (LSASS)** stores credentials in its memory for active Windows sessions. This avoids the hassle of users entering credentials for each and every service they access. It also stores Kerberos tickets. This allows attackers to perform a pass-the-hash attack and retrieve locally stored credentials. Decentralized management of admin accounts makes this process easier.

 There are features and security best practices that can be used to prevent pass-the-hash attacks in an identity infrastructure. I will explain them in detail in Chapter 15, *Active Directory Security Best Practices*.

Another problem with these types of accounts is once they become service admin accounts, they can eventually become Domain or Enterprise Admin accounts. I have seen engineers create service accounts and, when they can't figure out the exact permissions required for the program, add them to the Domain Admin group as an easy fix. It's not only infrastructure attacks that can expose such credentials. Service admins are attached to the application too, so compromising the application can also expose identities. In such a scenario, it will be easy for attackers to gain the keys to the kingdom:

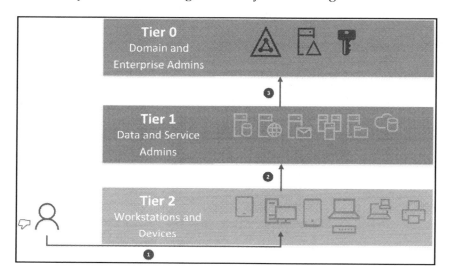

Tier 0 is where the **Domain Admins and Enterprise Admins** operate. This is what the ultimate goal of an identity infrastructure attack is; once they obtain access to **Tier 0**, they own your entire identity infrastructure. The latest reports show that after the initial breach, it takes less than 48 hours to gain **Tier 0** privileges. According to the reports, once attackers gain access, it takes up to 7-8 months at least to identify the breach, because once they have the highest privileges, they can make backdoors, clean up logs, and hide forever if needed. The systems we use always treat administrators as trustworthy people. This is no longer in the modern world. How many times do you check systems logs to see what your Domain Admins are doing? Even though engineers look at logs of other users, rarely do any of them check Domain Admin accounts. The same thing applies to an internal security breach too: as I said, most people are good, but you never know. Many high-profile identity attacks have proven this already.

When I have a discussion with engineers and customers about identity infrastructure-security, these are the common comments I hear:

- "We have too many administrator accounts."
- "We do not know how many administrator accounts we've got."
- "We have fast-changing IT teams, so it's hard to manage permissions."
- "We do not have visibility over administrator account activities."
- "If there is an identity infrastructure breach or attempt, how do we identify it?"

The answer to all these issue is PAM. As I said in the beginning, this is not one product; it's a workflow and a new way of working. The main steps and components of this process are as follows:

1. Apply pass-the-hash prevention features to the existing identity infrastructure (Chapter 15, *Active Directory Security Best Practices*).
2. Install Microsoft Advanced Threat Analytics to monitor the domain controller traffic to identify potential real-time identity infrastructure threats (Chapter 15, *Active Directory Security Best Practices*).
3. Install and configure Microsoft Identity Manager 2016—this product enables us to manage privilege access to an existing AD forest by providing task-based time-limited privilege access. I will explain this in detail later in this chapter with examples.

What is it to do with AD DS 2016?

AD DS 2016 now allows time-based group membership, which makes this whole process possible. A user is added to a group with a TTL value, and once it expires, the user is removed from the group automatically. For example, let's assume your CRM application has administrator rights assigned to the CRMAdmin security group. The users in this group only log in to the system once a month to do some maintenance. But the admin rights for the members in that group remain untouched for the remaining 29 days, 24/7. This provides enough opportunity for attackers to try and gain access to privileged accounts. So if it's possible to grant access privileges for a shorter time period, isn't that more useful? Then we can rest assured that for the majority of the days in a month, the CRM application does not run the risk of being compromised by an account in the CRMAdmin group.

What is the logic behind PAM?

PAM is based on the **just-in-time** (**JIT**) administration concept. Back in 2014, Microsoft released the PowerShell tool kit, which allows **just enough administration** (**JEA**). Let's assume you are running a web server in your infrastructure. As part of the operation, every month you need to collect some logs to make a report. You've already set up a PowerShell script for it. Someone in your team needs to log in to the system and run it. In order to do so, you require administrative privileges. Using JEA, it is possible to assign the required permissions for the user to run only that particular program. In this way, there's no need to add the user to the Domain Admin group. The user will not be allowed to run any other program with the permission assigned as it is, and it will not apply for another computer either. JIT administration is bound in *time*. Users will have the required privileges only when they need it; they will not hold privileged access rights all the time.

PAM operations can be divided into four major steps, as shown in the following diagram:

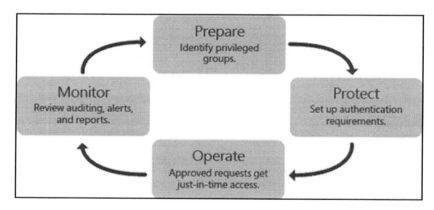

Source: https://docs.microsoft.com/en-gb/microsoft-identity-manager/pam/privileged-identity-management-for-active-directory-domain-services

Let's look at these following four major steps:

- **Prepare**: The first step is to identify the privileged access groups in your existing AD forest and start to remove users from them. You may also need to make certain changes to your application infrastructure to support this setup. For example, if you assign privileged access to user accounts instead of security groups (in applications or services), this will need to change. The next step is to set up equivalent groups in a *bastion forest* without any members.

When setting up MIM, a bastion forest will be used to manage privileged access in an existing AD forest. This is a special forest and cannot be used for other infrastructure operations. This forest runs on a minimum of Windows Server 2012 R2 AD forest functional level. When an identity infrastructure is compromised and attackers gain access to Tier 0, they can hide their activities for months or years. How can we be sure our existing identity infrastructure has not been compromised already? If we implement this on the same forest, it will not achieve its core targets. Also, domain upgrades are painful, requiring time and money. But with a bastion forest, this solution can be applied to your existing identity infrastructure with minimum changes.

- **Protect**: The next step is to set up a workflow for authentication and authorization. Define how a user can request privileged access when required. This can be done using an MIM portal or existing support portal (with integrated MIM REST API). It is possible to set up a system to use **multi-factor authentication (MFA)** during this request process to prevent any unauthorized activity. Also, it's important to define how the requests will be handled. It can be an automatic or manual approval process.

- **Operate**: Once the privileged access request is approved, the user account will be added to the security group in the bastion forest. The group itself has an SID value. In both forests, the group will have the exact same SID value. Therefore, the application or service will not see a difference between the two groups in two different forests. Once the permission is granted, it will only be valid for the time defined by the authorization policy. Once it reaches the time limit, the user account will be removed from the security group automatically.

- **Monitor**: PAM provides visibility over privilege-access requests. On each and every request, events will be recorded, and it is possible to review and also generate reports for audits. This helps fine-tune the process and also identify potential threats.

Let's see how it really works:

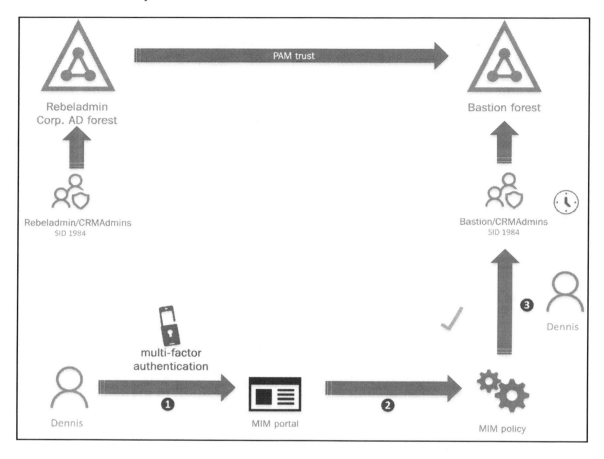

Rebeladmin Corp. uses a CRM system for its operations. The application has the administrator role and **Rebeladmin/CRMAdmins** security group assigned to it. Any member of that group will have administrator privileges to the application. Recently, PAM has been introduced to Rebeladmin Corp. As an engineer, I have identified **Rebeladmin/CRMAdmins** as a privileged group and am going to protect it using PAM. The first step is to remove the members of the **Rebeladmin/CRMAdmins** group. After that, I set up the same group in the bastion forest. It's not only that the name is the same; both groups have the same SID value: **1984**.

User **Dennis** used to be a member of the **Rebeladmin/CRMAdmins** group and was running monthly reports. At the end of a month, he tried to run it and figured he did not have the required permissions. The next step for him was to request the required permission through the MIM portal. According to the policies, as part of the request, the system wants **Dennis** to use MFA. Once Dennis verifies the PIN, the request is logged in the portal. As an administrator, I received the alert about the request, and I log in to the system to review the request. It's a legitimate request, and I approve his access to the system for 8 hours. Then the system automatically adds the user account for Dennis to the **Bastion/CRMAdmins** group. This group has the same SID value as the production group. Therefore, a member of the **Bastion/CRMAdmins** group will be treated as an administrator by the CRM application. This group membership contains the TTL value too. After it passes 8 hours from approval, Dennis's account will automatically be removed from the **Bastion/CRMAdmins** group. In this process, we didn't add any member to the production security group, which is **Rebeladmin/CRMAdmins**. So, the production forest stays untouched and protected.

Here, the most important thing we need to understand is that the legacy approach to identity protection is no longer valid. We are up against human adversaries. Identity is our new perimeter in the infrastructure, and to protect it, we need to understand how our adversaries are doing it and stay a step ahead. PAM with AD DS 2016 is a new approach in the right direction.

Time-based group memberships

In the previous section, I explained PAM features in the new AD DS 2016. Time-based group membership is a part of that broader topic. It allows administrators to assign temporary group membership, which is expressed by a **time-to-live** (TTL) value. This value will be added to the Kerberos ticket. It is also called the **expiring links** feature. When a user is assigned to a temporary group membership, their login Kerberos **ticket-granting ticket** (TGT) lifetime will be equal to the lowest TTL value they have. For example, let's assume you grant temporary group membership to user A to be a member of the Domain Admin group. It is only valid for 60 minutes. But the user logs in 50 minutes after the original assignment and only has 10 minutes left to be a member of the Domain Admin group. Based on this, the domain controller will issue a TGT valid only for 10 minutes to user A.

This feature is not enabled by default. The reason is that to use this feature, the forest function level must be Windows Server 2016. Also, once this feature is enabled, it cannot be disabled.

Let's see how it works in the real world:

1. I have a Windows domain controller installed and it is running with the Windows Server 2016 forest functional level. This can be verified using the following PowerShell command:

   ```
   Get-ADForest | fl Name,ForestMode
   ```

2. Then, we need to enable the expiring links feature. It can be enabled using the following command:

   ```
   Enable-ADOptionalFeature 'Privileged Access Management Feature'
   -Scope ForestOrConfigurationSet -Target rebeladmin.com
   ```

   The domain name rebeladmin.com can be replaced with your FQDN.

3. This is the output you'll get with the previous command:

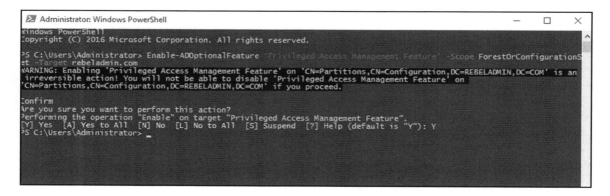

4. I have a user called Adam Curtiss to whom I need to assign Domain Admin group membership for 60 minutes. Take a look at this command:

   ```
   Get-ADGroupMember "Domain Admins"
   ```

5. It lists the current members of the Domain Admin group:

6. The next step is to add Adam Curtiss to the Domain Admin group for 60 minutes:

```
Add-ADGroupMember -Identity 'Domain Admins' -Members 'acurtiss'
-MemberTimeToLive (New-TimeSpan -Minutes 60)
```

7. Once it has run, we can verify the remaining TTL value for the group membership using the following command:

```
Get-ADGroup 'Domain Admins' -Property member
-ShowMemberTimeToLive
```

8. Once I log in as the user and list the Kerberos ticket, it shows the renew time as less than 60 minutes as I've logged in after a few minutes of being granted permission:

```
Administrator: Windows PowerShell

Windows PowerShell
Copyright (C) 2016 Microsoft Corporation. All rights reserved.

PS C:\Windows\system32> klist

Current LogonId is 0:0x5d58c0

Cached Tickets: (1)

#0>     Client: acurtiss @ REBELADMIN.COM
        Server: krbtgt/REBELADMIN.COM @ REBELADMIN.COM
        KerbTicket Encryption Type: AES-256-CTS-HMAC-SHA1-96
        Ticket Flags 0x40e10000 -> forwardable renewable initial pre_authent name_canonicalize
        Start Time: 1/10/2017 21:45:03 (local)
        End Time:   1/10/2017 22:38:28 (local)
        Renew Time: 1/10/2017 22:38:28 (local)
        Session Key Type: AES-256-CTS-HMAC-SHA1-96
        Cache Flags: 0x1 -> PRIMARY
        Kdc Called: REBEL-PDC-01
```

Once the TGT renewal period is crossed, the user will no longer be a member of the Domain Admin group.

Microsoft Passport

The most common way of protecting access to a system or resources is to introduce authentication and authorization processes. This is exactly what AD does as well. When a user logs in to a domain-joined device, AD first authenticates the user to see whether they're the user they claim to be. Once authentication is successful, it then checks what the user is allowed to do (authorization). To do that, we use usernames and passwords. This is what all identity infrastructure attackers are after. They need some kind of username and password to get into the system. Passwords are a rather weak authentication method. They are breakable, and it's just a matter of time and methods used. As a solution, organizations are tightening password policies, but when they are forcibly made complex, more and more people start to write down. I have seen a few people who just use sticky notes and stick them on the monitor. So, if it's a weak authentication method, what is the solution?

With Windows 10, Microsoft introduced its new biometric sign-in system. Windows Hello allows us to use face, fingerprint, or PIN for authentication. But this does not allow the user to use any service or apps. It is an additional layer of security to allow the device to identify its correct user. After the system identifies its legitimate user, the user still needs to authenticate to be allowed access to resources. Microsoft Passport provides strong two-factor authentication instead of passwords. The user needs a specific device and biometric authentication/PIN to be allowed access.

In the process of Microsoft Passport setup, it will generate a new public-private key pair and store a private key in the device's **Trusted Platform Module (TPM)**. If the device doesn't have TPM it will save in software. The private key will stay on the device all the time. The public key can be stored in AD (on-premises) or Azure AD (cloud). AD DS 2016 is supporting Microsoft Passport configuration.

In the process of authentication using Microsoft Passport, first the user needs to authenticate to the device using Hello. Then the user needs to prove their identity using MFA, smart cards, or gesture. This information will be passed to AD. Then the device generates a unique key, attests the key, isolates the public key part, and sends it to AD to register it. Once AD DS registers the public key, it asks the device to log in using the private key. Once the device successfully logs in with the private key, AD DS validates it and generates the authentication token. This token will allow the user and the device to use resources.

This feature eliminates the traditional method of using a username and password and provides a robust, secure, future-proof way of authentication.

Active Directory Federation Services improvements

Active Directory Federation Services (AD FS) allows the sharing of identities among trusted business partners (federated) with minimum identity infrastructure changes. AD FS 2016 added many new features to protect federated environments with rising identity infrastructure threats. In Chapter 13, *Active Directory Federation Services*, I will explain AD FS in detail. Right now, I am going to summarize the shiny new features it has.

In the previous section about Microsoft Passport, I explained why the traditional username/password method is no longer an option against modern identity threats. This is applicable to federated environments as well. Most federated environments use MFA as another layer of security, but we still use usernames and passwords for the initial authentication process. AD FS 2016 supports three new methods to authenticate without usernames and passwords.

Microsoft Azure provides Azure MFA as a service to protect cloud workloads from unauthorized access. If on-premises AD is federated with Azure AD, it can also be used to protect on-premises workloads. AD FS 2016 supports Azure MFA integration. If you need to set up AD FS 2012 R2 and integrate with Azure MFA, you need an on-premise MFA server. With AD FS 2016, no additional components are required as it comes with an in-built Azure MFA adapter, which makes it seamless. If Azure MFA is configured as primary authentication, the user needs to provide a username and OTP from Azure Authenticator for authentication.

AD FS 2016 also supports passwordless access from compliant devices. This is combined with conditional access policies, which is another big feature of AD FS 2016. Azure conditional access policies can be used with devices registered with Azure AD or Intune (an enterprise mobility suite). AD FS 2016 allows us to use the same conditional policies to manage access to on-premise resources. If the devices are not managed or compliant, we can force MFA for access using policies.

AD FS 2016 also supports access using Microsoft Hello and Microsoft Passport. Using these new authentication methods, users can access AD FS protected workloads from an intranet or extranet.

Some organizations use non-Microsoft directory services for operations. AD FS 2016 now supports LDAP v3-based directories. This allows us to federate identities between AD and non-AD environments. This also allows corporations to federate their identities with Azure services even if they use third-party directory services.

In the previous version of AD FS, if you needed to upgrade it to the latest version, you needed to build a separate AD FS farm and then export/import the configuration. But with AD FS 2016, it's no longer needed. You can introduce an AD FS 2016 server to an existing AD FS 2012 R2 farm. Then, it will operate on the AD FS 2012 R2 level. Once the last AD FS 2012 R2 server is removed from the farm, the farm's functional level can be raised to AD FS 2016.

In previous AD FS versions, we only had limited customization options for the login pages. With AD FS 2016, we are able to change text, images, logos, and themes to provide a more personalized GUI experience for organizations.

The rest of the AD FS operational enhancements will be explained in detail in Chapter 13, *Active Directory Federation Services*.

Time sync improvements

Time accuracy is important for AD infrastructures to maintain Kerberos authentication between users and domain controllers. Currently, the time accuracy between two parties should be less than 5 minutes. In an AD environment, domain members sync time with domain controllers (PDC or domain controller in the root forest or a domain controller with the **good time server** (**GTIMESERV**) flag) to maintain accurate time across the environment.

But sometimes, this doesn't work as expected. Virtual servers sync time with their hosts, which can cause accuracy issues. Depending on the network topology, the reply packets for time requests can take longer to reach the requester. This also can cause accuracy issues between the DC and client. Mobile devices and laptops may not connect with the domain very often, which can also lead to time accuracy issues.

Time accuracy impacts an organization's business and operations in different ways:

- AD replications between domain controllers is the primary requirement of a healthy AD infrastructure. Inaccurate time syncs create replication issues.
- Credit card processing requires 1-second accuracy, according to industry standards.
- There are government regulations enforced for stock trades (50 microseconds accuracy from FINRA).
- It can result in inaccurate data for reports, log analytics and threat analysis, and troubleshooting in infrastructures.
- It impacts distributed systems such as clusters, SQL farms, and database farms.

With Windows Server 2016, Microsoft made several improvements to maintain accurate time synchronization across infrastructures. Its improved algorithms will mitigate the impact of NTP data accuracy, resulting in network congestion and network latency. It also uses an improved API for accurate time references. With these improvements, it can provide 1 microsecond time accuracy.

The Hyper-V 2016 time sync service has also improved to provide accurate time for virtualized environments. It will provide the initial accurate time on VM start and then interrupt with corrections for w32time samples. This allows us to have a time accuracy between 10-15 microseconds.

With Windows Server 2016, new performance monitor counters have also been implemented to monitor and troubleshoot time-accuracy issues in infrastructures.

Summary

In this chapter, we looked at the new features and enhancements that come with AD DS 2016. One of the biggest improvements was Microsoft's new approach toward privilege access management. This is not just a feature that can be enabled via AD DS and is just part of the border solution. It helps protect identity infrastructures from adversaries as traditional techniques and technologies are no longer valid with rising threats. We also saw the new types of advanced authentication methods allowed by AD DS. Typical username/password combinations are the weaker option with current infrastructure-security challenges. AD FS 2016 also has additional security enhancements to protect identities in a federated environment. Last but not least, we saw the improvements made to time synchronization to maintain time accuracy across the AD domain.

In the next chapter, we are going to look into designing AD infrastructures. The correct design is key for a productive, highly available, and secure identity infrastructure.

3
Designing Active Directory Infrastructure

The Active Directory deployment process in the infrastructure has been made easy over the years. Even if you do not have advanced knowledge of Active Directory, with a few wizards, you can install AD DS on a server. I've written articles on my blog with step-by-step guides on how to install each and every version of Active Directory, and lots of people still follow those to do the installations. But will a clean installation of Active Directory in your environment make it a good design too? Let's figure it out.

In this chapter, we will cover the following topics:

- Designing a forest structure
- Designing a domain structure
- Designing an OU structure
- Designing the physical topology of Active Directory
- Global catalog server placement

What makes a good system?

When I was 15 years old, my dad bought me my first bicycle. It was brand new and I jumped on it and cycled round the house fast a few times before I crashed into my grandmother—even though it was brand new, the brakes didn't work properly. Luckily, she wasn't hurt. Then my dad came to me and said even if it was brand new, it hadn't been *tuned* yet. The same day, my dad took the bike to a shop. The mechanics in there removed the parts of the cycle one by one and then started to fit them in again after applying oil and grease. While they were doing this, they asked questions about what kind of seat I would like and whether I needed different lights, different pedals, and so on. Based on my answers, some parts were added and some parts were fine-tuned. In this way, from a brand-new bicycle, they made me a bicycle that was fit for my unique requirements. I liked it even before they'd tuned it, but after, I liked it more. For a few years, I maintained it properly: I washed it, oiled it, changed parts when needed, and upgraded as new things came in. When I went to high school, I had to leave it at home, so I didn't have time to take care of it. Within a few years, it wasn't usable at all. There are a few things I want to emphasize here. A perfect product does not make for a perfect solution. In this story, the bike was much better when it was tuned. Also, it worked as intended when I maintained it properly. When I couldn't maintain it properly, after a while, it was unusable. This applies to any system we use.

What makes a good system?

- A good design: fundamentals need to be strong
- Correct implementation according to plan
- Monitoring the system to find possible issues
- Maintaining the system by fixing issues and performing upgrades as required

This theory applies to an Active Directory infrastructure as well. Design is the key requirement for any identity infrastructure. As engineers, we are rarely assigned to build an identity infrastructure from scratch. We're usually assigned to expand or maintain an existing infrastructure. But it's important to know the foundation of the design; then, even if it has to be extended or changed, you know whether that is possible or not. For example, let's consider a house. I have a two-bedroom, one-storey house. If I need to add more space, I can only add it on the same level. I cannot go for two storeys as my house's foundations are meant to hold only one storey. I know for a fact you can't just build two storeys—you need a foundation that will support that weight. This is a rule, and it's not going to change. Therefore, knowing the fundamentals allows us to make the right decision at the right time.

When I work on Active Directory projects, one of the common questions I get from customers is "Do you think our design is correct?" On most occasions, I can't give a yes or no answer. It will be a yes *and* no answer. The reason is that it may not be valid for the current business with respects to the requirements of the organization, but it was a valid design for the same organization some time ago. If I ask their IT managers or engineers questions such as "Why did you put this domain controller here?" or "Why did you configure this domain controller like this?", most of the time, they have a valid reason to justify it. It is difficult to draw the line between the right and wrong design unless the design's fundamentals are right or wrong.

If it's not a fresh design, there are occasions on which you may need to revise or redesign the existing Active Directory topology.

New business requirements

Business goals are targets that change from time to time. When you start designing the Active Directory infrastructure for an organization from the ground up, if management can confirm what it will become in 20 years' time, that's perfect. Then, you know what to do. But this only happens in a perfect world. When organizational changes happen, most of the time, it affects the identity infrastructure too. It can be a change such as introducing a new department, hiring more people, a new business acquisition, or business merges. Some of these changes may be easy to implement, and some may require larger organization-wide changes. This usually happens when you need to extend the security boundaries of the identity infrastructure. Your Active Directory forest is your security boundary for the identity infrastructure. If your requirement is beyond that, it always involves a design change. As an example, if Rebeladmin Corp. merges with My-Learning Inc., the management of Rebeladmin Corp. needs centralized IT administration and sharing of resources between the two organizations. Both organizations maintain their own Active Directory forests. So definitely, the My-Learning Inc. forest is beyond the Rebeladmin Corp. identity infrastructure security boundary. In order to merge them, we need to create a forest trust or domain trust relationship between the two infrastructures. With these changes, the Rebeladmin Corp. identity infrastructure will have new security boundaries. Your operations and security also change accordingly.

Correcting legacy design mistakes

These kinds of situations are pricier for organizations. Most of the time, they end up with restructuring domain infrastructures. A year ago, I was talking to a company about a domain restructure. It's a multimillion dollar trading company with branches across the world. So, the problem was that when they designed the AD infrastructure a long time ago, they used a single-label domain name as the primary domain. SLDs are domain names that do not have DNS suffixes such as `.com`, `.org`, or `.net`. After some time, they realized the limitations of SLDs and didn't fix them as that required some *administrative* changes. No one wanted to take the responsibility, either. The company kept growing, and instead of fixing the fundamental problem, they kept introducing new forests and new domains. At the end, it became almost unmanageable, with multiple domains and forests, which doesn't make sense. Therefore, they had no option other than redesigning the whole Active Directory structure as the organization had decided to move a majority of workloads to Azure Cloud. But it was a very costly and painful change. If you can snip off the weeds growing in your garden with your hands, do it right away; don't wait until you have to use a saw.

Gathering business data

Before starting to figure out how many forests, domains, and domain controllers to create, we need to gather some critical data to help us make an accurate design that agrees with the core business requirements.

Understanding the organizational structure correctly is vital to designing an identity infrastructure. An organizational chart is a good place to start. It will give you an idea of who you need to ask questions of in order to collect the specific data that will help in your design. For example, if you need to know what your software development department requires in directory services, the best person to ask will be the technical lead or architect of the team. They will be able to give you the exact answer you are looking for. If you ask the same question to the managing director, the answer may not be that accurate. So before you seek the answers to your questions, you need to find the correct source.

Defining security boundaries

The next step in the process is to define the security boundaries. If you purchase empty land to build a house, what will be the first thing you do? You need to clearly identify the plot's boundaries. Your building/development can't go beyond it. What kind of information do we need to gather in order to identify an identity infrastructure's boundaries? Understanding business operations is vital for this. For example, Rebeladmin Corp. owns a group of companies. The operations of each business are completely different. One is a hosting company and the other one is an IT training institute. They also have a pharmaceutical company. Operations and business requirements are different for each of those companies. In such scenarios, multiple forests will be ideal as none of the companies depend on each other's resources for its operations. Sometimes, even if it's a single company, some business units may need logical separation at least from the directory service point of view. For example, Rebeladmin Corp. has a research and development department. Engineers in that department keep testing new software and services, and most of them are Active Directory-integrated. Their security requirements rapidly change as well. They need to test different group policies for testing purposes. If it's the same Active Directory forest, the activities of these tests will impact the entire directory. Therefore, the best option will be to isolate their activity to a separate forest.

Identifying the physical computer network structure

Once we identify the organizational structure and security boundaries, the next thing is to identify the physical computer network structure. It's important to identify how many branch networks there are, how they are connected together, and what kind of bandwidth there is between sites. This information helps design the domain structure. Domains help partition the directory and define the replication boundaries for efficiency. Network diagrams are the best place to start. Also, it's important to identify potential issues and bottlenecks between physically separated networks. In network diagrams, it may look nice with links connected between sites, but if these connections have reliability and bandwidth issues, that's also going to impact your design. Gather uptime bandwidth utilization reports for these links at least for 3 months and review them. In Chapter 1, *Active Directory Fundamentals*, I explained **read-only domain controllers** (RODC). These have been used on branch networks when they cannot guarantee security and a reliable connection. Even the branch offices connected together and linked is not reliable, or if the links have already been fully utilized, we need to fix that bottleneck first or place RODC instead of the fully blown domain controller. Gathering this information will help you make that call.

It is also important to gather information about the company road map and the company products road maps, as that will also impact the identity infrastructure design. For example, if a company is in the process of business acquisition or merging in the next 6 months, your design should be future-proof to address that requirement to another company. In the same way, if the company is going to downsize or sell the product they developed in another company, that's also going to impact the design. So, it's best to discuss this with the relevant people and get a better understanding of road maps. As I mentioned earlier, identity infrastructure changes are costly and involve a lot of work. By understanding the company's future, you will prevent this kind of awkward situation.

The company IT administration model is also important for identity infrastructure design. It can be either centralized or decentralized. Rebeladmin Corp. has a group of companies. Each of these companies has its own IT department. So, each company's IT teams are responsible for their own infrastructures. In this case, maintaining separate forests is helping to divide the responsibilities for IT operations. Also, some companies may outsource their IT operations to a third-party company. This will change the security requirements in the identity infrastructure from in-house IT operations. Some of the workloads may need to be isolated from them due to data protection and businesses, legal requirements. The design will need to match these types of IT operation requirements.

Businesses are subject to specific government regulations. For example, banks and hedge funds need to follow specific rules in their operations to protect the customer data and the trade data. Businesses that process credit cards need to be PCI-compliant and follow specific regulations. Also, if organization operations are aligned with ISO standards, it's another set of rules and best practices to follow. If an organization has branch offices in different countries, the government rules and regulations applied to those will be different from the rules applied to the headquarters. It is important to gather this data as it can also make an impact on the design.

Modern identity infrastructure requirements are complicated. Some organizations have already extended their identity infrastructures to the cloud. Some organizations have been fully moved to Azure Active Directory managed domains. Most application vendors have moved their products to the public cloud. So, businesses need to collaborate with technology changes happening around them. Some products and services are not going to continue anymore as in-house services and customers need to move to the cloud version. The identity infrastructure design should be future-proof as far as possible. Therefore, it's important to research and evaluate new technologies and services that can improve the organization's identity infrastructure and adopt them to the design as required.

In any project, the implementation phase is relatively easy. The design and planning process is complicated and time-consuming. But it is vital for business satisfaction. Once you collect data as described, go through it a few times and understand it properly. If you have doubts, go and gather more data to clear it. When Johnathan Ive designed Apple Mac, do you think he designed it in one go? I am sure he must have used an eraser. But in the end, everyone loved the Apple designs. No one bothered about how hard it was or how much time he spent. The end result was the ultimate success. Therefore, don't be afraid to use an eraser in the design phase.

Designing the forest structure

The Active Directory design starts with designing the forest structure. The Active Directory forest is the security boundary for the identity infrastructure. When you deploy the first domain controller in your infrastructure, it creates a forest as well. So, every Active Directory infrastructure has at least one forest.

There are two types of forest implementations:

- Single forest
- Multiple forest

Single forest

Single forest deployment is the default deployment mode. Most business models fit into the single forest model. Complexity and cost of implementation are low in this model. One of the main things you need to consider in this mode is replication. Domains are used to partition the directory and manage the replication. But forest-wide data, such as schemas, still needs to be replicated across all domains. If replication involves with branch offices, you need to make sure forest-wide replications are handled properly.

Multiple forest

The multiple forest model is a complex implementation process. The cost of implementation is also higher as it requires additional resources (hardware, software, and maintenance). There are several reasons why you might need the multiple forest model:

- **Business operations isolations**: Businesses can have groups of companies or departments that are required to operate independently. Their dependence on other departments and partner companies may be minimum. In such scenarios, it is good to create a separate forest for them.

- **Rapid changes in directory services**: Business may have some departments or business units that involve rapid directory changes. For example, R&D, DevOps test environments, and software development departments may require AD schema changes, Active Directory integrations, group policy changes to test or develop the products and services. It is best to keep them in a separate forest in order to minimize the impact on the entire identity infrastructure.

- **IT operation mode**: Some organizations have decentralized IT operations. Groups of companies are an example for this. Each company may have its own IT staff and be required to operate independently. A separate forest will define the security and operation boundary for each of those companies.

- **Resource isolation**: This is an ideal solution for service providers or organizations with multiple separate forests that like to share resources. For example, Rebeladmin Corp. has a group of companies with separate AD forests. Each company has its own IT department. But the mother company still likes to share some common systems among all the companies, such as payroll, email, CMS. Creating a separate forest for these resources will allow the organization to manage them in an efficient, secure way. Other forests can have the forest trust to the resource forest and use the systems hosted in there. Service providers can create resource forests to isolate their products and services.

- **Legal requirements**: Businesses are bound to government rules and regulations. Also, they may have business agreements with partners and merged companies. Based on that, they may be required to create a separate forest to isolate data, services, and identities.

- **Business acquisitions or divestiture**: Business acquisitions or divestiture will require extended security boundaries or isolated resources and identities. The best way to do that will be to use the multiple forest model. If there is a requirement to share data or resources between forests, the cross-forest trust can be established.

Creating the forest structure

Once the forest mode is decided, the next step is to create the forest structure. In order to do that, we need to decide whether we are going to achieve autonomy or isolation.

Autonomy

Autonomy gives independent control over resources. The Active Directory environment that is focused on autonomy will help administrators manage the resources independently, but there will be more privileged administrators who can manage the resources and privileges of other administrators.

There are two types of autonomy:

- **Service autonomy**: This will provide privileges to an individual or a group of administrators to control the service level of AD DS fully or partially. For example, it will allow administrators to add or remove domain controllers, modify Active Directory schema, and modify DNS without the forest owner.
- **Data autonomy**: This will provide privileges to an individual or a group of administrators to control data stored in Active Directory or domain-joined computers. This also allows you to perform any administrative task regarding data without approval from a higher, privileged account. This autonomy will not prevent forest service administrators from accessing the data.

Isolation

Isolation gives independent and privileged control over the resources. Administrators can control resources independently and no other accounts can take control.

There are two types of isolations:

- **Service isolation**: This will prevent any other control or interference with AD DS other than the administrators defined in it. In other words, it will provide full control over identity infrastructure. Service isolations happen mainly due to operations or legal requirements. As an example, Rebeladmin Corp. has three different services that are built in-house. Each service has its own customer base. Operations in one product should not impact others. Service isolation will allow the organization to isolate the operation for each service.

- **Data isolation**: This will provide ownership of the data that is stored in Active Directory or domain-joined computers to individuals or groups of administrators. However, data administrators cannot prevent the service administrator from accessing the resource they control. In order to isolate a subset of data completely, they will need to create a separate forest.

The number of forests needed for an infrastructure depends on the autonomy or isolation requirements.

Selecting forest design models

Once the forest structure and the number of forests are decided, the next step is to select forest design models. There are three forest design models.

Organizational forest model

In an organizational forest model, resources, data, and identities will stay on separate forests and will be managed independently. This model can be used to provide service autonomy, service isolation, or data isolation:

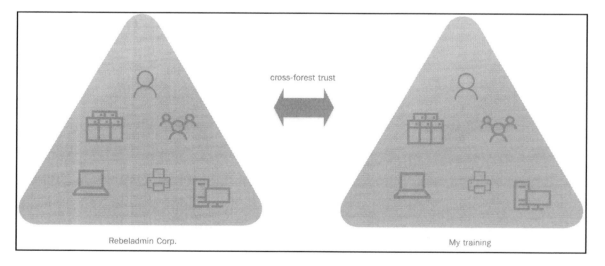

In the preceding example, **Rebeladmin Corp.** and **My training** are two companies under the same mother company. Due to the operation requirements, it needs service isolation. In order to do that, engineers have created two separate forests. Each company has its own IT department and manages resources and identities independently. If resources need to be shared between two forests, that can be done via **cross-forest trust**.

Resource forest model

In a resource forest model, a separate forest is used for resources. A resource forest does not contain any user accounts; rather, it contains service accounts and resource forest administration accounts. All the identities for the organization will be in a separate forest. The cross-forest trust created between forests and users for an organization forest can access resources in the resource forest without additional authentication. Resource forest models provide service isolation:

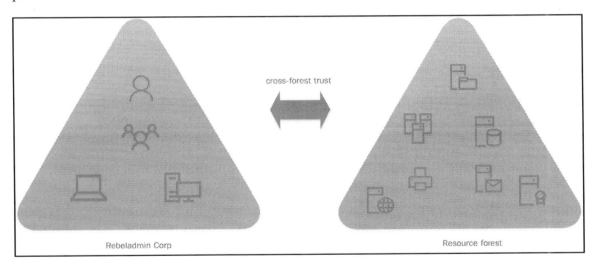

In the preceding example, **Rebeladmin Corp** wanted to isolate services into **Resource forest** as it's about to merge with another IT-service-providing company in the next 6 months. Once the merge is completed, the other company can use the resource forest to access the services and resources as well. It will only need the cross-forest trust to be established between the company forest and **Resource forest**.

Restricted access forest model

In the restricted access forest model, a separate forest is created to isolate identities, and data must be separated from the other organization's data and identities. There is no trust created between the two forests, so identities in one forest will not be able to access the resources in another. To access the resources in each forest, we need to have separate user accounts. The **Restricted access forest** model provides data isolation:

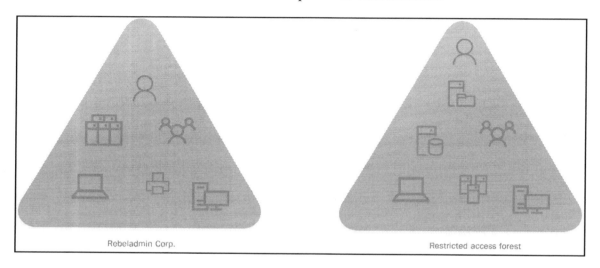

In the preceding example, **Rebeladmin Corp.** is involved with a corporate divestiture process. For some of the assets, data and identities need to be isolated completely there. In order to do that, the company introduced **Restricted access forest**.

Once the forest structure, the number of forests, and the design model are finalized, the next step will be to design the domain structure.

Designing the domain structure

Every AD DS forest has at least one domain. When you set up your first domain forest, it is also set up as a default domain. There are a few reasons why you will need to consider having multiple domains in a forest:

- **Smaller administrative boundaries**: Active Directory is capable of managing nearly 2 billion objects. Having a large directory creates administrative nightmares. Imagine managing a large herd of sheep. As it grows, shepherds need to put in more and more effort to manage it. Predators will also take advantage of it, and sometimes, shepherds may not notice missing sheep as they are too busy managing the herd. Instead of managing a large number of sheep together, isn't it easy if each shepherd manages smaller herds? Domains will help set smaller administrative boundaries and smaller management targets. This will help manage organization resources efficiently.

- **Replication**: Every domain in the Active Directory forest shares the same schema. It needs to be replicated to all the domain controllers. But each domain has its own domain partition, which will only need to be replicated to the domain controllers inside the domain. This allows you to control the replication within the Active Directory forest. Rebeladmin Corp. has branches in different countries. These branches are connected together with leased lines. Each of these branches also has domain controllers set up. So, if it's a single-forest-single-domain setup, each and every domain controller will need to be replicated with each other. Leased lines between countries are not cheap, and they're not always high-speed links. The same bandwidth is also used for the other company operations. If we create different domains to represent each branch office, it will eliminate unnecessary replications as the domain partition only needs to be replicated within domain boundaries.

- **Security**: In the previous section, we talked about data and service isolations based on forests. These are due to operational and legal requirements in the business. Domains help isolate resources and objects based on the security requirements within the forest. My-Learning Inc. is an IT training company. It has mainly two types of students. Some are academic students who are studying the HND program, and others are students who are taking professional exams. Both groups have separate labs, software, and resource access. Both groups have their own data, resources, and identity security requirements. Some of these requirements are only achievable via domain-wide security settings. Therefore, having two separate domains will allow them to apply different security standards without interaction.

There are two models we can use for domains' structure design.

Single domain model

A single domain model contains the single-domain-single-forest structure. It is easier to administer and has a lower cost to implement. When we set up the Active Directory infrastructure the first time, it will be in this single domain model by default. The domain will become the root domain for the forest by default and all the objects will be stored in there:

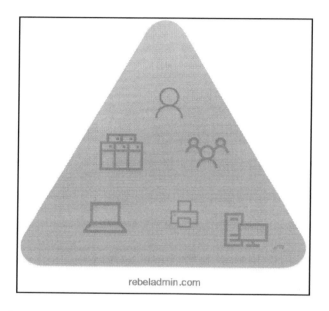

In this mode, all the directory data will need to be replicated to all the available domain controllers. It doesn't matter even if it's in a different geographical location. The user can use any available domain controller to authenticate into any system or resources. All domain controllers in the domain can act as global catalog servers. The downside of this model will be administrative overhead and the less-controlled replication traffic.

Regional domain model

In the regional model, the AD DS forest will contain the forest root domain and multiple domains that are connected via **wide area networks (WANs)**. This is mainly applicable to branch offices and sub-companies located in different geographical locations:

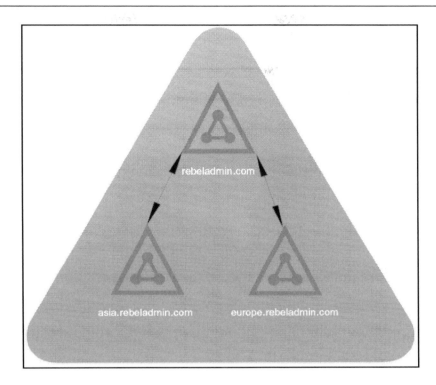

This model is complex to implement compared to the single domain model and will require additional hardware and resources. In this model, the domain partition data will be replicated only to the domain controllers inside the domain, and it will allow you to reduce the replication traffic flow between WAN links. This model will also help isolate the security requirements. Note that this will not provide data or service isolation. If it's the requirement, it needs to be done on the forest level.

The number of domains

After deciding on the domain structure model, the next step is to identify the number of domains required. The number of domains depends on the number of objects that will be managed, the number of geographical locations, administrative requirements, and the bandwidth of links.

In the following table, I have listed down the number of users that can be maintained in a domain against the replication bandwidth:

Bandwidth	If 1% of bandwidth is allowed for replication	If 10% of bandwidth is allowed for replication
128kbps	25,000	100,000
256kbps	50,000	100,000
512kbps	80,000	100,000
T1	100,000	100,000

Bandwidth between locations is not the only reason for multiple domains. Administrative requirements and security requirements are also valid reasons for it.

When the number of domains increases, the complexity, cost of implementation and maintenance, and the management of diverse security settings increase as well. Therefore, decide the number of domains in a meaningful manner. I have seen people create domains in places where they can achieve the same thing using an OU or some different group policies.

Deciding domain names

Every domain in the forest needs to have a unique name. There are mainly two types of names. NetBIOS names are used for Windows (SMB)-based sharing and messaging. DNS names are able to be resolved by the internet and different systems. When promoting the domain, it asks for the DNS name as well as the NetBIOS name.

When considering the naming, keep the following points in mind:

- Do not use names that you do not legally own; if it's a fully qualified domain name, make sure you have authority over it with the internet registrar.
- Do not use numbers and special characters that can easily confuse users.
- Do not use names associated with products and operating systems, for example, NT and Windows.
- Avoid using longer domain names or suffixes.
- Be careful with the spellings. I have seen people who deployed the entire domain structure and then realized they made a mistake with the spelling.

Once the domain name is assigned, it will not be able to be changed without redeployment, domain rename process, or domain migration. When planning names for the domain tree, try to define a standard. For example, it can be based on a continent, country, product, or service name. You can use the forest root domain name as a prefix, but it is not a must.

Forest root domain

The first domain set up in the forest becomes the forest root domain. This root domain contains two important privileged groups, which are Enterprise Admins and Schema Admins. Members of these security groups can add/remove domains and modify the Active Directory schema.

In the multiple domain model, there are two types to define the forest root domain:

- **Dedicated forest root domain**: A separate domain to operate as the forest root domain. It will not contain any regular user accounts, objects, or resources. It will contain only the service administrator accounts. All other domains in the forest will be child domains for this root domain. In a single domain environment, domain administrators can add themselves to the Enterprise Admin or the Schema admin group. But when you have a separate root domain, child domain administrators will not be able to add them to these privileged groups without doing that from the forest root domain level. The dedicated forest root domain should not share a geographical naming convention, and it should stand with a separate name from the rest of the child domains. For example, `rebeladmin.com` can be a root domain name instead of `Europe.rebeladmin.com`.
- **Regional forest root domain**: If you're not going to use a separate forest domain, the regional domain can also be selected as the forest root domain. It will be the parent domain for all other regional domain controllers. For example, `HQ.rebeladmin.com` can be the regional root domain. This domain can contain regular user accounts, groups, and resources.

By now, we have all the required information to design the domain structure. The next step will be to determine domain and forest functional levels.

Deciding domain and forest functional levels

Once the domain and forest designs are ready, the next step is to decide the forest and domain functional levels. Forest and domain functional levels define the AD DS features that can be used in the identity infrastructure. You cannot have AD DS 2016 features if your organization level is running on Windows Server 2012 domain and forest functional levels. When you add the domain controller to the existing forest or domain, it will automatically match the existing forest and domain functional level.

There are a few things you need to consider when deciding the forest and domain functional levels:

- **Existing domain controllers**: It is always good to run the latest and greatest functional levels, but it is not always practical. If you are extending the existing identity infrastructure, the lowest domain controller (the operating system) in the domain decides the maximum forest and domain functional you can have without an upgrade. As an example, in your domain, if you are running a Windows Server 2008 domain controller, the maximum forest and domain functional level you can have is Windows Server 2008. It will not prevent you from adding a domain controller to Windows Server 2016, but until you decommission the Windows Server 2008 domain controller, it is not possible to upgrade forest and domain functional levels.
- **Application requirements**: Sometimes, legacy applications support only certain domain and forest functional levels. This happened to me on several occasions when planning domain upgrades for customers. Most of the time, it happens when companies have custom-made applications. Therefore, check with application vendors whether they're going to be compatible and supported before deciding the forest and domain functional levels.

Once you define the forest and domain functional levels, the lower domain controller version will not be able to be introduced to the system. If you are running the Windows Server 2016 domain and forest functional levels, you cannot introduce the Windows Server 2012 R2 domain controller to the same forest.

 Before AD DS 2012 R2, if the domain and forest functional levels are raised, it will not be able to be downgraded again. After AD DS 2012 R2, you can downgrade forest and domain functional levels if required.

In order to find the current domain and forest functional levels, you can run the following commands from any domain controller:

To find the domain functional level, run the following command:

```
Get-ADDomain | fl Name,DomainMode
```

To find the forest functional level, run the following command:

```
Get-ADForest | fl Name,ForestMode
```

```
Administrator: Windows PowerShell
Windows PowerShell
Copyright (C) 2016 Microsoft Corporation. All rights reserved.

PS C:\Users\Administrator> Get-ADDomain | fl Name,DomainMode


Name       : REBELADMIN
DomainMode : Windows2016Domain


PS C:\Users\Administrator> Get-ADForest | fl Name,ForestMode


Name       : REBELADMIN.COM
ForestMode : Windows2016Forest


PS C:\Users\Administrator> _
```

Designing the OU structure

In Active Directory, there are different types of objects, such as user accounts, groups, and devices. It is important to manage them effectively. Organizational units can group objects that have similar administrative and security requirements within the domain. Organizational units are used to delegate the administration of objects and apply group policies.

OU design changes are less complex compared to domain- and forest-level structure changes. As OUs are bound to group policies, when you change the structure, you need to make sure the correct group policies are still applied. When you move objects from one OU to another, object will inherit the security settings and group polices that are applied to the destination OU. It will not move any settings it has in the source OU level.

The forest owner can delegate permission to users to become OU administrators. OU administrators can manage objects and manage policies within the OU. They can also create child OUs and delegate permissions to another user/users to manage child OU objects. OU administrators will not have control over the directory services operations, and it is another way of managing privilege access within the identity infrastructure.

There are two types of organization units:

- **Account OU**: Account OU contains the user, group, and computer objects. It is the forest owner's responsibility to create the OU structure and delegate the administration over the objects.
- **Resource OU**: Resource OU contains resources and user accounts which used to manage resources. The forest owner must create the OU structure and delegate permissions as required.

It is important to follow up some standards when defining the OU tree. These standards can be specific for the organization requirements. In the following list, I have mentioned a few methods that can be used to organize an OU tree:

- **Based on the organization structure**: The OU tree can match the same organization structure; this will be easy to follow in most cases, but it will make the boundaries larger.
- **Based on geographical locations**: This method can be used to build the OU structure if the organization has branch offices. It can further be broken down using departments or teams existing in each branch office.
- **Based on departments**: This is the most commonly used method to create the OU structure. It can be further categorized based on geographical location. For example, sales OU can have child OUs to represent branch offices such as Dallas, London, and Toronto.

- **Based on security requirements**: Group policies can be used to apply security policies and settings to objects in the OU. Based on the same objective, we can build the OU structure. For example, tier-1 support engineers in the IT team who will have a different set of security polices from tier-3 engineers. To accommodate that, we can create a tier-1 OU and a tier-3 OU. This method is suitable for small business.
- **Based on the resource type**: The OU tree can be structured based on server roles, applications, and device types.

It is possible to use a mixture of all of these methods as well. There is no limit to the number of child OUs you can create, but for administration and manageability, Microsoft recommends that you not have more than 10 levels.

Once you finalize the OU structure, make sure that you document it properly. Also, provide guidelines to follow the method you used to structure it. This will help other engineers follow the same practice. When I work on the projects, I notice that some OU structures do not make any sense at all, as over time, different engineers use their own methods to structure the OUs. Organizations should have a specific standard to follow.

Designing the physical topology of Active Directory

In the previous sections of this chapter, I explained how we can design the Active Directory logical topology. The next step is to design the physical topology of the Active Directory design.

Physical or virtual domain controllers

Most of the workloads we have in modern infrastructures are virtualized. Domain controllers can also be virtualized, but based on the virtualization vendor, the best practices will be different. Therefore, if you plan to deploy virtual domain controllers, refer to your software vendor and find out what the recommendations for virtual domain controllers are. The guidelines in this section will focus on the Microsoft Hyper-V virtualization platform.

It is not recommended that you use only virtual domain controllers. In fact, it is recommended that you balance it between physical and virtual domain controllers for availability and integrity. This is especially applicable if virtual domain controllers and Hyper-V clusters use the same domain. As an example, Rebeladmin Corp. uses `rebeladmin.com` as its primary domain. When the company started, it was using physical servers to host the server roles. The company was running two physical Active Directory domain controllers. After some time with the virtualization era, the company created a Hyper-V cluster. This cluster was also joined to the `rebeladmin.com` domain. The company was moving workloads from physical servers to virtual servers. With the new release of Active Directory, they set up virtual domain controllers and moved FSMO roles to virtual domain controllers. The Hyper-V cluster service needs to maintain 50% and more host availability in order to maintain the quorum. In hardware failure, if system lost quorum, the cluster will be down and workloads will not live-migrate properly. Since all the domain controllers are virtualized in such an event, when the Hyper-V host boots up, it will have a problem with cluster authentication as virtualized domain controllers are down. Therefore, make sure that you use physical domain controllers on appropriate occasions.

In a virtualized environment, make sure that you distribute the domain controllers among hosts. This will help maintain availability in a disaster.

In the following table, I have listed the dos and don'ts when considering the virtualized domain controllers:

Dos	Don'ts
Run domain controllers in different virtualized clusters in different data centers in order to avoid a single point of failure.	Do not save the Active Directory database and log files in virtual IDE disks. For durability, save them on VHD attached to a virtual SCSI controller.
Virtual hard disks (VHDs) security is important as copied VHDs can map to a computer and read the data inside it. If someone unauthorized gains access to `ntds.dit`, it will expose the identities. Hyper-V 2016 provides the shielded VM feature to encrypt the VHDs and prevent unauthorized access.	In a virtualized environment, engineers use templates to deploy the operating systems faster. Do not install the domain controller on an operating system that is not prepared with Sysprep.

Disable time synchronization between the virtual domain controller and the host. This will allow domain controllers to sync time with PDC.	Do not use a copy of the already deployed domain controller VHD to create additional domain controllers.
N/A	Do not user the Hyper-V export feature to export the virtual domain controller (rollback or restore purposes).
N/A	Do not pause or stop domain controllers for longer periods of times (longer than the tombstone lifetime).
N/A	Do not take snapshots of virtual domain controllers.
N/A	Do not use differencing disk VHD as it decreases the performance.
N/A	Do not copy clone Active Directory VHDs.

Domain controller placement

Domain controller placement in the infrastructure is dependent on a few things:

- **Network topology**: Organizations can have different buildings, branch offices, and data centers connected together. Services and resources will be hosted in those locations that will require domain controller integration. Replication is key for domain controllers. The placement of the domain controllers in the network will depend on whether it's possible to achieve successful replication or not. Network segmentations can prevent relevant traffic from passing through networks in order to have successful replications. It is important to adjust the network topology to support the Active Directory design you have in place.
- **Security**: Physical security is important for domain controllers as its holds the identity infrastructure footprint. In places that you cannot guarantee physical security in your network, it is recommended that you do not place the domain controller. In such scenarios, instead of the domain controller, it is possible to deploy a RODC.
- **Link reliability between sites**: As I mentioned earlier, replication is key for the health domain controller infrastructure. If the connectivity between sites is not stable, it is not possible to place the domain controller and maintain healthy replication. In such scenarios, it's advisable that you use RODC.

- **Active Directory sites**: We covered Active Directory sites in `Chapter 1`, *Active Directory Fundamentals*. It is important in the physical topology design. In the later chapters, I will demonstrate how to set up site links and how to manage them.

Global catalog server placement

Global catalog servers are responsible for keeping a fully writable copy of objects in its own domain and a partial copy of all other domains objects in the forest. It facilitates querying about objects in the entire forest. Global catalog service is part of the domain controller services, and it cannot be separated.

In a single-forest-single-domain environment, all the domain controllers can be global catalog servers as it will not be different from domain replication. But in a multi-domain environment, global catalog server placement involves planning as it increases the amount of data to be replicated and the bandwidth.

There are certain things that you need to consider when placing a global catalog server:

- **Number of users**: It is recommended that you place a global catalog server on any site that is over 100 users. This will help maintain site availability in the event of WAN link failure.
- **WAN link reliability**: If you are struggling with link availability between sites, it's recommended that you place global catalog servers in a remote site, and enable universal membership caching.
- **Roaming users**: Roaming users are required to connect to the global catalog server when they log in for the first time from any location in the infrastructure. Therefore, if users are using roaming profiles in remote sites, it's important that you place the global catalog server.
- **Application requirements**: Applications such as Microsoft Exchange heavily depend on global catalog servers. If similar applications are hosted on remote sites, they will be required to have a global catalog server.

 When the universal membership caching feature is enabled in the domain, any domain controller can process any logon request locally without going through a global catalog server. This will provide a faster logon experience and reduced traffic when users use it over WAN.

Once the global catalog server placement is determined, the Active Directory design phase is completed. Now we have the logical and physical design for the Active Directory infrastructure ready.

Summary

Design, implementation, and maintenance are key stages for any successful service deployment. In this chapter, you learned how to design the Active Directory infrastructure according to industry standards and best practices. There are two main parts of the process, which are designing a logical structure and designing a physical structure. Designing domain and forest structures, designing the OU structure, and global catalog server placements fall under logical structure design, and domain controller placements and site design fall under the physical topology design. In the next chapter, we are going to look into **Domain Name System (DNS)**, which is the naming system for infrastructures.

4
Active Directory Domain Name System

Domain Name System (**DNS**) and AD DS live in each other's pockets. Since Windows Server 2003, DNS has become the primary name resolution service. Before that, Windows was using NetBIOS, the **Windows Internet Name Service** (**WINS**) name service that it still continues to use. But DNS became the ruler.

WINS and DNS are both TCP/IP networks' name resolution services. There are legacy systems that still use WINS instead of DNS, for example, bar code scanners. That's the reason why WINS still continues with the latest operating systems.

DNS helps locate resources via the internet and intranet. DNS can run as an independent server role on the intranet, perimeter network, or public network. There are different vendors who provide DNS server software other than Microsoft, such as Linux/Unix BIND. There are mainly two categories of DNS infrastructure. One category is organizations that host their own DNS servers to facilitate the name resolution requirements. Another category is organizations that sell DNS as a service, such as Azure DNS, DynDNS, and Amazon Route 53.

In this chapter, our main focus will be to understand how AD-integrated DNS works in the infrastructure. Throughout the chapter, you will be learning about the following:

- Hierarchical naming structure
- How DNS works
- DNS records
- DNS zones
- Zone transfers
- DNS delegation

What is DNS?

In mobile phones, we have phone books. If we need to save someone's phone number, how we do that? Do we just enter the number and save it? No, we attach the number to a person name or something we can remember. So, the next time we open the contact list, we can easily find it. In Boaz Yakin's film *Safe*, there was a little Chinese girl who could remember long numeric codes. But if I had such a memory, I have a lot of other things I would like to remember rather than a bunch of numbers. It is the same with when you are dealing with IP addresses. I remember a few of the most commonly used IP addresses in infrastructure. But I do not remember most others. I remember lots of servers by their hostnames rather than IP addresses. This is because hostnames are more user friendly and easy to remember than IP addresses. This is what exactly DNS does. It maps IP addresses to domain names or common terms that are user friendly.

As I stated, there will be no functioning AD domain infrastructure without DNS. There are two main reasons why AD DS needs DNS:

- **Maintaining hierarchical infrastructure design**: In the previous chapters, I talked about designing the AD infrastructure. I mentioned implementing multiple forests, domains, and child domains. We use domain namespaces to separate them with each other and build the AD hierarchy. The only way you can reflect that logical structure infrastructure is using DNS.
- **To locate domain controllers**: Devices in infrastructure need to communicate with AD domain controllers for authentication. If it's a remote site, it needs to locate its closet domain controller for authentication. This process is done using DNS **service** (**SRV**) records. Also, if an application or service needs to locate a host or resources, DNS will help resolve that.

Before DNS, systems were using LMHOSTS and host files to map IP addresses to friendly names. This is still done in small networks. The LMHOSTS file helps find NetBIOS names in TCP/IP networks. The host file helps find domain names in TCP/IP networks. This is also used to override the DNS entries because in name resolution, the host file still gets priority.

The LMHOSTS and host file will be located at `C:\Windows\System32\drivers\etc`:

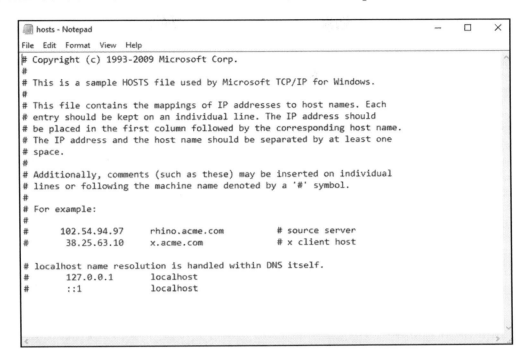

DNS was invented to support email communication in **Advanced Research Projects Agency Network (ARPANET)**. Earlier, people were using the LMHOSTS and hosts file, and as networks grew, it wasn't a practice to maintain large host files. The first conversation to start a better, centralized name resolution system started with RFC 606 in December, 1973. It took almost a decade with several RFCs to decide on the technology outline for modern DNS, and the final RFCs were released on November, 1983 (RFC 881, 882, 883).

DNS maintains a database that contains various DNS data types (A, MX, SRV, AAAA). This database can be distributed among multiple servers. This also provides control over the DNS infrastructure and enables administrators to add/edit/delete DNS entries. DNS allows you to delegate administration over the DNS domain. It also allows you to share a read-only copy of the database, where we cannot guarantee the infrastructure security.

Hierarchical naming structure

In Chapter 1, *Active Directory Fundamentals*, we looked into *domain trees* and explored how domain trees can be used to organize the domain structure in the hierarchical method. DNS allows you to translate that logical structure into the domain namespace. Similar to a tree, it starts from the root and is spread into different layers, such as branches and leaves. In the domain tree, the root is represented by a dot (.). The actual tree branch contains many leaves. In the domain tree, a branch represents a collection of named resources. A leaf in a branch represents a single named entry. In a tree, branch and leaves depend on each other. Branches or leaves are part of one system until everything is attached together. When we describe a leaf or a branch, we explain it with the tree. For example, if I need to show someone a leaf of an apple tree, I explained it as an *apple leaf*. Then the person knows it's part of the apple tree. In the same way, when we represent a domain leaf, it should be represented in a way to describe its relationship with the branch and the root. In a fully qualified domain, each level is separated by a dot (.):

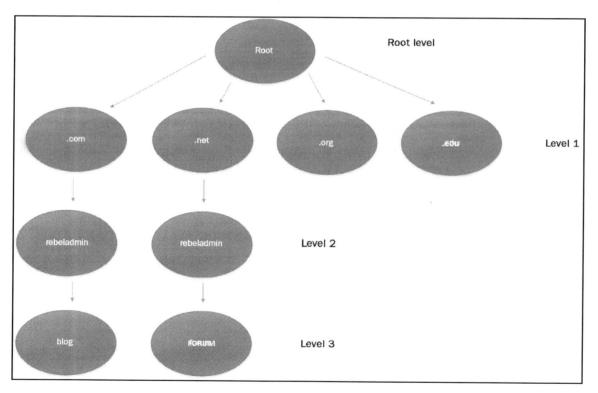

In the preceding diagram, level 1 represents the **top-level domains** (TLD). These are managed by the internet name registration authority according to international standards.

The following table describes common domain suffixes:

DNS Name	Description
.com	This is the most commonly use **top-level domain** (TLD) and it is mainly used to register the businesses that are focused on profits. This is also used to register sites such as personal websites, blogs, community websites, and so on. It is open for any person to register.
.org	This is mainly used by non-profit organizations and communities. It is open for any person to register.
.net	This is used to represent distributed computer networks. It is open for the public and anyone can register a name under it.
.edu	This is limited registration for educations institutes.
.gov	This is limited to government entities.
.ca, .co.uk	These are used to represent the countries. The registration of a domain under these depend on the rules and regulations of its country domain registrar authority.

> The complete list of TLDs can be viewed at `http://data.iana.org/TLD/tlds-alpha-by-domain.txt`.

Level 2 in the hierarchy is controlled by the organization. In my example, I need two domain names called `rebeladmin.com` and `rebeladmin.net` for my organization. I can go to the domain name registrar and register the names (for example, GoDaddy or Dotster). Once I register it, no one else can have the same name without my authority or unless it expires. As the domain owner, I can create any sub-domain (child domain) under `rebeladmin.com` and `rebeladmin.net`. In DNS, there are some records that need to be publish on the internet. For example, if I need a website hosted under my domain that people can access via the internet, I need to map my web server IP address to the `www.rebeladmin.com` DNS record. In order to do that, I need an authoritative server. This needs to be highly available as well. When you register the domain name, the domain registrar will use their own DNS servers as authoritative DNS servers by default. But if need to, we can have our own DNS servers and point to them using **nameserver** (NS) records.

In level 3, domain owners have complete authority to create any sublevel DNS namespace. In my example, there are `blog.rebeladmin.com` and `forum.rebeladmin.net`. With each dot (`.`), it represents each level of the domain tree:

The left-most part represents the lowest level in the domain tree and the right-most part shows the domain root.

If you own a domain name, you can use the same domain as your AD domain name, but there are a few things you need to consider:

- **Manually set up DNS records to match public DNS records**: As an example, I am going to use `rebeladmin.com` as my AD domain name. I am using domain registrar DNS servers to set up the public DNS records. I have a website `www.rebeladmin.com`, and it points to the `1.1.1.1` public IP address. I also use AD-integrated DNS servers to maintain local infrastructure DNS records. But when I go to access the `www.rebeladmin.com` website from a domain PC, it does not load. The reason is when I ping to the domain name, it doesn't resolve anything. This is because my AD DNS server does not know anything about `www.rebeladmin.com`. So, in order to resolve this, I need to set up a relevant DNS record in the AD domain DNS.
- **Modify DNS records to use lowest routing path**: In my previous example, the web server public address is `1.1.1.1`. This web server can also be accessed via local IP address `192.168.0.100`. If I traceroute to `www.rebeladmin.com` with DNS record `1.1.1.1`, it takes nearly 10 network hop to reach the web server. But if I use the local IP address `192.168.0.100`, it gets resolved with one network hop. Therefore, if your domain name has public and private DNS entries, make sure that you make adjustments and help users use the lowest routing path in order to improve performance and accessibility.

Maintaining the same domain namespace on two infrastructures is called a **split-brain DNS structure**. This will require manual record adjustments in both infrastructures in order to maintain service availability and integrity. The recommended setup for a similar infrastructure is a **whole-brain DNS structure**. Linking both DNS namespaces into one using a standard DNS name resolution mechanism will reduce manual user interaction.

How DNS works

DNS-related service tickets are common in any helpdesk. Some of them can be easily fixed with simple DNS flush (`ipconfig /flushdns`), and some may require DNS server level troubleshooting. Even if the DNS issues are small or critical, it is important to know how DNS works in order to troubleshoot any DNS-related issue.

A few days ago, I posted a birthday card to my mother, who lives in Sri Lanka. I posted it from the local post office in Kingston upon Thames, England. Once I put it inside the post box, the delivery process started, and now it was the postal service's responsibility to deliver it to the correct person. So, the local post office worker who picked up my letter, did he/she know my parents' house location exactly? No, they don't, but at the end of my address, it said the country was *Sri Lanka*. They then knew that if this letter goes to Sri Lanka, then the postal service there will be able to deliver it. So, the next stop of the mail was Sri Lanka. Once the card reached the main postal sorting facility in Sri Lanka, would the worker who picked up the letter know the exact address location? Maybe not, but if they don't, they could look for the city it should be delivered to. Then someone in that city would know what to do. Once the letter reached the city's mail sorting facility, the worker would know which sub-post-office this letter should be delivered to. Once it reached the sub-post-office in my parents' city, the postman there would definitely know where my parents' house is located. In the end, even though my local post office did not know where my parents live, the letter got delivered. How did they really do it? Even though they did not know the end delivery location, they knew someone who could figure it out in each stage. This is exactly how DNS resolves addresses too. Your DNS server in the infrastructure isn't aware of billions of websites on the internet and their IP addresses. When you type a domain name and press Enter, your DNS server will try to resolve it, but if it doesn't know how, it will work with other DNS servers that may know about it and work with them to find the correct destination.

In the following example, my friend William is trying to access the `www.rebeladmin.com` website from his laptop. This device is a domain-joined device and the user logs in to the device using the domain username and password.

In order to get the IP address of the `rebeladmin.com` web server, the DNS client in William's PC needs to perform a *DNS query* from its DNS server.

A *DNS query* can happen between the DNS client and the DNS server or between DNS servers.

There are two types of DNS queries:

- **Recursive**: A recursive query is usually sent by DNS clients. Once the query is processed, it expects a success or failure response from the DNS server. It is the DNS server's responsibility to work with other DNS servers in order to provide an answer if it cannot process the query by itself.
- **Iterative**: Once the DNS server receives an iterative query, it will respond with the best answer it has by looking at its DNS zones and caching. If it cannot resolve the query, it will respond with a negative answer:

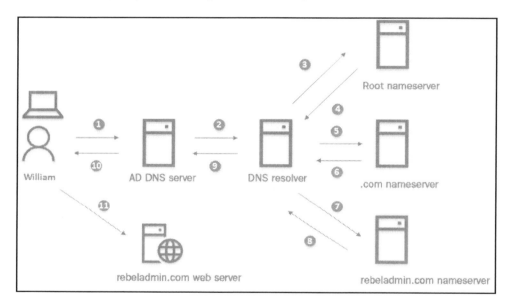

The following steps explain the preceding diagram:

1. **William**'s laptop sends the recursive DNS query to the **AD DNS server** in order to resolve the IP address for the `www.rebeladmin.com` website. This DNS server info is defined in the IP configuration of the laptop. It will use either DHCP or static.
2. The AD-integrated DNS server tries to resolve the name to an IP address, but it cannot. It doesn't have relevant DNS record configured for it. However, it knows a DNS server that can help resolve this. This is defined as DNS forwarders in DNS server configuration. Normally, system will be the ISP DNS server or public DNS server, such as Google.

In order to check the DNS forwarder address in your DNS server, you can use the following PowerShell command:

```
Get-DnsServerForwarder
```

The following screenshot shows the output for the preceding command:

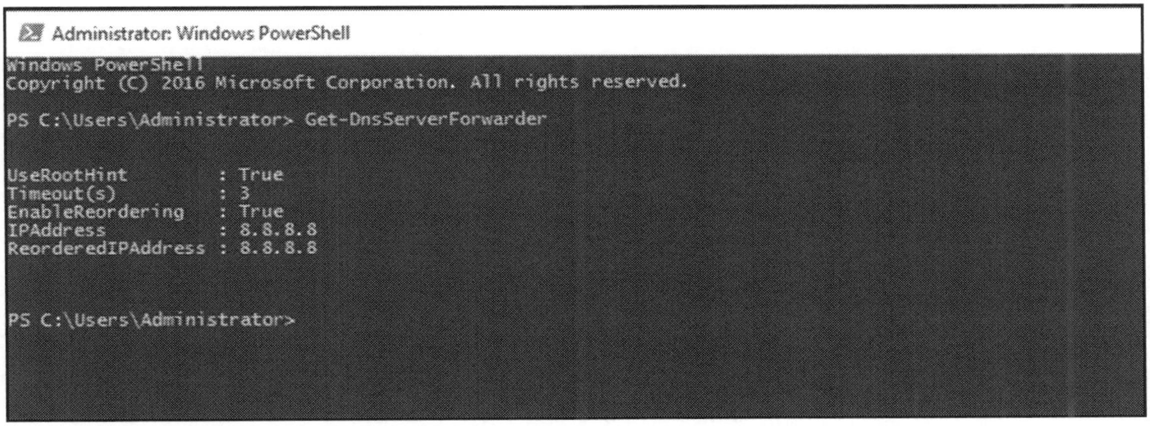

```
Administrator: Windows PowerShell
Windows PowerShell
Copyright (C) 2016 Microsoft Corporation. All rights reserved.

PS C:\Users\Administrator> Get-DnsServerForwarder


UseRootHint        : True
Timeout(s)         : 3
EnableReordering   : True
IPAddress          : 8.8.8.8
ReorderedIPAddress : 8.8.8.8


PS C:\Users\Administrator>
```

3. If the **DNS resolver** does not have a record in its cache or local zone, then it will send an iterative query to root server. There are 13 root servers clustered and operating from different geographical locations. They are controlled by IANA.

   Microsoft DNS, uses an option called **root hints**. By default, this contains all 13 root servers. If you do not have the forwarder setup in your DNS server, it will use these root servers to resolve DNS queries:

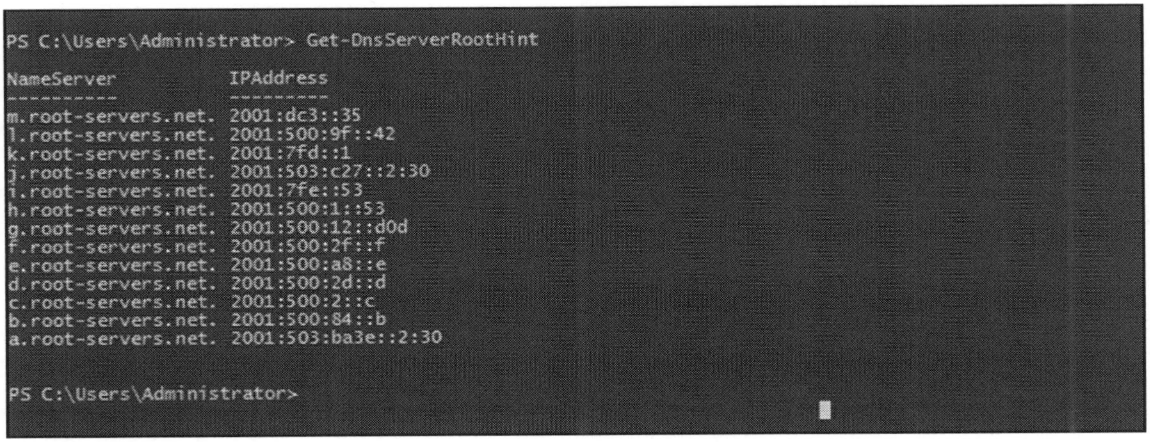

```
PS C:\Users\Administrator> Get-DnsServerRootHint

NameServer          IPAddress
----------          ---------
m.root-servers.net. 2001:dc3::35
l.root-servers.net. 2001:500:9f::42
k.root-servers.net. 2001:7fd::1
j.root-servers.net. 2001:503:c27::2:30
i.root-servers.net. 2001:7fe::53
h.root-servers.net. 2001:500:1::53
g.root-servers.net. 2001:500:12::d0d
f.root-servers.net. 2001:500:2f::f
e.root-servers.net. 2001:500:a8::e
d.root-servers.net. 2001:500:2d::d
c.root-servers.net. 2001:500:2::c
b.root-servers.net. 2001:500:84::b
a.root-servers.net. 2001:503:ba3e::2:30


PS C:\Users\Administrator>
```

4. Since its iterative query root server will look it and respond saying *I do not know about rebeladmin.com but I know someone who knows about .com*, it attaches the information about the `.com` TLD nameservers to the response.

5. Based on the response from root server, the **DNS resolver** sends an iterative query to the `.com` TLD nameservers.

6. TLD nameservers look into the query and respond saying *I do not know about the IP address of rebeladmin.com but I know nameserver information for rebeladmin.com, go and check with them they may be able to help you.*

7. Now **DNS resolver** knows about the **rebeladmin.com nameserver** and sends an iterative query to the `rebeladmin.com` nameserver by asking for IP address for `www.rebeladmin.com` (A record).

8. Finally, a question is asked from the right person. The **rebeladmin.com nameserver** responds with the IP address for `www.rebeladmin.com`.

9. Now the **DNS resolver** knows the answer, and it responds to the **AD DNS server**.

10. Then, the DNS client on William's laptop gets the response for its recursive query with the IP address for `www.rebeladmin.com`.

11. **William**'s laptop connects to the **rebeladmin.com web server** and views the website.

This is how the DNS request will be processed from top to bottom in an infrastructure. This will not be exactly the same on each and every request, as DNS servers will cache the data. If DNS servers can find the answer from their cache, the process will be quicker.

DNS essentials

In a Windows Server environment, the DNS service can be run as an individual service or as an AD-integrated service. Either way, there are core DNS components, methodologies, and terms, which will be applied to both scenarios.

DNS records

The DNS database holds various types of resource records. In an AD-integrated DNS setup, some of these records will be created automatically when adding resources to the domain, when change settings in resources, and when installing/removing domain controllers (SRV records, A and AAAA records). Other types of resource records will need to be added to the DNS server (static) based on infrastructure requirements.

Start of authority record

Each DNS zone must have a **start of authority (SOA)** record, and it is created when a zone is created for the first time. This record provides lots of general information for the DNS zones, such as the following:

- **Primary server**: The best DNS source for the zone.
- **Responsible person**: The email address of the zone administrator.
- **Serial number**: A number that is used to track the zone changes. If there is a secondary DNS zone on another server, when it checks the updates with the master zone, it will compare this serial number. If the secondary zone has a lower serial number than the master zone, it will update its copy.
- **Refresh interval**: This value is defined when the secondary server should check with the master server for zone updates.
- **Retry interval**: This value defines after how long the secondary server should try for updates if the first request is unsuccessful.
- **Expires after**: If the secondary server can't refresh the zone before the value defined here, it will no longer consider it as self-authoritative.
- **Minimum (default) TTL**: If the TTL value is not defined in the resource records, it will use this default TTL value. This TTL value is attached to the response of DNS-resolved queries.

The following PowerShell command can be used to view the properties of an SOA record:

```
Get-DnsServerResourceRecord -ZoneName "REBELADMIN.COM" -RRType "SOA" |
Select-Object -ExpandProperty RecordData
```

In the preceding command, REBELADMIN.COM can be replaced with any zone. Select-Object -ExpandProperty RecordData is used to expand the output.

A and AAAA records

Host records are used to map FQDN to an IP address. These records are used for IPv4 and AAAA records are used for IPv6. In AD and integrated DNS, every device will have an A or AAAA record when it is added to the domain. If the IP addresses get changed, the system will automatically update its DNS record too. The following commands can be used to add, remove, or list the A records:

To add an A record, run the following command:

```
Add-DnsServerResourceRecordA -Name "blog" -ZoneName "REBELADMIN.COM" -
IPv4Address "192.168.0.200"
```

To remove an A record, run the following command:

```
Remove-DnsServerResourceRecord -ZoneName "REBELADMIN.COM" -RRType "A" -Name
"blog"
```

To list A records in a zone, run the following command:

```
Get-DnsServerResourceRecord -ZoneName "REBELADMIN.COM" -RRType "A"
```

In the preceding commands, REBELADMIN.COM can be replaced with any zone name.

NS records

NS records will be used to list authoritative DNS servers for the zone. In an AD-integrated DNS setup, all the domain controllers with the DNS role installed will be added to the nameserver records in the zone file. Having multiple nameservers will add redundancy to the DNS setup.

The following command can list down the nameservers for a zone. REBELADMIN.COM can be replaced with any zone name:

```
Get-DnsServerResourceRecord -ZoneName "REBELADMIN.COM" -RRType "NS"
```

MX records

MX records specify the mail exchanger server for a domain. The mail exchanger can be any email server (Microsoft Exchange, Exim, and Office 365). A domain can have multiple MX records and the *mail server priority* number will be used to maintain the priority order. The lowest number will get the highest priority.

Canonical name record

Canonical name (CNAME) records are aliases for FQDN. They work like *nicknames*. For example, I have an `A` record setup for `blog.rebeladmin.com`; there is a blog running under it. Some time ago, I used the `my.rebeladmin.com` URL and changed it to a new one. If users still use `my.rebeladmin.com`, I need them to still see my blog at `blog.rebeladmin.com`. To do that, I can create CNAME records.

PTR record

Pointer resource records are used to map IP addresses to FQDN. Some call it reverse DNS records as well. The reverse lookup zone will not be created when the DNS is set up with AD. It will need to be created manually. If you have multiple address spaces, you will need to create separate reverse lookup zones to represent each address space.

SRV records

SRV records are used to specify the location of a service inside an infrastructure. For example, if you have a web server in the infrastructure, using an SRV record, you can specify the protocol, service, and domain name and define the service location. In an AD environment, SRV records are important as they have been used to locate the domain controllers in the infrastructure. In the previous chapters, I explained AD *sites*; if you have multiple sites when a user logs in, system needs to point the user to site's local domain controller instead of the domain controller in the hub. This is done via SRV records.

In an SRV record, the following information can be specified:

- **Service**: This will define the service this SRV record is assigned with.
- **Protocol**: This will define the protocol it will use. It can be either TCP or UDP.
- **Priority**: This will define the service priority if the service supports this function.
- **Weight**: This will help define the order it should serve along with the similar type of records.
- **Port number**: This will define the service port number.
- **Host offering this service**: This will define the server offering this particular service. It needs to use FQDN.

The AD-integrated DNS environment has a set of default SRV records created.

SRV records can be listed using the following command:

```
Get-DnsServerResourceRecord -ZoneName "REBELADMIN.COM" -RRType "SRV"
```

Detailed output can be viewed using the following command:

```
Get-DnsServerResourceRecord -ZoneName "REBELADMIN.COM" -RRType "SRV" |
Select-Object -ExpandProperty RecordData
```

 In the preceding commands, REBELADMIN.COM can be replaced with any zone name.

Zones

The Microsoft DNS server supports four types of zone. Each of these zones has different responsibilities and characteristics within the DNS namespace.

Primary zone

Primary zone is a read/write container that contains the DNS records for a domain. When you create the first domain controller with integrated DNS in a domain, it will create a primary zone by default. It holds a master copy of the zone and stores it in AD DS. Primary zones will be the source for secondary zones. It is allowed to create primary zones and integrate them with AD DS even though they are not related to the AD DS domain name.

In an AD-integrated DNS setup, primary zone can be created using the following command:

```
Add-DnsServerPrimaryZone -Name "rebeladmin.net" -ReplicationScope "Forest"
-PassThru
```

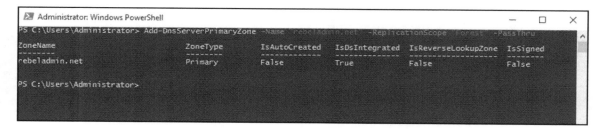

This will create an AD-integrated primary DNS zone for the
`rebeladmin.net` domain. Its replication scope is set to the forest, which means it will
replicate to any DNS servers running on domain controllers in the `rebeladmin.net` forest.
If you use the wizard to create the primary zone, the replication scope is set to the
`rebeladmin.net` domain by default, which refers to any DNS servers running on domain
controllers in the `rebeladmin.net` domain:

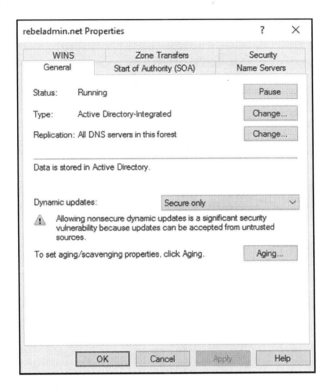

Secondary zone

A secondary zone keeps a read-only copy of a primary zone. It needs to refresh the zone
data by contacting the primary zone hosted on another server. Network connectivity and
zone transfer permissions are used to maintain a secondary zone. Secondary zones cannot
be stored in AD DS.

I have an AD-integrated primary zone running. I have a standalone DNS server, and for application requirement, I need to set up a secondary zone in it.

Before the secondary zone setup, I need to adjust the permission for zone transfer. By default, zone transfer is not allowed in AD DS-integrated zones:

```
Set-DnsServerPrimaryZone -Name "rebeladmin.net" -SecureSecondaries
TransferToSecureServers -SecondaryServers 192.168.0.106
```

In the preceding command, `rebeladmin.net` is my zone and `TransferToSecureServers` defines that the transfer will be allowed only for the listed secondary server `192.168.0.106`.

If needed, configuration can be modified with `-TransferAnyServer` to allow transfer to any server and `-TransferToZoneNameServer` to allow transfer only to nameservers:

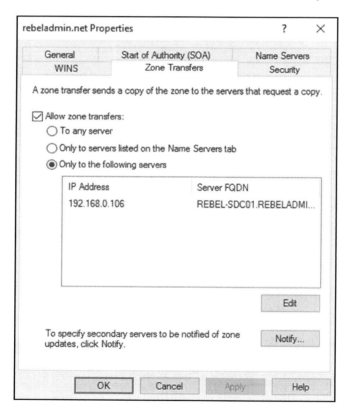

Now I can set up a secondary zone from the server `192.168.0.106`.

In the following command, `-MasterServers` defines the IP address of the master server. The `-ZoneFile` parameter is there only for file-backed DNS servers:

```
Add-DnsServerSecondaryZone -Name "rebeladmin.net" -ZoneFile
"rebeladmin.net.dns" -MasterServers 192.168.0.105
```

The following figure shows `Forward Lookup Zones`:

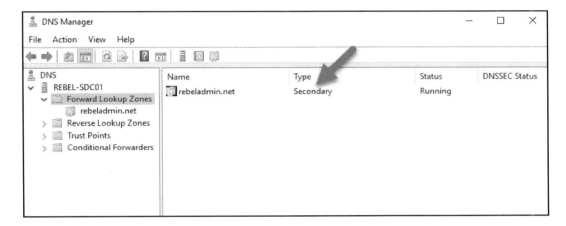

Stub zone

Stub zone is a read-only copy of a master zone but contains only SOA records and NS records. It is not an authoritative DNS server for that zone. Stub zones are not a replacement for secondary zones, and they cannot be used for load sharing or redundancy purposes. Some think stub zones and conditional forwarder do the same thing. But it is completely different. Conditional forwarder has a list of DNS servers which can help your DNS server to resolve DNS queries for a specific domain. Once DNS server receives a query for that domain, DNS server forwards the query to the servers list in the conditional forwarder. This may or may not include all the authoritative DNS servers for the domain. Stub zone is aware of all the authoritative DNS servers for its domain. When DNS server receives a query for stub zone it goes ahead and queries directly from servers listed on the zone and retrieves the result.

Reverse lookup zone

Reverse lookup zones hold PTR records. Reverse lookup zone can also be a primary zone, a secondary zone, or stub zone. Reverse lookup zones will need to match the organization network segment. Even it is AD DS-integrated, the system will not create a default reverse lookup zone. It needs to be created manually.

As an example, I need to create a reverse lookup zone for my `10.10.10.0/24` network . I can use the following command to do that:

```
Add-DnsServerPrimaryZone -NetworkID "10.10.10.0/24" -ReplicationScope
"Domain"
```

In the preceding command, `-ReplicationScope` is set to `Domain`. This means that it will be replicated to all domain controllers with integrated DNS in the domain:

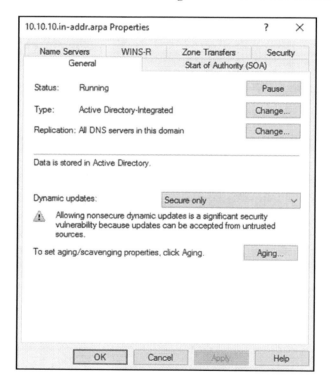

DNS server operation modes

There are three types of DNS server operation modes. These modes are not something we can choose during the setup process. These are listed based on their characteristics:

- **Dynamic**: AD DS-directory-integrated DNS uses the **Dynamic DNS (DDNS)** by default. DDNS allows hosts and users to register, update, and remove DNS records from DNS servers. Let's assume we have an AD environment with 200 computers. It uses DHCP to maintain the IP assignment. So, every three days, each device will renew its IP allocation. Some may have the same IP address, but some may receive a new one. But if the system uses static DNS every three days, administrators will need to update the DNS list to match IP allocations. Also, AD will not be able to find the devices to establish authentication or handle resource access requests. Thanks to DDNS, this is no longer manual work, and it allows the environment to maintain up-to-date DNS information without user interaction.

- **Read/Write**: This is applicable when DNS zones run without AD DS integration. For example, one of the Rebeladmin Corp. clients wants to host his/her own web server. So, as a service provider, we need to provide a solution. DNS design is part of it. The client likes the cost to a minimum, and since it's a testing environment, they do not worry about high availability. For their web server DNS requirement, we can set up a standalone DNS server in the same web server and use it as an authoritative DNS server. Records there are not going to change often, so there is no need for DDNS. If records need to be updated, an authorized user can update them manually.

- **Read-only**: If the DNS server only keeps a read-only copy of a master zone, it operates in a read-only mode. There are two types of read-only DNS servers. Some DNS servers keep only secondary zones for security, load balancing, or disaster recovery purposes. This can typically be seen in web server farms. Read-only DNS servers will check with master DNS servers for DNS updates periodically.

With Windows Server 2008, Microsoft introduced read-only domain controllers. Read-only domain controllers can be used in infrastructures where physical security and connectivity cannot be guaranteed. RODC runs AD DS-integrated primary DNS zones in the read-only mode.

These operation modes can be used in infrastructures in order to meet their DNS requirements. It is possible to mix DNS servers with different operation modes. But it's important to clearly understand each operation mode capability for DNS troubleshooting.

Zone transfers

Healthy DNS replication is a key requirement for service and infrastructure integrity. In the previous section, I explained the different zones. I also mentioned how to set the zone transfer permissions.

There are two types of zone file replications:

- **Full zone transfer (AXFR)**: When setting up a new secondary zone, the system will replicate a full copy of the zone file from the master server. It is not just for the secondary zone; it's applicable to other zones too. In the event of DNS replication issues, the administrator may require you to request a full zone transfer from its master server time to time.
- **Incremental zone transfer (IXFR)**: After the initial full zone transfer, it will replicate only those records that have been modified. It reduces the replication traffic as well as provides faster replication.

When there is a change in the master DNS zone, the system will send a notification to secondary servers about the change. Then, the secondary servers will request for a zone update. If secondary servers lose connection to the primary server or after the service is restarted, the system will still query (based on SOA refresh intervals) from master DNS servers for zone updates.

DNS delegation

In the previous chapter, when we were looking at the AD DS design, I explained child domain controllers and how they can be used to organize the company's AD hierarchy. When you create a child domain in a forest, it also creates its own DNS namespace. In a DNS infrastructure, sometimes, it is required that you divide the DNS namespace to create additional zones. DNS delegation allows organizations to achieve this without the need for changing the domain structure.

In AD-integrated DNS, you are allowed to create any DNS zone, and it will be replicated to other domain controllers. But there are situations where this can lead to administration overhead. Rebeladmin Corp. uses `rebeladmin.com` as its AD DS domain name. They have a software development department that develops web-based applications. In order to test these applications, they have to use a web URL. Each time they need to test something, they open a support ticket and the IT team creates a record in the DNS server for it. Of late, these requests have been too frequent, and sometimes due to the workload, the IT team faces delays in processing these requests. This starts making an on software release deadlines. What can we do in order to overcome the situation and provide a better solution? If there is a way to allow the software development team to create DNS A records when they are required, they do not need to wait for the IT team. But at the same time, it shouldn't be complex as it will still create additional administration tasks for the IT team. With the help of the DNS delegation feature, we can deploy a DNS server and create a DNS zone called `dev.rebeladmin.com`. Then, we can allow the software development team to manage the DNS record under it. They can create A records for apps such as `app1.dev.rebeladmin.com` and `app2.dev.rebeladmin.com`. Also, all the users under `rebeladmin.com` will still be able to access these URLs without additional changes, as the `rebeladmin.com` DNS zone knows which DNS server is authoritative for the `dev.rebeladmin.com` DNS entries.

DNS delegation can also be used to divide the DNS workloads into additional zones in order to improve the performance and create a fault-tolerant setup.

Before we start the delegation process, the second DNS server needs to be installed and create the primary DNS zone.

In my example, I have a new DNS server called `REBEL-SDC01.rebeladmin.com`. I have installed the DNS role in it and created a primary DNS zone called `dev.rebeladmin.com`:

```
Add-DnsServerPrimaryZone -Name "dev.rebeladmin.com" -ZoneFile
"dev.rebeladmin.com.dns"
```

I have also created an A record in the zone called `app1`:

```
Add-DnsServerResourceRecordA -Name "app1" -ZoneName "dev.rebeladmin.com" -
AllowUpdateAny -IPv4Address "192.168.0.110"
```

In order to set up the DNS delegation, I log in to the domain controller REBEL-PDC-01.rebeladmin.com and run the following command:

```
Add-DnsServerZoneDelegation -Name "rebeladmin.com" -ChildZoneName "dev" -
NameServer "REBEL-SDC-01.rebeladmin.com" -IPAddress 192.168.0.110
```

In the preceding command, ChildZoneName defines the zone name in the other DNS server.

Now when I go to DNS manager and expand the tree, I can see the delegated zone entry for dev.rebeladmin.com:

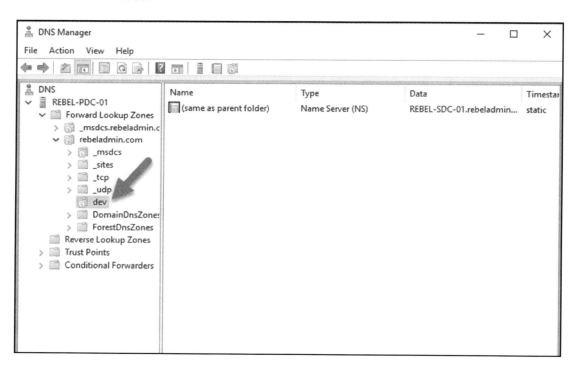

When I ping `app1.dev.rebeladmin.com` from a PC in `rebeladmin.com`, I can successfully reach it:

Summary

The DNS service is key for modern infrastructures. Maintaining a healthy DNS infrastructure ensures service and resource availability. In this chapter, we covered the basics of DNS and you learned why it's important. Then, we moved on to the hierarchical naming structure and saw how it helps translate organization logical structure to the domain namespace. We also learned how exactly DNS works behind the scene. Then, we looked at DNS records and DNS zones. This also included some explanation on how to create different zones. At the end of the chapter, you learned about different DNS operation modes and replications. I hope this information helps you understand the importance of DNS in an infrastructure and how to use it properly.

In next chapter, we will look at the AD FSMO roles and explore how to place them correctly in an infrastructure.

5
Placing Operations Master Roles

Rebeladmin Corp. is a managed IT service provider. They have introduced a new client management system where clients can open service tickets, check their billings, track the project progress, and so on. Every customer and every employee gets an account in it. Each of these user accounts gets certain privileges based on their roles and responsibilities. Support engineers are allowed to open tickets, edit tickets, and close tickets. But they are not allowed to change the schedules, delete tickets, change the appearance of the portal, or change the system database settings. Only operation manager Sean can do similar system level changes. What if everyone is allowed to do these kinds of system-level changes? Will the system be able to maintain its integrity for long? Keeping system-level change permissions limited to certain roles will prevent unnecessary structural changes and data modifications.

Active Directory infrastructures are built upon multi-master databases. This means that any writable domain controller in the domain can update the database values. But there are some operations that need to be controlled in a sensible manner in order to maintain the integrity of AD DS. These operations are better managed in a single-master mode rather than a multi-master mode. These special roles are called **Flexible Single Master Operation (FSMO)** roles. These roles can run from one domain controller or be distributed among multiple domain controllers (according to guidelines). But each role can appear only once in a domain or forest. It makes the operation master holder important in an AD DS infrastructure and in the event of its failure, it will prevent changes. In such a catastrophe, if the operation master holder cannot recover, another domain controller will have to forcefully regain control over its operation master roles.

In this chapter, we are going to look into the following topics:

- FSMO roles and duties
- FSMO role placement
- Moving FSMO roles
- Seize FSMO roles

FSMO roles

There are five flexible single master operations roles in the Active Directory infrastructure. Each of them will be performing specific Active Directory tasks that other domain controllers in the infrastructure are not permitted to perform. These five FSMO roles are divided into two categories based on their operation boundaries:

Forest Level	Domain Level
Schema operations master	The **primary domain controller (PDC)** emulator operations master
Domain naming operations master	The **relative identifier (RID)** operations master
N/A	The infrastructure operations master

When we create the first Active Directory forest and the first Active Directory domain, all these FSMO roles will be installed in the domain's first domain controller (obviously there's no other place to place them). A majority of the Active Directory infrastructures leave the default configuration as it is even though they keep adding domain controllers. Keeping them in one domain controller makes it easier to manage them, but there are certain guidelines on how to place them correctly in the infrastructure in order to get the best benefits, which we will discuss later in this chapter. This will not only improve the performance, it will also remove the risk of a single point of failure. It's always good not to put all our eggs in one basket.

Schema operations master

This role boundary is the forest. This means that an Active Directory forest can have only one schema master. The owner of this role is the only domain controller in the forest who can update the Active Directory schema. In order to make schema changes in the forest, it also needs to have a user account that is a member of the Schema Admins group. Once the schema changes are done from the schema master role owner, they will be replicated to other domain controllers in the forest.

In an Active Directory forest, the schema master role owner can be found using the following command:

```
Get-ADForest | select SchemaMaster
```

 When you add a new version of Active Directory to the domain the first time, it will need a schema modification. If you run the Active Directory configuration wizard with a user account that has the Domain Admin permission, it will fail. You need an account with Schema Admin privileges.

Domain naming operations master

The domain naming operations master role holder is responsible for adding domain controllers and removing domains controllers from the Active Directory forest. When you add or remove a domain controller for the forest, it will contact the domain naming operation master role holder via the **Remote Procedure Call** (**RPC**) connection, and if it fails, it will not allow you to add or remove the domain controller from the forest. This is a forest-wide role, and only one domain naming operations master role holder can exist in one forest.

In the Active Directory forest, the domain naming operations master role owner can be found using the following command:

```
Get-ADForest | select DomainNamingMaster
```

Primary domain controller emulator operations master

The PDC operations master role is a domain-wide setting, which means each domain in the forest will have a PDC operations master role holder. One of the common Active Directory interview questions is this: *what FSMO role is responsible for time synchronization?* The answer is *PDC!* In an Active Directory environment, it allows a maximum of five minute time difference (time skew) by default. If it's more than 5 minutes, devices will not be able to add to the domain, users will not be able to authenticate, and the Active Directory-integrated application will start throwing authentication-related errors.

It is important that domain controllers, computers, and servers in the Active Directory domain controller agree on one clock:

Computers and servers in a domain will sync their time with the domain controller they are authenticated with. Then, all of the domain controllers will sync their time with their **domain PDC** role holder. All the **domain PDC** role holders will sync the time with the forest **root domain PDC** role holder. In the end, the **root domain PDC** role holder will sync the time with an **external time source**.

Apart from time synchronization, the PDC role holder is also responsible for maintaining password change replications. Also, in the event of authentication failures, PDC is responsible for locking down the account. All the passwords changed in other domain controllers will be reported back to the PDC role holder. If any authentication failure occurs in a domain controller before it passes the authentication failure message to the user, it will check the password saved in the PDC, as that will prevent errors that can occur due to password replication issues. The PDC is also responsible for managing the **Group Policy Object (GPO)** edit. Every time the GPO is viewed or updated, it will be done from the copy stored in the PDC's SYSVOL folder.

In the Active Directory domain, the PDC role owner can be found using the following command:

```
Get-ADDomain | select PDCEmulator
```

Relative ID operations master role

The RID master role is a domain-wide setting, and each domain in the forest can have RID role owners. It is responsible for maintaining a pool of relative identifiers that will be used when creating objects in the domain. Each and every object in a domain has a unique **security identifier (SID)**. The RID value is used in the process of SID value creation. SID is a unique value to represent an object in Active Directory. RID is the incremental portion of the SID value. Once RID value is being used to generate a SID, it will not use again. Even after deleting an object from AD, it will not able to reclaim the RID value back. This ensure the uniqueness of the SID value. The RID role owner maintains a pool of RIDs. When the domain has multiple domain controllers, it will assign a block of 500 RID values for each domain controller. When they are used more than 50%, domain controllers will request another block of RID for the RID role owner.

In the event of an RID role owner failure, its impact will be almost unnoticeable until all domain controllers run our of allocated RID values. . It will also not allow you to move objects between domains.

In the Active Directory domain, the RID role owner can be found using the following command:

```
Get-ADDomain | select RIDMaster
```

Infrastructure operations master

This role is also a domain-wide setting, and it is responsible for replicating SID and distinguished name value changes to cross-domains. SID and DN values get changed based on their location in the forest. So if objects are moved, their new values need to be updated in groups and ACLs located in different domains. This is taken care of by the infrastructure operations master. This will ensure that the changed objects have access to their resources without interruptions.

The infrastructure operation master role owner checks its database periodically for foreign group members (from other domains) and once it finds those objects, it checks its SID and DN values with the global catalog server. If the value in the global catalog is different from the local value, it will replace its value with the global catalog server value. Then, it will replicate it to other domain controllers in the domain. By design, the global catalog server holds a partial copy of every object in the forest. It does not have the need to keep a reference of cross-domain objects. If the infrastructure master is in place in a global catalog server, it will not know about any cross-domain objects. Therefore, the infrastructure operations master role owner should not be a global catalog server. However, this is not applicable when all the domain controllers are global catalogs in a domain because that way, all the domain controllers will have up-to-date information.

In the Active Directory domain, the infrastructure operations master role owner can be found using the following command:

```
Get-ADDomain | select InfrastructureMaster
```

FSMO roles placement

The first domain controller in the first Active Directory forest will hold all five FSMO roles. All these roles are critical in the Active Directory infrastructure. Some of them are heavily used and some roles are only used only on specific occasions. Some role owners will not be able to afford any downtime, and some roles will still be able to have downtime. So, based on characteristics, impact, and responsibilities, these can be placed on different domain controllers. FSMO roles placements are based on certain facts that are listed in the next section.

Active Directory logical and physical topology

If it's a single forest-single domain environment, it is not hard to keep all the FSMO roles in one domain controller. The infrastructure master role should not be in the global catalog server, but in the single forest-single domain environment, on most occasions, all servers are global catalog servers too. Therefore, it will not make any difference. In the following example, in the rebeladmin.com single forest-single domain environment, there are three domain controllers in the infrastructure:

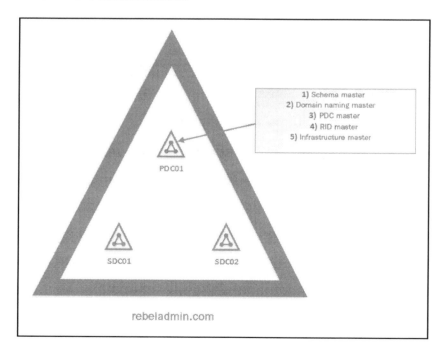

PDC01 is recognized as the most powerful (capacity) and most reliable domain controller. Therefore, **PDC01** holds all five FSMO roles. **SDC01** and **SDC02** are also two global catalog servers. In this case, just moving the infrastructure master role to one of the domain controllers will not make a significant impact. In the event of a **PDC01** failure, secondary domain controllers will be able to claim ownership of FSMO roles (this process is called **seizing FSMO roles** and will be described later in the chapter).

In a multiple-domain environment, this will change. Forest-wide roles and domain-wide roles will need to be placed properly in order to maintain high availability and performance.

In the following example, Rebeladmin Corp. has three domains. The `rebeladmin.net` domain is the forest root domain. The `rebeladmin.com` domain is used in its headquarters in USA and `rebeladmin.ca` is used in its Canadian branch:

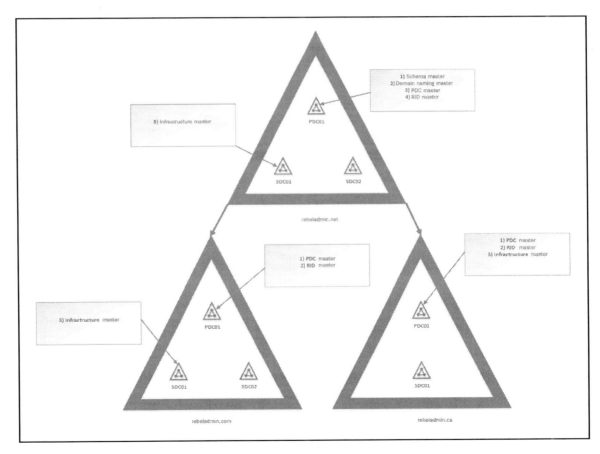

All these three domains share one forest. Therefore, forest-wide roles, which are the **schema master** and the **domain naming master**, will be placed in the forest root domain. In the rebeladmin.net forest root domain, it has three domain controllers. **PDC01** is identified as the most reliable domain controller. The **Schema master** and the domain name master use relatively less amount of processing power as forest-wide changes will not happen frequently. But high availability is a must as other domain activities will depend on it. PDC is the most consumed FSMO role as it will replicate password changes, control time synchronization, and manage GPO edits. So, it's important for PDC to run on the domain controller that has the most processing power. The PDC role holder is the biggest customer of the **RID master**. Therefore, reliable communication between two role holders is crucial. It is advised that you keep PDC and RID together in one domain controller in order to avoid network-latency-related issues. So, in the end, we can place four FSMO roles in **PDC01**. In a multi-domain environment, cross-domain referencing is important. If the user account in the forest root domain changes its name, it will immediately be replicated to all the domain controllers in the forest root domain. But if the user is a part of group in the other domains, they also need to know about these new values. Therefore, **SDC01** is made as non-global catalog server and it holds **infrastructure master** role. **SDC02** is kept as a backup domain controller; if any of the FSMO role holders is dead, it can claim role ownership. In some infrastructures, the forest root domain is not used for active operations. In such situations, keeping multiple domain controllers is a management overhead.

In the rebeladmin.com domain, it only holds domain-wide FSMO roles. The PDC and RID masters run from the **PDC01** and **SDC01** runs the **infrastructure master** role. It is also not a global catalog server. **SDC02** is the domain controller that can be used as an FSMO role holder in the event of an existing role owner failure.

In rebeladmin.ca, the domain is hosted in a regional office. It has less than 25 users, and most of them are sales peoples. Therefore, keeping multiple domain controllers cannot be justified based on capacity or reliability facts. The setup is limited to two domain controllers, and **PDC01** hosts all three domain-wide **FSMO** roles. **SDC01** is kept as a backup domain controller, to be used in a DR scenario.

In the previous chapters, I explained read-only domain controllers and their responsibilities in an infrastructure. By design, RODC cannot hold any FSMO roles.

Connectivity

Healthy replication between domain controllers is a must for the Active Directory infrastructure. FSMO role holders are designated to do specific tasks in the infrastructure. Other domain controllers, devices, and resources should have a reliable communication channel with FSMO role holders in order to get these specific tasks done for them when required.

In Active Directory infrastructures, there can be regional offices and remote sites that are connected using WAN links. Most of the time, these WAN links have limited bandwidth. These remote sites can have domain controllers hosted too. If replication traffic between sites is not handled in an optimized way, it can turn out to be a bottleneck. Rebeladmin Corp. is a managed services provider and it has two offices. The HQ is located in Toronto and the operation center is based in Seattle, USA. It is connected via a 512 KB WAN link. In the Toronto office, there are 20 users and in the Seattle office, there are 500 users. It runs on a single domain Active Directory infrastructure. As I mentioned earlier, among all these FSMO roles, the PDC is the most highly used FSMO role. Devices and users keep communicating with PDC more frequently than other FSMO role holders. In this scenario, if we place the PDC in the Toronto office, 500 users and associated devices and the other workloads will need to go through the WAN link in order to communicate with the PDC. But if we place it in the Seattle site, then the traffic that will pass through the WAN link to connect to the PDC will be lower. In a regional office scenario, make sure you always place the PDC near the site that hosts the most number of users, devices, and resources.

Network topology use for inter-site connectivity also makes an impact on the FSMO role placement:

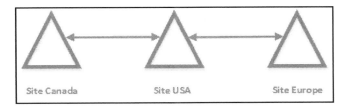

In the preceding example, Active Directory setup has three Active Directory sites with a single domain infrastructure. **Site Canada** connects to **Site USA** and **Site USA** connects to **Site Europe**. But **Site Canada** does not have a direct connection with **Site Europe**. Now if the FSMO roles are placed in **Site Canada**, **Site Europe** will have issues communicating with it. **Site Europe** will not be able to perform any FSMO-related tasks. According to the network topology, the best option will be to place the FSMO roles in **Site USA** as both sites have a direct connection to it.

The number of domain controllers

The number of domain controllers that can be deployed on an Active Directory infrastructure depends on the budget and available resources (computer resources, space, power, and connectivity). Based on the number of domain controllers, engineers will need to decide to either run all FSMO roles together or distribute them among domains controllers. It is recommended that you have at least two domain controllers in a site. One will be holding the FSMO roles, and other one will be kept as a standby domain controller. In the event of a primary server failure, FSMO roles can be hosted on standby domain controller.

Capacity

The capacity of the Active Directory infrastructure also affects the FSMO roles placement. When the number of users, devices, and other resources increases, it also increases FSMO role-related activities. If it's a multi-site environment, it's recommended that you place FSMO roles on sites that run with a high capacity of Active Directory objects in order to lower the impact of replication and latency issues.

FSMO role holders are also involved in typical Active Directory tasks such as user authentication. In large Active Directory environments (10,000+ objects), it is important to prioritize FSMO-related tasks over regular Active Directory tasks. This mainly impacts the PDC emulator as it is the most active FSMO role. It is possible to prioritize domain controller operations by editing the *weight* value of the DNS SRV record. The default value is *100*, and reducing it will reduce the number of user authentication requests. The recommended value is *50*.

This can be done by adding a new registry key under `HKLM\SYSTEM\CurrentControlSet\Services\Netlogon\Parameters`. Key should have a `DWORD` value with the entry name `LdapSrvWeight`.

Moving FSMO roles

In the Active Directory infrastructure, on certain occasions, FSMO roles will need to be moved from one domain controller to another. Here, I have listed a few scenarios where it will need to consider FSMO roles transfers:

- **Active Directory upgrades**: When the infrastructure needs to be upgraded from one Active Directory version to another, the way to do that is to introduce the new domain controllers to the existing infrastructure and then move the FSMO roles. After that, the domain controllers that run older versions can decommission and then increase the forest and domain functional levels to the latest. This will make the migration smooth with minimum identity infrastructure operations impact.

- **Active Directory logical and physical topology**: When installing the first domain controller in the infrastructure, it will automatically hold all five FSMO roles. But based on the Active Directory topology design, the roles can be transferred to ideal locations, as discussed in the previous section. This can be based on the initial design or an extended design.

- **Due to performance and reliability issues**: FSMO role owners are responsible for specific tasks in an Active Directory infrastructure. Each role can appear in only one domain controller in a domain. Some of these roles are focused on more processing power and some roles are more concerned about the uptime. Therefore, in general, FSMO roles should be running on the most reliable domain controllers in the infrastructure. If the allocated resources are not enough for the FSMO role operations or if the servers have reliability issues, it will need to move on to another host. This happens mainly when these roles are running on physical servers. If it's a virtual server, it will just be a matter of increasing the allocated resources. Some businesses also have infrastructure refreshment plans, which will kick off every 3 or 5 years. In such situations, the FSMO roles will need to move into the new hardware.

Let's look at how we can transfer the FSMO roles.

Before we start, we need to check the current FSMO role holder. This can be done by running the following command:

```
netdom query fsmo
```

The following screenshot shows output for the preceding command:

```
Administrator: Windows PowerShell

Windows PowerShell
Copyright (C) 2016 Microsoft Corporation. All rights reserved.

PS C:\Users\Administrator> netdom query fsmo
Schema master                 REBEL-PDC-01.REBELADMIN.COM
Domain naming master          REBEL-PDC-01.REBELADMIN.COM
PDC                           REBEL-PDC-01.REBELADMIN.COM
RID pool manager              REBEL-PDC-01.REBELADMIN.COM
Infrastructure master         REBEL-PDC-01.REBELADMIN.COM
The command completed successfully.

PS C:\Users\Administrator> _
```

In the infrastructure, there is a new domain controller added with the name `REBEL-SDC02`, and I'd like to move the domain-wide FSMO roles, which are the PDC, RID, and infrastructure roles, to the new server:

```
Move-ADDirectoryServerOperationMasterRole -Identity REBEL-SDC02 -
OperationMasterRole PDCEmulator, RIDMaster, InfrastructureMaster
```

The following screenshot shows output for the preceding command:

```
Administrator: Windows PowerShell                                                    —   □   ×

PS C:\Users\Administrator> Move-ADDirectoryServerOperationMasterRole -Identity REBEL-SDC02 -OperationMasterRole PDCEmula
tor, RIDMaster, InfrastructureMaster

Move Operation Master Role
Do you want to move role 'PDCEmulator' to server 'REBEL-SDC02.REBELADMIN.COM' ?
[Y] Yes  [A] Yes to All  [N] No  [L] No to All  [S] Suspend  [?] Help (default is "Y"): A
PS C:\Users\Administrator>
```

> FSMO role transfer commands need to be run with the required privileged accounts. If you need to move domain-wide roles, the minimum you need to have are Domain Admin privileges. If they are forest-wide roles, they need to be Enterprise Admin privileges. To move the schema master role, Schema Admin privileges are the minimum requirement.

Once the move is completed, we can check the role owners again:

```
Administrator: Windows PowerShell                                          —    □    ×
PS C:\Users\Administrator> netdom query fsmo
Schema master              REBEL-PDC-01.REBELADMIN.COM
Domain naming master       REBEL-PDC-01.REBELADMIN.COM
PDC                        REBEL-SDC02.REBELADMIN.COM
RID pool manager           REBEL-SDC02.REBELADMIN.COM
Infrastructure master      REBEL-SDC02.REBELADMIN.COM
The command completed successfully.

PS C:\Users\Administrator> _
```

If we need to move all five FSMO roles to a new host, we can use the following command:

```
Move-ADDirectoryServerOperationMasterRole -Identity REBEL-SDC02 -
OperationMasterRole SchemaMaster, DomainNamingMaster, PDCEmulator,
RIDMaster, InfrastructureMaster
```

The following screenshot shows the output for the preceding command:

```
Administrator: Windows PowerShell                                          —    □    ×
PS C:\Users\Administrator> Move-ADDirectoryServerOperationMasterRole -Identity REBEL-SDC02 -OperationMasterRole SchemaMa
ster, DomainNamingMaster, PDCEmulator, RIDMaster, InfrastructureMaster

Move Operation Master Role
Do you want to move role 'SchemaMaster' to server 'REBEL-SDC02.REBELADMIN.COM' ?
[Y] Yes  [A] Yes to All  [N] No  [L] No to All  [S] Suspend  [?] Help (default is "Y"): A
PS C:\Users\Administrator> _
```

The following screenshot shows the output for the `netdom query fsmo` command:

```
Administrator: Windows PowerShell                                          —    □    ×
PS C:\Users\Administrator> netdom query fsmo
Schema master              REBEL-SDC02.REBELADMIN.COM
Domain naming master       REBEL-SDC02.REBELADMIN.COM
PDC                        REBEL-SDC02.REBELADMIN.COM
RID pool manager           REBEL-SDC02.REBELADMIN.COM
Infrastructure master      REBEL-SDC02.REBELADMIN.COM
The command completed successfully.

PS C:\Users\Administrator>
```

If we need to move a single FSMO role, the `Move-ADDirectoryServerOperationMasterRole` command can be used with the individual role.

Once the transfer is completed, the system will create an event in the event viewer under the directory service log with the event ID `1458`.

Seize FSMO roles

In the previous section, I explained how to transfer FSMO roles from one domain controller to another. But there are certain situations where we will not be able to transfer the FSMO roles, such as the following:

- **Hardware failures**: If the domain controller that holds the FSMO roles failed due to hardware issues and there is no other way to bring it back online, it is possible to seize the FSMO roles. However, if the failed server is protected by a backup DR solution, it's still worth going through that process than the seize process because it will still be able to recover the domain controller in the most up-to-date, usable status.
- **System operation issues**: If the domain controller has issues such as operating system corruptions, viruses, malware, file corruptions, it may not be allowed to transfer the FSMO role to another domain controller, which will also lead to FSMO role seize.
- **Forcefully removed domain controller**: If the FSMO role holder is forcefully decommissioned using the `/forceremoval` command, in order to keep infrastructure operations running, FSMO roles will need to seize.

The FSMO role seize process should be used only in a disaster where you cannot recover the FSMO role holder. Some of the FSMO roles (RID, domain naming master, schema master) can still afford a few hours of downtime with minimum business impacts. Therefore, we do not use the seize option as the first option if the FSMO role holder can still be recovered or fixed.

Once the seize process is completed, the old FSMO role holder should not be brought online again. It is recommended that you format and remove it from the network. At any given time, it is not possible to have the same FSMO role appear in two servers in the same domain.

In the following example, there are two domain controllers in the infrastructure. REBEL–SDC02 is the FSMO role holder and REBEL–PDC–01 is the additional domain controller. Due to hardware failure, I cannot bring REBEL–SDC02 online and I need to seize the FSMO roles:

In order to seize the roles, the following command can be used:

```
Move-ADDirectoryServerOperationMasterRole –Identity REBEL–PDC–01 –
OperationMasterRole SchemaMaster, DomainNamingMaster, PDCEmulator,
RIDMaster, InfrastructureMaster –Force
```

This command will take a few minutes to complete as in the background, it will try to connect to the original FSMO role holder.

The only change in the command from the FSMO role transfer is the `-Force` parameter at the end. Otherwise, it's the exact same command. You also can seize the individual role using `Move-ADDirectoryServerOperationMasterRole -Identity REBEL-PDC-01 -OperationMasterRole <FSMO Role> -Force`.

`<FSMO Role>` can be replaced with the actual FSMO role value.

Once the command is completed, we can test the new FSMO role holder:

As we can see, `REBEL-PDC-01` becomes the new FSMO role holder.

Summary

This is the end of another Active Directory infrastructure design chapter that was focused on FSMO role placements. FSMO roles are designated to do specific tasks in an Active Directory infrastructure in order to maintain integrity. In this chapter, you learned about FSMO roles and their responsibilities. Then, we moved on to FSMO role placement in the infrastructure, where you learned about techniques and best practices that need to be followed in order to maintain the best performance and availability. After that, we looked at how to transfer the FSMO roles from one domain controller to another using PowerShell, followed by how to seize FSMO roles in the event of a disaster where you cannot recover the original FSMO role holder.

In the next chapter, we will look at actual Active Directory deployment scenarios and explore how to migrate from older versions of Active Directory to AD DS 2016.

6
Migrating to Active Directory 2016

In the previous chapters, we looked at Active Directory infrastructure components and how to design an identity infrastructure using these components, as well as different technologies and methodologies. Now it's time to look at Active Directory Domain Service installation and migrations. It would be perfect if we could design and implement an identity infrastructure from scratch, but a majority of organizations require the ability to migrate from one version of Active Directory to a newer version to use the new features or enhancements. At the same time, it is expected that they fix the existing issues in the identity infrastructure. On some occasions, this is also followed with extending the existing infrastructure to meet the new business requirements.

This chapter is mainly focused on gaining hands-on experience of different deployment scenarios of Active Directory Domain Service. It will cover the following:

- Active Directory Domain Service installation prerequisites
- Active Directory Domain Service deployment scenarios
- How to plan an Active Directory migration
- How to migrate to Active Directory Domain Service 2016
- How to confirm successful installation and migration

Active Directory Domain Service installation prerequisites

Before we look into **Active Directory Domain Service (AD DS)** service installation, there are certain prerequisites which need to be fulfilled. Without these, even if we have a good design, we would still not be able to achieve the core objectives.

Hardware requirements

In modern infrastructures, most of the workloads are running as virtualized environments. Active Directory Domain Services also can deploy in virtualized platforms, but there are certain scenarios where physical domain controllers should be used. In such situations for AD DS 2016, following are the minimum hardware requirements:

- 1.4 GHz 64-bit processor
- 2 GB RAM
- Storage adapter which supports PCI Express architecture (Windows Server 2016 does not support IDE/ATA/PATA/EIDE for boot and data)
- 32 GB of free space
- 1 x network adapter
- DVD drive or support for network, USB boot

 This is the minimum requirement to install the AD DS 2016 service; it doesn't mean it can accommodate organization's identity infrastructure requirements. The system needs to be size-based on the AD DS roles it will host, number of objects and operation requirements.

Virtualized environment requirements

Today, virtualization solutions allow organizations to build their own private cloud or use public cloud providers such as Microsoft Azure and Amazon AWS. AD DS 2016 provides support for both scenarios. If it's private cloud, it will give more control over resource allocation, but in public cloud, it will depend on the subscription plans and the amount the organization is capable of spending.

I have listed the minimum requirements for virtualized environment, as follows:

- 1.4 GHz 64-bit processor
- 2 GB RAM
- Virtual SCSI storage controller
- 32 GB free space
- 1 x virtual network adapter

Based on your virtualization service provider, there will be specific guidelines for virtualized domain controllers. Always follow these recommendations to get the best out of them.

In Chapter 3, *Designing Active Directory Infrastructure*, we saw the dos and don'ts when deploying virtualized domain controllers. Refer to it for more details.

Microsoft Advanced Threat Analytics is an application which allows administrators to find Active Directory infrastructure security threats. This will be covered in Chapter 15, *Active Directory Security Best Practices*. As part of that solution, it will require a standalone gateway or Lightweight Gateway which can be installed in domain controllers. To install it on domain controller, minimum RAM requirements for service is 6 GB. Therefore, if you are going to use ATA in infrastructure, domain controllers at least need to have 8 GB RAM allocated.

Additional requirements

Apart from the physical or virtual resources requirements, there are other factors to consider before installing the first domain controller:

- **Operating system version and installation mode**: Windows Server 2016 has standard and data center versions. Based on the version, its capabilities will be decided. AD DS is a core functionality and it does not have dependencies on the version, but it is important to arrange the required licenses in advance for the Active Directory domain controllers.

- Windows Server 2016 supports three installation modes. A server with desktop experience is the standard installation method with GUI. Server roles and operations can be managed by using GUI or commands. Server core method also supports AD DS. Server core doesn't have GUI and it reduces the operating system footprint. It also reduces the attack surface of the identity infrastructure. Nano Server mode was introduced with Windows Server 2016. It is similar to server core but optimized from private clouds. Its OS footprint is lower than Windows Server core and only allows 64-bit applications. It also only allows remote administration. At the time of writing this book, Microsoft Nano Server does not support AD DS. Before installing the domain controller, it's important to decide the server operating system version and installation mode. Based on that, system prerequisites and licensing will change as well.

- **Design document**: Documentation is crucial in any system implementation. Before starting the installation process, produce a document including the Active Directory physical and logical topology, risks, technologies in use, and so on.

> It is recommended to get the documentation approved by authorized people before deployment. It helps everyone to agree on one design and refer to it whenever required. It also creates a starting point for future identity infrastructure changes.

- **Domain and forest names**: During the AD DS installation, we need to specify the domain name and the forest name. In an organization, it's important to agree about these names with management before starting the installation process. This information can be added to your Active Directory design document and submitted for approval. A year ago, I wrote an article in my blog about the Active Directory domain rename process. Engineers write to me if they require any further guidance regarding the rename process, and I am always curious to find out the reason for a domain rename as it's not *normal*. One of the instances was very interesting. It was a large organization, with nearly 500 users. They changed their business name and wanted to create a separate forest and domain structure, and move users over to it along with resources in a merged company. They hired an engineer to do it. The engineer created a new Active Directory structure and moved more than 400 users and devices over to the new structure. After a few weeks, the management came back and said that instead of using .com in the primary domain, they would prefer to use the .ca domain name. Even after long discussions, the company still didn't change its mind and wanted to remove the .com domain name. Although this sounds like a small task, it can have a big operational impact.

- **Dedicated IP address**: Domain controllers are recommended to operate with static IP addresses. Before installation begins, assign static IP addresses to domain controllers and test the connectivity. Active Directory domain controller IP addresses can be changed later if required, but it is recommended to avoid that as much as possible.
- **Monitoring**: Once AD DS service is installed, we need to monitor system performance, replication health, and component and services integrity to identify potential service impacts and bottlenecks. Microsoft **System Center Operation Manager (SCOM)** and Microsoft **Operation Management Suite (OMS)** are the recommended monitoring tools, as they include modules especially designed to identify both service level and security issues.
- **Backup/disaster recovery**: High availability of identity infrastructure is a must for organizational operations as many services, applications, and other business components depend on it. Therefore, we need to plan how to keep identity infrastructure functioning in a disaster with minimum operations impact. There are different technologies and services which can be used to backup Active Directory domain controllers, and some of those will be evaluated later on in this book. After deciding the solution, also plan for periodic DR tests to verify solution validity.
- **Virus protection in domain controllers:** As with any other system, domain controllers also can get infected by malicious codes. There is debate about whether Active Directory domain controller should have antivirus software installed or not, but in Microsoft documentations, I have never found anything saying it should not have antivirus software. Always refer to your antivirus solution provider and check if the solution is supported to protect Active Directory domain controllers.

  Once I was working on an Active Directory upgrade project for a world-leading bank. Everything went smoothly, and after project closure, one morning I received a call from their support team about the domain controller's replications. When I checked, I found out that they had installed antivirus software on the domain controllers and it was preventing DFS SYSVOL replication between domain controllers. Therefore, follow the relevant guidelines from your service provider before antivirus installations.

Active Directory Domain Service installation methods

There are two methods we can use to install the Active Directory domain controllers:

- **Using Windows GUI**: After Microsoft introduced Server Manager with Windows Server 2008, the installation process of AD DS became simplified. In order to install the AD DS using Windows GUI, we first need to install the AD DS role using Server Manager. Once it is completed, we can run the AD DS configuration wizard:

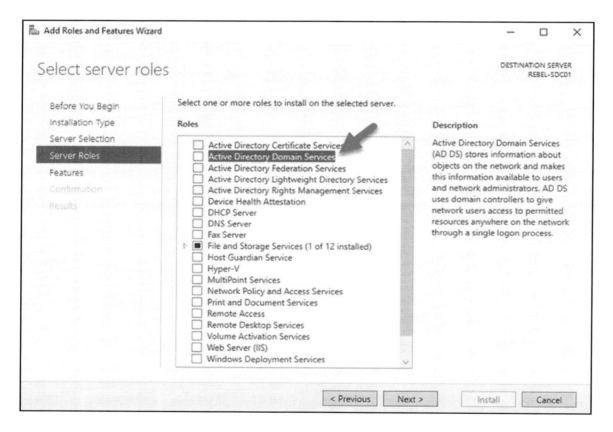

The following screenshot shows the **Active Directory Domain Services Configuration Wizard**:

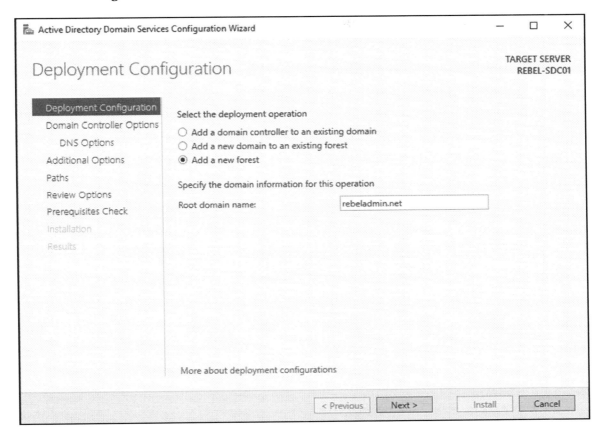

- **Using PowerShell**: Before Windows Server 2012, AD DS were able to be configured using *Dcpromo unattended* files. The Dcpromo tool was used to configure the AD DS, and using a text file it was possible to pass the configuration values required. It removed the user interaction for the AD DS configuration. With Windows Server 2012, Dcpromo got replaced by PowerShell. Now we can use PowerShell script to install and configure AD DS. In this chapter, we will be using PowerShell for deployments.

Active Directory Domain Service deployment scenarios

In this section, we are going to look into different installation scenarios of AD DS.

Setting up a new forest root domain

As the first scenario, I am going to demonstrate how to setup the new Active Directory forest. This will be the first domain controller of a new identity infrastructure. You can use the following checklist to make sure you have done your homework before clicking on the installation button.

Active Directory Domain Service installation checklist for first domain controller

The following checklist can be used for fresh AD DS installation:

- Produce Active Directory design document
- Prepare physical/virtual resources for domain controller
- Install Windows Server 2016 Standard/Datacenter
- Patch servers with latest Windows updates
- Assign dedicated IP address to domain controller
- Install AD DS role
- Configure AD DS according to design
- Review logs to verify the healthy AD DS installation and configuration
- Configure service and performance monitoring
- Configure AD DS backup/DR
- Produce system documentation

Design topology

As explained in the following diagram, in this scenario `rebeladmin.com` will be the forest root domain:

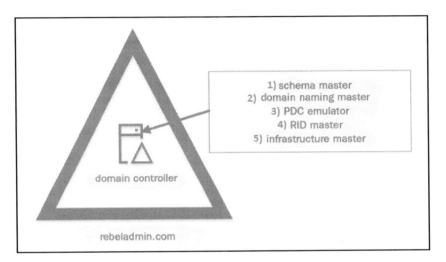

The first domain controller installed on the forest will hold all five FSMO roles. In the previous chapter, we learned about FSMO roles placement, and once additional domain controllers are added to the domain, these roles can migrate to the best location.

Installation steps

Next, I will be demonstrating how to install first domain controller in the forest. These demonstration steps are done based on Windows Server 2016:

1. Log in to the server as a member of the local administrator's group.
2. As a first step, verify the static IP address allocation by using `ipconfig /all`.
3. Launch the PowerShell console as an administrator.
4. Before the configuration process, we need to install the AD DS role in the given server. In order to do that, we can use the following command:

```
Install-WindowsFeature -Name AD-Domain-Services
   -IncludeManagementTools
```

This does not require a reboot to complete the role service installations:

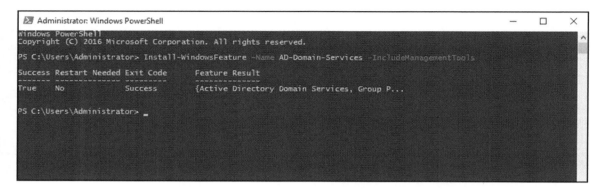

5. Now that we have the AD DS role installed, the next step is to proceed with the configuration:

```
Install-ADDSForest
-DomainName "rebeladmin.com"
-CreateDnsDelegation:$false
-DatabasePath "C:\Windows\NTDS"
-DomainMode "7"
-DomainNetbiosName "REBELADMIN"
-ForestMode "7"
-InstallDns:$true
-LogPath "C:\Windows\NTDS"
-NoRebootOnCompletion:$True
-SysvolPath "C:\Windows\SYSVOL"
-Force:$true
```

There are no line breaks for the command; I have listed it as shown in the preceding example to allow readers to see the parameters clearly. In the preceding command, the -DomainName and -DomainNetbiosNames values can be replaced with the domain name and NetBIOS name applying for your environment.

6. The following table explains the PowerShell commands and what they do:

Cmdlet	Description
`Install-WindowsFeature`	This cmdlet allows us to install Windows roles, role services, or Windows features in a local server or remote server. It is similar to using Windows Server Manager to install them.
`Install-ADDSForest`	This cmdlet allows us to setup a new Active Directory forest.

7. Following table explains the arguments for the commands and what they do:

Argument	Description
`-IncludeManagementTools`	This installs the management tools for the selected role service.
`-DomainName`	This parameter defines the FQDN for the Active Directory domain.
`-CreateDnsDelegation`	Using this parameter, we can define whether to create a DNS delegation that references Active Directory integrated DNS.
`-DatabasePath`	This parameter defines the folder path to store Active Directory database file (`ntds.dit`)
`-DomainMode`	This parameter will specify the Active Directory domain's functional level. In the aforementioned example, I used mode 7, which is Windows Server 2016.
`-DomainNetbiosName`	This defines the NetBIOS name for the forest root domain.
`-ForestMode`	This parameter will specify the Active Directory forest's functional level. In the aforementioned example, I used mode 7, which is Windows Server 2016.
`-InstallDns`	Using this can specify whether DNS role needs to be installed with Active Directory domain controller. For new forest, it is default requirement to set it to `$true`.
`-LogPath`	Log path can be used to specify the location to save domain log files.

-SysvolPath	This is to define the SYSVOL folder path. The default location for it will be C:\Windows.
-NoRebootOnCompletion	By default, the system restarts the server after domain controller configuration. Using this command can prevent the automatic system restart.
-Force	This parameter will force command to execute by ignoring the warning. It is typical for the system to pass the warning about best practices and recommendations.

8. Once executed, the command will prompt for **SafeMode**AdministratorPassword. This is to use in **Directory Services Restore Mode (DSRM)**. Make sure to use a complex password (according to Windows password complexity recommendations). Failure to do so will stop the configuration:

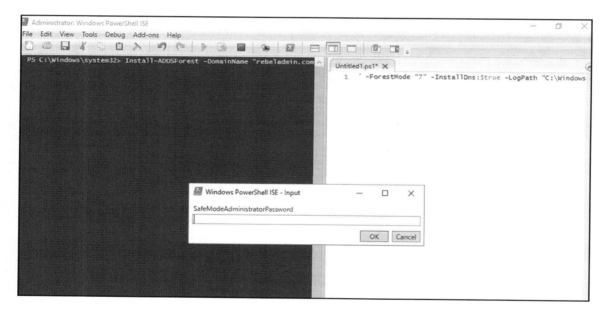

9. Once the configuration is complete, reboot the domain controller and log back in as domain administrator.
10. Let's do a further check to confirm the successful installation of the services:

```
Get-Service adws,kdc,netlogon,dns
```

The preceding command will list the status of the Active Directory related services running on the domain controller:

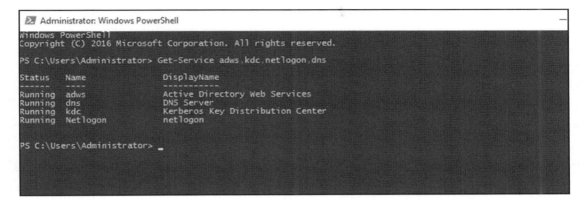

11. The following command will list all the configuration details of the domain controller:

```
Get-ADDomainController
```

The following screenshot demonstrates the output for the preceding command:

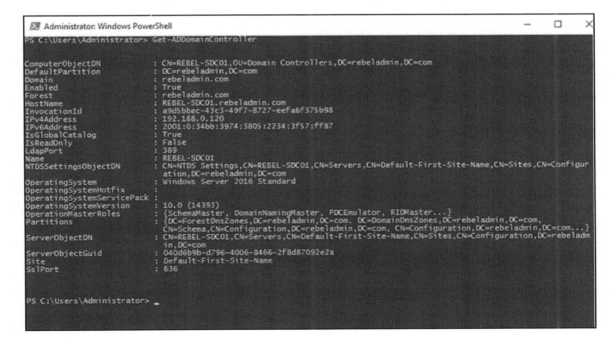

12. The following command will list down the details about the Active Directory domains:

```
Get-ADDomain rebeladmin.com
```

The following screenshot shows the output for the preceding command:

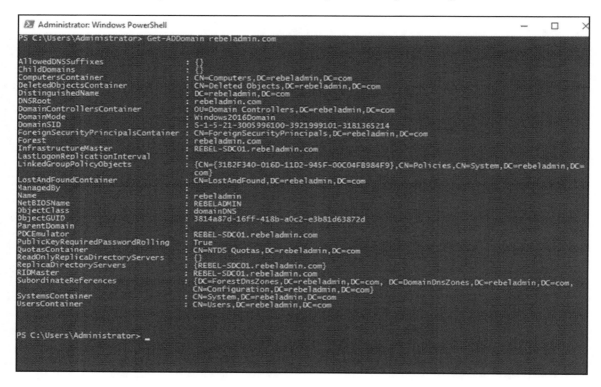

13. In the same way, `Get-ADForest rebeladmin.com` will list the Active Directory forest details.

14. The following command will show whether the domain controller shares the SYSVOL folder:

```
Get-smbshare SYSVOL
```

The following screenshot shows the output for the preceding command:

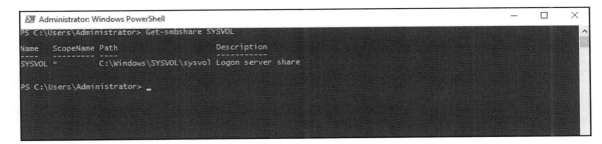

As we can see, AD DS components are installed and configured successfully. Now we have a new root domain installed, and in the next phase, let's see how to extend it further.

Setting up an additional domain controller

In this scenario, we are going to look into the installation of an additional domain controller in an existing Active Directory domain. Before we look into this installation, there are few prerequisites that need to be fulfilled:

- **Environment setup**: The physical server or VM, which is going to be used as the additional domain controller, needs to be added to the existing Active Directory domain. If the additional domain controller is going to be a DNS server, set its own IP address as the primary DNS server in the NIC settings and the existing domain controller IP address as secondary DNS server. During the installation process, it needs to have connectivity to existing domain controllers (via LAN or WAN) to replicate the Active Directory data.

 By default, during the installation, the system will try to replicate the Active Directory partitions from the available domain controller. If this is via a slow WAN link, it is going to affect the installation process. Therefore, in such a scenario, Active Directory can be installed using installation media. This is similar to an Active Directory backup from an existing domain controller. Then, the system will use local media to replicate the initial Active Directory data. This will be explained in detail in Chapter 11, *Active Directory Services.*

- **Existing infrastructure information**: In order to add an additional domain controller, we need to know certain information about the existing Active Directory infrastructure such as:
  - Active Directory domain name
  - Active Directory site
  - Whether the additional domain controller needs to be a global catalog server, DNS server or RODC
  - Active Directory initial data sync source (a specific Active Directory domain controller or media installation)
- **Schema preparation and domain preparation**: Let's assume we have an Active Directory infrastructure based on Windows Server 2012 R2. Now we need to add a domain controller, but we need it to use Windows Server 2016. Each version of Active Directory version has different schema. So by default, AD DS 2012 R2 schema will not recognize the domain controller running on Windows Server 2016. Before actual configuration begins, the existing schema needs to be modified to support this new requirement. This is done by using the `adprep.exe` application, which comes with the *operating system source files*. Before Windows Server 2012, this file had to be copied to the schema master, and we needed to run `/domainprep` and `/forestprep` to prepare the domain and forest. But now it comes as part of the AD DS configuration and it will run these commands in the background. In order to do that, configuration process of the domain should run as Schema Admin or Enterprise Admin.

Active Directory Domain Service installation checklist for an additional domain controller

The following checklist can be used for fresh AD DS installation for an additional domain controller:

- Prepare physical/virtual resources for the domain controller
- Install Windows Server 2016 Standard/Datacenter
- Patch servers with latest Windows updates
- Assign dedicated IP address to the domain controller
- Add the domain controller to the existing Active Directory domain as a domain member
- Find information about existing domain sites and the initial replication method
- Log into the server with a privileged account (Schema Admin, Enterprise Admin)
- Install AD DS role

- Configure AD DS
- Review logs to verify the healthy AD DS installation and configuration
- Configure service and performance monitoring
- AD DS backup/DR configuration

Design topology

As per the following diagram, we are going to add an **additional domain controller** to the `rebeladmin.com` domain:

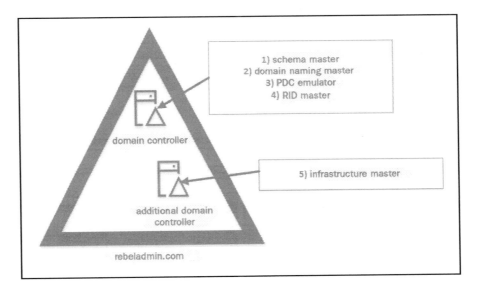

This domain controller is not going to be a global catalog server, and therefore at the end, we need to move the infrastructure master FSMO role over to it.

Installation steps

The following steps demonstrate how to add an additional domain controller to an existing domain:

1. Log in to the server as a member of Schema or Enterprise Admins group.
2. As a first step, verify the static IP address allocation by using `ipconfig /all`.
3. Launch the PowerShell console as an administrator.

4. Install the AD DS role service:

```
Install-WindowsFeature -Name AD-Domain-Services
   -IncludeManagementTools
```

5. After successful role service installation, the next step is to configure the domain controller:

```
Install-ADDSDomainController
-CreateDnsDelegation:$false
-NoGlobalCatalog:$true
-InstallDns:$true
-DomainName "rebeladmin.com"
-SiteName "Default-First-Site-Name"
-ReplicationSourceDC "REBEL-SDC01.rebeladmin.com"
-DatabasePath "C:\Windows\NTDS"
-LogPath "C:\Windows\NTDS"
-NoRebootOnCompletion:$true
-SysvolPath "C:\Windows\SYSVOL"
-Force:$true
```

There are no line breaks for the command. I have listed the parameters in the following as shown in the preceding example to allow readers to identify the parameters clearly:

Argument	Description
`Install-ADDSDomainController`	This cmdlet will install the domain controller in Active Directory infrastructure.
`-NoGlobalCatalog`	If you do not want to create the domain controller as a global catalog server, this parameter can be used. By default, the system will enable the global catalog feature.
`-SiteName`	This parameter can be used to define the Active Directory site name. The default value is `Default-First-Site-Name`.
`-DomainName`	This parameter defines the FQDN for the Active Directory domain.
`-ReplicationSourceDC`	Using this parameter can define the Active Directory replication source. By default, it uses any available domain controller. But if needed, we can be specific.

6. Once executed, the command will ask for **SafeModeAdministratorPassword**. Use a complex password to proceed. This will be used for DSRM.

7. After the configuration has completed, restart the system and log back in as administrator to check the AD DS status.

8. The following command will confirm the status of the AD DS service:

```
Get-Service adws,kdc,netlogon,dns
```

9. The following command will list the domain controllers, along with their IP addresses and the sites they belong to:

```
Get-ADDomainController -Filter * |  Format-Table Name,
   IPv4Address, Site
```

The following screenshot shows output for the preceding command:

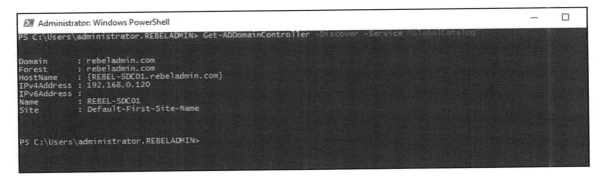

10. The following command will list the global catalog servers available in the domain and confirm this new domain controller server is not a global catalog server:

```
Get-ADDomainController -Discover -Service "GlobalCatalog"
```

The following screenshot shows output for the preceding command:

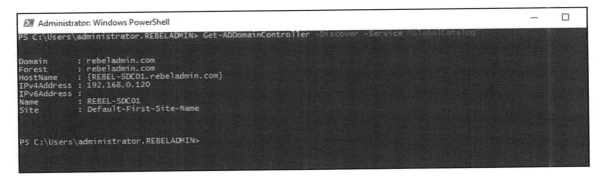

11. As per plan, the next step is to move the infrastructure master role to the new additional domain controller:

```
Move-ADDirectoryServerOperationMasterRole
 -Identity REBEL-SDC-02
 -OperationMasterRole InfrastructureMaster
```

12. By using the `netdom query fsmo` command, we can confirm the change:

```
PS C:\Users\administrator.REBELADMIN> netdom query fsmo
Schema master               REBEL-SDC01.rebeladmin.com
Domain naming master        REBEL-SDC01.rebeladmin.com
PDC                         REBEL-SDC01.rebeladmin.com
RID pool manager            REBEL-SDC01.rebeladmin.com
Infrastructure master       REBEL-SDC-02.rebeladmin.com
The command completed successfully.

PS C:\Users\administrator.REBELADMIN>
```

13. This is the end of this scenario, and the next step will be to extend the domain further by adding an additional domain.

Setting up a new domain tree

Active Directory **domain tree** is a collection of domains which share a contiguous namespace. An Active Directory forest can have multiple domain trees which use different namespaces. In one forest, each of these domain trees have explicit trust among them by default. In this scenario, we are going to create a new domain tree in an existing Active Directory forest.

Before we start with the installation, we need to consider a few things:

- **Environment setup**: The new physical server or the VM which is going to be set up should have network reachability to the existing forest root domain. It can be in different network segments, but in order to add it to the existing forest, a connection is required. In order to proceed with the configuration, the administrator should have a local administrator account for the server, and a Schema Admin or Enterprise Admin account log in details for the existing forest.

- **Information**: In order to set up the new domain tree, we need to gather the following information:
  - FQDN for the new domain
  - Forest name
  - Schema Admin or Enterprise Admin credentials for the existing *forest root domain*
- **Schema preparation**: If the new domain controller is going to be a newer version than the existing AD DS version, it needs the forest schema modified with `adprep /forestprep` to support the new version. As I explained in the previous scenario, this is now a part of the Active Directory configuration process. However, we need Schema Admin privileges to do it.

Active Directory Domain Service installation checklist for a new domain tree

The following checklist covers all the steps which need to considered for a new domain tree deployment:

- Prepare physical/virtual resources for the domain controller
- Install Windows Server 2016 Standard/Datacenter
- Patch servers with the latest Windows updates
- Assign dedicated IP address to the domain controller
- Find information about AD forest and Schema Admin/Enterprise Admin login details for the existing forest root domain
- Log into the server as local administrator
- Install AD DS role
- Configure AD DS new domain tree
- Review logs to verify the healthy AD DS installation and configuration
- Configure service and performance monitoring
- AD DS backup/DR configuration

Design topology

As per the following diagram, in this scenario we are going to add `rebeladmin.net`, a new domain tree. The `rebeladmin.com` domain is the existing forest tree which was created in the first scenario. Both domain trees will be under one **Active Directory forest**. The system will automatically create **two-way trust** between the two domain trees:

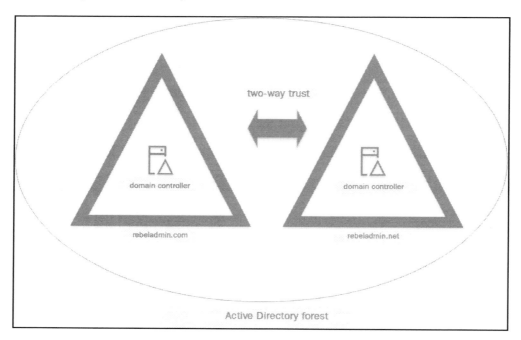

Installation steps

The following steps demonstrate how to add a new domain tree to an existing Active Directory forest:

1. Log in to the server as a local administrator.
2. As a first step, verify the static IP address allocation by using `ipconfig /all`.
3. Launch the PowerShell console as an administrator.
4. Install the AD DS role service:

```
Install-WindowsFeature -Name AD-Domain-Services
 -IncludeManagementTools
```

5. After successful role service installation, the next step is to set up the new domain tree:

```
Install-ADDSDomain
-Credential (Get-Credential)
-ParentDomainName "rebeladmin.com"
-NewDomainName "rebeladmin.net"
-NewDomainNetbiosName "REBELNET"
-DomainMode "WinThreshold"
-DomainType "TreeDomain"
-CreateDnsDelegation:$false
-NoGlobalCatalog:$false
-InstallDns:$true
-SiteName "Default-First-Site-Name"
-DatabasePath "C:\Windows\NTDS"
-LogPath "C:\Windows\NTDS"
-NoRebootOnCompletion:$true
-SysvolPath "C:\Windows\SYSVOL"
```

6. In the following table, I have listed down the descriptions of new PowerShell arguments:

Argument	Description
Install-ADDSDomain	This cmdlet installs the new Active Directory domain.
-Credential (Get-Credential)	This parameter allows us to pass the credentials which need to connect to the parent domain.
-ParentDomainName	This parameter defines the existing parent domain in the AD forest.
-NewDomainName	This defines the FQDN for the new AD domain name.
-NewDomainNetbiosName	This parameter defines the NetBIOS name for the new domain.
-DomainType	Using this parameter defines the type of the domain. The options will be child domain or domain tree. The default value for the parameter is Child Domain.

7. Once it is processed, it will prompt you to provide the credentials for Schema Admin/Enterprise Admin to connect to the parent domain. If this is not defined in the command, it will use the account user that is already logged in:

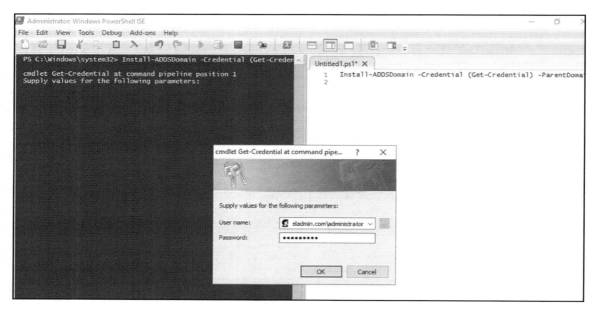

8. It will also ask for **SafeModeAdministratorPassword**. Use a complex password to proceed. This will be used for DSRM.

9. Once the configuration is complete, reboot the domain controller and log in as the new Domain Admin.

10. After login, we can do some testing to confirm the successful configuration.

11. The following command will list the FSMO role holders, and as we can see the forest root domain controller is the forest-wide FSMO role holder:

```
netdom query fsmo
```

The following screenshot shows output for the preceding command:

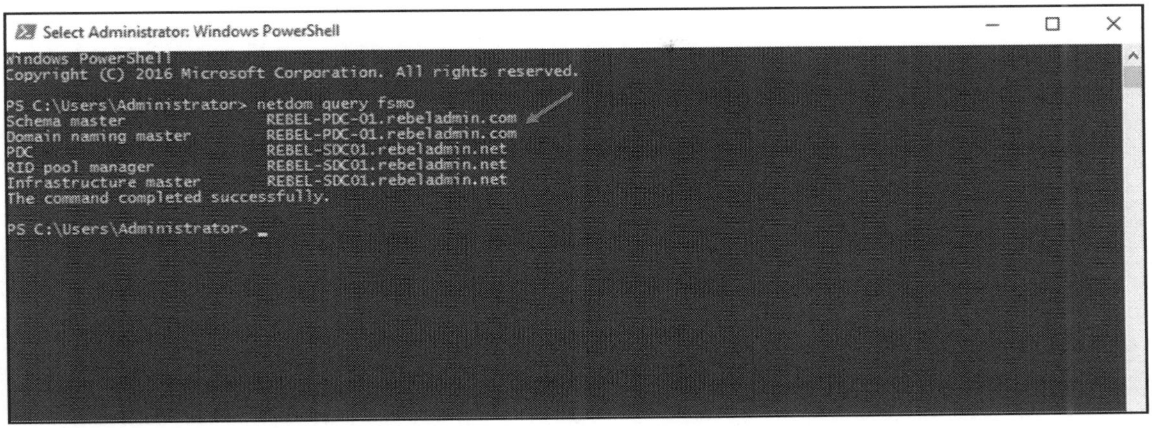

12. This next command lists the AD trust information between the two domain trees:

```
Get-ADTrust -Filter *
```

The following screenshot shows output for the preceding command:

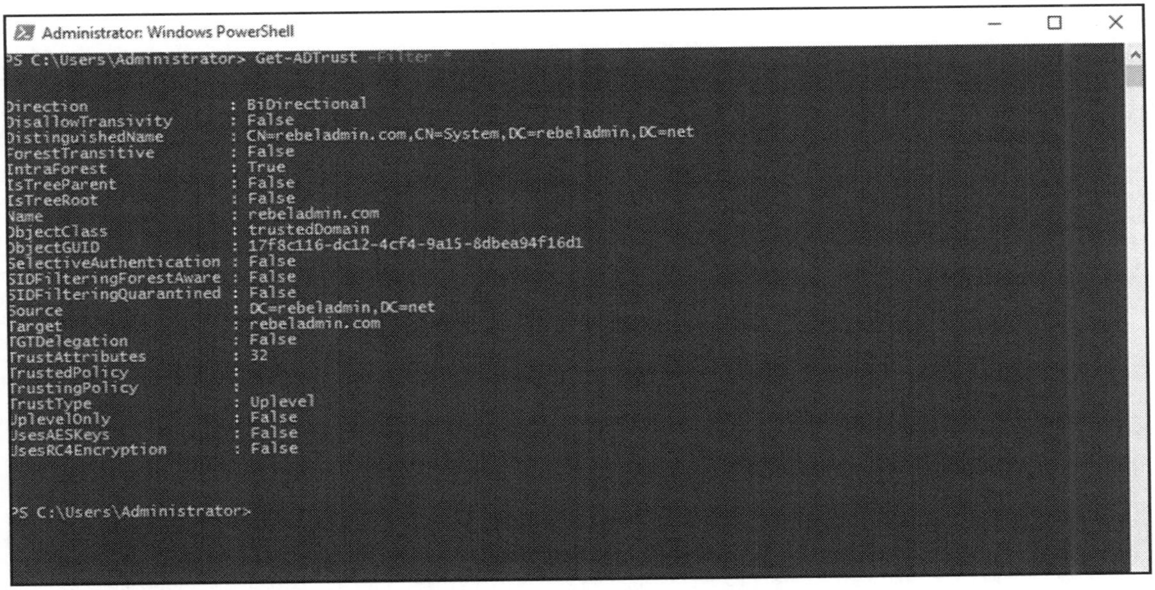

13. This following command confirms the domain controllers under the new domain tree:

```
Get-ADDomainController -Filter * | Format-Table Name,
    IPv4Address
```

The following screenshot shows output for the preceding command:

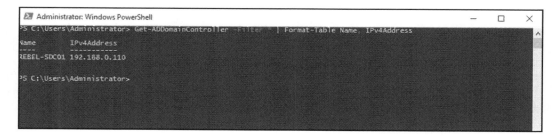

14. The following command lists the details about the new Active Directory domain:

```
Get-ADDomain
```

The following screenshot shows output for the preceding command:

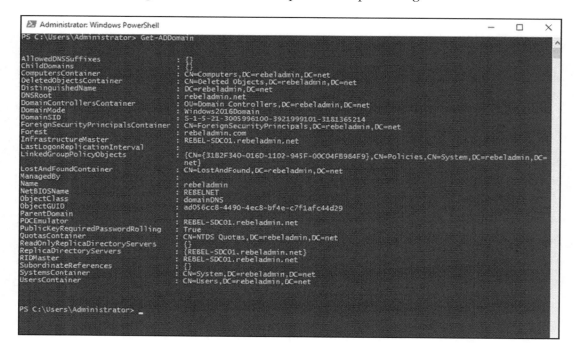

The commands used in the previous two scenarios can be used to test the domain setup further. In the next scenario, you will learn how to extend the domain trees further using child domains.

Setting up a new child domain

In a domain tree, domains maintain a contiguous namespace. The domains in a domain tree have a parent domain and all other domains under it are called **child domains**. As children use their parents' surname, child domains also use the name from their parent domain. For example, if the parent domain is `rebeladmin.com`, the child domains can look like `europe.rebeladmin.com` or `asia.rebeladmin.com`. Child domains help organizations to structure the resources and provide flexible IT management.

Before we start the installation, let's look into a few prerequisites, which are as follows:

- **Information**: In order to set up a child domain, we need to gather the following information:
  - FQDN for the child domain
  - Forest name
  - Schema Admin or Enterprise Admin credentials for the existing forest root domain
- **Environment setup**: The resources requirement for the installation is very much similar to creating a new domain tree. The server should not connect to the existing domain but during the installation, it needs connectivity to the parent domain. It also needs the credential for the Schema Admin or Enterprise Admin account from the parent domain in order to modify the schema.
- **Schema preparation**: As explained in the previous scenarios, if the new domain controller is going to be newer than the existing AD DS version, it needs the forest schema modified with `adprep.exe /forestprep` and `adprep.exe /domainprep` to support the new version. This action is now part of the Active Directory configuration process. But we need Schema Admin/Enterprise Admin privileges to do it.

Active Directory Domain Service installation checklist for a new child domain

The following checklist covers all the steps you need to follow when deploying a new child domain:

- Prepare physical/virtual resources for the domain controller
- Install Windows Server 2016 Standard/Datacenter
- Patch servers with the latest Windows updates
- Assign dedicated IP address to the domain controller
- Find information about AD forest and Schema Admin/Enterprise Admin login details for the existing forest root domain
- Log into the server as a local administrator
- Install AD DS role
- Configure AD DS new child domain
- Review logs to verify the healthy AD DS installation and configuration
- Configure service and performance monitoring
- AD DS Backup/DR configuration

Design topology

As per the following diagram, we are going to add a new child domain to the `rebeladmin.com` **domain tree**:

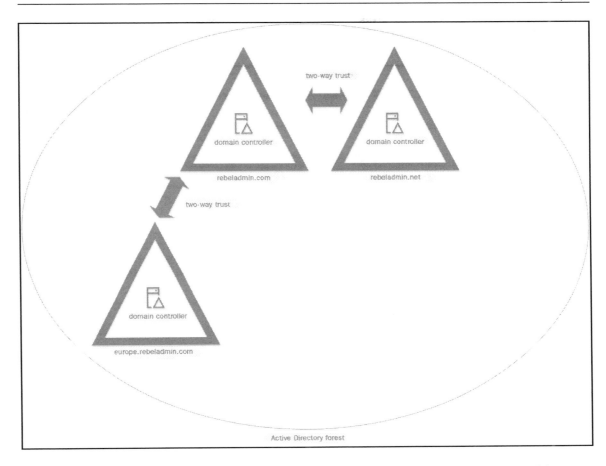

The name of the new child domain will be `europe.rebeladmin.com`. This will still be under the same **Active Directory forest**. Similar to new domain tree, the child domain and parent domain will have two-way domain trust created automatically. This domain controller is going to be the first domain controller on the child domain, therefore it cannot be a RODC.

Installation steps

The following steps demonstrate how we can add a new child domain to the existing domain:

1. Log in to the server as a local administrator.
2. As a first step, verify the static IP address allocation by using `ipconfig /all`.

3. Launch the PowerShell console as an administrator.

4. Install the AD DS role service:

```
Install-WindowsFeature -Name AD-Domain-Services
  -IncludeManagementTools
```

5. After successful role service installation, the next step is to set up the new child domain:

```
Install-ADDSDomain
-Credential (Get-Credential)
-ParentDomainName "rebeladmin.com"
-NewDomainName "europe"
-NewDomainNetbiosName "EUROPE"
-DomainMode "WinThreshold"
-DomainType "ChildDomain"
-CreateDnsDelegation:$true
-NoGlobalCatalog:$false
-InstallDns:$true
-SiteName "Default-First-Site-Name"
-DatabasePath "C:\Windows\NTDS"
-LogPath "C:\Windows\NTDS"
-NoRebootOnCompletion:$true
-SysvolPath "C:\Windows\SYSVOL"
```

6. In the following table, I have listed down the descriptions of some PowerShell arguments:

Argument	Description
-DomainType	Using this parameter the type of the domain can be defined. The options will be child domain or domain tree. For this scenario the default ChildDomain type is selected.
-CreateDnsDelegation	When a child domain is set up, DNS delegation is a must with its parent domain. Delegation records must be created in the parent domain DNS zone to provide correct referrals to the DNS servers to server client's DNS queries.

7. After executing the commands, it will prompt for the credentials. We need to provide Schema Admin/Enterprise Admin account details for the parent domain.

8. It will also ask for **SafeModeAdministratorPassword**. Use a complex password to proceed. This will be used for DSRM:

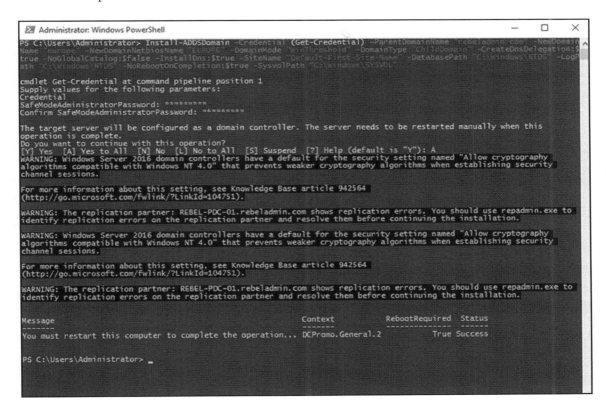

9. Once the configuration is complete, reboot the domain controller and log in as the new Domain Admin.

10. Let's do some tests to verify the configuration. I have logged in to the parent domain controller, and in DNS I can see that the new zone delegation is set up for the child domain:

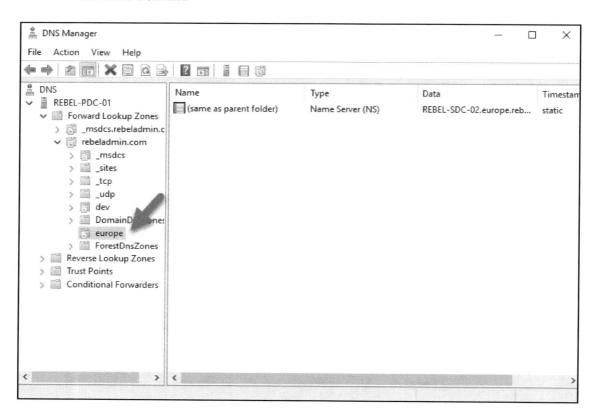

11. We can use the following command to verify the FSMO role placement for the new child domain:

```
netdom query fsmo
```

The preceding command is recommended to be executed on the child domain controller.

12. I ran the following command to verify the two-way trust between the parent domain and the child domain. This is processed from the parent domain controller:

```
Get-ADTrust -Identity europe.rebeladmin.com
```

The following screenshot shows output for the preceding command:

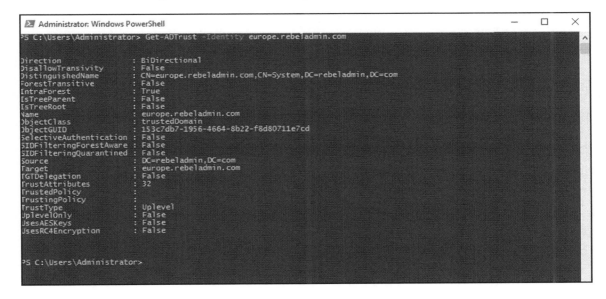

13. The following command will list the details about the new subdomain:

```
Get-ADDomain europe
```

The following screenshot shows output for the preceding command:

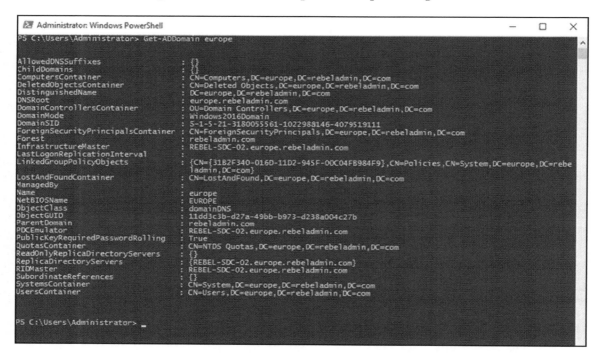

14. We can use the following to verify the status of the AD DS:

```
Get-Service adws,kdc,netlogon,dns
```

According to the test results, the child domain is functioning properly. This is the end of AD DS installation scenarios, and in the next section, we are going to look into AD DS migration.

How to plan Active Directory migrations

Active Directory migration from an older version to a new version is a common challenge for identity infrastructures. In some documents, this is called **Active Directory upgrades**, but I prefer to call it **Active Directory migration**. In this process, a new AD DS version will install in a new server or an existing server. Then the FSMO roles will migrate to the new domain controllers. Once it's completed, the older version of AD DS will be decommissioned. Afterwards, the domain and forest function level will be raised to match the new AD DS version. Even though each AD DS version has core functions that are the same, newer versions always have new features and enhancements which apply at domain or forest level. Therefore, it's more of a *migration* than an *upgrade*. The **migration** term is also used for migrating Active Directory objects from one forest to another, or one domain to another. In there, it may or may not have Active Directory version change. But in this section, we are only going to look at the migration from one version to another.

There can be many reasons why organizations may consider Active Directory migrations. I have listed a few main reasons that I usually see in my projects, and they are as follows:

- **To implement new features in the identity infrastructure**: Every new version of Active Directory comes with new features and enhancements. Some of these changes are game changers. As an example, AD DS 2016 privilege management is a turning point for identity infrastructures. In order to implement these new features, companies look for AD DS migrations. It's only been a few months since the AD DS 2016 release, and I have already finished a few large projects to migrate to the new version, which is a good trend. I am a geek and I always prefer to run the latest and the greatest. At the same time, I see that some organizations just like to run the latest but do not worry much about implementing any new features. Just migrating to a new version is not going to give any benefits if it's not used properly. There's no point buying a Ferrari just to drop your kids to school. Therefore, as organizations, it's important to evaluate the objectives thoroughly before Active Directory migration.

- **To address support issues and compliance issues**: Back in 2015, Microsoft ended its support for Windows Server 2003. At that time, organizations which were running AD DS 2003 have no choice but to migrate to new version. Some businesses need to comply with compliance in order to run their operations. Business in the financial sector is a good example of that. These compliances have standards related to IT systems. As an example, the businesses subject to **Payment Card Industry (PCI)** compliance had rules that it couldn't use end-of-life operating systems for operations. Thus, these kind of business requirements force organizations to migrate from one AD DS version to another.

- **To fix existing issues**: The health of identity infrastructure is key for an organization's operations and security. As in any other system, it is possible for identity infrastructure to have issues. These could be due to bad design, configuration issues, system corruptions, and so on. Fixes for these problems may lead to migrations as well. When I bring my car for servicing, sometimes they tell me that some parts need to be replaced. But before replacement, mechanics normally give me a few options to choose from. Some parts are of the same make and model but others are for a new version. So, the mechanic makes sure to explain the advantage of the new model and explain what it can give me, rather than just fix the problem. Most of the time, I end up using the new model, as it doesn't just fix the existing issue, it fixes it in a better way.
So, if existing identity infrastructure issues can be fixed in a *better way* by migrating to a new version, do not hesitate to go for it. But at the same time, there are some basic AD health requirements that need to be fulfilled before performing the migration. This will be covered later in this chapter.

- **Operation requirements**: In business, there can be other operational requirements which can lead to AD migrations. New application implementations are a good example of this. Some applications only support certain AD DS schema versions. In such situations, even businesses don't have plans for migrations, so it creates new requirements where reconsideration will have to be made. There is another scenario which applies to organizations that run AD forest with multiple domain trees. As an example, Rebeladmin Corp. has three domain trees with one forest. Each domain tree represents a separate sub company with its own IT department. One company has business requirements to upgrade its domain and forest function level to a newer version. But in order to do that, the other two domains also need to upgrade their AD DS versions. So, it isn't an operational requirement for two of the companies, but to support the forest level upgrade, there is no option but to upgrade their AD DS.

Migration life cycle

Based on the steps in the AD DS migration process, I have come up with the following life cycle:

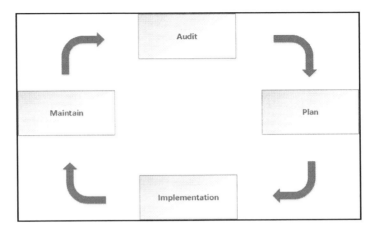

Following this will ensure that every aspect of the migration process is covered.

Audit

In the migration process, auditing and planning are the most important stages. When you have proper auditing and a plan, the implementation process is quite easy. It minimizes the post implementation issues. In the audit stage, we review the current Active Directory infrastructure and get a clear understanding about the logical and physical topology and health status, and identify potential risks in migration.

Active Directory logical and physical topology

A few years ago, I needed to add an additional room to my house. So I went to meet an architect and explained my requirement. When I explained, I mentioned the house structure, where it's located, why I needed this extension, and where I thought it suited best. Even though I explained the structure, one of the initial requests from the architect was to show him the current house plan. My verbal explanation about the house wasn't enough for him to provide me with a new plan. That is because my explanation was still missing some critical information, such as length, width, door and window locations, and so on. But the current house plan indicates all this information, which helps him to make an accurate new plan.

Similarly, in Active Directory migration projects, one of my initial requests to customers is to provide an Active Directory topology diagram. However, most of the time, I only get the basic information, such as the number of domain controllers, the number of sites, and so on. But that is not enough to get an understanding of domain trees, replication topology, site links, and FSMO role placements. In most cases, I have to create an Active Directory topology diagram from scratch as part of the exercise. Microsoft Active Directory Topology Diagrammer is a tool that can be used to automatically generate a diagram with a lot of important data, such as domain trees, sites, server system info, and organization units. It connects to the Active Directory using LDAP connection and generates a Visio diagram. In order to run this, we need a domain-joined computer with Microsoft Visio installed. This tool doesn't have many updates, but it still can do the job. It can be downloaded from `https://www.microsoft.com/en-gb/download/details.aspx?id=13380`. The diagram it generates can be modified as per other requirements.

Apart from the topology diagram, network diagrams also help the engineers to understand the physical placement of the Active Directory components. The topology diagram includes data about physical structure, such as site links, number of domain controllers, and number of sites, but it doesn't give much of an overview about how traffic flows (network segments) and what kind of connections and bandwidth each site has. Network diagrams provide help to gather this data.

Some organizations always keep these diagrams up to date with all the changes. But it's not the same for the majority. Lots of companies either do not have any of these diagrams, or even if they have them, they may not be up to date. Depending on the project scope, it may not be your responsibility to create a topology diagram and network diagram, but at least collect the data which is vital for the AD DS migration project. If you are dealing with fragmented data, you can use other techniques, such as interviews and questionnaires with engineers, managers, and team leaders to clear up doubts. Also, you can refer to the asset changes if the company has a change-tracking system.

I have shortlisted the types of data we need to gather during this exercise:

- Active Directory logical topology
- Active Directory physical topology
- Organization's network topology
- Links between Active Directory sites
- Bandwidth between Active Directory sites

Active Directory health check

My first car was a white Honda Civic 2004 model (I loved that little beast). After I bought the car, I saw little rust spots on the bonnet. I took it to a paint shop and the man who checked it said that it needed a fresh coat of paint. So I agreed and got it done. After a few months, I started to see some bubbles again on the bonnet. I took it back to the shop, as I had 6 months warranty for the job they had done. They said they would redo the paint. But guess what—after a few months, again the same issue. I did not want to waste my time any more and I took it to another place which specialized in paint jobs. When I explained the issues, the engineers there performed some tests and said that they needed to remove the whole paint and apply anti-rust first. So they did that and applied the paint layers over it. After that, there were no more bubbles on the bonnet. Just applying a new coat of paint didn't fix the issue. It was only a waste of time and money.

If Active Directory infrastructure has got existing issues related to its core operations (such as replications, DNS, and site links), then those need to be identified and fixed before migration. Otherwise, they will not allow the objectives of the migration to be achieved. There is no specific, predefined sequence for Active Directory health checks. You can have your own checklist which covers the evaluation of each Active Directory components health. I am going to list down some key areas which need to be covered in any Active Directory health check:

- **Replication health**: A healthy replication is important for any Active Directory infrastructure. All domain controllers in the infrastructure need to be aware of every change to the Active Directory database. There are tools and techniques we can use to identify the replication issues between Active Directory domain controllers. `Repadmin.exe` is a Microsoft-built tool which can be used to diagnose Active Directory replication issues. Since Windows Server 2008, it has come built into the operating system, and it can be used if the AD DS role is installed. This tool needs to run as Enterprise Admin. If it runs as Domain Admin, it can only be used to review domain-level replications:

    ```
    Repadmin /showrepl
    ```

    The preceding command will display the status of the last inbound replication of the Active Directory partition. This will only list the replication status of the domain controller this command executes from.

If you need to check the replication status of a specific domain controller, you can use a command similar to the following. The REBEL-SDC-03 section of the command can be replaced by the name of the domain controller:

```
Repadmin /showrepl REBEL-SDC-03
```

The /replicate parameter can be used to trigger a replication between the domain controllers to see the real-time results:

```
Repadmin /replicate REBEL-SDC-03.rebeladmin.com
    REBEL-PDC-01.rebeladmin.com DC=rebeladmin,DC=com
```

The preceding command will initiate replication of the rebeladmin naming context from REBEL-PDC-01 to REBEL-SDC-03.

The following commands will initiate full replication of all the changes from REBEL-PDC-01 to REBEL-SDC-03:

```
Repadmin /replicate REBEL-SDC-03.rebeladmin.com
    REBEL-PDC-01.rebeladmin.com DC=rebeladmin,DC=com /full
```

The /replsummary parameter can be used to see the summary of the replication status of all domain controllers:

```
Repadmin /replsummary
```

The preceding command will provide a summary of all the domain controllers in the infrastructure:

```
PS C:\Users\Administrator> repadmin /replsummary
Replication Summary Start Time: 2017-02-05 14:53:08

Beginning data collection for replication summary, this may take awhile:
.......

Source DSA        largest delta    fails/total %%    error
REBEL-PDC-01           54m:10s      0 /   6    0
REBEL-SDC-02      02d.15h:05m:56s   4 /   4   100   (1908) Could not find the domain controller for this domain.
REBEL-SDC-03           58m:42s      0 /   6    0

Destination DSA   largest delta    fails/total %%    error
REBEL-PDC-01      02d.15h:05m:56s   4 /  10   40   (1908) Could not find the domain controller for this domain.
REBEL-SDC-03           54m:10s      0 /   6    0

Experienced the following operational errors trying to retrieve replication information:
        58 - 9a145fff-4ea2-4595-ba37-1df8ddaf98ba._msdcs.rebeladmin.com
      8341 - REBEL-SDC-02.europe.rebeladmin.com
PS C:\Users\Administrator>
```

The following command will only list the domain controllers which have replication issues with partners:

```
Repadmin /replsummary /errorsonly
```

- **Event Viewer**: **Event Viewer** can also be used to evaluate the replication health of the Active Directory environment. There are certain event IDs you can use to filter the data. You can find these events under **Event Viewer** | **Application and Service Logs** | **Directory Services**.

I have listed down some key event IDs which will show the replication problems:

Event ID	Cause
1925	The attempt to establish a replication link for a writable directory partition failed. This can be caused by network issues, domain controller failures, or DNS issues.
1988	The local domain controller has attempted to replicate an object from a source domain controller that is not present on the local domain controller because it may have been deleted and already garbage-collected. Replication will not proceed for this directory partition with this partner until the situation is resolved. This happens when a domain controller is down for a long time (more than the tombstone lifetime) before being brought back online. It could then have non-existing objects (lingering objects). They need to be cleaned to initiate the replication again.
2087	AD DS could not resolve the DNS hostname of the source domain controller to an IP address, and replication failed. This will show up in the destination domain controller when it cannot resolve the DNS name for its source domain controller. If DNS lookup fails in the first place, it will also try FQDN and NetBIOS to resolve the name. It will prevent replication until it's been resolved.
2088	AD DS could not resolve the DNS host name of the source domain controller to an IP address, but replication succeeded. In this situation, destination domain controller failed to resolve the source name using DNS lookup but it was able to connect to it using the FQDN or NetBIOS name.
1311	The replication configuration information in AD DS does not accurately reflect the physical topology of the network. This usually occurs due to misconfiguration of Active Directory site links. It may have wrong subnets assigned.

Once an object is deleted from the Directory, it will not delete right away from the Active Directory database. It will be removed by the garbage collector once it passes the tombstone lifetime value. The default value is 180 days.

- **Domain controller health**: In the previous section, we had to evaluate the replication health and the next step is to check the health of domain controllers. Similar to Repadmin, Microsoft has tools which can be used for this task.

The Dcdiag.exe tool can be used to run predefined tests to evaluate the health of the domain controllers:

```
Dcdiag /e
```

This command will test the domain controllers in the forest:

```
Dcdiag /s:REBEL-SDC-03
```

The preceding command will run the test on domain controller REBEL-SDC-03.

Instead of running all the tests, the following command will run only a replication test on REBEL-SDC-03:

```
Dcdiag /test:replications /s:REBEL-SDC-03
```

It will run tests to check Active Directory services on the local domain controller:

```
Dcdiag /test:Services
```

- **DNS health**: We cannot talk about Active Directory health without healthy DNS infrastructure. Active Directory heavily depends on DNS functionalities.

To start with, I prefer to review the DNS server-related events in domain controllers. It can access the DNS logs from **Event Viewer** | Application and Service Logs | **DNS Server**:

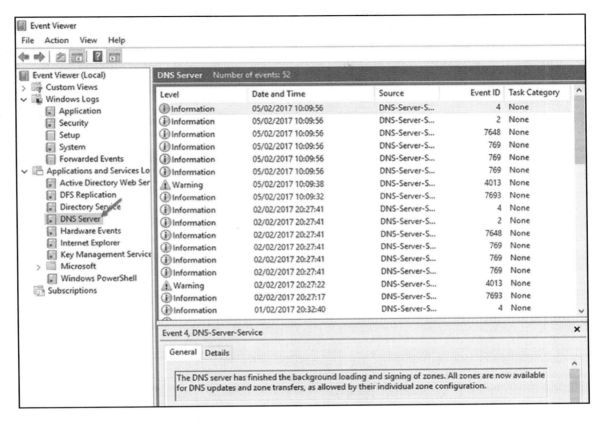

The `Dcdiag` utility can also be used to test the DNS health:

```
Dcdiag /test:DNS /DNSBasic
```

The preceding command will run the basic DNS check to ensure DNS services are running, resource records are registered, and DNS zones are presented.

The following command will test if the DNS forwarders are functioning properly:

```
Dcdiag /test:DNS /DnsForwarders
```

The following command will test the registration of DC locator records:

```
Dcdiag /test:DNS /DnsRecordRegistration
```

System Center Operation Manager and Operation Management Suite

SCOM have Active Directory Management Packs and DNS Management Packs which monitor the application level health events. OMS has modules which evaluate the health and security of the Active Directory environment and the replication health. If organizations have these tools configured, they provide real-time data about the AD health, and also, if there are any issues detected, they provide guidelines on how to fix them (OMS AD assessment).

In the following section, I have listed down the Active Directory health checklist I use with the projects.

Active Directory health checklist

The following is the Active Directory health checklist:

- Review connection status between domain controllers
- If the organization has a monitoring system, review the reports and latest events about domain controllers, AD DS roles, replication health, and DNS services
- Review the latest backup reports
- Review DNS issues and events
- Review Active Directory domain controller's health
- Test Active Directory replications
- Review Active Directory logs to find any re-occurrence issues
- Review the existing domain controller's performance
- Review bandwidth utilization between site links

Application audit

If organizations are running AD DS, it's obvious they have Active Directory integrated applications. Some of those may use it just for LDAP authentication and some may use advanced integration with a modified Active Directory schema. With Active Directory migration, some of these applications may require modifications or upgrades to match the new AD DS version.

Therefore, before the implementation process, it is important to recognize these Active Directory integrated applications and evaluate their impact on the migration:

- **LDAP connection string modifications**: In order to use **single sign-on (SSO)** with applications, it may use LDAP connections to domain controllers. Sometimes, applications use hardcoded hostnames or IP addresses of domain controllers to define the connections. If domain migration involves IP address changes and hostname changes, alternation to these records will need to be planned.

- **Schema version changes**: Some legacy applications only support certain versions of Active Directory schema. This is specific to custom-made Active Directory-integrated applications. This is very rare but I have faced these issues in my Active Directory migrations projects. Therefore, if it's not a well known application, check with the application vendor whether it supports the new AD DS schema version.

- **Application migrations**: Some organizations have legacy application versions which are no longer supported or developed by their vendors. There are occasions when these types of issues turn out to be bottlenecks for AD Migration projects. Once I was working on an AD DS 2003 to AD DS 2012 R2 migration project. The organization had a legacy application which ran on the Windows Server 2000 system. AD DS 2012 R2 does not support Windows Server 2000-member servers. The vendor who created the application was no longer in business. As a result we had to use to a similar type of application which supported the new operating systems before we started with the Active Directory migrations.

- **Server roles/applications installed on domain controllers**: In the majority of cases, once the FSMO roles are migrated to new domain controllers, the old domain controllers are decommissioned. Even though Microsoft recommends not to install applications or other server roles in domain controllers, people still do it. Some of the common roles installed in domain controllers are DHCP, file servers, and licensing servers. If existing domain controllers are subject to decommissioning, these applications and server roles need to migrate to new servers. Some of these roles or application versions may not be on the market anymore. For example, Windows **Internet Authentication Service (IAS)** in Windows Server 2003 was replaced by **Network Policy Server** (**NPS**). Therefore if you cannot use the same versions in migration, you will need to plan for upgrades or replace it with an equivalent application.

Plan

After a successful auditing phase, we have a lot of data and insight about the existing Active Directory infrastructure. In the planning process, I usually re-evaluate the collected data and make a blueprint to follow in the implementation process. This can be presented as a document so that each party involved in the project is aware of it.

The following information needs to be covered in the plan:

Data	Description
Overview of existing AD DS infrastructure	Based on the collected data from the audit, it is required to provide an overview of the existing infrastructure. It should include information about Active Directory logical and physical topology.
Overview of the proposed solution	Based on the collected data from the audit and the business requirements, we can provide a detailed design of the proposed solution. It should include data about the topology changes, new domain controller placements, FSMO role placements, new site links, IP addresses, hostnames, required hardware or virtual machined resources, required firewall rule changes, and so on.
Risks	One main objective of the audit exercise is to identify the potential risks which can impact the AD DS migration. These can be due to wrong design, bad health of the Active Directory services, or other infrastructure or application issues. The recognized risks can be categorized based on impact (for example: high, medium, low).
Risk mitigation plan	Once the risks are identified, we need to provide a plan to describe what action can be taken to address them. If it's possible, include a task list, estimated time frame, and budget in the plan.
Service interruptions	During the implementation process, there can be service interruptions. This can be due to events such as application migrations or server IP changes. In this section, make a list of these service interruptions, along with the expected time range, so that the relevant parties can be informed prior to the migration process.
Recommendations	During the audit process, you may have found things that you could do to improve AD DS performance, security, or manageability. What wasn't covered in the initial business requirements can be listed as recommendations. Note that these should not make any direct impact on the AD DS migration process. If this is done, it should be listed in the proposed solution section.

Task list and schedule	The plan should have a detailed task list and schedule for the AD DS migration implementation process. It should also include roles and responsibilities for completing each task.
Test plan	It is also required to have a detailed test plan to test the Active Directory functions after the AD DS migration process, to verify the health and integrity. This must be used during the implementation process and should include evidence to prove successful completion of each test task (screenshots, events, reports).
Recovery plan	After a successful audit and planning process, there is a very low possibility of project failure. But the plan still needs to provide a recovery plan to use in the event of a failure. It also should include a process to test the existing DR or backup solution which will be used in the recovery prior to starting the project.

Once the plan is produced, explain it to everyone involved in the project. Also, explain their roles and responsibilities in the project. It is also required to get the plan approved from the required authorized people before implementation.

Implementation

After a successful audit and planning process, the next step is to perform the implementation. If you have done your homework correctly in the previous phases, this process will be straight forward and end with a successful result.

Based on the previous phases, I have created the following checklist that you can use for the Active Directory migration process.

Active Directory migration checklist

The following is the Active Directory migration checklist:

- Evaluate business requirements for Active Directory migration
- Perform an audit on the existing Active Directory infrastructure
- Provide a plan for the implementation process
- Prepare physical/virtual resources for the domain controller
- Install Windows Server 2016 Standard/Datacenter
- Patch servers with the latest Windows updates

- Assign a dedicated IP address to the domain controller
- Install AD DS role
- Migrate application and server roles from the existing domain controllers
- Migrate FSMO roles to the new domain controllers
- Add new domain controllers to the existing monitoring system
- Add new domain controllers to the existing DR solution
- Decommission the old domain controllers
- Raise the domain and forest functional level
- On going maintenance (Group Policy review, new-feature implementations, identifying and fixing Active Directory infrastructure issues)

Here as part of the exercise, I am going to demonstrate how to perform migration from AD DS 2012 R2 to AD DS 2016.

Design topology

As per the following diagram, `rebeladmin.com` domain has two domain controllers:

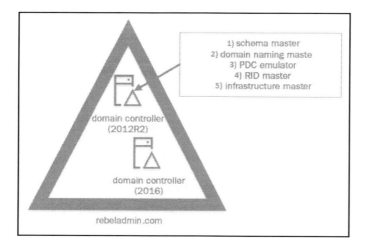

The FSMO role holder is running a domain controller based on Windows Server 2012 R2. The domain and forest functional levels currently operate in Windows Server 2012 R2. A new domain controller with Windows Server 2016 will be introduced and it will be the new FSMO role holder for the domain. Once the FSMO role migration is complete, the domain controller running Windows Server 2012 R2 will be decommissioned. After that, the forest and domain function levels are raised to Windows Server 2016.

In the demonstration, `REBEL-WIN-DC01` is the domain controller with Windows Server 2012 R2 and `REBEL-SDC01` is the domain controller with Windows Server 2016.

 When you introduce new domain controllers to existing infrastructure, it is recommended to introduce to the forest root level first and then go to the domain tree levels.

Installation steps

Using the following steps, we can install the new domain controller and migrate FSMO roles to it:

1. Log in to the server as a member of the local administrator's group.
2. Add the server to the existing domain as a member.
3. Log in to the domain controller as Enterprise Admin.
4. Verify the static IP address allocation by using `ipconfig /all`.
5. Launch the PowerShell console as an administrator.
6. Before the configuration process, we need to install the AD DS role in the given server. In order to do that, we can use the following command:

```
Install-WindowsFeature -Name AD-Domain-Services
  -IncludeManagementTools
```

7. Configure the new server as an additional domain controller. (The steps were covered earlier in this chapter).
8. Migrate all five FSMO roles to the new domain controller by using the following command:

```
Move-ADDirectoryServerOperationMasterRole -Identity REBEL-SDC01
  -OperationMasterRole SchemaMaster, DomainNamingMaster,
PDCEmulator, RIDMaster, InfrastructureMaster
```

In the preceding command, `REBEL-SDC01` is the domain controller running with Windows Server 2016.

9. Once it's completed, we can verify the new FSMO role holder using the following command:

```
netdom query fsmo
```

The following screenshot demonstrates the output of the preceding command:

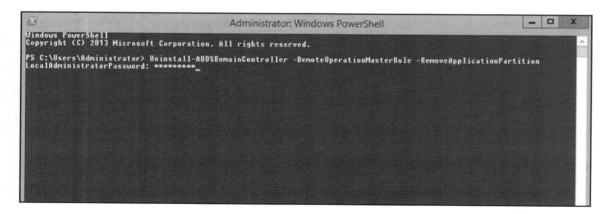

10. The next step of the process is to decommission the old Windows domain controllers running on Windows Server 2012 R2. To do that, execute the following command as Enterprise Admin from the relevant DC:

```
Uninstall-ADDSDomainController -DemoteOperationMasterRole
    -RemoveApplicationPartition
```

11. After executing the command, it will ask you to define a password for the local administrator account:

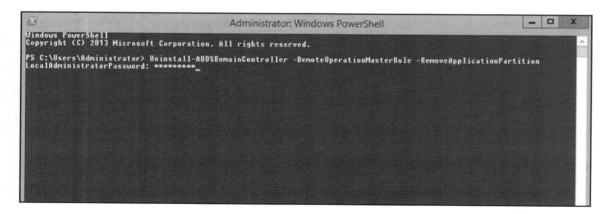

Once it's completed, it will be a member server of the rebeladmin.com domain.

12. The next step is to raise the domain and forest functional level to Windows Server 2016. To do that, you can use the following commands. To upgrade domain functional levels:

```
Set-ADDomainMode -identity rebeladmin.com
  -DomainMode Windows2016Domain
```

To upgrade forest function levels:

```
Set-ADForestMode -Identity rebeladmin.com
  -ForestMode Windows2016Forest
```

Now we have completed the migration from AD DS 2012 R2 to AD DS 2016. The same steps apply when migrating from Windows Server 2008, Windows Server 2008 R2, and Windows Server 2012.

Verification

After the migration completes, we still need to verify whether it's completed successfully. The following command will show the current domain functional level of the domain after the migration:

```
Get-ADDomain | fl Name,DomainMode
```

The following command will show the current forest functional level of the domain:

```
Get-ADForest | fl Name,ForestMode
```

Also, you can use the following command:

```
Get-EventLog -LogName 'Directory Service' | where {$_.eventID -eq 2039 -or
$_.eventID -eq 2040} | Format-List
```

The following screenshot shows the search of event ID 2039 and 2040 in the Directory Service log, which shows the forest and domain functional level updates:

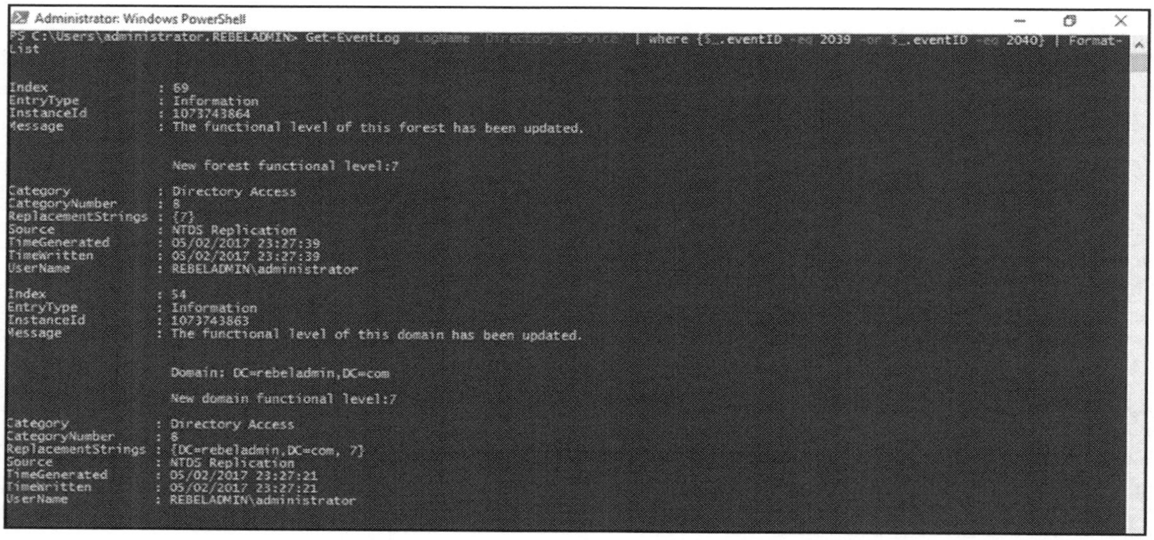

Event ID 1458 will verify the transfer of the FSMO roles:

```
Get-EventLog -LogName 'Directory Service' | where {$_.eventID -eq 1458} |
Format-List
```

You can use the following command to verify the list of domain controllers and make sure the old domain controller is gone:

```
Get-ADDomainController -Filter * | Format-Table Name, IPv4Address
```

Apart from these, you can also go through directory service and DNS logs to see if there are any issues recorded.

Maintain

I am a petrol head; I love the smell of burning fuel. I always service my car at the right time, wash it regularly, put in the best oil which is recommended, and do all the tune ups when required. Because of that, my little beast never gets me in trouble when I am on the wheels, touch wood!

Likewise, it doesn't matter how good your Active Directory infrastructure is today; if you do not maintain and tune it, you are not going to get much out of it. Following, I have listed things you need to do after Active Directory migration to get the most out of it:

- **Add to the monitoring system**: The new domain controllers now hold the responsibilities of your identity infrastructure. It is important to get notified if there is any failure of the hardware or system service which will affect company operations. For that task, I prefer to use an advanced application layer monitoring system, such as SCOM or OMS, which not only alerts about service and system failures, but also predicts issues in advance and allows engineers to rectify them. OMS also provides guidance based on Microsoft best practices to improve the performance and security in the identity infrastructure.

- **Add to the DR solution**: In the event of hardware failure or natural disaster, the company should be able to recover its workloads to continue its operations. It can be backed up, or you can use any other DR solution. My preference for this is to keep additional domain controllers in DR sites, along with backup. In a disaster, it will allow the other application to continue its operations with minimum impact. Once you add new domain controllers to the backup or DR solution, make sure to test them periodically to verify the validity.

- **Implement new features**: Once the domain and forest functional levels are updated, you can start implementing or start using the new features of AD DS 2016, that I described in `Chapter 2`, *Active Directory Domain Services 2016*. Applying new features is one main objective of any AD DS migration project. When applying features, try to apply them first to test devices or a group of test users before applying them organization-wide. It will minimize the impact if you need to alter it or completely remove it. The features you can use for your organization depend on the organization's business model and operations.

- **Group Policy reviews**: Group policies can be used to manage systems, application and security settings for users, devices, and other resources in the Active Directory infrastructure. As the system migrates from one AD DS version to another, Group Policy capabilities change too. In an infrastructure, there can be group policies which contain legacy settings no longer valid for the organization's operations. Or else, the newer AD DS version may have a *better way* of doing things. Therefore, after AD DS migrations, review your group policies and make any required amendments or implementations. For Group Policy testing, always try it against a test group and test devices before applying it to production.

- **Documentation**: Documentation is required for any system implementation. Once the migration process is complete, prepare a document including data about design, implementation steps, configuration changes, test results, resources that have been used, Group Policy changes, new feature configurations, and so on. It will be a good starting point for engineers and management to plan future AD DS migrations. Also, it will help engineers in maintenance and system troubleshooting.

Summary

The first few chapters of this book were focused on understanding AD DS and its capabilities. This chapter is different from those as it was more focused on *implementation* of AD DS. In the first part of the chapter, we saw the implementation of domain controllers to different identity infrastructures. The second part of the chapter was focused on AD DS migration from an older version of AD DS to AD DS 2016. There, we understood what we need to consider with respect to a domain migration project and what steps to follow. We also looked at the migration life cycle and what is covered in each stage. Last but not the least, we learnt how to migrate from AD DS 2012 R2 to AD DS 2016.

In the next chapter, we are going to learn about managing Active Directory objects.

7
Managing Active Directory Objects

I started my career as a web developer. I still remember my first day at work. It was a software development company with 20 engineers. My team lead, Indika, showed me my desk and passed me a piece of paper with a username and password to log in to my computer. I didn't know anything about Active Directory back then as I was too focused on being a *software engineer*. So I turned on the computer and typed in my username and password to log in. Then it said I needed to set a new password. My team lead asked me to type in a new password but be sure to make it *complex*. So I typed the most complex password I could think of. After that, I logged in and started working. It was a pretty busy morning with learning new things. I took a quick 20-minute lunch break in the late afternoon and came back to my seat to continue my work. I typed my complex password to log in but failed. Tried it again but had the same result. I kept on trying, and after a few attempts came the famous *account lockout* message. It felt so embarrassing. I informed my team lead who told me to go and talk to our system admin to get the account unlocked. I walked into the server room next to the office kitchen and mentioned my account situation to the admin. He gave me the typical admin look and opened up a kind of console on his screen. Then, he expanded some folders in a folder tree and selected something that had my name. After a few clicks, he opened a small box and asked me to type in a new password. Then, he said everything was okay and I should be able to log in. What magic! After a few years (when I changed careers), I realized that was the famous Active Directory Users and Computers **Microsoft Management Console** (**MMC**), which can manage Active Directory objects. I am sure all of you had similar excitement when you saw this Active Directory console for the first time. It is impossible to explain Active Directory without these tools, which manage Active Directory objects as *visual* components of the Active Directory infrastructure.

As explained in `Chapter 1`, *Active Directory Fundamentals*, the things we need to represent in Active Directory are created and saved as **objects**. These can be users, computers, printers or groups. **Attributes** are used to describe these objects. It's similar to the way we use characteristics to describe a person or things. There are different tools and methods we can use to add, modify, or remove objects from the Active Directory database.

In this chapter, we will cover the following:

- Tools and methods to manage Active Directory objects
- Creating, modifying, and removing objects in Active Directory
- Finding objects in Active Directory

Tools and methods to manage objects

As we saw before, there are different tools and methods we can use to manage Active Directory objects. When you install AD DS on a server, it will also enable access to these management tools. There are other vendors who build different Active Directory management tools as well. But in this chapter, we only will be using built-in tools on Windows Server systems.

Active Directory Administrative Center

The *Active Directory Users and Computers* MMC is the most commonly used tool to manage Active Directory environments. This tool is built in to the system from the early version of Active Directory and has continued to the latest. With AD DS 2008 R2, Microsoft introduced the **Active Directory Administrative Center (ADAC)**, which is a built-in PowerShell command-line interface technology. It provides an enhanced GUI, which can be used to manage Active Directory objects in an efficient way. With AD DS 2012, the Microsoft introduced the PowerShell history viewer, which helps administrators learn about PowerShell commands associated with Active Directory objects. I do not even now see a majority of engineers use this interface compared to the Active Directory Users and Computers MMC. This tool comes with the AD DS role. Once you complete the role installation, it will be available for operations without any additional configuration.

To access the ADAC console, you can type `dsac.exe` in a PowerShell command line or the **Run** box:

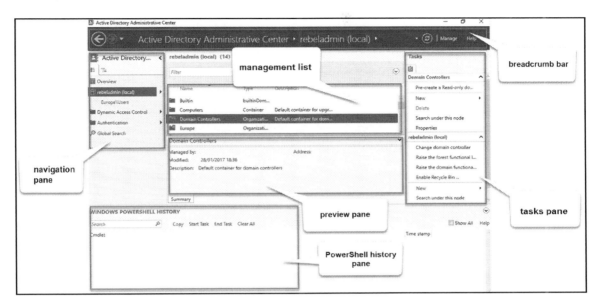

The preceding figure shows the default interface for ADAC and its components, which can be used to manage Active Directory objects. The following are the components:

- **Breadcrumb bar**: This can be used to navigate to different containers directly. In order to navigate to a specific container, you need to use its distinguished name. It can also be used the other way around, to find out the distinguished name of a container.

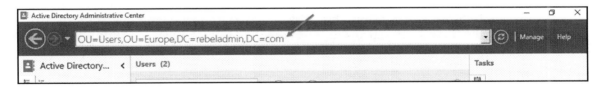

Using the **Manage** option allows us to add navigation nodes to the navigation pane. Basically, it's similar to adding a shortcut to specific containers.

- **Management list**: In this section will be listed the containers, objects contained in the containers, object search results, and so on. Data display in this section will change based on the options selected in the navigation pane.
- **Preview pane**: This section shows the summary of the object you selected in the management list. The summary contains certain attribute values, such as description, DNS name, and username as well as the time the object was modified:

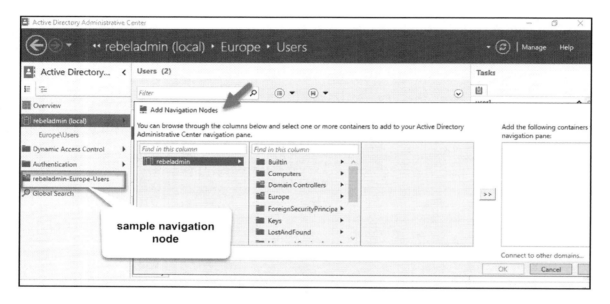

- **Navigation pane**: This is similar to the navigation pane in the Active Directory Users and Computers MMC. Using it, you can navigate to different containers in your domain. This can also be used to upgrade the domain and forest functional levels and enable the Active Directory Recycle Bin. Using the navigation pane, we can add objects such as users, groups, organizational units, or computers to the directory:

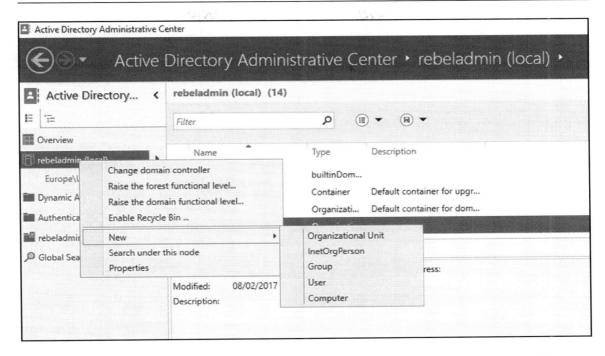

The navigation pane also lists the **Global Search** option, which can be used to locate Active Directory objects in the directory. Once the search returns an object, it also provides options to perform administrative tasks:

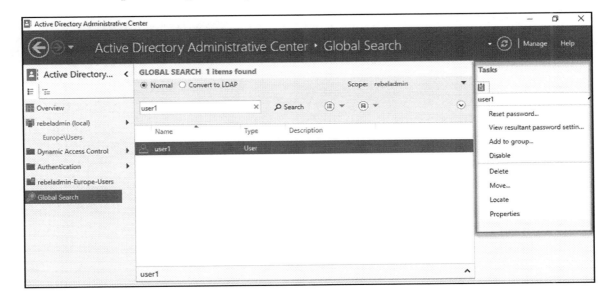

- **Tasks pane**: The tasks pane will list down the administrative tasks associated with the objects you select, such as moving objects, password resets, properties, and deletion. The list of administrative tasks will change based on the object type.
- **PowerShell history pane**: ADAC is built based on PowerShell command-line interface technology, so each and every task performed in ADAC is executed as a PowerShell command. In this pane will be listed all executed PowerShell commands. Engineers can copy these commands and reuse or develop them further to manage Active Directory objects via PowerShell directly. It also allows us to search for commands, if required.

When you open ADAC for the first time, you will not see the PowerShell history pane in expanded mode as shown in the following screenshot. You need to click on the **WINDOWS POWERSHELL HISTORY** bar to expand it.

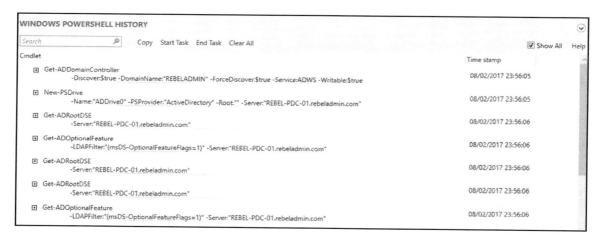

ADAC also allows us to manage objects from other domains. It can also be opened using **Server Manager | Tools | Active Directory Administrative Center**. If domains have one-way or two-way trust between them, it will allow us to add them to the same ADAC console. In order to do that, you need to go to the breadcrumb bar and click on **Manage | Add Navigation Nodes** and then click on **Connect to other domains...** in the window:

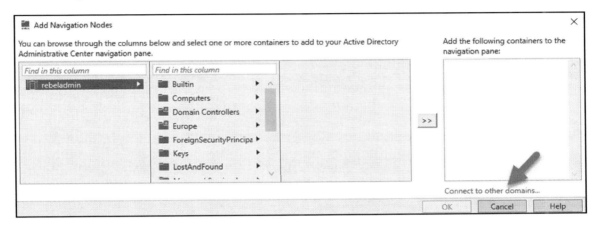

Another advantage of ADAC is the advanced object property window. If you've used the Active Directory Users and Computers MMC before, you may already know that in order to view object properties, we need to go through lots of different tabs. But with ADAC advanced object properties window, we can view a lot of data in one window. If required, you can easily navigate to different sections.

Using the same window, you can run administrative tasks related to objects. Not only that, it also allows us to modify the list of sections in the properties page as we want:

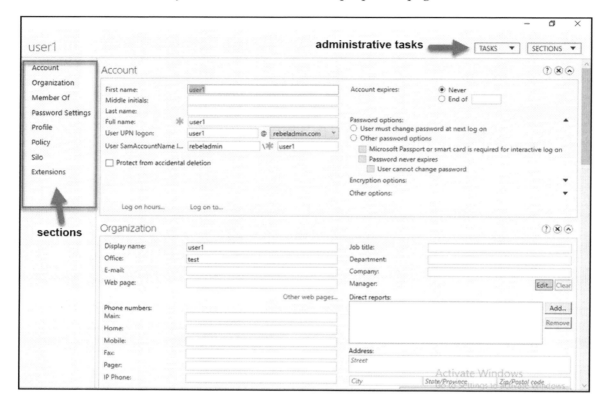

ADAC capabilities can be listed as follows:

- Creating users, groups, computer accounts, and organization units
- Managing users, groups, computer accounts, and organization units
- Removing users, groups, computer accounts, and organization units
- Managing Active Directory objects from other trusted domains
- Filtering Active Directory objects using queries

The Active Directory Users and Computers MMC

The Active Directory Users and Computers MMC is the most commonly used tool to manage Active Directory objects. This tool is available from AD DS 2000 onward, and over the years hasn't changed much in interface and features. This MMC comes with the AD DS role, and it can also be installed using **Remote Server Administration Tools (RSAT)** on desktop computers or member servers.

It can be opened using `dsa.msc` in PowerShell Command Prompt, or the **Run** box from the Start menu:

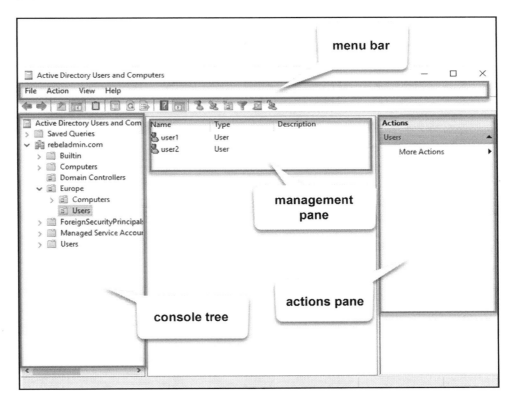

- **Menu bar**: This contains menus with different options. Most of the options mentioned in the menus can also be executed using icons beneath the menu bar or actions pane.

- **Console tree**: The console tree lists down the structure of Active Directory components and helps us navigate through containers and find objects.
- **Management pane**: This displays the objects inside the selected container in the console tree. It can display different objects types, such as users, groups, and devices. The content will change based on the selected container.
- **Actions pane**: The actions pane contains the administrative tasks related to selected Active Directory objects. As an example, if a user object is selected, the actions pane will list administrative tasks, such as moving the object, deleting it, password reset, and disabling the account.

We won't be looking at its functions too much here as it's the most commonly used tool by any administrator. But I am going to list down some of the main features:

- **Advanced features**: By default, the MMC will not list down all the containers and object properties related to advanced system administration. In order to access these options, you need to enable them using **View** | **Advanced Features**.
- **Saved queries**: Using the MMC, we can create custom queries to filter Active Directory objects and save these queries to rerun at a later time. This saves time as administrators do not need to spend time navigating through containers to find objects.

  To create a query, right-click on **Saved Queries** and select **New Query**. In this window, we can build a query using the **Define Query...** option:

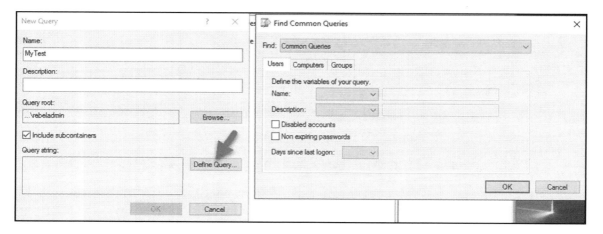

- **Access different domains**: If a domain has trust relationships with other domains, the same console can be used to access them and manage the objects:

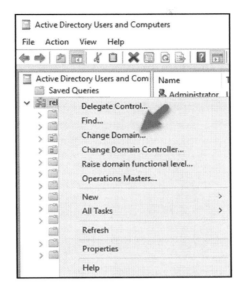

The capabilities of the Active Directory Users and Computers MMC can be listed as follows:

- Adding, editing, and removing users, groups, computers, and organization units
- Managing objects in different domains (needs two-way or one-way trust)
- Building queries to filter objects
- Searching for objects in directories
- Changing object properties

Active Directory object administration with PowerShell

By introducing the PowerShell scripting language, Microsoft provided more control over Windows system functions and operations. PowerShell also allows engineers to use extra features that cannot be used via GUI. There is the Active Directory PowerShell module, which can be used to manage Active Directory Domain Services, **Active Directory Lightweight Directory Services** (**AD LDS**), and objects. Active Directory objects can still be managed using Command Prompt, but PowerShell provides advanced, centralized control over Active Directory components and operations.

Any server that runs AD DS or AD LDS role services has the Active Directory PowerShell module by default. It can also be enabled on a desktop computer or member server by installing RSAT.

 If RSAT tools are installed on computers running PowerShell 2, you need to run `Import-Module ActiveDirectory` before using commands to manage Active Directory.

In this book, I have used PowerShell commands and scripts mostly to manage Active Directory. Therefore, we will not see its capabilities in detail here. In the next section, there will be more examples with PowerShell commands to mange Active Directory objects.

Creating, modifying, and removing objects in Active Directory

Creating, modifying, and removing objects are the most commonly performed management tasks in an Active Directory environment. Using the different tools and methods described in the previous section, we can perform these tasks. Each tool and method has its own pros and cons. By comparing GUI capabilities, the complexity of performing an administrative task, and the time it takes to execute a task, you can choose the tool that is best for you. My recommendation is to use a mix of tools as not every tool is good for every administrative task.

Creating Active Directory objects

Each and every object type has a different set of attributes. When you create objects, you need to provide values for those attributes. Some of these are mandatory and some are not. Based on the company's operations and preferences, some custom attributes may need to be added to the object types.

Creating user objects

In order to create a user object in Active Directory, we can use the `New-ADUser` cmdlet in PowerShell. You can view the full syntax of the command along with the accepted data types using this command:

```
Get-Command New-ADUser -Syntax
```

In order to create a new user account using PowerShell, the minimum value you need to pass is `-Name`. It will create a disabled user account, and you can define values for other attributes later.

This is an example that can be used to create a user account:

```
New-ADUser -Name "Talib Idris" -GivenName "Talib" -Surname "Idris" -
SamAccountName "tidris" -UserPrincipalName "tidris@rebeladmin.com" -Path
"OU=Users,OU=Europe,DC=rebeladmin,DC=com" -AccountPassword(Read-Host -
AsSecureString "Type Password for User") -Enabled $true
```

This command has the following parameters:

- `-Name`: This parameter defines the full name.
- `-GivenName`: This parameter defines the first name.
- `-Surname`: This parameter defines the surname.
- `-SamAccountName`: This parameter defines the username.
- `-UserPrincipalName`: This parameter defines the UPN for the user account.
- `-Path`: This defines the OU path. The default location is `CN=Users,DC=rebeladmin,DC=com`. If you do not define the `-Path` value, it will create the object under the default container.
- `-AccountPassword`: This will allow the user to input a password for the user, and the system will convert it to the relevant data type.
- `-Enabled`: This defines whether the user account status is enabled or disabled.

The following screenshot shows output for the preceding command:

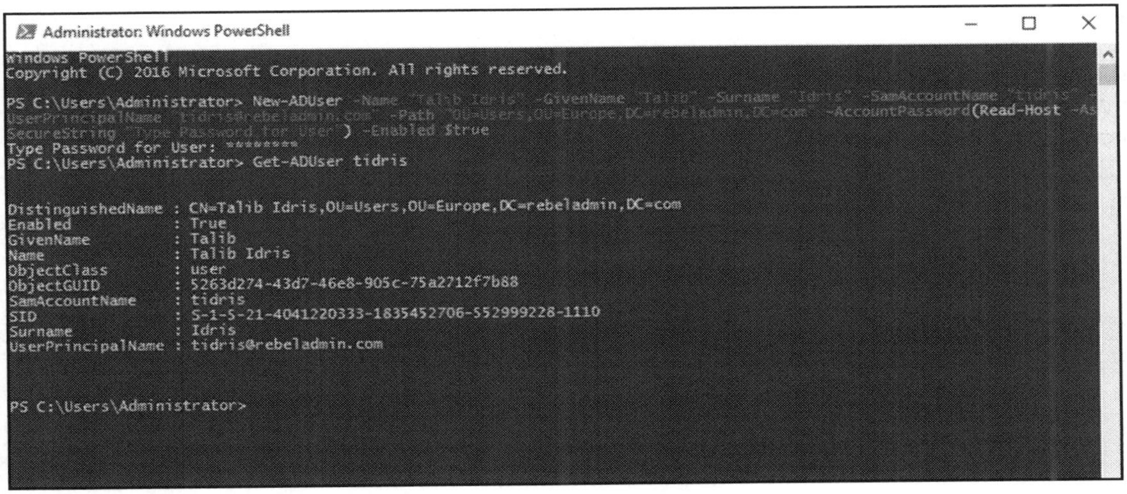

You can create a user account with the minimum attributes, such as name and UPN. Later, you can define a password and enable the account. A user account cannot be enabled without a password. To define a password, you can use the `Set-ADAccountPassword -Identity` cmdlet, and to enable an account, you can use the `Enable-ADAccount -Identity` cmdlet.

Instead of executing multiple commands to create multiple user objects, we can create a **comma-separated values (CSV)** file that includes data for attributes and use it to create accounts in one go.

For demonstration, I am using the following CSV file:

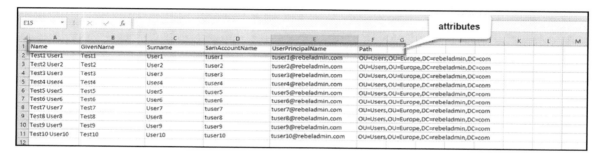

I have used data for some of the attributes in the CSV file, and some common values will be passed through the following script:

```
Import-Csv "C:\ADUsers.csv" | ForEach-Object {
$upn = $_.SamAccountName + "@rebeladmin.com"
New-ADUser -Name $_.Name `
 -GivenName $_."GivenName" `
 -Surname $_."Surname" `
 -SamAccountName $_."samAccountName" `
 -UserPrincipalName $upn `
 -Path $_."Path" `
 -AccountPassword (ConvertTo-SecureString "Pa$$w0rd" -AsPlainText -force) -
Enabled $true
 }
```

In this script, the `Import-Csv` cmdlet is used to import the CSV file created. I have defined the `$upn = $_.SamAccountName + "@rebeladmin.com"` parameter to be used for the `-UserPrincipalName` value. In the script, I have defined a common password for all the accounts using `-AccountPassword (ConvertTo-SecureString "Toronto@1234" -AsPlainText -force)`:

Creating computer objects

When a desktop computer or member server is joined to a domain, it will create a *computer object* in Active Directory.

This computer object can be created before being added to the domain. This will not add the device to the domain, but it can be used with offline domain joins and RODC domain joins.

In order to create a computer object, we can use the `New-ADComputer` cmdlet. To view the complete syntax of the command, use this:

```
Get-Command New-ADComputer -Syntax
```

The minimum attribute you need to define in order to create a computer object is `-Name`:

```
New-ADComputer -Name "REBEL-PC-01" -SamAccountName "REBEL-PC-01" -Path
"OU=Computers,OU=Europe,DC=rebeladmin,DC=com"
```

In the preceding example, the command will create the computer object REBEL-PC-01 in the OU=Computers, OU=Europe, DC=rebeladmin, DC=com OU. If you do not define the path, it will create the object under the default computer container CN=Computers, DC=rebeladmin, DC=com:

```
Administrator: Windows PowerShell                                          —  □  ×
PS C:\Users\Administrator> New-ADComputer -Name REBEL-PC-01 -SamAccountName REBEL-PC-01 -Path "OU=Computers,OU=Europe,DC=rebeladmin,DC=com"
PS C:\Users\Administrator> Get-ADComputer REBEL-PC-01

DistinguishedName : CN=REBEL-PC-01,OU=Computers,OU=Europe,DC=rebeladmin,DC=com
DNSHostName       :
Enabled           : True
Name              : REBEL-PC-01
ObjectClass       : computer
ObjectGUID        : ac14fdc2-e637-4330-93da-c01006a40d61
SamAccountName    : REBEL-PC-01S
SID               : S-1-5-21-4041220333-1835452706-552999228-1181
UserPrincipalName :


PS C:\Users\Administrator>
```

We very rarely need mass computer-object creation in an organization. In case it's required, though, it can be done using a CSV method similar to user-object creation.

 I am not going to explain group object administration here, which will instead be covered in detail in Chapter 8, *Managing Users, Groups, and Devices*.

All these objects can also be created using ADAC or ADUC, presented as a wizard in which you can define values for attributes:

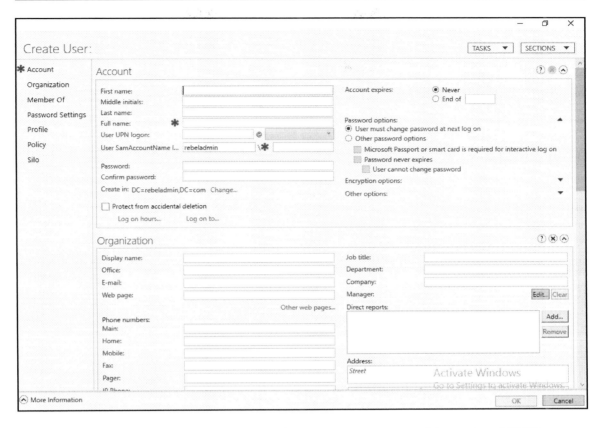

The following screenshot shows the wizard to create a computer object using ADUC:

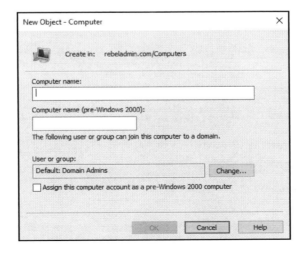

Modifying Active Directory objects

When we create objects, we define values for different attributes. After we've created the objects, there may be situations in which we need to edit the values of those attributes or add values to empty attributes.

We can use the `Set-ADUser` cmdlet to change and add attribute values to existing AD user objects:

```
Set-ADUser tidris -OfficePhone "0912291120" -City "London"
```

In the preceding sample command, we're adding values for the `-OfficePhone` and `-City` attributes for user `tidris`.

There are occasions where you may need to change the existing value of an attribute:

```
Set-ADUser tidris -OfficePhone "0112291120"
```

In the preceding command, I'm replacing the existing value with a new one.

In the aforementioned commands, I have defined the exact user account, but it's not practical if you need to do this for a large number of accounts. To do that, we need to combine the `Set-ADUser` cmdlet with the `Get-ADuser` cmdlet. It will allow us to search for objects first and push the changes to those:

```
Get-ADUser -Filter * -SearchBase 'OU=Users,OU=Europe,DC=rebeladmin,DC=com'
| Set-ADUser -City "London"
```

In the preceding command, we search for all the user objects located in `OU=Users,OU=Europe,DC=rebeladmin,DC=com` and set the `City` value to `London`:

```
Get-ADUser -Filter {City -like "London"} | Set-ADUser -City "Kingston"
```

In the preceding example, I search for all the users in the directory who have the `City` value defined as `London` and change it to `Kingston`.

Combining a search query with object modification saves a lot of manual work, and it's not something we can do easily using other GUI tools.

Computer object values can also be added/changed using a similar method. In order to do so, we need to use the `Set-ADComputer` cmdlet:

```
Set-ADComputer REBEL-PC-01 -Description "Sales Computer"
```

The preceding command sets the `Description` object value of the computer named `REBEL-PC-01`.

This cmdlet also can be combined with a search query using the `Get-ADComputer` cmdlet:

```
Get-ADComputer -Filter {Name -like "REBEL-PC-*"} | Set-ADComputer -Location
"M35 Building"
```

In the preceding command, it searches for computers that start with the name `REBEL-PC` and sets the location value for all those objects to `M35 Building`.

In the ADAC and ADUC GUI tools, it's just a matter of double-clicking and editing the attribute values. This also allows us to select multiple object and edit a particular attribute value in one go. I am not going to explain GUI tool capabilities as most of you already use it.

Removing Active Directory objects

Removing Active Directory objects can easily be compared to the creation or editing process. For removal, all you need to worry about is finding the exact object you need to remove.

In order to remove AD user objects, we can use the `Remove-ADUser` cmdlet. We can find the complete syntax information using the following command:

```
Get-Command Remove-ADUser -Syntax
```

When using the cmdlet, we need to pass the `-Identity` parameter to specify the account. We can use a distinguished name, GUID, SID, or the `SamAccountName` value to identify the name. If in an LDS environment, we need to define the object partition parameter too:

```
Remove-ADUser -Identity "dzhang"
```

The preceding command will remove the AD user object called `dzhang` from the directory. It will ask for confirmation before it removes the object.

This cmdlet can also be combines with the search query to find objects before removing them:

```
Get-ADUser -Filter {Name -like "Test1*"} | Remove-ADUser
```

In the preceding command, we search for the user whose name starts with `Test1` in the entire directory and remove it.

The `Remove-ADComputer` cmdlet can be used to remove computer objects from the directory:

```
Remove-ADComputer -Identity "REBEL-PC-01"
```

The preceding command will remove the `REBEL-PC-01` computer object from the directory. We can also combine it with a search query:

```
Get-ADComputer -Filter * -SearchBase
'OU=Computers,OU=Europe,DC=rebeladmin,DC=com' | Remove-ADComputer
```

In the preceding command, we search for the computer objects in the given OU and then remove those from the directory.

ADAC and ADUC tools can also be used to remove objects from a directory. They can also be used with a search function to locate specific objects and then delete them.

Finding objects in Active Directory

Active Directory holds different types of objects in its database. The most common way to locate an object in Active Directory is to use ADAC or ADUC and browse through the containers. As the number of objects increases, so does the difficulty of locating objects in Active Directory. In this section, we are going to look into more efficient ways of locating objects in an Active Directory environment.

ADAC has enhanced query and filter capabilities. Since it's used via a GUI, it helps us retrieve results faster compared to PowerShell.

In its management list, there is a filter box in the top section (once you click on the domain name in the navigation pane). It doesn't change the view as you navigate through the containers. It helps you filter the data displayed in the management list quickly. It doesn't search for objects at multiple levels (child containers):

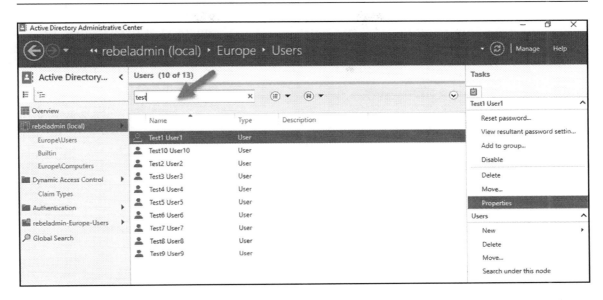

ADAC has a feature called **Global Search**, which can be used to search for objects in the entire directory. This allows a typical text-based search or advanced LDAP-based queries:

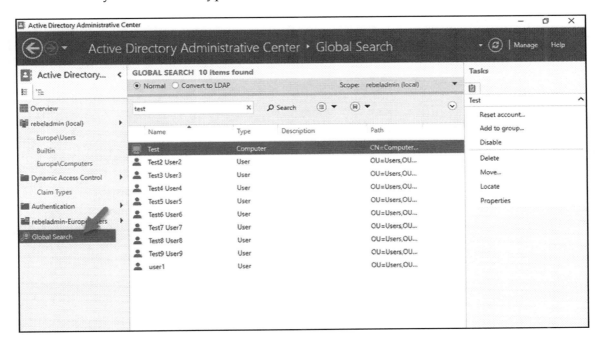

Let's now look at how to perform LDAP-based searches. The method also allows us to define the search scope:

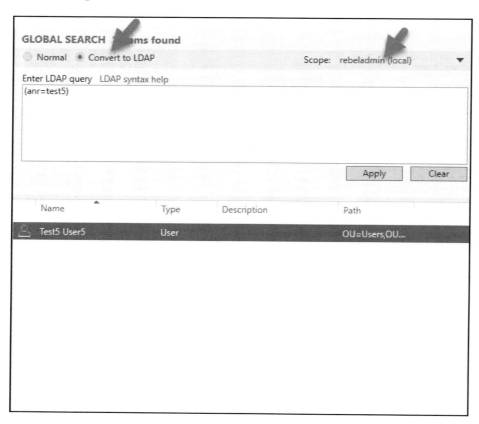

In a **Normal** search, you can use any text pattern. This can be a complete or partial value. In an LDAP search, we need to use exact syntax. Using the **Convert to LDAP** option, we can generate an LDAP query from a **Normal** search. Also, using **LDAP syntax help**, you can learn about the LDAP syntax and ways to use it.

This **Global Search** function can also be accessed from the overview page.

In ADUC, object search functions are very limited compared to ADAC and PowerShell. It does have the **Find...** option, which allows us to locate objects in the directory. It can be accessed by right-clicking on any container:

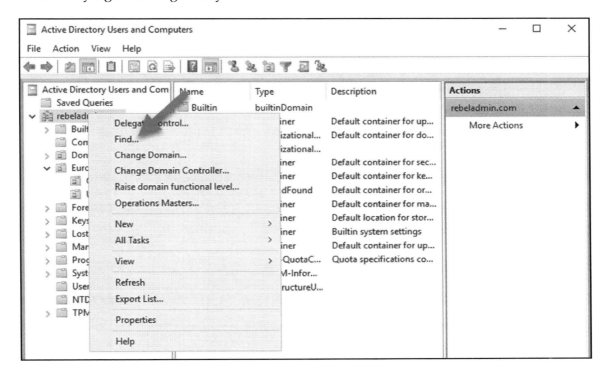

It allows us to do a text-based search as well as an advanced search based on attributes and their values. It also allows to define the search scope:

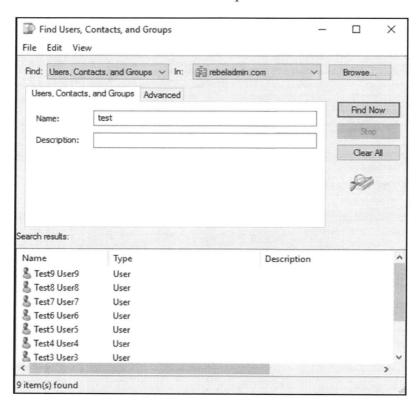

Finding objects using PowerShell

In the previous section, we learned about the Get-ADUser and Get-ADComputer cmdlets and how they can be used with other commands to filter out objects from Active Directory and perform administrative tasks. They can also be used to retrieve specific attribute values from filtered objects:

```
Get-ADUser -Identity user1 -Properties *
```

The preceding command will list down all the attributes and values associated with `user1`. This helps us find the exact attribute names and common values, which be can used for further filtering.

I need to know the values for `Name`, `UserPrincipalName`, and `Modified` for all the users. The following command will create a table with attributes and their values:

```
Get-ADUser -Filter * -Properties Name,UserPrincipalName,Modified | ft
Name,UserPrincipalName,Modified
```

The following screenshot shows output for the preceding command:

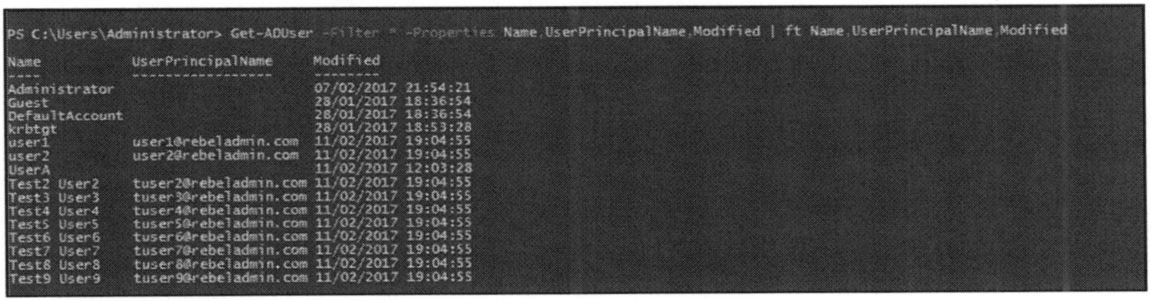

I can see some accounts in the list that are service and administrator accounts. I only want to see the accounts in the `Kingston` office:

```
Get-ADUser -Filter {City -like "Kingston"} -Properties
Name,UserPrincipalName,Modified | ft Name,UserPrincipalName,Modified
```

The preceding command filters further based on the `City` value.

Now I have the list of data I need, and I'd like to export it to a CSV file for future use, like so:

```
Get-ADUser -Filter {City -like "Kingston"} -Properties
Name,UserPrincipalName,Modified | select-object
Name,UserPrincipalName,Modified | Export-csv -path C:\ADUSerList.csv
```

This example demonstrates how a search query can be built up from a granular level to find the exact information needed from objects.

The `Search-ADAccount` cmdlet can also be used to search for Active Directory objects based on account and password status. The full syntax of the cmdlet can be retrieved using the following command:

```
Get-Command Search-ADAccount -Syntax
```

As an example, it can be used to filter accounts that are locked out:

```
Search-ADAccount -LockedOut | FT Name,UserPrincipalName
```

This command will list down all the locked-out accounts with name and UPN.

Unlike the graphical tools, PowerShell queries can be built to filter exact objects and data from Active Directory.

Summary

There are lots of different tools out there to manage Active Directory objects. In this chapter, we looked into tools built by Microsoft to manage Active Directory objects. Each and every tool has different characteristics, and we learned how we can use them to add, edit, and remove Active Directory objects effectively. We also learned how we can use different tools and technologies to search for specific Active Directory objects and attribute values.

In the next chapter, we will dive deep into Active Directory objects and attributes. In there, we will evaluate different types of objects and their roles in an Active Directory environment.

8
Managing Users, Groups, and Devices

In the previous chapter, we learned about the main AD object types and how we can add, edit, and remove them. We also learned about the different management tools and technologies which help us to do these tasks. Last but not the least, we learned how we can locate AD objects or the value of an attribute when required, using different tools and techniques. This chapter is an extension to that and here we going to talk about *objects* and *attributes* further.

In this chapter, we are going to look into the following areas:

- Object attributes
- Different types of user accounts and their actions
- Different types of groups and their actions
- Different types of devices and other objects which can be managed via AD
- Object management best practices

Object attributes

My daughter Selena loves Julia Donaldson's books, especially the books about the *Gruffalo*. So every time I take her to the library, she picks at least one of her books. Last night, I was reading her one of the Gruffalo series books, *Gruffalo's Child*. In that book, Gruffalo's child asks about the big bad mouse who lives in the snowy forest. Gruffalo describes the mouse, saying he is strong, his eyes are big, his tail is very long, and he has got whiskers thicker than wires. Then Gruffalo's child goes out to find this mouse in a snowy night.

During his journey, he finds animals that match one or a few of the characteristics that his father had described; but none matches all of them. At the end, only a *shadow* matches all these characteristics of the big bad mouse. If I compare it with objects, the big bad mouse is an object. Gruffalo describes it to his kid using characteristics which are similar to attributes of an object. When Gruffalo's kid goes to find it, he also finds other animals that have similar characteristics. Similarly, objects can have attributes which are common for other objects in the same class. At the end, however he finds the best match for all characteristics because some of those couldn't match with the characteristics of any other animal. Similarly, some attributes have unique values which make objects unique under the same class.

In the following screenshot, I have opened a user object via ADUC MMC. In there, under the **Attribute Editor**, we can see all the attributes associated with this object, including the values:

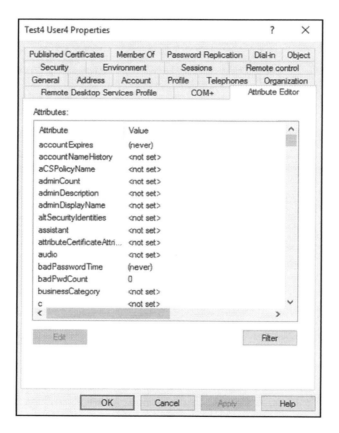

Using this window, we can add, edit, or remove values from some attributes. Most of these attribute names do not match with the names in the wizard you get when you create the object. As an example, the attribute `givenName` (LDAP name) maps to the first name (display name) in the user account creation wizard.

All the user accounts in the AD will have the same set of attributes. This is defined by *class* in AD schema:

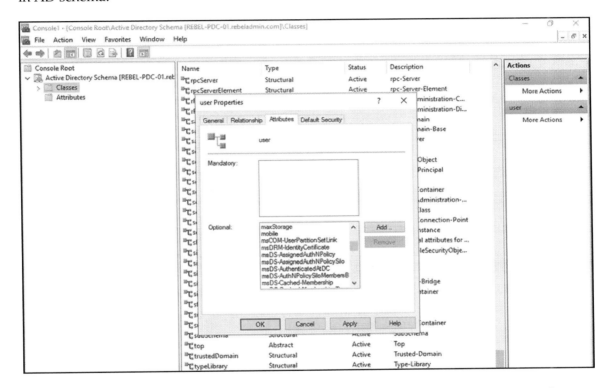

In order to open the AD schema snap-in, you need to run the command `regsvr32 schmmgmt.dll` from the domain controller. After that, you can use MMC and add the AD schema as snap-in.

In the preceding figure, I have opened AD schema snap-in and opened the **user** class. In order to open snap-in, go to **Run** | **MMC** | **File** | **Add/Remove Snap-in**, then select **Active Directory Schema** from the list, and click **Add** to complete and click **OK**. In there, we can see the list of attributes which associate with objects under the **user** class. The same attributes can be a part of different classes too. As an example, the **mail** attribute is part of the **user** and **group** class:

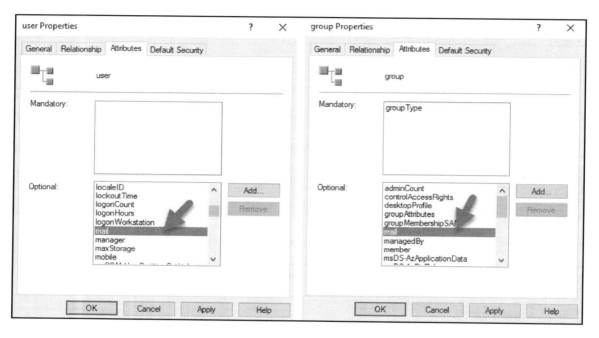

We can review the attribute details by opening attributes from the `Attributes` container:

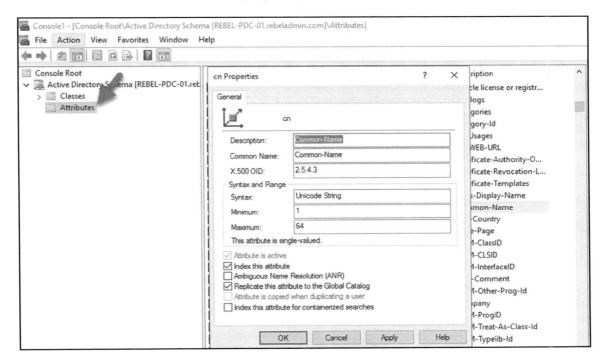

In the preceding figure, I opened the attribute **cn**, and in the window it shows details such as common-name, syntax, and values accepted.

Custom attributes

In AD schema, you are allowed to add custom attributes. In organizations, there are situations where this option is useful. Most of the time, it is related to application integration requirements with AD infrastructure. In modern infrastructures, applications are decentralizing identity management. Organization's identities can sit on AD as well as applications. If these applications are integrated with AD it still provides central identity management but that's not always the case. Some applications have their own way of handling their user accounts and privileges. Similar to AD attributes, these applications can also have their own attributes defined by their database systems to store the data. Most of the time, these application attributes will not match the attributes on AD.

As an example, HR system uses *employee ID* to identify an employee record uniquely from others. But AD uses *username* to identify a unique record. Each system's attributes hold some data about the objects even if they are referring to the same user or device. If there is another application which requires you to retrieve data from both systems' attributes, how can we facilitate that without data duplication?

Once a customer was talking to me regarding a similar requirement. They had AD infrastructure in place. They were also maintaining an HR system that was not integrated with AD. They got a new requirement for an employee collaboration application, which required data input in a specific way. It had defined its fields in the database and we needed to match the data in that order. Some of these require data about users which can be retrieved from AD and some of the user data can be retrieved from the HR system. Instead of keeping two data feeds to the system, we decided to treat the AD as the trustworthy data source for this new system. If AD needs to hold all the required data, it somehow needs to store the data that comes from the HR system as well. The final solution was to add *custom attributes* to AD schema and associate it with the *user class*. Instead of both systems operating as data feeds, now the HR system passes the filtered values to AD and it exports all the required data in CSV format to the application.

In order to create custom attributes, go to **Active Directory Schema** snap-ins, right-click on the `Attributes` container, and select the **Create Attribute...** option.

Then, the system will give a *warning* about the schema object creation. Click **OK** to continue.

It will open up a form and this is where we need to define the details about custom attribute:

- **Common Name**: This is the name of the object. It is only allowed to use letters, numbers, and hyphens for the CN.
- **LDAP Display Name**: When an object is referring to a script, program or command-line utility, it needs to be called using **LDAP Display Name** instead of **Common Name**. When you define the CN, it will automatically create **LDAP Display Name**.
- **Unique X500 Object ID**: Each and every attribute in AD schema has a unique OID value. There is a script developed by Microsoft to generate these unique OID values. It can be found at https://gallery.technet.microsoft.com/scriptcenter/Generate-an-Object-4c9be66a#content. It includes the following script which will generate the object ID:

```
#---
$Prefix="1.2.840.113556.1.8000.2554"
$GUID=[System.Guid]::NewGuid().ToString()
$Parts=@()
$Parts+=[UInt64]::Parse($guid.SubString(0,4),
  "AllowHexSpecifier")
$Parts+=[UInt64]::Parse($guid.SubString(4,4),
  "AllowHexSpecifier")
$Parts+=[UInt64]::Parse($guid.SubString(9,4),
  "AllowHexSpecifier")
$Parts+=[UInt64]::Parse($guid.SubString(14,4),
```

```
 "AllowHexSpecifier")
$Parts+=[UInt64]::Parse($guid.SubString(19,4),
 "AllowHexSpecifier")
$Parts+=[UInt64]::Parse($guid.SubString(24,6),
 "AllowHexSpecifier")
$Parts+=[UInt64]::Parse($guid.SubString(30,6),
 "AllowHexSpecifier")
$OID=[String]::Format("{0}.{1}.{2}.{3}.{4}.{5}.{6}.{7}",
 $prefix,$Parts[0],$Parts[1],$Parts[2],$Parts[3],$Parts[4],
 $Parts[5],$Parts[6])
$oid
#---
```

- **Syntax**: It defines the storage representation for the object. It is only allowed to use a syntax defined by Microsoft. One attribute can only associate with one syntax. In the following table, I have listed a few commonly used syntax in attributes:

Syntax	Description
Boolean	True or false
Unicode String	A large string
Numeric String	String of digits
Integer	32-bit numeric value
Large Integer	64-bit numeric value
SID	Security identifier value
Distinguished Name	String value to uniquely identify object in AD

Along with the syntax, we can also define the minimum or maximum values. If it's not defined, it will take the default values.

In the following demo, I would like to add a new attribute called `nINumber` and add it to the **user** class:

As the next step, we need to add it to the **user** class. In order to do that, go to the `Classes` container, double-click on the **user** class, and click on the **Attributes** tab. In there, by clicking the **Add** button, we can browse and select the newly added attribute from the list:

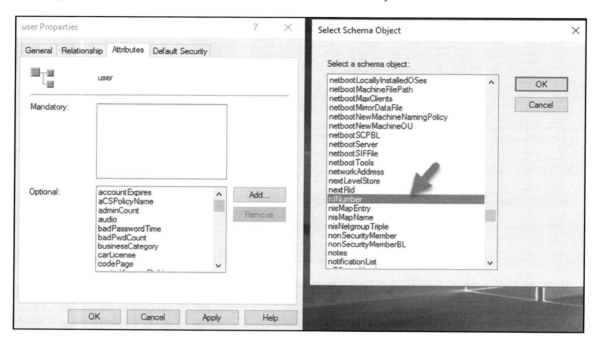

Now when we open a user account, we can see the new attribute and we can add the new data to it:

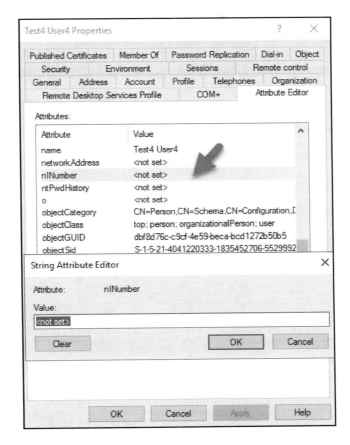

Once the data has been added, we can filter out the information as required:

```
Get-ADuser "tuser4" -Properties nINumber | ft nINumber
```

The following screenshot shows the output for the preceding command:

```
PS C:\Users\Administrator> Get-ADUser "user4" -Properties nINumber | ft nINumber

nINumber
--------
2234553786
```

To add the attributes to the schema, you need to have Schema Admin privileges or Enterprise Admin privileges. After adding new attributes, it's recommended to reboot the system in order to reflect the new changes to the schema.

User accounts

In AD infrastructure, what is the most common administrative task? Obviously, it's creating and managing user accounts. A user account does not only hold a username and password, it also holds data such as group memberships, roaming profile path, home folder path, login script info, remote dial in permissions, and many more. Every time we set up a new account, we need to define values for these attributes. When it increases the number of attributes and features that need to adjust on the account creation process, it also increases the number of mistakes that can happen. Here, however, we are dealing with identities, and even a small mistake can cost organization lot. As an example, if you add a user to the wrong user group accidentally, he/she will have access to some resources which they are not supposed to have.

When I create a SOW or implementation plan for a customer, I always start it based on a *template*. It contains sections that I need to change according to each customer's requirements and solution, but it has lots more information that is common for each customer. When I use a template, it not only saves my time, it also eliminates any mistake that can happen during manual data copy by typing or document formatting. Similarly, in the AD environment, user accounts may have common attributes and privilege levels. As an example, users under the sales department will be members of the same security groups. They also would have the same log on scripts to map the network shares. Therefore, instead of creating a sales user account from scratch, I can create a template with all the common attribute values and use it to creates a new account. From Windows NT onwards Microsoft supports the creation of user accounts templates.

Even though there are common attribute values in user accounts, some attributes still need to have unique values or not a null value:

Attribute	Description	Value
First Name	User's first name	Unique within OU
Last Name	User's last name	Unique within OU
User logon name (`UserPrincipleName` and `SamAccountName`)	User's logon name	Unique
Password	User's password	No need to be unique
Profile path	User's roaming profile path	Recommended to be unique

There are few things to consider when creating user templates:

- **Do not copy user accounts as templates**: I've seen a lot of engineers just randomly select a user under the same OU and use it as template for a new user account. Templates should be a baseline. Other user accounts may have some unique privileges and attribute values, even if they are all under the same OU. Therefore, always keep separate user account templates.
- **Disable Account**: No one should use template accounts to authenticate. When creating templates, make sure to set them as disabled accounts. During the new user creation process, the status of the account can change.

To demonstrate, I am going to create a user template for Technical Department users. The command I will use is as follows:

```
New-ADUser -Name "_TechSupport_Template" -GivenName "_TechSupport" -Surname
"_Template" -SamAccountName "techtemplate" -UserPrincipalName
"techtemplate@rebeladmin.com" -Path
"OU=Users,OU=Europe,DC=rebeladmin,DC=com" -AccountPassword(Read-Host -
AsSecureString "Type Password for User") -Enabled $false
```

The preceding command creates a user account called _TechSupport_Template. It is also set as a disabled account.

I'm also going to add it to the Technical Department security group:

```
Add-ADGroupMember "Technical Department" "techtemplate"
```

Now when we go to ADUC, we can see the new template. In order to create a new account from it, right-click and click **Copy...**:

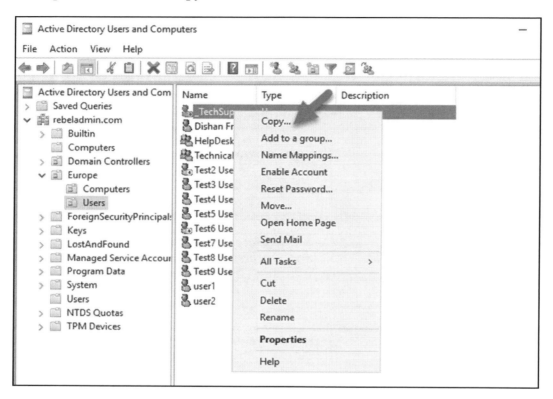

Then go and fill the information in the wizard and complete the user account creation process. The following screenshot shows an account created based on the template created:

```
PS C:\Users\Administrator> Get-ADUser "sbrewer" -Properties * | ft Name,Memberof,Enabled

Name          Memberof                                                            Enabled
----          --------                                                            -------
Scott Brewer  {CN=Technical Department,OU=Users,OU=Europe,DC=rebeladmin,DC=com}    True
```

Managed Service Accounts

Service accounts are recommended to use when installing application or services in infrastructure. It is a dedicated account with specific privileges which are used to run services, batch jobs, and management tasks. In most of the infrastructures, service accounts are typical user accounts with the **Password never expire** option. Since these service accounts are not used regularly, administrators have to keep track of these accounts and their credentials. I have seen many occasions where engineers face issues due to outdated or misplaced service account credential details. The trouble is, if you reset the password of service accounts, you will need to update the services, databases, and application settings to get the application or services up and running again. Apart from that, engineers also have to manage the **service principal name** (**SPN**), which helps to identify service instances uniquely.

After considering all these challenges, Microsoft has introduced Managed Service Accounts with Windows Server 2008 R2. These accounts have got the following features and limitations:

- There is no more password management. It uses a complex, random, 240-character password and changes that automatically when it reaches the domain or computer password expiry date.
- It cannot be locked out or used for interactive login.
- Only one Managed Service Account can be used in one computer. It cannot be shared between multiple computers.
- It provides simplified SPN management; the system will automatically change the SPN value if the `SamAccountName` details of the computer change or DNS name property changes.

In order to create Managed Service Account, we can use the following command. I am running this from the domain controller:

```
New-ADServiceAccount -Name "MyAcc1" -RestrictToSingleComputer
```

In the preceding command, I have created a service account called `MyAcc1` and I have restricted it to one computer.

The next step is to associate the service account with the host `REBEL-SRV01`, where I am going to use this service account:

```
Add-ADComputerServiceAccount -Identity REBEL-SRV01 -ServiceAccount "MyAcc1"
```

The next step is to install the service account in the REBEL-SRV01 server. We need the AD PowerShell module for this. We can install it using RSAT tools. This can be done by running the Install-WindowsFeature RSAT-AD-Tools command. Once it's ready, run the following command:

```
Install-ADServiceAccount -Identity "MyAcc1"
```

Once it's done, we can test it using the following command:

```
Test-ADServiceAccount "MyAcc1"
```

It returns the value True, which means the test was successful:

```
Administrator: Windows PowerShell
PS C:\Users\administrator.REBELADMIN> Install-ADServiceAccount -Identity "MyAcc1"
PS C:\Users\administrator.REBELADMIN> Test-ADServiceAccount "MyAcc1"
True
PS C:\Users\administrator.REBELADMIN>
```

From the AD server, we can verify the service account by running the following command:

```
Get-ADServiceAccount "MyAcc1"
```

The following screenshot shows the output for the preceding command:

```
PS C:\Users\Administrator> Get-ADServiceAccount "MyAcc1"

DistinguishedName : CN=MyAcc1,CN=Managed Service Accounts,DC=rebeladmin,DC=com
Enabled           : True
Name              : MyAcc1
ObjectClass       : msDS-ManagedServiceAccount
ObjectGUID        : e72809fe-2b55-41d6-98de-85c62c9f5fc6
SamAccountName    : MyAcc1$
SID               : S-1-5-21-4041220333-1835452706-552999228-1203
UserPrincipalName :
```

 When configuring the Managed Service Account in service, make sure to leave the password empty. You do not need to define any password as the system autogenerates the password.

Group Managed Service Accounts

In the previous section, we talked about Managed Service Accounts. One Managed Service Account can be used with one computer only. But there are operation requirements which require the same service account to be shared in multiple hosts. Microsoft's network load balancer, the IIS server farm, is a good example of this. All the hosts in these server groups are required to use the same service principal for authentications. **Group Managed Service Accounts (gMSA)** provides the same functionalities as Managed Service Accounts, but it extends its capabilities to host group levels. This was first introduced with Windows Server 2012.

The gMSA has got the following capabilities:

- No password management
- Supports sharing across multiple hosts
- Can be used to run scheduled tasks (Managed Service Accounts do not support running scheduled tasks)
- It uses Microsoft **Key Distribution Center (KDC)** to create and manage the passwords for the gMSA.

Key Distribution Service (KDS) was introduced with Windows Server 2012. KDS shares a secret (root key ID) among all the KDS instances in the domain. This value changes periodically. When gMSA requires a password, the Windows Server 2012 domain controller generates a password based on a common algorithm which includes root key ID. Then all the hosts which share the gMSA will query from the domain controllers to retrieve the latest password.

Requirements for gMSA:

- Windows Server 2012 or higher forest level
- Windows Server 2012 or higher domain member servers (Windows 8 or upper domain joined computers are also supported)
- 64-bit architecture to run PowerShell command to manage gMSA

 gMSA is not supported for the failover clustering setup. But it is supported for services which run upon failover clusters.

In order to start the configuration process, we need to create a KDS root key. This needs to be run from the domain controller with Domain Admin or Enterprise Admin privileges:

```
Add-KdsRootKey -EffectiveImmediately
```

Once this is executed, there is a default 10 hours time limit to replicate it to all the domain controllers and start the response to gMSA requests. In a testing environment with one domain controller, it can be forced to remove this waiting time and start to response gMSA immediately. This is *not* recommended for a production environment:

```
Add-KdsRootKey -EffectiveTime ((get-date).addhours(-10))
```

After that we can create the first gMSA account. I have created an AD group IISFARM and added all my IIS servers to it. This farm will be using the new gMSA account:

```
New-ADServiceAccount "Mygmsa1" -DNSHostName "web.rebeladmin.com"
-PrincipalsAllowedToRetrieveManagedPassword "IISFARM"
```

In the preceding command, Mygmsa1 is the service account and web.rebeladmin.com is the FQDN of the service. Once it's processed, we can verify the new account using the following command:

```
Get-ADServiceAccount "Mygmsa1"
```

The following screenshot shows the output for the preceding command:

```
PS C:\Users\Administrator> Get-ADServiceAccount Mygmsa1

DistinguishedName : CN=Mygmsa1,CN=Managed Service Accounts,DC=rebeladmin,DC=com
Enabled           : True
Name              : Mygmsa1
ObjectClass       : msDS-GroupManagedServiceAccount
ObjectGUID        : 6b39efa1-19b8-4690-a477-858873f0aa40
SamAccountName    : Mygmsa1$
SID               : S-1-5-21-4041220333-1835452706-552999228-1205
UserPrincipalName :
```

The next step is to install it on the server in IIS Farm. It needs the AD PowerShell module to run it. It can be installed using RSAT:

```
Install-ADServiceAccount -Identity "Mygmsa1"
```

If you created the server group recently and added the host, you need to restart the host computer to reflect the group membership. Otherwise, the aforementioned command will fail.

Once it's executed, we can test the service account by running the following command:

```
Test-ADServiceAccount " Mygmsa1"
```

The following screenshot shows the output for the preceding command:

```
Administrator: Windows PowerShell                                      —   □   ×
PS C:\Users\administrator.REBELADMIN> Install-ADServiceAccount –identity Mygmsa1
PS C:\Users\administrator.REBELADMIN> Test-ADServiceAccount  Mygmsa1
True
PS C:\Users\administrator.REBELADMIN> _
```

Similar to Managed Service Account, when you configure the gMSA with any service, leave the password blank.

Uninstalling Managed Service Account

There can be requirements for removing the Managed Service Accounts. This can be done by executing the following command:

```
Remove-ADServiceAccount –identity "Mygmsa1"
```

The preceding command will remove the Managed Service Account Mygmsa1. This applies to both types of Managed Service Accounts.

Groups

In general, a **group** is a collection of individuals or resources which share the same characteristics and responsibilities. In an organization, individual identities get added and deleted, but roles and responsibilities do not change much. Therefore, the best way to manage privileges in organizations is based on roles and responsibilities rather than individuals. For example, in a sales department, sales persons will change quite often but their operational requirements will not change frequently. They all will access the same file shares, have the same permissions to CRM application, and have the same privileges to access each other's calendars. AD groups allow you to isolate identities based on the privileges requirements.

In an AD environment, there are two categories of groups:

- **Security groups**: This type is used to assign permissions to the resources. As an example, Rebeladmin Corp. has a team of 10 sales persons. They use a shared folder called `Sales` in the file server. Everyone in the sales team has the same access permissions to it. If the permission would be managed at the user level, the ACL for the `Sales` folder would have 10 entries to represent each user. If a new sales person joins the team, his account will need to be added to the ACL and match with the permission manually by comparing existing users in the ACL. Since this is a manual process, there is a possibility that the wrong privileges are applied by mistake. If it's based on security groups, we can create group such as sales department and then add that to the `Sales` folder ACL with the relevant privileges. After that, we can remove individual entries for each sales user from ACL. Thereafter, access to the `Sales` folder will be controlled by adding or removing users from sales department group.
- **Distribution group**: This is to be used with an email system, such as Microsoft Exchange, to distribute one email to a group. These groups are not security enabled, so you cannot use them to assign permissions.

Group scope

Group scope helps to define the operation boundaries within the AD forest. There are three predefined scopes to choose from, when creating AD groups:

- **Domain local**: Domain local groups can be used to manage privileges to resources in a single domain. This doesn't mean that the group can only have members within the same domain. It can have the following types as members as well:
  - User accounts from any trusted domain
  - Computer accounts from any trusted domain
  - Universal groups from any trusted forest
  - Domain local groups from the same domain
  - Global groups from any trusted domain

  Domain local group objects and their membership data will be replicated to every domain controller in the same domain.

- **Global**: Global groups can be used to manage privileges to resources in any domain under the same forest, such as:
  - User accounts from the same domain
  - Computer accounts from the same domain
  - Global groups from the same domain

    Global group objects and membership data will be replicated to every domain controller in the same domain. This group had the limited membership but it not high availability as it's available for other domains in the forest. This is ideal when categorizing privileges based on roles and responsibilities.

- **Universal**: Similar to global groups, universal groups can be used to manage privileges in any domain in the forest. However, it allows you to have members from any domain. As an example, the `rebeladmin.com` and `rebeladmin.net` domains under the same forest can have one universal group called **Sales Managers**, with members from both the domains. Then, I can use it to assign permissions to the folder in `rebeladmin.org` in the same forest. It can have the following types of members:
  - User accounts from any trusted domain
  - Computer accounts from any trusted domain
  - Global groups from any trusted domain
  - Universal groups from any domain in the same forest

Universal group objects and membership data will be replicated to all the global catalog servers. Universal groups give flexibility to apply permissions to any resource in any domain under the same forest.

 Groups are supported to have other groups as members. These are called **nested groups**. This reduces the ACL changes further. In the preceding points, we have listed what type of groups are allowed to add as nested groups under each scope.

Converting groups

Group scope needs to be defined during the group setup process. But with operational requirement or infrastructure changes, there can be occasions where this already defined scope is not valid anymore. In such a situation, instead of setting up a new group, it can be converted into a different scope. It doesn't mean you can convert any scope to any group. There are some rules to follow:

Group Scope	Domain local	Global	Universal
Domain local	N/A	X	√(only if there are no other domain local groups as members)
Global	X	N/A	√(only if it's not a member of other global groups)
Universal	√	√(only if there are no other universal groups as members)	N/A

Setting up groups

Similar to user accounts, there are several methods we can use to create and manage groups:

- **Active Directory Administrative Center (ADAC)**
- **Active Directory Users and Computers (ADUC)** MMC
- PowerShell cmdlets

In this section, I am going to use PowerShell cmdlets to setup and manage AD groups.

The `New-ADGroup` cmdlet can be used to add a new group to the AD environment. We can review the full syntax for the command using:

```
Get-Command New-ADGroup -Syntax
```

I have a requirement to create a new security group called `Sales Team`. For the task, I am using the following command:

```
New-ADGroup -Name "Sales Team" -GroupCategory Security -GroupScope Global -Path "OU=Users,OU=Europe,DC=rebeladmin,DC=com"
```

In the previous command:

- −GroupCategory: This defines the type of the group (security or distribution).
- −GroupScope: This defines the scope of the group.
- −Path: This defines the path for the group object. If it's not used the path option it will use the default container Users.

Due to the importance of the group, I want to protect this group object from *accidental deletion*:

```
Get-ADGroup "Sales Team" | Set-ADObject -
ProtectedFromAccidentalDeletion:$true
```

This can also be set using the group properties window:

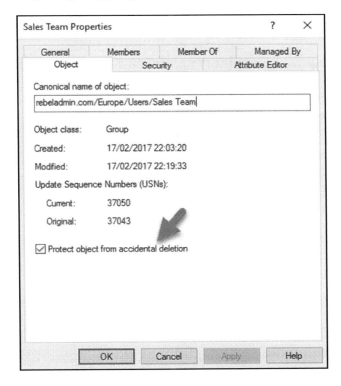

The next step for the task is to add members to the group. For that, we can use:

```
Add-ADGroupMember "Sales Team" tuser3,tuser4,tuser5
```

The previous command will add users `tuser3`, `tuser4`, and `tuser5` to the group.

If we need to remove a user from the group, we can use the following command:

```
Remove-ADGroupMember "Sales Team" tuser4
```

We can search for group properties using the `Get-ADGroup` cmdlet:

```
Get-ADGroup "Sales Team"
```

This can also be used to retrieve specific values from the group:

```
Get-ADGroup "Sales Team" -Properties DistinguishedName,Members | fl
DistinguishedName,Members
```

The preceding command will list down the DN and members of the `Sales Team` security group:

```
Administrator: Windows PowerShell                                        —    □    ×
PS C:\Users\Administrator> Get-ADGroup "Sales Team" -Properties DistinguishedName,Members | fl DistinguishedName,Members

DistinguishedName : CN=Sales Team,OU=Users,OU=Europe,DC=rebeladmin,DC=com
Members           : {CN=Test8 User8,OU=Users,OU=Europe,DC=rebeladmin,DC=com, CN=Test7
                    User7,OU=Users,OU=Europe,DC=rebeladmin,DC=com, CN=Test5
                    User5,OU=Users,OU=Europe,DC=rebeladmin,DC=com, CN=Test4
                    User4,OU=Users,OU=Europe,DC=rebeladmin,DC=com...}


PS C:\Users\Administrator>
```

If we need to change the scope of the group, it can be done using the following command:

```
Set-ADGroup "Sales Team" -GroupScope Universal
```

This will change the group scope from global to universal:

```
PS C:\Users\Administrator> Set-ADGroup "Sales Team" -GroupScope Universal
PS C:\Users\Administrator> Get-ADGroup "Sales Team"

DistinguishedName : CN=Sales Team,OU=Users,OU=Europe,DC=rebeladmin,DC=com
GroupCategory     : Security
GroupScope        : Universal
Name              : Sales Team
ObjectClass       : group
ObjectGUID        : a70e28d9-be49-4f6a-9c88-2ca0dbd4bcbf
SamAccountName    : Sales Team
SID               : S-1-5-21-4041220333-1835452706-552999228-1208


PS C:\Users\Administrator> _
```

Last but not the least, a group can be removed using the `Remove-ADGroup` cmdlet:

```
Remove-ADGroup "Sales Team"
```

The preceding command will remove the group `Sales Team`.

> If you have the accidental deletion option enabled in the group, you need to remove it, before executing the `Remove-ADGroup` command. Otherwise, it will fail to execute. To remove the accidental deletion option, we can use the `Get-ADGroup "Sales Team" | Set-ADObject –ProtectedFromAccidentalDeletion:$false` command.

Devices and other objects

Apart from the computers, AD supports other devices and objects types as well. In this section, we will look into these different object types:

- **Printers**: Printers are one of the most commonly shared resources in an office network. We can use several methods to configure shared printers in user computers. We can set them up using the printer setup wizard in Windows and connect to a printer via an IP Address. We also can use log on scripts to map and install printers in workstations. If an organization uses printer servers, we can connect to it and install the printers too. In the AD environment, we can register the printer as an object in AD. It will allow the users to browse the AD and find the relevant printer quickly, without going through different printer servers.

This can be integrated with a directory from the printer properties. To register a printer with AD, go to **Printer properties** and then to the **Sharing** tab. There you can put tick on the **List in the directory** checkbox to list it on AD:

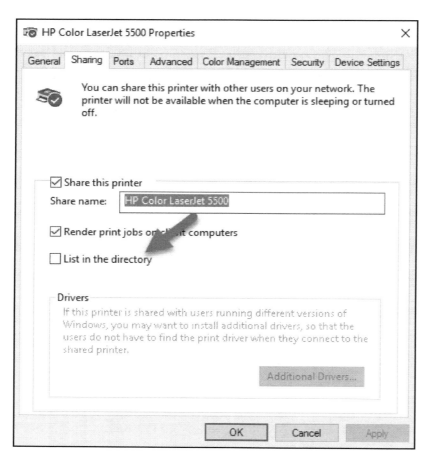

Then in workstation, we need to select the option to list printers from the directory during the printer setup process. It will list down the AD integrated printers:

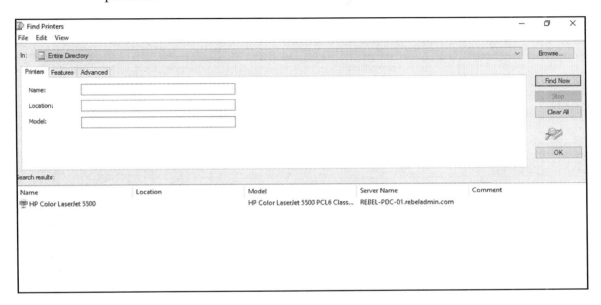

- **inetOrgPerson**: This object is defined in RFC 2798. This object type is used by other directory services which are based on LDAP and X.500. This is existing in AD in order to support migration from non-Microsoft directory service and support applications that requires inetOrgPerson objects. This object can be converted into regular a AD user.

  In order to add this object, we can use ADAC, ADUC, or PowerShell.

  In PowerShell, it will be using the same cmdlet `New-ADUser`, which will be used to add a regular AD user:

```
New-ADUser -Name "Inet User1" -GivenName "Inet"
  -Surname "User1" -SamAccountName "inetuser1"
  -UserPrincipalName "isuer1@rebeladmin.com"
  -AccountPassword (Read-Host -AsSecureString
    "Type Password for User")
  -Enabled $true -Path "OU=Users,OU=Europe,DC=rebeladmin,DC=com"
  -Type iNetOrgPerson
```

The preceding command will add an inetOrgPerson object called `Inet User1`. The only difference in the command from a regular AD user is `-Type iNetOrgPerson`, which defines the account type as `iNetOrgPerson`.

We can convert the `inetOrgPerson` object to a regular AD user object using the following command:

```
Set-ADUser "inetuser1" -Remove @{objectClass='inetOrgPerson'}
```

The following screenshot shows the output for the preceding command:

```
PS C:\Users\Administrator> Set-ADUser "inetuser1" -Remove @{objectClass="inetOrgPerson"}^M
PS C:\Users\Administrator> Get-ADUser "inetuser1"

DistinguishedName : CN=Inet User1,OU=Users,OU=Europe,DC=rebeladmin,DC=com
Enabled           : True
GivenName         : Inet
Name              : Inet User1
ObjectClass       : user
ObjectGUID        : 7c4ba922-b0f7-495a-977f-e62e4f181177
SamAccountName    : inetuser1
SID               : S-1-5-21-4041220333-1835452706-552999228-1210
Surname           : User1
UserPrincipalName : isuer1@rebeladmin.com


PS C:\Users\Administrator> _
```

Best practices

Here we will look into some of the best practices that can be used to manage AD object:

- **Housekeeping**: It is important to review the validity of AD objects from time to time. There can be objects no longer active in operations. They can be computer objects, group objects, or user objects. There are several ways to handle these types of objects:
  - If it's possible to verify objects are not in use for 100% of the time, objects can be completely deleted from the AD.
  - If it's not possible to confirm, the object can be disabled and monitored for events. If there no events occur based on the action, it can be removed from the AD after sometime.

  In order to manage disabled objects, it is advised to create a different OU and move the disabled objects to that. This will allow us to keep track of them and allow easy access when required.

In AD, there can be objects that are only been used for a limited time. As an example, there can be contractors who only work on a projects. These user accounts are only used during a project. These types of objects can be kept disabled and only enabled when required. Past employee accounts also fall into the same category.

- **Adding description**: In AD objects, there is an option attribute where you can add a description about the object. It is advised to add a description to object if its cannot describe the object using its given name. This mostly applies to services accounts and groups objects. It allows other engineers to locate an object quickly and understand the purpose of it.
- **Protecting objects from accidental deletion**: This feature was introduced with AD DS 2008. It can be enabled on user, computer, and group objects. This prevents the objects from being accidentally deleted. It can be enabled at an individual object level or the OU/Directory level as well. This feature needs to be disabled if you need to delete an object on purpose.
- **Object naming conversion**: When defining names, usernames for the objects always follow a standard. As an example, some organizations prefer to use the first letters of the first name and last name as the username. Some may prefer the `firstname.lastname` format. These standards can be different from business to business. It is recommended to document these standards so other team members can also follow the same processes. If there is no such existing document in the AD infrastructure to refer to, go and review similar type objects to understand the standards being used.

Summary

In this chapter, we learnt about AD objects and attributes, and how they have been defined in the AD schema. We also learnt how to define custom attributes in AD schema. Then we looked into creating user account templates and the different types of Managed Service Accounts, followed by different computer groups and their actions. Later, we focused at other objects that we can add to the AD. Last but not the least, we discussed some of the best practices which can be used to manage the AD objects.

In the next chapter, we will be learning about designing and managing the **organizational units (OU)** structure.

9

Designing the OU Structure

My local library in Kingston has a collection of nearly 10,000 books. These books cover many different subjects. When I walk into the library, I can see that there are signs hanging from the ceiling to guide you to the different book sections, such as novels, politics, arts, technology, cooking, and so on. So, if you know the type of the book you looking for, you can easily go to the relevant section. Most of the time, I end up in the cooking or history sections. Each of these sections has multiple bookshelves. These bookshelves are further categorized into subcategories. At the top of each bookshelf, there is a sign to describe which subcategory it belongs to. As an example, the history section has bookshelves with categories such as Europe History, Asia History, World History, and so on. This makes book selection even easier, as now you know exactly which bookshelves to look for. When you go to the bookshelf, the books are usually organized in alphabetical order. Each book has a small label indicating the first character of the book title. If I am looking for a book on *British History*, I can look at the books with the label *B*. So out of 10,000 books, within a few minutes, I can locate a book I need. If it's not *structured*, I will have to spend hours to find books. This doesn't benefit only the members; when the library receives new books, employees know exactly where to rack those up as there is a defined *system* in place for everyone to follow.

The Kingston library for children is in a different building from the main one. I usually have to bring my daughter there. But in there, the books are not categorized in the same way as it's obvious that kids' books are mostly stories. Books there are mainly divided based on age groups. Then, bookshelves are further categorized based on alphabetical order. When I go there, I spend more time in book selection than main library because a category contains more books. Plus, there is another problem: the children's library has a reading corner, so children can pick books from the shelves and read them there. But when they return the books to the shelves, they do not follow the same rules as they are too young to understand these. Therefore books end on up different shelves than where they should be. Both libraries have their own ways of categorizing books. In the main library, it was easier to locate a book than in the children's library. So, just having a *structured* system is not going to give the same output. It depends on the way it was designed and, more importantly, the way it was *maintained*.

In Active Directory, there can be hundreds or thousands of objects based on the organization size. Each of these objects has different operation and security requirements. We do not manage a user object in the same way as we manage computer objects. In the preceding library example, the structured environment helped locate a book easily from lots of a similar type of objects. It also helps the administration maintain the library service with integrity. In the Active Directory environment, **organizational units (OUs)** allow engineers to categorize objects into smaller administrative boundaries based on the object class and administration requirements. In this chapter, we are going to look into the following topics:

- What needs to be considered when designing the OU structure?
- How to choose the OU structure model needed for a business
- How to manage the OU structure

OUs in operations

In Chapter 3, *Designing Active Directory Infrastructure*, you learned how we can represent an organization based on domains. But this hierarchical design has border boundaries. There, we do not consider object class requirements. Organizations units help you define the hierarchical structure for objects within the domain boundaries based on the company requirements.

There are mainly three reasons for creating an OU:

- Organizing objects
- Delegating control
- Group policies

Organizing objects

An Active Directory domain controller supports holding nearly 2 billion objects. As the number of objects increases in the infrastructure, the effort we need to put in, in order to manage it also increases. If we have a proper structure to group these objects into small groups, then we have more control over it and we know at a glance where we can find the specific object:

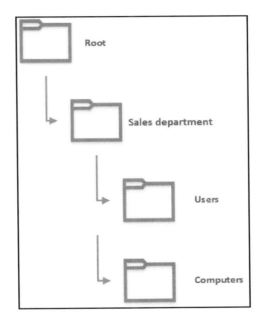

In the preceding example, Rebeladmin Corp. has nearly 100 salespersons. They are also using nearly 150 desktops and laptops. There is no problem putting all these objects into the root of the hierarchy (under default containers). But it will not be easy to identify **Sales department** objects from other Active Directory objects. Instead of that, we can create the OU for **Sales department**. It can be further categorized into two OUs: **Users** and **Computers**. Both of these OUs are in the same hierarchical level. Now if we need to locate a user object in **Sales department** in Active Directory, we definitely know it should be under the **Users** OU of the **Sales department** OU. In the same way, if we need to add a new Active Directory object under **Sales department** now, we have a predefined structure in which we place it. Every engineer in the IT department should follow the same structure when managing objects, and it will not change based on the individual's preferences.

Delegating control

OUs can be used to delegate the administration of a set of objects to individuals or groups. These individuals have control over managing objects in that OU, under the privileges defined by the Domain Admins or Enterprise Admins. Later on in this chapter, we will look into the configuration steps.

Group policies

We cannot think of an Active Directory without group policies. Using group policies, we can apply rules to manage application settings, security settings, and system settings of Active Directory objects. Each and every object in Active Directory has different operation and security requirements. As an example, sales computer security requirements are different from a server that hosts the database system. Group policies can be bound to the organizational units. Therefore, objects that have different Group Policy requirements can be placed into different OUs with relevant policy settings added. Even though this is the most common reason for OUs, this is where things mostly go wrong as well. If you do not consider Group Policy inheritance and how parent Group Policy settings will affect group policies in child OUs, eventually, you can end up with Group Policy conflicts or not applying policies:

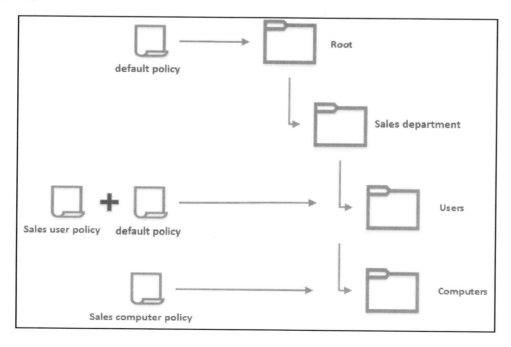

In the preceding example, the structure has a **default policy**, which applies to the majority of the objects in the AD structure. Therefore, it is created at the top of the hierarchy. It is inherited to the child OU levels by default. Therefore, **Sales department** and **Users** under **Sales department** will have the **default policy** inherited by default. But the organization would like to add specific sales user settings via a Group Policy. For that, a new Group Policy is created with the name **Sales user policy** and is mapped to the **Users** OU of **Sales department**. By default, the **Computers** OU under **Sales department** will also have inherited **default policy**, but due to operational requirements, it should block that policy and should have only **Sales computer policy**, which is linked to the **Computers** OU. In order to do that, OU inheritance is blocked. It will no longer apply any inherited policy from parents OUs and only apply the policies that are linked to the OU. This explains how we can use OUs to facilitate Group Policy requirements.

Before we implement the OU structure, we need to decide why we need each of these OUs. This needs to be evaluated based on the preceding three points; if the requirement does not fall under these three points, we should not set up an OU. Most engineers do not pay attention to designing the OU structure because OU structures are easy to change compared to domain structures. If the OU structure does not match your needs, it can be replaced with a completely new structure. But it is followed by moving objects and the Group Policy hierarchy restructure. Even though OUs have flexibility to adopt structure changes, it's important to get the initial requirements correct and design a structure with improved manageability and extensibility in mind.

Containers versus OUs

When you open the ADUC MMC with the advanced view, there will be pre-setup folders. But not all of these are OUs. Most of these are **containers**:

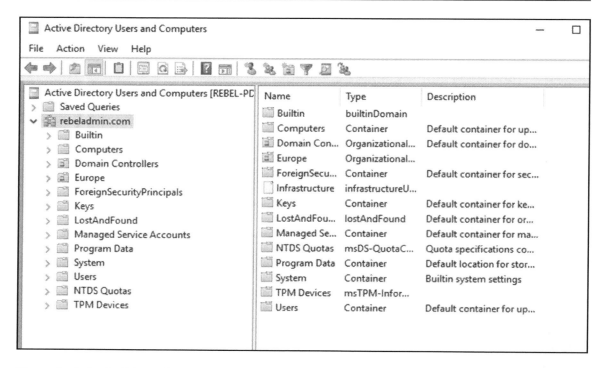

The *only* default OU in the AD environment is the `Domain Controllers` OU. All other folders in the tree are containers. Containers can also contain objects. The `Computers` and `Users` containers are good examples of that. By default, any computer object will be stored in the `Computers` container. All the default user accounts and security groups are stored in the `Users` container. Similar to OUs, containers can also be used to delegate administration control. The only difference between containers and OUs is that group policies cannot apply to containers. Group policies can be assigned only to OUs. The system also does not allow you to create new containers other than containers created by the system.

OU design models

In this section, we are going to look into different design models that you can use for your infrastructure. This doesn't mean every design should be one of these. Modern infrastructure requirements are complex and challenging. These models will guide you to create a design that suits your organization's requirements.

The container model

In the previous section, I explained what a container is. One of the characteristics of this container is that it has large administrative boundaries. As an example, the `Computers` container will contain any computers added to the Active Directory by default. It can be a physical server, virtual server, desktop computer, or laptop. The container model is based on a similar concept. This is mainly applicable to small businesses where there are limited administrative and security requirements over the Active Directory objects. When OU boundaries are large, it is not possible to apply tailored group policies or precise delegated control as each OU can contain different classes of objects as well:

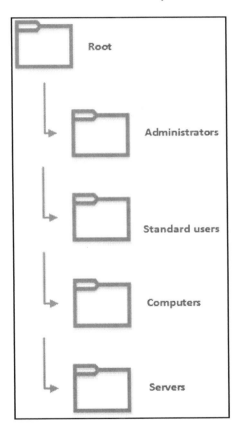

In the preceding example, the organization has four main OUs. In the container model, there will not be any child OUs. As we can see, each OU covers a large boundary. As an example, the **Standard users** OU will contain objects from each and every department. This is not going to apply different policies or delegate control based on each department. In here, the user object's OU will be decided based on its privileges. If a user object has administrator privileges, it will be in the **Administrators** OU, and if not, it will be in the **Standard users** OU.

The following table discusses the advantages and disadvantages of the container model:

Advantages	Disadvantages
Easy to implement: No child OUs; no granular-level security and administrative boundary design required.	**Less control**: It will not categorize objects in detail. Therefore, administrators will have less control over the objects. Since administrative boundaries are large, it is not practical to implement delegated control either.
Fewer group policies: When OUs contain a large number of objects from different classes, it's hard to be specific about system or security settings. Therefore, each OU will have a smaller number of group policies. Even on those, the settings will be more high level than complex tune-ups.	**Less security**: It is difficult to apply different group policies to match the security requirements of objects and workloads as the OU structure doesn't help group the relevant objects together.
Easy to change: Since each OU doesn't contain many group policies and complex inheritance, if needed, the structure can be changed completely with minimum impact.	**Less extensibility**: This is not a future-proof design. As the business grows, object management requirements will change as well. If further categorization is required, it will be difficult to implement without a complete structural change.

The object type model

Active Directory contains different types of objects, such as users, groups, and computers. It is possible to group these different types of objects into separate OUs and manage them. Each of these types can be further categorized into child OUs based on geographical locations or roles and responsibilities:

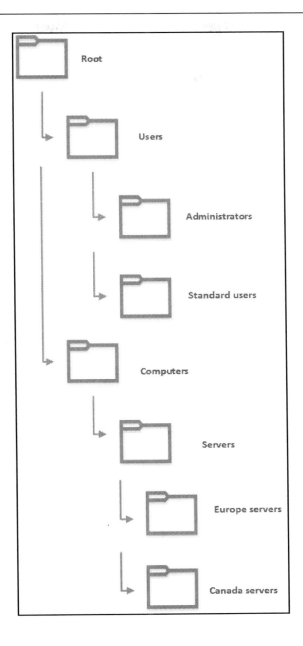

In the preceding example, OUs are mainly categorized based on object types **Users** and **Computers**. The **Users** OU is further categorized into **Administrators** and **Standard users**. These were based on privileges level, and each object's responsibilities within the organization. The **Computers** OU got the child OU for **Servers**. It plays a different role than other computer objects, such as desktops/laptops. It was further categorized based on workloads' geographical locations.

The following table lists the advantages and disadvantages of the object type model:

Advantages	Disadvantages
Flexibility: It gives greater flexibility into categorizing objects. Under each object type, you can categorize objects further based on roles, responsibilities, geographical locations, teams, departments, and so on.	**Complexity**: As this model gives freedom to engineers to categorize objects using many options, the structure can get complex to maintain. There is no limit to the number of levels OUs can break into, but when the number of levels increases, management gets complex too.
Easy management of AD objects: The core value behind this model is the manageability. That's why it can use many methods to categorize objects. When objects are categorized into small administrative boundaries, it's easy to manage the objects in every aspect.	**Structural changes are difficult**: If there is a requirement to change the structure of OUs, it will be difficult as more tailored settings and delegated control are applied to the objects. In structural changes, these specific settings will need to move with objects as well.
Extensibility: Since the model allows you to use a large number of options to categorized objects, it has greater extensibility to implement future organization requirements easily with minimum impact.	N/A
Use of group policies: More tailored group policies can be applied to objects as categorization is more granular.	N/A

The geographical model

This is one of the most common models for large organizations. The OU structure will be based on the geographical location of the branch offices. Each of these branch offices may also have its own IT team. So, the main idea behind this model is to delegate administration control:

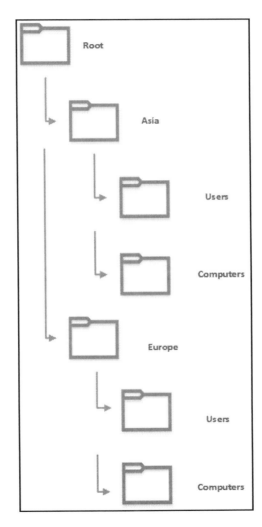

In the preceding example, the organization has two branches in Asia and Europe. The first level of the OUs will start based on geographical location and then be further categorized based on the object types. **Asia** and **Europe** both have **Users** and **Computers** child OUs in their second level. In this model, on most occasions, each geographical location will follow the same structure in its child OUs. This allows you to delegate control for a group of administrators to manage branch office objects easily. This will improve infrastructure management and the productivity of IT operations.

The advantages and disadvantages of the geographical model are listed as follows:

Advantages	Disadvantages
Delegated control: As explained earlier, the core value of this model is *easy delegated control*. Each object related to each branch is located in one structure, and it provides more control for administrators to delegate control.	**Extensibility**: Limited extensibility compared to the object type model. Most of the time, each branch structure should follow predefined standards. Therefore, if structural changes are required, it will have limitations based on these standards.
Repetitive: Most of the time in this model, each branch office will have similar administrative, operational, and security requirements. Therefore, most of the Group Policy settings used in one branch will be able to apply for another branch too.	**Operation limitations**: Each branch office IT team will have delegated control to manage the branch office's objects. But these privileges are limited. It is possible that in order to perform certain tasks, they still need to depend on the HQ IT team.
Maintain standards: This model allows you to maintain administrative and security standards across the organization even if it has different branches. Even though branch IT teams have delegate control to perform certain tasks, at any time, privileged administrators can change or revoke these delegated controls.	N/A

The department model

In the organization, departments help represent the hierarchical order as well as responsibilities. The same structure can be converted into the Active Directory OU structure. Users and asserts related to each department will be categorized together:

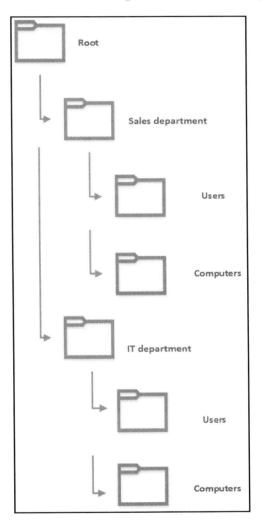

In the preceding example, the OU structure starts with the departments. Each department has its own OU, and its objects are further categorized based on the class and responsibilities. This allows you to delegate control to objects in each department easily. As an example, managers in each department can be set up with delegated control to add or modify objects under their own departments.

The advantages and disadvantages of the department model are listed as follows:

Advantages	Disadvantages
Distributed delegated control: Under the department, objects are grouped together based on object classes, and responsibilities. This allows administrators to delegate control to individuals or groups in order to manage objects in their own department operation boundaries. Administrators do not need to change the structure based on delegation requirements as the model will group it the way it is needed by default.	**Object locations will be difficult to match with the structure**: Not all objects can match with this structure. In organizations, there are asserts and services that are shared by different departments. As an example, printers, file servers, and mail servers are shared by all the departments in the organization. This will need to be represented under the common OU, which is not going to match the organization structure.
Minimum structure changes: Since the model matches the company operation's structural design, the changes to the OU structure will be minimal compared to other models.	**Limitation of applying company-wide settings**: In an organization, there are operational and security requirements that are not dependent on the departments. For example, an organization's data security policies, network security policies, identity protection measures, and so on are common for every department and every user in the organization. Since objects are grouped based on department levels, we will have limitations of targeting objects to apply these different policies.
Less complex: The organization's operational structures (departments) are not complex usually. Departments have a well-defined structure to manage their asserts and responsibilities. Since the OU structure is going to be almost a replica of that model, the OU structure also will be less complex to manage.	N/A

These different types of models can be used as guidelines to design your OU structure. Maybe none of these models match your business requirements. It is absolutely fine to create a mixed model using all of these, but make sure that you validate the design considering easy object management, GPO requirements, and appropriate delegated control.

 There is no limitation to how many sublevels OUs can have. Having more sublevels helps categorize objects in the granular level, but at the same time, it will add to the complexity of managing the structure. This is especially effective in Group Policy management. Therefore, try to keep it under three sublevels.

Managing the OU structure

Similar to any other Active Directory object, the OU structure can be managed using **Active Directory Administrative Center (ADAC)**, **Active Directory Users and Computers (ADUC)** MMC, and PowerShell. In this section, I am going to demonstrate how to manage the OU structure using PowerShell.

A new OU can be created using the `New-ADOrganizationalUnit` cmdlet. The complete syntax can reviewed using the following command:

```
Get-Command New-ADOrganizationalUnit -Syntax
```

As the first step, I am going to create a new OU called `Asia` to represent the Asia branch:

```
New-ADOrganizationalUnit -Name "Asia" -Description "Asia Branch"
```

In the preceding command, `-Description` defines the description for the new OU. When there is no path defined, it will create the OU under the root. We can review the details of the new OU using the following command:

```
Get-ADOrganizationalUnit -Identity "OU=Asia,DC=rebeladmin,DC=com"
```

```
Administrator: Windows PowerShell                                          —    □    ×
PS C:\Users\Administrator> Get-ADOrganizationalUnit -Identity "OU=Asia,DC=rebeladmin,DC=com

City                     :
Country                  :
DistinguishedName        : OU=Asia,DC=rebeladmin,DC=com
LinkedGroupPolicyObjects : {}
ManagedBy                :
Name                     : Asia
ObjectClass              : organizationalUnit
ObjectGUID               : bd86da23-eabf-4f57-abb0-21993afa4c51
PostalCode               :
State                    :
StreetAddress            :
```

We can add/change values of OU attributes using the following command:

```
Get-ADOrganizationalUnit -Identity "OU=Asia,DC=rebeladmin,DC=com" | Set-
ADOrganizationalUnit -ManagedBy "Asia IT Team"
```

The preceding command will set the ManagedBy attribute to Asia IT Team.

> When you use the ManagedBy attribute, make sure that you use an existing Active Directory object for the value. It can be an individual user object or a group object. If you don't use these, the command will fail.

ProtectedFromAccidentalDeletion for the OU object is a nice small safeguard we can apply. It will prevent accidental OU object deletion. This will be applied by default if you create an OU using ADAC or ADUC:

```
Get-ADOrganizationalUnit -Identity "OU=Asia,DC=rebeladmin,DC=com" | Set-
ADOrganizationalUnit -ProtectedFromAccidentalDeletion $true
```

As the next step, I am going to create a sub-OU under the Asia OU called Users:

```
New-ADOrganizationalUnit -Name "Users" -Path "OU=Asia,DC=rebeladmin,DC=com"
-Description "Users in Asia Branch" -ProtectedFromAccidentalDeletion $true
```

The preceding command will create an OU called Users under the OU=Asia,DC=rebeladmin,DC=com path. It is also protected from accidental deletion.

Now we have the OU structure created, and the next step is to move objects to it. For that, we can use the Move-ADObject cmdlet:

```
Get-ADUser "tuser3" | Move-ADObject -TargetPath
"OU=Users,OU=Asia,DC=rebeladmin,DC=com"
```

The preceding command will find the user tuser3 and move the object to OU=Users,OU=Asia,DC=rebeladmin,DC=com.

We can also move multiple objects to the new OU:

```
Get-ADUser -Filter 'Name -like "Test*"' -SearchBase
"OU=Users,OU=Europe,DC=rebeladmin,DC=com" | Move-ADObject -TargetPath
"OU=Users,OU=Asia,DC=rebeladmin,DC=com"
```

The preceding command will first search all the user accounts that start with Test in OU=Users,OU=Europe,DC=rebeladmin,DC=com and then move all objects it found to the new OU path.

If you have `ProtectedFromAccidentalDeletion` enabled on objects, it will not allow you to move objects to a different OU. It needs to be removed before the object is moved.

If we need to remove the OU object, it can be done using the `Remove-ADOrganizationalUnit` cmdlet:

```
Remove-ADOrganizationalUnit "OU=Laptops,OU=Europe,DC=rebeladmin,DC=com"
```

The preceding command will remove the `OU=Laptops,OU=Europe,DC=rebeladmin,DC=com` OU.

Delegating control

Administrators can delegate control based on OUs. This will provide control to individuals or groups to manage objects within OUs.

In my demo, I am going to provide delegated control for `Asia IT Team` members to manage objects under the `Asia` OU:

1. To do that, log in to the domain controller as the Domain Admin and open ADUC. Then, right-click on the relevant OU and click on **Delegate Control...**:

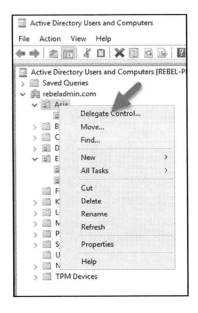

2. Then, it will open up the wizard; there, select the individuals or group that you'd like to provide delegated control to. In this demo, this is **Asia IT Team (REBELADMIN\Asia IT Team)**:

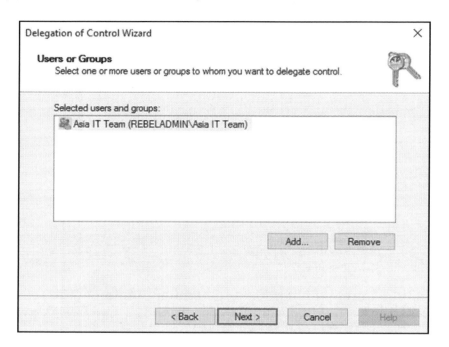

3. In the next window, system will provide the option to select what kind of control to provide. These are sets of permissions predefined by Microsoft, and they cannot be changed. But it also provides the option to create custom tasks. After selecting the options needed, click **Next** to proceed:

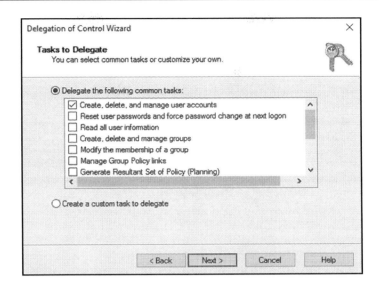

4. After the wizard completes configuration, the team will have delegated control over the objects under `OU=Asia,DC=rebeladmin,DC=com`.

We can review the delegated permission under the OU security settings:

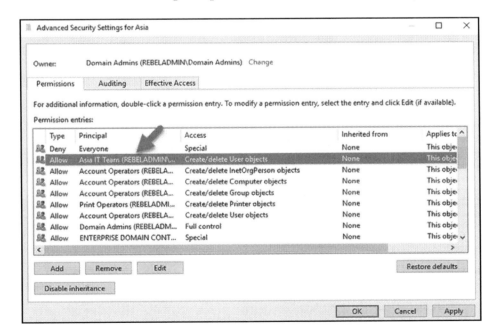

When required, delegated permission can be removed through these security settings.

Summary

OUs play a crucial role by allowing engineers to create a hierarchical structure within domain boundaries. The hierarchical structure will be created considering object management, delegating control, or applying group policies to manage applications, services, and security settings. In this chapter, you learned why the OU design is important and what needs to be considered when designing the OU structure. After that, we moved on to different OU models that can be used as guidelines to design OU structures. In the end, you learned how to manage OUs in the Active Directory infrastructure and how to delegate control for OUs.

In the next chapter, we will look into group policies, which are one of the core features of Active Directory.

10
Managing Group Policies

Before I started writing these words in this chapter, many things were going through my head about this topic because there's a lot of things to cover in just one chapter. Group policies is a broader topic to discuss, and it is possible to even write a whole book about it. It will be challenging, but I will make sure that I cover a majority of it.

My council tax is going to increase by 5% in April (thanks to Brexit). It is a rule and whether I like it or not, I have to pay it every month. If not, I will have to face the consequences. This particular rule has a clear audience. It will only apply to houses under the Kingston council. We can consider Group Policy as an authority that executes a rule or set of rules against a clearly identified audience. This is similar to the council in my example.

It is impossible to describe Active Directory benefits without mentioning group policies. It is one of the main reasons why Active Directory becomes so important in infrastructure management. Group policies are a double-edged sword. It has lots of advantages as it helps manage various types of security, application, and system settings. But at the same time, if it has not been configured properly or not been used properly according to best practices, it can cost you a lot in many ways. Group Policy troubleshooting is one of the most common types of support calls for IT helpdesks. That said, in this chapter, we will cover the following topics:

- Understanding group policies and their capabilities
- Guidelines to use group policies appropriately in the infrastructure

Benefits of group policies

A Group Policy mainly has two types of settings: computer settings and user settings. Based on the purpose—rules, configurations, and scripts will push under these two categories. These will provide non-tangible but more valued benefits for businesses. Let's review some of these benefits in detail.

Maintaining standards

I assume most of you have heard about **International Organization for Standardization (ISO)** standards. It allows organizations to run their operations as per industry standards. In return, it will provide a certification to prove the organization's commitment. Even though organizations pass the ISO certification, the relevant authority will perform a yearly evaluation to make sure they *maintain* the standards. Most companies follow these standards throughout the year, but for some, it comes to mind only when the evaluation is due. This is because the implementation of standards is easy but maintaining it is challenging.

Our infrastructures are also subject to many standards. These standards can be based on the nature of the business, application and services' best practices, business preferences, and industry standards. Defining these standards within the organization is relatively easy when compared to the efforts required to maintain it. The best way to maintain the standard is to enforce it. As an example, a common security standard for a password is to use *complex* passwords. But whenever you're asked to define a password, by nature, people go for the easiest password they can remember. But in the system, if we can *enforce* not accepting a non-complex password, users do not get any choice. If the user needs to define the password, they must comply with the password standards.

Group Policy allows you to enforce the infrastructure standards. It can be based on either user standards or computer standards. This ensures that the company follow these standards with minimum maintenance efforts because once a policy setting is applied, the target group of the user or devices will have to comply with it and not allow you to opt out. It's almost like converting a standard into a *rule*.

Automating administration tasks

I started my career as a web developer and later moved on to system administration. My job title at that time was *associate system administrator*. I was training under a senior engineer. It was a software development company. So, one of the common service requests from the development team manager was to deploy software to the software engineer's computers. There were around 20 people in the company, and since I was a *junior* person, I always had to go and install those software on all 20 computers. It was painful, but since it was just 20 computers, it was somewhat manageable. But imagine if it was hundreds of computers; I would be spending days of doing boring, repetitive tasks. From a company point of view, it is still at the cost of operations. This was just an example, but a regular helpdesk usually gets requests which are small but repetitive, such as mapping shared folders, printer installations, customized application settings, and so on. Group policies allow engineers to automate these types of common, repetitive administration tasks. As an example, group policies can be used to push application installations, push new printer deployments, and map drives when the user logs in, and so on. This reduces the cost of operations as well as allows you to allocate IT resources for more important tasks.

Preventing users from changing system settings

The Windows system does have a software firewall by default to prevent hosts from threats, but sometimes this prevents access to certain application traffic. Most of the time, the reaction to this will be either to disable the firewall or allow application traffic via the custom rule. But if it happens without the IT team knowing about it, it can put the entire infrastructure at risk. Group policies allow you to force these types of sensitive settings and prevent users from modifying them. Not only firewall settings, group policies can also be used to prevent modifying services, preventing access to control panel features, preventing changes to applications, and much more.

Flexible targeting

In the beginning of this section, I explained how group policies can be used to enforce standards. In a business, some of these standards apply to the entire organization, and some can be specific to departments, business units, or users/device group. Group policies allow you to apply different policies based on AD sites, domains, organization units, or groups. As an example, devices in the IT department can have different firewall settings than Sales department firewall settings.

We can create two group policies to cover these requirements and link them to a relevant organization unit. Not only the standards, but this flexible targeting also allows you to apply different system settings for a specific audience. As an example, the Sales department's map drives can be different from the HR department's map drives requirements. Group policies also has *item level targeting*, which can be used to go granular in finding the exact target and applying the group policies to it.

No modifications to target

Group Policy also uses the server-client architecture when applying the group policies. Active Directory domain controllers hold the group policies and publish them to client devices. In order to apply Group Policy to a client, it doesn't have to have any system or profile modification. If the target meets the Group Policy criteria, it will process the Group Policy settings. It simplifies the Group Policy processing process as there are less dependencies.

Group Policy capabilities

Group policies can be used to perform many different tasks in an infrastructure. Here, I have listed some of their capabilities:

- Group policies can be linked to sites, domains, and organization units. It allows you to match the Group Policy requirements with the Active Directory structure.
- Group policies allow you to use security filtering to target specific groups, users, or computers.
- WMI filters are capable of filtering the Active Directory objects based on criteria such as OS version, roles, system configuration, and so on. Group policies allow you to use WMI filters for targeting.
- The GPO status can change based on the operational requirements. If required, Group Policy can disable completely or disable user or computer settings individually.
- Group Policy management tasks can be delegated to individuals or groups.
- It can be used to install, redeploy, or remove programs from computers.
- It can be used to publish scripts to be executed on computer start-up or to shut down a process.

- It can be used to deploy printers to computers.
- Group policies are capable of applying different security policies, such as password policies, lock-out policies, Kerberos policies, firewall policies, public key policies, and much more.
- It can be used to define system audit settings and enable/manage advanced system audit capabilities, which allows you to capture more data about the roles and their activities.
- Group Policy can be used to add registry keys to systems.
- Group policies can be used to define software restriction policies and application control policies to control the application behaviors in computer systems.
- It can be used to set up policy-based QoS rules to define **Differentiated Services Code Point (DSCP)** and throttle values for the outgoing network traffic. It will allow you to prioritize/manage network traffic in a system.
- Group Policy administrative templates can be used to define the registry-based policies' targeting system, applications, and service settings.
- Group Policy can be used to apply preference settings to computers and users. For example, it can be used to define mapped drives, printers, power options, Internet Explorer settings, regional settings, local users and groups, and so on.
- Using group policies, it is possible to manage end user roaming profile settings, including folder redirection. It will automatically save user data to a network location instead of a local computer. It allows you to access the same profile data from any workstation in the domain.

Group Policy objects

When new Active Directory objects are added, system saves the object data inside the Active Directory database. But the GPO store procedure is different from the typical Active Directory object. GPO object contents are stored in two locations in the Active Directory infrastructure.

Group Policy container

As with any other object, the Active Directory database also holds GPO information. This information is more related to system settings and the path reference for the other dataset. When GPO is created, as with any other AD object, it will also have the **globally unique identifier (GUID)** value; this is important as this value is used by both datasets to refer to each other. This value is used in **Common-Name (CN)** too. Before we look into datasets, we need to find the GUID value for the GPO. This can be done using the following command:

```
Get-GPO -name "Test Users"
```

The preceding PowerShell command will list the default properties of the `Test Users` GPO:

In the preceding figure, the `Id` attribute represents the GUID value of the `Test Users` GPO.

Now we have the GUID info, the next step is to review the **Group Policy container (GPC)** information for the given GPO. This information can be accessed using ADSI Edit MMC or `Ldp.exe`. On this occasion, I am going to use `Ldp.exe` to review the data.

In order to open `Ldp.exe`, type `Ldp.exe` in the domain controller's **Run** box. Then, go to the **Connection** menu and select **Bind**. Select the default options if the logged in account has relevant privileges (Schema or Enterprise Admin). In the next step, click on **Tree** under **View** and select the domain DN. As an example, in my demo, DN value is `DC=rebeladmin,DC=com`. GPC values are located under `CN=Policies,CN=System,DC=rebeladmin,DC=com`:

The policy object is further divided into two sections, which represent the **Computer Configuration** (machine) and the **User Configuration** (user):

The preceding screenshot shows details about the GPO we selected, including certain attribute values:

- `displayName`: This attribute contains the name of the Group Policy, defined during the GPO setup process.
- `gPCFileSysPath`: This attribute value represents the path to the other dataset of the GPO. This is called the Group Policy template path. It is always under the `SYSVOL` folder.
- `gPCMachineExtensionNames`: This attribute lists all the **client-side extensions (CSE)** that need to process the GPO computer settings. This is all listed with GUIDs, and `https://blogs.technet.microsoft.com/mempson/2010/12/01/group-policy-client-side-extension-list/` can be used as a reference to most of the known CSEs.

The Group Policy template

When I explained the Group Policy capabilities, I mentioned that they can be used to publish applications, run startup/shutdown scripts, and so on. From the Active Directory objects' point of view, all these settings are attributes and all these files and scripts will need to be saved in the Active Directory database somehow. But instead of doing that, all these policy-related files and settings are saved in the `SYSVOL` folder. It will sync to all domain controllers. The default path for the **Group Policy template (GPT)** data is `\\rebeladmin.com\SYSVOL\rebeladmin.com\Policies`. In here, `rebeladmin.com` can be replaced with your domain FQDN:

```
PS Microsoft.PowerShell.Core\FileSystem::\\rebeladmin.com\SYSVOL\rebeladmin.com\Policies\{721DA008-AB1B-4DA1-A456-5C0BED
0B45A5}> dir


    Directory: \\rebeladmin.com\SYSVOL\rebeladmin.com\Policies\{721DA008-AB1B-4DA1-A456-5C0BED0B45A5}


Mode                LastWriteTime         Length Name
----                -------------         ------ ----
d-----        25/02/2017     11:55                Machine
d-----        20/02/2017     00:18                User
-a----        25/02/2017     11:55             59 GPT.INI
```

Inside the policy folder, there are two subfolders called `Machine` and `Users`. These folders contain files and settings related to the GPO's **Computer Configuration** and **User Configuration**. There is another file called `GPT.INI`, and it contains the version number of the Group Policy. In every Group Policy editing version number will increase automatically and it will be used as a reference to sync the Group Policy changes from one domain controller to another:

```
GPT - Notepad
File  Edit  Format  View  Help
[General]
Version=6
displayName=New Group Policy Object
```

Inside the `Machine` and `User` folders, there are a number of folders that will include the data according to GPO configuration. As an example, the `Applications` folder will contain the software installation files if the GPO is set to publish applications. The `Scripts` folder will contain any startup/shutdown scripts that are published via GPO:

```
PS Microsoft.PowerShell.Core\FileSystem::\\rebeladmin.com\SYSVOL\rebeladmin.com\Policies\{721DA008-AB1B-4DA1-A456-5C0BED
0B45A5}\Machine> dir


    Directory: \\rebeladmin.com\SYSVOL\rebeladmin.com\Policies\{721DA008-AB1B-4DA1-A456-5C0BED0B45A5}\Machine


Mode                LastWriteTime         Length Name
----                -------------         ------ ----
d-----        25/02/2017     09:52                Applications
d-----        25/02/2017     09:53                Microsoft
d-----        25/02/2017     09:52                Scripts
-a----        25/02/2017     11:55           8046 Registry.pol

PS Microsoft.PowerShell.Core\FileSystem::\\rebeladmin.com\SYSVOL\rebeladmin.com\Policies\{721DA008-AB1B-4DA1-A456-5C0BED
0B45A5}\Machine> cd
PS Microsoft.PowerShell.Core\FileSystem::\\rebeladmin.com\SYSVOL\rebeladmin.com\Policies\{721DA008-AB1B-4DA1-A456-5C0BED
0B45A5}> cd User
PS Microsoft.PowerShell.Core\FileSystem::\\rebeladmin.com\SYSVOL\rebeladmin.com\Policies\{721DA008-AB1B-4DA1-A456-5C0BED
0B45A5}\User> dir


    Directory: \\rebeladmin.com\SYSVOL\rebeladmin.com\Policies\{721DA008-AB1B-4DA1-A456-5C0BED0B45A5}\User


Mode                LastWriteTime         Length Name
----                -------------         ------ ----
d-----        25/02/2017     12:35                Applications
d-----        25/02/2017     12:17                Documents & Settings
d-----        25/02/2017     12:17                Scripts
```

In order to process a Group Policy successfully, GPT data synchronization between domain controllers is crucial. `SYSVOL` replication issues will make an impact on GPO policy processing. Before Windows Server 2008 domain services, `SYSVOL` replication used **File Replication Service (FRS)**. After AD DS 2008, it was replaced by **Distributed File System (DFS)**, which provides more efficiency and redundancy in replication.

Group Policy processing

When evaluating Group Policy requirements for an organization, we can identify some settings that are common for objects in the entire domain. But at the same time, some settings are unique to departments or specific groups. Any Group Policy that is applied at the root level will be inherited by other organization units by default. Therefore, organization units can have inherited group policies as well as directly linked group policies. In that case, which Group Policy will be processed? Will it prevent any group policies? If the same setting is applied to different policies, which one will win? To answer all these questions, it's important to understand how Group Policy processing works.

There are mainly two types of policies in the Active Directory environment:

- **Local policies**: Windows systems are supported to set up local security policies. These policies are not similar to domain GPOs, and they contain limited features that are more focused on security settings. It is applied to any user who logs in to the system.
- **Non-local policies**: These policies are Active Directory-based policies that we will be discussing throughout this chapter. These policies will apply only to the domain-joined computers and Active Directory users. These policies are feature-rich compared to local policies.

Group Policy can be applied to three levels in the Active Directory environment:

- **Site**: Group Policy can be linked to an Active Directory site. Any site-level Group Policy will apply to all domains in that site.
- **Domain**: Any Group Policy applied at the domain level will apply to all users and computers' Active Directory objects under that domain. By default, the system creates a Group Policy called **Default Domain Policy** at the domain level. Most of the time, domain-level policies will be used to publish security policies that are applicable to the entire infrastructure.
- **Organization units**: Group Policy at the OU level will be apply to any user or computer object under it. By default, the system creates an OU-level Group Policy called **Default Domain Controllers Policy**, which applies to the domain controller's OU. Group Policy settings applied at the OU level are more specific as the target audience is small.

The following diagram illustrates the policy levels in Active Directory:

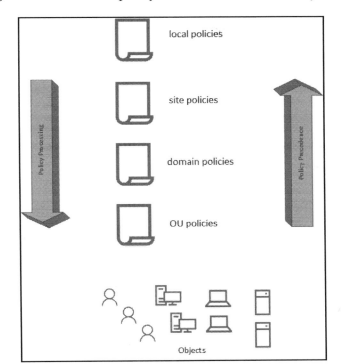

In the Active Directory environment, group policies will be processed in this order:

- **Local policies**
- **Site policies**
- **Domain policies**
- **OU policies**

In general, this order is called **LSDOU**. The first policy to be processed is the local policy, and the last one to be processed is the OU policy. This doesn't mean that the most preferred policy is the local policy. Of all four policies, the policy that holds least precedence value will be the winning GPO, which is the OU policy. This processing order is important when policies have conflicting values. The policy at the OU level will be the *closest* policy to the object. As I said earlier, OU-level policy settings are more specific according to organization requirements. Therefore, they hold the most accurate policy setting for the targeted objects. This order is the default processing order, and based on the requirements, it is possible to change the precedence order. We will be looking into this later on in this chapter.

The local policies processing can be completely turned off if required. This will prevent applying non-recommended settings that administrators do not have control over or awareness of. This can be disabled by using a Group Policy setting. The policy setting is located at `Computer Configuration\Administrative Templates\System\Group Policy\Turn off Local Group Policy Objects Processing`; to disable policy processing, the value should be set to `Enable`.

In order to apply computer Group Policy settings successfully, the device should have a valid connection to domain controllers, and to apply user Group Policy settings, a user (the domain account) should log in to the domain-joined computer that has an active connection to domain controllers.

Group policies are mainly processed in two different modes. By default, Group Policy's computer settings will start to process during the startup process before the user log-on box prompts. Once the user enters the username and credentials, Group Policy's user settings start to process. This pre-processing mode is called **foreground processing**. During the foreground process, some policies will finish processing but some will not. They will be processed in the **background** after login and network connection is initialized. Also, once the user logs in, every 90 minutes, the group policies will run in the *background* by default. This is the second mode of Group Policy processing.

Foreground processing can be further divided into two sub-modes. Before Windows XP was introduced, all the policy settings that ran in the foreground mode finished before the user saw the desktop after the login process. This is called a **synchronous** mode. But after Windows XP, the default mode of processing is **asynchronous**, which means it doesn't wait until the Group Policy process finishes or before the user starts to use the computer. When the computer is presented with the login screen, in the background, the computer settings part of the policies will still be processing. After the user logs in, system will start to process user settings as part of the policies, by the time computer loads into initial home screen, the group policies may still be processing in the background. There are four policy settings that are defined by Microsoft that are always processed in the asynchronous mode. If any policy has folder redirection, software installation, disk quota, and drive mapping enabled, it will be processed in the synchronous mode. Not only that, all the startup scripts also run in the foreground in synchronous mode.

This default behavior of processing provides a faster logon time for users, but at the same time, some policy settings can take up to two logon cycles to apply the changes fully. This behavior makes an impact on security settings. As an example, if we want to block access to control panel settings and if the policy setting not processed in the synchronous mode, when the user logs in, there is a possibility for them to have access to the **Control Panel**. Then, it is not going to give the expected results. This default mode is useful when users are connected through a *slow link*. Because if it's not, it can take an awful amount of time to finish the Group Policy processing. If there is no specific reason, it is recommended that you use synchronous mode always. This can be changed using Group Policy. The policy settings are located at `Computer Configuration\Administrative Templates\System\Logon\Always wait for the network at computer startup and logon`. One disadvantage of this is that even when there is slow link detection, system will still process it in the synchronous mode.

As I explained earlier, there are four Group Policy settings defined by Microsoft that always run in the synchronous mode. Even if systems are connected via slow link, it will process these Group Policy settings in synchronous mode. Therefore, it is recommended that you enable the following two Group Policy settings to force the asynchronous mode when you log in via slow link and remote desktop services. Forcing the asynchronous mode for slow links can be enabled via `Computer Configuration\Administrative Templates\System\Group Policy\Change Group Policy Processing to run asynchronously when a slow link is detected`. Forcing the asynchronous mode for remote desktop services can be enabled via `Computer Configuration\Administrative Templates\System\Group Policy\Allow asynchronous user Group Policy processing when logging on through Remote Desktop Services`.

Group Policy inheritance

Any Group Policy applied in the upper level of the structure is inherited by a lower level. The order of the inherited policies is based on the LSDOU model that I have explained in a previous section. Group Policy inheritance for each OU can be reviewed using **Group Policy Management** MMC.

Once you click on the OU, click on the tab called **Group Policy Inheritance**:

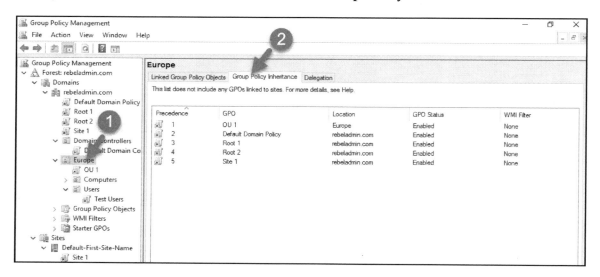

The Group Policy inheritance details can also be viewed using the `Get-GPInheritance` cmdlet. So, the same information listed in the preceding figure can be viewed using the following command:

```
Get-GPInheritance -Target "OU=Users,OU=Europe,DC=rebeladmin,DC=com"
```

In this example, I have one site-linked Group Policy called **Site 1**. There are two domain-linked group policies called **Root 1** and **Root 2**. I also have an OU-linked Group Policy called **Test Users**:

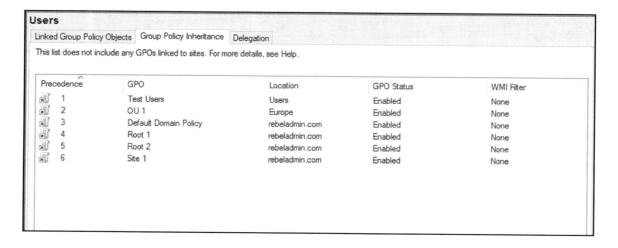

In the list, the first precedence goes to the **Test Users** Group Policy that is closest to the OU. It is the OU-linked Group Policy. Then, precedence order **2** goes to the Group Policy linked to the parent OU. Precedence order **3**, **4**, and **5** go to the domain-linked group policies. The last in the order is the **Site 1** Group Policy, which is linked to the AD site.

This inheritance is not useful in every scenario. There can be situations where the OU needs to have very specific settings and should not be disturbed by any other inherited policy. When the number of group policies increases, the time it needs for processing also increases. For example, when I need a chicken burger, if someone offered me a chicken burger and a beef burger, I'd still say okay. But I would eat only the chicken burger as I don't eat beef. If my Group Policy OU requirements can be achieved using one Group Policy that is linked to the OU, why should I still apply inherited policies that are not going to help me anyway? In a similar scenario, Group Policy inheritance can be blocked at the OU level. This can be done using the **Group Policy Management** MMC or the PowerShell cmdlet `Set-GPinheritance`:

```
Set-GPInheritance -Target "OU=Users,OU=Europe,DC=rebeladmin,DC=com" -
IsBlocked Yes
```

The preceding command will block the Group Policy inheritance in `OU=Users,OU=Europe,DC=rebeladmin,DC=com`:

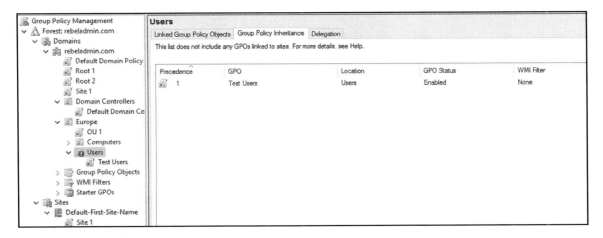

After the Group Policy inheritance block, the only policy in the inheritance list is the policy that is linked to the OU.

Group Policy conflicts

Group policies' precedence order LSDOU and Group Policy inheritance also decide which policy will win when we have some conflicting settings. Let's look at this further with an example:

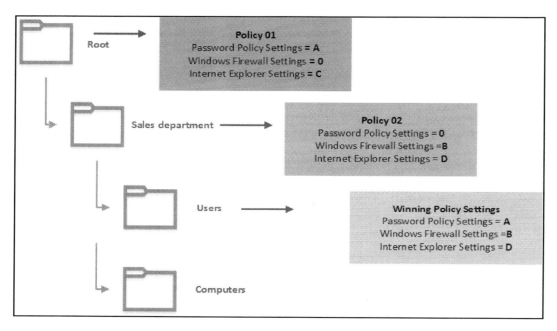

As per the preceding diagram, we have two policies inherited to **Users** OU. **Policy 01** is the domain-linked Group Policy. **Policy 02** is the OU-linked Group Policy. Each of the Group policies has its own values defined for the three selected settings. Based on the default Group Policy inheritance, the **Users** OU will have both policies applied. According to LSDOU, **Policy 02** will have the lowest precedence value as it is the closest policy for the **Users** OU. For **Password Policy Settings,** only **Policy 01** has a value defined. Therefore, even though it's the least preferred Group Policy, that value will apply to the **Users** OU. For **Windows Firewall Settings,** only **Policy 02** has a value. It will also apply to the **Users** OU. When it comes to **Internet Explorer Settings**, both policies have values. This makes a conflict. The winning value of conflicting policy settings will be decided based on LSDOU. Therefore, the winning value will be from **Policy 02**.

Microsoft allows you to change this default policy winning procedure by *enforcing* policies. When Group Policy has been enforced, it will have the lowest precedence value regardless of where it's been linked. Another advantage of the enforced policy is that it will apply even though OU has blocked inheritance. If the domain-linked policy is enforced, it will apply to any OU under the domain, and it will hold the lowest precedence. If multiple policies are enforced, all of them will take the lowest precedence numbers in order.

To enforce a policy, load GPMC, right-click on the selected Group Policy, and then select the **Enforced** option. This will enforce the policy and change the policy icon with a small padlock mark. This allows you to identify enforced policies quickly from the policy list:

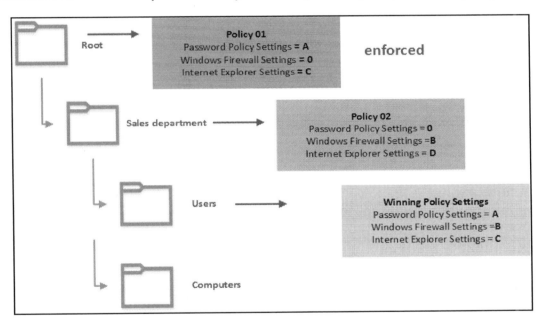

In the preceding example, **Policy 01** was **enforced**. It is the domain-linked Group Policy. In normal circumstances, **Policy 02** will get the lowest precedence value when it's applied to the **Users** OU. But when the policy is **enforced**, **Policy 01** will have the lowest precedence value. When we look into winning policy values of the **Users** OU, for **Password Policy Settings**, system will process the **Policy 01** value as it is the only one with any value for it. For **Windows Firewall Settings**, **Policy 01** does not have any value defined. So even if policy has been **enforced**, the winning policy setting will be from **Policy 02** as it's the only one with a value defined. **Policy 01** and **Policy 02** both have values for **Internet Explorer Settings**. But the **enforced Policy 01** is on top of the policy list and the winning policy setting will be from it.

So far, we talked about conflicting policy settings from different levels in the domain structure. How will it work if it's at the same level? Policies at the same level also apply according to the precedence order. When policies are at the same level, the *LSDOU* process is of no use. The winning policy will be decided based on its position in the policy list. The order of the list is decided based on the **Linked Group Policy Objects** list. This list can be viewed using the **Linked Group Policy Objects** tab in the OU detail window in GPMC:

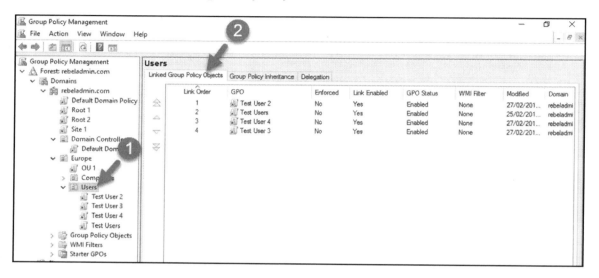

The order of the policy in the same level can be changed using two methods. One method is to enforce the policy. When the policy is enforced, it will take priority from the other policies in the same level. But it will not change the **Link Order** of the policy. The order of the list can be changed using the up and down buttons in the **Linked Group Policy Objects** tab. The link order will match the precedence order of the group policies:

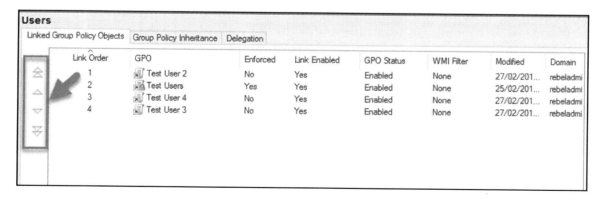

Group Policy mapping and status

There are a few things we need to consider when we create and link a Group Policy object to a site, domain, or OU:

- If it's a new GPO, it can be created directly under the relevant OU or domain using GMPC.
- In sites, it's only allowed to link to an existing GPO; therefore, if the new GPO needs to link to the site, it needs to add a new GPO using GPMC or a PowerShell cmdlet.
- An already added GPO can link to any OU, domain, or site. As an example, if policy A is created and linked under OU A, it can be reused in any other OU, domain, or site.

A new GPO object can be created using the New-GPO PowerShell cmdlet:

```
New-GPO -Name GPO-Test-A
```

The preceding command will create a GPO called GPO-Test-A. By default, it will not link to any OU, domain, or site. In GPMC, it can be viewed under the Group Policy Objects container.

After an object is created, it can be linked to an OU, domain, or site using the New-GPLink cmdlet:

```
New-GPLink -Name GPO-Test-A -Target
"OU=Users,OU=Europe,DC=rebeladmin,DC=com"
```

```
PS C:\> New-GPLink -Name GPO-Test-A -Target "OU=Users,OU=Europe,DC=rebeladmin,DC=com"

GpoId         : ca25a48f-9e9a-43c7-85eb-83c5ff824d3c
DisplayName   : GPO-Test-A
Enabled       : True
Enforced      : False
Target        : OU=Users,OU=Europe,DC=rebeladmin,DC=com
Order         : 5


PS C:\> _
```

The preceding command links a GPO called `GPO-Test-A` to `OU=Users,OU=Europe,DC=rebeladmin,DC=com`.

Both cmdlets can be combined to create and link a GPO at the same time:

```
New-GPO -Name GPO-Test-B | New-GPLink -Target
"OU=Users,OU=Europe,DC=rebeladmin,DC=com"
```

The preceding command will create a new GPO called `GPO-Test-B` and link it to `OU=Users,OU=Europe,DC=rebeladmin,DC=com` at the same time.

There are occasions where the link to the group policies needs to be disabled. This is useful when you do Group Policy troubleshooting. When the link to Group Policy is disabled, it will remove it from the Group Policy precedence list. But it will not remove it from the **Link Order** list or from its location. This can be done via GMPC or using the PowerShell cmdlet `Set-GPLink`:

```
Set-GPLink -Name GPO-Test-B -Target
"OU=Users,OU=Europe,DC=rebeladmin,DC=com" -LinkEnabled No
```

The preceding command will disable the link between the `GPO-Test-B` GPO and `OU=Users,OU=Europe,DC=rebeladmin,DC=com`. This is usually used to temporarily disable a policy. It can be enabled at any time using the `-LinkEnabled Yes` option.

But if this requirement is permanent, this GPO link can be completely removed using the `Remove-GPLink` cmdlet. This will remove the link, but it will not delete the GPO. It will also not affect any other existing links in GPO:

```
Remove-GPLink -Name GPO-Test-B -Target
"OU=Users,OU=Europe,DC=rebeladmin,DC=com"
```

This command will remove the `GPO-Test-B` policy from `OU=Users,OU=Europe,DC=rebeladmin,DC=com`. It will remove the GPO from the **Precedence** list as well as the **Link Order** list.

If GPO needs to be deleted completely, we can use the `Remove-GPO` cmdlet for that:

```
Remove-GPO -Name GPO-Test-A
```

The preceding command will delete the mentioned GPO completely from the system. If it was linked, it will forcefully remove it at the same time.

Without disabling links, removing links, or deleting the GPO, it is possible to disable GPO settings only. This feature provides options to disable computer settings, user settings, or both. Once the settings are disabled, it will not remove it from the **Link Order** or **Precedence** list. It will disable only the applied settings:

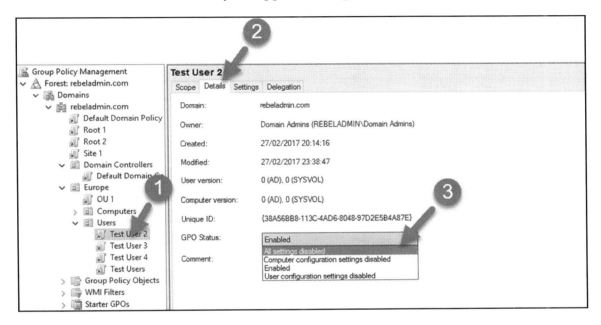

Administrative templates

Group policies allow you to manage computer settings and user settings in many ways. However, infrastructure operation requirements often change in businesses. They can be based on new application versions, new security requirements, new business policy requirements, and so on. We know that group policies can be used to manage organization-wide settings but not all the requirements will be supported by default. As an example, by the time AD DS 2008 was released, it was not possible to have group policies that could manage settings in the Office 2016 application. Application vendors and developers can develop administrative templates and publish them via group policies to customize, manage, and optimize their products and services. Administrative templates contain registry-based changes to the system. They can be divided into two sections. **Administrative Templates** under **Computer Configuration** in the GPO can be used to modify the registry entries under the HKEY_LOCAL_MACHINE key.

Administrative Templates under **User Configuration** in the GPO can be used to modify registry entries under the HKEY_CURRENT_USER key. Microsoft also has predeployed administrative templates that can be used to edit more than 1,000 individual registry settings. Administrative templates are not just from the application vendors; if needed, we can also create custom administrative templates to address unique requirements.

Before Windows Server 2008, administrative templates came as unicode-formatted text file with the .adm file extension. But it does have some drawbacks. It saves the .adm file as part of the Group Policy inside SYSVOL. If it is used in different GPOs, it will save a copy of .adm with each and every GPO. It increases the size of SYSVOL. Also, if you need to change a setting in the .adm file, it needs to be edited in each copy of .adm. One .adm file has support for only one language. If you need to use multiple languages, for each language, you need a copy of .adm.

After Windows Server 2008, administrative templates were presented as two XML files. The file with the .admx extension is responsible for publishing registry settings and the file with the .adml extension is responsible for providing language-specific interface settings. This allows administrators to edit and manage policies in multiple languages. Unlike .adm files, if you need to edit the ADMX file, it needs to be edited in one place only, and it will map the relevant ADML file to provide multi-language support if required.

The .adm file is part of the GPO, so it's always stored in the SYSVOL folder. But by default, for ADMX/ADML, Group Policy holds the settings only for the policy, and when it needs editing, it will pull the ADMX and ADML files from the local workstation. It is possible to change this behavior and save these files in a central location where everyone can pull the templates files when required. This provides easy access and better management for administrative templates.

We can move administrative templates to the SYSVOL folder using the following steps:

1. Log in to the domain controller as the Domain Admin or higher.
2. Create a folder called PolicyDefinitions under \\rebeladmin.com\SYSVOL\rebeladmin.com\Policies. The rebeladmin.com domain can be replaced by your own domain FQDN:

```
mkdir \\rebeladmin.com\SYSVOL\rebeladmin.com\Policies
\PolicyDefinitions
```

3. After that, copy the policy definition data to this new folder:

```
Copy-Item C:\Windows\PolicyDefinitions\*
\\rebeladmin.com\SYSVOL\rebeladmin.com\Policies
\PolicyDefinitions -Recurse -Force
```

This will also move ADML files into
`\\rebeladmin.com\SYSVOL\rebeladmin.com\Policies\PolicyDefinitions` with its
language name. As an example, US English will be in
`\\rebeladmin.com\SYSVOL\rebeladmin.com\Policies\PolicyDefinitions\en-US`. The language to use in policy editing will be decided based on the language used in the
workstation.

Group Policy filtering

As you learned earlier, Group Policy can map to sites, domains, and OUs. If Group Policy is
mapped to the OU, by default, it will apply to any object under it. But within an OU,
domain, or site, there are lots of objects. The security, system, or application settings'
requirements covered by group policies not always applied to broader target groups. Group
Policy filtering capabilities allow you to further narrow down the Group Policy target to
security groups or individual objects.

There are a few different ways in which we can do the filtering in Group Policy:

- Security filtering
- WMI filtering

Security filtering

Before you apply the security filtering, the first thing to make sure is that Group Policy is
mapped correctly to the site, domain, or OU. The security group or the objects you are
going to target should be at the correct level where the Group Policy is mapped.

We can use the GMPC or PowerShell cmdlets to add the security filtering to GPO:

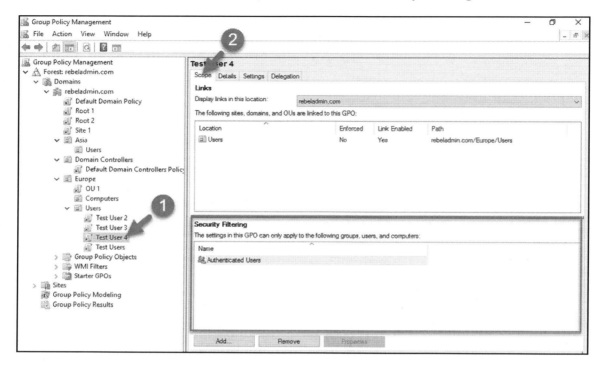

As you can see, by default, any policy with the **Authenticated Users** group is added to the **Security Filtering**. This means that by default, the policy will apply to any authenticated user in that OU. When we add any group or object to security filtering, it also creates an entry under delegation. In order to apply a Group Policy to an object, it needs a minimum of the following:

- **Read**
- **Apply group policy**

Any object added to the **Security Filtering** section will have both of these permissions set by default. In the same way, if an object is added directly to the delegation section and applies both permissions, it will list down those objects under the **Security Filtering** section.

Now, before we add custom objects to the filtering, we need to change the default behavior of the security filtering with **Authenticated Users**. Otherwise, it doesn't matter what security group or object you add; it will still apply Group Policy settings to any authenticated user. Before Microsoft released security patch MS16-072 in the year 2016, we could simply remove the **Authenticated Users** group and add the required objects to it. With these new security patch changes, group policies will now run within the computer security context. Earlier, it was executed within the user's security context. In order to accommodate these new security requirements, one of the following permissions must be available under Group Policy **Delegation**:

- **Authenticated Users**: Read
- **Domain Computers**: Read

In order to edit these changes, go to the Group Policy and then go to the **Delegation** tab. Click on **Advanced**, select **Authenticated Users**, and then remove the **Apply group policy** permissions:

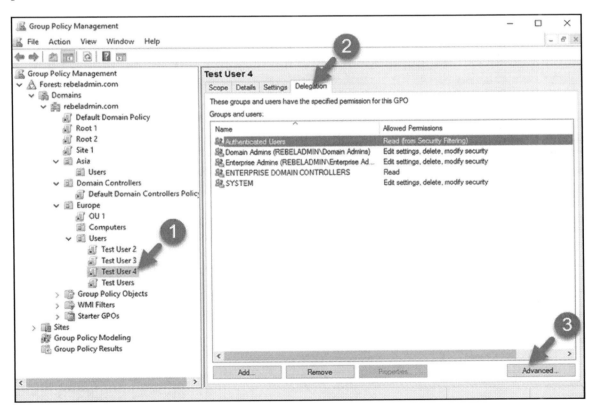

Now we can go back to the **Scope** tab and add the required security group or objects to the **Security Filtering** section. It will automatically add the relevant **Read** and **Apply group policy** permissions:

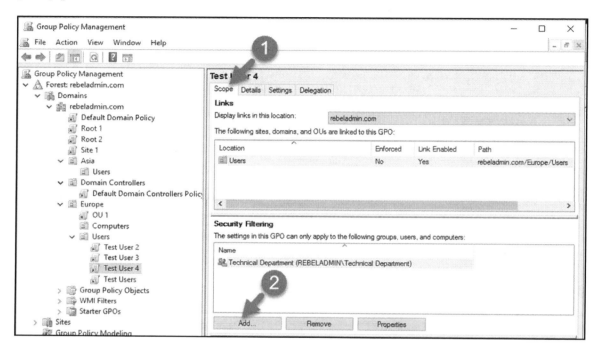

In here, we are looking at how to apply Group Policy to a specific target, but it also allows you to explicitly allow it to a large number of objects and *block* groups or objects by applying it. As an example, let's assume we have an OU with a few hundred objects from different classes. From all these, we have 10 computer objects that we do not need to apply to a given Group Policy. Which one is easy? Go and add each and every security group and object to **Security Filtering** or allow everyone for Group Policy and block it only for one security group. Microsoft allows you to use the second method in filtering too. In order to do that, Group Policy should have default security filtering, which is **Authenticated Users** with **Read** and the **Apply group policy** permissions. Then, go to the **Delegation** tab and click on the **Advanced** option. In the next window, click on the **Add** button and select the group or object that you need to block access to:

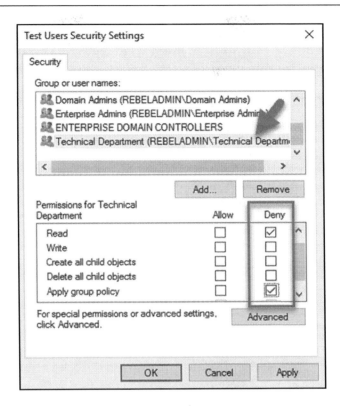

Now in here, we are denying **Read** and **Apply group policy** permissions to an object. So it will not be able to apply the Group Policy and all other object under that OU will still be able to read and apply Group Policy. Easy, huh?

WMI filtering

Windows Management Instrumentation (WMI) filters is another method that we can use to filter the Group Policy target. This method can be used to filter only the computer objects, and it is based on computer attribute values. As an example, WMI filters can be used to filter different operating system versions, processor architecture (32 bit/64 bit), Windows Server roles, registry settings, event ID, and so on. WMI filters will run against WMI data of the computers and decide whether it should apply the policy or not. If it matches the WMI query, it will process the Group Policy, and if it's false, it will not process the Group Policy. This method was first introduced with Windows Server 2003.

We can use GPMC to create/manage WMI filters. Before applying a filter to a GPO, first, we need to create it. A single WMI filter can be attached to many GPOs, but a GPO can have only a single WMI filter attached.

To create a WMI filter, open GPMC, right-click on **WMI Filters**, and click on **New**:

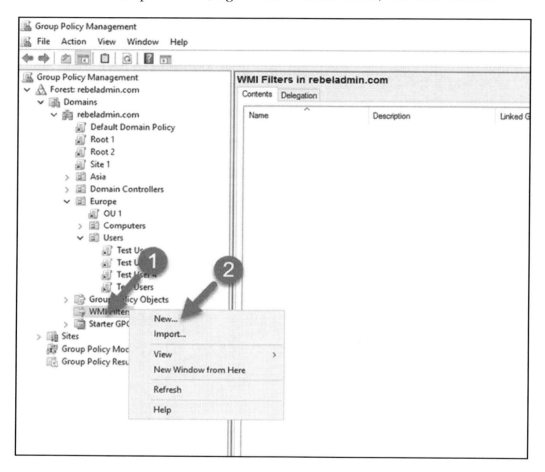

It will open up a new window where we can define the WMI query:

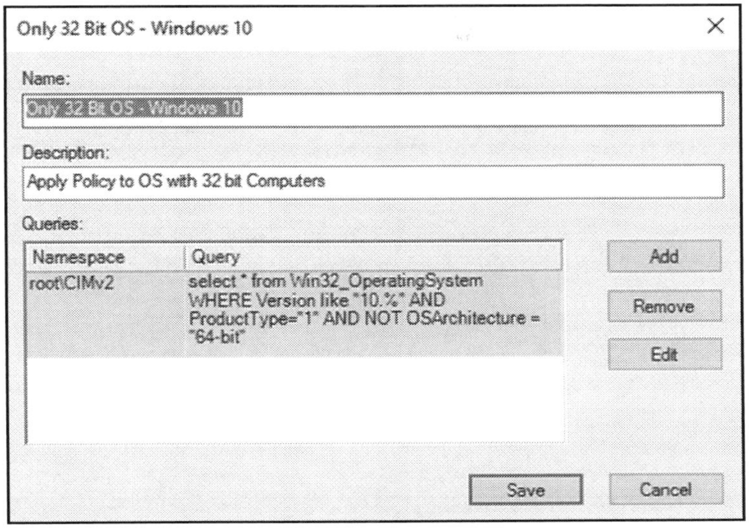

By clicking on the **Add** button, we can define **Namespace** and WMI **Query**. As an example, I have created a WMI query to filter the Windows 10 operating system running the 32-bit version:

```
select * from Win32_OperatingSystem WHERE Version like "10.%" AND
ProductType="1" AND NOT OSArchitecture = "64-bit"
```

In the following commands, you can find a few examples of commonly used WMI queries:

To filter OS—Windows 8—64bit, use the following command:

```
select * from Win32_OperatingSystem WHERE Version like "6.2%" AND
ProductType="1" AND OSArchitecture = "64-bit"
```

To filter OS—Windows 8—32 bit, use the following command:

```
select * from Win32_OperatingSystem WHERE Version like "6.2%" AND
ProductType="1" AND NOT OSArchitecture = "64-bit"
```

To filter any Windows Server OS—64bit, use the following command:

```
select * from Win32_OperatingSystem where (ProductType = "2") OR
(ProductType = "3") AND  OSArchitecture = "64-bit"
```

To apply a policy to a selected day of the week, use the following command:

```
select DayOfWeek from Win32_LocalTime where DayOfWeek = 1
```

Day 1 is Monday.

Once WMI Filter is created, it needs to be attached to the GPO. To do that, go to GPMC and select the required GPO. Then, under the **WMI Filtering** section, select the required WMI filter from the drop-down box:

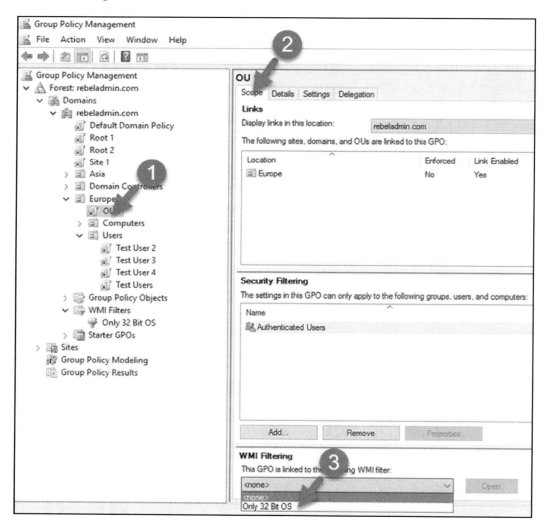

Now it is time for testing. Our test query is to target 32-bit Windows 10 operating systems. If I try to run it over a 64-bit operating system, it should not apply. We can check this by running `gpupdate /force` to apply a new Group Policy and `gpresult /r` to check the results:

```
Administrator: Windows PowerShell

Site Name:                    Default-First-Site-Name
Roaming Profile:              N/A
Local Profile:                C:\Users\administrator
Connected over a slow link?:  No


COMPUTER SETTINGS
------------------
    CN=REBEL-PC01,OU=Europe,DC=rebeladmin,DC=com
    Last time Group Policy was applied: 02/03/2017 at 23:52:28
    Group Policy was applied from:      REBEL-PDC-01.rebeladmin.com
    Group Policy slow link threshold:   500 kbps
    Domain Name:                        REBELADMIN
    Domain Type:                        Windows 2008 or later

    Applied Group Policy Objects
    -----------------------------
        Default Domain Policy

    The following GPOs were not applied because they were filtered out

        OU 1
            Filtering:  Denied (WMI Filter)
            WMI Filter: Only 32 Bit OS - Windows 10

        Local Group Policy
            Filtering:  Not Applied (Empty)

    The computer is a part of the following security groups
    -------------------------------------------------------
        BUILTIN\Administrators
        Everyone
        BUILTIN\Users
        NT AUTHORITY\NETWORK
        NT AUTHORITY\Authenticated Users
        This Organization
        REBEL-PC01$
        Domain Computers
        Authentication authority asserted identity
        System Mandatory Level
```

The test was successful and the policy was blocked as I was running Windows 10—64-bit OS version.

Now we know how we can apply these different filtering options to target a specific object for GPO. But in what order will all these apply?

- **LSDOU**: The first filtering option will be based on the order in which policies are placed in the domain structure. This has been covered in an earlier section of this chapter in detail.

- **WMI filters**: The next filtering it will look for is the WMI filtering, which you learned in this section. If it's true, it will go to the next step. If the result is false, the Group Policy does not apply.

- **Security settings**: As a last step, it will look into security filtering and check whether the given security criteria have been met. If they are met, it will process the Group Policy.

Group Policy preferences

Group Policy preferences were introduced with Windows 2008 to publish administrative preference settings to Windows desktop operating systems and server operating systems. These preference settings can apply only to domain-join computers. Group Policy preferences provide granular-level targeting and also provide easy management via enhanced GUI. Group Policy preferences have replaced many Group Policy settings that required registry edits or complex logon scripts. Group Policy preferences are capable of adding/updating/removing settings such as the following:

- Drive maps
- Internet Explorer settings
- Registry entries
- Printers deployment
- Start menu items
- Power management
- Local users and groups
- File replication
- Managing VPN connections
- Schedule tasks

Group Policy settings and Group Policy preferences are processed in two different ways. Group Policy settings are applied during the boot-up process and the user logon process. After that, settings are refreshed every 90 minutes (default). Once the Group Policy setting is applied, its values cannot change easily. It is required to push new values via Group Policy. Otherwise, even if it's changed, it will be overwritten in the next policy refresh cycle. But Group Policy preferences will not be enforced. They allow users to alter them if required. This also allows you to configure applications that are not Group Policy-aware.

Group Policy preferences are also divided into **Computer Configuration** and **User Configuration**. We can use GPMC to manage preference settings. To access preference settings, select the Group Policy, right-click on **Edit...**, and expand **Computer Configuration** or **User Configuration**. In there, we can see the `Preferences` container:

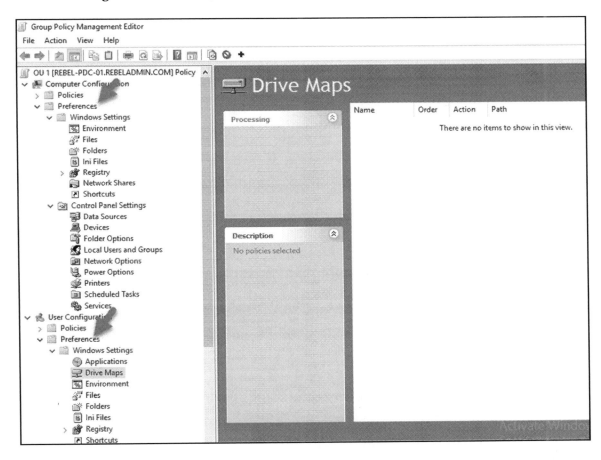

As an example, we can see how we can configure Internet Explorer settings. This is one of the commonly used preference settings in organizations, specifically to publish proxy settings. Before IE 10, Internet Explorer settings managed using **Internet Explorer Maintenance (IEM)** in Group Policy. If your organization has IE settings published using IEM, it will not be applicable to IE 10 and IE 11 anymore. Internet Explorer settings can also be applied via registry edits; Group Policy preferences made this easy as it can use a GUI similar to an actual IE settings window.

In order to configure the settings, open the Group Policy settings and then go to **User Configuration** | Preferences | Control Panel Settings | **Internet Settings**. Then, right-click and select **New**. In there, we can select the settings based on the IE version. There is no option for IE 11. But any setting that applies to version 10 will apply to IE 11 too:

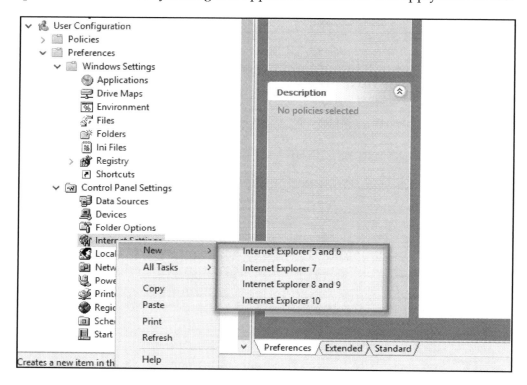

Once you open the relevant configuration, you will see that it is very similar to the setting window we see in the application itself. Complex registry entries to configure IE settings are no longer needed. One thing you need to make sure is once you input the changes, press the *F6* key to apply the changes. If it works fine, the *red* dotted line will change to a *green* dotted line. It doesn't matter what changes you put; if you do not activate it by pressing the *F6* key, it will not publish:

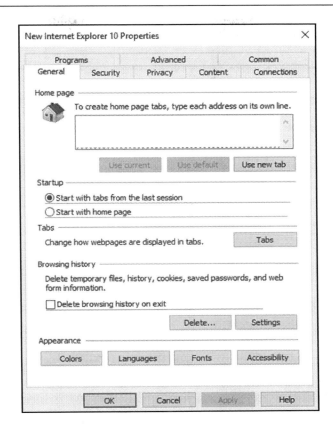

These preference settings will not prevent users from changing it. If it still needs to control editing settings, then it needs to control them via Group Policy settings.

Item-level targeting

In the previous section, I explained how we can use WMI filters for granular-level Group Policy targets. In a similar way, item-level targeting can be used to target Group Policy preference settings based on application settings and properties of users and computers at the granular level. We can use multiple targeting items in preference settings and make selections based on logical operators (AND, OR, IS, IS NOT).

Item-level targeting in Group Policy preferences can be set up/managed using GPMC. To do that, open the Group Policy settings, go to relevant preference settings, and right-click and select **Properties**.

As per the previous example (IE 10 Settings), the path should be **User Configuration** | Preferences | **Internet Settings** | **Internet Explorer 10**. Then, right-click and select **Properties**.

From the **Properties** window, select the **Common** tab, tick **Item-level targeting**, and then click on the **Targeting...** button:

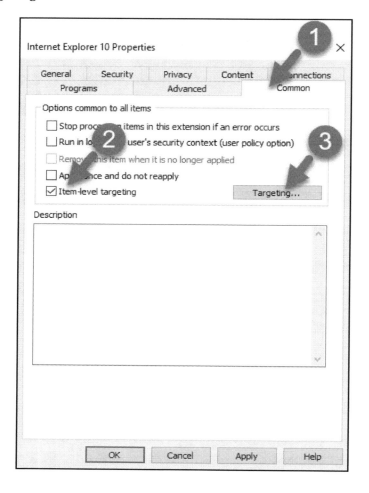

In the next window, we can build granular-level targeting based on one item or multiple items with logical operators:

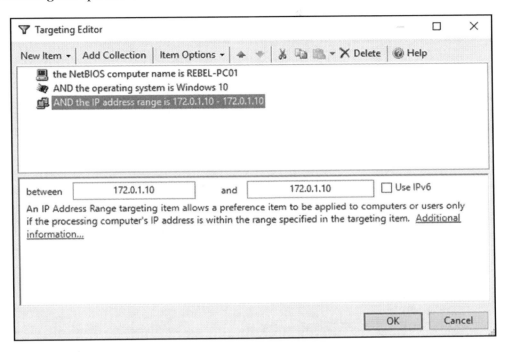

In the preceding example, I built a query based on three settings, which are the NetBIOS name, the operating system, and the IP address. In order to apply the preference settings, all three statements should provide the `true` value as a result as I used the *AND* logical operator. If it's the *OR* logical operator, the result can have `true` or `false` values.

In the window, the **New Item** menu contains items we can use for targeting. **Add Collection** allows you to create a parenthetical grouping. The **Item Options** menu is responsible for defining logical operators.

Loopback processing

Group Policy mainly has two configurations. One is targeted computer settings, and the other is targeted user configuration. When we apply user configuration to a user located in OU, it doesn't matter which computer they log in to; their policy settings will follow them. As an example, let's assume user Liam is located under the `Sales` OU. The computer he usually logs in to is also located under the same OU. But he occasionally logs in to the meeting room laptop that is located under the `IT operations` OU. The `IT operations` OU has its own **Computer Configuration** and **User Configuration** policies assigned. But when Liam logs in to it, he still has the same settings he had in the `Sales` OU PC. This is the normal behavior of group policies. But there are situations where it needs to apply user policy settings based on the computer the user logs in to. **Remote Desktop Services** (RDS) and Citrix Xenapp/XenDesktop solutions are one of the greatest examples of this scenario. These solutions are mostly open for login from remote networks. Therefore, its security and operation requirements are different from a computer in LAN. If users who log in from different OUs are going to have different settings, it's hard to maintain the system with the required level of protection. Using *loopback processing*, we can force users to only have user policy settings that are linked to the OU where computers are located.

There are two modes of loopback processing:

- **Replace mode**: In the replace mode, user settings attached to the user from the original OU will be replaced by the user settings attached to the destination OU. If loopback processing replaces the mode enabled in my previous example, when Liam logs in to the meeting room laptop, he will get the same settings as the user in the `IT operations` OU.

- **Merge mode**: If the merge mode is enabled, in my example, Liam will have his sales user settings apply when he logs in to meeting room laptop first, and after it is processed, it will also add the user settings from the `IT operations` OU. If there are any conflicting settings, the `IT operations` OU user policy settings will win.

To enable loopback processing for Group Policy, go to the Group Policy edit mode: **Computer Configuration**| `Policies`| `Administrative Templates` | `System` | `Group Policy`| **Configure user Group Policy loopback processing mode**:

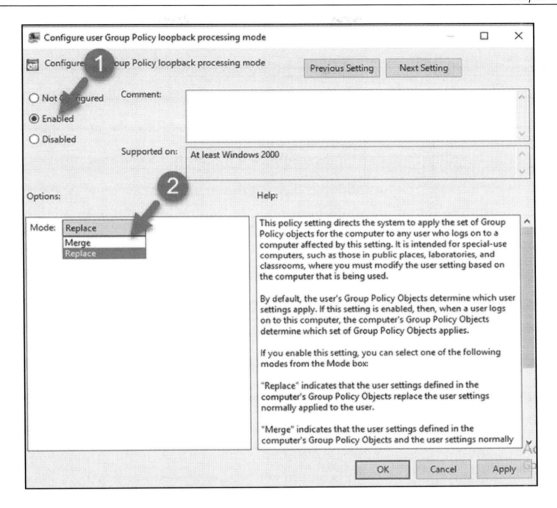

Group Policy best practices

In Sri Lanka, there is a common saying: *eating curd from a knife*. Curd with honey is amazing, but if you have to eat it using a sharpened knife, there is a risk you may cut your tongue if you're not careful. But it's still worth taking the risk (if you ever tasted curd and honey before). Group policies are also like that; they can do so many things but only if you use them correctly. In the Active Directory environment, Group Policy-related issues are the most painful and time-consuming task as there are so many things that can go wrong.

Here, I have listed a few tips that will be useful for Group Policy designing:

- **Identify the best place to link the Group Policy**: Group Policy can be linked to the site, domain, or OU. Organizations have different Group Policy requirements that can also map with the aforementioned components. It is important to understand the best place in the hierarchy to publish each Group Policy setting. This will prevent repetition and Group Policy conflicts. As an example, password complexity settings are common for all the objects under the domain, so the best place to link the policy for the password setting is the domain root, not the OU.

- **Standardize settings**: Today, infrastructure requirements are complex. Each business unit has its own operation and security requirements to address group policies. When designing group policies, always try to summarize the changes as much as possible. If two business units have almost the same user settings requirements, discuss it with the relevant authorized people (line manager, team leads, and so on) and try to use the standard settings. This will allow you to use one Group Policy and link it to two business units instead of creating two separate group policies. Always try to reduce the number of group policies that will be used in the system as when the number of group policies increases, it also increases the time to process during the login process.

- **Use meaningful names**: This is a small suggestion, but I have seen people use Group Policy with names that don't explain anything. In such a scenario, when you go for troubleshooting, it can take an awful amount of time to find the relevant Group Policy. Make sure that you name the Group Policy to reflect the settings in there. It doesn't need to have details, but at least have something that you and your colleagues can understand.

- **Avoid mixing user settings and computer settings**: Group Policy has two main configuration sets that will apply to users and computers. Always try to avoid mixing these settings in the same Group Policy. Try to use separate group policies for computer settings and user settings. This will make it easy to organize policies. After that, disable the unused configuration section in the Group Policy to avoid processing. This can be done using GPMC:

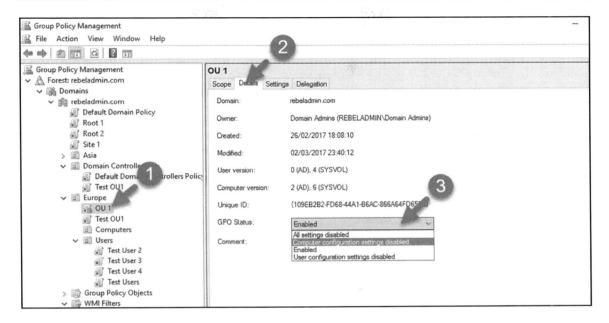

- **Use Group Policy enforcing and block inheritance appropriately**: These features are a good way to manage the default Group Policy inheritance, but use it carefully as this can prevent users/system from applying critical policy settings applied from the top of the hierarchy. Because most policy settings come from the domain level, parent OU levels are related to security- and system-related settings. In the same way, by enforcing policies, you may enforce settings to users and computers that should not be a target. Therefore, always measure the impact before using enforce or blocking inheritance features.

- **Do not edit default policies**: There are two default group policies: **Default Domain Policy** and **Default Domain Controllers Policy**. It is highly recommended that you not use these to publish the Group Policy settings. These can be used as the baseline when you design the group policies and also allows you to revert to the original settings with minimum effect. These can also be used as a reference to troubleshoot inheritance issues and replication issues.

- **Be careful with using loopback processing**: Lots of issues related to loopback processing are due to lack of knowledge, especially related to replace and merge modes. In this chapter, before I explain both of these modes, we will use an example that you can use as a reference. If you are enabling loopback processing, always use separate Group Policy and name it correctly so that everyone understands it when it comes to troubleshooting. My recommendation is that you use it in a situation where you can use the *replace* mode. The merge mode can create lots of hassles with combined group policies plus conflicted settings.

- **Win or lose**: Earlier in this chapter, I explained which policy settings will win when there is a settings conflict. But in theory, there should not be any conflicts at all if the design is correctly done. Therefore, in design, always avoid repeating values in a hierarchical structure. If different values are used for the same setting, use filtering options and block inheritance to prevent the policy conflicts.

- **Housekeeping:** Last but not least, it is important that you review the group policies periodically and remove the policies that have not been used. Also, remove the legacy policy settings if they have been replaced by new policies or methods. Audit and make sure that the hierarchical order is maintained and objects are getting the expected group policies applied to them.

Summary

Group policies are one of the core values of the Active Directory environment. As long as they are designed and maintained properly, they can be used to manage computer and user settings effectively. In this chapter, you learned about Group Policy components and their capabilities. This was followed by explaining features that can be used to design and maintain a healthy Group Policy structure. Last but not least, you learned about Group Policy designing best practices that can be used as a reference.

With the next chapter, we are moving into the third part of this book, which will focus on Active Directory server roles. In this part, you will learn about Active Directory Domain Service's advanced features, including schema, replication, RODC, and Active Directory recovery.

11
Active Directory Services

With this chapter, we are moving towards the third part of this book, which focuses on the Active Directory server roles. There are mainly five Active Directory server roles:

- **Active Directory Domain Services (AD DS)**
- **Active Directory Lightweight Directory Services (AD LDS)**
- **Active Directory Federation Services (AD FS)**
- **Active Directory Rights Management Services (AD RMS)**
- **Active Directory Certificate Services (AD CS)**

We have already looked into many Active Directory components, features, and capabilities, but we are not quite done yet. This chapter is mainly focused on covering AD DS and the AD LDS related topics such as the following:

- AD LDS overview
- Active Directory replication
- Active Directory sites
- Active Directory database maintenance
- Read-only domain controllers in action
- AD DS backup and recovery

The AD LDS overview

When we talk about Active Directory, we refer to it as a single service, but AD DS is attached to many other components as well. DNS, group policies, and the SYSVOL folder replication are a few example. Each of these components need to operate well in order to run a healthy Active Directory environment. It doesn't come easy; it involves investment on resources, time, and skills. In the Active Directory service, the core values are centralized identity management, authentication, and authorization capabilities. All these extra components make it easy to archive its core values, but at same time, it also opens up risks such as dependencies and security. The failure or compromise of these components/services will make impact on the entire Active Directory infrastructure.

Microsoft Windows Core and Nano Servers also count as *operating systems*. These don't have fancy GUIs or sparkly applications running. But they are still doing the job of an operating system. It allows users to build them from scratch according to their requirements. It also increases the server up time (less updates), reliability, performance, and security. Soon after Microsoft released the first Active Directory version, IT engineers, application developers, IT professional start requesting a *cut down* version of AD DS with pure LDAP capabilities. They wanted to eliminate all these dependencies and management requirements, so they could focus on application development upon core AD functions. After Windows Server 2003, Microsoft released **Active Directory Application Mode (ADAM)**, which allowed administrators to run *cut down* version of Active Directory without group policies, file replication, and so on. It can run on a desktop computer or a member server similar to any other Windows service. Simultaneously, it was providing all the core values of the Active Directory service. With Windows Server 2008, Microsoft renamed it *Active Directory Lightweight Directory Services* and allowed users to install the role using Server Manager. This version provided more control and visibility to administrators to deploy and manage LDS instances. This was continued with all the AD DS versions after that and was included in Windows Server 2016 too.

Where to use LDS?

Less dependencies, and less management of LDS extended its operation capabilities and in the following sections, I have listed several scenarios where we can use LDS.

Application developments

This is the area that has benefited most from AD LDS capabilities. Application developments involve lots of experiments, tests, and demo systems. If these applications are Active Directory *integrated*, it is obvious that they need to be developed and tested within the Active Directory environment. During the process, it may be required to build many test environments. If it's full-blown AD DS instances, it will take resources, time, and efforts to deploy and maintain it. AD LDS allows you to run multiple instances of it within the same system independently. Each instance will have its own schema, and engineers can maintain the instance for each application test environments. Even it looks like *cut down* version and gives the same AD DS authentication and management capabilities so that engineers can easily adopt it. Since AD LDS instance allows to run on a desktop or server version of the operating system, it does have less prerequisites. Therefore, applications can also release with integrated LDS; for example, not every business runs Active Directory. Even though application functions are based on Active Directory features, it is still not easy to convince that everyone should have the Active Directory environment in order to run the application. Instead of this, the application installation can have an integrated LDS instance, and it will install it in the guest system as part of the installation process.

Hosted applications

Nowadays, hosted applications, **Software as a Service (SaaS)**, are a common business operation mode for lots of businesses. These services are normally deployed in the perimeter or in a public network. These applications also can have authentication requirements. But it is not recommended to install AD DS in the perimeter or public network. In such a situation, it is recommended to deploy AD FS to provide the federated access. But it still needs additional resources and skills to deploy and maintain. Instead of this, we can set up the AD LDS instance inside the perimeter/public network and provide the directory-enabled authentication service to applications. It doesn't have any connection with LAN or the other LDS instance in the perimeter network and provides a secured environment by design.

Distributed data stores for Active Directory integrated applications

Most of the Active Directory integrated applications also require schema modifications. After this, the application will store certain datasets in the Active Directory database. If it's multiple applications, Active Directory schema and data continues to grow, it will make a significant impact on Active Directory replication. Especially if it's via slow links. Instead of storing data in Active Directory database, additional datasets of applications can be stored in LDS instance. It will still use AD DS for authentication. Additional datasets stored in the LDS instance will not replicate to any other domain controllers.

Migrating from other directory services

There can be environments and applications, which use legacy X.500 based directory services that like to migrate to AD DS. In such scenarios, AD LDS can be used as a middle man, which also can support X.500 based applications. It also allows to clean up the junk and only move filtered data to AD DS. AD LDS allows to run the instances alongside AD DS; and privileged identity solutions, such as MIM, can sync data between LDS and AD DS instances.

The LDS installation

In the Windows Server 2016 operating system, LDS can be installed using Server Manager. In order to install LDS, a user needs to log in with *local administrator* privileges.

Once logged into **Server Manager**, click on **Add Roles and Features**. Then, follow the wizard, select **Active Directory Lightweight Directory Services** under **Server Roles**, and proceed with enabling the role:

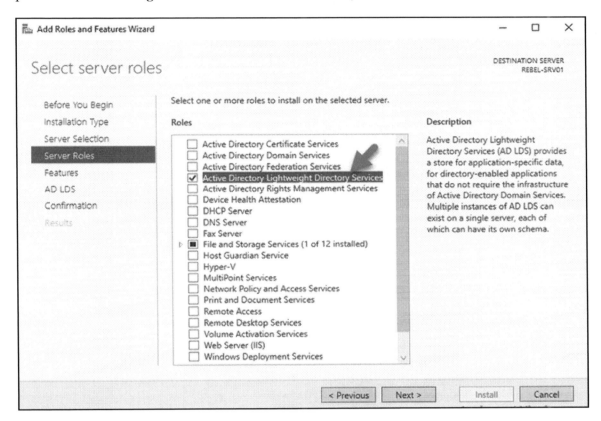

Once the role is installed, click on the **Post-Deployment Configuration** wizard in **Server Manager**. LDS can be set up in two ways: one is as **A unique instance** and other one as **A replica of an existing instance**. The replica option is similar to the clone copy of an existing instance. This is useful especially in application development environment where engineers can maintain the number of application versions:

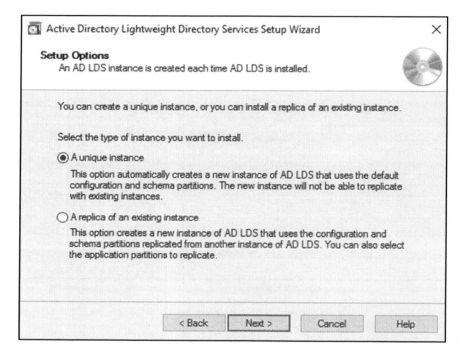

In the next window, we can define the name and description for the LDS instance:

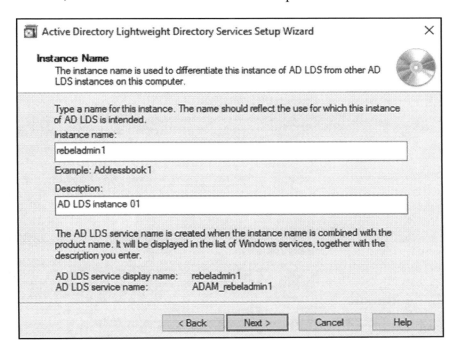

In the next window, we can define the LDS port. By default, the LDAP port is set to 389 and the SSL port is set to 636. If you run multiple instances, these can be changed accordingly.

After this, we can create the application directory partition. This allows applications to use this partition as a data repository to store the application-related data. If the application is capable of creating a partition, this step is not necessary and we can create relevant partition during the application deployment process. When defining the application's **Partition name**, we need to provide it in distinguished name format:

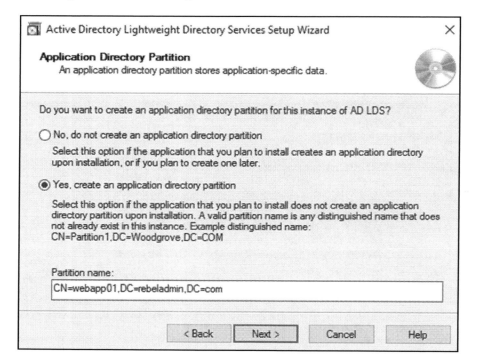

The next step is to define a location to store the LDS data files. After this, it gives the option to specify a service account for LDS. If it's a workgroup environment, you can use the **Network service account** or local user account for it. If its a domain environment, it can be any the AD user account:

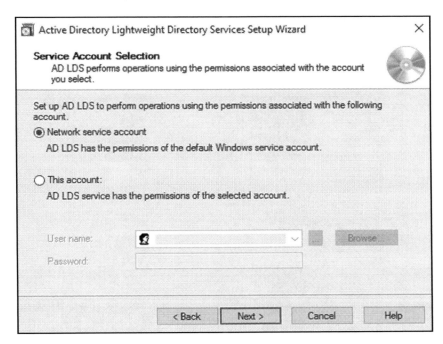

After that, we need to define the AD LDS administrator account. By default, it selects the user account that it used for the installation. If required it can be changed to a different account or group.

Once we define the administrator account, the next step is to define which LDIF file to import. This is a text file that represent data and commands, which will be used by LDAP instance. It can contain one or more LDIF file. These files are depending on application requirements. For example, if it's user account functionalities, the relevant LDIF file will be MSUser:

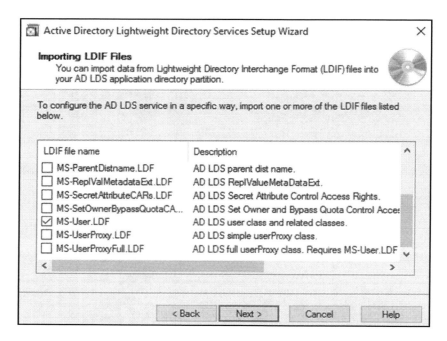

This will complete the AD LDS installation; and once it is completed, we can create relevant objects and manage them. There is a two-way method to connect to it. One way is to connect using the ADSI Edit tool:

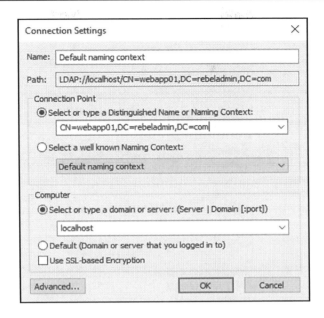

LDS objects can manage using PowerShell cmdlets. They are the same commands which we use for AD DS user object management and the only difference being the need to define the DN and server:

```
New-ADUser -name "tidris" -Displayname "Talib Idris" -server
'localhost:389' -path "CN=webapp01,DC=rebeladmin,DC=com"
```

The preceding command will create a user account called `tidris` on the local LDS instance that runs on `389`. Its DNS path is `CN=webapp01,DC=rebeladmin,DC=com`:

```
Get-ADUser -Filter * -SearchBase "CN=webapp01,DC=rebeladmin,DC=com" -server
'localhost:389'
```

The preceding command is going to list all the user accounts in the LDS instance, `CN=webapp01,DC=rebeladmin,DC=com`. If you'd like to know about more commands, please refer to `Chapter 7`, *Managing Active Directory Objects*:

```
PS C:\Users\Administrator> Get-ADUser -Filter * -SearchBase "CN=webapp01,DC=rebeladmin,DC=com" -server 'localhost:389'

DistinguishedName : CN=tidris,CN=webapp01,DC=rebeladmin,DC=com
Enabled           : False
GivenName         :
Name              : tidris
ObjectClass       : user
ObjectGUID        : bfb4aa5e-3af6-4cfa-8934-c5b468a07326
SID               : S-1-378946516-2781328988-2354691366-1218222115-2413536430-3425642021
Surname           :
UserPrincipalName :
```

AD LDS can be installed in desktop operating system using the Windows features option under **Program and Features**. The installation steps are similar to the server version. Once AD LDS enabled, the setup wizard can be found under **Administrative Tools**:

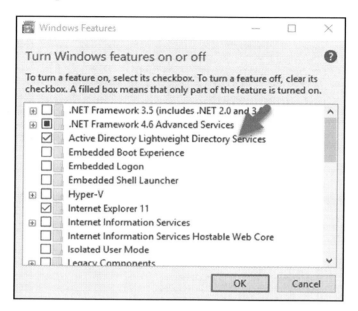

 This option is available on a desktop operating systems after Windows Vista. If it's Windows 7, it needs to be downloaded from the Microsoft site. In order to manage objects, you need to install RSAT tools or use PowerShell to manage them.

The Active Directory replication

Healthy replication is the key to the healthy Active Directory environment. Active Directory uses multi-master database, so every domain controller in the environment should be aware of any changes made to any of the Active Directory databases. It is not only that, it should also know about changes in group policies, startup scripts, preferences settings, and so on, which will also be saved in the SYSVOL folders. When it comes to replication, it is not only the replication service responsible for it. There should be an uninterrupted *communication* between domain controllers. This communication media can be copper cables, fiber cables, or even via a **Software Defined Network (SDN)**. In this section, we are going to look at how we can use the Active Directory integrated features to maintain a healthy replication.

FRS versus DFSR

Windows Server 2000 and 2003 uses **File Replication Service (FRS)** to replicate the SYSVOL folder content to other domain controllers. With Windows Server 2008, it deprecated the FRS and introduced **Distributed File System (DFS)** for the SYSVOL folder replication:

File Replication Service	Distributed File System Replication
FRS is an outdated protocol and no development or investment was made after the release of Windows Server 2003 R2. There wasn't any bug fixes or updates released. Outdated protocols can make security threats to systems, as they will not be tested against modern security threats.	Continuous improvements and investments were made towards the DFSR protocol and continuously tested against emerging threats.
FRS uses last write wins algorithm. When system detects a file change in one of the SYSVOL folders, it becomes the authoritative server and will replicate the *entire* file to other domain controllers. It will not merge the changes. It doesn't matter how small the change is. It always copies entire file, which can cause performance issues especially if the domain controllers are connected via slow-links.	DFSR allows to replicate the partial file changes using the block-level replication. It supports the asynchronous file replication via slow links. If you are running Enterprise edition, it can use cross-file **Remote Differential Compression (RDC)** to create files on the client side using common blocks used by similar files. It will reduce the amount of data that needed to transfer via the links.
FRS uses NTFS file compression in the staging folder.	File compression can be controlled based on the file type.
There is no interface for monitoring (API or WMI) and GUI tools to manage service are very limited. GUI tools are no longer available after Windows Server 2003. They do not support monitoring using the System Center Operation Manager.	There is an enhanced GUI tool to manage related services and it can use WMI to monitor health of the service. It also has management packs developed to monitor via the System Center Operation Manager.
FRS does not have a reporting system to generate diagnostic reports if required. It will only be based on events. It also has limited counters to review performances using PerfMon.	DFRS supports to generate health reports in XML or HTML format. It also includes many counters to review the performance stats using PerfMon.

FRS does not have system to auto-heal if there is a file corruption.	DFSR is capable of auto-healing when it detects a data corruption.
FRS does not fully support the RODC environment, and it can have data synchronization issues.	DFSR is fully supported for RODC replication.
It does not have advanced audit capabilities, as it only contains limited event log and debug logs.	DFSR generates data rich events and logs that can be used to audit, troubleshoot, and debug.

Even though FRS is deprecated with new Windows Server operating systems, it can still be used for replication if you have migrated from Windows Server 2000 or 2003. Most of the time, engineers forget to migrate to DFRS as part of the upgrade projects. This cannot migrate automatically and a few manual steps are involved. This can be done using the `Dfsrmig.exe` utility. In order to perform the migration from FRS to DFRS, your domain and forest functional level should be minimum of Windows Server 2008.

Before we start, we can check the current replication method using the following command:

```
dfsrmig /getglobalstate
```

If it passes the status as `Eliminated`, it is using DFRS for replication. If it's `Start` that means it is still using FRS for replication:

FRS to DFRS migration is based on four states:

- **state 0** (`Start`): By initiating this state, FRS will replicate the `SYSVOL` folder among the domain controllers. It is important to have an up-to-date copy of the `SYSVOL` folder before beginning the migration process to avoid any conflicts.

- **state 1** (Prepared): In this state, while FRS continues replicating the SYSVOL folder, DFSR will also replicate a copy of the SYSVOL folder. It will be located in %SystemRoot%SYSVOL_DFRS. But this SYSVOL folder will not respond to any other domain controller service requests.

- **state 2** (Redirected): In this state, the DFSR copy of SYSVOL starts a response for the SYSVOL folder service requests. FRS will continue the replication of its own SYSVOL copy but will not be involved with the replication from production SYSVOL (DFRS) folders.

- **state 3** (Eliminated): In this state, DFS will continue its replication and serve the SYSVOL folder requests. Windows will delete the original SYSVOL folder used by the FRS replication and stop the FRS replication.

In order to migrate from FRS to DFSR, it must to go from state 1 to state 3.

Prepared state

The following steps demonstrate the prepared state:

1. Log into the domain controller as the Domain Admin or Enterprise Admin.
2. Launch the PowerShell console.
3. Type dfsrmig /setglobalstate 1:

```
Administrator: Windows PowerShell

Windows PowerShell
Copyright (C) 2013 Microsoft Corporation. All rights reserved.

PS C:\Users\administrator.CONTOSO> dfsrmig /setglobalstate 1

Current DFSR global state: 'Start'
New DFSR global state: 'Prepared'

Migration will proceed to 'Prepared' state. DFSR service will
copy the contents of SYSVOL to SYSVOL_DFSR
folder.

If any domain controller is unable to start migration, try manual polling.
Or run with option /CreateGlobalObjects.
Migration can start anytime between 15 minutes to 1 hour.
Succeeded.
PS C:\Users\administrator.CONTOSO> _
```

4. Type `dfsrmig /getmigrationstate` to confirm all the domain controllers have reached the `Prepared` state:

```
PS C:\Users\administrator.CONTOSO> dfsrmig /getmigrationstate

All domain controllers have migrated successfully to the Global state ('Prepared').
Migration has reached a consistent state on all domain controllers.
Succeeded.
PS C:\Users\administrator.CONTOSO> _
```

Redirected state

The following steps demonstrate the redirected state:

1. Type `dfsrmig /setglobalstate 2` and press the *Enter* key:

```
Administrator: Windows PowerShell

Windows PowerShell
Copyright (C) 2013 Microsoft Corporation. All rights reserved.

PS C:\Users\administrator.CONTOSO> dfsrmig /setglobalstate 2

Current DFSR global state: 'Prepared'
New DFSR global state: 'Redirected'

Migration will proceed to 'Redirected' state. The SYSVOL share
will be changed to SYSVOL_DFSR folder,
which is replicated using DFSR.

Succeeded.
PS C:\Users\administrator.CONTOSO> _
```

2. Type `dfsrmig /getmigrationstate` to confirm all the domain controllers have reached the `Redirected` state:

```
PS C:\Users\administrator.CONTOSO> dfsrmig /getmigrationstate

All domain controllers have migrated successfully to the Global state ('Redirected').
Migration has reached a consistent state on all domain controllers.
Succeeded.
PS C:\Users\administrator.CONTOSO> _
```

Eliminated state

The following steps demonstrate the eliminated state:

1. Type `dfsrmig /setglobalstate 3` and press the *Enter* key:

```
Administrator: Windows PowerShell
Windows PowerShell
Copyright (C) 2013 Microsoft Corporation. All rights reserved.

PS C:\Users\administrator.CONTOSO> dfsrmig /setglobalstate 3

Current DFSR global state: 'Redirected'
New DFSR global state: 'Eliminated'

Migration will proceed to 'Eliminated' state. It is not possible
to revert this step.

If any read-only domain controller is stuck in the 'Eliminating' state for too long
 run with option /DeleteRoNtfrsMember.
Succeeded.
PS C:\Users\administrator.CONTOSO> _
```

If you need to revert back to FRS, you need to do so before this state. When it eliminates the state, it will not be possible to go back.

2. Type `dfsrmig /getmigrationstate` to confirm all the domain controllers have reached the `Eliminated` state:

```
PS C:\Users\administrator.CONTOSO> dfsrmig /getmigrationstate

All domain controllers have migrated successfully to the Global state ('Eliminated').
Migration has reached a consistent state on all domain controllers.
Succeeded.
PS C:\Users\administrator.CONTOSO> _
```

By this stage, it is successfully migrating from FRS to DFSR. To verify this, we can run *net share*. It will list down the shares, and we should be able to see the `SYSVOL_DFSR` share.

Once all is confirmed, we need to *stop* the FRS service and *disable* it:

 Once DFSR is enabled, related firewall ports also need to open for successful DFS replication. TCP 137, 139, 389, 135, and 445 and UDP ports 137, 138, 389, and 445 need to be allowed. In some occasions, antivirus software will also block DFS traffic. Therefore, make sure the traffic is not interrupted.

Active Directory sites and replication

Active Directory components are representing the physical and logical structure of a business. Active Directory forests, domains, organization units, and Active Directory objects, such as computers and users, are representing logical structure of the business. Active Directory features and capabilities, such as group policies, can be used to represent the organization's operation and security requirements. In an infrastructure, all these components are connected together using physical connections such as copper or fiber. Without the physical connection, there is no possibility for these Active Directory components to communicate with each other and perform a logical structure. Based on the business requirements, these network connections may require to be extended to remote geographical locations. It can be from different buildings located in same location into locations in different continents. These remote networks may use various connection methods to maintain the connectivity between each other. It can be VPN, copper leased lines, fiber connections, or even satellite connections. When we build Active Directory infrastructure based on such network topology, its components will be placed on these different networks as well. By default, Active Directory will not understand the network topology underneath it. If we consider the **Open Systems Interconnection (OSI)** model, Active Directory is operated in the Application layer and physical connections are represented by the Network layer. There are mainly three reasons why Active Directory should also be aware of this physical network topology, which are as follows:

- Replication
- Authentication
- Service location

Replication

The Active Directory infrastructure depends on a healthy replication. Every domain controller in the network should be aware of every change it has made. When a domain controller triggers a sync, it passes the data through the physical network to the destination. It consumes *bandwidth* of the wire for the data. Based on the used media and available bandwidth, the impact made by this replication traffic will vary. If it has high-speed links such as 40 Gbps, 10 Gbps, 1 Gbps, 100 Mbps, then the impact made by replication traffic will be very low. But in slow link such as 128 Kbps, 256 Kbps, the impact will be significantly high.

Most of the time, links between remote networks are slow links and come with big bill. Therefore, there should be a way to control the replication based on available bandwidth and Active Directory should be aware of it.

Authentication

When an identity tries to authenticate, the request should be processed by a domain controller. If all the domain controllers are located in one geographical location, it doesn't matter which available domain controller processes the request. But if it's between remote networks, the time it takes to process the request will depend on the available link bandwidth and the number of hops it needs to travel through.

As an example, let's assume Rebeladmin Corp. do have an Active Directory infrastructure and it is stretched across two offices in London and Seattle. It has domain controllers located in both the locations. If a user logs in to a PC in the London office, it doesn't make sense to process the authentication request by a domain controller in the Seattle office. This is because the request needs to pass through a few network hops and a slow link. If large numbers of requests are processed, majority of the slow link bandwidth will be used by these requests. Ideally, it should process by the closest domain controller, which is located at the same location. Then, there are no additional hops to pass and no bandwidth limitations. Also, it will not depend on the status of the link between two locations in order to process the requests. Therefore, Active Directory should force identities located in remote networks to authenticate via its closest domain controllers.

Service locations

This is the extension to the things I explained in the previous reason. In a remote network, there can be different server roles and Active Directory integrated applications running. Similar to authentication requests, when users or computers try to use a service or application, it should process by the closest application server. It will improve the user experience and the reliability of the application or the services. When it's via slow link, it does have lots of dependencies and performance-related limitations. In order to do this, there should be a system, which can process these service requests and point users to the closest servers.

The answer for all the aforementioned requirements are the Active Directory sites and related components. These allow us to represent the physical network topology within the Active Directory infrastructure. Then, Active Directory will be aware where its components are located and how it's connected with each other. Based on this data, Active Directory will allow to control the replication over slow links and point the authentication and service requests to the closest servers.

Let's look into Active Directory site and its related components.

Sites

Sites can be explained as physical locations, which contain various objects. They should be able to be described using their boundaries. As an example, users, computers, and network devices located in an office location in London can be treated as a site, and they can be identified uniquely from similar objects located in the Seattle office. The Active Directory site topology can be mainly divided into four designs:

- **Single domain-single sites**: This is the most common setup for small and medium site businesses. In this setup, there will be one site and one domain. When we set up the first domain controller in the infrastructure, it is set up as single domain-single site by default. This is easy to maintain.
- **Single domain-multiple sites**: In this setup, the infrastructure has only one domain, and it's been extended to multiple sites. It can be based on different buildings, data centers, or geographical locations. Sites are interconnected using physical network links. This can be via VPN, leased lines, or satellite connections.
- **Multiple domain-single sites**: In one physical site, there can be multiple domain setups. Replications between domains will depend on the logical topology. The replication bandwidth impact is minimal as domain controllers communicate with each other using fast LAN connections.
- **Multiple domain-multiple sites**: In this setup, multiple domains will be placed in multiple sites. In this setup, replication will depend on the logical topology as well as the physical topology. In some setups, domains will be limited to sites; and in others, domains will be extended to multiple sites.

Subnets

Subnets are representing associated IP address ranges in each site. This is equal to subnets allocated in network devices, but does not need to be exactly the same. For example, if a site uses 10-20 class C subnets, then instead of adding all these to Active Directory sites subnet, we can summarize all those into a class B subnet and use them. Based on this subnet information, it allows objects to locate the closest domain controller. When physical subnets are added or removed, they should be updated in the Active Directory site configuration as well. Otherwise, they will pass unwanted traffic via slow links.

Site links

Site links represent the physical connection between sites. But it doesn't control the network level routing or the connectivity between sites. It's been still handled by the underlying WAN links and network devices. Site links allow to schedule the replication and control the bandwidth (link cost).

Site link bridges

Site link bridges contain multiple site links. These allow transitive communication between each site link under the bridge. By default, all site links are treated as bridges. In some cases, not all sites links need to talk to each other. But they are controlled by the routing rules in the network devices. If it's set up that way, the default behavior of the link bridges needs to modify and disable **Bridge all site links**:

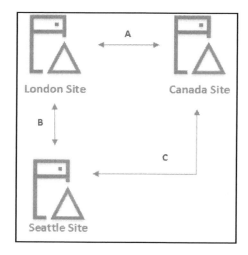

The best way to explain about site link bridges is by using this simple example. According to the preceding diagram, for the **London Site** to reach **Canada Site**, there is two paths: one is using **A** and the other one is using **B** + **C**. Therefore, on the **Seattle Site**, we can create a site link bridge and include site links **B** and **C** and preset them as an alternative path to reach the **Canada Site**.

Managing Active Directory sites and other components

There are two ways to manage Active Directory sites and related components. One option is to use the Active Directory Sites and Services MMC, and other-one is to use PowerShell cmdlets. In order to add/edit/remove sites and related configurations, we need to have Domain Admin/Enterprise Admin privileges.

The Active Directory Sites and Services MMC will be available in any server which has AD DS service enabled or any server/computer that has **Remote Server Administration Tools (RSAT)** installed. The Active Directory PowerShell module also will be available in any server, which has AD DS role enabled or has the RSAT tools installed.

Managing sites

When the first domain controller is introduced into the infrastructure, the system creates its first site as `Default-First-Site-Name`. This can be changed based on the requirements. We can review the existing sites configuration using the following PowerShell cmdlet:

```
Get-ADReplicationSite -Filter *
```

It will list down the sites information for the AD infrastructure.

In our example, it only has the default Active Directory site. As the first step, I need to change it to a meaningful name, so we can assign objects and configurations accordingly. In order to do that, we can use the `Rename-ADObject` cmdlet:

```
Rename-ADObject -Identity "CN=Default-First-Site-
Name,CN=Sites,CN=Configuration,DC=rebeladmin,DC=com" -NewName "LondonSite"
```

The preceding command will rename the `Default-First-Site-Name` site to `LondonSite`. In the existing site, we can change the values using the `Set-ADReplicationSite` cmdlet:

```
Get-ADReplicationSite -Identity LondonSite | Set-ADReplicationSite -
Description "UK AD Site"
```

The preceding command changed the site description to `UK AD Site`.

We can create a new AD site using the `New-ADReplicationSite` cmdlet. The full description of the command can be viewed using `Get-Command New-ADReplicationSite -Syntax`:

```
New-ADReplicationSite -Name "CanadaSite" -Description "Canada AD Site"
```

The preceding command will create a new AD site called `CanadaSite`:

```
PS C:\Users\Administrator> Get-ADReplicationSite -Filter *

Description                        : UK AD Site
DistinguishedName                  : CN=LondonSite,CN=Sites,CN=Configuration,DC=rebeladmin,DC=com
InterSiteTopologyGenerator         : CN=NTDS Settings,CN=REBEL-SDC-02,CN=Servers,CN=LondonSite,CN=Sites,CN=Configuration,DC=rebeladmin,DC=com
ManagedBy                          :
Name                               : LondonSite
ObjectClass                        : site
ObjectGUID                         : fbef3a2c-2de8-44d2-bde9-c37403c9f3a9
ReplicationSchedule                : System.DirectoryServices.ActiveDirectory.ActiveDirectorySchedule
UniversalGroupCachingRefreshSite   :

Description                        : Canada AD Site
DistinguishedName                  : CN=CanadaSite,CN=Sites,CN=Configuration,DC=rebeladmin,DC=com
InterSiteTopologyGenerator         :
ManagedBy                          :
Name                               : CanadaSite
ObjectClass                        : site
ObjectGUID                         : 1bc04b4a-0f69-4ef5-8083-98d9bb0e88ca
ReplicationSchedule                :
UniversalGroupCachingRefreshSite   :
```

Once sites are created, we need to move the domain controllers to the relevant site. By default, all the domain controllers are placed under the default site, `Default-First-Site-Name`.

 Even if you do not want to place a domain controller in a site, it can be assigned to the site aware services, such as DFS and exchange services. Placing a domain controller on site depends on the number of users and link reliability as well.

In the following command, I am listing down all the domain controllers in the Active Directory infrastructure with filtered data to show the `Name`, `ComputerObjectDN`, `Site` attributes values:

```
Get-ADDomainController -Filter * | select Name,ComputerObjectDN,Site | fl
```

Now, we have the list of domain controllers, and as the next step, we can move the domain controller to the relevant site:

```
Move-ADDirectoryServer -Identity "REBEL-SDC-02" -Site "CanadaSite"
```

The preceding command will move the `REBEL-SDC-02` domain controller to `CanadaSite`.

During the additional domain controller setup, we can define which site it will be allocated to. If the site already has domain controllers, it will do the initial replication from those. But if it doesn't, it will replicate from any selected domain controller or, if not, from any available domain controller. If the link bandwidth is an issue, it's recommended to promote the domain controller from a site that has fast links, and then move the domain controller to the relevant site.

Managing site links

Now, we have the sites set up, the next step is to create site links. Using site links, we can manage the replication schedule and the bandwidth.

The site cost

The site link cost defines the nearest resources, if the on-site resource is not available. In a network topology, the site link is mainly based on the link's bandwidth. But here, a site link is decided based on the bandwidth, latency, and reliability. For example, let's assume site A and site B are connected via a 100 Mbps link. Site A and site C are connected via the 512 Kbps link. If we only consider the bandwidth, site A will prefer site B as the closest site. But this link had a few failures last month and 512 Kbps is more reliable. By changing the site link cost, I can force site A to use site C as the preferred closest resource site. In the following example, we have three sites, and each site has two site links to connect to each other:

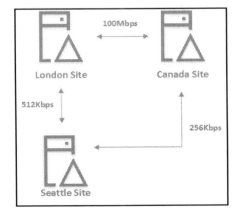

If the line latency and availability has a problem, then for **London Site**, the first preferred site should be **Canada Site**. In that link failure, it still uses **Seattle Site**. For **Canada Site**, the **London Site** will be the first preference and next the **Seattle Site**. For the **Seattle Site**, the first preference will be **London Site** and the next is the **Canada Site**. But here, we consider only the bandwidth. The link preferences can be modified by changing the site cost. By default, every site link gets the cost of 100. The site link which holds lowest site cost value will be the first preference. When the system determines the code to a destination, it does not consider about the direct links. It is the same way, a network topology will find its best route. In the preceding example, if **London Site** to wants to reach **Canada Site**, there are two paths; one is the direct link and other one is via **Seattle Site**. So, when it considers the best path, it will calculate the cost value of the direct link against the cost value of the **London Site** > **Seattle Site** > **Canada Site**.

The following list includes the preferred site cost value based on the bandwidth:

Available bandwidth	Cost
9.6 Kbps	1,042
19.2 Kbps	798
38.4 Kbps	644
56 Kbps	586
64 Kbps	567
128 Kbps	486
256 Kbps	425
512 Kbps	378
1,024 Kbps	340
2,048 Kbps	309
4,096 Kbps	283
10 Mbps	257
100 Mbps	205
1,000 Mbps	171

Inter-site transport protocols

There are two transport protocols, which can be used for replication via site links. Replication uses the **Remote Procedure Call (RPC)**, and it can either be the IP or SMTP transport protocol. The default protocol used in site link is IP, and it performs synchronous replication between available domain controllers. The SMTP method can be used when the link between sites is not reliable. It will use mail messages to replicate Active Directory partition data including the schema changes between domain controllers. If it uses the SMTP method, it needs to have certification authority to encrypt the traffic.

Replication intervals

By default, in a default site link, a replication is occurring *every 180 minutes* via the site link. Based on the requirement, it can be changed to the value we need. If required, it also allows to disable the replication, and then it will be based on a manually triggered replication.

Replication schedules

By default, the site replication is happening 24/7. Based on the site bandwidth consideration, this can be changed. For example, if it's a slow link, it is best to set the replication in after operation hours and in lunch hours. It will control the replication traffic impact on slow links and allow the organization to use the link bandwidth for other mission critical traffic. It's important to evaluate the consequences of changing the replication schedule. If you add/modify objects and policies, those will not replicate between sites unless they match replication intervals and the replication schedule.

In order to set up the site links, we can use the `New-ADReplicationSiteLink` cmdlet:

```
New-ADReplicationSiteLink -Name "London-Canada" -SitesIncluded
LondonSite,CanadaSite -Cost 205 -ReplicationFrequencyInMinutes 30 -
InterSiteTransportProtocol IP
```

The preceding command creates a new site link called `London-Canada` and it includes `LondonSite` and `CanadaSite`. The site cost is set to `205`, and the replication intervals are set to every `30` minutes. Its transport protocol is set to `IP`.

We can create and also modify the settings using the **Active Directory Sites and Services** MMC:

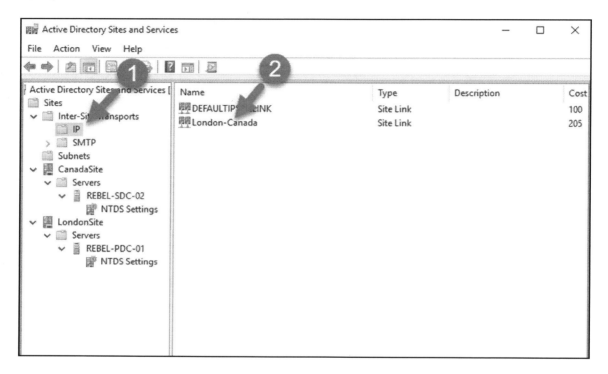

We can change the replication schedule using the `-ReplicationSchedule` option or GUI. In order to change it using GUI, click on the **Change Schedule...** button. Then in the window, you can change the replication schedule. In this demo, I changed the replication to happen Monday to Friday from 6 a.m. to 10 a.m.:

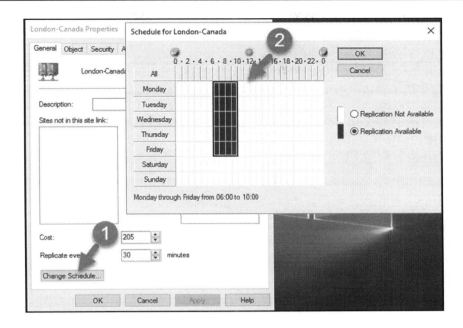

Site link bridge

We can create the site link bridge using the `New-ADReplicationSiteLinkBridge` cmdlet:

```
New-ADReplicationSiteLinkBridge -Name "London-Canada-Bridge" -
SiteLinksIncluded "London-Canada","London-CanadaDRLink"
```

The preceding command creates new site link bridge called `London-Canada-Bridge` using two site links: `London-Canada`, `London-CanadaDRLink`.

Using the `Set-ADReplicationSiteLinkBridge` cmdlet, the existing site link bridge value can change:

```
Set-ADReplicationSiteLinkBridge -Identity "London-Canada-Bridge" -
SiteLinksIncluded @{Remove='London-CanadaDRLink'}
```

The preceding command will remove the `London-CanadaDRLink` site link from the existing site link bridge, `London-Canada-Bridge`:

```
Set-ADReplicationSiteLinkBridge -Identity "London-Canada-Bridge" -
SiteLinksIncluded @{Add='London-CanadaDRLink'}
```

The preceding command will add the given site link to the existing site link bridge.

Bridgehead servers

In the Active Directory infrastructure, the **Knowledge Consistency Checker** (**KCC**) is an in-built process which runs on domain controllers and it is responsible for generating replication topology. It will configure the replication connection between domain controllers. When it comes to replication between sites, KCC selects a domain controller as a *bridgehead server*, which will send and receive replication traffic for its site. If you have multiple domains in multiple sites, each domain should have its own bridgehead server. A site can have multiple bridgehead servers for same domain, but at a given time, only one will be active. It is decided based on the domain controller's lowest GUID value. In the Active Directory environment, if it involves an intra-site replication, Active Directory automatically selects the bridgehead servers. However, there are situations where you may prefer a specific server to act as a bridgehead server.

By opening the properties of the domain controller, you can choose what you want to set as bridgehead server. The best practice is to set the most reliable domain controller as the bridgehead server:

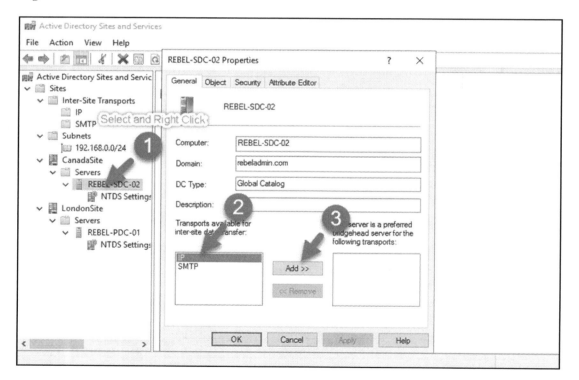

Managing subnets

Now, we have sites and site links set up. The next step is to assign the subnets to each site. This can be set up using the `New-ADReplicationSubnet` cmdlet:

```
New-ADReplicationSubnet -Name "192.168.0.0/24" -Site LondonSite
```

The preceding PowerShell command will create new subnet, `192.168.0.0/24`, and will assign it to `LondonSite`.

Using `Set-ADReplicationSubnet`, we can change value of the existing subnet:

```
Set-ADReplicationSubnet -Identity "192.168.0.0/24" -Site CanadaSite
```

The preceding command will change the site of the `192.168.0.0/24` subnet into `CanadaSite`.

We can use the `Get-ADReplicationSubnet` cmdlet to find the subnet data:

```
Get-ADReplicationSubnet -Filter {Site -Eq "CanadaSite"}
```

The preceding command will list all the subnets under `CanadaSite`:

```
PS C:\Users\Administrator> Get-ADReplicationSubnet -Filter {Site -Eq "CanadaSite"}

DistinguishedName : CN=192.168.0.0/24,CN=Subnets,CN=Sites,CN=Configuration,DC=rebeladmin,DC=com
Location          :
Name              : 192.168.0.0/24
ObjectClass       : subnet
ObjectGUID        : 1e84b584-7bcf-4c08-b29b-ac96aaab4eb7
Site              : CN=CanadaSite,CN=Sites,CN=Configuration,DC=rebeladmin,DC=com
```

How does replication work?

By now, we know the logical and physical components involved with the Active Directory replication process. It is time to put all these together and understand how exactly the Active Directory replication happens.

In the Active Directory environment, there are mainly two types of replication:

- Intra-site replications
- Inter-site replications

Intra-site replications

As the name implies, this covers the replications happening within a site. By default, (according to Microsoft) any domain controller will be aware of any directory update within 15 seconds. Within the site despite the number of domain controllers, any directory update will be replicated in less than a minute:

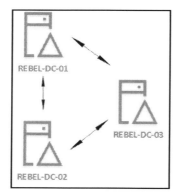

Within the site, the replication connections are performing in a ring topology, which means any given domain controllers have two replication links (of course, if there are minimum of three domain controllers). This architecture will prevent domain controllers from having endless replication loops.

For example, if there are five domain controllers and if all are connected to each other with one-to-one connection, each domain controller will have four connections and when there is an update in one of the domain controllers, it will need to advertise it to four domain controllers. Then, the first one to receive update will advertise to its four connected domain controllers, and it goes on and on. There will be too many replication processes to advertise, listen, and sort out the conflicts.

But in a ring topology, despite the number of domain controllers in the site, any given domain controller only needs to advertise or listen to two domain controllers in any given time. With this replication topology, there is no need for manual configuration, and Active Directory will automatically determine the connections it needs to make. When the number of domain controllers grow, the replication time can grow as well as it's in ring topology. But to avoid latency, Active Directory will create additional connections. This is also determined automatically, and we do not need to worry about these replication connections.

Inter-site replications

If the Active Directory infrastructure contains more than one site, a change in one site needs to be replicated over to other sites. This is called as **inter-site replication**, and its topology is different from the intra-site replication. Replication within the site always benefits from the high-speed links. But when it comes to connection between sites, facts such as bandwidth, latency and reliability makes impact. In the previous section, we discussed about site links, site costs, and replication schedules which we can use to control intra-site replications:

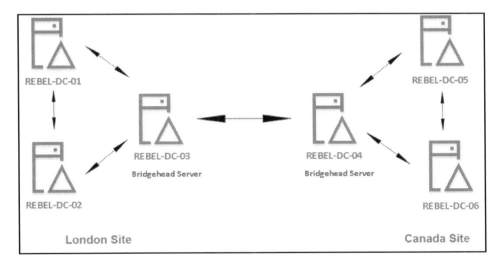

When it comes to inter-site, the replication will happen via *site links*. The replication within each site still uses the ring topology. In the preceding example, let's assume an object has been added to **REBEL-DC-02** in **London Site**. Now, based on the topology, it will be advertised to **REBEL-DC-03** too. But apart from being the domain controller, this particular domain controller is a bridgehead server as well. So, it is this server's responsibility to advertise the updates it received into the bridge server in **Canada Site,** which is **REBEL-DC-04**. Once it receives the update it will advertise to other domain controllers in the site. The replication between sites still needs to obey the rules applied to control the replication.

AD DS automatically selects the bridgehead server for a site. But there are situations where engineers want to select a server they prefer to be the bridgehead server. In the previous section, I have explained how we can force a domain controller to become *preferred bridgehead server*.

Knowledge Consistency Checker

When I explained about the replication, I mentioned *Active Directory automatically creates replication links, select bridgehead servers…*, and so on. But how does it really do it? KCC is the one responsible for all these. The KCC is a built-in service in Active Directory domain controllers, and is responsible for generating and maintaining the replication topology for intra- and inter-site replications. Every 15 minutes, KCC will revalidate its existing replication topology and make the topology changes if required. It gives enough time for domain controllers to replicate the changes if the existing replication topology is valid.

When it comes to inter-site, KCC selects a single KCC holder in a remote site to act as **intersite topology generator (ISTG),** and its ISTG's responsibility is to select the bridgehead servers for replication. ISTG creates the view of replication topology for all the sites it is connected to. ISTG is responsible for deciding topology for the site; and individual domain controllers (KCC) are responsible for making topology decisions locally.

The best way to understand KCC is to compare it with a network routing protocol. A network routing protocol is responsible for maintaining a routing path for connected networks. If network A needs to communicate with network B, routing table will tell it what path to go to. In the same way, the topology created by KCC will tell how the domain controller A can replicate the changes in the domain controller B. When I work on AD projects, I have seen engineers create manual replication links between domain controllers. But I really doubt if someone can be smarter than KCC on deciding replication topology.

How update occurs ?

Now, we know how the replication topology works, but how exactly does a domain controller know when an update is occurring? And how does the connected domain controllers know if it's an update? In order to understand this, we need to understand a few terms.

The update sequence number

The **update sequence number** (**USN**) is a 64-bit number, which is allocated to the domain controller during the Dcpomo process. When there is any object update, the USN allocated to the domain controller will be increased. For example, let's assume the domain controller A had initial USN 2000 assigned to it. If we add five user objects, the new USN will be 2005. This number is only increases. It cannot be decreased. The USN is only valid for the its own domain controller. There is no technical possibility for two domain controllers in the site to have the same USN assigned.

Directory Service Agent GUID and invocation ID

Domain controllers involved in the replication process are identified using two unique identifiers. First one is **Directory Service Agent** (**DSA**) GUID, and it is generated during the Dcpromo process; and it will never change in the life time of the domain controller. Then, the next is invocation ID. It will only change when an Active Directory restore happens. In a restore process, it will change; the otherwise, the existing domain controllers will identify it as an existing domain controller and will not replicate the data over.

The high watermark vector table

The **high watermark vector** (**HWMV**) table is maintained locally by each domain controller to keep the track of the last change from its's replication partner for the given naming context. As you are aware, domain controllers have three naming contexts, which are schema NC, configuration NC, and domain NC. There will be an HWMV table for each naming context. The table contains the latest USN value it received from its replication partner for a given naming context. Based on that, the domain controller will decide where to start the replication process.

The up-to-dateness vector table

The **up-to-dateness vector (UTDV)** table is maintained locally by each domain controller to prevent unneeded replications. UTDV also per naming context and each domain controller has a minimum of three UTDV tables. The UTDV table contains the highest UPN value it learned from any connected domain controller per NC basis. This will prevent domain controllers from replicating the same changes over and over. For example, if a domain controller A received a domain NC from domain controller B, it will update the UTDV table and update the UPN value for it. Based on that, it will not retrieve the same update from the other connected domain controllers. Because of UTDV, domain controllers will not send any data to their replication partners if they have already received them from someone else. This is called **propagation dampening**:

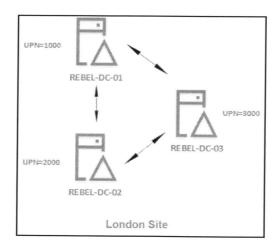

In order to summarize the replication, let's follow a scenario. In the preceding example, we had three domain controllers connected. Each had an initial UPN value assigned. Now let's assume, using **REBEL-DC-01** a new user object has been added. So now, its UPN is increased to **1001**. At this point domain controller know about its connected replication partners based on DSA GUID and invocation ID. **REBEL-DC-02 is** already aware of the last UPN value it received from **REBEL-DC-01** as it is stored on the HWMV table. Before it updates, it will check the UTDV to make sure it didn't receive the same update via **REBEL-DC-03**. If not that, then it replicates and increases its UPN and values in HWMV and UTDV tables. I hope this explains exactly what is happening with the Active Directory replication.

The read-only domain controllers

The **read-only domain controllers** (**RODCs**) are a great feature introduced with Windows Server 2008 in order to maintain a low-risk domain controller in locations where it cannot guarantee physical security and the maintenance. Throughout the chapter we have discussed possible scenarios where we required a domain controller in a remote site. When considering a domain controller in a remote site, the link between sites is not the only thing we need to focus on. When we deploy a domain controller, by default, it will be aware of any changes in the Active Directory structure. Once an update triggers, it updates its own copy of the Active Directory database. This `ntds.dit` file contains everything about the Active Directory infrastructure, including the identity data of the user objects. If it falls into wrong hands, they can retrieve data related to identities and compromise the identity infrastructure.

When considering information security, the physical security is also important. That's why the data centers have all sorts of security standards. So, when deploying a domain controller in a remote site, physical security is also consideration as we do not want to have loose ends. If you have a requirement for domain controller in a remote site and yet you cannot confirm its security, then RODC is the answer. RODC does not store any password in its database. All the authentication requests against an object will be processed by the closest writable domain controller. So, if people manage to get copy of the database, they will not be able to do much.

 In its virtual environment, Windows allows you to map the VHD file to any computer and view the data on it. So, even if you are not the Domain Admin and if you have privileges in the virtual environment, the database files can be retrieved. In order to prevent this, Microsoft has introduced the *shielded VMs* with Hyper-V 2016. It will allow to encrypt the virtual machine using a bit locker, and no one will be able to use the copied VHD.

Other advantages of RODC include its one-way replication. When considering remote sites, you also need to consider how they will be maintained. Every organization cannot maintain IT teams for remote offices. Most of the maintenance tasks still can be carried out remotely, but there are certain situations where you will need to delegate some permissions to persons in remote sites. Most of the time, these people can be less experienced on IT. So, a simple mistake made by them can replicate to other domain controllers and make a mess. RODC's one-way replication will prevent this and no change will be replicated over to other domain controllers. Nice, huh?

By default, RODC does not save any passwords (except RODC objects) for Active Directory objects. Every time when authentication happens, it will need to retrieve the data from the closest domain controller. Using **Password Replication Policy (PRP)**, we can allow certain passwords for objects to be cached. In that case, if the connection between a remote site and the closest domain controller is interrupted, RODC will be able to process the request. One thing to remember is, in order to process Kerberos request, it needs to cache the password for the user object as well as the computer object.

RODC deployment process involves the following stages. In this process, we can use a preselected account and promote the RODC using it instead of using a Domain Admin or an Enterprise Admin account:

1. Set up computer account for RODC domain controller.
2. Attach that account to the RODC during the promo process.

In order to create a RODC computer account, we can use the `Add-ADDSReadOnlyDomainControllerAccount` cmdlet:

```
Add-ADDSReadOnlyDomainControllerAccount -DomainControllerAccountName REBEL-RODC-01 -DomainName rebeladmin.com -DelegatedAdministratorAccountName "rebeladmindfrancis" -SiteName LondonSite
```

The preceding command will create the RODC domain controller account for `REBEL-RODC-01`. The domain name is defined using `-DomainName`, and `-DelegatedAdministratorAccountName` defines which account to delegate the RODC installation. The new RODC will be placed in `LondonSite`:

```
PS C:\Users\Administrator> Add-ADDSReadOnlyDomainControllerAccount -DomainControllerAccountName REBEL-RODC-01 -DomainNa
e rebeladmin.com -DelegatedAdministratorAccountName rebeladmindfrancis -SiteName LondonSite
WARNING: Windows Server 2016 domain controllers have a default for the security setting named "Allow cryptography
algorithms compatible with Windows NT 4.0" that prevents weaker cryptography algorithms when establishing security
channel sessions.

For more information about this setting, see Knowledge Base article 942564
(http://go.microsoft.com/fwlink/?LinkId=104751).

WARNING: Windows Server 2016 domain controllers have a default for the security setting named "Allow cryptography
algorithms compatible with Windows NT 4.0" that prevents weaker cryptography algorithms when establishing security
channel sessions.

For more information about this setting, see Knowledge Base article 942564
(http://go.microsoft.com/fwlink/?LinkId=104751).


Message                          Context              RebootRequired  Status
-------                          -------              --------------  ------
Operation completed successfully DCPromo.General.1                    False Success
```

Now, we can see the newly added object under the Active Directory domain controllers:

```
ComputerObjectDN           : CN=REBEL-RODC-01,OU=Domain Controllers,DC=rebeladmin,DC=com
DefaultPartition           : DC=rebeladmin,DC=com
Domain                     : rebeladmin.com
Enabled                    : False
Forest                     : rebeladmin.com
HostName                   : REBEL-RODC-01.rebeladmin.com
InvocationId               : 00000000-0000-0000-0000-000000000000
IPv4Address                :
IPv6Address                :
IsGlobalCatalog            : True
IsReadOnly                 : True
LdapPort                   : 389
Name                       : REBEL-RODC-01
NTDSSettingsObjectDN       : CN=NTDS Settings,CN=REBEL-RODC-01,CN=Servers,CN=LondonSite,CN=Sites,CN=Configuration,DC=re
                             beladmin,DC=com
OperatingSystem            :
OperatingSystemHotfix      :
OperatingSystemServicePack :
OperatingSystemVersion     :
OperationMasterRoles       : {}
Partitions                 : {CN=Schema,CN=Configuration,DC=rebeladmin,DC=com, CN=Configuration,DC=rebeladmin,DC=com,
                             DC=rebeladmin,DC=com}
ServerObjectDN             : CN=REBEL-RODC-01,CN=Servers,CN=LondonSite,CN=Sites,CN=Configuration,DC=rebeladmin,DC=com
ServerObjectGuid           : 2fc5dc79-dbc8-4ffb-a708-656b8c2c9875
Site                       : LondonSite
SslPort                    : 636
```

Now, we have things ready for the new RODC and the next step is to promote it:

```
Install-WindowsFeature -Name AD-Domain-Services -IncludeManagementTools
```

The preceding command will install the AD DS role in the RODC. Once it's completed, we can promote it using the following command:

```
Import-Module ADDSDeployment
Install-ADDSDomainController `
-Credential (Get-Credential) `
-CriticalReplicationOnly:$false `
-DatabasePath "C:WindowsNTDS" `
-DomainName "rebeladmin.com" `
-LogPath "C:WindowsNTDS" `
-ReplicationSourceDC "REBEL-PDC-01.rebeladmin.com" `
-SYSVOLPath "C:WindowsSYSVOL" `
-UseExistingAccount:$true `
-Norebootoncompletion:$false `
-Force:$true
```

Once this is executed, it will prompt for the user account, and we need to input user account information, which was delegated for RODC deployment. The command is very similar to a regular domain promotion.

Now, we have the RODC and next steps to look in to PRPs.

The default policy is already in place, and we can view the allowed and denied lists using the following command:

```
Get-ADDomainControllerPasswordReplicationPolicy -Identity REBEL-RODC-01 -
Allowed
```

The preceding command will list the allowed objects for password caching. By default, a security group called **Allowed RODC Password Replication Group** is allowed for the replication. This doesn't contain any members by default. If we need caching, we can add object to the given group:

```
Get-ADDomainControllerPasswordReplicationPolicy -Identity REBEL-RODC-01 -
Denied
```

The preceding command lists the denied objects for password caching. By default, following security groups are in the denied list:

- **Denied RODC Password Replication Group**
- **Account Operators**
- **Server Operators**
- **Backup Operators**
- **Administrators**

These are high privileged accounts in the Active Directory infrastructure; these should not be cached at all. By adding objects to **Denied RODC Password Replication Group**, we can simply block the replication.

Apart from the use of predefined security groups, we can add objects to allow and denied list using the Add-ADDomainControllerPasswordReplicationPolicy cmdlet:

```
Add-ADDomainControllerPasswordReplicationPolicy -Identity REBEL-RODC-01 -
AllowedList "user1"
```

The preceding command will add the user object `user1` to the allowed list as shown in the following screenshot:

```
PS C:\Users\Administrator> Get-ADDomainControllerPasswordReplicationPolicy -Identity REBEL-RODC-01 -Allowed

DistinguishedName : CN=user1,OU=Users,OU=Europe,DC=rebeladmin,DC=com
Name              : user1
ObjectClass       : user
ObjectGUID        : edd1f313-f14d-48cc-bd27-e6f8e57a5fc4
SamAccountName    : user1
SID               : S-1-5-21-4041220333-1835452706-552999228-1104

DistinguishedName : CN=Allowed RODC Password Replication Group,CN=Users,DC=rebeladmin,DC=com
Name              : Allowed RODC Password Replication Group
ObjectClass       : group
ObjectGUID        : 89f5a011-391f-49d2-9238-8bebdb80c1ce
SamAccountName    : Allowed RODC Password Replication Group
SID               : S-1-5-21-4041220333-1835452706-552999228-571
```

The following command will add the user object named `user2` to the denied list:

> **Add-ADDomainControllerPasswordReplicationPolicy -Identity REBEL-RODC-01 -DeniedList "user2"**

The following screenshot illustrates the preceding command:

```
PS C:\Users\Administrator> Add-ADDomainControllerPasswordReplicationPolicy -Identity REBEL-RODC-01 -DeniedList "user2"
PS C:\Users\Administrator> Get-ADDomainControllerPasswordReplicationPolicy -Identity REBEL-RODC-01 -Denied

DistinguishedName : CN=user2,OU=Users,OU=Europe,DC=rebeladmin,DC=com
Name              : user2
ObjectClass       : user
ObjectGUID        : 679ec55b-fb62-427f-b828-bd0ec31d7e30
SamAccountName    : user2
SID               : S-1-5-21-4041220333-1835452706-552999228-1105
```

> To improve the security further, it is recommended to install RODC in the Windows Core operating system. Nano Servers introduced with Windows Server 2016 is not yet supported for RODC.

Active Directory database maintenance

Active Directory maintains a multi-master database to store schema information, configuration information, and domain information. Normally, when we say *database*, first thing which comes to our mind is a software like Microsoft SQL, MySQL, or Oracle. But here it's quite different. Active Directory database uses the **Extensible Storage Engine (ESE)**, which is an **indexed and sequential access method (ISAM)** technology.

Here, a single system works as the client and server. It uses record-oriented database architecture, which provides extremely fast access to records. ESE indexes the data in the database file. This database file can grow up to 16 terabytes and hold over 2 billion records. Typically ESE is used for the application which requires fast structured data storage. ESE is used for many other Microsoft applications including Microsoft Exchange, DHCP, FRS, and so on.

As the part of the domain controller installation process, it creates the database under `C:\Windows\NTDS` unless we select a custom path. It is recommended to use separate partition/disk with higher speed to increase the database performances as well as the data protection:

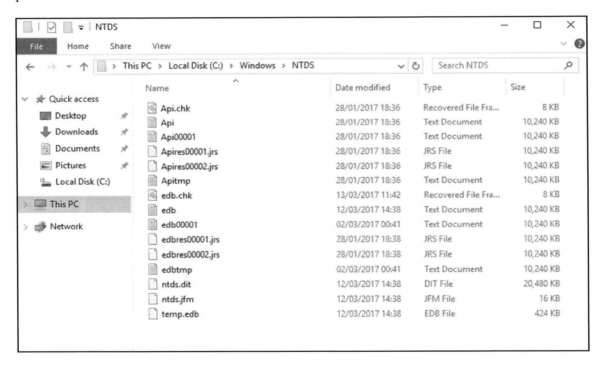

In this folder, we can see few different files. Out of those, the following files are important.

The ntds.dit file

This is the actual Active Directory database file. This database mainly contains three tables. The **schema** table includes data regarding the object classes, attributes, and the relationship between those. The **link** table includes the data about values referring to another object. Group membership details are a good example of this. The **data** table includes all the data about users, groups, and any other data integrated with Active Directory. In the table, rows represent the object and columns represent the attributes.

The edb.log file

In here, we can see that a few log files starts with `edb*`. Each of them are 10 MB or less in size. It is the transaction log maintained by the system to store the directory transaction before writing into the database file.

The edb.chk file

This file is responsible to keep track of the data transaction committed into the database from log files (`edb*.log`).

The temp.edb file

This file will be used during the Active Directory database maintenance to hold data and also to store information about large in-progress AD data transactions.

Every domain controller in the Active Directory infrastructure needs to be aware of the changes made in each domain controller. In that case, you may think it is the database being synced. But it is not the database, it is only the changes being synced. Therefore, each domain controller in the domain will not have the same size.

Most of the database systems have their own automatic data grooming techniques to maintain the efficiency of the system. This also gives administrators a chance to perform custom maintenance tasks to perform granular maintenance. The Active Directory database system is a self-maintained system. It does not required daily maintenance. However, there are situation where it requires manual intervention:

- If the default database partition is running out of space or notices a potential hardware failure
- To free up unused space in Active Directory database after mass object deletion

In order to move Active Directory, we can use a command-line tool called `ntdsutil`. When moving the database files, it is also recommended to move the log files, so it will not need to refer to two different disks. The minimum space requirement for the database file is 500 MB or the database file size along with 20% of the database file size (which ever is greater). The log file space requirement is also the same.

The database and log files cannot be moved while AD DS is running. So, the first step of the action is to stop the service:

```
net stop ntds
```

This will also stop the associated services such as KDC, DNS, and DFS.

The Active Directory database and log files cannot be moved to a non-existing folder. So before move the files, the folder needs to be created.

In my demo, I will be moving it to a folder called ADDB in a different partition:

```
ntdsutil
activate instance ntds
files
move db to E:\ADDB
move logs to E:\ADDB
integrityquit
quit
```

In the preceding command `ntdsutil`, initiate the utility. `move db to E:ADDB` moves the database files to the new location and `move logs to E:ADDB` moves the log files to new directory. The `integrity` part will verify the integrity of the database and log files in the new location:

```
PS E:\> ntdsutil
C:\Windows\system32\ntdsutil.exe: activate instance ntds
Active instance set to "ntds".
C:\Windows\system32\ntdsutil.exe: files
file maintenance: move db to E:\ADDB

Successfully updated the backup exclusion key.
Copying NTFS security from C:\Windows\NTDS to E:\ADDB...
The previous NTDS database location C:\Windows\NTDS\dsadata.bak is unavailable. The default NTFS security will be applie
d to NTDS folders.
Default NTFS security on NTDS folders will be set on reboot.
Copying NTFS security from C:\Windows\NTDS to E:\ADDB...

Drive Information:

        C:\ NTFS (Fixed Drive  ) free(28.8 Gb) total(39.4 Gb)
        E:\ NTFS (Fixed Drive  ) free(1.9 Gb) total(1.9 Gb)

DS Path Information:

        Database    : E:\ADDB\ntds.dit - 20.0 Mb
        Backup dir  : E:\ADDB\DSADATA.BAK
        Working dir : E:\ADDB
        Log dir     : C:\Windows\NTDS - 50.0 Mb total
                      edbtmp.log - 10.0 Mb
                      edbres00002.jrs - 10.0 Mb
                      edbres00001.jrs - 10.0 Mb
                      edb00001.log - 10.0 Mb
                      edb.log - 10.0 Mb

Move database is successful.
Please make a backup immediately else restore will not retain the new file
location.
file maintenance: move logs to E:\ADDB
Successfully updated the backup exclusion key.

Copying NTFS security from C:\Windows\NTDS to E:\ADDB...

Drive Information:

        C:\ NTFS (Fixed Drive  ) free(28.9 Gb) total(39.4 Gb)
        E:\ NTFS (Fixed Drive  ) free(1.8 Gb) total(1.9 Gb)

DS Path Information:

        Database    : E:\ADDB\ntds.dit - 20.0 Mb
        Backup dir  : E:\ADDB\DSADATA.BAK
        Working dir : E:\ADDB
        Log dir     : E:\ADDB - 50.0 Mb total
                      edbtmp.log - 10.0 Mb
                      edbres00002.jrs - 10.0 Mb
                      edbres00001.jrs - 10.0 Mb
                      edb00001.log - 10.0 Mb
                      edb.log - 10.0 Mb

If move log files was successful,
please make a backup immediately else restore
will not retain the new file location.
```

Once it's completed, we need to start the AD DS using the following command:

```
net start ntds
```

As soon as this process is completed, it is recommended to make a full backup of the AD as the path changes. The previous backup, which was taken, will not be valid anymore.

Offline defragmentation

In any database system, the data will be added, modified, and deleted as it goes. When new data is added, it will require *new* space inside the DB. When the data is removed, it will *release* space to the DB. When it is modified, it can be either need new space or release space. In the Active Directory database, once an object has been deleted, it will release the space it used to the database and not to the filesystem. So, that free space will be used for the new objects. This process is called **online defragmentation** because it does not need to stop the AD services. By default, it runs every 12 hours.

However, when there is large number of objects removed or when global catalog server is being removed, its worth releasing this free space to the filesystem as it may not use that space for long time if it's just stay inside the database. In order to do that, we need to perform *offline defragmentation*, and it is required to stop the Active Directory services.

Once the service stops (`net stop ntds`), we can run the defragmentation using the following command:

```
ntdsutil
activate instance ntds
files
compact to E:\CompactDB
quit
quit
```

In the preceding process, it needs a temporally folder location to save the compact `ntds.dit` file. In my demo, I created folder `E:\CompactDB` for it:

```
PS E:\> ntdsutil
C:\Windows\system32\ntdsutil.exe: activate instance ntds
Active instance set to "ntds".
C:\Windows\system32\ntdsutil.exe: files
file maintenance: compact to E:\CompactDB
Initiating DEFRAGMENTATION mode...
    Source Database: E:\ADDB\ntds.dit
    Target Database: E:\CompactDB\ntds.dit

            Defragmentation  Status (% complete)

        0    10   20   30   40   50   60   70   80   90  100
        |----|----|----|----|----|----|----|----|----|----|
        ..................................................

It is recommended that you immediately perform a full backup
of this database. If you restore a backup made before the
defragmentation, the database will be rolled back to the state
it was in at the time of that backup.

Compaction is successful. You need to:
    copy "E:\CompactDB\ntds.dit" "E:\ADDB\ntds.dit"
and delete the old log files:
    del E:\ADDB\*.log

file maintenance: quit
C:\Windows\system32\ntdsutil.exe: quit
PS E:\>
```

Once it is completed, the compact database should copy to original `ntds.dit` location. It can be done using the following command:

```
copy "E:\CompactDB\ntds.dit" "E:\ADDB\ntds.dit"
```

After that, we need to delete the old log file too:

```
del E:\ADDB\*.log
```

After that we can start the AD DS using `net start ntds`.

This completes the two scenarios where we will need manual intervention for Active Directory database maintenance.

Active Directory backup and recovery

Active Directory domain controllers are the main components responsible for the organization's identity infrastructure. The failure of domain controllers and their services impact the entire identity infrastructure. Therefore, as with any other critical system, Active Directory server's high availability is crucial. There are two types of disaster which can occur related to Active Directory domain controllers.

The first one is when there is a complete system crash due to the faulty hardware. Apart from the Active Directory backup, maintaining multiple domain controllers will help organizations to recover from such situation easily without a backup restore. If it's not the FSMO role holder, we can forcefully remove the crashed domain controller's related records and introduce a new domain controller. If it is the FSMO role holder, we can *seize* the FSMO role and make it available from any other live domain controller. On the other hand, most of the workloads are operating in a virtualized environment today including domain controllers. These virtualized solutions are built considering the fault tolerance and disaster recovery. They can be based on a clustered environment or advanced recovery solution such as the Azure site recovery. Therefore, in modern infrastructures, I rarely see any one who has had to restore a domain controller from backup.

However, the second type of disaster, which is due to Active Directory objects deletion or configuration alternations, are more visible. Restoring a system from backup is not always a *no-impact* disaster recovery. It can take *time* to recover it to a *latest* working condition. It can be followed by some data loss or operation impact due to the time taken by recovery process. If you want to recover an object you deleted in Active Directory, it doesn't make sense if you have to restore whole domain controller itself from a backup. Therefore, Microsoft uses different tools and methodologies to recover from both scenarios. In this section, we are going to look into these in detail.

Preventing accidental deletion of objects

With AD DS 2008, Microsoft has introduced a small but important feature to prevent accidental AD object deletion. This is not a solution to recover from disaster, but it is to prevent a disaster. In every Active Directory object under the **Object** tab, there is small checkbox to enable this feature. This can be enabled when we create objects using PowerShell. If it's not PowerShell, it still can enable using the **Object** properties window at any time. When creating OU using GUI, it allows users to enable this option and that's the only object allowed to do so during the setup:

When it is enabled, it will not allow to delete the object unless you disable this option:

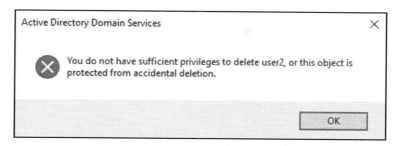

In PowerShell, it can be done using the `-ProtectedFromAccidentalDeletion $true` parameter. It can be set in an individual object level or a mass object level.

Active Directory Recycle Bin

The most common Active Directory related disasters are due to accidentally deleted objects. Once the object is deleted from Active Directory, it is not permanently deleted. As soon as an object is deleted, it will set the `isDeleted` object value to `True` and move the object under `CN=Deleted Objects`:

Then, it stays there until system reaches the *tombstone lifetime* value. By default, it is 180 days, and this can be change if required. As soon as the object passes the tombstone lifetime, it is available for permanent deletion. When I explained about the Active Directory database in the previous section, I mentioned online defragmentation. It uses the garbage collector service to remove the deleted objects from the Active Directory database and release that space to database. This service runs every 12 hours. Once the deleted object exceeds the tombstone lifetime value, it will be permanently removed in next garbage collector service cycle. The problem with this one is, during the tombstone process, most of the object values are striped off. So even if you were able to recover, these objects values will need to be re-entered.

With Windows Server 2008 R2, Microsoft introduced *Active Directory Recycle Bin* feature. When this feature is enabled, once the object is deleted, it still sets the `isDeleted` object value to `True` and moves the object under `CN=Deleted Object`. But instead of the tombstone lifetime, now it's controlled by **deleted object lifetime (DOL)**. Object attributes will remain the same in this stage, and it is easily recoverable. By default, the DOL value is equal to the tombstone lifetime. This value can be changed by modifying the `msDS-deletedObjectLifetime` object value. Once it's exceeded the DOL, it is moved into the `Recycled` state and the `isRecycled` object value is set to `True`. By this state, it will not be able to recover, and it will be in that state until the tombstone lifetime value is exceeded. After it reaches the value, it will be permanently deleted from the AD.

 The Active Directory Recycle Bin feature requires a minimum of Windows Server 2008 R2 domain and a forest functional level. Once this feature is enabled, it cannot be disabled.

This feature can be enabled using the following command:

```
Enable-ADOptionalFeature 'Recycle Bin Feature' -Scope
ForestOrConfigurationSet -Target rebeladmin.com
```

In the preceding command, `-Target` can be changed with your domain name:

```
PS C:\Users\Administrator> Enable-ADOptionalFeature 'Recycle Bin Feature' -Scope ForestOrConfigurationSet -Target rebeladmin.com
WARNING: Enabling 'Recycle Bin Feature' on 'CN=Partitions,CN=Configuration,DC=rebeladmin,DC=com' is an irreversible action! You will not be
able to disable 'Recycle Bin Feature' on 'CN=Partitions,CN=Configuration,DC=rebeladmin,DC=com' if you proceed.

Confirm
Are you sure you want to perform this action?
Performing the operation "Enable" on target "Recycle Bin Feature".
[Y] Yes  [A] Yes to All  [N] No  [L] No to All  [S] Suspend  [?] Help (default is "Y"): A
PS C:\Users\Administrator>
```

Once it is enabled, we can revive the objects, which are deleted using the following command:

```
Get-ADObject -filter 'isdeleted -eq $true' -includeDeletedObjects
```

It will search for the objects where the `isdeleted` attributes are set to true.

Now, we know the deleted object, and it can be restored using the following command:

```
Get-ADObject -Filter 'samaccountname -eq "dfrancis"' -IncludeDeletedObjects
| Restore-ADObject
```

The preceding command will restore the user object, `dfrancis`:

```
PS C:\Users\Administrator> Get-ADObject -Filter samaccountname -eq dfrancis -IncludeDeletedObjects | Restore-ADObject
PS C:\Users\Administrator> Get-ADUser -identity dfrancis

DistinguishedName : CN=Dishan Francis,OU=Users,OU=Europe,DC=rebeladmin,DC=com
Enabled           : True
GivenName         : Dishan
Name              : Dishan Francis
ObjectClass       : user
ObjectGUID        : 276f06a4-b457-4daf-a503-6092300cae70
SamAccountName    : dfrancis
SID               : S-1-5-21-4041220333-1835452706-552999228-1186
Surname           : Francis
UserPrincipalName : dfrancis@rebeladmin.com
```

Active Directory snapshots

When we are working with virtual servers, we understand how *snapshots* are important in a faster recovery process. Snapshots allow to revert the system to a previous working state with minimum impact.

 It is not recommended to take snapshots and restore domain controllers using this method, as it will create integrity issues with other existing domain controllers and their data.

With Windows Server 2008, Microsoft introduced Active Directory snapshot feature. Here, it will take snapshot of Active Directory in a given time. Later, it can be used to compare object value changes and export and import objects, which have been deleted or modified. Do not mistake this as a typical snapshot. This is happening inside the Active Directory, and we cannot use it to complete AD overwrite. It allows to mount snapshot while the existing AD DS configuration is running. However, it is not allowing to move or copy objects between snapshots and a working AD DS instance.

We can create the AD DS snapshot using `ntdsutil`. In order to run this, we need domain administrator privileges:

```
ntdsutil
snapshot
activate instance ntds
create
quit
quit
```

Now, we have a snapshot, and at a later time, it can be mounted. To mount it, we need to use the following command:

```
ntdsutil
snapshot
activate instance ntds
list all
mount 1
quit
quit
```

The preceding command will mount snapshot called 1 from the list and it is listed under the given mount points:

The next step is to mount the snapshot, and it can be done using the following command:

```
dsamain -dbpath C:$SNAP_201703152333_VOLUMEE$ADDBntds.dit -ldapport 10000
```

In the preceding command, `-dbpath` defines the AD DS database path, and `-ldapport` defines the port used for the snapshot. It can be any available TCP port.

Once it's mounted, we can connect to the mounted snapshot using server name and the LDAP port, `10000`:

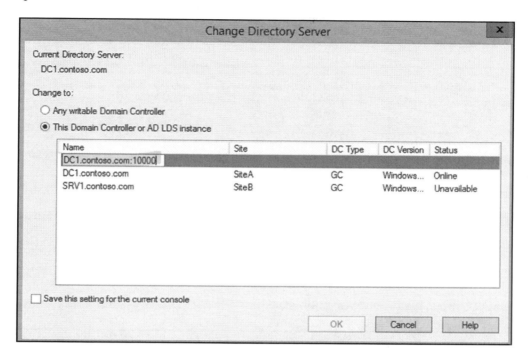

Once the work is finished, it needs to be unmounted as well. To do that, we can use the following command:

```
ntdsutil
snapshot
activate instance ntds
list all
unmount 1
quit
quit
```

 If you need to move an object from a snapshot to leave the database, the first object needs to export, and then import it over.

Active Directory system state backup

Active Directory system state backup is required in order to restore Active Directory in a disaster, which cannot be recovered using the previously explained object level recovery options. Windows backup is supported to make the system state backup; there are many third-party backup tools, which backup Active Directory using similar technology.

In a system state backup the following files are included:

- Active Directory DC database file (`ntds.dit`)
- The `SYSVOL` folder and its files
- The certificate store
- User profiles
- IIS metabase
- Boot files
- DLL cache folder
- Registry info
- COM+ and WMI info
- Cluster service info
- Windows Resource Protection system files

After Windows Server 2008, the system state backup also included Windows system files, so the system state backup is larger than Windows Server 2003 system states backups. It is recommended to take a system state backup for every domain controller for successful backup.

The first step to proceed with configuration is to install the Windows backup feature in AD server:

```
Install-WindowsFeature -Name Windows-Server-Backup -IncludeAllSubFeature
```

Next, create a backup policy using the following command:

```
$BKPolicy = New-WBPolicy
```

Next, let's add system state to the policy:

```
Add-WBSystemState -Policy $BKPolicy
```

It also needs the backup volume path:

```
$Bkpath = New-WBBackupTarget -VolumePath "F:"
```

Now, we need to map policy with the path:

```
Add-WBBackupTarget -Policy $BKPolicy -Target $Bkpath
```

We can run the backup using the following command:

```
Start-WBBackup -Policy $BKPolicy
```

Active Directory recovery from system state backup

When the system needs to recover from the system state backup, it needs to be done via **Directory Services Restore Mode (DSRM)**.

The first system needs to be rebooted; press the *F8* key and select **Directory Services Restore Mode**.

Once it's loaded to safe mode, we can use the following command:

```
$ADBackup = Get-WBBackupSet | select -Last 1

Start-WBSystemStateRecovery -BackupSet $ADBackup
```

This will restore the last backup the system has taken.

 If you are using the Active Directory backup software other than Windows, the recovery options will be different from the aforementioned options and refer to vendor guidlines.

Summary

It is the end of a quite long chapter. In this chapter, we have focused on AD DS architecture and features to improve the AD infrastructure further to match with business requirements. We started the chapter by looking into AD LDS and its capabilities. Then, we moved on to Active Directory replication. In that section, we focused on the physical and logical components involved with Active Directory replication and how they can be used to optimize complex replication requirements. More importantly, we also looked into how Active Directory replication happens behind the scene. Then, we moved on to the read-only domain controllers and looked into their features and deployment scenarios. Later, we looked into Active Directory database maintenance. In there, we looked into different tools and techniques used to optimize the Active Directory database performance. Last but not least, we have looked at the Active Directory recovery options.

In the next chapter, we are going to look into another important Active Directory role service which is important in enterprise infrastructures, namely which is AD CS.

12

Active Directory Certificate Services

The two-man rule in security is used to secure high-valued assets and operations. As an example, many banks provide a safety box facility. People can rent these safety boxes to store valuable asserts they have. Most of these safety boxes are designed to support a two-man rule. This means each safety box has two locks. One key to the lock is held by the bank and the key for the second lock is issued to the customer. In order to open it, customers and bank agents need to agree to open it and use their keys at same time. As soon as a customer shows up at the bank, he/she can't just go to the place where lockers are located. There is a certain process for that. Banks will verify their *identity* first. They will ask for passport and driving license to verify their identity. After a successful verification, they will assign a bank agent to go with the customer and open it using the bank and customer keys. But the end goal of these layers of security is to verify that the customer is the exact same person he/she *claims to be* in order to allow access to the high valued assets in the locker box.

The role of the **public key infrastructure (PKI)** is similar to this. PKI is responsible for verifying objects and services that are genuine using digital certificates. When we apply for visas or jobs, sometimes they ask to verify our identity using police certificates. We may have already provided a copy of passport and identity cards with the application forms. However, the police department is a well-known authority, which anyone can trust. Therefore, a police certificate, which verifies our identity will confirm that we are the same person we claim to be. On the other hand, the police department is now responsible for the certificate they issued about us. Before providing certificates, it's their responsibility to verify the identity using different procedures.

Modern businesses are increasingly using PKI to counter the modern infrastructure threats. As an example, they use digital certificates to verify their web services, to authenticate their web applications, billing systems, service URLs and so on. They use digital certificates to encrypt network traffics between networks or hosts, so no other unauthorized party can decrypt them. AD CS allows organizations to set up and maintain their own PKI in their own infrastructure boundaries to create, manage, store, renew, and revoke digital certificates. In this chapter, we are going to look at the following topics:

- What is a certificate service and how PKI works?
- How to design your PKI?
- Different PKI deployment models in action

PKI in action

Sometimes when I talk to customers and engineers about encrypted traffic, most of them know SSL is *more secure* for communication and works with the TCP port, 443. But most of them do not really know what a certificate is and how this encryption and decryption works. It is very important to know how it works, and then the deployment and management becomes easy. Most of the PKI related issues I have worked on are related to the misunderstandings of core technologies, components and concepts related to it, rather than service-level issues.

Symmetric keys versus asymmetric keys

There are two types of cryptographic methods used to encrypt the data in computer world. Let's now look at them:

- **Symmetric keys**: Symmetric methods work exactly the same way your door lock works. You have one key to lock or open the door. This is also called **shared secret** and **private key**. VPN connections and backup software are some of the examples, which still use symmetric key to encrypt data.
- **Asymmetric keys**: This method, on the other hand, uses *key pair* to do the encryption and decryption. It includes two keys: one is a *public key* and the other one is a *private key*. Public keys are always distributed to public and anyone can have them. Private keys are unique for the object and will not be distributed to others. Any message encrypted using a public key can be decrypted only using its private key. Any message encrypted using a private key can be decrypted only using a public key. PKI uses the asymmetric key method for digital encryption and digital signatures.

Digital encryption

Digital encryption means the data transfer between the two parties will be encrypted, and the sender will ensure it can only be opened by the expected receiver. Even if an unauthorized party gains access to that encrypted data, it will not be able to decrypt the data. The best way to explain it will be through the following example:

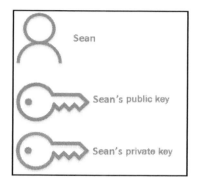

We have an employee in an organization called **Sean**. In the PKI environment, he owns two keys: a public key and a private key. Sean can use these keys for encryption and signature process. Now, he has a requirement to receive a set of confidential data from the company account manager, **Chris**. He doesn't want anyone else to have this confidential data. The best way to do this is to encrypt the data, which is going to be sent from **Chris** to **Sean**:

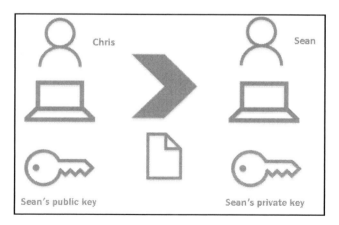

In order to encrypt the data, **Sean** sends his public key to **Chris**. There is no issue with providing the public key to any party. Then, **Chris** uses this public key to encrypt the data he is sending over to **Sean**. This encrypted data can only be opened using the private key of **Sean**. He is the only one who has this private key. This verifies the receiver and his authority over the data.

Digital signatures

The digital signature verifies the authenticity of the service or data. It is similar to signing a document to prove its authenticity. As an example, before buying anything from Amazon, we can check its digital certificate and will verify the authenticity of the website and confirm it's not a phishing website. Let's look into it further with a use case. In the previous scenario, **Sean** successfully decrypted the data he received from **Chris**. Now, **Sean** wants to send some confidential data back to **Chris**. It can be encrypted using the same method using Chris's public key. But the issue is **Chris** is not a part of the PKI setup, and he does not have a key pair. The only thing **Chris** needs to verify is that the sender is legitimate and it's the same user he claims to be. If **Sean** can certify it using the digital signature, and if **Chris** can verify it, the problem is solved:

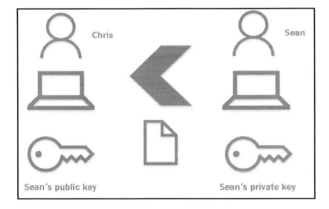

Now in here, **Sean** encrypts the data using his private key. The only key it can be decrypted is by the public key of **Sean**. **Chris** already has this information. When **Chris** receives the data, he decrypts it using **Sean's public key**, and it confirms the sender is definitely **Sean**.

Signing, encryption, and decryption

In the previous two scenarios, I have explained how digital encryption and digital signatures work with PKI. But both of these scenarios can be combined together to provide the encryption and signing at the same time. In order to do that, we use two additional techniques:

- **Symmetric keys**: A one-time symmetric key will be used for the message encryption process, as it is faster than the asymmetric key encryption algorithms. This key needs to be available for the receiver, but to improve the security, it will still be encrypted using the receiver's public key.

- **Hashing**: During the signing process, the system will generate a one-way hash value to represent the original data. Even if someone manages to get that hash value, it will not be possible to reverse engineer to get the original data. If any modification is done to the data, the hash value will be changed; and the receiver will know this straight away. These hashing algorithms are faster than encryption algorithms and also the hashed data will be smaller than the actual data values.

Let's look into this based on a scenario. We have two employees, **Simran** and **Brian**, and both are using a PKI setup. Both have their private and public keys assigned:

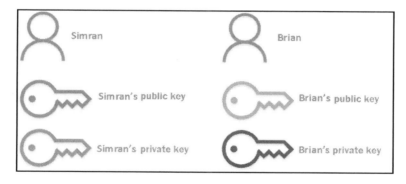

Simran wants to send an encrypted and signed data segment to **Brian**. Processes mainly can be divided into two stages: **data signing** and **data encryption**. It will go through both stages before the data sent to **Brian**:

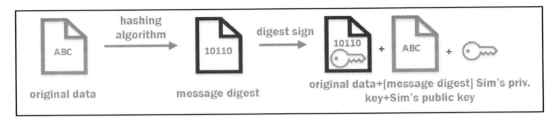

The first stage is to sign the data segment. The system receives the data from **Simran**, and the first step is to generate **message digest** using **hashing algorithm**. This will ensure data integrity; and if it's altered, once it leaves the senders system; the receiver can easily identify it using the decryption process. This is a one-way process. Once **message digest** is generated, in next step, **message digest** will encrypt using Simran's private key in order to digitally sign. It will also include Simran's public key, so **Brian** will be able to decrypt and verify the authenticity of the message. Once the encrypt process finishes, it will be attached with the **original data** value. This process will ensure data was not altered and was sent from exact expected sender (genuine):

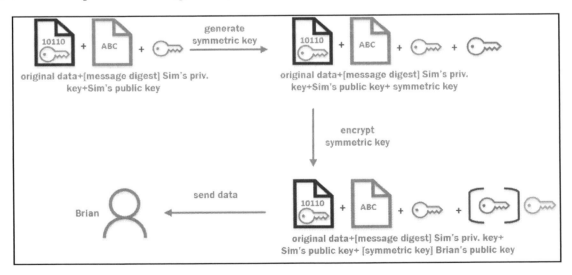

The next stage of the operation is to encrypt the data. The first step in the process is to generate a one-time symmetric key to encrypt the data. An asymmetric algorithm is less efficient compared to symmetric algorithms to use with long data segments. Once a symmetric key is generated, the data will encrypt using it (including message digest and signature). This symmetric key will be used by **Brian** to decrypt the message. Therefore, we need to ensure it is only available for **Brian**. The best way to do it is to encrypt the symmetric key using **Brian's public key**. So, once he receives it, he will be able to decrypt it using his private key. This process is only encrypting a symmetric key in itself, and rest of the message will stay same. Once it is completed, the data can be sent to **Brian**.

The next step of the process is to see how the decryption process will happen on Brian's side:

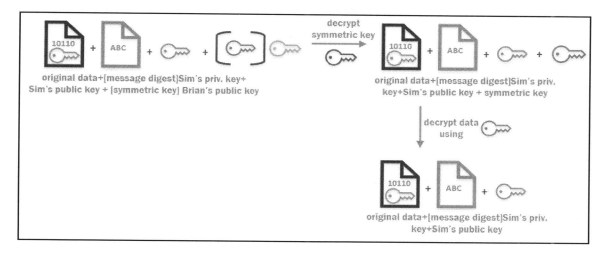

The message decryption process starts with decrypting the symmetric key. Brian needs symmetric to go further with the decryption process. It can only be decrypted using Brian's private key. Once it's decrypted, a symmetric key can be used to decrypt the **message digest** along with signature. Once the decryption is done, the same key information cannot be used to decrypt similar messages as it's a one-time key:

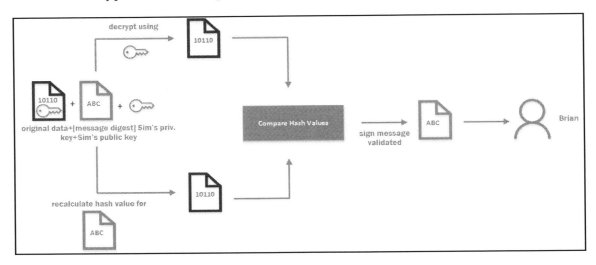

Now we have the decrypted data, and the next step is to verify the signature. At this point, we have the message digest, which is encrypted using Simran's private key. It can be decrypted using Simran's public key, which is attached to the encrypted message. Once it's decrypted, we can retrieve the message digest. This digest value is one way. We cannot reverse engineer it. Therefore, the retrieved original data digest value will be recalculated using exact same algorithm used by sender. After that, this newly generated digest value will be compared with the digest value attached to message. If the value is equal, it will confirm the data wasn't modified during the communication process. When the value is equal, the signature will be verified and the original data will be issued to Brian. If the digest values are different, the message will be discarded, as it's been altered or not signed by Simran.

This explained how the PKI environment works with the encryption/decryption process as well as the digital signing/verification process.

Secure Sockets Layer certificates

So far, we have talked about how asymmetric key pairs and symmetric keys work in PKI. But when we talk about PKI, we talk about **Secure Sockets Layer** (**SSL**) certificates. So, what is the responsibility of the certificates?

I travel regularly between London and Seattle. My original passport is still one issued from Sri Lanka. When I reach Seattle-Tacoma International Airport, nice folks in border asks for my passport to put the stamp and allow me into the country. They do not know me personally, but the passport I hold is issued from an authority, which operates under international migration laws; and they certify the person who owns the passport is Dishan Francis. If they want to check the authenticity of it, they can confirm with the authority it was issued. So, they have a proof of identity, and they can further check the visa status to decide my entry to the country.

Similarly, when looking into a PK cryptography, we know a public key can be used by many. But how exactly can it be published and how can the receiver confirm the authenticity of it? This is done using *digital certificates* issued by a **certification authority** (**CA**), which can be trusted by the receiver. This digital certificate will include the public key of the object it was issued. The receiver can retrieve the public key of the object or the service it accesses via a digital certificate; and it can be verified by the *trusted* authority, which can be trusted by the receiver. These digital certificates follow similar structure, so everyone can understand it. It is similar to the way the passport works; folks in border agency know where to look even it's a passport they have never seen before. These certificates are also time-bound and they are only valid for a certain period of time. Once it has exceeded the validity period, it needs to be reissued, similar to a passport renewal.

 The validity period is defined by the certificate template used by the object or service. In the event of exceeding the validity period, one needs to contact the certification authority and request a renewal. It can either be an automatic renewal process or a manual renewal process.

The certificate includes the following data:

- **Version**: X.509 standards define the format of the certificate. It was first introduced in 1988 and currently, it uses version 3.
- **Serial number**: A unique identifier used by the CA to identify the certificate.
- **Signature algorithm**: The type of the algorithm used by the CA to sign the digital certificate.
- **Signature hash algorithm**: The type of hash algorithm used by the CA.

- **Issuer**: The name of the CA who issued the certificate.
- **Valid from**: The day certificate was issued by the CA.
- **Valid to**: The day certificate will expire.
- **Subject**: To whom the certificate was issued.
- **Public key**: The public key of the certificate owner. It will be the object or the service it was issued to.

The following screenshot shows a sample certificate:

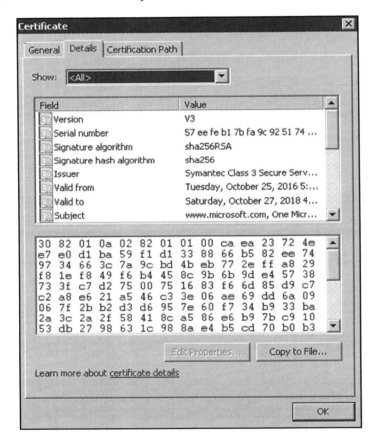

Types of certification authorities

There are two types of certification authorities:

- **Private CAs**: This is what we are covering in this chapter. This type of CA is mainly for the internal infrastructures, and it can be used to issue, manage, renew, and revoke certificates for internal objects and services. This will be a less of a cost to maintain. It is Active Directory integrated service, however if necessary AD CS components can also be installed in a workgroup environment (stand-alone CA). If objects in the external network likes to use certificates from the internal CA, the certificate must be first requested within the internal network; and once it's issued, it needs to export and import it into the external network along with the *root certificate,* which certifies the issuer itself.
- **Public CAs**: Public CAs are available for anyone, and users can pay the associate fees and generate certificates. These certificates come with a different level of insurance as well to confirm the protection. Internal CAs can trust internal objects as it's one of *our*. But if you provide internet-facing services, it doesn't make sense to use internal CA-issued certificates, as not everyone will *trust* the issuer. Instead of that, we can use a certificate issued by well-known CA, which everyone can trust.

How do certificates work with digital signatures and encryption?

In the previous section, we followed a scenario where Simran sends encrypted and digitally signed data to Brian. During the process, we used each other's private and public keys. A public key has to be shared between two parties. Now, the problem we have is how exactly does the system know the public key of Brian is exactly from him and not from someone that is pretending to be Brian? Therefore, we can use certificates to verify the shared public keys are exactly from the person it claims to be. It is certified by the CA, which is trusted by Simran and Brian.

Digital signature process the following occurs:

- Simran's private key will be used to encrypt the message digest. This private key will be retrieved from Simran's digital certificate. It verifies it is issued from a valid authority and it's authentic.
- Simran's public key is also attached to the message as it can be used by Brian to verify the signature. This will be available to Brain via Simran's digital signature.

Data encryption process the following occurs:

- A one-time symmetric key is used to encrypt the whole message; and after that, the key itself will be encrypted using Brian's public key. This public key will be retrieved using Brian's digital certificate as it confirms it is exactly from Brian. It is certified by a CA which Simran also trusts.

 During the certificate validation process, the system will verify the certificates using CA's public key as it will confirm the authenticity of the CA. It also checks the validity period of the certificates using the **Valid to** value in certificate.

Data decryption process the following occurs:

- The first step is to decrypt the one time symmetric key using Brian's private key. It will be retrieved using Brian's digital certificate. Once key is retrieved, the key will be decrypted, and it will be used to decrypt the entire message.

Signature verification process the following occurs:

- The message digest (hash) is encrypted using Simran's private key. It can be decrypted using Simran's public key. This public key can be retrieved from Simran's digital certificate. This certificate is issued by a CA, which is trusted by Brian.

The rest of the steps in the process stay the same.

What can we do with certificates?

The previous scenario is not the only way we can use a certificate. Let's look into some of the scenarios where we can use certificates:

- When networks extend their network boundaries to allow remote **virtual private networks (VPNs)**, it is important to protect the data transfer between two networks. Intercepted network traffic can cause serious infrastructure security issues. **IPSEC** is a network protocol used to encrypt the network traffic using cryptographic keys. Therefore, we can use certificates to encrypt the traffic between two peers.

- The physical security of the data also matters when considering data security. People are moving into mobile computing, and we need a way to protect the data inside these laptops and tablets if they are stolen. **Encrypted File System (EFS)**, which is based on certificates, can be used to encrypt and decrypt files. It will prevent any unauthorized access to data even if it is physically available for them.

- Wireless networks do have less control over connections compared to physical cable connections. Anyone who is aware of the wireless password can connect to the network. Instead of using passwords, it can use certificates to authenticate into wireless network and communication will be only allowed from trusted devices.

- In the Active Directory environment, the main authentication method is the username and password. In addition to that, certificates can be used to verify the authenticity of the users and computer authentication requests.

- Some services and applications have multiple roles and subservices integrated in order to provide one integrated solution. The communication between these role services or subservices are unique and crucial for the system operations. Therefore, those services use certificates to verify the connectivity to each component and encrypt the communication between those to ensure the protection of application-related traffic. As an example, the communication between the System Center Operations Manager management pool and gateway servers is based on certificates.

- The **Secure/Multipurpose Internet Mail Extensions (S/MIME)** protocol can be used to encrypt and digitally sign email messages. When it digitally signs email, it ensures the authenticity of the message, and no alternation has been made after it leaves the sender. This is done based on certificates. If you have Exchange Server 2013 SP1 or later, you can use S/MIME. Office 365 also supports this protocol.

- When we search for applications or drivers on the internet, sometimes we can notice fake installation files, which pretend to be from the original vendor. But at the end, it includes malware or viruses, which can harm the infrastructure. Therefore, application vendors and manufacturers use certificates to digitally sign their applications, drivers, and code to confirm the authenticity of them. So, as users, we know it's definitely from the genuine vendor.

- The most common use of certificate is with websites. A certificate of websites proves few things. One is, it proves its authenticity and it is not a phishing site. The other thing is the user of the website knows the communication between user and the web server is secure and any information passed between is encrypted. This is important when users involves with online transactions. I will never use my credit cards with a website, which doesn't have a certificate. If it's an internet-facing website, it is recommended to use public CA to maintain the visibility and trust.

- Non-repudiation is another benefit from the certificates. If an object or service signed set of data, they cannot deny that they are not the private key holder. It is signed using a private key, and its public key is attached to the data segment. These keys were retrieved from the certificate, which was issued by a trusted CA. The CA and the object is responsible for signed data and cannot deny it. This is why public CA provide an insurance, and they are bound to pay fee to customers if there is any key compromise. This is important for online businesses and businesses which accept internet payments.

Active Directory Certificate Service components

AD CS is a collection of role services, and they can be used to design the PKI for your organization. Let's look into each of these role services and their responsibilities.

The certification authority

CA role service holders responsible for issue, store, manage, and revoke certificates. The PKI setup can have multiple CAs. There are mainly two types of CA, which can be identified in PKI:

- **The root CA**: The root CA is the most trusted CA in the PKI environment. The compromise of the root CA will possibly compromise entire PKI. Therefore, the security of the root CA is critical, and most organization only bring those online when they need to issue or renew a certificate. This is also capable of issuing certificates to any object or services, but considering security and hierarchy of the PKI, it is used to issue certificates only to subordinate CAs.

- **Subordinate CAs**: In PKI, subordinate CAs are responsible for issuing, storing, managing, and revoking certificates for objects or services. Once CA receives a request, it will process it and issue the certificate. PKI can have multiple subordinate CAs. Each subordinate server should have its own certificate from the root CA. The validity period of these certificates is normally longer than ordinary certificates. It also needs to renew its certificate from root CA when it reaches the end of the validity period. Subordinate CAs can have more subordinate CAs under them. In such situations, subordinate CAs are also responsible for issuing certificates for their more subordinate CAs. These subordinate CAs, which have more subordinate CAs, are called **intermediate CAs**. These will not be responsible for issuing certificates to users, devices, or services. The subordinate
servers which issues certificates will be called **issuing CAs**:

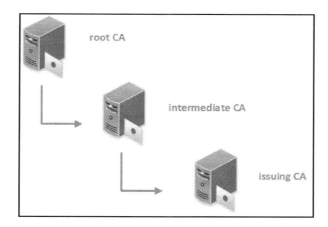

Certificate Enrollment Web Service

Certificate Enrollment Web Service allow users, computers, or services to request a certificate or renew a certificate via web browser, even it is not domain-joined or is temporally out of corporate network. If it is domain-joined and in corporate network, they can use auto enrollments or template-based request process to retrieve certificate. This web service will remove the dependencies to use other enrollment mechanisms.

Certificate Enrollment Policy Web Service

This role service works with Certificate Enrollment Web Service and allows user, computers, or services to perform policy-based certificate enrollment. Similar to the enrollment web services, the client computers can be non-domain joined computer or domain-joined devices, which are out of the company's network boundaries. When a client requests for policy information, the enrollment policy web service queries the AD DS using LDAP for the policy information, and then deliver it to the client via HTTPS. This information will be cached and used for similar requests. Once the user has the policy information, then he/she can request the certificate using Certificate Enrollment Web Service.

Certification Authority Web Enrollment

This is similar to a web interface for CA. Users, computers, or services can request certificates using web interface. Using the interface, users also can download the root certificates and intermediate certificates in order to validate the certificate. This can be used to request **certificate revocation list** (**CRL**). This list includes all the certificates expired or revoked within its PKI. If any presented certificate matches entry in the CRL, it will be automatically refused.

Network Device Enrollment Service

Network devices such as routers, switches, and firewalls can have device certificates to verify authenticity of traffic pass through it. Majority of these devices are not domain-joined, and their operation systems are also very unique and do not support typical Windows computer functions. In order to request or retrieve certificates, it uses **Simple Certificate Enrollment Protocol** (**SCEP**). It allows network devices to have X.509 version 3 certificates similar to other domain-joined devices. This is important as if the devices are going to use IPSEC, it must have an X.509 version 3 certificate.

Online Responder

Online Responder is responsible for producing information about certificate status. When I explained about Certification Authority Web Enrollment, I explained about how CRL includes the entire list of certificates, which are expired and revoked within the PKI. The list will keep growing based on the number of certificates it managed. Instead of using bulk data, Online Responder will respond to individual requests from users to verify status of a particular certificate. This is more efficient than the CRL method as the request is focused to find out the status of one certificate at a given time.

The types of CA

Based on the installation mode, the CAs can be divided into two types: the **stand-alone CA** and the **enterprise CA**. The best way to explain capabilities of both types is to compare them:

Feature	Stand-alone CA	Enterprise CA
AD DS dependency	Does not depend on AD DS, it can be installed on member server or standalone server in workgroup	Only can be installed on member server
Operate offline	Can stay offline	Cannot be offline
Customized certificate templates	Does not support, only supports standard templates	Supported
Supported enrollment methods	Manual or web enrollment	Auto, manual or web enrollment
Certificate approval process	Manual	Manual or automatic based on the policy
User input for the certificate fields	Manual	Retrieved from AD DS
Certificate issuing and managing using AD DS	N/A	Supported

Stand-alone CAs are mostly used as the root CA. In the previous section, I have explained how important a root CA security is. The stand-alone CA supports to keep the server offline and brings it online when it needs to issue a certificate or renew a certificate. Root CAs are only used to issue certificates to a subordinate CA. So, the manual processing and approval are manageable, as this task may only have to do it every few years. This type is also valid for public CAs. Issuing CAs are involved with day-to-day CA tasks such as issuing, managing, storing, renewing, and revoking certificates. Depending on the infrastructure size, there can be hundreds or thousands who use these issuing CAs. If the request and approval process is manual, it may take much manpower to maintain it. Therefore, in corporate networks, it is always recommended to use an enterprise CA type. Enterprise CAs allow engineers to create certificate templates with specific requirements and publish these via AD DS. End users can request the certificates based on these templates. Enterprise CAs are installed on Windows Server Enterprise Edition or the Datacenter Edition only.

Planning PKI

By now, we understand what PKI is and how it works. You also learned about AD CS components and their capabilities. The next thing is to plan the deployment of PKI. In this section, we will look into things we need to consider during the PKI planning process.

Internal or public CAs

AD CS is not just a role that we can install on a server and leave it to run. It needs resources to run the role services. It needs knowledge to set up and operate it. It needs to be maintained as any other IT system. It also needs solutions for backup and high availability. All these come with a cost. On the other hand, public CA certificates need to be purchased through a service provider. Each provider has many different types of certificates with different price ranges. It is important to evaluate these associated costs against the company requirements. If its regarding a few web service certificates, there is no point to maintain few servers internally just for that. If a public CA can offer same thing for $15, it makes sense to invest on that rather than wasting resource and money by maintaining an internal CA. However, it's not only the cost we need to evaluate. Internal CA provides greater flexibility administrations. It allows to create templates and policies according to organization requirements. Public CAs are only given limited control. All you can do is pay for the certificate, submit the signing request, and then download the certificate once it's issued. But public CAs do have a reputation. If a user outside the corporate network needs to trust a certificate issued by the internal CA, user needs to trust the issuing CA and the rest of the CAs in the chain. But not everyone would like to do that. But if it's from a reputed CA, it gives confident about the certificate and the content protected by it. When you use public CA, customers can get professional support via vendor whenever required. No need to have advanced knowledge to request and retrieve a digital certificate. On the other hand, internal CA requires advanced knowledge about PKI to deploy, manage, and maintain. Therefore, considering all these pros and cons, we need to decide which CA model is best suited for the origination requirements.

Identifying the object types

Certificates can be issued to users, computers, services or network devices. User certificates are mainly used for authentication process. Certificates can also be used with application or service. User certificates will be installed under a user certificate store. Computer certificates allow to uniquely identify the device and based on certificate, application or services can decide if it should allow to connect. Computer certificates will be stored in a computer certificate store. Network devices are allowed to use X.509 certificates, and it can be used to certify the device and encrypt the traffic passing through it. Services, such as web and email, can use certificates to authenticate or encrypt data. Service itself will not have a certificate, but it will use a computer certificate or user certificate, which is associated with the service. It is important to understand what types of objects will have certificates as the configuration of the CA will be based on it. As an example, if network devices need certificates, we need to install Network Device Enrollment Service and configure it. Certificate templates should be modified to support the object type.

Cryptographic provider

With CA, we can use Microsoft's default cryptographic provider, which is **RSA Microsoft Software Key Storage Provider** or other advanced providers, such as ECDSA_P256, ECDSA_P521, or ECDSA_P384. Based on the used provider, the length of the cryptography key and hash algorithm will also change. Unless there are specific reasons, it is always recommended to use Microsoft RSA.

The cryptography key length

When the size of the cryptographic key is increased, it increases the security further. The minimum recommended key size is 2048 and this size can change based on the cryptographic provider. When the key size is increased, the encryption/decryption process takes more system resources.

Hash algorithms

We can decide the hash algorithm standard, which will be used by CA to sign the certificates. By default, it is SHA256, and it can change into SHA384, SHA512, or MD5. SHA1 is no longer recommended to use as it is proved to be a weaker hash algorithm.

The certificate validity period

Certificates are time bound. Using certificate templates, we can specify the validity period of the certificate. It can be months or years. Before certificate expires, it will need to renew (the certificate template will define how many days or weeks in advance it can renew). The expiry date of an issued certificate cannot be changed unless there is a renew or reprocess.

The CA hierarchy

Root CA in PKI can have more subordinate CAs. It will create a PKI hierarchy and number of subordinate based on the organization requirements. There are mainly two type of hierarchy design which is two-tier and three-tier. These will be explained in the next section in detail but in here what I want to emphasize is selecting correct hierarchy model will reduce operation cost and resource wastage.

High availability

Based on the operation requirements, we will have to decide what the best solution to maintain the high availability is. If it's a highly used PKI, the availability of the CA role services is important. Workload's up time can be guaranteed by running it on a clustered environment or using advanced site recovery solutions such as Azure Site Recovery. Based on the maximum downtime an organization can afford, investment on high availability products, technologies, and approach will also change.

Deciding certificate templates

Not every user, computer, or service needs the same type of certificates. If you purchase certificates from public CA, they have lots of different types of certificates with different prices. Each of these certificates have different options and value added services. Certificate templates allow to create custom templates that can match the different certificate requirements. As an example, user certificates may need to renew in every year due to staff changes while computer certificates renew in every 5 years' time. As part of the planning process, we need to evaluate certificate requirements so we can create new templates to match it.

The CA boundary

Before starting the deployment, it is important to decide on the operation boundaries as the PKI design can reflect it. We need to decide under which domain, forest, or network segment it will operate. Once the boundaries are defined, it can be hard to extend it later without any physical or logical network layer changes. As an example, if you have a CA in the perimeter network and if you need to extend the boundary to corporate network it will require network boundary changes. In another example, if a partner company or third party wants to use the corporate CA, it will require the AD CS role changes, firewall changes, network routing changes, DNS changes, and so on. Therefore, it's important to evaluate these types of operation requirements in the planning process.

PKI deployment models

In several places in this chapter, I have mentioned about the PKI hierarchy and components, such as root CAs, intermediate CAs, and issuing CAs. Based on the business and operation requirements, PKI topology will also change. There are three deployments models we can use to address the PKI requirements. In this section, we will look into these models and their characteristics.

The single-tier model

This model is also called as **one-tier model**, and it is the simplest deployment model for PKI. This is not recommended to use in any production network, as its single point of failure of entire PKI:

root and issuing CA

In this model, a single CA will act as **root CA and issuing CA**. As I explained before, the root CA is the highest trusted CA in PKI hierarchy. Any compromise to the root CA will compromise the entire PKI. In this model, it's a single server, so any compromise on the server will easily compromise the entire PKI, as it doesn't need to spread through different hierarchy levels. This model is easy to implement and easy to manage. Because of that event, it's not recommended; this model exists in corporate networks.

Some CA aware applications require certificates in order to function. **System Center Operations Manager** (**SCOM**) is one of those examples. It uses certificates to secure web interfaces, authenticate management servers, and many more. If the organization doesn't have an internal CA, the option is to purchase certificates from vendor or to deploy a new CA. In similar situations, engineers usually use this single-tier model as its only use for a specific application or task:

Advantages	Disadvantages
Less resources and low cost to manage as it's all running from a single server. It also reduces the license cost for the operating systems.	High possibility of getting compromise as root CA is online and running the entire PKI-related roles from one single server. If someone gets the access to a private key of the root CA, he has complete ownership over the PKI.
Faster deployment and it is possible to get the CA running in a short period of time.	Lack of redundancy as certificate issuing and management all depend on single server and availability of it will decide the availability of PKI.
N/A	It is not scalable, and it will need to restructure the hierarchy if need to add more role servers.
N/A	All the certificate issuing and management is done by one server and all the work requests have to be handled by it. It creates a performance bottleneck.

The two-tier model

This is the most commonly used PKI deployment model in corporate networks. By design, the root CA needs to keep offline, and it will prevent the private key of the root certificate from being compromised. Root CAs will issue certificates for subordinate CAs, and subordinate CAs are responsible for issuing certificates for objects and services:

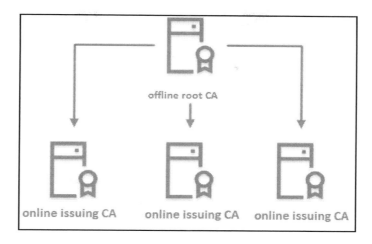

If a subordinate CA's certificate expires, the **offline root CA** will need to bring online to renew the certificate. Root CA doesn't need to be a domain member, and it should be operating in a work-group level (a stand-alone CA). Therefore, the certificate enrollment, approval, and renewal will be a manual process. This is a scalable solution and the number of issuing CAs can be increased based on workloads. This allows to extend the CA boundaries to multiple sites too. In a single-tier model if PKI got compromised, in order to recover all the issues certificates, need to be manually removed from the devices. In a two-tier model, revoke the certificates issued by CA, publish CRL, and then reissue the certificates:

Advantages	Disadvantages
Improved PKI security as the root CA is offline and it's been protected by private key been compromised.	High maintenance—needs to maintain multiple systems and needs skills to process the manual certificates request/approval/renewal between the root and subordinate CAs
Flexible scalability—can start small and expand by adding additional subordinate CAs when required.	Cost—the cost of resources and licenses are high compared to a single-tier model
Restrict the issuing CA impact in CA hierarchy by controlling certificates scope. It will prevent issuing the *rouge* certificates.	The manual certificate renewal process between root CA and subordinate CAs adds additional risks; if administrators forget to renew it on time, it can bring the whole PKI down.

Improved performances as workloads can be shared among multiple subordinate CAs.	N/A
Flexible maintenance capabilities as less dependencies.	N/A

Three-tier models

The three-tier model is the highest in the model list, which operates with greater security, scalability, and control. Similar to a two-tier model, it also has an offline root CA and online issuing CAs. In addition to that, there will be offline intermediate CAs, which operates between the root and subordinate CAs. The main reason for it is to operate intermediate CAs as policy CAs. In larger organizations, different departments, different sites, and different operation units can have different certificate requirements. As an example, a certificate issued to a perimeter network will required manual approval process while others users in the corporate network prefer auto approval. IT teams prefer to have advanced cryptographic provider for its certificates and large keys while other users operate with the default RSA algorithms. All these different requirements are defined by the policy CA, and it publishes relevant templates and procedures to the other CAs:

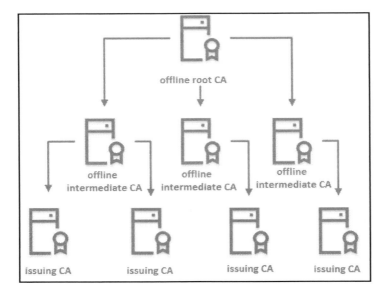

This model adds another layer of security to the hierarchy. However, if you are not using CA policies, the intermediate tier will be of no use. It can be a waste of money and resources. Therefore, most of the organizations prefer a two-tier model to start with and then expand as required.

In this model, both the root CA and intermediate CAs operates as stand-alone CAs. Root CA only will issue certificates to intermediate CAs and those will only issue certificate to issuing CAs:

Advantages	Disadvantage
Improved security as it adds another layer of CAs to the certificate verification.	Cost—the cost of resources and licenses are high as its need to maintain three layers. It also increases the operation cost.
Greater scalability as each tier can span horizontally.	High maintenance—when the number of servers increases, the efforts needed to maintain those also increases. Both the tiers that operates stand-alone CAs require additional maintenance as it's not supported for automatic certificate request/approval/renewal.
In the event of a compromise of the issuing CA, the intermediate CA can revoke the compromised CA with minimum impact to the existing setup.	The implementation complexity is high as compared to other models.
High-performance setup as workloads are distributed and administrative boundaries are well defined by intermediate CAs.	N/A
Improved control over certificate policies and allows enterprises to have tailored certificates.	N/A
High availability as dependencies are further reduced.	N/A

Setting up PKI

Now, we have finished the theory part of this chapter and are moving on to the deployment part. In this section, I am going to demonstrate how we can set up a PKI using the two-tier model. I have used this model as it is the most commonly user model for mid and large organizations:

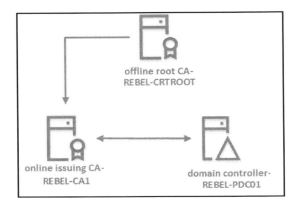

The preceding diagram explains the setup I am going to do. In there I have one domain controller, one stand-alone root CA, and one issuing CA. All are running with Windows Server 2016 with the latest patch level.

Setting up a stand-alone root CA

The first step is to set up the stand-alone root CA. This is not a domain member server, and it is operating in the workgroup level. By configuring it on separate VLAN will add additional security to the root CA, as it will not be able to talk to each other directly even if it is online.

Once the server is ready, log into the server as the member of local administrator group. The first task is to install the AD CS role service. It can be done using the following command:

```
Add-WindowsFeature ADCS-Cert-Authority -IncludeManagementTools
```

Once the role service is installed, the next step is to configure the role and get the CA up and running:

```
Install-ADcsCertificationAuthority -CACommonName "REBELAdmin Root CA" -
CAType StandaloneRootCA -CryptoProviderName "RSA#Microsoft Software Key
Storage Provider" -HashAlgorithmName SHA256 -KeyLength 2048 -ValidityPeriod
Years -ValidityPeriodUnits 20
```

The preceding command will configure the CA. In the -CACommonName command, define the common name for the CA. -CAType defines the CA operation type. In our case, it is -StandaloneRootCA. The option for it will be EnterpriseRootCA, EnterpriseSubordinateCA, or StandaloneSubordinateCA. -CryptoProviderName specifies the cryptographic service provider and in the demo; I am using the Microsoft default service provider. -HashAlgorithmName defines the hashing algorithm used by the CA. The option for it will be changed, based on the CSP we choose. SHA1 is no longer counted as secure algorithm; it is recommended to use SHA256 or more. -KeyLength specifies the key size for the algorithm. In this demo, I am using the 2048 key. -ValidityPeriod defines the validity period of CA certificates. It can be hours, days, weeks, months, or years. -ValidityPeriodUnits is followed by -ValidityPeriod and specifies how many hours, days, weeks, months, or years it will be valid for. In our demo, we are using 20 years:

Now, we have the root CA up and running. But before we use it, we need to do certain configuration changes.

DSConfigDN

As I mentioned earlier, this is a stand-alone root CA, and it is not part of the domain. However, **CRL Distribution Points (CDP)** and **authority information access** (AIA) locations, which are required by the CA, will be stored in DC. Since they use DN names with a domain, the root CA needs to be aware of the domain information to publish it properly. It will retrieve this information via a registry key:

```
certutil.exe -setreg ca\DSConfigDN CN=Configuration,DC=rebeladmin,DC=com
```

CDP locations

CDP is defined as the location where CRL can be retrieved from. This is web-based location and should be able to access via HTTP. This list will be used by the certificate validator to verify the given certificate is not in revocation list.

Before we do this, we need to prepare the web server for that task. It should be a web server in domain as the issuing CA also in a domain.

In my demo, I am going to use the same issue CA as the CDP location.

The web server can be installed using the following command:

```
Install-WindowsFeature Web-WebServer -IncludeManagementTools
```

Next, create a folder and create share so that can be use as the virtual directory:

```
mkdir C:\CertEnroll
New-smbshare -name CertEnroll C:\CertEnroll -FullAccess
SYSTEM,"rebeladmin\Domain Admins" -ChangeAccess "rebeladmin\Cert
Publishers"
```

As part of the exercise, it will set share permissions to rebeladmin\Domain Admins (full access) and rebeladmin\Cert Publishers (change access).

After that load the IIS manager and add a virtual directory `CertEnroll` with the aforementioned path:

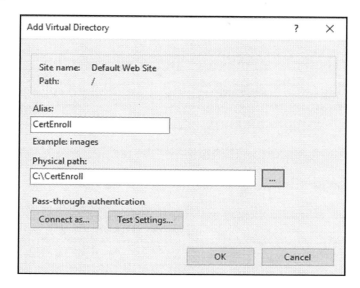

Last but not the least, we need to create a DNS record to use this publication point using FQDN. In this demo, I am using `crt.rebeladmin.com`. This will allow to access the new distribution point using `http://crt.rebeladmin.com/CertEnroll`.

Now, everything is ready, and we can publish the CDP settings using the following command:

```
certutil -setreg CA\CRLPublicationURLs
"1:C:\Windows\system32\CertSrv\CertEnroll\%3%8%9.crl
\n10:ldap:///CN=%7%8,CN=%2,CN=CDP,CN=Public Key
Services,CN=Services,%6%10\n2:http://crt.rebeladmin.com/CertEnroll/%3%8%9.c
rl"
```

The single numbers in the command refer to the options and numbers with % refers to the variables:

Option	Details
0	No changes
1	Publish CRL to the given location
2	Attach CDP extensions of issued certificates

4	Include in CRL to find the delta CRL locations
8	Specify if need to publish all CRL info to AD when publishing manually
64	Delta CRL location
128	Include the IDP extension of issued CRL

All these settings can be specified using GUI. In order to access it, go to the **Server Manager** | **Tools** | **Certification Authority**, right-click, and select **Properties** of the server and go to the **Extension** tab.

There you can add all the preceding using GUI:

Variable	GUI Reference	Details
%1	<ServerDNSName>	The DNS name of the CA server
%2	<ServerShortName>	NetBIOS name of the CA server
%3	<CAName>	Given name for the CA
%4	<CertificateName>	Renewal extension of the CA
%6	<ConfigurationContainer>	DN of the configuration container in AD
%7	<CATruncatedName>	Truncated name of the CA (32 Characters)
%8	<CRLNameSuffix>	Inserts a name suffix at the end of the filename before publishing a CRL
%9	<DeltaCRLAllowed>	When this called, this will replace the CRLNameSuffix with a separate suffix to use the delta CRL
%10	<CDPObjectClass>	Object class identifier for CDP
%11	<CAObjectClass>	Object class identifier for a CA

AIA locations

AIA is an extension, which is in the certificate and defines the location where the application or the service can retrieve issuing CA's certificate. This is also a web-based path, and we can use the same location we used for the CDP.

This can be set using the following command:

```
certutil —setreg CA\CACertPublicationURLs
"1:C:\Windows\system32\CertSrv\CertEnroll\%1_%3%4.crt\n2:ldap:///CN=%7,CN=A
IA,CN=Public Key
Services,CN=Services,%6%11\n2:http://crt.rebeladmin.com/CertEnroll/%1_%3%4.
crt"
```

The options are very much similar to the CDP with a few smaller changes:

Option	Details
0	No changes
1	Publish CA certificate to given location
2	Attach AIA extensions of issued certificates
32	Attach **Online Certificate Status Protocol (OCSP)** Extensions

CA time limits

When we set up the CA, we have defined the CA validity period as 20 years. But it doesn't mean every certificate it issues will have 20 years' valid period. Root CAs will issue certificates only to the issuing CAs. Certificate requests, approval, and renewal processes are manual. Therefore, these certificates will have longer validity periods. In the demo, I will set it for 10 years:

```
certutil —setreg ca\ValidityPeriod "Years"
certutil —setreg ca\ValidityPeriodUnits 10
```

CRL time limits

CRL also has some time limits associated:

```
Certutil —setreg CA\CRLPeriodUnits 13
Certutil —setreg CA\CRLPeriod "Weeks"
Certutil —setreg CA\CRLDeltaPeriodUnits 0
Certutil —setreg CA\CRLOverlapPeriodUnits 6
Certutil —setreg CA\CRLOverlapPeriod "Hours"
```

In the preceding commands:

- `CRLPeriodUnits`: This specifies the number of days, weeks, months or years CRL will be valid.
- `CRLPeriod`: This specifies whether CRL validity period is measured by days, weeks, months or years.
- `CRLDeltaPeriodUnit`: This specifies the number of days, weeks, months or years delta CRL will be valid. For offline CA, this should be disabled.
- `CRLOverlapPeriodUnits`: This specifies the number of days, weeks, months, or years that CRL can overlap.
- `CRLOverlapPeriod`: This specifies whether the CRL overlapping validity period is measured by days, weeks, months, or years.

Now, we have all the settings submitted; and in order to apply the changes, the certificate service need to be restarted:

```
restart-service certsvc
```

The new CRL

The next step is to create a new CRL, and it can be generated using the following command:

```
certutil -crl
```

Once it's done, there will be two files under `C:\Windows\System32\CertSrv\CertEnroll`:

```
PS C:\Users\Administrator> cd C:\Windows\System32\CertSrv\CertEnroll
PS C:\Windows\System32\CertSrv\CertEnroll> dir


    Directory: C:\Windows\System32\CertSrv\CertEnroll


Mode                LastWriteTime         Length Name
----                -------------         ------ ----
-a----        22/03/2017     21:05            793 REBEL-CRTROOT_REBELAdmin Root CA.crt
-a----        22/03/2017     23:00            694 REBELAdmin Root CA.crl


PS C:\Windows\System32\CertSrv\CertEnroll>
```

Publishing the root CA data into the Active Directory

In the preceding list, we have two files on of which ends with `.crt`. This is the root CA certificate. In order to be trusted by other clients in the domain, it needs to publish to the Active Directory. To do that, copy this file from the root CA to Active Directory server. Then, log into AD as the Domain Admin or Enterprise Admin and run the command:

```
certutil -f -dspublish "REBEL-CRTROOT_REBELAdmin Root CA.crt" RootCA
```

The next file ends with `.crl`. This is the root CA's CRL. This also needs to publish to AD. So, everyone in the domain is aware of that too. In order to do that, copy the file from root CA to domain controller and run the command:

```
certutil -f -dspublish "REBELAdmin Root CA.crl"
```

Setting up the issuing CA

Now that we finished with the root CA setup, the next step is to set up the issuing CA. Issuing CAs will be running from a domain member server and will be AD integrated. In order to perform the installation, log into the server as the Domain Admin or Enterprise Admin.

First task will be to install the AD CS role:

```
Add-WindowsFeature ADCS-Cert-Authority -IncludeManagementTools
```

I will use the same server for the web enrollment role service from the same service. So, it can be added using the following command:

```
Add-WindowsFeature ADCS-web-enrollment
```

After that, we can configure the role service using the following command:

```
Install-ADcsCertificationAuthority -CACommonName "REBELAdmin IssuingCA" -
CAType EnterpriseSubordinateCA -CryptoProviderName "RSA#Microsoft Software
Key Storage Provider" -HashAlgorithmName SHA256 -KeyLength 2048
```

In order to configure the web enrollment role service, use the following command:

```
Install-ADCSwebenrollment
```

Issuing a certificate for the issuing CA

In order to get AD CS running on the issuing CA, it needs the certificate issued from the parent CA, which is the root CA we just deployed. During the role configuration process, it automatically creates the certificate request under C:\, and exact filename will be listed in command output from the previous command:

```
PS C:\Users\administrator.REBELADMIN> Install-ADcsCertificationAuthority -CACommonName REBELAdmin IssuingCA -CAType En
terpriseSubordinateCA -CryptoProviderName RSA#Microsoft Software Key Storage Provider -HashAlgorithmName SHA256 -KeyLe
ngth 2048

Confirm
Are you sure you want to perform this action?
Performing the operation "Install-AdcsCertificationAuthority" on target "REBEL-CA1".
[Y] Yes  [A] Yes to All  [N] No  [L] No to All  [S] Suspend  [?] Help (default is "Y"): A
WARNING: The Active Directory Certificate Services installation is incomplete. To complete the installation, use the
request file "C:\REBEL-CA1.rebeladmin.com_REBELAdmin IssuingCA.req" to obtain a certificate from the parent CA. Then,
use the Certification Authority snap-in to install the certificate. To complete this procedure, right-click the node
with the name of the CA, and then click Install CA Certificate. The operation completed successfully. 0x0 (WIN32: 0)

ErrorId ErrorString
------- -----------
    398 The Active Directory Certificate Services installation is incomplete. To complete the installation, use the ...
```

The file needs to copy from the issuing CA to the root CA and execute the command:

```
certreq –submit "REBEL–CA1.rebeladmin.com_REBELAdmin IssuingCA.req"
```

As I explained before, any request to root CA will be processed manually, and this request will be waiting for a manual approval. In order to approve the certificate, go to **Server Manager** | **Tools** | **Certification Authority** | Pending Requests; right-click on the certificate and select **All Tasks** | **Issue**:

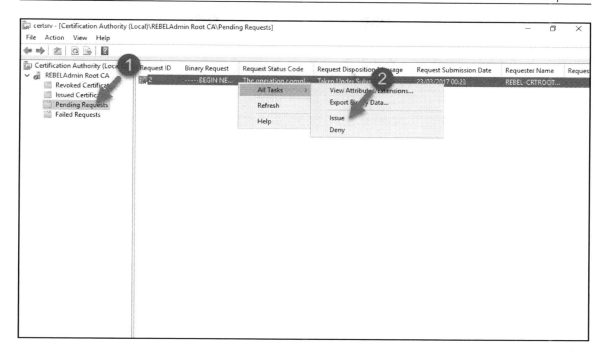

Once it is issued, it needs to be exported and imported into issuing CA:

```
certreq -retrieve 2 "C:\REBEL-CA1.rebeladmin.com_REBELAdmin_IssuingCA.crt"
```

The preceding command will export the certificate. The number 2 is the *request ID* in the CA MMC.

Once it exports, move the file to the issuing CA, and from there, run this command:

```
Certutil -installcert "C:\REBEL-
CA1.rebeladmin.com_REBELAdmin_IssuingCA.crt"
start-service certsvc
```

Post configuration tasks

Similar to the root CA, after the initial service set up, we need to define some configuration values.

CDP locations

The CDP location is similar to the root CA, and I am going to use the already created web location for it:

```
certutil -setreg CA\CRLPublicationURLs
"1:%WINDIR%\system32\CertSrv\CertEnroll\%3%8%9.crl\n2:http://crt.rebeladmin
.com/CertEnroll/%3%8%9.crl\n3:ldap:///CN=%7%8,CN=%2,CN=CDP,CN=Public Key
Services,CN=Services,%6%10"
```

AIA locations

In a similar way AIA location also can be specified using the following command:

```
certutil -setreg CA\CACertPublicationURLs
"1:%WINDIR%\system32\CertSrv\CertEnroll\%1_%3%4.crt\n2:http://crt.rebeladmi
n.com/CertEnroll/%1_%3%4.crt\n3:ldap:///CN=%7,CN=AIA,CN=Public Key
Services,CN=Services,%6%11"
```

CA and CRL time limits

CA and CRL time limits also need to be adjusted. This can be done using the following command:

```
certutil -setreg CA\CRLPeriodUnits 7
certutil -setreg CA\CRLPeriod "Days"
certutil -setreg CA\CRLOverlapPeriodUnits 3
certutil -setreg CA\CRLOverlapPeriod "Days"
certutil -setreg CA\CRLDeltaPeriodUnits 0
certutil -setreg ca\ValidityPeriodUnits 3
certutil -setreg ca\ValidityPeriod "Years"
```

Once all this is done, in order to complete the configuration, restart the certificate service using the following command:

```
restart-service certsvc
```

Last but not the least, run the following command:

```
certutil -crl
```

Once all done, to generate CRLs, we can run `PKIView.msc` to verify the configuration:

 `PKIView.msc` was first introduced with Windows 2003, and it gives visibility over enterprise PKI configuration. It also verifies the certificates and CRL for each CA to maintain the integrity.

Certificate templates

Now, we have the working PKI, and we can turn off the stand-alone root CA. It should only be brought online if the issuing CA certificates are expired or PKI is compromised to generate new certificates.

Once the CA is ready, then objects and services can be used for certificates. The CA comes with the predefined **Certificates Templates**. These can be used to build custom certificate templates according to the organization requirements and publish it to AD.

The **Certificate Templates** MMC can be accessed using **Run** | **MMC** | **File** | **Add/Remove Snap-in...** | **Certificate Templates**.

To create a custom template, right-click on a template and click on **Duplicate Template**:

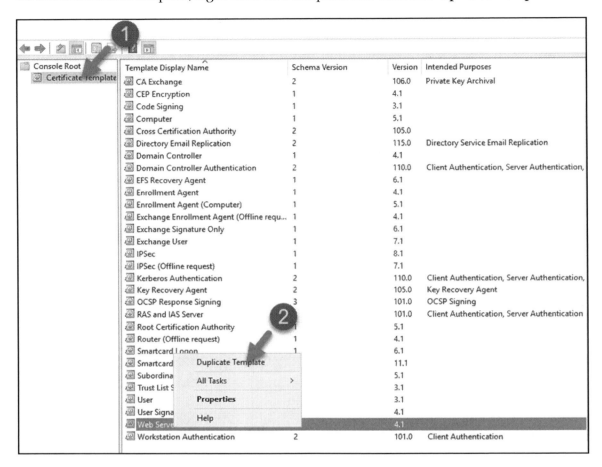

Then, it will open up the properties window and can change the settings of the certificate template to match the requirements. Some common settings to change in templates are:

- **Template display name** (the **General** tab): Display name of the template
- **Template name** (the **General** tab): Common name of the template
- **Validity period** (the **General** tab): Certificate validity period

- **Security**: Authenticated users or groups must have **Enroll** permission to request certificates:

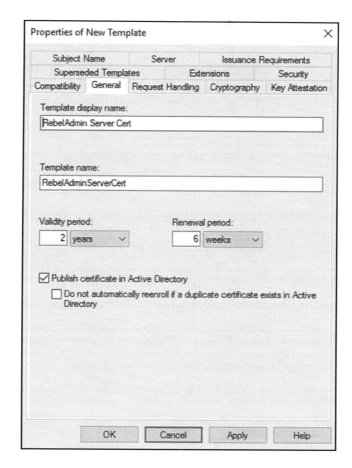

Next step before use it to issue the certificate template. Then, the members of the domain can request certificates based on that.

To do so, go to the **Certification Authority** MMC | **Certificate Templates**, right-click on it and select **New** | **Certificate Template to Issue**.

Then, from the list, select the template to issue and click on **OK**:

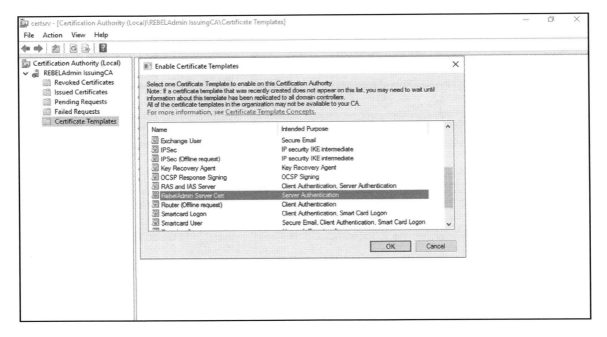

Requesting certificates

Based on the published certificates templates, users can request certificates from the issuing CA. I have logged into an end user PC and am going to request a certificate based on the template we just created in the previous step.

Go to **Run**, type MMC | **Add/Remove Snap-in...** | **Certificates**, click on the **Add** button.

From the list, select the computer account to manage certificates for computer object. This is depended on the template. Once selected, in next window, select **Local computer** as the target.

> If the user is not an administrator, with default permission, it will only allow to open the **Current User** snap in. To open the computer account, MMC needs to **Run as administrator**.

Once MMC is loaded, go to the `Personal` container, right-click, and then follow **All Tasks | Request New Certificate**.

It will open a new window and click next until it reaches the request certificate window. In there, we can see the new template. Click on the checkbox to select the certificate template, and then click on link with yellow warning sign to provide additional details, which are required for the certificate:

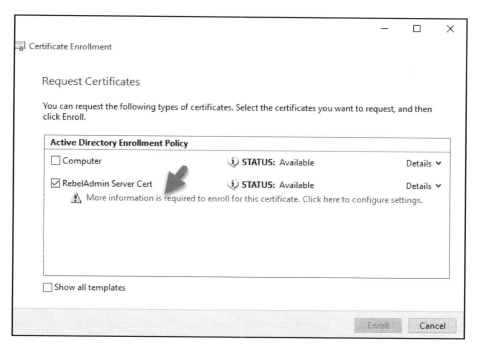

Provide the required fields and click on **OK** to proceed. Most of the times, its **Common name** which required if its computer certificate:

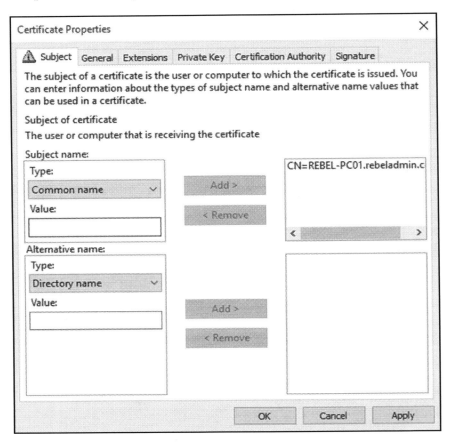

Once it's done, click on **Enroll** to request the certificate. Then, it will automatically process the certificate request and issue the certificate. Once it's issued, it can be found under the `Personal` | `Certificate` container:

We can see a valid certificate is issued. At the same time, information about this issued certificate can be found under the issuing CA's **Certification Authority** MMC | **Issued Certificate**.

In this exercise, you learned how to set up a two-tier PKI from top to bottom. After the setup, as any other system, regular maintenance is required to keep up the good health. Also, it is important to have proper documentation about the setup, certificate templates, and procedures to issue, renew and revoke different types of certificates.

Summary

Digital certificates are more and more used in modern infrastructure as additional layers of security to prove the objects and services are genuine, and they are the same objects and services they claim to be. In this chapter, you learned what PKI is and how it exactly works in the infrastructure. Then, we looked into AD CS components and their duties. Later, we moved into the PKI planning and discussed what needs to be considered when building PKI. Then, we further looked into PKI deployment models and evaluated their advantages and disadvantages. Last but not the least, we went through a step-by-step guide to set up two-tier PKI successfully.

In the next chapter, you are going to learn about another Active Directory role service—Active Directory Federation Service, and see how identities have been handled in a federated environment.

13

Active Directory Federation Services

My city is famous around the globe because of Hampton Court Palace. It was redeveloped by Cardinal Thomas Wolsey, and in 1529, the famous king Henry VIII seized the palace; and until 1760, it used to be a royal residence for kings and queens. One side of the palace is protected by the river Thames and the palace itself is further surrounded by high walls. Life in the palace is protected by these strong walls. In and out to the palace been controlled by guards. Even in an attack, it is not easy to bring down a castle as they always get the benefits of strong walls. Castles create a big gap between the outside world and the life inside.

The days of castles are gone now, we no longer live in the similar small world. We are living in a society where everyone is connected. In cities, we no longer see the high, strong walls like in the castles before. The well-connected society gives a lot of benefits to human beings, but it's not the only outcome. I am writing this chapter just less than 48 hours after the London Westminster terrorist attack. London is a city where we welcome everyone. It's a great, strong city, but this connected society brings vulnerabilities from time to time.

Modern businesses operation boundaries are no longer in a closed or isolated mode. As an example, from on-premises applications, organizations are moving into cloud-based versions. Computer workloads are moving to public or hybrid cloud infrastructures. All these different systems are also bounds to authentication and authorization.

In the AD environment, most of the systems or applications can be integrated with it, and they use one username and password to access systems (single sign-on). When we extend the identity infrastructure boundaries, we may start to loose control over it, as these system identities are managed by vendors or other organizations.

Therefore, it usually can ends up having different user accounts and passwords to log in to different systems. From the end user's perspective, it's just different accounts for different systems, but from the service provider's perspective, it's more than that.

Imagine that we have an application developed in-house, and we want to sell it as a service. External users need to access it and in order to authenticate, we have to create a username and password for every one of them. Setting an account is not the only thing we need to consider; when we create account, it becomes a part of our identity infrastructure. We need to make sure it's secured and only has access to that particular application. All of a sudden, the identity management got new challenges, and if it's not handled appropriately, it can bring vulnerabilities to the whole system. Instead of mixing identities in such scenarios, **Active Directory Federation Services (AD FS)** allows businesses to manage their own identity infrastructures and use *claim*-based authentication to the resources. So, users do not need to use a separate login to access, and the resource owners do not need to keep managing identities for external users. In this chapter, you are going to learn about the following:

- What is AD FS and how does it work?
- AD FS components and how to use them in the AD FS setup
- AD FS deployment and management
- MFA in action
- Integrating with Microsoft Azure

How does AD FS work?

Rebeladmin Inc. is an IT service provider. There are many customers who use different IT and cloud services from the company. Recently, the company introduced a new web-based control panel where customers can access their resources. The same application also used internal staff to manage the infrastructure services. Rebeladmin Inc. uses **Active Directory Domain Service (AD DS)** to manage identities. When the internal IT staff logs into the portal, it doesn't ask for any login details. It is because the web application uses **integrated Windows authentication (IWF)** to allow access. This is also called **NTLM authentication** or **domain authentication**. It doesn't prompt for the login information initially and transfer hashed data about the current logged in user to the web server and check if it's allowed. This web server is domain-joined and the application in itself is AD integrated. Now, users from the Depache solution also like to get access to the same portal to manage their workloads, which is hosted with Rebeladmin Inc.

There are two ways to facilitate this:

- **Using a user account in Rebeladmin Inc. AD**: When external users try to access the web portal, the initial IWF will fail as the application doesn't understand the external users' accounts. Then, it will prompt for login details. If a user has an account in Rebeladmin Inc., AD instance, it can be used to authenticate into the portal. This involves several security-related issues. When users have an account in AD, by default, it allows users to access any resources, which have *everyone* or *authenticated users*. In the internal network, it is possible to force users to follow policies and best practices to protect their identities. But it is not possible to apply the same standard to an external party. So, these accounts have a high possibility of getting compromised. As an example, if an internal user resigns, normally his/her AD user login will be reset and disabled, but if it's an account which is shared with external, even the relevant user resigns, he/she may still have access to portal (until it is informed). Some vendors use **Active Directory Lightweight Directory Services (AD LDS)** for each customer to minimize the security impact. But this still adds management overhead to keep different instances running.

- **AD trust between two infrastructures**: When there is AD trust, resources access can be allowed from remote infrastructures. In order to have successful trust, there should be a physical connection between two infrastructures and it will be based on TCP/UDP ports such as 389 (LDAP), 53 (**Domain Name System (DNS)**) and so on. These ports need to be allowed via firewalls in both the infrastructures. It adds additional management tasks for both the infrastructures to protect their confidential data from being exposed to each other.

As we can see, even though both the options can allow *access* from the external infrastructures, both struggle with security and management related challenges.

Federation trust will be the answer for all these concerns. In simple English, the federation service is a web service, which authenticates users from the **Identity Provider (IdP)** and provides access to claim-based applications from the **Service Provider (SP)**. There are many federation service providers and the Microsoft federation service is called **Active Directory Federation Service**:

In the preceding example, Rebeladmin Inc. is using the AD DS to manage the identities. Its users are going to use a hosted web application (**MyHostedApp1**) from a cloud service provider. Rebeladmin Inc. uses AD FS in order to create federation trust between Rebeladmin Inc. and the SP. It will allow the Rebeladmin Inc. users to launch **MyHostedApp1** using the same Windows credentials. In this setup, the federation service is hosted in the Rebeladmin Inc. infrastructure and it becomes the IdP. In AD FS' point of view, it also called **Claims Provider (CP)**. It is because that's where the actual authentication happens. The vendors who host the application also have their own identity infrastructure. The application vendor becomes the SP, also known as the **Relying Party (RP),** in federation trust; and it depends on the claims provided by the federation service to allow/deny access to the application from the Rebeladmin Inc. users. This setup does not need to open additional firewall rules either. This is based on a secure connection via TCP port 443.

Even if it is called *trust*, it cannot be used to replace AD domain or Forest Trusts. If the AD trust is in place, administrators can manage access to resources from remote users in the exact same way it was done for internal users. Users can be allowed to access folders and files based on NTFS permissions. Users can be allowed to log in to devices. Any application's work with internal users can be allowed for remote users too. But in a federated environment, the access can only be allowed to *claims aware* applications. Claims is simply an attribute and a relative value. As an example, claim can have attribute usernames and its value, dfrancis. Federation Service will request access from the SP based on the claims. If the SP's application doesn't understand *claims,* it cannot decide whether to allow or deny access:

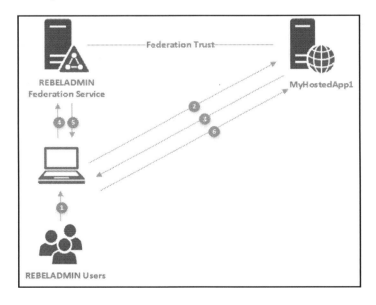

Let's revisit the previous example with a detailed explanation to understand how exactly it works behind the scenes:

1. In the first step, the Rebeladmin Inc. user logs in to a computer in the Rebeladmin Inc. infrastructure. This is a domain-joined device. The user used his domain credentials to log in to the device.

2. Once the user is logged into the device successfully, the user launches his web browser and types the URL for **MyHostedApp1**. This application is hosted in the remote infrastructure.

3. As soon as the application receives the access request from the Rebeladmin Inc. user, it first checks the data passing through the browser (Integrated Windows Authentication). Then, it realizes it is not from the internal infrastructure, but it's an account from the identity infrastructure, which the SP have federated relationship. If it's from a federate environment, the user access rights need to be decided based on claims. Therefore, the SP sends a redirect response to redirect users to the Rebeladmin Inc. federation service web interface.

4. Users are automatically redirected to the Rebeladmin Inc. federation service web interface. In the web interface, users have to type in their login details.

5. Once the user provides their credentials, it will be validated with Rebeladmin Inc. AD DS and will retrieve its access rights. Then, the Federation service will create a security token including user claims, such as name, group memberships, UPN, and email address. This security token will be signed by the issuer's digital certificate. At the end of the process, federation services send responses back to the user with a generated security token plus a `redirect` command to redirect the user browser back to MyHostedApp1.

6. The user browser is redirected to the hosted application, and this time, its present with the security token it received from the federation service. Then, the web server claims-aware agent decrypts the security token and looks into the claims it provided. Based on the claims, it will decide whether the user is allowed to access the application or not. If the claims are accepted, the user will be able to see the initial page of the application successfully.

In the preceding scenario, the federation trust is made directly with the application. But in some scenarios, the SP will also have the federation service environment on its end. This is mainly when the service provider has multiple clients with federation trusts. In such situation:

- When the application finds out that user needs to log in via the federation, the user will initially redirect to the service provider's federation service.

- Then, the SP's federation service will redirect the user to Rebeladmin's federation service.

- Once the user receives the security token, it will present it to the SP's federation service. It will decrypt the token and retrieve the claims inside it. Then, it will map claims to the SP's claims and filter it to match with application claims requirements.
- Based on the filtered claims, the SP's federation service creates a new security token and it signed using the SP's federation service digital certificate. This new security token is the one will forward to the application server.

AD FS also supports many industry standards, which are used to build third-party, claim-based solutions. It guarantees the interoperability with many cloud-based or hosted applications in the market today.

Security Assertion Markup Language (SAML)

In the federated environment, the IdP and the SP need to exchange the authentication and authorization data. SAML is a XML-based standard format to present the data. This standard was first introduced in 2001 by OASIS Security Services Technical Committee and the latest version available is 2.0. This is a commonly used standard by many federation service providers and application developers to provide a **single sign-on** (**SSO**) experience. Claims request and processing of it is exactly the same as the example used in the previous section and the only difference will be the format of the token request and response. It will use signed XML files as the token. In the SAML terminology, generated security tokens in IdP end are called **asserts** and the decryption and processing of the assert in the SP end is called **assertion**.

WS-Trust

This is part of many the WS* standards including WS-Security, WS-Federation, and the WS-Security policy. **WS** stands for **Web Services**. WS-Trust defines protocols used in requesting and issuing security token by WS-Security. **Security Token Service** (**STS**) is a big feature in WS-Trust, and it can be uses to convert locally issued security tokens into another security token formats, which can be understood by the application. It also can convert incoming security tokens into supported token formats.

WS-Federation

WS-Federation is also a part of WS* standards. While SAML only works with the SAML token, WS-Federation supports to use many token types including SAML. Basically, WS-Federation provides a mechanism to simplify the communication between an IdP and a service provider. The fundamental goal of WS-Federation is to simplify the development of federated services through cross-realm communication and management of Federation Services by reusing the WS-Trust Security Token Service model and protocol. More information about WS-Federation can be found at `http://download.boulder.ibm.com/ib mdl/pub/software/dw/specs/ws-fed/WS-FederationSpec05282007.pdf?S_TACT=105AGX 04&S_CMP=LP`.

AD FS components

When the AD FS role is installed, there are few related components we need to be aware of. Before Windows Server 2012 R2, there were four AD FS roles services: the federation service, the federation service proxy, the claim-aware agent, and windows token-based agent (to support the AD FS 1.x interoperability). These are no longer available as role services; and when go to install AD FS, it will only have the Federation Service role.

Federation Service

This is the main role service for the AD FS, and it can work on IdP as well as the SP end. In order to install the AD FS role service, system needs to be a member server of an AD domain. Depending on the workload, multiple federation servers can be installed under the same domain, and it is called as **AD FS Farm**. The federation server is responsible for generating security tokens and signing them with its signing certificate. There have been very few versions of AD FS so far.

AD FS 1.0

AD FS first introduced with Windows Server 2003 R2. This version of AD FS is no longer available as Windows Server 2003 is end of life. This provided basic SSO capabilities, but it mainly suffered because of less compatibility with other federation service providers in the market.

AD FS 1.1

This was introduced with Windows 2008, and it did continue to Windows Server 2008 R2. It doesn't have much changes from 1.0. It suffered from limited support to other federation services. It only supported the WS-Federation passive requester profile and SAML 1.0.

AD FS 2.0

This version was released after Windows Server 2008 R2 but as a separate installation (download via web). All other versions came as part of the operating system. Before version 2.0, it was supported to use AD LDS as the authentication store. This means users can authenticate with AD LDS similar to AD. With version 2.0, it no longer supports LDS to act as the account store. It can work as the attribute store, which can store AD FS data but it cannot be used for authentication. AD FS 2.0 also supports a parent-child domain environment, so users in child domain can use AD FS in another domain for the federation. It reduces the management overhead. It also improved support for federation trusts with the use of industry-standard metadata formats. It allows organizations to create trust between federation partners quickly. Systems that run with version 1.x can have an in-place upgrade to 2.0 (if still trust).

AD FS 2.1

This version comes with Windows Server 2012 and did not have major changes from the 2.0. This is also available to download from the web and install in Windows Server 2008 and 2008 R2.

AD FS 3.0

This version was introduced with Windows Server 2012 R2. This removed a few role services from the AD FS 2.0. AD FS Proxy service provided interface between the internet and AD FS servers. It operates from the **demilitarized zone (DMZ)** and doesn't need to be domain joined. The idea of it is to protect the identity infrastructure with bogus token. This was replaced by Web Application Proxy, which comes under remote access role. This is not used by AD FS anymore. It also removed the AD FS web agents 1.x, which provided connections with other systems.

Workspace Join is one of the greatest features that came up with this. It allows to register mobile devices (even non-windows) with corporates to access application and data with SSO. AD FS 3.0 does not require IIS anymore and is installed as a separate role. It also supports **Group Managed Service Account (gMSA)**. This is a new type of service account, which supports automatic password changes. The creation and management of this accounts is explained in `Chapter 8`, *Managing Users, Groups, and Devices*. This version also supports the OAuth 2 standard access tokens. Those are JSON format tokens and are easy to use with modern applications. This version also gives more control over customizing AD FS web interface to match with company themes.

AD FS 4.0

AD FS 4.0 is the latest version available with Windows Server 2016. This is what we will be using throughout this chapter. This version is supported for modern hybrid cloud requirements. If you are already using Azure AD, this version allows to use Microsoft **Azure Multi-Factor Authentication (Azure MFA)** without additional components' installation and configuration. Before, it needed an additional server to configure. With the new version, AD FS have Azure MFA adapter built-in. Similar to AD FS 3.0, the new version also supports mobile device registration to maintain the organization compliance requirements. If it's in Azure AD environment, using AD FS, it can apply conditional access policies to on-premises components. This version also supports modern authentication standards, such as OpenID Connect and OAuth 2.0. It provides enhanced user experience with Windows 10 and latest Android and iOS apps. AD FS 4.0 also supports authentication with LDAP v3.0 compliant directories. It allows people to use AD FS more and more even when they are not running AD DS. Windows 10 introduced the new password-less log in methods: Windows Hello and Microsoft Passport. These are based on PIN and biometric input, such as fingerprint or facial recognition. AD FS 4.0 supports these new sign-in methods.

Migration from AD FS 2012 R2 process is been simplified as well. Before if we need to migrate from one version to another, we needed to build a parallel farm and then migrate the configuration over. But with the new version, we can simply add it to the existing Windows Server 2012 R2 farm, and it will start to work in Windows Server 2012 R2 operation level. Once all the Windows Server 2012 R2 servers are removed from the farm, the operation level can upgrade to Windows Server 2016.

The Web Application Proxy

We use proxy servers to access the internet, because it does the required communication with the internet on behalf of the internal users and protects them from external threats. Web application proxy allows to publish web applications (including AD FS) to public without exposing the backend of it. This role is no longer a part of AD FS, and it comes as a part of remote access role. AD FS does not require Web Application Proxy to work, but it is recommended to use if users log in from external networks. It also provides the basic **Denial of Service (DoS)** protection by throttling and quieting connections. The communications between proxy server and web clients are encrypted (based on SSL). Web application proxy is not supported to install on the same AD FS server. It doesn't have built-in load balancing capabilities. If load balancing is required, it can be done using any software or hardware based load balancer, which supports HTTP/HTTPS.

AD FS configuration database

AD FS configuration needs to save in a database. AD FS supports two types of databases. The simple method is to use the **Windows Internal Database (WID)** and it comes with the AD FS installation. This is not a standalone database installation, and it is capable of providing high availability by copying it to other servers in the AD FS farm. When we go for AD FS configuration, it gives two deployment options:

- Creating the first federation server in a federation server farm
- Adding the federation server to a federation server farm

If WID is used with first option, WID will be deployed with scalability, which allows servers to be added to the farm later and replicate WID. The first server will select Primary Server and it hosts the read/write copy of the database.

When we use option 2, the newly added server will replicate the copy of WID from the primary server, and it maintains as a read-only copy. Any configuration change should be replicated from the primary server. In the event of a primary server failure, other servers in the farm continue to process requests as normal, but any configuration change will not be possible until the primary server is brought online. If it's not possible to bring it online, a secondary server can be forcefully nominated as a primary server.

It allows to use Microsoft SQL as the database service provider. This enhances the performance of the AD FS farm if its deals with high traffic as it can do faster read/write to database. The high availability of the database will be based on the SQL setup. If it's set up with the SQL high availability, such as SQL cluster or Always On, the availability will be according to that. This removes the primary server / secondary server concept with WID and every server in the farm has read/write access to the database. If you use SQL database, it also enables support for features such as SAML artifact resolution and SAML/WS-Federation token replay detection. Both the features require a configuration stored in the shared SQL database instead of WID.

AD FS deployment topologies

There are a few different deployment models we can consider on planning AD FS deployment. In this section, let's look into different topologies and their characteristics.

Single Federation Server

This is the simple AD FS deployment using single AD FS server with WID. It will not have high availability (unless in host level). This is ideal for a lab environment or staging environment:

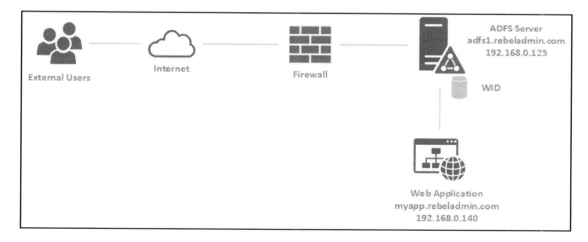

In the preceding example, we have web application, `myapp.rebeladmin.com`, which needs to allow access via AD FS. We have one AD FS server in the setup with WID. It is behind the firewall and there is NAT and access rules setup to do the following:

- Map external IP address to `myapp.rebeladmin.com`, so users can make initial request from external networks. It is recommended to use TCP 443.
- Map external IP address to `secure.rebeladmin.com`, map it to the IP address of `adfs1.rebeladmin.com`, and open TCP 443 from the external to allow access.

It should also have relevant external DNS records set up, and in the internal network, it should have DNS records map to the local IP addresses. That way, when internal users log in, it will only communicate via the internal network.

My recommendation for this setup is to configure the AD FS server with **Network Load Balancer** (**NLB**). It is only going to cost you one additional IP address for the NLB cluster IP. But when we need to expand the AD FS farm, all we need to do is configure another server and add it to the NLB. The cluster IP will map to external IP, and it will be used with external DNS entry for the AD FS. In this setup, no Web Application Proxy has been used:

Advantages	Disadvantages
Low cost to implement. Only one server required for AD FS and no SQL licenses been used as it uses WID.	No redundancy or single point of failure.
Easy to manage	Poor performance as no way to share workloads
No additional service role integration and therefore fewer dependencies.	Less secure as it is not possible to relay the requests to AD FS server, and it will be a direct connection point to process the requests. (no Web Application Proxy)
Still can configure to support future expands and can add servers to the AD FS farm whenever required.	N/A

Single federation server and single Web Application Proxy server

This will be ideal setup to start with. This removes the security concern we had with the single federation server. The Web Application Proxy server will be the initial contact from the external network and it will relay requests in and out from the internal AD FS server. This is still not going to provide high availability as each role holder only runs one server:

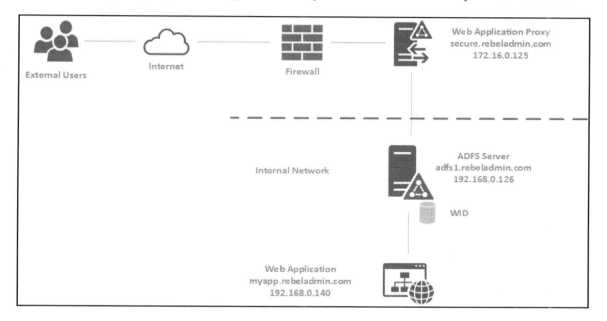

In this setup, we can separate the network functionality into perimeter and corporate networks. In the firewall, there will be following NAT and access rules:

- Map external IP address to myapp.rebeladmin.com so users can make initial request from external networks. It is recommended to use the TCP 443.
- Map external IP address to secure.rebeladmin.com and map it to IP address of Web Application Proxy server and open the TCP 443 from external to allow access.
- Allow access from Web Application Proxy server to AD FS server in the TCP port 443.

In the preceding example, once the external user accesses the application URL, it will redirect to the Web Application Proxy server. This doesn't need to be domain join as it operates from perimeter network. Proxy servers should be able to resolve the DNS name for the AD FS servers from the perimeter network. It can be done using a DNS server or a hosts file.

Similar to the previous model, this can be implemented with NLB to allow future expansion with minimum impact. We need two NLB clusters for that. The first cluster is for the Web Application Proxy and the second NLB cluster is for AD FS servers. The only change will be in the DNS records. Instead of pointing DNS and firewall rules to the server IP addresses, it needs to point to NLB cluster IP addresses:

Advantages	Disadvantages
Improved security as the Web Application Proxy act as an intermediate layer between external users and corporate network.	No redundancy and single point of failure.
Basic DoS protection by throttling and queuing connections.	The implementation cost is high compared to the single server model as additional servers need to be added.
This setup support future expands. Easily can add servers to the AD FS farm and Web Application Proxy group, when required.	Adding more roles also means more dependencies. Both the roles need to function correctly to complete the process.

Multiple federation servers and multiple Web Application Proxy servers with SQL Server

So far, we have looked into models, which suit for easy implementation and improved security. But this model is focused for high availability. Each role will be configured with NLB clusters. The AD FS database will be hosted in the SQL Always On cluster environment. This model is ideal for the SPs and other businesses, which deal with high volume AD FS requests.

The NLB cluster is a software-based load balancing solution that comes with Microsoft. It is easy to implement with no additional licenses. However, hardware load balancers provide high performance and fewer dependencies.

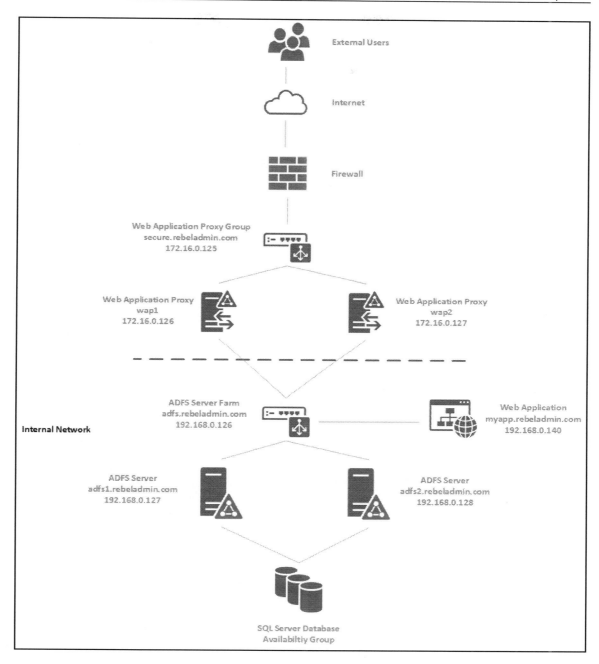

Similar to the previous model, this model's operations are clearly divided into two networks: perimeter and corporate. The firewall will have following NAT and access rules to support the setup:

- Map external IP address to `myapp.rebeladmin.com` so that users can make initial request from external networks. It is recommended to use TCP 443.
- Map external IP address to `secure.rebeladmin.com`, map it to the IP address of Web Application Proxy server group's NLB cluster IP, and open TCP 443 from the external to allow access.
- Allows access from Web Application Proxy servers to AD FS Farm NLB cluster IP in TCP port 443.

For both the NLB clusters, the initial connection point will be NLB cluster IP and the external and internal DNS records should have entry for it. Apart from the application's external URL, the only external published URL will be Web Application Proxy's URL. In the preceding example, `secure.rebeladmin.com` is a map to Web Application Proxy NLB cluster IP.

AD FS servers are using Microsoft SQL Always On availability group to host the AD FS database. This is a read/write database for both the hosts.

 SQL Always On is a high availability solution which runs on top of the Windows cluster. Windows Server 2016 support a two-node cluster with Azure Cloud Witness. It reduces the number of servers which need to be used in a SQL Always On setup.

Advantages	Disadvantages
High availability: Each component hosts multiple servers with load balancer. AD FS database also using SQL high availability environment.	**High cost**: It needs multiple servers and licenses (OS, SQL Servers). It also increases the management cost.
High performance: Workloads are distributed between multiple hosts using load balancers.	**Complex setup**: The implementation will be time consuming and needs advanced skills for planning and configuration.
Support for features such as SAML artifact resolution and SAML/WS-Federation token replay detection.	Troubleshooting an issue will be time consuming and complex as there are many systems and application dependencies.

AD FS deployment

In this section, we are going to look into the AD FS deployment using single federation server and single Web Application Proxy server model. Before we setup, we need a few prerequisites to fulfill.

DNS records

We need few DNS records (internal and external) set up prior to start the deployment:

DNS Record	External	Internal
Application URL	Yes	Yes
WAP URL	Yes	N/A
AD FS URL	N/A	Yes

In the test environment, the following URLs will be used:

- `myapp.rebeladmin.com` will be the application, and it will have the external DNS record created and map it to the external IP address. It will NAT to the application server IP address using firewall. It will also have the internal DNS entry and point to the internal IP address of the application server.
- `secure.rebeladmin.com` will be the WAP connection point from the external. WAP servers are in the perimeter network; it is not necessary to have the internal DNS record unless there are multiple WAP servers.
- `adfs.rebeladmin.com` will be the AD FS server DNS entry; and it does not need to have the external DNS entry. However, WAP servers need to connect to AD FS servers via the SSL certificate. Since it's one server, there is no point deploying a DNS server in the perimeter network, and it can be done using the HOSTS file entry.

SSL certificates

AD FS deployment requires a few SSL certificates. In this demo, we will be using the following:

- `*.rebeladmin.com`: This is a wildcard SSL certificate for external URLs. This is used for application and WAP.

- `rebeladmin.com`: This SSL is for AD FS service communication.

 In the lab environment, these certificates can create using internal CA. If the domain name is the same, wildcard certificates are used internally and externally as well. It will simplify the certificate management.

Installing the AD FS role

Before starting the installation, the SSL certificate for `adfs.rebeladmin.com` needs to be installed in the computer account as it is required during the AD FS installation. This can be checked using the following command:

```
dir Cert:\LocalMachine\My
```

 The AD FS server should be a member server of the domain and should log in as the domain administrator or the Enterprise admin to do the installation.

Next, install the AD FS role service, and it can be done using the following PowerShell command:

```
Install-WindowsFeature ADFS-Federation -IncludeManagementTools
```

Once it is completed, configure AD FS. I am going to use the following configuration for the demo setup:

```
Import-Module ADFS
$credentials = Get-Credential
Install-AdfsFarm `
-CertificateThumbprint:"938E369FA88B2F884A5BBC495F2338BE9FA0E0BB" `
-FederationServiceDisplayName:"REBELADMIN INC" `
-FederationServiceName:"adfs.rebeladmin.com" `
-ServiceAccountCredential $credentials
```

In this setup, we are using WID for AD FS, so no need for the SQL configuration. In the preceding command, `CertificateThumbprint`, specify the SSL certificate (`adfs.rebeladmin.com`), `FederationServiceDisplayName`, and specify the display name of the federation service. `FederationServiceName` is the service name, and it should match the SSL we used. `ServiceAccountCredential` is used to define the service account details for the AD FS setup. At the end, the system needs to restart to apply the configuration:

```
PS C:\Windows\system32> Import-Module ADFS
$credentials = Get-Credential
Install-AdfsFarm `
-CertificateThumbprint:"938E369FA88B2F884A5BBC495F2338BE9FA0E0BB" `
-FederationServiceDisplayName:"REBELADMIN INC" `
-FederationServiceName:"adfs.rebeladmin.com" `
-ServiceAccountCredential $credentials
cmdlet Get-Credential at command pipeline position 1
Supply values for the following parameters:
WARNING: A machine restart is required to complete ADFS service configuration. F
or more information, see: http://go.microsoft.com/fwlink/?LinkId=798725
WARNING: The SSL certificate subject alternative names do not support host name
'certauth.adfs.rebeladmin.com'. Configuring certificate authentication binding o
n port '49443' and hostname 'adfs.rebeladmin.com'.
WARNING: The SSL certificate does not contain all UPN suffix values that exist i
n the enterprise. Users with UPN suffix values not represented in the certifica
te will not be able to Workplace-Join their devices. For more information, see
http://go.microsoft.com/fwlink/?LinkId=311954.

Message                          Context             Status
-------                          -------             ------
The configuration completed successfully. DeploymentSucceeded Success


PS C:\Windows\system32> |
```

The error about alternative SSL name `certauth.adfs.rebeladmin.com` is regarding the certificate authentication. Before Windows Server 2016, this was an issue as it wasn't supporting different bindings for certificate authentication and device authentication on the same host. The default `443` is used by the device authentication and couldn't have multiple bindings in the same channel. In Windows Server 2016, this is possible and now it supports two methods. The first option is using the same host (`adfs.rebeladmin.com`) with different ports (`443`, `49443`). The second option is to use different hosts (`adfs.rebeladmin.com` and `certauth.adfs.rebeladmin.com`) with the same port (`443`). This will require an SSL certificate to support `certauth.adfs.rebeladmin.com` as an alternate subject name.

Once the reboot completes, we can check whether the installation was successful:

```
Get-WinEvent "AD FS/Admin" | Where-Object {$_.ID -eq "100"} | fl
```

This will print the event 100, which confirms the successful AD FS installation.

Installing WAP

The next step of the configuration is to install WAP. This doesn't need to be a domain-joined server and should be placed on the perimeter network. Before the installation process, install the required SSL certificates. In my demo, it is for `*.rebeladmin.com`. We can verify this using this:

```
dir Cert:\LocalMachine\My
```

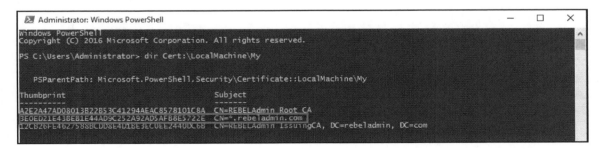

Before proceeding, we also need to check whether a server can resolve to `adfs.rebeladmin.com` as WAP needs to connect to AD FS.

Once everything is confirmed, we can install the WAP role:

```
Install-WindowsFeature Web-Application-Proxy -IncludeManagementTools
```

```
PS C:\Users\Administrator> Install-WindowsFeature Web-Application-Proxy -IncludeManagementTools

Success Restart Needed Exit Code      Feature Result
------- -------------- ---------      --------------
True    No             Success        {RAS Connection Manager Administration Kit...
WARNING: To finish configuring this server for the Web Application Proxy role service using Windows PowerShell, see
http://go.microsoft.com/fwlink/?LinkId=294322.
```

Once it's completed, we can proceed with configuration using the following:

```
$credentials = Get-Credential
Install-WebApplicationProxy
-FederationServiceName "adfs.rebeladmin.com"
-FederationServiceTrustCredential $credentials
-CertificateThumbprint "3E0ED21E43BEB1E44AD9C252A92AD5AFB8E5722E"
```

In the preceding commands, `FederationServiceName` is used to define the AD FS service name, and it needs to match the name provided on the AD FS setup. `FederationServiceTrustCredential` is used to provide an account, which is authorized to register a new proxy server with AD FS. The account which is used here should have permissions to manage AD FS. The `CertificateThumbprint` parameter is used to define the certificate for WAP. In our demo, it's the certificate, `*.rebeladmin.com`. At the end of the system, restart to apply the changes:

```
PS C:\Windows\system32> $credentials = Get-Credential
Install-WebApplicationProxy -FederationServiceName "adfs.rebeladmin.com" -FederationServiceTrustCredential $credentials -CertificateThum
cmdlet Get-Credential at command pipeline position 1
Supply values for the following parameters:
WARNING: Given SSL certificate does not match the STS certificate. Requests doin
g NTLM authentication over the proxy will fail.
WARNING: A machine restart is required to complete ADFS service configuration. F
or more information, see: http://go.microsoft.com/fwlink/?LinkId=798725

Message                         Context         Status
-------                         -------         ------
The configuration completed successfully. DeploymentSucceeded Success
```

Once the reboot is completed, we can confirm the health of the configuration using the following event log in AD FS server:

```
Get-WinEvent "AD FS/Admin" | Where-Object {$_.ID -eq "396"} | fl
```

```
PS C:\Users\administrator.REBELADMIN> Get-WinEvent "AD FS/Admin" | Where-Object {$_.ID -eq "396"} | fl

TimeCreated   : 30/03/2017 00:37:38
ProviderName  : AD FS
Id            : 396
Message       : The trust between the federation server proxy and the Federation Service was renewed successfully.

                Proxy trust certificate subject: CN=ADFS ProxyTrust - REBEL-CRTROOT.
                Proxy trust certificate old thumbprint: 0A191B3E42B8B9B826F8ED1AE6BEC2C142B0CABA.
                Proxy trust certificate new thumbprint: D0CA59939D1427A95FA1EEE09DAD2B950040E4A0.

TimeCreated   : 30/03/2017 00:36:37
ProviderName  : AD FS
Id            : 396
Message       : The trust between the federation server proxy and the Federation Service was renewed successfully.

                Proxy trust certificate subject: CN=ADFS ProxyTrust - REBEL-CRTROOT.
                Proxy trust certificate old thumbprint: 0A191B3E42B8B9B826F8ED1AE6BEC2C142B0CABA.
                Proxy trust certificate new thumbprint: D465695A3D4BE6137903645177E2569ADB8411BE.

TimeCreated   : 30/03/2017 00:27:56
ProviderName  : AD FS
Id            : 396
Message       : The trust between the federation server proxy and the Federation Service was renewed successfully.

                Proxy trust certificate subject: CN=ADFS ProxyTrust - REBEL-CRTROOT.
                Proxy trust certificate old thumbprint: 0A191B3E42B8B9B826F8ED1AE6BEC2C142B0CABA.
                Proxy trust certificate new thumbprint: F4C1680F09C36C278B2F8981BFD5FC2415C8E06E.

TimeCreated   : 30/03/2017 00:26:55
ProviderName  : AD FS
Id            : 396
Message       : The trust between the federation server proxy and the Federation Service was renewed successfully.

                Proxy trust certificate subject: CN=ADFS ProxyTrust - REBEL-CRTROOT.
                Proxy trust certificate old thumbprint: 0A191B3E42B8B9B826F8ED1AE6BEC2C142B0CABA.
                Proxy trust certificate new thumbprint: FA394B73302BD662407A374FCADC183069648B2.
```

Configuring the claim aware app with new federation servers

At the start, we saw not every application can use the AD FS environment. It should be a Claim aware application. I have an application called `myapp.rebeladmin.com` already set up. In the configuration, I set it up to use the existing STS and added new AD FS server's metadata URL, which is
`https://adfs.rebeladmin.com/federationmetadata/2007-06/`
`federationmetadata.xml`.

If it's successful AD FS install the metadata XML should be able to view using web browser. If it cannot load, you need to check it before this step.

Once the application is configured, when I go to my application, which is `https://myapp.rebeladmin.com/myapp` (internally), I can see the following error. It was expected as the AD FS setup does not know about my application yet:

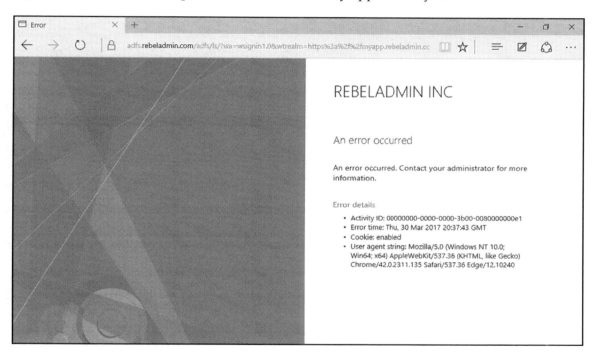

Creating a relaying party trust

We need to create a relay party trust with the application and the AD FS. Then, AD FS is aware about the application.

In order to do that, perform the following:

1. Log into the AD FS server as administrator.
2. Go to **Server Manager** I **Tools** I **AD FS Management**.
3. Go to **Relying Party Trusts**, and then click on **Add Relying Party Trust**:

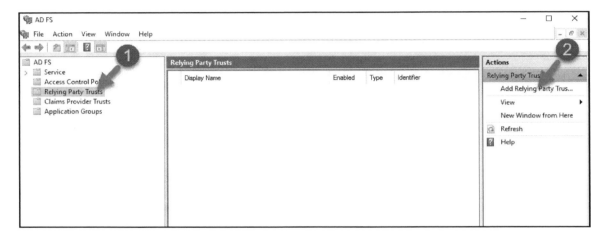

4. It will open the **Add Relay Party Trust Wizard**; select **Claims Aware**, and click **Start**.
5. In the **Select Data Source** page, select **Import data about the relying party published online or on a local network** and enter the metadata URL for the application. For my application, I have created the metadata file under `https://myapp.rebeladmin.com/myapp/federationmetadata/2007-06/federationmetadata.xml`:

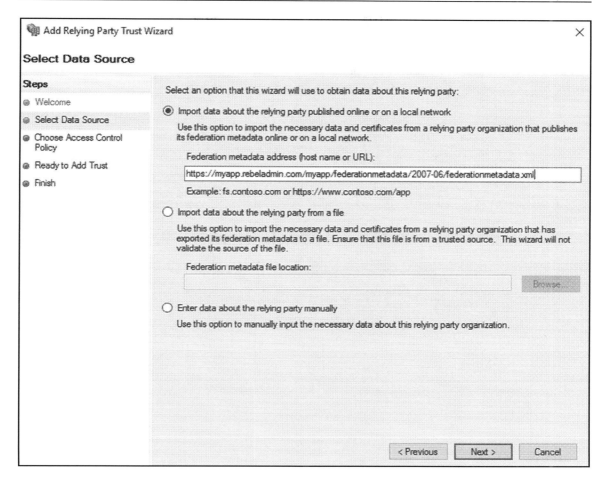

6. On the next page, **Specify Display Name** for the claim and click on **Next**.

7. On the **Choose an access control policy** page, select **Permit Everyone** and click on **Next**.

This is a new feature of AD FS 2016, and it allows to create access policies easily. It is possible to add customer access policies as well. In this demo, I am not going to use any MFA as it's a test lab:

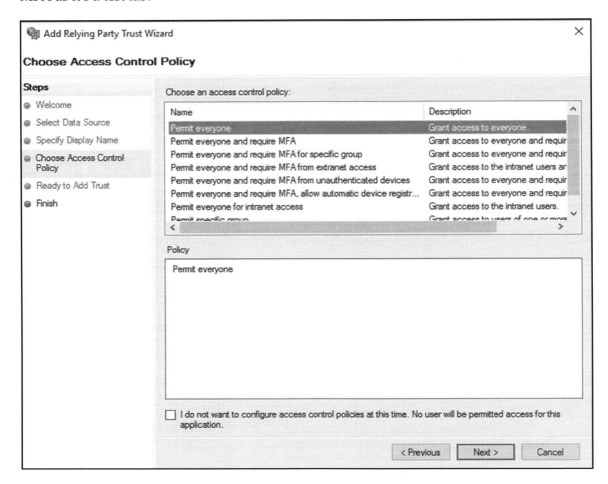

8. In the next window, we can review the settings and click on **Next** to continue.
9. In the **Finish** page, keep the tick for **Configure claims issuance policy for this application** and click on **Close**:

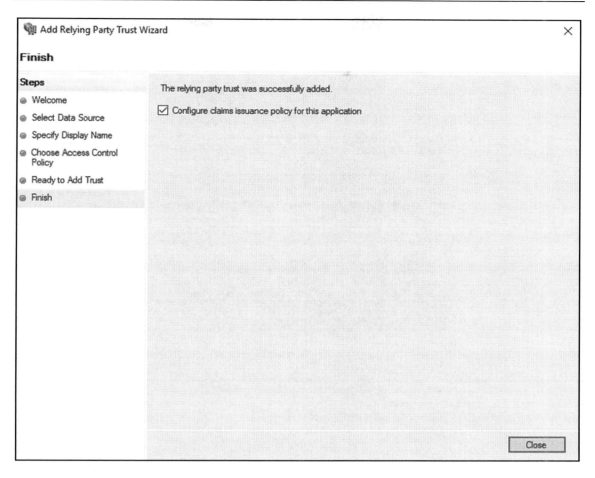

10. It will open the **Edit Claim Issuance policy** window; if it does not, click on **Edit Claim Issuance policy** from the action pane. Once the window is opened, click on the **Add Rule** button.

11. In **Add Transform Claim Rule Wizard,** select **Send Claims Using a Custom Rule** and click on **Next:**

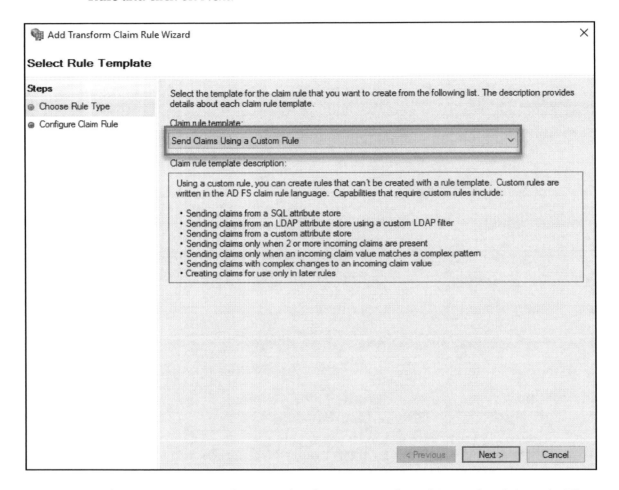

12. In the next page, type the name for the custom rule and input the claim rule. The claim rule is depends on the application requirement. Most of application vendors specify what kind of claim rule you need to have. Once complete, click on **Finish**.

13. Once finished, click **OK** to exit from the wizard.

Configuring the Web Application Proxy

Now, we have the application configured with AD FS. But our requirement is to use the Web Application Proxy to publish the application to the public.

In order to do that, log into the Web Application Proxy server as administrator and execute the following command:

```
Add-WebApplicationProxyApplication
-BackendServerUrl 'https://myapp.rebeladmin.com/myapp/'
-ExternalCertificateThumbprint '3E0ED21E43BEB1E44AD9C252A92AD5AFB8E5722E'
-ExternalUrl 'https://myapp.rebeladmin.com/myapp/'
-Name 'MyApp'
-ExternalPreAuthentication AD FS
-ADFSRelyingPartyName 'myapp.rebeladmin.com'
```

In the preceding command, `ExternalUrl` specifies the external URL for the application. `BackendServerUrl` specifies the internal URL for the application. `ExternalCertificateThumbprint` is the certificate to use from external networks. The `Name` parameter specifies the custom name for the app, which will display on the proxy page. `ExternalPreAuthentication` defines the authentication mode. On our setup, we use the AD FS mode. It also supports the pass-through mode. `ADFSRelyingPartyName` specifies the AD FS relying party name, which will use for this application.

 The Web Application Proxy can translate hostnames used in the external URL and the backend URL. But it cannot translate paths.

Once all is done, when I access the app from the external `https://myapp.rebeladmin.com` `/myapp/`, it successfully proxies to AD FS; and after a successful authentication, the app page is displayed. Yippee!

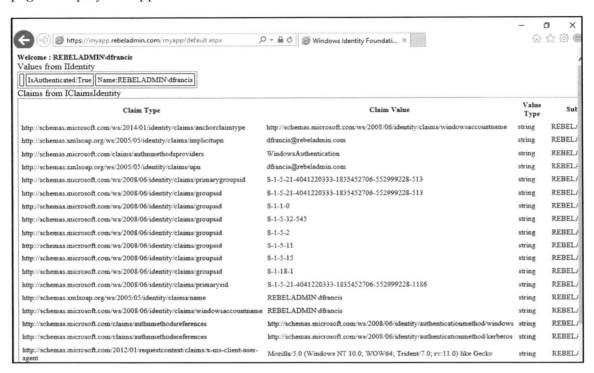

This confirms an AD FS setup using a single AD FS server and a single Web Application Proxy server.

Integrating with Azure MFA

The **multi-factor authentication (MFA)** is a common requirement today for online services. It can be for any hosted solution in organizations such as Citrix, RDS, or other web applications. MFA is used in hybrid cloud environments where a company uses cloud-based applications. In both the scenarios, AD FS helps to integrate the traditional authentication with MFA.

There are many MFA service providers in the market. Some of those are on premises solutions, where we can install an appliance and use MFA services. In today's market, the majority of them are cloud-based solution providers and sell it as subscriptions. Customers can simply install agent on premises and get it connected with these cloud based solutions. Azure MFA first was introduced to use with Azure services and later developed further to support on-premises workload protections too. Users can use mobile text, calls, or PIN generated on mobile app to authenticate. Most of the MFA SPs have a separate agent, which needs to be installed in the AD FS servers in order to get it connected with the MFA services.

The Azure MFA integration was complicated in Windows Server 2012 R2 environments, as it needed an agent as well as an Azure MFA server installed on separate server. A big change with AD FS 2016 was Azure MFA integration enhancement. With AD FS 2016, we no longer need to install these components, and Azure Adapter is integrated with Azure AD to pull the configuration. In this section, we are going to look how we can integrate the AD FS set up we have with Azure MFA.

Prerequisites

In order to configure Azure MFA, we need a few things:

- A valid Azure subscription.
- Azure Global Administrator Privileges.
- Azure AD Federated Setup–Azure AD needs to integrate with AD FS on premises and synchronize identities to Azure. This will be covered in `Chapter 17`, *Azure Active Directory for Hybrid Setup.*
- Windows Server 2016 AD FS in local infrastructure.
- Enterprise Admin privileges for AD FS servers to configure MFA.
- Azure Multi-Factor Authentication Enabled–the users sync from on-premises AD need to have MFA enabled. I wrote an article about this before and you can refer to it at `http://www.rebeladmin.com/2016/01/step-by-step-guide-to-config ure-mfa-multi-factor-authentication-for-azure-users/`.
- Windows Azure AD module for Windows PowerShell in AD FS servers–this can be downloaded from `http://go.microsoft.com/fwlink/p/?linkid=236297`.

Before installing the Azure PowerShell module, the system needs Microsoft online services sign-in assistant installed. It can be downloaded from `https://www.microsoft.com/en-us/download/details.aspx?dis playlang=en&id=28177`. Once it is installed, we need to install the Azure Resource Manager cmdlet using `Install-Module AzureRM`. This allows to manage azure resources.

Creating a certificate in an AD FS farm to connect to Azure MFA

As the first step, we need to create a certificate, which will be used by the AD FS farm and Azure MFA to connect. This needs to run from the AD FS server:

```
$certbase64 = New-AdfsAzureMfaTenantCertificate -TenantID
05c6f80c-61d9-44df-bd2d-4414a983c1d4
```

The preceding command will generate the new certificate. TenantID is the subscription ID you have from Azure. This can be found out by running this:

```
Login-AzureRmAccount
```

It will ask for the credentials for Azure and once we provide them, it will list down the Tenant ID:

This will create a certificate under Local Computer:

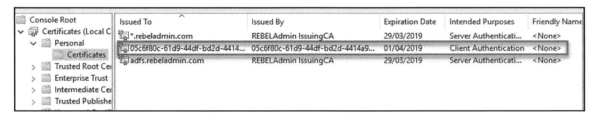

Enabling AD FS servers to connect with Azure Multi-Factor Auth Client

Now, we have the certificate, but we need to tell Azure Multi-Factor Auth Client to use it as a credential to connect with AD FS.

Before that, we need to connect to the Azure AD using Azure PowerShell. We can do that using this:

```
Connect-MsolService
```

Then, it will prompt for login and use your Azure Global Administrator account to connect.

After that, we can pass the credentials using this:

```
New-MsolServicePrincipalCredential -AppPrincipalId 981f26a1-7f43-403b-a875-
f8b09b8cd720 -Type asymmetric -Usage verify -Value $certbase64
```

In the preceding command, `AppPrincipalId` defines the **globally unique identifier (GUID)** for Azure Multi-Factor Auth Client.

Enabling AD FS farm to use Azure MFA

The next step of the configuration is to enable AD FS farm to use Azure MFA. This can be done using this:

```
Set-AdfsAzureMfaTenant -TenantId 05c6f80c-61d9-44df-bd2d-4414a983c1d4 -
ClientId 981f26a1-7f43-403b-a875-f8b09b8cd720
```

In the preceding command, `TenantId` refers to the Azure Tenant ID. `ClientId` represents the Azure Multi-Factor Auth Client GUID.

Once the command successfully runs, we need to restart the AD FS service in each server in the farm:

```
PS C:\Users\administrator.REBELADMIN\Desktop> Set-AdfsAzureMfaTenant -TenantId 05c6f80c-61d9-44df-bd2d-4414a983c1d4 -Cli
entId 981f26a1-7f43-403b-a875-f8b09b8cd720
WARNING: PS0177: The authentication provider configuration data was successfully updated.  Before your changes take
effect, you must restart the AD FS Windows Service on each server in the farm.
PS C:\Users\administrator.REBELADMIN\Desktop>
```

Enabling Azure MFA for authentication

The last step of the configuration is to enable Azure MFA globally for the AD FS server.

In order to do that, log into the AD FS server as the Enterprise Admin. Then, go to **Server Manager** | **Tools** | **AD FS Management**.

Then, in the console, navigate to **Service** | **Authentication Methods**. Then in the **Actions** panel, click on **Edit Primary Authentication Method**:

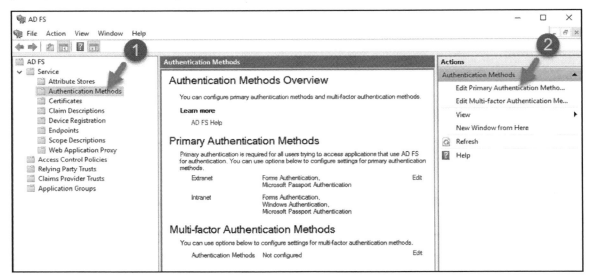

This opens up the window to configure global authentication methods. It has two tabs, and we can see Azure MFA on both. If Azure MFA used as primary method by removing other options, it will not ask for logins and will use MFA as the only authentication method. Its operation boundaries can be set to intranet or extranet:

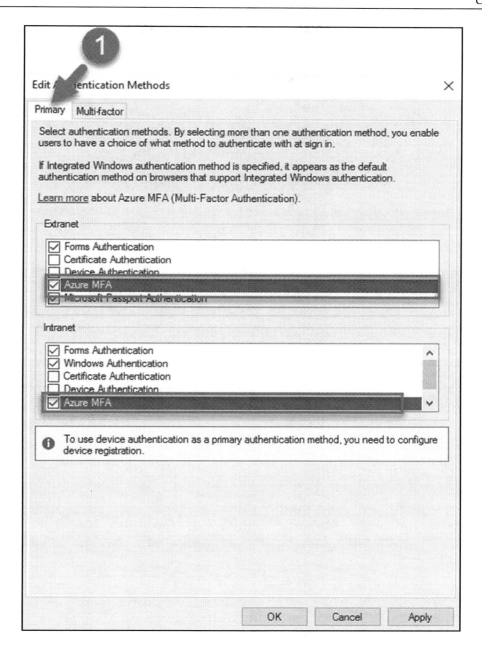

Another option is to select MFA as the secondary authentication method:

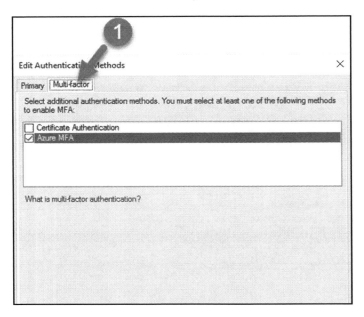

This finishes the Azure MFA integration, and users can use MFA based on the option selected in the preceding wizards. There is still lots to talk about AD FS, and it is hard to cover everything in a chapter. I have selected the most suitable configuration for any business to explain the AD FS deployment.

Summary

We are living in a *connected* world. Businesses are using cloud-based applications and B2B connections more and more. Microsoft AD FS allows engineers to handle identity requirements for such scenarios in an effective and secure manner, which we cannot get from traditional methods.

In this chapter, you learned what AD FS is, and how it works in the infrastructure. We also looked into the AD FS components and their characteristics. Later, we moved into the AD FS deployment and learned how to configure AD FS and integrate it with the Web Application Proxy. Last but not least, we looked into the Azure MFA integration with on-premises AD FS.

In the next chapter, we will look into another AD role service *Active Directory Rights Management Service*, which we can use to safeguard sensitive data in corporation.

14

Active Directory Rights Management Services

After the computer was invented, people started to transform the data and information into the digital format. It transformed the way that people *accessed* data as well. With easy access and high availability of data, people started to get their hands on data that they were not supposed to have. That's where people start to talk about data security and data governance. It's still a hot topic, especially in the last decade. When the wrong people have access to the wrong data, it can come back to people, organizations, or even on countries with bigger consequences.

The famous WikiLeaks phenomenon is a good example of it. WikiLeaks got access to state secrets. Some of that data was in the digital format, such as emails and scanned files. Someone with authority over that data had passed on the data to WikiLeaks, or they stole that data illegally. Either way, it's obvious that WikiLeaks should not have had access to that data originally. Even now, they keep releasing data to the public, and some of that data is even strong enough to make an impact on foreign affairs between countries.

The other concern of data security is related to intellectual properties. As an example, let's consider a software vendor. They spend a lot of money and time on developing a product and release it for the public to purchase. After a month, someone publishes the software with valid license keys on torrent sites. So, what will happen to the expected revenue?

We all know there are laws to protect companies from similar situations, but companies still have to constantly fight to protect their product data from being exposed. The same thing is applicable to films, music tracks, drama, and so on. I've been maintaining my own technical blog (`http://www.rebeladmin.com`) for the last 7 years and written more than 400 articles. I also write for Microsoft TechNet. I maintain that blog just to share my experience and knowledge with the public. I do not make money from it in any form. Over the years, I have seen people using my articles on their own websites without saying a word to me. So far, I have never written a single email to any of those people as I do not maintain my blog to make money.

Two months ago, a gentleman sent me a very interesting email. In his email, he complained that I was copying other people's blog posts. He even said I was copying posts including the same text. If I include anything in my blog post, I always include the reference. So, I was very interested to find out more about it. I asked him for more details and he sent me a few links to a post from a website. When I checked, yes, it was exactly the same, but the gentlemen who made the complaint didn't check the published dates. This site had copied my articles and published them as their own articles. These articles even included the same screenshots that I used. In the end, I explained and proved I was the original author. But that wouldn't be necessary if those people didn't use my posts without my permission. It's just another side of modern data theft.

Governments, data security agencies, application vendors, IT communities, and professionals came up with laws, rules, applications, services, methodologies, and best practices to protect digital data, but one thing we need to understand is that none of the solutions are going to protect all the data in the infrastructure 100%. These data security threats come from human advisories. They keep changing their tactics, and there can be a breach somewhere. But these solutions will help improve data security and prevent breaches as much as possible. Active Directory **Rights Management Services (RMS)** is a server role that helps protect sensitive data that has been forwarded, printed, or copied without permission. It also allows you to do that using corporate policies to ensure data governance. In this chapter, we are going to cover the following topics:

- What is AD RMS?
- AD RMS components
- How does AD RMS work?
- How do we deploy AD RMS?

What is AD RMS?

Microsoft had taken their first approach to **Information Rights Management (IRM)** by introducing Windows RMS with Windows Server 2003. This was fully compliant with **Federal Information Processing Standard (FIPS)** 140-1. The updated version of Windows RMS was renamed as AD RMS and reintroduced with Windows Server 2008. It continued to grow with features and was included with every new Windows Server version after that. Microsoft also released Azure RMS (included in Azure Information Protection), which can be used in a hybrid cloud environment to protect data.

As I stated earlier, AD RMS is not the solution for all data security requirements. In an infrastructure, there are other things attached to data security. The first step of protection is to decide who has access to corporate network and resources. This falls under perimeter defense and hardware/software firewalls can be used to define rules to manage traffic coming into the corporate network and traffic going out from the corporate network. Modern layer-7 firewalls and Next Generation Firewalls allow not only managing connections, but they also go further into analysis traffic based on applications and user accounts (AD integrated). If users are allowed to use the internet, it also can bring threats to corporate data. It can be via viruses, malware, phishing emails, and so on.

Similar threats can be eliminated using layer 7 firewalls or proxies. The next step in data protection is to control the data access for users and groups in the corporate network. This is done using NTFS and **access control lists (ACLs)**. These help control *who* has access to *what* data and resources. The challenge is to protect data once users and groups have access to it.

As an example, Rebeladmin Inc. has a sales department. The CEO creates a word document, which includes the previous year's total sales, and saves it in a network folder. The only people who have access to it are the CEO and sales manager. They send an email to the sales manager and inform him about the file. Access to the network share is protected by ACLs. However, if sales manager can access it, what will prevent him from emailing it to a person in the technical department or bringing it home with him and sharing it with third-party? AD RMS controls the behavior of data once users have access to it. But this will not prevent data leakage via digital photographs, third-party screen capturing, hard copies, or viruses and malware.

AD RMS can:

- **Follow data with policies (persistent usage rights and conditions)**: NTFS permission and ACLs can only manage data within their operation boundaries. In my previous example, when the report is inside the `Sales` folder, it can be accessed only by the CEO and the sales manager. However, if it's copied to a local disk and forwarded as an email, it will bypass the NTFS permissions and ACLs. AD RMS uses persistent usage policies that follow the data. Even when it's moved or forwarded, the policies will follow it.

- **Prevent confidential emails from getting into the wrong hands**: Emails are commonly involved with data leakage. Constant news comes out on media due to the wrong people having access to *confidential* emails. Once an email has left an outgoing email folder, we do not have control over the data and we do not have any guarantee whether this is only accessed by the recipient and whether it's not forwarded to another party that the original sender is not aware of. AD RMS can prevent the recipient from forwarding, modifying, copying, or printing confidential emails. It also guarantees that they can be opened only by the expected recipient.

- **Prevent data from being accessed by unauthorized people**: Similar to emails, AD RMS can also protect confidential files and reports from being modified, copied, forwarded, or printed by unauthorized users.

- **Prevent users by capturing content using the Windows print screen feature**: Even users who do not forward or copy methods to send data can still use the print screen option to capture the data in another format. AD RMS can prevent users from using the Windows print screen tool to capture data. However, this is not going to prevent users from using third-party screen capturing solutions.

- **File expiration**: AD RMS allows you to set a time limit to the files so that after a certain period of time, its content will not be able to be accessed.

- **Protect data on mobile devices and macOS**: People use mobile devices to access corporate services and data. AD RMS mobile extension allows you to extend its data protection capabilities to mobile devices that run on Windows, Android, or iOS. In order to do that, the device should have the latest RMS clients and RMS-aware apps installed as well. This also applies to macOS devices as long as they use Office 2016 for macOS and RMS-aware applications.

- **Integration with applications**: AD RMS not only supports Microsoft Office files, but it also supports a wide range of applications and file types. As an example, AD RMS can directly integrate with SharePoint (2007 onwards) to protect the documents published on the intranet site. There are third-party applications that support RMS too. RMS also supports file types such as `.pdf`, `.jpg`, `.txt`, and `.xml`. This allows corporates to protect more and more data types in the infrastructure.

AD RMS is supported to operate in three different operation boundaries:

- **Internal**: In this scenario, AD RMS is used only to protect data in an internal network. Policies are applied to internal applications, files, and users. It will not consider how the data will be protected when it leaves the company premises. This will not support corporate data in mobile devices. This mode is suited for testing environment or small businesses.
- **Partner networks**: Some businesses have a partnership with other companies. Based on the nature of the business requirements, there can be Active Directory trusts between multiple forests. In this scenario, the company will focus on protecting data that is exchanged between the partners. This can be one way or both ways. If it's both ways, both infrastructures will have to have their own RMS instances.
- **External**: In this scenario, AD RMS operations are focused on protecting the company's high valued data, which travels across infrastructures where companies do not have control. It can be either completely foreign networks or federated networks. Corporate data protection on mobile devices also needs this type of AD RMS deployment. In this mode, certain AD RMS components will need to be hosted in the perimeter network and allow service URLs to be accessed via the internet.

Even though there are three AD RMS deployment modes, it doesn't prevent organizations from setting up AD RMS environments to cover two or all three deployments modes. It is absolutely supported to extend AD RMS operation boundaries based on the organization's requirements. This means that organizations can start with protecting internal data and then extend it to protect data in a partner environment or external environments when required.

The following table lists the applications, file types, and scenarios we can protect using AD RMS:

Requirements	Application	Protected file types
Protect confidential files	Microsoft Outlook Windows (version 2003 or more) Office for macOS 2016: • Word • Excel • PowerPoint PDF Image processing XPS Viewer Gaaiho Doc GigaTrust Desktop PDF Client for Adobe Foxit Reader Nitro PDF Reader Siemens JT2Go	`.doc, .docm, .docx, .dot, .dotm, .dotx, .potm, .potx, .pps, .ppsm, .ppsx, .ppt, .pptm, .txt, .xml, .jpg, .jpeg, .pdf, .png, .tif, .tiff, .bmp, .gif, .jpe, .jfif, .jt, .xps`
Protect confidential emails	Microsoft Outlook Windows (version 2003 and newer) Office for macOS 2016 Microsoft Exchange 2007 SP1	`.msg`
Protect content on the intranet	Microsoft SharePoint 2007 and newer	`.doc, .docm, .docx, .dot, .dotm, .dotx, .potm, .potx, .pps, .ppsm, .ppsx, .ppt, .pptm, .txt, .xml, .jpg, .jpeg, .pdf, .png, .tif, .tiff, .bmp, .gif, .jpe, .jfif, .jt, .xps`

| Protect mobile data | Microsoft Word
Microsoft Word app
Microsoft Excel app
Microsoft Outlook app
Microsoft PowerPoint app
WordPad
Office for macOS 2016
Word Online
TITUS Docs
Foxit Reader | `.doc, .docm, .docx, .dot, .dotm,`
`.dotx, .potm, .potx, .pps, .ppsm,`
`.ppsx, .ppt, .pptm, .txt, .xml,`
`.jpg, .jpeg, .pdf, .png, .tif,`
`.tiff, .bmp, .gif, .jpe, .jfif,`
`.jt, .msg, .xps` |

AD RMS components

AD RMS has its own role services and related components that need to work together in order to maintain a healthy AD RMS environment. Let's look at these components in detail.

Active Directory Domain Services

AD RMS is one of the Active Directory role services. AD RMS can be installed only in an AD DS environment, and it must be on the member servers. It is also used to publish a **service connection point (SCP)**, where internal users can automatically discover the URL for the AD RMS environment.

The AD RMS cluster

The AD RMS **cluster** is a single RMS server or a group of servers that share certificates and licensing requests from their clients. Even though it is named as a *cluster*, it is different from a typical Windows failover cluster term. The failover cluster needs at least two nodes. However, with RMS even though it has single server it becomes a cluster. But there is one requirement for the AD RMS cluster if there are multiple servers involved. AD RMS supports two types of databases similar to AD FS. By default, it uses the **Windows Internal Database (WID)**, and it also supports the Microsoft SQL Server database. If the AD RMS cluster is going to have multiple servers, it must use the MS SQL database on a separate server.

There are two types of clusters in AD RMS:

- **The root cluster**: When you first set up the AD RMS server in the infrastructure, it becomes the root cluster. By default, it responds to both licensing and certificates requests from clients. When required, additional RMS servers can be added to the cluster. There is only one root cluster that can exist in one AD DS forest.
- **Licensing cluster**: If an organization has multiple Active Directory sites, there are situations where remote sites prefer to use servers on their own site whenever possible. It prevents users from connecting sites through slow links. In such scenarios, organizations can deploy licensing-only cluster on remote sites. It only responds to licensing requests from clients.

When the new RMS server is added to the infrastructure, based on installed roles, it will automatically make it part of the relevant cluster. However, it is recommended that you use the root cluster *only*, as it will automatically load balance both certificates and licensing requests. When it has two clusters, load balancing is handled by each cluster separately even though they are components of one system.

Web server

AD RMS requires the web service for its operations. Therefore, it requires IIS 7.0 or higher, with the following role services:

- Web server (IIS)
- Web server:
    - Common HTTP features:
        - Static content
        - Directory browsing
        - HTTP errors
        - HTTP redirection
    - Performance:
        - Static content compression
    - Health and diagnostics:
        - HTTP logging
        - Logging tools
        - Request monitor
        - Tracing

- Security:
  - Windows authentication

- Management tools:
  - IIS Management Console
  - IIS 6 Management Compatibility:
    - IIS 6 Metabase Compatibility
    - IIS 6 WMI Compatibility

SQL Server

AD RMS supports WID and the Microsoft SQL Server database. If an AD RMS cluster is going to have multiple servers, its database must be in the MS SQL Server. It supports SQL Server 2005 onward. AD RMS has three databases:

- **Configuration database**: This includes configuration data related to the AD RMS cluster, Windows users identities, and the AD RMS certificate key pair that is used to create a cluster.
- **Logging database**: This contains the logging data for the AD RMS setup. By default, it will install it in the same SQL Server instance that hosts the configuration database.
- **Directory service database**: This database maintains cached data about users, SID values, group membership, and related identifiers. This data is collected by the AD RMS licensing service from LDAP queries that run against the global catalog server. By default, it's refreshed every 12 hours.

AD RMS supports SQL high availability solutions, including SQL failover clustering, database mirroring, and log shipping. It is *not* supported by SQL Server Always On.

In the previous section, I mentioned mobile device extensions that can be used to extend AD RMS to manage corporate data in mobile devices. It does not support WID, and if you are going to use this feature, AD RMS databases must run from a separate SQL Server.

AD RMS client

The AD RMS client is required to communicate with the AD RMS cluster and protect data. This is included in all the recent operating systems that were released after Windows XP. However, this still needs to be installed on macOS and mobile devices in order to use AD RMS.

Active Directory Certificate Service

AD RMS uses several certificates to protect communication between AD RMS components and clients. Most of these can be issued using corporate trusted CA. As an example, the AD RMS cluster can be built using the SSL certificate to protect communication between servers in a cluster. If the AD RMS setup is required to publish service URLs externally, then it will require a certificate from public CA.

AD RMS itself uses various **eXtensible rights Markup Language (XrML)**-based certificates to protect communication between components and data. These certificates are different from AD CS certificates.

How does AD RMS work?

Now we know the components of the AD RMS and its capabilities. In this section, we are going to understand in detail how all these components work together to protect corporate data.

Before we start the data protecting process, we need to have a healthy AD RMS cluster, AD RMS clients (author and recipient), and a reliable connection between those components. Once these prerequisites are fulfilled, the data protection process will happen in three main stages: protect content by the author, publish the protected content, and access the protected content by the recipient.

Let's assume Peter is trying to protect a document using AD RMS. He is going to send it to Adam and he does not want him to edit or print it. This is the first time he is going to use AD RMS. In an AD RMS environment, the user Peter will be referred to as an **information author**. In his first authentication into the AD RMS cluster, it creates a **rights account certificate (RAC)**, and it will be the user's identity in AD RMS. This is a one-time process. This certificate contains the public key and private key of Peter, which is encrypted by his computer's public key. When Peter registers with the AD RMS cluster, it also creates another certificate called the **Client Licensor Certificate (CLC)**. This CLC includes the CLC's public key and private key, which are protected by the public key of Peter. It also includes the AD RMS cluster public key, which is signed by the AD RMS private key.

Peter decides what data needs to be protected first. Then, it generates a symmetric key (random) and encrypts the data that needs to be protected. It uses AES-256 standards to encrypt the data. When the first AD RMS server is added to the cluster, it creates another certificate called the **server licensor certificate (SLC)**. This represents the identity element of the AD RMS server. This is shared with clients so that they can be used to exchange confidential data in a secure way. SLC includes the public key of the AD RMS server. As a next step, the system will encrypt the symmetric key used for the data encryption using the AD RMS server public key. So only the AD RMS cluster can open it.

After that, the RMS client creates the **publishing license (PL)**. This PL is used to indicate to the allowed recipients what rights they have and what conditions will apply toward the protected data. The PL includes an encrypted symmetric key that can be used to decrypt the protected data. All this data is then encrypted with SLC's public key. Apart from that, the AD RMS client also will sign encrypted data with the private key of the SLC. In the end, this protected data will be attached to the PL. It also includes the copy of the symmetric key that is encrypted with the SLC public key. This confirms Peter's authority over the protected document, so he can decrypt the document without using another license. Once all these encryptions and signings are done, the document is ready to be sent over to Adam.

Once Adam receives the document, his AD RMS-aware application tries to open it and finds out that it is a protected document. Similar to Peter, Adam already has his RAC and CLS from the AD RMS cluster. In order to open the protected document at once, does it need to encrypt it or sign with any of Adam's certificates? No, it does not. But his AD RMS client knows who needs to be contacted in order to sort it out for him. To open the protected document, Adam should have a **use license (UL)**. This is issued by the RMS cluster. So, the AD RMS client request for the license also included the encrypted PL, the encrypted symmetric key, Peter's CLC, and the public key of Adam's RAC. The protected document will not be sent over with this request to the RMS cluster.

To decrypt the protected document, Adam needs the symmetric key that is used by Peter to encrypt the document. As a first step, the server needs to know whether Adam is permitted to access the document; if he is permitted, what sort of conditions and rights will apply? This information is in the PL. It is encrypted using the public key of the SLC. The AD RMS server is the private key owner for it, and he can easily extract it. If Adam is not allowed in the PL, it will be declined access to it. If it's allowed, it creates a list mentioning Adam's rights to the document.

The most important part of the decryption process is to retrieve the symmetric key. This is also encrypted by SLC's public key. Once it is extracted, it will be re-encrypted using Adam's RAC public key. It was a part of the UL request. This ensures that the only one who can see the key is Adam's system. Since the server has all the required information, it generates the UL, including the permission list and encrypted symmetric key. Then, it sends it over to Adam's RMS client. Once it reaches Adam's system, it can decrypt the symmetric key using RAC's private key. Then, the RMS-aware application will decrypt the document and attach the rights information retrieved from the UL. In the end, voila! Adam can see the content of the document.

In the preceding example, we saw different certificates, licenses, data encryption, and decryption. I thought it's still better to explain it on a high level in order to recap the things you learned:

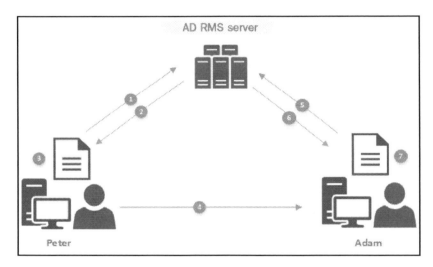

Peter wants to send the protected document to **Adam**. **Adam** should have only read permission to the document and should not be able to modify or print it:

- This is the first time **Peter** is going to use **AD RMS server**. As soon as he tries to protect the document, the RMS client initiates a connection to the **AD RMS server** (cluster)
- The **AD RMS server** replies with RAC and CLC. This is a one-time process.

- In **Peter**'s system, a random symmetric key is generated, and it encrypts the document using it. Then, this symmetric key is encrypted using SLC's public key. After that, it is attached to a PL, which includes **Adam's** rights for the protected document. After that, the PL is attached to the encrypted document.
- **Peter** sends the protected document (along with this additional info) to **Adam**.
- **Adam**'s RMS-aware application tries to open it and finds that it needs the UL from the **AD RMS server**. Then, the RMS client requests it from the RMS server.
- The RMS server decrypts the symmetric key and the PL. After that, the server checks whether the requester matches the PL. In our scenario, it matches, so it goes ahead and creates the UL. This includes the symmetric key (it re-encrypts using **Adam**'s RAC public key) and a list that contains the rights describes in the PL. Then, it delivers it to **Adam**'s system.
- Once **Adam**'s system receives the UL, it retrieves the symmetric key and decrypts the document. Then, **Adam** opens the document and uses it according to the rights described in the PL.

AD RMS deployment

AD RMS deployment topologies are a bit different from other AD role service deployments. Other AD role service deployment topologies are mostly focused on high availability or scalability. But AD RMS deployments are more about addressing different types of business requirements. Let's look at those topologies in detail.

Single forest – single cluster

This is the most commonly used deployment topology. AD RMS operation boundaries are limited to their own forest. The deployment will have only one AD RMS cluster to process certificates and licensing requirements. The cluster can contain any number of servers, and load balancing is handled in the cluster level. If it has multiple servers, the AD RMS cluster should use the MS SQL Server database instead of WIDs. This deployment model will not consider extending to non-corporate networks.

Following are the advantages and disadvantages of single forest—single cluster:

Advantages	Disadvantages
Easy to implement. A fewer number of resources (servers and licenses) are used.	Can protect data only within a limited environment.
System maintenance and management is easy due to smaller operation boundaries.	N/A
Support for extending into any other deployment topologies.	N/A

Single forest – multiple clusters

This is the extended configuration of a single forest—a single cluster topology. There are two types of AD RMS clusters. The AD RMS root cluster is the default cluster, and it answers for both certificates and licensing requests. The licensing-only cluster can also be deployed in the same forest, and it will respond to licensing requests only. This suits infrastructures that have sites in different geographical locations. Then, it will rule out the requirement of contacting RMS clusters via slow links. Instead, it will use a license-only cluster on each site for licenses. There is only one root cluster for the forest. But it can have multiple licensing-only clusters.

Based on the role installed in the AD RMS server, it will decide which cluster it will be part of. However, unless there is a special requirement, it is recommended that you use the root cluster only. Load balancing between member servers is handled on the cluster level, and its configurations are independent. It cannot be shared between different clusters. In this topology, it will also need to consider MS SQL high availability and see how it can be used with multiple sites.

The following table lists the advantages and disadvantages of this topology:

Advantages	Disadvantages
Remote sites do not need to depend on the site links and bandwidth. The local RMS license-only cluster will process the licenses request from the site resources.	Complexity—deployment needs advanced planning and conflagration.
Complies with government rules to use localized encryption tools and technologies.	High cost—need to use additional resources and licenses for the deployment. Also increases the maintenance cost.
N/A	Distributed management—when placing clusters on remote sites, it may also need to grant privileges to the site's IT team in order to manage and maintain the system. This can make an impact on security and system integrity.

AD RMS in multiple forests

If the organization has multiple forests and if AD RMS needs to use between them to protect data, this deployment method can be used. One forest can have only one RMS root cluster. Therefore, in multiple forest environments, each domain should have their own AD RMS cluster. The AD RMS cluster uses AD DS to query an object's identities. When there are multiple forests, it needs to have contact objects of users and groups for the remote forest. The following are required for AD RMS deployment in multiple forests:

- AD RMS root cluster in each forest
- Setting up contact objects for remote users and groups (from the different forests)
- Schema extension in place to trace back to the mother forest of the contact objects
- Attribute values of contact objects needed to sync with the mother forest so that when required, it can be used to trace back to the original object

Active Directory trust between forests is not a must. It can have two-way trust, one-way trust, or no trust at all. If there is trust, it will simplify the process of managing permissions and validations of cross-forest objects.

The following table lists the advantages and disadvantages:

Advantages	Disadvantages
Extended data protection boundaries	Complexity—deployment needs advanced planning and conflagration.
Standardized data protection with partners to protect confidential data	Dependencies—success of the solution depends on the system configuration and availability of the AD RMS components of the partner's forest. It also can have dependencies, where the primary forest does not have control.

In this topology, AD RMS trust policies control how it handles licensing requests and data protection between different AD RMS clusters. There are two types of trust policies:

- **Trusted AD RMS domains**: This allows the AD RMS root cluster to process requests for the CLC or UL from users who have RAC issued by a different AD RMS root cluster. We can add a trusted AD RMS domain by importing the SLC of the AD RMS cluster to trust.
- **Trusted publishing domains**: This allows one AD RMS cluster to issue ULs for PLs that were issued by a different AD RMS cluster. We can add a trusted publishing domain by importing the SLC and the private key of the server to trust.

AD RMS with AD FS

As I explained in the previous topology, in order to be set up, it needs the AD RMS root cluster in each forest. Most of these forests also have two-way trust between them. But not every partner or business agrees to do so. They may want to use AD RMS but they may not want to maintain the AD RMS cluster or create trust between forests. AD FS allows companies to use the already deployed AD RMS cluster in a remote forest. AD FS allows user accounts to use their own credentials established by a federated trust relationship. When one organization trusts an AD RMS-trusted domain from a federated organization, first, it should import it using the trust federated users option as AD FS trusts are not transitive by default. Then, once the user contacts it for the first time, the RAC is issued (for federated users). But its validity period is specified in Federated Identity Support settings.

Before we set it up, certain prerequisites are required between federated infrastructures. Refer to `https://technet.microsoft.com/en-us/library/dn758110(v=ws.11).aspx` for more details on the configuration.

The following table lists the advantages and disadvantages:

Advantages	Disadvantages
No need to maintain multiple AD RMS clusters between organizations. It can use an already existing federation trust to use AD RMS in other forests.	There are security concerns, as its possible to spoof someone's user account and access protected data through a federation proxy.
Extended data protection boundaries and implementation are less complex.	If an internal CA is used to make SSL-based trusts (AD RMS and AD FMS), the federated domain should configure to trust the root CA (using GPO to publish the root cert). Or else, they may need to invest on using public certificates.
Fewer system dependencies between infrastructures.	N/A

AD RMS in extranet, including RMS mobile extensions, is also considered another deployment model, but in modern workloads, it acts as part of other topologies mentioned in the preceding table as users have started using mobile devices to access corporate data more and more.

AD RMS configuration

In this section, let's look at how we can set up AD RMS 2016 and see how it really works on protecting confidential data. The environment it uses for the demo is built based on Windows Server 2016 with the latest updates. The AD DS forest and domain function levels are also set to Windows Server 2016.

Setting up AD RMS root cluster

AD RMS only can install in a domain member server. I have a demo server setup and its already a member server of the domain. First AD RMS server added to the forest creates the AD RMS cluster.

Installing the AD RMS role

The following are the steps to install the AD RMS role:

1. Log into the server as Enterprise Admin.
2. Install the AD RMS role and related management tools using the following command:

   ```
   Install-WindowsFeature ADRMS -IncludeManagementTools
   ```

   The following screenshot shows the output for the preceding command:

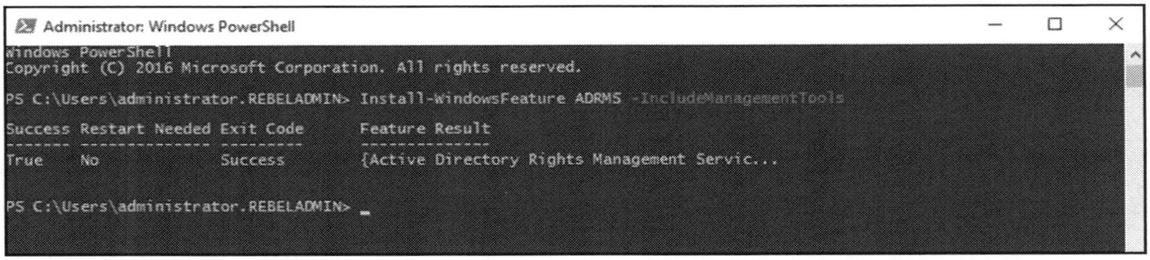

Configuring the AD RMS role

The following are the steps to configure the AD RMS role:

1. Launch **Server Manager** and go to the notifications icon and by navigating to **Configuration required for Active Directory Rights Management Services | Perform additional configuration.**; this will open the AD RMS configuration wizard. Click on **Next** to start the configuration:

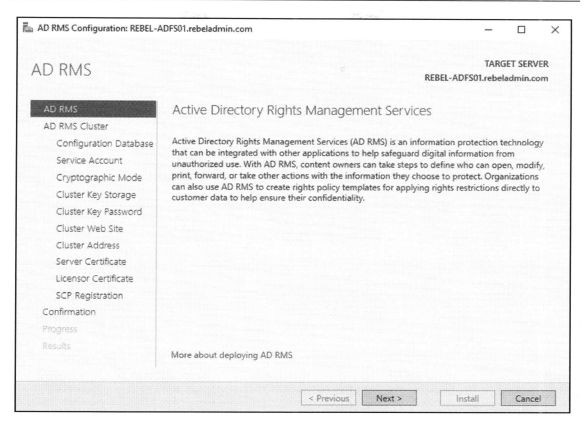

2. On the next screen, there is the option to create a new AD RMS root cluster or join it to the existing AD RMS cluster. Since it is a new cluster, select the **Create a new AD RMS root cluster** option and click on **Next**.

3. The next screen is to define the AD RMS database configuration. If it's going to use MS SQL Server, select **Specify a database server and a database instance**, or else select **Use Windows Internal Database on this server**. Note that if WID is used, it cannot have any more AD RMS servers and cannot have the AD RMS mobile extension either. Since it's a demo, I am going to use WID. Once the selection is made, click on **Next** to move to the next step:

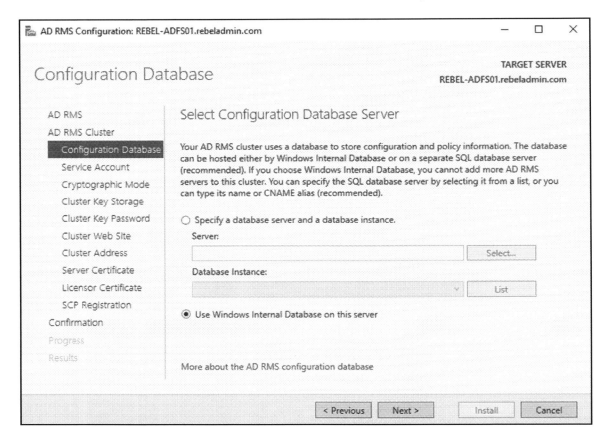

4. In the next window, we need to define the service account. It is used to communicate with other services and computers. This doesn't need to have Domain or Enterprise Admin rights. Click on **Specify...** and provide the username and password for the account. Then, click on **Next** to proceed to the next window.

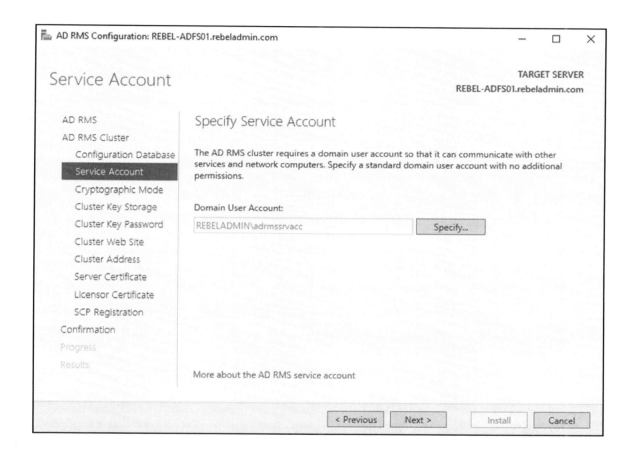

5. On the next screen, we need to select the cryptographic mode. This defines the strength of the hashes. This supports two modes, which are SHA-1 and SHA-256. It is highly recommended that you use **Cryptographic Mode 2 (RSA 2048-bit keys/SHA-256 hashes)**, which is SHA-256 for stronger hashing. However, this needs to be matched with the other RMS cluster it deals with. In our setup, I am going to use the default SHA-256. Once the selection is made, click on **Next** to proceed:

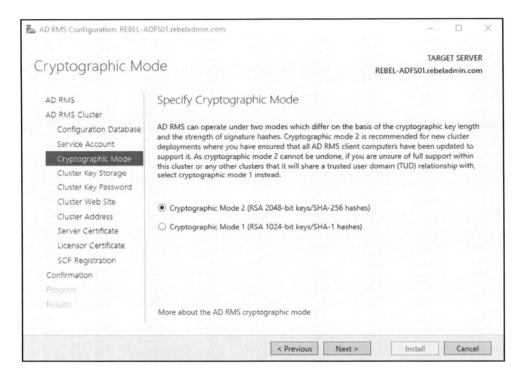

6. AD RMS uses the cluster key to sign the certificate and licenses it issues. This is also required when AD RMS is restored or when the new AD RMS server adds to the same cluster. It can be saved in two places. The default method is to use AD RMS in a centrally managed key storage. So, it doesn't need any additional configurations. It also supports the use of the **cryptographic service provider (CSP)** as storage. But this requires manual distribution of a key when adding another AD RMS server to the cluster. In this, we will use the **Use AD RMS centrally managed key storage** option. Once the selection is made, click on **Next** to proceed.

7. AD RMS also uses a password to encrypt the cluster key described earlier. This is required to be provided when adding another AD RMS server to the cluster or when restoring AD RMS from the backup. This key cannot be reset. Therefore, it is recommended that you keep it recorded in a secure place. Once you define the AD RMS cluster key password, click on **Next** to proceed.

8. In the next step, we need to define the IIS virtual directory for the AD RMS website. Unless there is a specific requirement, always use the default and click on **Next**:

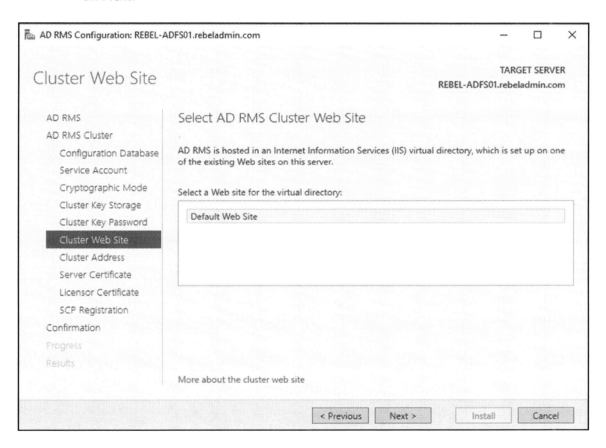

9. In the next step, we need to define an AD RMS cluster URL. This will use by AD RMS clients to communicate with the AD RMS cluster. It is highly recommended that you use SSL for this even if it allows to use it with the HTTP only method. The related DNS records and firewall rules need to be adjusted in order to provide a connection between AD RMS clients and this URL (internally or externally). Once configuration values are provided, click on **Next** to proceed. One thing you need to note is that once this URL is specified, it cannot be changed. In this demo, the RMS URL is `https://rms.rebeladmin.com`:

10. In the next step, we need to define a server authentication certificate. This certificate will be used to encrypt the network traffic between RMS clients and the AD RMS cluster. For testing, it can use a self-signed certificate, but this is not recommended for production. If it uses an internal CA, client computers should be aware of the root certificate. In the wizard, it automatically takes the list of SSL certificates installed on the computer, and we can select the certificate from there. It is also allowed to configure this setting at a later time. Once settings are defined, click on **Next** to proceed:

11. On the next window, it asks you to provide a **Name** for the SLC. This certificate is used to define the identity of the AD RMS cluster, and it used in the data protection process between clients to encrypt/decrypt symmetric keys. Once you define a meaningful name, click on **Next** to proceed.

12. The last step of the configuration is to register AD RMS SCP with the AD DS. If needed, this can be configured later too. This needs Enterprise Admin privileges to register it with AD DS. In this demo, I have already logged as Enterprise Admin, so I am using **Register the SCP now**. Once the option is selected, click on **Next**:

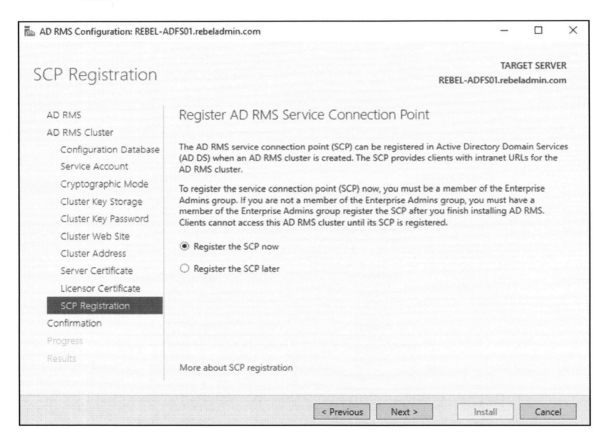

13. After the confirmation, the installation will begin; wait for the result. If all is successful, log out and log back in to the AD RMS server.

14. Once logged back in, select **Server Manager** and navigate to **Tools | Active Directory Rights Management Service** in order to access the AD RMS cluster:

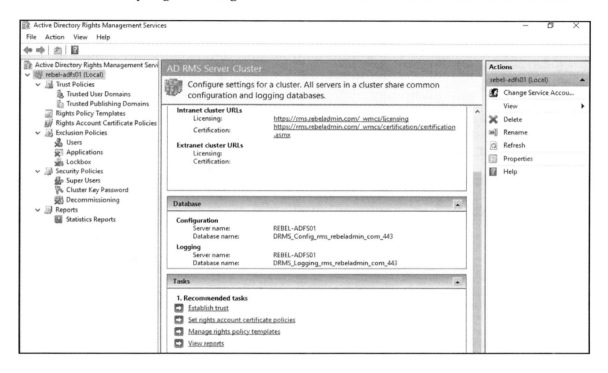

Testing by protecting data using the AD RMS cluster

The next step of the demo is to test the AD RMS cluster by protecting the data. For that, I am using two user accounts, as shown in the following table:

User	Email Address	Role
Peter	peter@rebeladmin.com	Author
Adam	adam@rebeladmin.com	Recipient

The email account field is a must, and if the user doesn't have an email address defined, they will not be allowed to protect the document.

The end user computers must add `https://rms.rebeladmin.com` to the Internet Explorer and the local intranet's trusted site lists. This can be done via GPO. If it's not added, when you go to protect the document, you will get the following error:

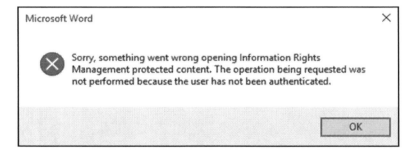

In this demo, as the user, Peter is going to create a protected document using Word 2013. The recipient will be the user Adam only, and he will have only the read permission.

To protect the document

Following are the steps that need to be performed in order to protect the document:

1. Log in to the Windows 10 (domain member) computer as the user Peter.
2. Open Word 2013 and type some text.
3. Then, go to **File** | **Protect Document** | **Restrict Access** | **Connect to Digital Rights Management Servers and get templates**:

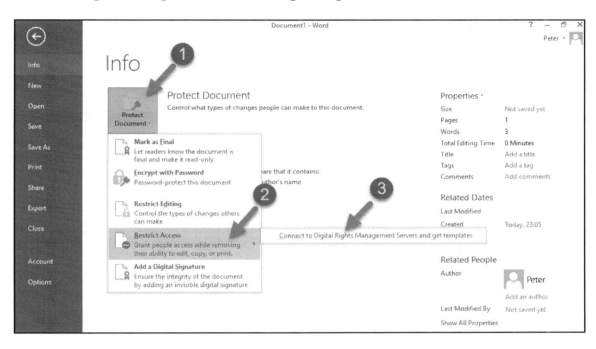

4. Once you have successfully retrieved the templates, go back to the same option and select **Restricted Access**:

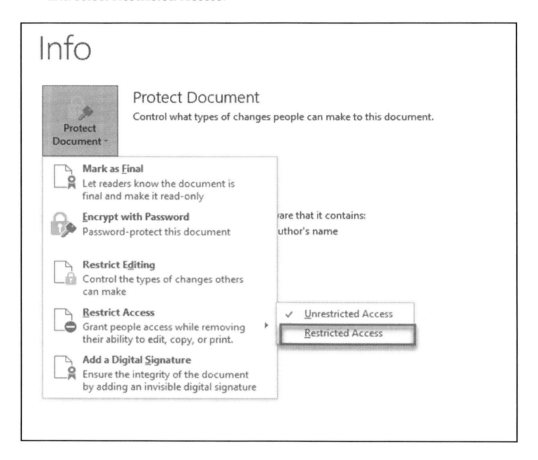

5. Then, it will open a new window. Once there, for the read permissions, type `adam@rebeladmin.com` to provide read-only permission to the user Adam. Then, click on **OK**:

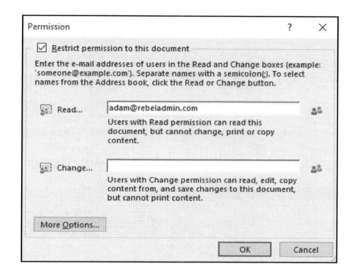

6. After that, save the document. In the demo, I used a network share that the user Adam also has access to.

7. Now log in to another Windows 10 computer as the user Adam.

8. Then, browse to the path where the document was saved and open it using Word 2013.

9. In the opening process, it asks to authenticate to the RMS to retrieve the licenses. After that, it opens the document. At the top of the document, it says the document has limited access. When you click on **View Permission...**, it lists down the allowed permissions and matches what we set on the author side:

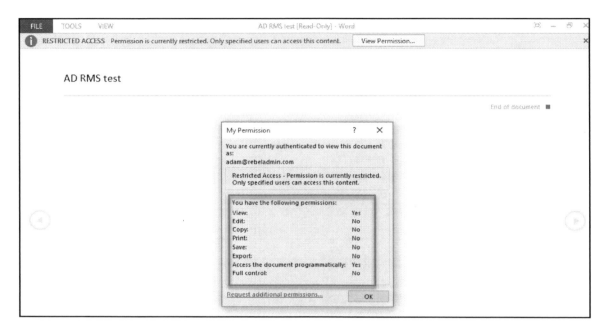

10. Further into testing, I log in to the system as another user (Liam), and when I access the file, I get the following dialog box:

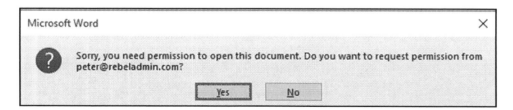

This ends the configuration and testing of the AD RMS cluster. In this demo, I explained how we can set up the AD RMS cluster with minimum resources and configuration. I used only the default configuration of the AD RMS cluster and no custom policies applied. Understanding the core functions allows you to customize it to meet your organization's requirements.

Summary

Digital data protection has been important from the day the computer was invented. There are different laws, products, technologies, and methodologies to improve the data protection in infrastructures. AD RMS is Microsoft's solution, which can be used to control things users can do once they have access to confidential data.

In this chapter, you learned what AD RMS and its components are. Then, we moved on to understanding how AD RMS works and how it protects data. After that, we looked at different AD RMS deployment topologies and their characteristics. Last but not least, we worked on AD RMS installation, configuration, and testing.

This ends the third part of this book, and we are moving on to the last part. The fourth part of the book is to start with a chapter that is focused on Active Directory security best practices.

15
Active Directory Security Best Practices

With this chapter, we are moving on to section four (the last section) of this book. This section includes chapters that cover Active Directory best practices, Active Directory troubleshooting, and extending an on-premises Active Directory infrastructure in Azure.

Infrastructure security is a very broad topic to discuss. It is not just security in Active Directory; it covers only a part of infrastructure security that is related to *identities*. At the same time, it is dependent on other security facts. As an example, before we protect the identities, we need to tighten the perimeter defense by setting up edge firewall rules to protect the internal network from outside threats.

Based on *2016 Internet Security Threat Report* (`https://www.symantec.com/security-center/threat-report`) by Symantec, for a majority of the identity attacks, the main reason is still phishing attacks, viruses, or malware. In the end, adversaries authenticate into user accounts, which are managed by Active Directory, but the first *security breach* is the result of an incident not related to the Active Directory service. In an infrastructure, there can be many Active Directory-integrated applications. These directly query AD DS databases in order to authenticate users. The compromise of these applications or a bug also can make a backdoor to adversaries to get into the Active Directory infrastructure.

From Windows Server 2000, Microsoft kept releasing new AD DS versions with each Windows Server release. All of these versions included new security enhancement and features, but to date compromises of the Active Directory infrastructure are still reported. This is because improving Active Directory security is not the only thing that is going to protect identities and data in the infrastructure. Infrastructure security is related to all seven **Open Systems Interconnection model (OSI)** layers.

In this chapter, we are going to discuss many different Active Directory features that can be used to improve the security of the Active Directory infrastructure. The chapter will cover the following topics:

- How does Active Directory authentication work?
- Delegating permissions
- Active Directory Protected Users security group
- Restricted RDP mode
- Authentication policies and authentication policy silos
- The **just-in-time (JIT)** administration and **just enough administration (JEA)**

Active Directory authentication

In the infrastructure, there can be different types of authentication protocols in use. Active Directory uses Kerberos version 5 as the authentication protocol in order to provide authentication between the server and the client. Kerberos v5 became the default authentication protocol for Windows Server from Windows Server 2003. It is an open standard, and it provides interoperability with other systems that use the same standards. Before we look into improvements in AD DS security, it is important to understand how Active Directory authentication works with Kerberos.

The Kerberos protocol is built to protect authentication between the server and the client in an open network where other systems are connected as well. The main concept behind authentication is that two parties have agreed on a password (secret), and both use it to identify and verify their authenticity:

In the preceding example, **Dave** and **server A** have regular communications. They exchange confidential data between them more often. In order to protect this communication, they agreed on a common secret code **1234** to be used to verify their identities before exchanging data. When **Dave** makes initial communication, he passes his secret to **server A** and says **Hay! I'm Dave**. Then **server A** checks the secret to see whether it's true. If it's correct, it identifies him as **Dave** and allows further communication:

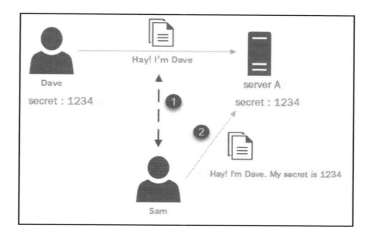

Communication between **Dave** and **server A** happens in an open network, which means there are other connected systems. **Sam** is a user connected in the same network where **Dave** is. He is aware of the communication between **Dave** and **server A**. He has an interest in data exchange between them and would like to get his hands on the data. He starts listening to the traffic between these two hosts to find out the secret they use. Once he finds it, he starts to communicate to **server A** and says he is **Dave** and also provides the secret code **1234**. From the **server A** point of view, system doesn't see a difference between requests from **Dave** and **Sam**, as both provide the correct secret.

Kerberos solved this security challenge using the shared symmetric cryptographic key instead of secrets. It uses the same key for encryption and decryption. The Kerberos name comes from a three-headed strong dog in Greek mythology. As the three-headed dog, the Kerberos protocol has three main components:

- A client
- A server
- A trusted authority to issue secret keys

This trusted authority is called the **Key Distribution Center (KDC)**. Before we look into Kerberos in detail, it's better to understand how a typical key exchange works:

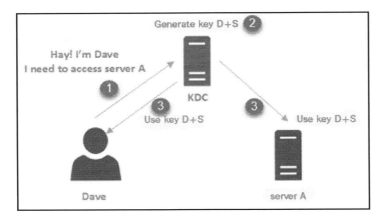

If we revisit our scenario, now we have a **KDC** in place. Instead of communicating to **server A** directly, **Dave** goes to the **KDC** and says he needs to access **server A**. It needs a symmetric key to start communication with **server A**. This key should be used only by **Dave** and **server A**. The **KDC** accepts the request and generates a key (**key D+S**) and then distributes it to **Dave** and **server A**. By the looks of it, this seems quite straightforward, but from the server point of view, there are a few challenges.

In order to accept a connection from **Dave**, the system needs to know **key D+S**, so it needs to keep this key stored in **server A**. We are considering only one connection in here. But if there are a hundred connections, it needs to store all the keys involved. This will cost resources for **server A**. However, the actual Kerberos protocol operation is more efficient than this.

In an Active Directory environment, the KDC is installed as part of the domain controller. The KDC is responsible for two main services: one is the **authentication service (AS)** and the other is the **Ticket-Granting Service (TGS)**.

In the preceding example, when Dave logs into the system, it needs to be proved to the KDC that he is exactly the same person that he claims to be. When he logs in, it sends username to the KDC along with a *long-time key*. The long-time key is generated based on Dave's password. The Kerberos client on Dave's PC accepts his password and generates the cryptographic key. The KDC also maintains a copy of this key in its database. Once the KDC receives the request, it checks its username and the long-term key with its records. If it's all good, the KDC responds to Dave with a *session key*. This is called a **ticket-granting ticket (TGT)**.

The TGT contains two things:

- A copy of a session key that the KDC uses to communicate with Dave. This is encrypted with the KDC's long-term key.
- A copy of a session key that Dave can use to communicate with the KDC. This is encrypted with Dave's long-term key so only Dave can decrypt it.

Once Dave receives this key, he can use his long-term key to decrypt the session key. After that, all future communication with KDC will be based on this session key. This session key is temporarily and has **time to live** (TTL) value.

This session key is saved in Dave's computer's volatile memory. Now it's time to request access to server A. Dave has to contact the KDC again, but this time, he uses the session key provided by the KDC. This request includes the TGT and the timestamp encrypted by the session key and the service ID (the service that is running on server A). Once the KDC receives it, it uses its long-term key to decrypt the TGT and retrieve the session key. Then, using the session key, it decrypts the timestamp. If the time difference is less than 5 minutes, it proves it came from Dave and is not the same request as the one from the previous time.

Once the KDC confirms it as a legitimate request, it creates another ticket, and this is called a **service ticket**. It contains two keys: one for Dave and one for server A. Both keys include the requester's name (Dave), the recipient, the timestamp, the TTL value, and a new session key (that will be shared between Dave and server A). One key of this is encrypted using Dave's long-term key. The other key is encrypted using server A's long-term key. In the end, both are encrypted together using the session key between the KDC and Dave. Finally, the ticket is ready and sent over to Dave. Dave decrypts the ticket using the session key. He also finds *his* key and decrypts it using his long-term key.

This process reveals the new session key that needs to be shared between him and server A. Then, he creates a new request including server A's key retrieved from the service ticket and the timestamp encrypted using the new session key created by the KDC. Once Dave sends it over to server A, it decrypts its key using its long-term key and retrieves the session key. Using the session key, it can decrypt the timestamp to verify the authenticity of the request. As we can see, in this process, it is not server A's responsibility to keep track of the key used by the client or it's not the client's responsibility to keep the relevant keys.

Let's go ahead and recap what we have learned about the Kerberos authentication:

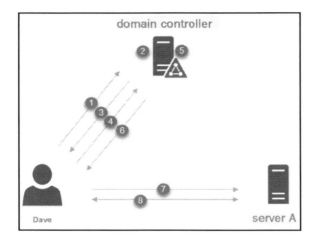

1. **Dave** sends the username and his long-term key to the KDC (**domain controller**).
2. The KDC checks the username and long-term key with its database and verifies the identity. Then, it generates a TGT. It includes a copy of a session key, which the KDC uses to communicate with **Dave**. This is encrypted with the KDC's long-term key. It also includes a copy of a session key **Dave** can use to communicate with the KDC.
3. KDC responds to Dave with its TGT.
4. **Dave** decrypts his key using his long-term key and the retrieved session key. His system creates a new request including the TGT and the timestamp encrypted by the session key and service ID. Once the request is generated, it is sent to the KDC.
5. The KDC uses its long-term key to decrypt the TGT and retrieve the session key. Then, the session key can be used to decrypt the timestamp. Then, it creates a service ticket. This ticket includes two keys. One for **server A** and one for **Dave**. **Dave**'s key is encrypted using his long-term key and **server A**'s key is encrypted using **server A**'s long-term key. In the end, both are encrypted using the session key used by the KDC and **Dave**.
6. KDC sends the service ticket to **Dave**.

7. **Dave** decrypts the ticket using the session key and retrieves his key. Then, he goes ahead and decrypts it to get a new key, which can be used to establish a connection with server A. In the end, it creates another request, including server A's key (which was created earlier) and the timestamp that is encrypted by the session key that Dave decrypted earlier in this step. Once everything is ready, the system sends it to **server A**.

8. **Server A** goes ahead and decrypts his key using its long-term key and the retrieved session key. Then, using it, **server A** can decrypt the timestamp to verify the request's authenticity. Once everything is green, it allows a connection between **Dave** and **server A**.

There are a few other things that need to be fulfilled in order to complete the process:

- **Connectivity**: The server, client, and KDC need to have a reliable connection between them in order to process requests and responses.
- **DNS**: Clients use DNS to locate the KDC and servers. Therefore, a functioning DNS with the correct records is required.
- **Time synchronization**: As we can see, the process uses the timestamp to verify the authenticity of the requests. It allows up to 5 minutes' time difference. Therefore, it's a must to have accurate time synchronization with the domain controllers.
- **Service principal names**: Clients use **service principal names** (**SPN**) to locate services in the AD environment. If there is no SPN for the services, the clients and the KDC cannot locate them when required. When setting up services, make sure that you set up SPN as well.

Delegating permissions

In an Active Directory environment, there are lots of management tasks. Managing domain controllers, adding / managing / removing users, adding / managing / removing groups, password resets, and adding devices to computers are just some of them. In a structured IT department, these management tasks can be bound to different roles. As an example, let's assume Rebeladmin Corp.'s IT department has first-line (first support contact), second-line (intermediate), and third-line (seniors) IT engineers.

When considering the Active Directory management tasks, first-line engineers are usually involved with user password resets, setting up new user accounts and groups, adding devices to domains, and so on. Second-line engineers are involved with additional tasks, such as Group Policy setup, Group Policy troubleshooting, and so on. Third-line engineers usually work on advanced troubleshooting, domain controller installations, schema changes, physical and logical design changes, and so on.

In this way, we can group engineers' Active Directory management tasks according to their role responsibilities. This helps different job roles take the *ownership* of different Active Directory management tasks. At the same time, if a certain job role got the ownership of a task, there should be a mechanism to prevent other job roles involved with that task. As an example, if third-line engineers are responsible for AD schema changes, there should be a way to prevent first-line and second-line engineers from doing it. If we need to prevent or allow users or groups to a folder in a file server, we do it using *permissions*. The same way, Active Directory also allows you to manage users'/groups' authority over objects or management tasks based on permissions. Managing permissions for the IT team is a difficult task, as it is not just a permission; it's a social fact too. There are a few ways to manage permissions for Active Directory management tasks:

- Using predefined Active Directory administrator roles
- Using object ACLs
- Using the delegate control method in AD

Predefined Active Directory administrator roles

Active Directory has predefined administrator roles, and it has predefined permissions attached to it. If a user account needs to grant these role permissions, it needs to be added to the relevant security group:

- **Enterprise Admins**: This is the highest Active Directory role permission which can be applied for in the AD forest. The accounts that are part of this group can modify the logical and physical topology of the Active Directory infrastructure. It also allows you to do schema change. This role is capable of managing other role memberships (Enterprise Admins, Schema Admins, and Domain Admins).
- **Schema Admins**: Members of this group can modify the Active Directory schema. This is included only in the forest root domain as the schema is handled on the forest level.

- **Domain Admins**: This is the highest Active Directory role permission which can be applied for in the AD Domain. When adding the first domain controller to the forest, the default administrator account will be part of the Domain Admin and Enterprise Admin group. The Domain Admin can add/remove Domain Admins from the Domain Admin group.

 These roles have high privileges in the Active Directory environment. Therefore, rather than keeping permanent memberships, it's recommended that you use PAM to provide time-based group memberships. This was described in detail in `Chapter 2`, *Active Directory Domain Services 2016*.

Using object ACLs

User or group access and permissions to a shared folder are controlled by the ACL. Similarly, we can define permissions to Active Directory objects. This can be applied to the individual object or the AD site/domain/OU and then inherit to lower-level objects.

As an example, I have a security group called `First Line Engineers`, and Liam is a member of this group. Liam is an engineer in the Europe office. In the Active Directory environment, he should allow to add user objects under any sub-OU in the `Europe` OU. But he should not be allowed to delete any object under it. Let's look at how we can do this using ACLs:

1. Log in to the domain controller as Domain Admin/Enterprise Admin.
2. Review the group membership using the following command:

    ```
    Get-ADGroupMember "First Line Engineers"
    ```

    The following screenshot shows output for the preceding command:

```
PS C:\Users\Administrator> Get-ADGroupMember "First Line Engineers"

distinguishedName : CN=liam,CN=Users,DC=rebeladmin,DC=com
name              : liam
objectClass       : user
objectGUID        : de876f8d-2737-4e3e-901b-a4abc5373677
SamAccountName    : liam
SID               : S-1-5-21-4041220333-1835452706-552999228-1230
```

3. Go to ADUC, right-click on the `Europe` OU, and click on **Properties**. Then, go to **Security**.

4. In the **Security** tab, click on **Add**.

5. In the new window, type `First Line Engineers` and click on **OK**. Afterwards, in the **Security** tab, select **First Line Engineers** and click on **Advanced**:

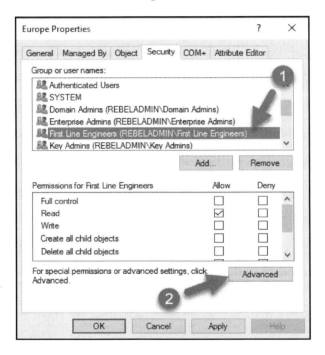

6. In the next window, select **First Line Engineers** from the list and click on **Edit**.

7. From the **Applies to** list, select **This object and all descendant objects** to apply permission to all child objects:

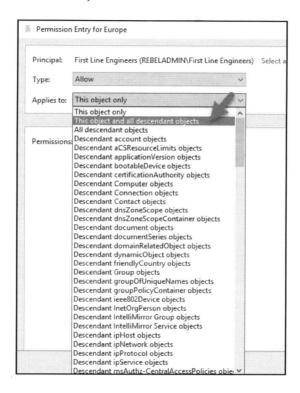

8. Under the **Permissions** section, tick **Create all child objects** and click **OK**.
9. Then, keep clicking on **OK** until all permission windows are closed.
10. Then, log in to the Windows 10 computer that has RSAT tools (`https://www.mic rosoft.com/en-gb/download/details.aspx?id=45520`) installed as the user Liam.
11. According to the permissions, he should be able to add the user account under the `Europe` OU:

```
New-ADUser -Name "Dale"
-Path "OU=Users,OU=Europe,DC=rebeladmin,DC=com"
```

12. This successfully adds the user. Let's see whether we can add another user on a different OU:

```
New-ADUser -Name "Simon"
-Path "OU=Users,OU=Asia,DC=rebeladmin,DC=com"
```

13. And as soon as I run it, I get an `Access is denied` error:

```
PS C:\Users\liam> New-ADUser -Name "Simon" -Path "OU=Users,OU=Asia,DC=rebeladmin,DC=com"
New-ADUser : Access is denied
At line:1 char:1
+ New-ADUser -Name "Simon" -Path "OU=Users,OU=Asia,DC=rebeladmin,DC=com ...
+
    + CategoryInfo          : PermissionDenied: (CN=Simon,OU=Use...beladmin,DC=com:String) [New-ADUser], UnauthorizedA
   ccessException
    + FullyQualifiedErrorId : ActiveDirectoryCmdlet:System.UnauthorizedAccessException,Microsoft.ActiveDirectory.Manag
   ement.Commands.NewADUser

PS C:\Users\liam> _
```

14. According to the applied permissions, Liam should not be able to delete any object under OU=Users,OU=Europe,DC=rebeladmin,DC=com either. Let's check this using the following command:

```
Remove-ADUser -Identity "CN=Dishan Francis,
OU=Users,OU= Europe,DC=rebeladmin,DC=com"
```

15. And as soon as I run it, I get an `Access is denied` error:

```
PS C:\Users\liam> Remove-ADUser -Identity "CN=Dishan Francis,OU=Users,OU=Europe,DC=rebeladmin,DC=com"

Confirm
Are you sure you want to perform this action?
Performing the operation "Remove" on target "CN=Dishan Francis,OU=Users,OU=Europe,DC=rebeladmin,DC=com".
[Y] Yes  [A] Yes to All  [N] No  [L] No to All  [S] Suspend  [?] Help (default is "Y"): A
Remove-ADUser : Access is denied
At line:1 char:1
+ Remove-ADUser -Identity "CN=Dishan Francis,OU=Users,OU=Europe,DC=rebe ...
+
    + CategoryInfo          : PermissionDenied: (CN=Dishan Franc...beladmin,DC=com:ADUser) [Remove-ADUser], Unauthoriz
   edAccessException
    + FullyQualifiedErrorId : ActiveDirectoryCmdlet:System.UnauthorizedAccessException,Microsoft.ActiveDirectory.Manag
   ement.Commands.RemoveADUser

PS C:\Users\liam>
```

This confirms that we can manage permissions for AD management tasks using ACLs.

Using the delegate control method in AD

This works similar to ACLs, but it simplifies the privilege management as it uses the following:

- The **Delegation of Control Wizard** can be used to apply delegated permissions
- Predefined tasks can be used and permissions are assigned to those tasks

This wizard contains the following predefined tasks, which can be used to assign permissions:

- Create, delete, and manage user accounts
- Reset user passwords and force a password change at the next logon
- Read all user information
- Create, delete, and manage groups
- Modify the membership of a group
- Manage Group Policy links
- Generate Resultant Set of Policy (Planning)
- Generate Resultant Set of Policy (Logging)
- Create, delete, and manage inetOrgPerson accounts
- Reset inetOrgPerson passwords and force a password change at the next logon
- Read all the inetOrgPerson information

This also allows you to create a custom task to delegate permissions if it's not covered in the common tasks list.

Similar to ACLs, permissions can be applied in the following levels:

- **Site**: Delegated permissions will be valid for all the objects under the given Active Directory site
- **Domain**: Delegated permission will be valid for all the objects under the given Active Directory domain
- **OU**: Delegated permissions will be valid for all the objects under the given Active Directory OU

As an example, I have a security group called `Second Line Engineers`, and Scott is a member of it. I like to allow members of this group to reset passwords for objects in `OU=Users,OU=Europe,DC=rebeladmin,DC`, and nothing else:

1. Log in to the domain controller as Domain Admin/Enterprise Admin.
2. Review the group membership using the following command:

   `Get-ADGroupMember "Second Line Engineers"`

   The following screenshot shows the output for the preceding command:

```
PS C:\Users\Administrator> Get-ADGroupMember "Second Line Engineers"

distinguishedName : CN=Scott Brewer,OU=Users,OU=Europe,DC=rebeladmin,DC=com
name              : Scott Brewer
objectClass       : user
objectGUID        : 717e5cb5-724d-4aa7-988a-de34ad7fb1e1
SamAccountName    : sbrewer
SID               : S-1-5-21-4041220333-1835452706-552999228-1200
```

3. Go to ADUC, right-click on the `Europe` OU, and then from the list, click on the **Delegate Control...** option.
4. This will open a new wizard in the initial page; click on **Next** to proceed.
5. On the next page, click on the **Add** button and add the `Second Line Engineers` group to it. Then, click on **Next** to proceed:

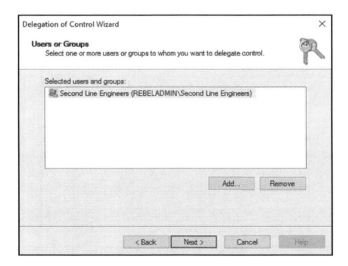

6. From the task, to delegate a window, select the **Delegate the following common tasks** option, and from the list, select **Reset user passwords and force password change at next logon**. On this page, we can select multiple tasks. If none of those work, we still can select **Create a custom task to delegate**. Once you complete the selection, click on **Next** to proceed:

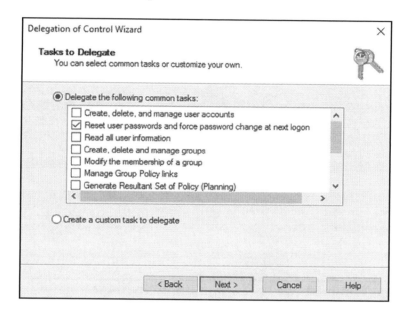

7. This completes the wizard; click on **Finish** to complete.
8. Now it's time for testing. I log in to the Windows 10 computer as user Scott that has RSAT tools (https://www.microsoft.com/en-gb/download/details.aspx ?id=45520) installed.
9. According to the permissions, Scott should be able to reset the password of an object under OU=Users,OU=Europe,DC=rebeladmin,DC:

   Set-ADAccountPassword —Identity dfrancis

10. This allows you to change the password successfully:

```
PS C:\Users\sbrewer> Set-ADAccountPassword -Identity dfrancis
Please enter the current password for 'CN=Dishan Francis,OU=Users,OU=Europe,DC=rebeladmin,DC=com'
Password: *********
Please enter the desired password for 'CN=Dishan Francis,OU=Users,OU=Europe,DC=rebeladmin,DC=com'
Password: ************
Repeat Password: ************
PS C:\Users\sbrewer>
```

11. However, it should not allow Scott to delete any objects. We can test it using the following command:

```
Remove-ADUser -Identity "CN=Dishan Francis,
OU=Users,OU=Europe,DC=rebeladmin,DC=com"
```

12. And as expected, it returns an `Access is denied` error:

```
PS C:\Users\sbrewer> Remove-ADUser -Identity "CN=Dishan Francis,OU=Users,OU=Europe,DC=rebeladmin,DC=com"

Confirm
Are you sure you want to perform this action?
Performing the operation "Remove" on target "CN=Dishan Francis,OU=Users,OU=Europe,DC=rebeladmin,DC=com".
[Y] Yes  [A] Yes to All  [N] No  [L] No to All  [S] Suspend  [?] Help (default is "Y"): A
Remove-ADUser : Access is denied
At line:1 char:1
+ Remove-ADUser -Identity "CN=Dishan Francis,OU=Users,OU=Europe,DC=rebe ...
+ ~~~~~~~~~~~~~~~~~~~~~~~~~~~~~~~~~~~~~~~~~~~~~~~~~~~~~~~~~~~~~~~~~~~~~~~~
    + CategoryInfo          : PermissionDenied: (CN=Dishan Franc...beladmin,DC=com:ADUser) [Remove-ADUser], Unauthoriz
   edAccessException
    + FullyQualifiedErrorId : ActiveDirectoryCmdlet:System.UnauthorizedAccessException,Microsoft.ActiveDirectory.Manag
   ement.Commands.RemoveADUser

PS C:\Users\sbrewer> _
```

Using all three methods, we can delegate permissions for Active Directory administrative tasks. This helps assign responsibilities to users or groups in order to keep the AD environment healthy and secure.

Fine-grained password policies

Password policy is a basic security setting that any administrator uses. In the Active Directory environment, password complexity settings and account lockout settings can be applied using GPO settings located at **Computer Configuration** | **Policies** | **Windows Settings** | **Security Settings** | **Account Policies**. Before Windows Server 2008, there was only one password policy and account lockout policy setting that could be applied to the users. With Windows Server 2008, Microsoft introduced fine-grained password policies. This allows administrators to apply different password and account lockout policy settings to individual users or groups. This allows you to protect privileged accounts using strong policies than regular user accounts. This feature continued with every AD DS version after 2008 and is available with AD DS 2016 as well.

Once, I was working on an AD audit for a hedge fund. As part of the report, I recommended that they use password policies with complexity as they were not doing so. After I explained things, the IT manager there agreed and I configured the password policy and the account lockout policy. After a few days, I went to the same site, and the IT Manager showed that after forcing the policy, the end users started to write down their complex passwords on sticky notes and papers. So even though it was a security setting, in the end, it led to bigger security issues as the users could see each other's passwords on sticky notes. Using fine-grained password policies, administrators can apply different settings based on the situation. As an example, while using a 5-character complex password for Sales department users, you can use a 12-character complex password for Domain Admins.

Limitations

Fine-grained password policies have the following limitations:

- Fine-grained password policies can be applied only to users and global security groups. They can't be applied to OUs.
- By default, only Domain Admin/Enterprise Admins can set up/manage/delete fine-grained password policies. It is possible to delegate permission to other users if required.
- The minimum domain functional level is Windows Server 2008.

Resultant Set of Policy

When you use fine-grained password policies, some objects may have multiple fine-grained password policies applied. However, only one password policy can be applied to an object. It is not possible to merge multiple policies either.

Resultant Set of Policy (RSoP) uses the attribute value of `msDS-PasswordSettingsPrecedence`, which is associated with each password to decide winning policy. A precedence value is an integer value that the administrator can define. A lower precedence value means higher priority. If multiple password policies are applied to the same object, the password policy with the lower precedence value wins.

Following list further explain how password policies works in an infrastructure:

- There are two ways in which an object can be linked to a password policy. The first method is via a directly linked policy. The second method is via group membership. If the policy targets a security group, its members will automatically have the password policy inherited. However, if a fine-grained password policy is linked to an object directly, it will be the winning policy.
- If there's no directly linked policy, object will consider the lowest policy precedence. These policies are inherited from its security groups.
- If both the settings are not applicable, the default GPO password policy setting is applied.

Configuration

There are two ways to apply fine-grained password policies. The first option is to use ADAC, and the second option is to use PowerShell cmdlets.

In ADAC, browse to **System | Password Settings Container**. Then, right-click and go to **New | Password Settings**. It will open up the window where we can define the policy settings:

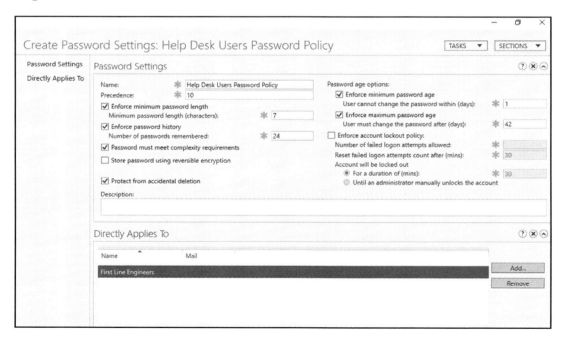

In the window, we can define the policy name, precedence, another password, and account lockout policy settings. **Directly Applies To** is the place where we can define the users or security groups this new policy applies to. In the preceding example, I added the `First Line Engineers` security group as the target.

This policy can also be created using PowerShell:

```
New-ADFineGrainedPasswordPolicy -Name "Domain Admin Password Policy" -
Precedence 1 `
-MinPasswordLength 12 -MaxPasswordAge "30" -MinPasswordAge "7" `
-PasswordHistoryCount 50 -ComplexityEnabled:$true `
-LockoutDuration "8:00" `
-LockoutObservationWindow "8:00" -LockoutThreshold 3 `
-ReversibleEncryptionEnabled:$false
```

In the preceding command, `New-ADFineGrainedPasswordPolicy` is the cmdlet to create a new policy. `-Precedence` defines the policy precedence. The `-LockoutDuration` and `-LockoutObservationWindow` values are defined in hours. The `-LockoutThreshold` value defines the number of login attempts allowed.

The policy settings can be viewed using ADAC or PowerShell:

```
Get-ADFineGrainedPasswordPolicy - Identity "Domain Admin Password Policy"
```

The preceding command will retrieve the settings for the given password policy:

```
PS C:\Users\Administrator> Get-ADFineGrainedPasswordPolicy -Identity "Domain Admin Password Policy"

AppliesTo                   : {}
ComplexityEnabled           : True
DistinguishedName           : CN=Domain Admin Password Policy,CN=Password Settings
                              Container,CN=System,DC=rebeladmin,DC=com
LockoutDuration             : 08:00:00
LockoutObservationWindow    : 08:00:00
LockoutThreshold            : 3
MaxPasswordAge              : 30.00:00:00
MinPasswordAge              : 7.00:00:00
MinPasswordLength           : 12
Name                        : Domain Admin Password Policy
ObjectClass                 : msDS-PasswordSettings
ObjectGUID                  : 81b80dc3-4243-41b2-8e2f-0fb54c24df74
PasswordHistoryCount        : 50
Precedence                  : 1
ReversibleEncryptionEnabled : True
```

Now we have a new policy and the next step is to assign objects to it. I need to add the Domain Admins security group to it:

```
Add-ADFineGrainedPasswordPolicySubject -Identity "Domain Admin Password
Policy" -Subjects "Domain Admins"
```

The preceding command will add the `Domain Admins` group to `Domain Admin Password Policy`. This can be verified using the following command:

```
Get-ADFineGrainedPasswordPolicy -Identity "Domain Admin Password Policy" |
Format-Table AppliesTo -AutoSize
```

This will confirm what the policy target is. This value is saved under the `AppliesTo` attribute.

Another useful command we can use is as follows:

```
Get-ADFineGrainedPasswordPolicy -Filter * | Format-Table
Name,Precedence,AppliesTo -AutoSize
```

This will list down all the fine-grained password policies along with `Name`, `Precedence`, and the targets.

This completes the configuration for the fine-grained password policies.

Pass-the-hash attacks

When the client and server uses the authentication system, in order to begin the communication, client needs to successfully prove his identity. This is done using a username and password. The client needs to present its username and password to the authentication server, and it will verify the identity. There are legacy protocols and systems that send this information in clear text even in an open network. Telnet is a good example. If someone is listening to traffic (packet capturing) for the telnet session, they can easily capture password as it is transmitted in clear text.

Modern authentication systems are well aware of these types of threats and use different technologies to encrypt credentials or create cryptographic hashes and then use them for identity verifications. The **cryptographic hash** means a password string transformed into a fixed-length digest using an algorithm.

Earlier in this chapter, we saw how Kerberos authentication works using hash values. When we use hash values, the authentication server compares the hash value submitted by the client with the hash value for the user password that is stored in its database. In the Windows environment, these password hashes are stored in three places:

- The **Security Account Manager (SAM)** database
- The **Local Security Authority Subsystem Service (LSASS)**
- The Active Directory database

The SAM database stores usernames and NT hashes in a `%SystemRoot%/system32/config/SAM` file. This contains all the hash values for accounts that are local to the computer. The current version of SAM does not store LM hashes in the database file.

The very first password hash schema introduced by Microsoft was **LAN Manager (LM)**. It uses the **Data Encryption Standard (DES)** algorithm for hashing. This is a legacy weak schema, and Microsoft highly recommends not to use it. It doesn't support passwords larger than 15 ASCII characters and passwords that are not case-sensitive. However, the new operating system after Windows Vista supports the **Advanced Encryption Standard (AES)** algorithm for hashing.

Compared to the clear text password, for an attacker, it is almost impossible to figure out the password based on the hash. Even if they are able to do it, it takes much compute power and time. But instead of retrieving the password, if they can find the hash value, it can be used to initiate a connection with the server on behalf of the original owner of the hash. This sounds easy, but in practice, it will be still be very difficult as these authentication protocols have their own mechanisms to prevent attackers using someone else's hash value. If you consider Kerberos, it uses timestamps along with requests and responses to verify the authenticity of those. LM and NTLM v1 and v2 also use similar challenge-response features to authenticate without revealing the password.

However, even hash values are not transmitted over directly. The LSASS stores credentials in memory on behalf of users with active sessions. LSASS can store credentials in multiple forms, such as NT hash, LM hash, and Kerberos tickets. This is required to maintain active sessions and do future authentications faster. It will clear up during the reboot, but it can be enough for the adversary to retrieve a hash value and use it to compromise the entire identity infrastructure. Microsoft introduced many features and techniques to protect the AD environment from pass-the-hash attacks, and in this section, we are going to look into them in detail.

Protected Users security group

The Protected Users security group was introduced with Windows Server 2012 R2 and continued in Windows Server 2016. This group was developed to provide better protection for high privileged accounts from credential theft attacks. Members of this group have non-configurable protection applied. In order to use the Protected Users group, PDC should be running with a minimum of Windows Server 2012 R2 and the client computers that member of this group log into should be running with a minimum of Windows 8.1 or Windows 2012 R2.

If a member of this group logs into Windows 8.1, Windows Server 2012 R2, Windows 10, or Windows Server 2016, we can expect the following:

- Members of this group cannot use NTLM, digest authentication, or CredSSP for authentication. Plain text passwords are not cached. So, any of the devices using these protocols will fail to authenticate to the domain.
- Kerberos long-term keys not cached. For accounts in this group, the Kerberos protocol verifies authentication at each request (the TGT acquired at log on).
- Sign-in is offline. A cached verifier is not created at sign-in.

For the Protected Users group feature, it is *not* a must to have a domain or forest functional level run on Windows Server 2012 R2 or higher (Windows Server 2008 is the minimum as Kerberos needs to use AES). The only requirement is to run the PDC emulator FSMO role in the Windows Server 2012 R2 domain controller.

 If required, after the Protected Users group object is replicated to all the domain controllers, the PDC emulator role can be transferred to a domain controller running a lower Windows Server version.

If the AD environment uses Windows Server 2012 R2 or Windows Server 2016 domain functional levels, it provides additional protections with Protected User groups, such as:

- No NTLM authentication
- No DES or RC4 encryption in Kerberos pre-authentication
- No delegation using the unconstrained or constrained method
- No Kerberos TGT valid more than 4 hours

Service accounts and computers cannot be members of the Protected Users' security group. These accounts can be protected using different features, such as policy silos, which I will explain later in this chapter.

To start with, we can review the `Protected Users` security group using the following command:

```
Get-ADGroup -Identity "Protected Users"
```

The following screenshot shows the output for the preceding command:

```
PS C:\Users\Administrator> Get-ADGroup -Identity "Protected Users"

DistinguishedName : CN=Protected Users,CN=Users,DC=rebeladmin,DC=com
GroupCategory     : Security
GroupScope        : Global
Name              : Protected Users
ObjectClass       : group
ObjectGUID        : 795da445-8143-41bf-93d5-e6cbc1aff863
SamAccountName    : Protected Users
SID               : S-1-5-21-4041220333-1835452706-552999228-525
```

We can add users to the `Protected Users` group using ADAC, ADUC MMC, and PowerShell. This group is located in the default `Users` container in AD.

In here, we are going to add the user account Adam in to the `Protected Users` group using the following command:

```
Get-ADGroup -Identity "Protected Users" | Add-ADGroupMember -Members
"CN=Adam,CN=Users,DC=rebeladmin,DC=com"
```

The first part of the command will retrieve the group and the second part will add the user Adam.

After the user is added to the group, we can verify group membership using the following command:

```
Get-ADGroupMember -Identity "Protected Users"
```

The following screenshot shows the output for the preceding command:

```
PS C:\Users\Administrator> Get-ADGroupMember -Identity "Protected Users"

distinguishedName : CN=Adam,CN=Users,DC=rebeladmin,DC=com
name              : Adam
objectClass       : user
objectGUID        : 7f628987-29b6-42a8-95a6-d90ba92b6128
SamAccountName    : adam
SID               : S-1-5-21-4041220333-1835452706-552999228-1229
```

In order to test this, we are going to use a tool called **mimikatz** (`https://github.com/gentilkiwi/mimikatz/blob/master/README.md`), which can be used to do experiments with Windows security.

I logged in as user the `liam`, and he is not part of the `Protected Users` group. When I list keys from LSASS for users, I can see Liam's NTLM hash clearly:

```
Authentication Id : 0 ; 3059384 (00000000:002eaeb8)
Session           : Interactive from 3
User Name         : liam
Domain            : REBELADMIN
Logon Server      : REBEL-PDC-01
Logon Time        : 15/04/2017 08:35:20
SID               : S-1-5-21-4041220333-1835452706-552999228-1230
        msv :
         [00010000] CredentialKeys
         * NTLM     : 947e1646ca81470d18fdb6d976ba8d6a
         * SHA1     : aabc44618a0645c7ddd29ca57f95bacc3f1871b6
         [00000003] Primary
         * Username : liam
         * Domain   : REBELADMIN
         * NTLM     : 947e1646ca81470d18fdb6d976ba8d6a
         * SHA1     : aabc44618a0645c7ddd29ca57f95bacc3f1871b6
        tspkg :
        wdigest :
         * Username : liam
         * Domain   : REBELADMIN
         * Password : (null)
        kerberos :
         * Username : liam
         * Domain   : REBELADMIN.COM
         * Password : (null)
        ssp :
        credman :
```

When I do the same thing for user the `adam`, who is a member of the `Protected Users` group, I cannot see the NTLM hash stored in the LSASS memory because members in the protected group do not use NTLM and don't save any credentials in the cache:

```
Authentication Id : 0 ; 3580277 (00000000:0036a175)
Session           : Interactive from 4
User Name         : adam
Domain            : REBELADMIN
Logon Server      : REBEL-PDC-01
Logon Time        : 15/04/2017 08:52:06
SID               : S-1-5-21-4041220333-1835452706-552999228-1229
        msv :
         [00010000] CredentialKeys
         * RootKey   : fc7b034be210b04c20921a5811dc1165fe4a6dcfddde33b3f939d2b41981b789
         * DPAPI     : c3ebcfb3a1e4b912d6ef928d8bd25c46
        tspkg :
        wdigest :
         * Username : adam
         * Domain   : REBELADMIN
         * Password : (null)
        kerberos :
         * Username : adam
         * Domain   : REBELADMIN.COM
         * Password : (null)
        ssp :
        credman :
```

Restricted admin mode for RDP

In a typical identity infrastructure attack, advisories target regular user accounts or endpoints for the initial breach. The reason is high privileged accounts and highly important systems have advanced protection compared to end user devices. These systems and accounts are constantly monitored and there is a high possibility that engineers recognize unauthorized login attempts or unusual behavior quickly. A typical end user account does not have privileges to do much damage, but the privileged account does, so the next thing they are looking for is to get their hands on the privileged account.

If they start to misbehave with the system, the user will contact the IT department for help. IT department engineers are usually members of Enterprise Admins, Domain Admins, or at least local administrators groups. In order to log in and troubleshoot, they have to use their privileged accounts. If the adversaries have programs running on the system for password harvesting, these privileged accounts credentials will be revealed.

In the previous section, we discussed how we can prevent credential hashes from being stored in LSASS. LSASS memory stores credentials when it:

- Logs in to a computer locally or using RDP
- Runs an application or a task using the **Run As** option
- Runs a Windows service on the computer with the service account
- Runs a scheduled task or a batch job on the computer
- Runs a task on the local computer using remote tools (system scans and installations)

RDP is used by engineers to access computers remotely. When engineering RDP, it sends credentials to the remote computer. This is a security issue if the remote computer is already compromised. Microsoft introduced the *restricted admin mode for RDP* with Windows Server 2012 R2. When this mode is used for RDP, it will not send credentials to the remote computer. Once the user is logged in via the restricted RDP session, they cannot connect to other resources, such as a shared network. This feature is also available in Windows Server 2016.

This mode can be used with Windows 7, Windows 8, Windows 8.1, Windows 10, Windows Server 2008 R2, Windows Server 2012, Windows Server 2012 R2, and Windows Server 2016.

By default, this mode is not enabled. Before you use it, it needs to be enabled in the target system. It can be done using the registry edit:

1. Log in to the target computer or server as the administrator.
2. Click on the Start menu, click on **Run**, type `regedit`, and then click on **OK**.
3. In **Registry Editor**, browse to `HKEY_LOCAL_MACHINE\System\CurrentControlSet\Control\Lsa`.
4. Create the following registry key:

```
Name: DisableRestrictedAdmin
Type: REG_DWORD
Value: 0
```

The following screenshot illustrates the preceding step:

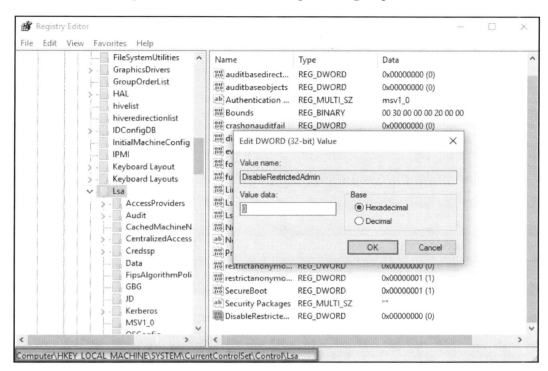

Once this is done, we can connect to the target computer using the restricted admin mode for RDP. In order to do that, the remote desktop client needs to run with the restricted mode. This can be done running the `mstsc /restrictedadmin` command:

In order to test this feature, we will connect to a Windows 10 member PC using the restricted RDP mode. The user account belongs to Peter, and he is the Domain Admin:

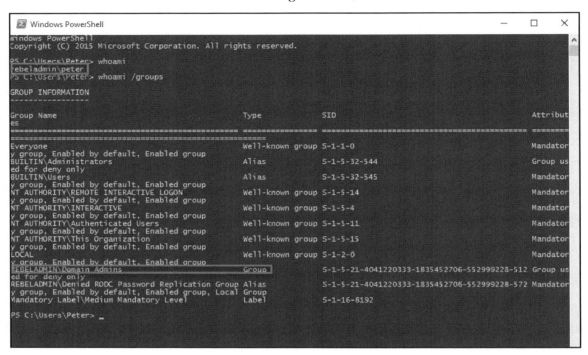

Now when I try to access another computer hard drive, it prompts with an **Access is denied** error. The user account is a Domain Admin, and it should not prevent access. This is due to the restricted RDP mode as it cannot be used to access resources through such a session:

Similarly, I tried to add the domain controller to the **Server Manager** in the remote computer. It issues an **Access denied** error as well:

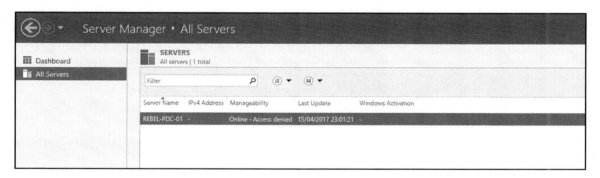

This confirms protection when using RDP to log in to remote systems. Even though these systems are already compromised, it minimize the risk of highly privileged accounts getting compromised.

The restricted RDP mode can be disabled by changing the value of the `DisableRestrictedAdmin` registry key to 1.

Authentication policies and authentication policy silos

A rule of thumb in pass-the-hash attack protection is to prevent trusted users from appearing on untrusted systems. Rebeladmin Corp. has the MS SQL farm to host its databases. When they were setting up the SQL services, engineers used service accounts. It is obvious that these SQL service accounts should be used only with SQL servers. If they appear on a receptionist's computer, something is definitely wrong. With Windows Server 2012 R2, Microsoft introduced authentication policies and policy silos that can be used to limit highly privileged accounts to highly valued systems.

Authentication policies

Authentication policies can be used to specify the Kerberos protocol TGT validity period and access control conditions to restrict user sign-on.

Authentication policy silos

Authentication policy silos are similar to containers where we can assign user accounts, computer accounts, and service accounts. Then, these accounts can be managed by the authentication policies.

This feature requires the following prerequisites:

- All domain controllers in the domain must be based on Windows Server 2012 R2 or Windows Server 2016
- The domain functional level must be Windows Server 2012 R2 or Windows Server 2016
- Domain controllers must be configured to support DAC
- Windows 8, Windows 8.1, Windows 10, Windows Server 2012, Windows Server 2012 R2, and Windows Server 2016 domain members must be configured to support DAC

Creating authentication policies

Before we create policies, we need to enable **Dynamic Access Control (DAC)** support for domain controllers and devices. DAC allows administrators to apply access control permissions and restrictions based on rules that can include the characteristics of the resources.

To enable DAC for domain controllers, perform the following steps:

1. Go to the **Group Policy Management** MMC.
2. Edit **Default Domain Controllers Policy**.
3. Go to **Computer Configuration** | Policies | Administrative Templates | System | KDC.
4. Click on **Enabled** to enable **KDC support for claims, compound authentication and Kerberos armoring**.
5. Under the options, select **Always provide claims** and click on **OK**. This will ensure it always returns claims for accounts and supports the RFC behavior to advertise the **Flexible Authentication Secure Tunneling (FAST)**:

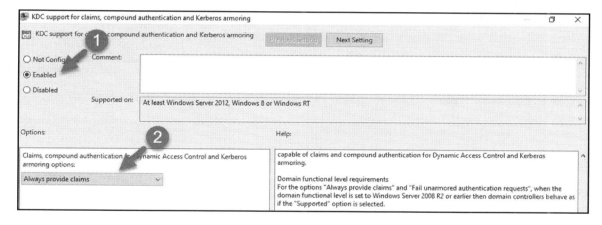

To enable DAC for computers, perform the following steps:

1. Go to the **Group Policy Management** MMC.
2. Edit **Default Domain Policy**.
3. Go to **Computer Configuration** | Policies | Administrative Templates | System | Kerberos.

4. Click on **Enabled** in **Kerberos client support for claims, compound authentication and Kerberos armoring**.

5. Once this is done, we can create a new authentication policy using the New-ADAuthenticationPolicy cmdlet. This can also be created using ADAC:

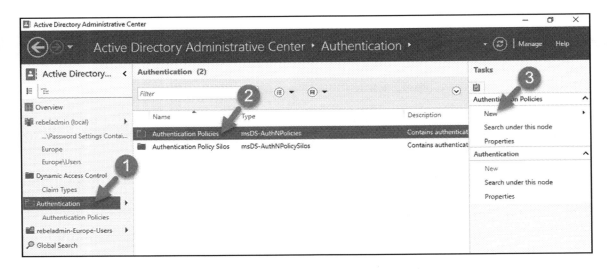

As an example, we will be creating a new authentication policy called AP_1hr_TGT with a TGT lifetime for 60 minutes:

```
New-ADAuthenticationPolicy –Name "AP_1hr_TGT" –UserTGTLifetimeMins 60 –
Enforce
```

In the preceding command, -UserTGTLifetimeMins defines the TGT lifetime for user accounts and the -Enforce parameter will enforce policy restrictions.

Creating authentication policy silos

Now that we have the authentication policy created. The next step is to create a new authentication policy silo. My requirement is to create a policy silo to prevent the user account Peter to REBEL-PC01.

Policy silos can be created using ADAC or the `New-ADAuthenticationPolicySilo` PowerShell cmdlet:

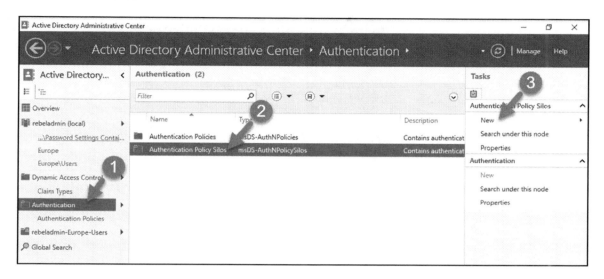

In the demo, we are going to create a new authentication policy silo called `Restricted_REBEL_PC01`:

```
New-ADAuthenticationPolicySilo -Name Restricted_REBEL_PC01 -
UserAuthenticationPolicy AP_1hr_TGT -ComputerAuthenticationPolicy
AP_1hr_TGT -ServiceAuthenticationPolicy AP_1hr_TGT -Enforce
```

In the preceding command, `-UserAuthenticationPolicy`, `-ComputerAuthenticationPolicy`, and `-ServiceAuthenticationPolicy` refer to the authentication policies that will be attached to the policy silo. For example, we are using only one policy, but if needed, the policy silo can be attached to multiple authentication policies that will cover the user, computer, and service classes.

The next step is to add the related objects as permitted accounts to the policy silo. In my demo, this is the user account `Peter` and the computer `REBEL-PC01`.

I can add these objects to the policy silos using the `Grant-ADAuthenticationPolicySiloAccess` PowerShell cmdlet:

```
Grant-ADAuthenticationPolicySiloAccess -Identity Restricted_REBEL_PC01 -
Account Peter
```

The preceding command will add the user account `Peter` to the `Restricted_REBEL_PC01` policy silo as a permitted account.

We also can combine it with a filter and then add the result to the policy silo:

```
Get-ADComputer -Filter 'Name -like "REBEL-PC01"' | Grant-
ADAuthenticationPolicySiloAccess -Identity Restricted_REBEL_PC01
```

In the preceding command, I search for the computer object and then pass the result to the policy silo.

Once this is completed, we need to assign policy silos and the authentication policy to `Peter` and `REBEL-PC01`. This can be done using `Set-ADAccountAuthenticationPolicySilo`:

```
Set-ADAccountAuthenticationPolicySilo -Identity Peter -
AuthenticationPolicySilo Restricted_REBEL_PC01 -AuthenticationPolicy
AP_1hr_TGT
```

The preceding command assigns the policy silo `Restricted_REBEL_PC01` and the authentication policy `AP_1hr_TGT` to the user account `Peter`.

These commands can also be attached to filters:

```
Get-ADComputer -Filter 'Name -like "REBEL-PC01"' | Set-
ADAccountAuthenticationPolicySilo -AuthenticationPolicySilo
Restricted_REBEL_PC01 -AuthenticationPolicy AP_1hr_TGT
```

In the preceding command, it filters for the AD computer object `REBEL-PC01` and then assigns the authentication policy and the policy silo.

The last step of the configuration is to define the access control condition for the authentication policy `AP_1hr_TGT`. This defines the condition of the device or host from which users log in. The condition that will be used for my demo will use the user's policy silo value:

```
Set-ADAuthenticationPolicy -Identity AP_1hr_TGT -
UserAllowedToAuthenticateFrom
"O:SYG:SYD:(XA;OICI;CR;;;WD;(@USER.ad://ext/AuthenticationSilo ==
`"Restricted_REBEL_PC01`"))"
```

In the preceding command, the condition is passed as an SDDL string. More about this SDDL can be found at `https://blogs.technet.microsoft.com/askds/2008/04/18/the-s ecurity-descriptor-definition-language-of-love-part-1/`.

This can also be modified using the authentication policy properties window in ADAC:

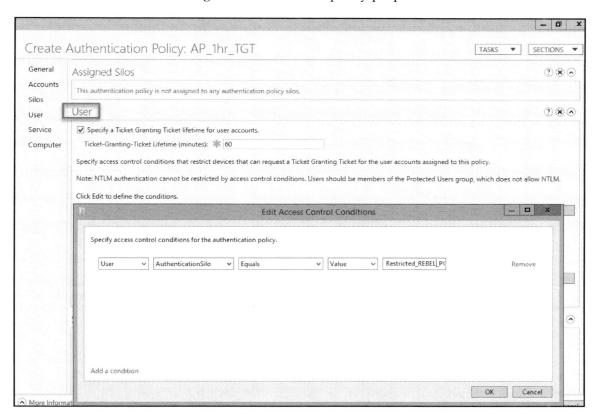

This finishes the configuration of the authentication policy silo and the authentication policy. Authentication policies and authentication policy silos provide greater flexibility in protecting highly valued accounts on highly valued systems.

Just-in-time administration and just enough administration

In the previous sections, you learned about new features and tools introduced by Microsoft to prevent pass-the-hash attacks. These types of attacks are still used by adversaries in identity infrastructure attacks. So, it's important to prevent these attacks whenever and wherever possible. But is this going to secure our identity infrastructures 100%? Software vendors, including Microsoft, release new products, features, security updates, and patches to protect systems, infrastructures, and workloads from various types of threats.

All these companies spend lots of money annually on R&D to protect their software, solutions, and customers from emerging threats. However, we still see constant news about identity infrastructure security breaches. For me, it is not a problem with technology. The myth of zero-day attacks is no longer valid. With all these technologies, we fight against human adversaries. If the method they used earlier is not working anymore, they will find another way to get in. We cannot close all the doors; we need to understand that there can be a breach anytime.

JIT and JEA are a different approach toward identity infrastructure security. In any identity infrastructure attack, advisories are after one common thing. In order to get control of the infrastructure, they need access to *privileged accounts*. This is what they are going after. JIT and JEA are about managing privileges effectively within the identity infrastructure. They limit what adversaries can do in the identity infrastructure even if there is a breach.

Just-in-time administration

In Chapter 2, *Active Directory Domain Services 2016*, you learned about JIT in detail and we discussed how AD DS 2016 features will help. Therefore, we are not going to look at it in detail in this chapter again, but I'd like to list down a few important facts:

- JIT administration allows you to assign administrative privileges to users whenever required. In this method, user accounts do not need to be members of privileged groups permanently.
- Privileges will be time-based. Privileged group memberships have TTL, and once it exceeds the allocated time, members will automatically fade away from groups.

- A bastion forest (the administrative forest) will introduce you to the existing infrastructure in order to manage privileges. This forest can run on the Windows Server 2016 or Windows Server 2012 R2 forest functional level.
- Minimal changes are required in the existing AD forest. They are not required for domain functional level and forest functional level upgrade.
- Microsoft Identity Manager 2016 is part of the solution. It is responsible for managing the bastion forest, managing group memberships, creating workflows, and producing reports.
- One bastion forest can manage privileges for multiple forests.
- Users can make requests for privileges, and it will be handled according to the policies in place. It can be either manual, or it can be an auto-approval process.
- All the incidents will be recorded and can be reported when required.
- The solution can be integrated with existing helpdesk systems or CMS using REST APIs.

Apart from that, AD DS 2016 supports time-based group memberships. This feature itself can be used to provide JIT administration.

Just enough administration

JEA was first introduced in 2014, and it was the first approach toward the JIT. JEA allows you to provide role-based privileges instead of full administrative privileges. As an example, the Rebeladmin Corp. IT team monthly runs a set of PowerShell scripts to generate reports for the monthly resource usage of its private cloud. A member of the IT team logs into a server monthly and runs these scripts. The individuals who run these reports are Domain Admins as they need administrative privileges. These users do not need Domain Admin privileges for their day-to-day helpdesk tasks. Using JEA, we can assign just enough privileges to run these scripts from specific hosts instead of providing Domain Admin privileges. This is a fully PowerShell-based solution. It can be used with anything that can be managed via PowerShell.

Microsoft AD DS already has some features that can be used to limit administrative permissions, such as role-based administration and delegated control. But these are still open to certain security concerns:

- First-line support engineers are involved with basic troubleshooting only. Log analysis, executing basic troubleshooting commands, and restarting services are some of their most common activities. They are not responsible for system- or service-level changes. But most of the time, they have Domain Admin, Enterprise Admin, or local administrator privileges.
- Software vendors and application support engineers require access to their systems to do installations, upgrades, patching, or provide supports. Their access requirements are not permanent and their activities are limited to a few servers. However, most of the time, these accounts end up as Domain or Enterprise Admins as it's easy for them to carry out the required tasks. With these permissions, nothing prevents them from accessing other critical systems or data.
- Built-in delegation control capabilities are limited. They cannot limit users and delegated permissions to hosts.
- Some service accounts are required to have local administrator privileges at least in order to run certain service-related tasks. But these tasks are application-specific. What will guarantee that these services accounts are not being used to change system settings or other services run in the system?

When using JEA, keep these points in mind:

- Users have only those permissions that are required to run tasks they are assigned for
- Users cannot copy the same permission to other users in the same system
- If user A is allowed to run task B on computer C, they cannot run task B on computer D even if it's the same task and the same privileges requirements
- Detail logging provides visibility of the activities in the environment

JEA is implemented as PowerShell session endpoints. It includes the following files:

- **PowerShell Session Configuration file**: This allows you to map users to the endpoint. We can map users and groups to specific management roles. We also can configure global settings, such as virtual accounts and transcription policies. The PowerShell Session Configuration file is system-specific. So, configuration settings can be applied on a per-machine basis.

- **Role Capability files**: These files specify what actions can be performed by users. This can be running a script, running certain cmdlets, running a program, and so on. These tasks can be grouped into roles and shared with other users. As an example, tasks performed by first-line engineers can be grouped into one role and shared with all the first-line engineers.

One of the disadvantages of JEA is that it is limited to PowerShell and is not compatible with typical GUI based tasks and functions.

JEA implementation will be covered in `Chapter 16`, *Advanced AD Management with PowerShell*.

Summary

Active Directory infrastructure security is a broad topic to cover in one chapter. Active Directory security is not just dependent on AD DS; it is related to every layer in the OSI 7-layer model. In the beginning of the chapter, I explained Kerberos authentication and what exactly happens behind the scene when a user tries to access a resource in the Active Directory environment. Then, we moved on to delegated permission control, and there, we learned how we can delegate permissions to users to do specific administrative tasks. After that, we moved to a new section, where I explained pass-the-hash attacks.

Microsoft has introduced new tools and features that can be used to prevent pass-the-hash attacks. The Protected User security group, restricted RDP mode, authentication policies, and authentication policy silos are some of those. In this chapter, you learned how these tools work and how we can implement them in the AD environment. Then, we moved on to JIT and JEA. Both technologies can be used to manage privileges in an effective, secure manner.

In the next chapter, we will look into AD management with PowerShell. JEA implementation will also be covered as a part of it.

16
Advanced AD Management with PowerShell

The very first **Active Directory (AD)** instance I set up was based on Windows Server 2003. It is a completely different approach from today's AD installations. In Windows Server 2003, there were a lot of prerequisites tasks, such as installing a DNS role, setting up DNS zones, adding the domain prefix, and so on. Even these tasks are directly related to **Active Directory Domain Services (AD DS)**, and I had to configure them separately prior to running the DCPORMO.exe command. But today, the AD installation process is very straightforward. With basic knowledge and resources, anyone can get the domain controller installed with a few clicks. Not only AD DS, Microsoft has made server role installations and configurations easy over the years. The main reason behind all these enhancements was to save time for engineers. Not only installations and configuration, repetitive tasks in infrastructure also take a majority of an engineer's time. In order to save time on repetitive administrative tasks, people started looking at automation technologies. In earlier days, we used DOS commands, VBScripts, and batch files to automate administrative tasks. But there were problems with that. Applications, server roles, and services had limitations on working with these automation technologies. Not every function available in the GUI supported the usage of commands or scripts. This lack of support and lack of flexibility was holding back engineers from automating tasks.

To bring automation to the next level, Microsoft promised to release a more flexible, more powerful, more integrated scripting language. PowerShell 1.0 was the initial release and was available to the public from November 2006. During the last decade, there have been a few versions released and now at version 5, it is arguably the most powerful scripting language on Windows systems. As with any other server role, AD DS also fully supported being managed via PowerShell. From the beginning of this book, I used PowerShell to install, configure, and manage AD DS roles. In this chapter, I will explain how we can use PowerShell to further improve the AD DS environment management.

The cmdlets and scripts used in this chapter were written and tested on an environment that has the following:

- Windows Server 2016
- AD domain and forest functional level set to Windows Server 2016
- PowerShell 5.0 (`https://msdn.microsoft.com/en-us/powershell/scripting /whats-new/what-s-new-in-windows-powershell-50`)

Therefore some of these are not supported on an environment that has older PowerShell versions and domain, forest functional levels.

In this chapter, we will cover the following topics:

- PowerShell scripts and commands that can be used to manage AD objects
- PowerShell scripts and commands that can be used to manage and troubleshoot AD replication
- Implementation and configuration guide for **Just Enough Administration (JEA)**

AD management with PowerShell – preparation

A PowerShell module can include assemblies, scripts, and functionalities. In order to use the functionalities covered by these factors, we need to import them. After that, we can call for the contents of the module to manage relevant server roles, services, or features. Before we start AD management with PowerShell, first, we need to import the `ActiveDirectory` module.

There are few ways to do it. Such as installing AD DS server role or by installing **Remote Server Administration Tools (RSAT)**:

- **AD DS Server Role**:
    1. If we install the AD DS server role using Server Manager, **Active Directory module for Windows PowerShell** is installed as a feature:

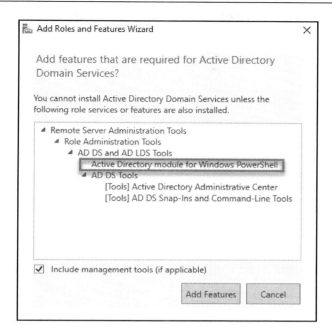

2. If the AD DS role is installed using PowerShell, we need to tell it to include the management tools, or use -IncludeManagementTools. Otherwise, by default, it will not install the module:

```
Install-WindowsFeature -Name AD-Domain-Services
-IncludeManagementTools
```

- **Remote Server Administration Tools**:
    1. Even if the server doesn't have the AD DS role installed, the existing domain environment can be managed using the AD DS PowerShell module. The AD PowerShell module is included with RSAT and can be installed using Server Manager or PowerShell.

2. On Server Manager, it can be found by navigating to **Features | Remote Server Administration Tools | Role Administration Tools | AD DS and AD LDS Tools | Active Directory module for PowerShell**, as shown in the following screenshot:

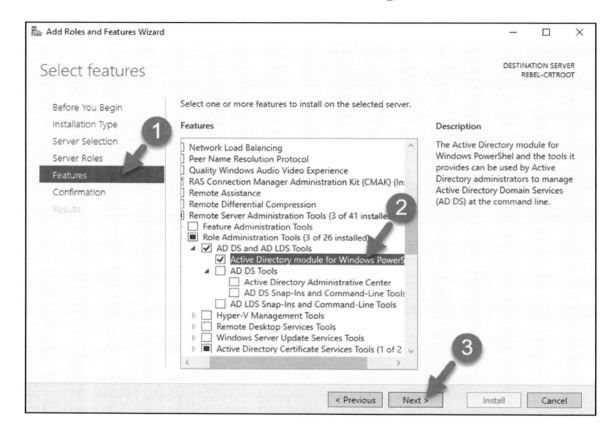

3. It also can be installed using PowerShell:

```
Add-WindowsFeature RSAT-AD-PowerShell
```

 It is also possible to install RSAT on the Windows desktop OS. As an example, RSAT for Windows 10 can be downloaded from https://www.microsoft.com/en-gb/download/details.aspx?id=45520.

Once the AD DS module is installed, we can list all the commands available under the module using the following command:

```
Get-Command -Module ActiveDirectory
```

There are about 147 commands under the module. The complete syntax for any command can be viewed using this command:

```
Get-Command commandname -Syntax
```

As an example, the following command will list the syntax for the New-ADUser command:

```
Get-Command New-ADUser -Syntax
```

The following screenshot show output for the preceding command:

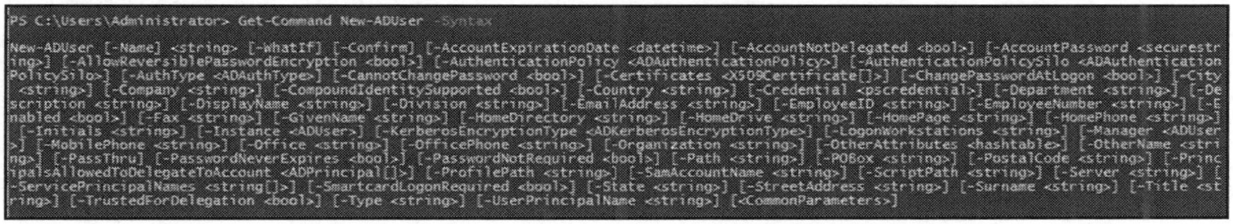

The Get-Help command provides help for any command. As an example, the following command provides help for the New-ADUser command:

```
Get-Help New-ADUser
```

The following screenshot show output for the preceding command:

```
PS C:\Users\Administrator> Get-Help New-ADUser

NAME
    New-ADUser

SYNOPSIS
    Creates a new Active Directory user.

SYNTAX
    New-ADUser [-Name] <String> [-AccountExpirationDate <DateTime>] [-AccountNotDelegated <Boolean>] [-AccountPassword <SecureString>]
    [-AllowReversiblePasswordEncryption <Boolean>] [-AuthenticationPolicy <ADAuthenticationPolicy>] [-AuthenticationPolicySilo
    <ADAuthenticationPolicySilo>] [-AuthType {Negotiate | Basic}] [-CannotChangePassword <Boolean>] [-Certificates <X509Certificate[]>]
    [-ChangePasswordAtLogon <Boolean>] [-City <String>] [-Company <String>] [-CompoundIdentitySupported <Boolean>] [-Country <String>]
    [-Credential <PSCredential>] [-Department <String>] [-Description <String>] [-DisplayName <String>] [-Division <String>] [-EmailAddress
    <String>] [-EmployeeID <String>] [-EmployeeNumber <String>] [-Enabled <Boolean>] [-Fax <String>] [-GivenName <String>] [-HomeDirectory
    <String>] [-HomeDrive <String>] [-HomePage <String>] [-HomePhone <String>] [-Initials <String>] [-Instance <ADUser>]
    [-KerberosEncryptionType {None | DES | RC4 | AES128 | AES256}] [-LogonWorkstations <String>] [-Manager <ADUser>] [-MobilePhone <String>]
    [-Office <String>] [-OfficePhone <String>] [-Organization <String>] [-OtherAttributes <Hashtable>] [-OtherName <String>] [-PassThru]
    [-PasswordNeverExpires <Boolean>] [-PasswordNotRequired <Boolean>] [-Path <String>] [-POBox <String>] [-PostalCode <String>]
    [-PrincipalsAllowedToDelegateToAccount <ADPrincipal[]>] [-ProfilePath <String>] [-SamAccountName <String>] [-ScriptPath <String>]
    [-Server <String>] [-ServicePrincipalNames <String[]>] [-SmartcardLogonRequired <Boolean>] [-State <String>] [-StreetAddress <String>]
    [-Surname <String>] [-Title <String>] [-TrustedForDelegation <Boolean>] [-Type <String>] [-UserPrincipalName <String>] [-Confirm]
    [-WhatIf] [<CommonParameters>]

DESCRIPTION
    The New-ADUser cmdlet creates a new Active Directory user. You can set commonly used user property values by using the cmdlet parameters.

    Property values that are not associated with cmdlet parameters can be set by using the OtherAttributes parameter.  When using this
    parameter be sure to place single quotes around the attribute name as in the following example.

    New-ADUser -SamAccountName "glenjohn"  -GivenName "Glen" -Surname "John" -DisplayName "Glen John" -Path 'CN=Users,DC=fabrikam,DC=local'
    -OtherAttributes @{'msDS-PhoneticDisplayName'="GlenJohn"}

    You must specify the SAMAccountName parameter to create a user.

    You can use the New-ADUser cmdlet to create different types of user accounts such as iNetOrgPerson accounts. To do this in AD DS, set the
    Type parameter to the LDAP display name for the type of account you want to create. This type can be any class in the Active Directory
    schema that is a subclass of user and that has an object category of person.

    The Path parameter specifies the container or organizational unit (OU) for the new user. When you do not specify the Path parameter, the
    cmdlet creates a user object in the default container for user objects in the domain.

    The following methods explain different ways to create an object by using this cmdlet.

    Method 1: Use the New-ADUser cmdlet, specify the required parameters, and set any additional property values by using the cmdlet
    parameters.
```

We also can view an example for the `New-ADUser` command using this:

```
Get-Help New-ADUser -Example
```

The following screenshot show output for the preceding command:

```
PS C:\Users\Administrator> Get-Help New-ADUser -Example
NAME
    New-ADUser
SYNOPSIS
    Creates a new Active Directory user.

    ----------------------- EXAMPLE 1 -----------------------
    C:\PS>New-ADUser GlenJohn -Certificate (new-object System.Security.Cryptography.X509Certificates.X509Certificate -ArgumentList
    "export.cer")

    Description
    -----------
    Create a new user named 'GlenJohn' with a certicate imported from the file "export.cer".
    ----------------------- EXAMPLE 2 -----------------------
    C:\PS>New-ADUser GlenJohn -OtherAttributes @{title="director";mail="glenjohn@fabrikam.com"}

    Description
    -----------
    Create a new user named 'GlenJohn' and set the title and mail properties on the new object.
    ----------------------- EXAMPLE 3 -----------------------
    C:\PS>New-ADUser GlenJohn -Type iNetOrgPerson -Path "DC=AppNC" -server lds.Fabrikam.com:50000

    Description
    -----------
    Create a new inetOrgPerson named 'GlenJohn' on an AD LDS instance.
```

More information on the command can be viewed using this:

```
Get-Help New-ADUser -Detailed
```

Technical information on the command can be viewed using the following:

```
Get-Help New-ADUser -Full
```

Online information about the command can be viewed using this:

```
Get-Help New-ADUser -Online
```

AD management commands and scripts

The module only has 147 commands, and they can be used in countless different ways to manage the AD environment. In this section, we will look at the capabilities of these commands and see how we can use them to improve AD management.

I'd like to start this section by explaining how we can review the existing configuration of an AD environment. The quick way to review the directory server configuration and capabilities is to use this:

```
Get-ADRootDSE
```

This command provides important information such as forest and domain functional levels, the default naming context, the current time, the currently logged-in domain controller, and so on:

```
PS C:\Users\administrator.REBELADMIN> Get-ADrootDSE

configurationNamingContext     : CN=Configuration,DC=rebeladmin,DC=com
currentTime                    : 19/04/2017 21:28:57
defaultNamingContext           : DC=rebeladmin,DC=com
dnsHostName                    : REBEL-SDC01.rebeladmin.com
domainControllerFunctionality  : Windows2016
domainFunctionality            : Windows2016Domain
dsServiceName                  : CN=NTDS Settings,CN=REBEL-SDC01,CN=Servers,CN=Default-First-Site-Name,CN=Sites,CN=Confi
                                 guration,DC=rebeladmin,DC=com
forestFunctionality            : Windows2016Forest
highestCommittedUSN            : 41039
isGlobalCatalogReady           : {TRUE}
isSynchronized                 : {TRUE}
ldapServiceName                : rebeladmin.com:rebel-sdc01$@REBELADMIN.COM
namingContexts                 : {DC=rebeladmin,DC=com, CN=Configuration,DC=rebeladmin,DC=com,
                                 CN=Schema,CN=Configuration,DC=rebeladmin,DC=com,
                                 DC=DomainDnsZones,DC=rebeladmin,DC=com...}
rootDomainNamingContext        : DC=rebeladmin,DC=com
schemaNamingContext            : CN=Schema,CN=Configuration,DC=rebeladmin,DC=com
serverName                     : CN=REBEL-SDC01,CN=Servers,CN=Default-First-Site-Name,CN=Sites,CN=Configuration,DC=rebel
                                 admin,DC=com
subschemaSubentry              : CN=Aggregate,CN=Schema,CN=Configuration,DC=rebeladmin,DC=com
supportedCapabilities          : {1.2.840.113556.1.4.800 (LDAP_CAP_ACTIVE_DIRECTORY_OID), 1.2.840.113556.1.4.1670
                                 (LDAP_CAP_ACTIVE_DIRECTORY_V51_OID), 1.2.840.113556.1.4.1791
                                 (LDAP_CAP_ACTIVE_DIRECTORY_LDAP_INTEG_OID), 1.2.840.113556.1.4.1935
                                 (LDAP_CAP_ACTIVE_DIRECTORY_V61_OID)...}
supportedControl               : {1.2.840.113556.1.4.319 (LDAP_PAGED_RESULT_OID_STRING), 1.2.840.113556.1.4.801
                                 (LDAP_SERVER_SD_FLAGS_OID), 1.2.840.113556.1.4.473 (LDAP_SERVER_SORT_OID),
                                 1.2.840.113556.1.4.528 (LDAP_SERVER_NOTIFICATION_OID)...}
supportedLDAPPolicies          : {MaxPoolThreads, MaxPercentDirSyncRequests, MaxDatagramRecv, MaxReceiveBuffer...}
supportedLDAPVersion           : {3, 2}
supportedSASLMechanisms        : {GSSAPI, GSS-SPNEGO, EXTERNAL, DIGEST-MD5}
```

The next step is to find about the domain controllers in the domain. We can use the following to list the domain controller name, the IP address, the status of global catalog server, and **Flexible Single Master Operation (FSMO)** roles:

```
Get-ADDomainController -Filter * | Select-Object
Name,IPv4Address,IsGlobalCatalog,OperationMasterRoles
```

It is also important to know about the AD site as it explains the AD physical topology:

```
Get-ADDomainController -Filter * | Select-Object Name,IPv4Address,Site
```

In an AD forest, it can have multiple domains. The following commands will list the forest names, domain name, domain controller, IP address, and AD site:

```
$Forestwide = (Get-ADForest).Domains | %{ Get-ADDomainController -Filter *
-Server $_ }
write-output $Forestwide -Filter * | Select-Object
Name,Forest,Domain,IPv4Address,Site
```

If we know the domain name, we can list the domain controllers and **read-only domain controller (RODC)** using the following command:

```
$Domain = Read-Host 'What is your Domain Name ?'
Get-ADDomain -Identity $Domain | select
ReplicaDirectoryServers,ReadOnlyReplicaDirectoryServer
```

In this command, system will ask user to input domain name. Once the user replies, it lists the domain controllers:

```
PS C:\Windows\system32> $Domain = Read-Host 'What is your Domain Name ?'
Get-ADDomain -Identity $Domain | select ReplicaDirectoryServers,ReadOnlyReplicaDirectoryServers

What is your Domain Name ?: rebeladmin.com

ReplicaDirectoryServers              ReadOnlyReplicaDirectoryServers
-----------------------              -------------------------------
{REBEL-PDC-01.rebeladmin.com}        {REBEL-RODC-01.rebeladmin.com}
```

In the preceding command, `ReplicaDirectoryServers` represents the read and write domain controllers and `ReadOnlyReplicaDirectoryServer` represents the read-only domain controllers.

Replication

Data replication is crucial for a healthy AD environment. For a given domain controller, we can find its inbound replication partners using this:

```
Get-ADReplicationPartnerMetadata -Target REBEL-SRV01.rebeladmin.com
```

The preceding command provides a detailed description for the given domain controller, including last successful replication, replication partition, server, and so on.

We can list all the inbound replication partners for the given domain using the following:

```
Get-ADReplicationPartnerMetadata -Target "rebeladmin.com" -Scope Domain
```

In the preceding command, the scope is defined as the domain. This can be changed to the forest to get a list of the inbound partners in the forest. The output is based on the default partition. If needed, the partition can be changed using `-Partition` into configuration or schema partition. It will list the relevant inbound partners for the selected partition.

Associated replication failures for a site, forest, domain, and domain controller can be found using the `Get-ADReplicationFailure` cmdlet:

```
Get-ADReplicationFailure -Target REBEL-SRV01.rebeladmin.com
```

The preceding command will list the replication failures for the given domain controller.

Replication failures for the domain can be found out using this:

```
Get-ADReplicationFailure -Target rebeladmin.com -Scope Domain
```

Replication failures for the forest can find out using the following:

```
Get-ADReplicationFailure -Target rebeladmin.com -Scope Forest
```

Replication failures for the site can find out using the following:

```
Get-ADReplicationFailure -Target LondonSite -Scope Site
```

In the command, `LondonSite` can be replaced with a relevant site name.

Using both `Get-ADReplicationPartnerMetadata` and `Get-ADReplicationFailure`, the following PowerShell script can provide a report against a specific domain controller:

```
## Active Directory Domain Controller Replication Status##
$domaincontroller = Read-Host 'What is your Domain Controller?'
## Define Objects ##
$report = New-Object PSObject -Property @{
ReplicationPartners = $null
LastReplication = $null
FailureCount = $null
FailureType = $null
FirstFailure = $null
}
## Replication Partners ##
$report.ReplicationPartners = (Get-ADReplicationPartnerMetadata -Target
$domaincontroller).Partner
$report.LastReplication = (Get-ADReplicationPartnerMetadata -Target
$domaincontroller).LastReplicationSuccess
## Replication Faliures ~#
$report.FailureCount = (Get-ADReplicationFailure -Target
$domaincontroller).FailureCount
```

```
$report.FailureType = (Get-ADReplicationFailure -Target
$domaincontroller).FailureType
$report.FirstFailure = (Get-ADReplicationFailure -Target
$domaincontroller).FirstFailureTime
## Format Output ##
$report | select
ReplicationPartners,LastReplication,FirstFailure,FailureCount,FailureType |
Out-GridView
```

 The aforementioned script is displayed in an easy way for readers to understand. When it is used in PowerShell make sure to prevent extra line spaces.

In this command, it will give an option for the engineer to specify the Domain Controller name:

```
$domaincontroller = Read-Host 'What is your Domain Controller?'
```

Then, it creates an object and maps it to the result of the PowerShell command outputs. Last but not least, it provides a report to display, including the following:

- Replication partner (**ReplicationPartners**)
- Last successful replication (**LastReplication**)
- AD replication failure count (**FailureCount**)
- AD replication failure type (**FailureType**)
- AD replication failure first recorded time (**FirstFailure**)

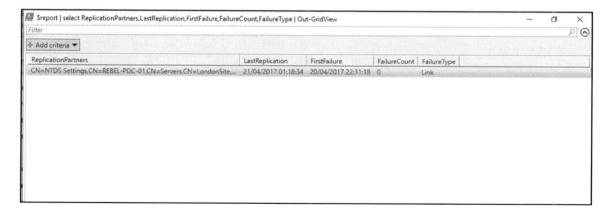

Further to AD replication topologies, there are two types of replications:

- **Intra-site**: Replications between domain controllers in the same AD site
- **Inter-site**: Replication between domain controllers in different AD sites

We can review AD replication site objects using the `Get-ADReplicationSite` cmdlet. The following command returns all the AD replication sites in the AD forest:

```
Get-ADReplicationSite -Filter *
```

The following screenshot show output for the preceding command:

```
PS C:\Users\Administrator> Get-ADReplicationSite -Filter *

Description                      : UK AD Site
DistinguishedName                : CN=LondonSite,CN=Sites,CN=Configuration,DC=rebeladmin,DC=com
InterSiteTopologyGenerator       : CN=NTDS Settings,CN=REBEL-PDC-01,CN=Servers,CN=LondonSite,CN=Sites,CN=Configuration,DC=rebeladmin,DC=com
ManagedBy                        :
Name                             : LondonSite
ObjectClass                      : site
ObjectGUID                       : fbef3a2c-2de8-44d2-bde9-c37403c9f3a9
ReplicationSchedule              : System.DirectoryServices.ActiveDirectory.ActiveDirectorySchedule
UniversalGroupCachingRefreshSite :

Description                      : Canada AD Site
DistinguishedName                : CN=CanadaSite,CN=Sites,CN=Configuration,DC=rebeladmin,DC=com
InterSiteTopologyGenerator       : CN=NTDS Settings\0ADEL:816b7b06-7427-4ccb-8303-ab229caa9931,CN=REBEL-SDC-02\0ADEL:1ed99178-bfb2-4717-80b2-c
                                   48d3c5f80ad,CN=Servers,CN=LondonSite,CN=Sites,CN=Configuration,DC=rebeladmin,DC=com
ManagedBy                        :
Name                             : CanadaSite
ObjectClass                      : site
ObjectGUID                       : 1bc04b4a-0f69-4ef5-8083-98d9bb0e88ca
ReplicationSchedule              :
UniversalGroupCachingRefreshSite :
```

We can review AD replication site links on the AD forest using the following:

```
Get-ADReplicationSiteLink -Filter *
```

In site links, the most important information is to know the site cost and the replication schedule. This allows you to understand the replication topology and expected delays in replications.

The following command lists all the replication site links, which includes the `CanadaSite` along with the site link name, link cost, and replication frequency:

```
Get-ADReplicationSiteLink -Filter {SitesIncluded -eq "CanadaSite"} |
Format-Table Name,Cost,ReplicationFrequencyInMinutes -AutoSize
```

A site link bridge can be used to bundle two or more site links and enable transitivity between site links.

Site link bridge information can be retrieved using the following:

```
Get-ADReplicationSiteLinkBridge -Filter *
```

AD sites uses multiple IP subnets that are assigned to sites for its operations. It is important to associate these subnets with AD sites so that domain controllers know which computer is located at which site.

The following command will list all the subnets in the forest in a table with the subnet name and AD site:

```
Get-ADReplicationSubnet -Filter * | Format-Table Name,Site -AutoSize
```

The following screenshot show output for the preceding command:

```
PS C:\Users\Administrator> Get-ADReplicationSubnet -Filter * | Format-Table Name,Site -A

Name           Site
----           ----
192.168.0.0/24 CN=LondonSite,CN=Sites,CN=Configuration,DC=rebeladmin,DC=com
10.11.0.0/24   CN=CanadaSite,CN=Sites,CN=Configuration,DC=rebeladmin,DC=com
```

Bridgehead servers operate as the primary communication point to handle replication data that comes in and goes out from the AD site.

We can list all the preferred bridgehead servers in a domain:

```
$BHservers = ([adsi]"LDAP://CN=IP,CN=Inter-Site
Transports,CN=Sites,CN=Configuration,DC=rebeladmin,DC=com").bridgeheadServe
rListBL
$BHservers | Out-GridView
```

In the preceding command, the attribute value `bridgeheadServerListBL` is retrieved via the ADSI connection.
We can list all of these findings using the following script:

```
## Script to gather information about Replication Topology ##
## Define Objects ##
$replreport = New-Object PSObject -Property @{
Domain = $null
}
## Find Domain Information ##
$replreport.Domain = (Get-ADDomain).DNSroot
## List down the AD sites in the Domain ##
$a = (Get-ADReplicationSite -Filter *)
Write-Host "########" $replreport.Domain "Domain AD Sites" "########"
$a | Format-Table Description,Name -AutoSize
## List down Replication Site link Information ##
```

```
$b = (Get-ADReplicationSiteLink -Filter *)
Write-Host "########" $replreport.Domain "Domain AD Replication SiteLink
Information" "########"
$b | Format-Table Name,Cost,ReplicationFrequencyInMinutes -AutoSize
## List down SiteLink Bridge Information ##
$c = (Get-ADReplicationSiteLinkBridge -Filter *)
Write-Host "########" $replreport.Domain "Domain AD SiteLink Bridge
Information" "########"
$c | select Name,SiteLinksIncluded | Format-List
## List down Subnet Information ##
$d = (Get-ADReplicationSubnet -Filter * | select Name,Site)
Write-Host "########" $replreport.Domain "Domain Subnet Information"
"########"
$d | Format-Table Name,Site -AutoSize
## List down Prefered BridgeHead Servers ##
$e = ([adsi]"LDAP://CN=IP,CN=Inter-Site
Transports,CN=Sites,CN=Configuration,DC=rebeladmin,DC=com").bridgeheadServe
rListBL
Write-Host "########" $replreport.Domain "Domain Prefered BridgeHead
Servers" "########"
$e
## End of the Script ##
```

The aforementioned script is displayed in an easy way for readers to understand. When it is used in PowerShell make sure to prevent extra line spaces.

The only thing we need to change is the ADSI connection with the relevant domain DN:

```
$e = ([adsi]"LDAP://CN=IP,CN=Inter-Site
Transports,CN=Sites,CN=Configuration,DC=rebeladmin,DC=com")
```

Replicating a specific object

Once an object is added to a domain controller, it needs to be replicated to all other domain controllers. Otherwise, users will face issues on login, using AD integrated applications and services. The replication is dependent on many different factors, such as the replication schedule and intra-site connectivity. However, sometimes, it is required to force the replication between domain controllers:

```
## Replicate Object to From Domain Controller to Another ##
$myobject = Read-Host 'What is your AD Object Includes ?'
$sourcedc = Read-Host 'What is the Source DC ?'
$destinationdc = Read-Host 'What is the Destination DC ?'
$passobject = (Get-ADObject -Filter {Name -Like $myobject})
```

```
Sync-ADObject -object $passobject -source $sourcedc -destination
$destinationdc
Write-Host "Given Object Replicated to" $destinationdc
```

The preceding script will ask a few questions:

- **Name of object**: This need not be a **Distinguished Name** (**DN**). All that is needed is that text be included in the object name field.
- **Source DC**: Hostname of source DC.
- **Destination DC**: Hostname of destination DC.

Once the relevant information is provided, the object will be forcefully replicated:

```
PS C:\Windows\system32> ## Replicate Objects to Domain Controllers ##
$myobject = Read-Host 'What is your AD Object Includes ?'
$sourcedc = Read-Host 'What is the Source DC ?'
$destinationdc = Read-Host 'What is the Destination DC ?'
$passobject = (Get-ADObject -Filter {Name -Like $myobject})
Sync-ADObject -object $passobject -source $sourcedc -destination $destinationdc
Write-Host "Given Object Replicated to" $destinationdc
What is your AD Object Includes ?: Adam
What is the Source DC ?: REBEL-PDC-01
What is the Destination DC ?: REBEL-SRV01
Given Object Replicated to REBEL-SRV01

PS C:\Windows\system32>
```

User and Groups

In this section, let's look in PowerShell commands and scripts that we can use to manage AD users and groups.

Last log on time

In certain occasions, we required to find when a user successfully log on to domain. it can be for audit purpose or troubleshooting purpose.

```
$username = Read-Host 'What is the User account you looking for ?'
   $dcs = Get-ADDomainController -Filter {Name -like "*"}
      foreach($dc in $dcs)
   {
     $hostname = $dc.HostName
     $user = Get-ADUser $userName -Server $hostname -Properties lastLogon
```

```
    $lngexpires = $user.lastLogon
    if (-not ($lngexpires)) {$lngexpires = 0 }
    If (($lngexpires -eq 0) -or ($lngexpires -gt
[DateTime]::MaxValue.Ticks))
    {
       $LastLogon = "User Never Logged In"
    }
     Else
    {
       $Date = [DateTime]$lngexpires
       $LastLogon = $Date.AddYears(1600).ToLocalTime()
    }
  }
  Write-Host $username "last logged on at:" $LastLogon
```

In preceding script, it will ask for the **username** of the account and once it is provided, system will search for the **lastLogon** attribute value in all available domain controllers. if its cannot find it will return **User Never Logged In** or if can find, it will return the last log on time stamp.

Last log in date report

Periodic housekeeping in AD is required for integrity. There can be user objects which not been used for years. If we can create report along with last login dates, we can use it as reference to clean up the objects.

```
## Script For Filter user with Last logon Time ##
$htmlformat = "<style>BODY{background-color:LightBlue;}</style>"
Get-ADUser -Filter * -Properties "LastLogonDate" | sort-object -property
lastlogondate -descending | Select-Object Name,LastLogonDate | ConvertTo-
HTML -head $htmlformat -body "<H2>AD Accounts Last Login Date</H2>"| Out-
File C:\lastlogon.html
Invoke-Expression C:\lastlogon.html
```

This script creates a HTML report which includes all the user accounts with their last log on date time stamps:

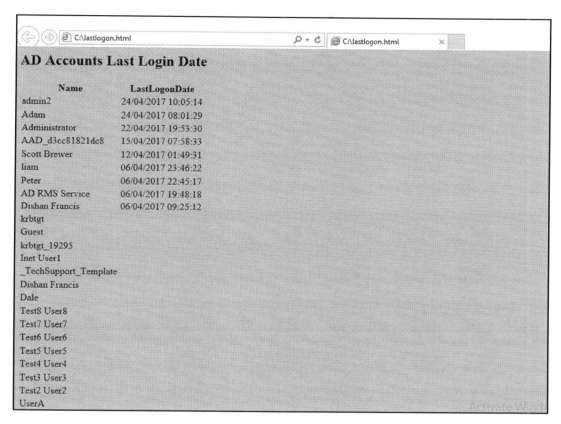

Login failures report

It is important to know about the failed login attempts to the DC, not just the successful attempts. These can be a result of potentially malicious activity.

The following script will create a report to indicate the login failures on given domain controller:

```
## Report for DC login Faliures ##
$failedevent = $null
$Date= Get-date
$dc = Read-Host 'What is the Domain Controller ?'
$Report= "C:\auditreport.html"
$HTML=@"
```

```
<title>Failed Login Report for $dc</title>
<style>
BODY{background-color :LightBlue}
</style>
"@
 $failedevent = Get-Eventlog security -Computer $dc -InstanceId 4625 -After
(Get-Date).AddDays(-7) |
 Select TimeGenerated,ReplacementStrings |
 % {
New-Object PSObject -Property @{
SourceComputer = $_.ReplacementStrings[13]
UserName = $_.ReplacementStrings[5]
SourceIPAddress = $_.ReplacementStrings[19]
Date = $_.TimeGenerated
 }
 }
 $failedevent | ConvertTo-Html -Property
SourceComputer,UserName,SourceIPAddress,Date -head $HTML -body "<H2>Failed
Login Report for $dc</H2>"|
 Out-File $Report
 Invoke-Expression C:\auditreport.html
```

 The aforementioned script is displayed in an easy way for readers to understand. When it is used in PowerShell make sure to prevent extra line spaces.

When you run the preceding script, it will ask the domain controller that you wish to run this report against. Then, in the background, it will search for event 4625 in the event viewer and then list the following data in a report:

- The source computer
- Username
- The source IP address
- Event time

The following screenshot shows the failed report for **REBEL-PDC-01**:

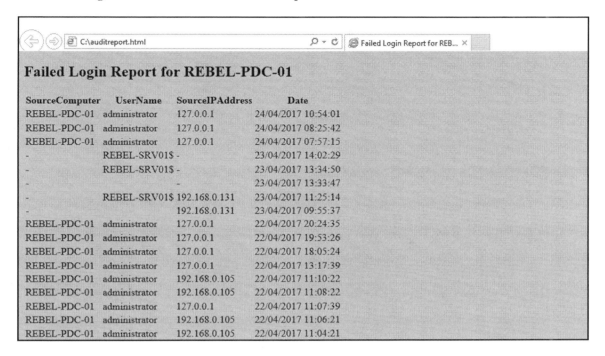

Finding the locked out account

If password policies are defined, accounts with a large number of login failures will be locked out. Locked out accounts in an AD environment can be found using the following:

```
Search-ADAccount -Lockedout | Select name, samAccountName, Lockedout
```

The following screenshot show output for the preceding command:

If any of those in list need to be unlocked, we can use the `Unlock-ADAccount` cmdlet to unlock the account.

For individual account, perform the following:

```
Unlock-ADAccount tuser4
```

For all the accounts on the list, perform the following:

```
Search-ADAccount -Lockedout | Unlock-ADAccount
```

Password expire report

Issues due to expired passwords are a common support call that helpdesks get. The following script can generate a report:

```
## Password Expire Report ##
$passwordreport = $null
$dc = (Get-ADDomain | Select DNSRoot).DNSRoot
$Report= "C:\passwordreport.html"
$HTML=@"
<title>Password Expire Report For $dc</title>
<style>
BODY{background-color :LightBlue}
</style>
"@
$passwordreport = Get-ADUser -filter * -Properties
"SamAccountName","pwdLastSet","msDS-UserPasswordExpiryTimeComputed" |
Select-Object -Property "SamAccountName",@{Name="Last Password
Change";Expression={[datetime]::FromFileTime($_."pwdLastSet")}},@{Name="Nex
t Password Change";Expression={[datetime]::FromFileTime($_."msDS-
UserPasswordExpiryTimeComputed")}}
$passwordreport | ConvertTo-Html -Property "SamAccountName","Last Password
Change","Next Password Change"-head $HTML -body "<H2>Password Expire Report
For $dc</H2>"|
Out-File $Report
Invoke-Expression C:\passwordreport.html
```

 The aforementioned script is displayed in an easy way for readers to understand. When it is used in PowerShell make sure to prevent extra line spaces.

This script will search for the attributes values for `SamAccountName`, `pwdLastSet`, and `msDS-UserPasswordExpiryTimeComputed` in every user object. Then, it will be presented in an HTML report:

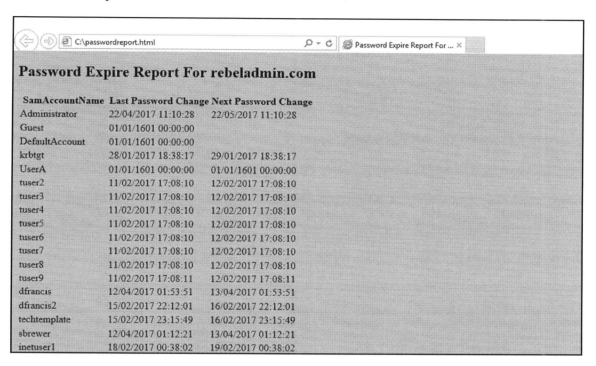

 All these reports can run as scheduled jobs and developed to be sent over as e-mail every week or month. This saves the time of administrators and also prevents the mistakes that can occur with manual tasks.

JEA

In the previous chapter, I explained how JEA can work in an infrastructure to secure the privileges associated with domain accounts. In a nutshell, we can create JEA endpoints and assign them to roles. Users do not need to have permissions such as domain admin or enterprise admin to run these. Users can use these endpoints with their regular AD user accounts. However, in the backend JEA, commands are executed using a JEA local administrator account. These login details need not be known by end users, and their passwords are reset on a daily basis—automatically.

As promised in the previous chapter, let's look at how to get JEA installed and configured.

In order to install JEA, first log in to the server from a user that has local administrator privileges, and open PowerShell:

```
Install-Module xJEA
```

The following screenshot show output for the preceding command:

```
PS C:\Windows\system32> Install-Module xJEA

NuGet provider is required to continue
PowerShellGet requires NuGet provider version '2.8.5.201' or newer to interact with NuGet-based repositories. The NuGet
 provider must be available in 'C:\Program Files\PackageManagement\ProviderAssemblies' or
'C:\Users\admin2\AppData\Local\PackageManagement\ProviderAssemblies'. You can also install the NuGet provider by
running 'Install-PackageProvider -Name NuGet -MinimumVersion 2.8.5.201 -Force'. Do you want PowerShellGet to install
and import the NuGet provider now?
[Y] Yes  [N] No  [S] Suspend  [?] Help (default is "Y"): Y

Untrusted repository
You are installing the modules from an untrusted repository. If you trust this repository, change its
InstallationPolicy value by running the Set-PSRepository cmdlet. Are you sure you want to install the modules from
'PSGallery'?
[Y] Yes  [A] Yes to All  [N] No  [L] No to All  [S] Suspend  [?] Help (default is "N"): A
PS C:\Windows\system32>
```

Once it is installed, we can confirm it using the following:

```
Find-Module -Name xJEA
```

The following screenshot show output for the preceding command:

```
PS C:\Windows\system32> Find-Module -Name xJEA | fl

Name                          : xJea
Version                       : 0.2.16.6
Type                          : Module
Description                   : Module with DSC Resources for Just Enough Admin (JEA).  Jea makes it simple to create
                                custom RBAC solutions using PowerShell.
Author                        : Microsoft Corporation
CompanyName                   : {PowerShellTeam, jsnover}
Copyright                     : (c) 2014 Microsoft Corporation. All rights reserved.
PublishedDate                 : 14/05/2015 19:51:23
InstalledDate                 :
UpdatedDate                   :
LicenseUri                    :
ProjectUri                    :
IconUri                       :
Tags                          : {PSModule}
Includes                      : {Function, RoleCapability, Command, DscResource...}
PowerShellGetFormatVersion    :
ReleaseNotes                  :
Dependencies                  : {}
RepositorySourceLocation      : https://www.powershellgallery.com/api/v2/
Repository                    : PSGallery
PackageManagementProvider     : NuGet
AdditionalMetadata            : {versionDownloadCount, ItemType, copyright, description...}
```

JEA configuration

Now we have JEA module installed, and the next step is to prepare the environment to use JEA. This can be done using a script that comes with JEA module. It is located at
`C:\Program Files\WindowsPowerShell\`
`Modules\xJea\0.2.16.6\Examples\SetupJEA.ps1`.

This script will do the following:

- Remove all existing endpoints from the computer
- Configure the DSC **Local Configuration Manager (LCM)** to apply changes and then check every 30 minutes to make sure the configuration has not been altered
- Enable the debug mode:

```
Configuration SetupJea
{
  Import-DscResource -module xjea Node localhost
  {
    xJeaEndPoint CleanAll
    {
      Name    = 'CleanALL'
      CleanAll = $true
    }
    LocalConfigurationManager
    {
      RefreshFrequencyMins = 30
      ConfigurationMode    = "ApplyAndAutoCorrect"
      DebugMode            = "ForceModuleImport"
      #This disables provider caching
    }
  }
}
SetupJea -OutputPath C:\JeaDemo
Set-DscLocalConfigurationManager -Path C:\JeaDemo -Verbose
Start-DscConfiguration -Path c:\JeaDemo -Wait -Verbose
#EOF
```

The aforementioned script is displayed in an easy way for readers to understand. When it is used in PowerShell make sure to prevent extra line spaces.

In order to run the script, move to `C:\Program Files\WindowsPowerShell\Modules\xJea\0.2.16.6\Examples\` folder and run `.\SetupJEA.ps1`:

Now we have completed the installation and the initial configuration.

Testing

JEA comes with three demo endpoint configurations, which we can use as references to create the endpoint. These demo files are also located at `C:\ProgramFiles\WindowsPowerShell\Modules\xJea\0.2.16.6\Examples` and `Demo1.ps1` which include the following:

```
cls configuration Demo1
{
   Import-DscResource -module xjea
   xJeaToolKit Process
```

```
  {
    Name           = 'Process'
    CommandSpecs = @"Name,Parameter,ValidateSet,ValidatePattern Get-Process
    Get-Service Stop-Process,Name,calc;notepad
    Restart-Service,Name,,^A"@
  }
  xJeaEndPoint Demo1EP
  {
    Name                     = 'Demo1EP'
    Toolkit                  = 'Process'
    SecurityDescriptorSddl =
      'O:NSG:BAD:P(A;;GX;;;WD)S:P(AU;FA;GA;;;WD)(AU;SA;GXGW;;;WD)'
    DependsOn                = '[xJeaToolKit]Process'
  }
}
Demo1 -OutputPath C:\JeaDemo

Start-DscConfiguration -Path C:\JeaDemo -ComputerName localhost -Verbose -
wait -debug -ErrorAction SilentlyContinue -ErrorVariable errors
if($errors | ? FullyQualifiedErrorId -ne 'HRESULT 0x803381fa')
{
    $errors | Write-Error
}

start-sleep -Seconds 30 #Wait for WINRM to restart

$s = New-PSSession -cn . -ConfigurationName Demo1EP
Invoke-command $s {get-command} |out-string
Invoke-Command $s {get-command stop-process -Syntax}
# Enter-pssession $s
Remove-PSSession $s
#EOF
```

The aforementioned script is displayed in an easy way for readers to understand. When it is used in PowerShell make sure to prevent extra line spaces.

As per the endpoint configuration, users are allowed to use only the following cmdlets:

- `Get-Process`
- `Get-Service`
- `Stop-Process,Name,calc;notepad`
- `Restart-Service,Name,^A`

According to the preceding `Stop-Process` cmdlet, it can only be used to stop calculator and notepad processes. But it allows you to use the `Restart-Service`, `Get-Process`, and `Get-Service` cmdlets without limitation.

In order to deploy the endpoint, we can use `.\Demo1.ps1`:

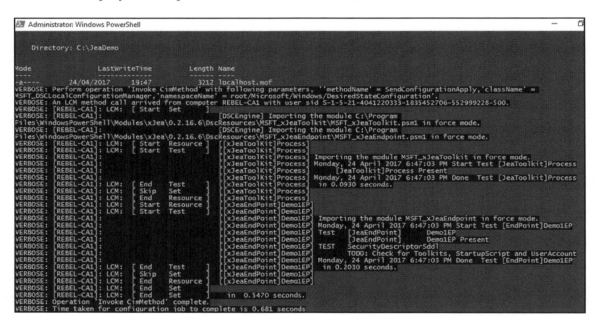

Once it's successfully executed, we can verify the new PowerShell session configuration using this:

```
Get-PSSessionConfiguration
```

The following screenshot show output for the preceding command:

```
PS C:\Program Files\WindowsPowerShell\Modules\xJea\0.2.16.6\Examples> Get-PSSessionConfiguration

Name          : Demo1EP
PSVersion     : 5.1
startupscript : C:\Program Files\Jea\StartupScript\Initialize-Demo1EP.ps1
RunAsUser     : JSA-Demo1EP
Permission    : Everyone AccessAllowed

Name          : microsoft.powershell
PSVersion     : 5.1
StartupScript :
RunAsUser     :
Permission    : NT AUTHORITY\INTERACTIVE AccessAllowed, BUILTIN\Administrators AccessAllowed, BUILTIN\Remote Management Users AccessAllowed

Name          : microsoft.powershell.workflow
PSVersion     : 5.1
StartupScript :
RunAsUser     :
Permission    : BUILTIN\Administrators AccessAllowed, BUILTIN\Remote Management Users AccessAllowed

Name          : microsoft.powershell32
PSVersion     : 5.1
StartupScript :
RunAsUser     :
Permission    : NT AUTHORITY\INTERACTIVE AccessAllowed, BUILTIN\Administrators AccessAllowed, BUILTIN\Remote Management Users AccessAllowed

Name          : microsoft.windows.servermanagerworkflows
PSVersion     : 3.0
StartupScript :
RunAsUser     :
Permission    : NT AUTHORITY\INTERACTIVE AccessAllowed, BUILTIN\Administrators AccessAllowed
```

The next step is to connect to a new endpoint. This can be done using the following:

```
Enter-PSSession -ComputerName localhost -ConfigurationName demo1ep
```

In the preceding command -ConfigurationName, defines the endpoint name.

As soon as we run the command, system is connected to the endpoint and changes the path to C:\Users\JSA-Demo1EP\Documents:

```
PS C:\Windows\system32> Enter-PSSession -ComputerName localhost -ConfigurationName demo1ep
[localhost]: PS C:\Users\JSA-Demo1EP\Documents>
```

This user is set up as part of the installation process by JEA. It is the PowerShell session account. This account is part of the local administrator group too:

```
PS C:\Windows\system32> get-localuser

Name             Enabled Description
----             ------- -----------
Administrator    True    Built-in account for administering the computer/domain
DefaultAccount   False   A user account managed by the system.
demo             True
Guest            False   Built-in account for guest access to the computer/domain
JeaSchTaskAccount True   This is a special Jea account to run the ResetJeaSessionAccountPasswords Scheduled task
JSA-Demo1EP      True    PowerShell Session Acount
```

The following figure confirms the members of the local Administrators security group:

```
PS C:\Windows\system32> Get-LocalGroupMember -Group "Administrators"

ObjectClass  Name                              PrincipalSource
-----------  ----                              ---------------
User         REBELADMIN\adam                   ActiveDirectory
User         REBELADMIN\Administrator          ActiveDirectory
Group        REBELADMIN\Domain Admins          ActiveDirectory
User         REBEL-CA1\Administrator           Local
User         REBEL-CA1\demo                    Local
User         REBEL-CA1\JeaSchTaskAccount       Local
User         REBEL-CA1\JSA-Demo1EP             Local
```

Once the session is connected, we can test it with an allowed command first. According to the configuration, we are allowed to run the `Get-Service` command without any limits:

```
PS C:\Windows\system32> Enter-PSSession -ComputerName localhost -ConfigurationName demo1ep
[localhost]: PS C:\Users\JSA-Demo1EP\Documents> get-service

Status   Name                DisplayName
------   ----                -----------
Stopped  AJRouter            AllJoyn Router Service
Stopped  ALG                 Application Layer Gateway Service
Running  AppHostSvc          Application Host Helper Service
Stopped  AppIDSvc            Application Identity
Running  Appinfo             Application Information
Stopped  AppMgmt             Application Management
Stopped  AppReadiness        App Readiness
Stopped  AppVClient          Microsoft App-V Client
Stopped  AppXSvc             AppX Deployment Service (AppXSVC)
Stopped  AudioEndpointBu...  Windows Audio Endpoint Builder
Stopped  Audiosrv            Windows Audio
Stopped  AxInstSV            ActiveX Installer (AxInstSV)
Running  BFE                 Base Filtering Engine
Stopped  BITS                Background Intelligent Transfer Ser...
Running  BrokerInfrastru...  Background Tasks Infrastructure Ser...
Stopped  Browser             Computer Browser
Stopped  bthserv             Bluetooth Support Service
Running  CDPSvc              Connected Devices Platform Service
Running  CDPUserSvc_32e3f2   CDPUserSvc_32e3f2
Running  CertPropSvc         Certificate Propagation
Running  CertSvc             Active Directory Certificate Services
Stopped  ClipSVC             Client License Service (ClipSVC)
Stopped  COMSysApp           COM+ System Application
Running  CoreMessagingRe...  CoreMessaging
Running  CryptSvc            Cryptographic Services
Stopped  CscService          Offline Files
Running  DcomLaunch          DCOM Server Process Launcher
Stopped  DcpSvc              DataCollectionPublishingService
Stopped  defragsvc           Optimize drives
Stopped  DeviceAssociati...  Device Association Service
Stopped  DeviceInstall       Device Install Service
Stopped  DevQueryBroker      DevQuery Background Discovery Broker
Running  Dhcp                DHCP Client
Stopped  diagnosticshub....  Microsoft (R) Diagnostics Hub Stand...
Running  DiagTrack           Connected User Experiences and Tele...
Stopped  DmEnrollmentSvc     Device Management Enrollment Service
Stopped  dmwappushservice    dmwappushsvc
Running  Dnscache            DNS Client
Stopped  dot3svc             Wired AutoConfig
Running  DPS                 Diagnostic Policy Service
Stopped  DsmSvc              Device Setup Manager
```

The user I logged in to this computer is a local administrator. So, I have enough privileges to restart the computer using the `Restart-Computer` cmdlet. But when I use the command through the endpoint, it should not allow me to do so according to the endpoint configuration:

```
[localhost]: PS C:\Users\JSA-Demo1EP\Documents> restart-computer
The term 'Restart-Computer' is not recognized as the name of a cmdlet, function, script file, or operable program.
Check the spelling of the name, or if a path was included, verify that the path is correct and try again.
    + CategoryInfo          : ObjectNotFound: (Restart-Computer:String) [], CommandNotFoundException
    + FullyQualifiedErrorId : CommandNotFoundException

[localhost]: PS C:\Users\JSA-Demo1EP\Documents>
```

So, it is working as expected. Users are allowed to use only the command permitted by the endpoint configuration. This configuration is not going to be valid for another computer unless the same endpoint configuration is used.

The `Demo2.ps1` endpoint configuration is focused on the file server administrator:

```
cls
configuration Demo2
{
    Import-DscResource -module xjea

    xJeaToolKit SMBGet
    {
        Name = 'SMBGet'
        CommandSpecs = @" Module,Name,Parameter,ValidateSet,ValidatePattern
            SMBShare,get-* "@
    }
    xJeaEndPoint Demo2EP
    {
        Name = 'Demo2EP'
        Toolkit = 'SMBGet'
        SecurityDescriptorSddl = 'O:NSG:BAD:P(A;;GX;;;WD)S:P(AU;FA;GA;;;WD)
            (AU;SA;GXGW;;;WD)'
        DependsOn = '[xJeaToolKit]SMBGet'
    }
}

Demo2 -OutputPath C:\JeaDemo
Start-DscConfiguration -Path C:\JeaDemo -ComputerName localhost -Verbose `
-wait -debug -ErrorAction SilentlyContinue -ErrorVariable errors
if($errors | ? FullyQualifiedErrorId -ne 'HRESULT 0x803381fa')
{
 $errors | Write-Error
}
```

```
start-sleep –Seconds 30 #Wait for WINRM to restart

$s = New-PSSession –cn . –ConfigurationName Demo2EP
Invoke-command $s {get-command} |out-string
# Enter-pssession $s

Remove-PSSession $s
#EOF
```

 The aforementioned script is displayed in an easy way for readers to understand. When it is used in PowerShell make sure to prevent extra line spaces.

As per the preceding script, system will allow you to use the following cmdlets list without restriction:

- SMBShare
- get-*

The following screenshot show output for the Get-PSSessionConfiguration command:

```
PS C:\Program Files\WindowsPowerShell\Modules\xJea\0.2.16.6\Examples> Get-PSSessionConfiguration

Name           : Demo1EP
PSVersion      : 5.1
startupscript  : C:\Program Files\Jea\StartupScript\Initialize-Demo1EP.ps1
RunAsUser      : JSA-Demo1EP
Permission     : Everyone AccessAllowed

Name           : Demo2EP
PSVersion      : 5.1
startupscript  : C:\Program Files\Jea\StartupScript\Initialize-Demo2EP.ps1
RunAsUser      : JSA-Demo2EP
Permission     : Everyone AccessAllowed

Name           : microsoft.powershell
PSVersion      : 5.1
StartupScript  :
RunAsUser      :
Permission     : NT AUTHORITY\INTERACTIVE AccessAllowed, BUILTIN\Administrators AccessAllowed, BUILTIN\Remote
                 Management Users AccessAllowed

Name           : microsoft.powershell.workflow
PSVersion      : 5.1
StartupScript  :
RunAsUser      :
Permission     : BUILTIN\Administrators AccessAllowed, BUILTIN\Remote Management Users AccessAllowed

Name           : microsoft.powershell32
PSVersion      : 5.1
StartupScript  :
RunAsUser      :
Permission     : NT AUTHORITY\INTERACTIVE AccessAllowed, BUILTIN\Administrators AccessAllowed, BUILTIN\Remote
                 Management Users AccessAllowed
```

We can connect to the second endpoint using the following:

```
Enter-PSSession -ComputerName localhost -ConfigurationName demo2ep
```

Once connected, `Get-Command` lists all the available commands in the endpoint:

```
PS C:\Windows\system32> Enter-PSSession -ComputerName localhost -ConfigurationName demo2ep
[localhost]: PS C:\Users\JSA-Demo2EP\Documents> get-command

CommandType     Name                                    Version    Source
-----------     ----                                    -------    ------
Function        A:
Function        B:
Function        C:
Function        cd..
Function        cd\
Function        Clear-Host
Function        D:
Function        E:
Function        F:
Function        format-list                             0.0        SafeProxy
Function        format-table                            0.0        SafeProxy
Function        G:
Function        Get-SmbBandwidthLimit                   0.0        SMBGet-Toolkit
Function        Get-SmbClientConfiguration              0.0        SMBGet-Toolkit
Function        Get-SmbClientNetworkInterface           0.0        SMBGet-Toolkit
Function        Get-SmbConnection                       0.0        SMBGet-Toolkit
Function        Get-SmbDelegation                       0.0        SMBGet-Toolkit
Function        Get-SmbMapping                          0.0        SMBGet-Toolkit
Function        Get-SmbMultichannelConnection           0.0        SMBGet-Toolkit
Function        Get-SmbMultichannelConstraint           0.0        SMBGet-Toolkit
Function        Get-SmbOpenFile                         0.0        SMBGet-Toolkit
Function        Get-SmbServerConfiguration              0.0        SMBGet-Toolkit
Function        Get-SmbServerNetworkInterface           0.0        SMBGet-Toolkit
Function        Get-SmbSession                          0.0        SMBGet-Toolkit
Function        Get-SmbShare                            0.0        SMBGet-Toolkit
Function        Get-SmbShareAccess                      0.0        SMBGet-Toolkit
Function        Get-Verb
Function        Group-Object                            0.0        SafeProxy
Function        H:
Function        help
Function        I:
Function        ImportSystemModules
Function        J:
Function        K:
Function        L:
Function        M:
Function        mkdir
Function        more
Function        N:
Function        O:
Function        oss
Function        P:
```

As expected, it is allowing you to run only the allowed cmdlets. In this test, we have used the `Get-SMBshare` cmdlet, which is allowed, and `Restart-Computer`, which isn't allowed:

```
[localhost]: PS C:\Users\JSA-Demo2EP\Documents> get-smbshare

Name          ScopeName  Path                                    Description
----          ---------  ----                                    -----------
ADMIN$        *          C:\Windows                              Remote Admin
C$            *          C:\                                     Default share
CertEnroll    *          C:\Windows\system32\CertSrv\CertEnroll  Active Directory Certificate Services share
IPC$          *                                                  Remote IPC


[localhost]: PS C:\Users\JSA-Demo2EP\Documents> restart-computer
The term 'Restart-Computer' is not recognized as the name of a cmdlet, function, script file, or operable program.
Check the spelling of the name, or if a path was included, verify that the path is correct and try again.
    + CategoryInfo          : ObjectNotFound: (Restart-Computer:String) [], CommandNotFoundException
    + FullyQualifiedErrorId : CommandNotFoundException

[localhost]: PS C:\Users\JSA-Demo2EP\Documents> _
```

`Demo3.ps1` provides the endpoint to manage and navigate through the filesystem:

```
cls configuration Demo3
{
    Import-DscResource -module xjea
    xJeaToolKit FileSystem
    {
        Name = 'FileSystem'
        CommandSpecs = @" Module,name,Parameter,ValidateSet,ValidatePattern,
            Get-ChildItem,Get-Item,Copy-Item,Move-Item,Rename-Item,
            Remove-Item,Copy-ItemProperty,Clear-ItemProperty,Move-ItemProperty,
            New-ItemProperty,Remove-ItemProperty,Rename-ItemProperty,Set-
ItemProperty,
            Get-Location,Pop-Location,Push-Location,Set-Location,Convert-Path,
            Join-Path,Resolve-Path,Split-Path,Test-Path,Get-PSDrive,New-PSDrive,
            out-file "@
        Ensure = 'Present'
    }

    xJeaEndPoint Demo3EP
    {
        Name = 'Demo3EP'
        ToolKit = 'FileSystem'
        Ensure = 'Present'
        DependsOn = '[xJeaToolKit]FileSystem'
    }
}

Demo3 -OutputPath C:\JeaDemo

Start-DscConfiguration -Path C:JeaDemo -ComputerName localhost -Verbose ` -
```

```
wait -debug -ErrorAction SilentlyContinue -ErrorVariable errors
if($errors | ? FullyQualifiedErrorId -ne 'HRESULT 0x803381fa')
{
 $errors | Write-Error
}

start-sleep -Seconds 30 #Wait for WINRM to restart
# This endpoint allows you to navigate the filesystem but not see
# the CONTENTS of any of the files
$s = New-PSSession -cn . -ConfigurationName Demo3EP
Invoke-command $s {dir 'C:\Program Files\Jea\Activity\ActivityLog.csv'}
Invoke-Command $s {get-content ` 'C:Program
FilesJeaActivityActivityLog.csv'}
# Enter-pssession $s

Remove-PSSession $s
#EOF
```

The aforementioned script is displayed in an easy way for readers to understand. When it is used in PowerShell make sure to prevent extra line spaces.

This endpoint configuration allows you to use the following cmdlets:

- Get-ChildItem
- Get-Item
- Copy-Item
- Move-Item
- Rename-Item
- Remove-Item
- Copy-ItemProperty
- Clear-ItemProperty
- Move-ItemProperty
- New-ItemProperty
- Remove-ItemProperty
- Rename-ItemProperty
- Set-ItemProperty
- Get-Location
- Pop-Location
- Push-Location

- Set-Location
- Convert-Path
- Join-Path
- Resolve-Path
- Split-Path
- Test-Path
- Get-PSDrive
- New-PSDrive
- out-file

This explains how we can use JEA endpoints to limit the use of privileges to specific tasks. These demo scripts can be used to build your own configuration. There are lots of examples can find in GitHub. You can access JEA GitHub page using `https://github.com/PowerShell/JEA`.

Summary

PowerShell has become the most powerful script language for Windows systems. PowerShell is very useful for systems management, but can also be an incredibly powerful tool for managing AD infrastructures. Throughout the book, I have used PowerShell for AD configuration and management. Furthermore, I have shared different commands and scripts that can be used to manage the AD environment efficiently. Towards the end of the chapter, you learned how to implement JEA and how it can be used to protect privileges AD environment. In the next chapter, we will look at Azure AD and understand how to manage identities in a hybrid environment.

17
Azure Active Directory Hybrid Setup

In 2006, I was working with a large Canadian managed-hosting service provider. Back then, people were using dedicated servers to host their workloads. Hardware, bandwidth, and management, all came at a high cost. When people were talking about virtualization, we were in a business where it could badly affect sales. Virtualization was able to bring the cost down for hosting. I still remember that there were all sorts of discussions, arguments, articles, blog posts, and summits where people were bringing the pros and cons of virtualization to the table. As with any technology, at the beginning, there were issues, but virtualization technologies developed rapidly, and it brought businesses to a point that they can't look away.

For us, it was the same: businesswise, we were always safe with dedicated server hosting, but with virtualization, customers were able to bring racks of dedicated servers into a few hypervisor hosts. Then the businesses in the hosting field started to find new ways of making money with virtualized technologies. This was the beginning of the cloud era. However, what I want to emphasize is similar to the technological shift from dedicated servers to virtualization, the majority of today's infrastructures are going through a very interesting phase of moving workloads from on-premises to public cloud. When Microsoft Azure was released, again the technology world was deluged with all sorts of discussions. Most of the points were related to data security, compliance, reliability, and cost.

Over the past few years, Microsoft has been addressing all those concerns and challenges, and it came to the point where organizations could not stay away from it anymore for the following reasons:

- The cloud pricing model (only pay for the resources you use) and operational model can bring down long-term infrastructure operation and maintenance costs.
- Software vendors started replacing their products with cloud-based versions and discontinued support for on-premises versions.
- Microsoft products have equivalent cloud versions as on-premises, and new features will only be available in the cloud versions. Also, cloud versions have frequent updates and bug fixes compared to on-premises versions.
- It removed dependencies (such as network connectivity, VPN, and firewall configuration) for mobile workers and provided seamless access to workloads from anywhere.
- The cloud adopts new technology changes quickly compare to on-premises infrastructures.
- A robust cloud infrastructure setup provides high availability for workloads, which may not be possible to achieve on-premises.

When an organization adopts cloud technologies, it's not easy to bring each and every workload to the public cloud at once. There are limitations for applications that still require some workloads to run on-premises. Even though workloads operate from two technologies, the user identities for the organization would stay the same. **Azure Active Directory (Azure AD)** helps to extend the on-premises identity infrastructure to Azure Cloud and use the same on-premises identities to authenticate with the application and services regardless of where they are running from.

In this chapter, we will look into the following:

- What is Azure AD?
- How to integrate Azure AD with on-premises AD?
- How to manage identities in a hybrid cloud model?

What is Azure AD?

Azure AD is a cloud-based Microsoft-managed multi-tenant directory and identity management service. Even if you do not have on-premises AD integration with Azure AD, if you are using cloud applications such as Office 365, Dynamic CRM, or applications from the Azure marketplace (most of them), you are already using Azure AD in the backend.

There are three main ways which we can handle identities in cloud-only or hybrid environments:

- **Windows AD only**: It's still a great tool. If you'd still like to manage organization identities only using on-premises solutions, it can be done using one of the following topologies:
  - Use site-to-site VPN or Azure ExpressRoute to connect on-premises networks with Azure directly and manage identities using a corporate AD setup.
  - Deploy additional domain controllers in an Azure virtual server and replicate on-premises AD changes periodically and manage them as an AD site.
  - Deploy domain controllers in Azure virtual servers and use those as **Flexible Single Master Operation (FSMO)** role holders. Additional domain controllers will be deployed in on-premises networks and will replicate changes from Azure servers via VPN or ExpressRoute.

  However, this solution still requires additional investment to ensure connectivity, and it will also not remove the operational costs of managing an on-premises AD environment.

 Azure ExpressRoute is similar to a leased line, and you can have a private link between your on-premises network and Azure datacenters. More details can be found at `https://azure.microsoft.com/en-gb/services/expressroute/`.

- **Cloud only**: If you do not have any workloads running on on-premises except for the endpoints, you can use a Microsoft-managed Azure AD instance to manage identities for the organization. All the user accounts and group memberships will be created, deleted, and managed by Azure AD. As long as it is on the same Azure virtual network, workloads and applications can use the same directory for authentication and authorization. By using Microsoft-managed Azure AD:

    - Administrators do not need to deploy, patch, or manage domain controllers.
    - Administrators do not need to plan for AD upgrades. Version upgrades will be seamless to tenants.
    - Administrators do not need to face issues related to AD replications.

> By default, Azure AD Domain service is only available for the virtual network it belongs to. However, if required virtual networks can connect together using Azure VNet-to-VNet connections. This is useful if company using Azure resources from different geographical locations or different subscriptions.

> However, since it's a managed solution, tenants will not have Domain Admin or Enterprise administrator privileges on the domain. Also, users and groups are created in a flat structure without **organizational units (OUs)** or **group policy objects (GPOs)**:

- **Hybrid setup**: If workloads are in Microsoft Azure and on-premises and both workloads need to be managed using the same identities, we can use Azure AD in a hybrid setup. When I explained Azure AD in a hybrid setup earlier, I mentioned that it allows us to *extend* our on-premises identity infrastructure to Azure, but it is not an *extension* to an on-premises Windows AD environment. Azure AD DS provides managed domain services such as domain join, Group Policy, LDAP, Kerberos/**NT LAN Manager (NTLM)** authentication that are fully compatible with Windows Server Active Directory. It is not similar to deploying an additional domain controller in Azure:

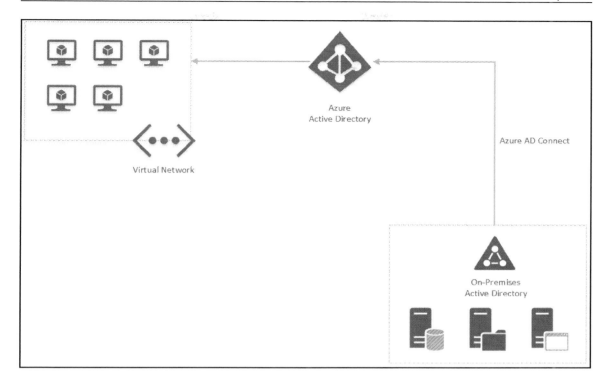

In a hybrid setup, the Azure AD instance is responsible for managing identities for its connected workloads; on-premises identities, group memberships, and credentials are synced to the Azure AD instance using Azure AD Connect. The Azure AD instance will be managed (patching and upgrades) by Microsoft, and engineers only need to manage Azure AD Connect.

Benefits of Azure AD

The following list describes why Azure AD is important for today's identity infrastructures:

- Azure AD can be enabled with a few clicks and we can start to manage identities. There's no need to deploy servers, install server roles, or configure roles.
- It is well integrated with Azure AD-aware applications, and users can authenticate to those with minimum application changes.
- Windows 10 devices can directly join Azure AD and be managed.

- Multifactor authentication and conditional access rules (`https://docs.microsof t.com/en-us/azure/active-directory/active-directory-conditional-acce ss`) can be used to protect identities and workload access.
- Advanced monitoring and auditing to understand identity usage and their actions is available.
- It provides self-service capabilities to reset forgotten passwords (when given conditions are met).
- It protects from modern identity-infrastructure threats: Microsoft security graph is equipped with cyber threat intelligence collected from many different sources. It allows Microsoft to identify modern identity infrastructure threats quickly and apply fixes and features directly without depending on customer interaction.
- Every time there is a new Windows Server version released, a new AD version is released too. In order to use new features associated with it, organizations need to upgrade their AD versions. It involves additional planning and costs. In comparison, Azure AD is managed by Microsoft, and if there is a new feature available, users can use it from day one.
- Azure AD keeps at least two additional copies of your directory data in different data centers. So even if the entire data center goes down, your Azure AD will not be affected in any way.

Azure AD limitations

Azure AD is a managed service, so we do not have some of the capabilities we have in on-premises AD:

- Tenants will not have domain admin or enterprise admin privileges
- Users and groups will be in a flat structure without support for advanced group policies and OU structure

Azure AD editions

There are four different Azure AD editions. Each edition has a different set of features and fees.

 This is only valid at the time this book was written. For the latest edition and pricing details, visit `https://azure.microsoft.com/en-gb/pricing /details/active-directory/`.

Azure AD free version

If you've subscribed to any Microsoft online service, such as Azure or Office 365, you will get the free Azure AD version along with it. It has limited features:

- Directory objects
- User/group management (add/update/delete), user-based provisioning, and device registration
- **Single sign-on (SSO)**
- Self-service password change for cloud users
- Connect (sync engine that extends on-premises directories with Azure AD)
- Security/usage reports

Azure AD Basic

Designed for task workers with cloud-first needs, this edition provides cloud centric application access and self-service identity management solutions. With the Basic edition of Azure Active Directory, you get productivity enhancing and cost reducing features like group-based access management, self-service password reset for cloud applications, and Azure Active Directory Application Proxy (to publish on-premises web applications using Azure Active Directory), all backed by an enterprise-level SLA of 99.9 percent uptime. -Microsoft

It has all the features available in the free edition and the following:

- Group-based access management/provisioning
- Self-service password reset for cloud users
- Company branding (logon pages/access panel customization)
- Application proxy
- A **service-level agreement (SLA)** of 99.9%

Azure AD Premium P1

Designed to empower organizations with more demanding identity and access management needs, Azure Active Directory Premium edition adds feature-rich enterprise-level identity management capabilities and enables hybrid users to seamlessly access on-premises and cloud capabilities. This edition includes everything you need for information worker and identity administrators in hybrid environments across application access, self-service identity and access management (IAM), identity protection and security in the cloud. It supports advanced administration and delegation resources like dynamic groups and self-service group management. It includes Microsoft Identity Manager (an on-premises identity and access management suite) and provides cloud write-back capabilities enabling solutions like self-service password reset for your on-premises users.
-Microsoft

It has all the features available in the Basic edition and the following:

- Self-service group and app management/self-service application additions/dynamic groups
- Self-service password reset/change/unlock with on-premises write-back
- Multi-factor authentication (cloud and on-premises (MFA Server))
- **Microsoft Identity Manager (MIM) Client Access License (CAL)** + MIM Server
- Cloud app discovery
- Connect health
- Automatic password rollover for group accounts

Azure AD Premium P2

Designed with advanced protection for all your users and administrators, this new offering includes all the capabilities in Azure AD Premium P1 as well as our new Identity Protection and Privileged Identity Management. Azure Active Directory Identity Protection leverages billions of signals to provide risk-based conditional access to your applications and critical company data. We also help you manage and protect privileged accounts with Azure Active Directory Privileged Identity Management so you can discover, restrict and monitor administrators and their access to resources and provide just-in-time access when needed.
-Microsoft

It has all the features available in Azure AD Premium P1 and the following:

- Identity protection
- Privileged identity management

Integrate Azure AD with on-premises AD

Before we start with the integration process, we need to get the following ready:

- **Valid Azure subscription**: You need to have a valid Azure subscription. It can be a pay-as-you-go subscription or a partner subscription, where you have credits applied. For testing purposes, you also can have a free Azure demo account with £150 credits. More info can found at `https://azure.microsoft.com/en-gb/off ers/ms-azr-0044p/`.

- **Global administrator account**: In order to set up Azure AD, you need to log in to Azure with an account that has global administrator account privileges.

- **Access to domain DNS**: As part of the Azure AD setup, we need to verify the domain name. This is done using a DNS record. Therefore, engineers need to have access to DNS servers. This is important if you using a public domain name (`.com`, `.org`, `.net`).

- **Enterprise administrator account**: In order to setup and configure Azure AD Connect, the engineers need to be members of the enterprise administrator group in the on-premises AD setup.

- **Connectivity**: The server running Azure AD Connect needs to have connectivity to Azure services. If your domain controllers do not have direct access to the internet, prior to deployment, firewall rules need to be modified to allow the Azure service access on recommended ports.

More information about ports can be found at `https://docs.microsoft. com/en-us/azure/active-directory/connect/active-directory-aadc onnect-ports`. The service URL and IP range information can found at `ht tps://support.office.com/en-gb/article/Office-365-URLs-and-IP- address-ranges-8548a211-3fe7-47cb-abb1-355ea5aa88a2?ui=en-US&r s=en-GB&ad=GB`.

Azure AD Connect

Azure AD Connect is the service responsible for integrating on-premises AD with Azure AD. Azure AD Connect replaces the previous versions of **Windows Azure Active Directory Sync (DirSync)** and Azure AD Sync components. Azure AD Connect has three main components:

- **Synchronization services**: This service checks whether Azure AD has the same identities as on-premises AD. If it doesn't, it will create the relevant objects in Azure AD.
- **Federation service**: Azure AD Connect can be configured to connect via an on-premises **Active Directory Federation Services (AD FS)** farm. This is used by organizations that use domain join SSO, third-party MFA, smart cards, and so on.
- **Monitoring**: Azure AD Connect Health monitors the health of Azure AD Connect and its components. These stats can be view using the Azure portal.

Azure AD Connect deployment topology

Azure AD Connect uses two different topologies to support on-premises AD deployments. However, there are certain limitations and unsupported configurations that we need to know about:

- **Single AD forest-single Azure AD**: This is the most commonly used deployment topology. When a user has a single AD forest, it can be synced to one Azure AD tenant. Even if it is has multiple domains, it still can be used with one AD tenant. The Azure AD Connect express setup only supports this topology.
  However, at any given time, only one Azure AD connect server can sync data to the Azure AD tenant. For high availability, staging server support is available, which will be explained later in this section.

- **Multiple AD forest-single Azure AD**: Some organizations have multiple AD forests for various reasons. Azure AD has support for syncing identities from all the forests into one Azure AD tenant. Each AD forest can have multiple domains as well. The AD connect server should be able to reach all the forests, but this doesn't mean it needs to have AD trust between forests. The Azure AD Connect server can be placed in a perimeter network and then allowed access to different forests from there. A rule of thumb in this model is to represent a user only once in Azure AD. If a user exists in multiple forests, it can be handled in two ways:

- We can set it to match the user's identity using the mail attribute. If Microsoft Exchange is available in one or more forests, it may also have on-premises GALSync solution. GALsync is a solution which use to share exchange mail objects between multiple forests. This will allow to represent each user object as a *contact* in other forests. If a user has a mailbox in one forest, it will be joined with the contacts in the other forests.

- If users are in an account-resource forest topology that has an extended AD schema with Exchange and Lync, they will be matched using the `ObjectSID` and `sExchangeMasterAccountSID` attributes.

These options can be selected during the AD Connect configuration. There is no support for having multiple AD Connect servers in each forest syncing to one Azure AD tenant.

Staging server

By design, it is not possible to have multiple Azure AD connect servers sync the same directory data to the same Azure AD tenant. However, Azure AD Connect supports maintaining a second server in staging mode. This is ideal for high availability. A server in staging mode reads data from all connected directories but will not sync it to the Azure AD tenant. It runs sync jobs as a normal Azure AD connect server, so in the case of a disaster, it already has the latest data. In the event of primary server failure, using the Azure AD Connect wizard, we can fail over to the staging server. This method can be used to replace the existing AD connect server. We can make all the relevant changes in staging mode, and when everything is ready, we can fail over to the newly implemented server. Maintaining multiple staging servers in an infrastructure is also supported.

Before installing the AD Connect server

Before installing the AD Connect server, we need to check whether the existing environment meets the following requirements. They can be found at `https://docs.micro soft.com/en-us/azure/active-directory/connect/active-directory-aadconnect-pr erequisites`:

- The AD forest functional level must be Windows Server 2003 or later.
- If you plan to use the password writeback feature, then the domain controllers must be on Windows Server 2008 (with the latest SP) or later. If your DCs are on 2008 (pre-R2), then you must also apply hotfix *KB2386717*.

- The domain controller used by Azure AD must be writable. Using a **read-only domain controller (RODC)** is not supported, and Azure AD Connect does not follow any write redirects.
- There is no support for using on-premises forests/domains using **Single Label Domains (SLDs)**.
- There is no support for using on-premises forests/domains using dotted NetBIOS names (names with a period in them).
- Azure AD Connect cannot be installed on Small Business Server or Windows Server Essentials. The server must use Windows Server Standard or better.
- The Azure AD Connect server must have the full GUI installed. There is no support for installing it on Server Core.
- Azure AD Connect must be installed on Windows Server 2008 or later. This server may be a domain controller or a member server when using express settings. If you use custom settings, then the server can also be standalone and does not have to be joined to a domain.
- If you install Azure AD Connect on Windows Server 2008 or Windows Server 2008 R2, then make sure to apply the latest hotfixes from Windows Update. The installation cannot be started with an unpatched server.
- If you plan to use the password synchronization feature, then the Azure AD Connect server must be on Windows Server 2008 R2 SP1 or later.
- If you plan to use a group-managed service account, then the Azure AD Connect server must be on Windows Server 2012 or later.
- The Azure AD Connect server must have .NET Framework 4.5.1 or later and Microsoft PowerShell 3.0 or later installed.
- If AD FS is being deployed, the servers where AD FS or Web Application Proxy are installed must be Windows Server 2012 R2 or later. Windows remote management must be enabled on these servers for remote installation.
- If AD FS is being deployed, you need SSL certificates.
- If AD FS is being deployed, then you need to configure name resolution.
- If your global administrators have MFA enabled, then the URL `https://secure.aadcdn.microsoftonline-p.com` must be in the trusted sites list. You are prompted to add this site to the trusted sites list when you are prompted for an MFA challenge and it has not been added before. You can use Internet Explorer to add it to your trusted sites.

- Azure AD Connect requires a SQL Server database to store identity data. By default, SQL Server 2012 Express LocalDB (a light version of SQL Server Express) is installed. SQL Server Express has a 10 GB size limit that enables you to manage approximately 100,000 objects. If you need to manage a higher volume of directory objects, you need to point the installation wizard to a different installation of SQL Server.
- If you use a different SQL Server version, then these requirements apply:
    - Azure AD Connect supports all flavors of Microsoft SQL Server from SQL Server 2008 (with the latest service pack) to SQL Server 2016. Microsoft Azure SQL Database is not supported as a database.
    - You must use a case-insensitive SQL collation. These collations are identified with a _CI_ in their name. There is no support for using case-sensitive collation, identified by _CS_ in the name.
    - You can only have one sync engine per SQL instance. There is no support for sharing a SQL instance with FIM/MIM Sync, DirSync, or Azure AD Sync.

Step-by-step guide to integrate on-premises AD environment with Azure AD

In this section, we are going to go through the Azure AD integration process. During the process, we are going to do the following:

- Create a virtual network
- Create an Azure AD instance
- Add DNS server details to the virtual network
- Create an AAD DC administrator group
- Create a global administrator account for Azure AD Connect
- Add a custom domain to Azure AD
- Set up Azure AD Connect

Creating a virtual network

In Azure, a virtual network is similar to the concept we use in virtualization. Azure AD and other workloads should use the same virtual network to be operated under same managed domain. If you already have a subscription and have your virtual network set up, this step can be skipped.

 Any virtual network created using the new Azure portal (ARM) cannot be seen using the classic portal and will not be able to be associated with the Azure AD instance.

Azure AD portal preview is available at the new Azure portal (`portal.azure.com`). However, at the time this book was written, the new portal didn't support all the functions available on the Azure classic portal (`manage.windowsazure.com`). Therefore, this configuration was done using the Azure classic portal:

1. Log in to Azure classic portal as global administrator (`https://manage.windowsa zure.com`).

2. Click on **Networks** from the left-hand navigation panel. Then click on **CREATE A VIRTUAL NETWORK:**

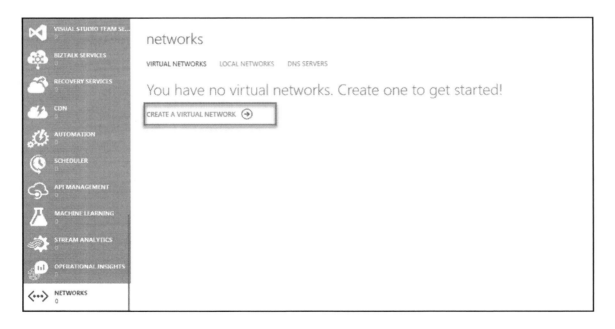

3. In the wizard, type the name of the virtual network and select the location, and then click on the proceed button to go to next step:

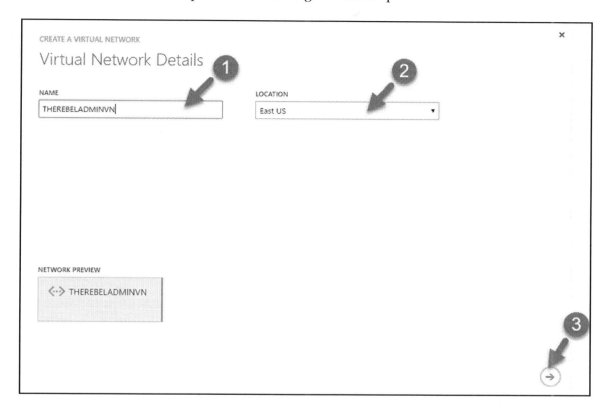

4. In the next window, it will ask you to define the DNS servers and also provide the option to configure VPN. These can be configure later as well if needed. Once done, click on the arrow button to go to the next window.

5. On the next page, we can define the address space and subnet info. The address range can have multiple subnets under it (as long as valid CIDR). In this demo, I have changed the address range to `192.168.0.0/24` and I am going to use the whole range as one subnet:

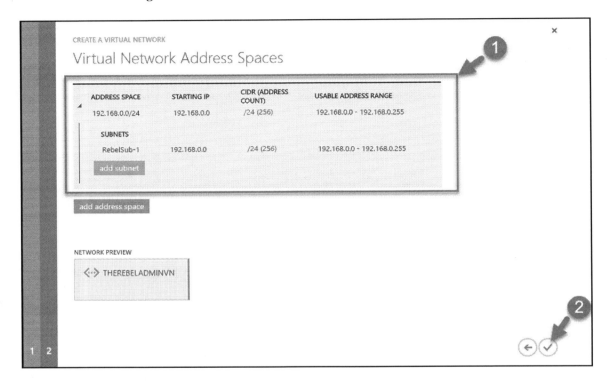

Creating an Azure AD instance

1. Log in to the Azure classic portal as global administrator (`https://manage.wind owsazure.com`).

2. Click on **NEW** | **App Services** | **ACTIVE DIRECTORY** | **DIRECTORY** | **CUSTOM CREATE**:

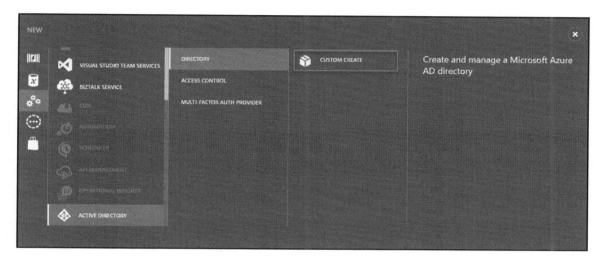

3. In the new window, we need to provide the following:
    - **NAME**: The organization name of the Azure AD tenant.
    - **DOMAIN NAME**: Azure AD needs an initial domain name, and it will have the UPN suffix `.onmicrosoft.com`. You can choose a name you like for this. Once our own domain is added, the default domain can be changed to it.
    - **COUNTRY OR REGION**: We can select the preferred country or region for resource placement.

4. Once the information has been provided, click on the checkmark button:

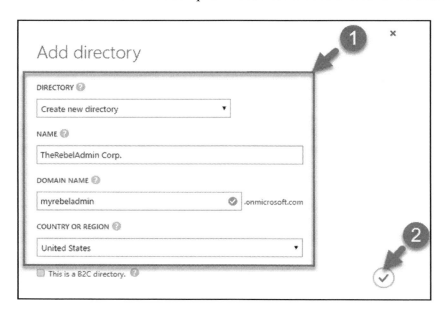

5. Once the directory is created, click on **Active Directory** from the left-hand side navigation panel. It will list down the Azure AD instance we created. Click on it to load the properties window.

6. Then click on the **CONFIGURE**:

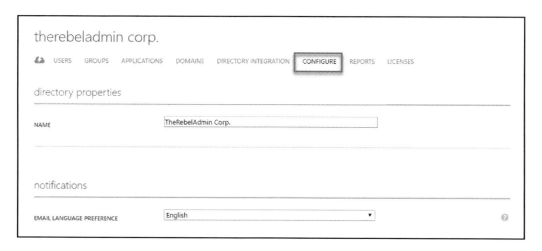

7. On the page, scroll down to **domain services**; there, click on **YES** to enable domain services for this directory. Then, from the dropdown in front of **CONNECT DOMAIN SERVICES TO THIS VIRTUAL NETWORK,** select the virtual network we created in the previous step:

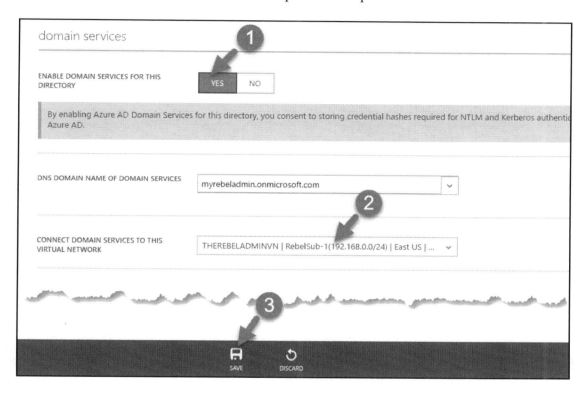

8. It takes about 30 minutes to enable the service and associate resources with the given virtual network. Once it is done, we can see it has the IP address assigned from the range we defined:

Add DNS server details to the virtual network

The IP address assigned to the domain service needs to be added to the virtual network as the DNS server. This will allow the domain to join servers created under the same virtual network:

1. Go to **Networks** in the left-hand navigation panel and click on the virtual network where the Azure AD instance is associated with.
2. Click on the **CONFIGURE** link, and in there, under the DNS server section, add the IP address that was assigned by the Azure AD configuration:

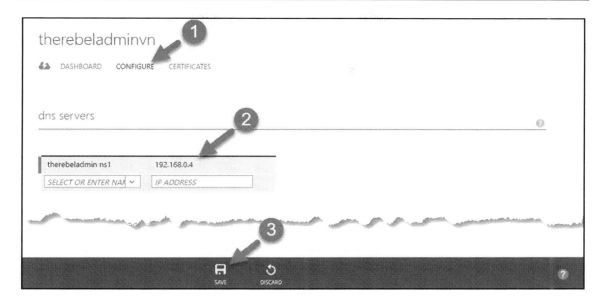

Create an AAD DC administrator group

Since the Azure AD Domain Services is a managed service, you will not get Domain Admin or Enterprise Admin privileges to the AD instance. But we are allowed to create a group called AAD DC administrators, and then all the members of this group will be granted administrator privileges to the domain-joined servers (this group will be added to the administrators group of the domain-join servers):

1. Click on the relevant Azure AD instance.
2. Navigate to the **GROUPS** link and then the **ADD A GROUP** option:

3. Then in the next window, type the group name `AAD DC Administrators` and select the type **Security**, and then click on the proceed button. Note that you must use the text in the same format in order to get this group created:

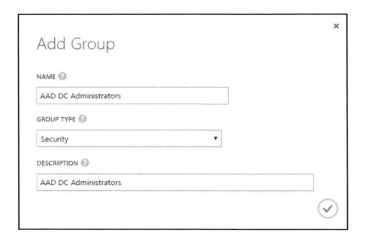

Creating a global administrator account for Azure AD Connect

During the Azure AD Connect configuration, we require an account having global administrator privileges (in Azure). It is recommended to use a separate account for this.

In order to create a new account, follow these steps:

1. Click on the relevant Azure AD instance.
2. Navigate to the **USERS** link and then the **ADD USER** option:

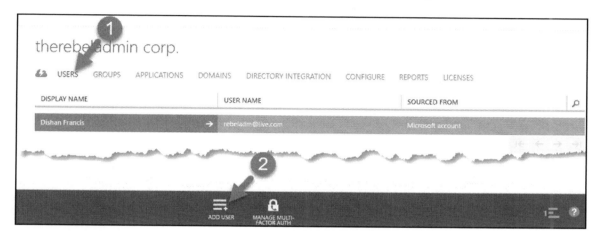

3. In the new window, it asks for a username for the new user. Type a username and click on the arrow button to proceed.
4. In the next window, you need to provide a **FIRST NAME, LAST NAME**, and **DISPLAY NAME** for the user account. More importantly, we need to select the Role as **Global Admin**. It is also required you provide an alternative email address for the account as it can be used to reset the password. Once all the info is provided, click on the arrow button to proceed.

The same window provides an option to enable MFA for additional security. For AD sync, however, it is not recommended.

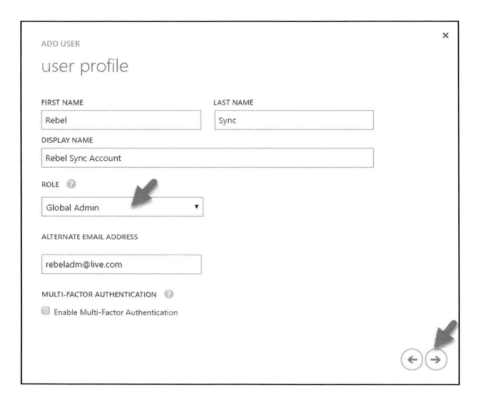

5. In the next window, it asks for confirmation to create the new account. At the end, it issues a temporary password for the account. You must log in to that account and set a new password before it is used in the Azure AD Connect configuration.

Add a custom domain to Azure AD

When we set up Azure AD, we initially defined a domain name ending in @onmicrosoft.com, but this is not the domain we have configured in the domain controllers. We can add our own domain name to Azure AD and assign usernames in a familiar format.

In order to add a custom domain, follow these steps:

1. Click on the relevant Azure AD instance.
2. Navigate to the **DOMAINS** link and click on **ADD A CUSTOM DOMAIN**:

3. In the next window, type the domain name and click on the **add** button. If you wish to enable SSO with a local AD FS farm, select the option **I plan to configure this domain for single sign-on with my local Active Directory**:

4. Once it is added, we need to verify the domain ownership. In order to do that, we need to create a **TXT record**. This should be created on the public DNS servers (if you use public domain name).

Azure also provides a DNS service. You can point the public name servers associated with the domain to Azure and use it from there. You can find more info about it on my blog post at `http://www.rebeladmin.com /2016/03/azure-dns/`.

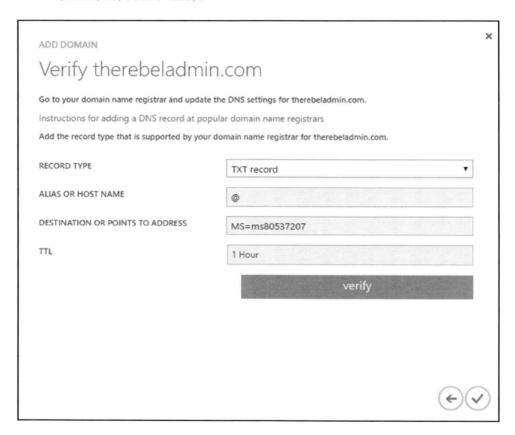

5. After the DNS record is added, you can click on the **verify** button and verify the domain ownership. Once it is verified, we can change the primary domain name to a custom domain name as well:

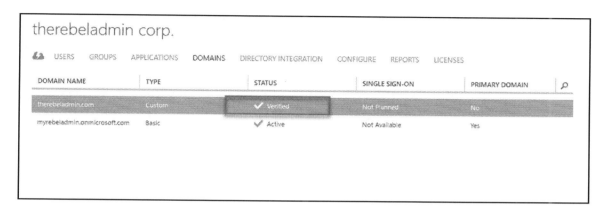

Setting up Azure AD Connect

Now we have everything ready to go ahead with the Azure AD Connect installation and configuration:

1. Log in to the server that you going to use as the Azure AD Connect server as enterprise administrator.
2. Download Azure AD Connect from `https://www.microsoft.com/en-us/downlo ad/details.aspx?id=47594`.
3. Run the setup, and after the installation, it will start the configuration wizard. On the first page, we need to accept the license and privacy terms and click on **Continue**.

4. On the next page, it will ask whether we'd like to use express settings or custom settings. If the current AD setup follows a single forest, single domain topology, it is recommended you use the express settings option:

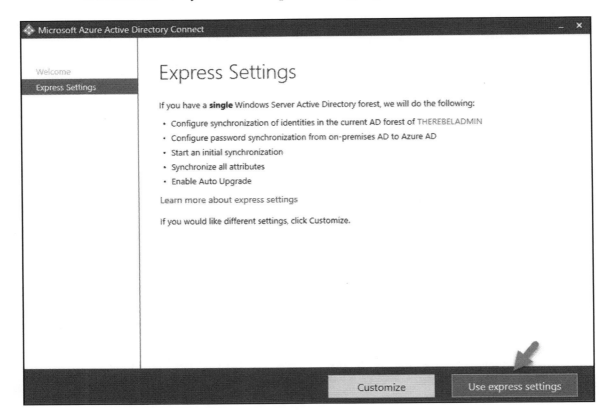

6. In the next window, it is asking for the credentials to connect to Azure AD. We need to use the global administrator account we created before for that:

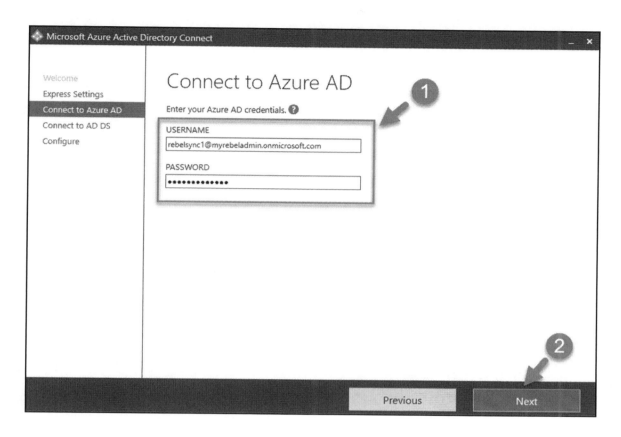

7. In the next window, it is asking us to provide the enterprise administrator credentials for the on-premises directory:

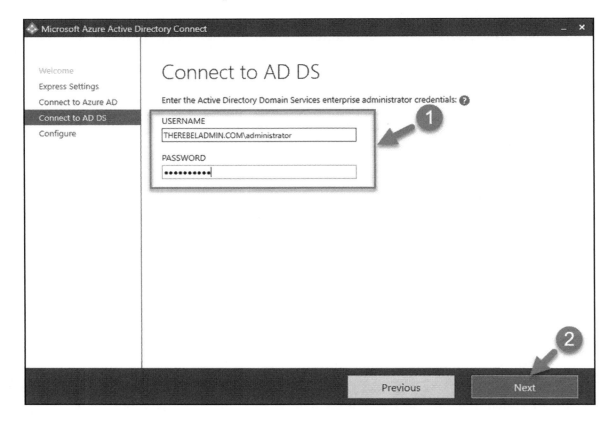

8. In the next window, it gives us a brief description of what it is going to be configured once we click on the **Install** button. Also, as soon as it finishes the configuration, it will start the initial synchronization with the Azure AD instance:

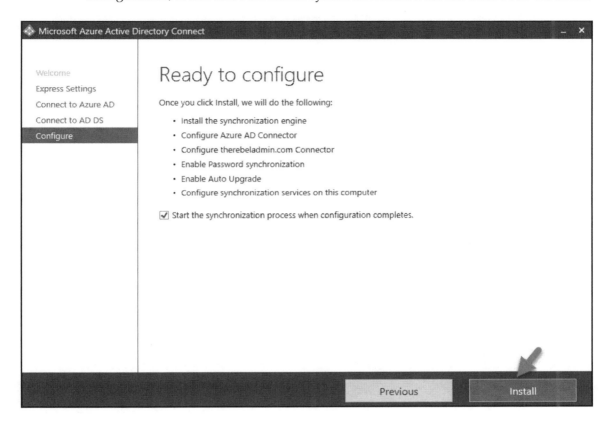

9. It will take a few minutes to finish the configuration and start the initial synchronization. We can review the synchronization status and health using Synchronization Service Manager. It is installed as part of the Azure AD Connect service:

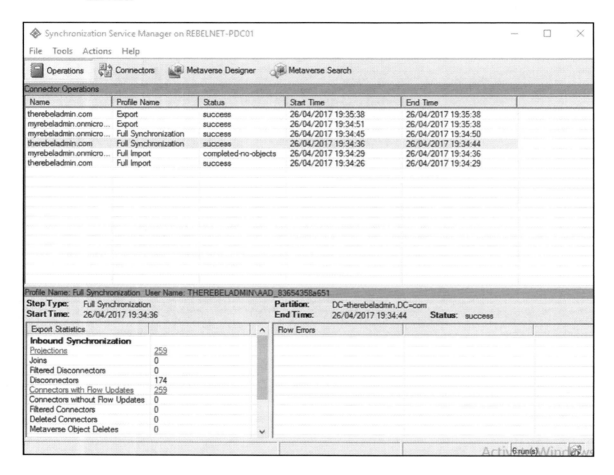

10. Once full synchronization completes, we can see that the identities are synced to the Azure AD instance:

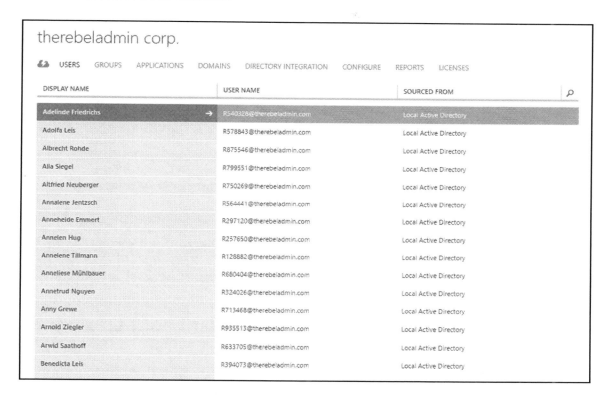

Password synchronization

If you use express settings for the AD Connect setup, by default, it enables password synchronization as well. This allows users to use the same AD password to authenticate to cloud-based workloads. It simplifies the user login experience and reduces helpdesk involvement.

As we discussed in Chapter 15, *Active Directory Security Best Practices*, AD uses hash values, which are generated by a hash algorithm, as passwords. They are not saved as clear text, and it is almost impossible to revert it to the original clear text password. There is misunderstanding about this as some people think Azure AD password sync uses clear text passwords. Every two minutes, the Azure AD connect server retrieves password hashes from the on-premises AD and syncs with Azure AD on a per user-basis in chronological order. This also involves an encryption and decryption process to add extra security to the password sync process. In the event of a password change, it will sync to Azure AD on the next password sync interval. In a healthy environment, the maximum delay to update password will be two minutes.

If the password was changed while the user has an open session, it will take effect on the next Azure authentication attempt. It will not log out the user from the existing session. Also, password synchronization doesn't mean SSO. Users always have to use corporate login details to authenticate to Azure services.

 You can find more information about SSO using `https://docs.microsof` `t.com/en-us/azure/active-directory/connect/active-directory-aa` `dconnect-sso`.

Syncing NTLM and Kerberos credential hashes to Azure AD

However, Azure AD Connect does not synchronize NTLM and Kerberos credential hashes to Azure AD by default. So, if you have an Azure AD directory setup and only enable Azure domain services recently, make sure you check the following:

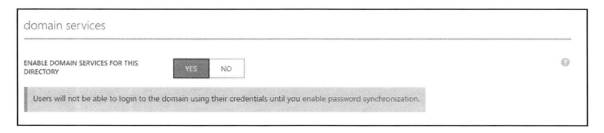

1. If there is an existing Azure AD Connect server, upgrade Azure AD connect to the latest version.
2. If there is an existing Azure AD Connect server, confirm that password synchronization is enabled in Azure AD Connect.

In order to do this, open Azure AD Connect and select the option to **view current configuration** and check whether password synchronization is enabled:

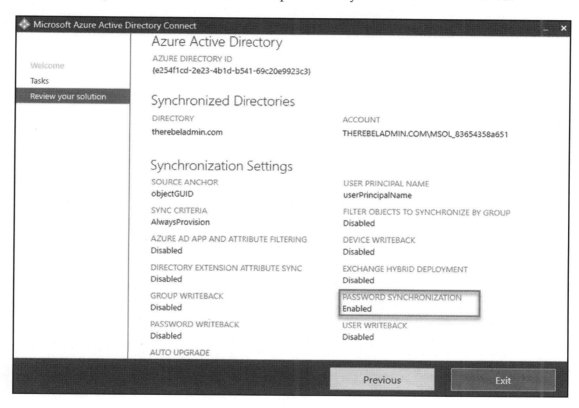

If its not, we need to go back to the initial page and select the option to **customize synchronization options** and, under optional features, select **password synchronization**:

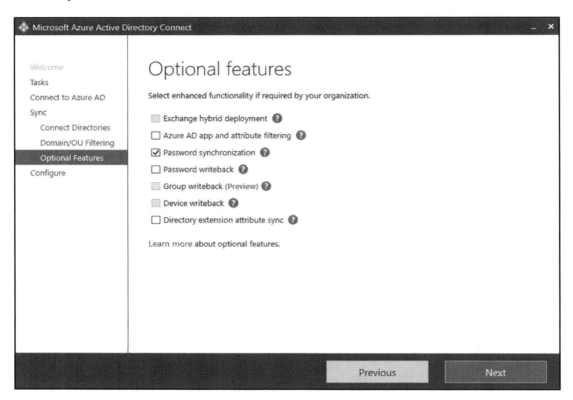

3. Run the following PowerShell script on local AD to force full password synchronization and set all on-premises users' credential hashes to sync to Azure AD:

```
$adConnector = "<CASE SENSITIVE AD CONNECTOR NAME>"
$azureadConnector = "<CASE SENSITIVE AZURE AD CONNECTOR NAME>"
Import-Module "C:\Program Files\Microsoft Azure AD Sync
\Bin\ADSync\ADSync.psd1"
$c = Get-ADSyncConnector -Name $adConnector
$p = New-Object Microsoft.IdentityManagement.PowerShell.
ObjectModel.ConfigurationParameter
"Microsoft.Synchronize.ForceFullPasswordSync",
String, ConnectorGlobal, $null, $null, $null
$p.Value = 1
$c.GlobalParameters.Remove($p.Name)
```

```
$c.GlobalParameters.Add($p)
$c = Add-ADSyncConnector -Connector $c
Set-ADSyncAADPasswordSyncConfiguration -SourceConnector
$adConnector -TargetConnector $azureadConnector -Enable $false
Set-ADSyncAADPasswordSyncConfiguration -SourceConnector
$adConnector -TargetConnector $azureadConnector -Enable $true
```

4. You can find the AD connector and Azure AD connector names at **Start** |
   Synchronization Service | **Connectors**:

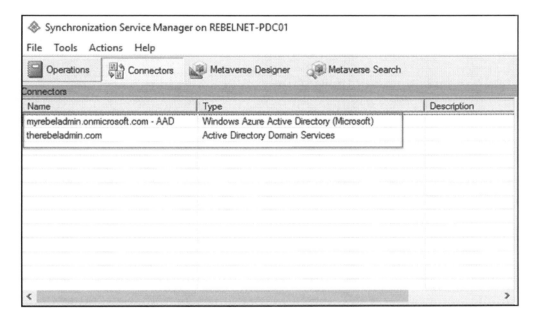

After that, you can try to log in to Azure as a user on the on-premises AD. If sync is
working properly, it should accept your corporate login.

Manage Azure AD Domain Services using virtual server

When Azure AD Domain Services is enabled and configured, we can add workloads to it
and make it part of the domain. We also can use Windows AD tools to manage the Azure
AD instance. In this section, we are going to learn how:

- Create virtual server in Azure under the same virtual network

- Join virtual server to Azure AD
- Install RSAT tools and manage Azure AD through virtual server

However, since it is a managed domain, we're only allowed to perform certain management tasks. Here's what Microsoft says (`https://docs.microsoft.com/en-gb/azure/active-di rectory-domain-services/active-directory-ds-admin-guide-administer-domain`):

- **Administrative tasks you can perform on a managed domain**: Members of the AAD DC Administrators group are granted privileges on the managed domain that enable them to perform tasks such as the following:
  - Join machines to the managed domain
  - Configure the built-in GPO for the *AADDC Computers* and *AADDC Users* containers in the managed domain
  - Administer DNS on the managed domain
  - Create and administer custom OUs on the managed domain
  - Gain administrative access to computers joined to the managed domain
- **Administrative privileges you do not have on a managed domain:** The domain is managed by Microsoft, including activities such as patching, monitoring, and performing backups. Therefore, the domain is locked down and you do not have privileges to perform certain administrative tasks on the domain. Some examples of tasks you cannot perform are as follows:
  - You are not granted domain administrator or enterprise administrator privileges for the managed domain
  - You cannot extend the schema of the managed domain
  - You cannot connect to domain controllers for the managed domain using remote desktop
  - You cannot add domain controllers to the managed domain

Creating virtual server in Azure in same virtual network

In the beginning of the previous section, we created a Azure virtual network and associated Azure AD with it. In order to add a server to the same managed domain, it needs to be part of the same virtual network. Any virtual network created using the Azure classic portal is only available for servers created using the same portal.

Therefore, we need to use the Azure classic portal to create our virtual machine:

1. Log in to the Azure classic portal as global administrator (`https://manage.wind owsazure.com`).

2. Go to **New** | **Compute** | **Virtual Machine** | **From Gallery** (because using this option, we can define the advanced options).

3. Then select the template from the list. I am going to use the Windows Server 2016 Datacenter version. After the selection, click on the arrow to proceed.

4. In the next window, provide the information for the new virtual machine (such as name, resources, and local admin account), and click on the proceed arrow:

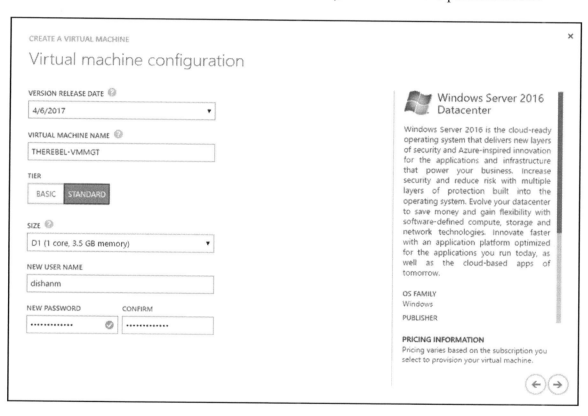

5. On the virtual machine configuration page, select the same virtual network as the one we set up the Azure managed domain. If we do not select the correct virtual network, we will not be able to connect this virtual machine to the managed domain. Once done, click on the button to proceed:

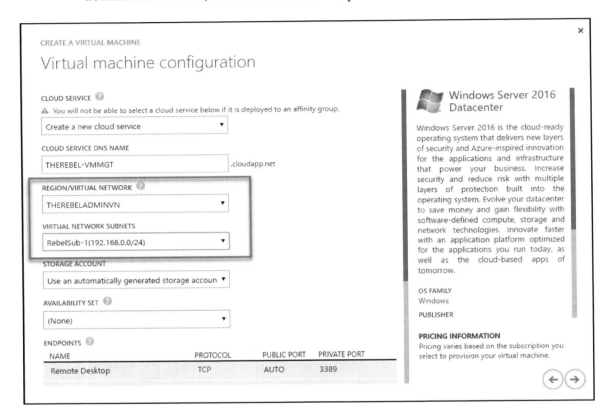

6. In the next window, we can add any add-on service from the list. Once you've made the relevant selections, click on the button at the bottom to proceed with the virtual machine setup.

Join virtual server to Azure AD

1. Once the virtual machine is created, log in to it as the local administrator.
2. Check the IP address and verify that it is from the address range we defined in the virtual network.
3. Go to the computer properties, and open the window to add the computer to the domain.
4. In the box, type the domain name associated with Azure AD. When clicking on **OK**, it will ask for the username and password. We need to use a user account that is a member of the AAD DC Administrators group:

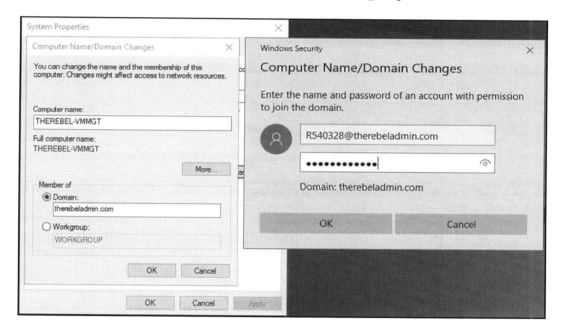

 DNS domain name is based on the name you specify when you enable Azure Domain Services. If you wish to use a custom name, it needs to be specified on the directory configuration page.

Following image shows where we can specify the DNS domain name for the directory:

5. Once the virtual machine is added to the domain, restart it to complete the action.

Install RSAT tools and managing Azure AD through a virtual server

1. Log in to the virtual machine as member of the AAD DC Administrators group.
2. Go to PowerShell and execute the following:

```
Add-WindowsFeature RSAT-AD-Tools
```

This will install the AD DS management tools.

3. Once this is completed, go to **Server Manager | Tools | Active Directory Administrative Center**.

4. In there, we can see the users synced from the local directory. Using this, we can manage the Azure AD objects:

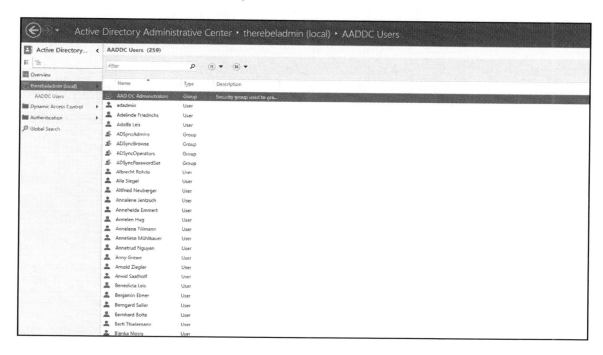

As I explained before, the management tasks we are allowed to do are limited. But basic functions such as password reset and group membership changes can be easily made using familiar AD DS management tools.

Summary

Azure AD is a Microsoft-managed, cloud-based multi-tenant directory service. It can be used in a cloud-only infrastructure or a hybrid infrastructure. When used in a hybrid infrastructure, it allows us to use the same identities to work with resources on-premises and in the cloud. It extends local AD infrastructure functionalities to the cloud.

In this chapter, we learned what Azure AD Domain Service is and its capabilities are. After that, we looked at a step-by-step guide to integrate our on-premises directory service with Azure AD. Last but not least, we learned how we can manage Azure AD using familiar AD management tools. In this chapter, I was able to demonstrate a very limited number of features and capabilities of Azure AD. You will find my blog at `www.rebeladmin.com` useful for more Azure AD-related topics.

In the next chapter, we will look at AD auditing and monitoring, which is crucial to maintaining a healthy AD infrastructure.

18

Active Directory Audit and Monitoring

The entire cybersecurity framework is based on three things: **protect, detect**, and **respond**. All these components are connected to one another. When we implement a system, we first need to understand what to protect and how to protect it. So far in this book, I've explained the importance of an identity infrastructure and how to protect it from emerging threats. Based on that, we can build a protected identity infrastructure, but we should understand that we cannot close all the doors. We need to expect a possible security breach at any time. But when it happens, we should have a system in place to detect and notify. This allows us to respond to the situation quickly and to minimize damage. In order to detect similar incidents, it is important to have proper systems and processes in place. This is where audit and monitoring come in. These help us to ensure the protected system we build is operating as expected and if there is any unexpected or unnatural behavior, it's recorded and reported. Incident response will be based on the outcome of the detection process.

Before I use the London Underground, I always check the **Transport for London (TfL)** website to see the status of the tube line services. It is a service provided by TfL to make sure its users are planning their journey properly and avoid delays. The system TfL has in place to monitor the line status gives us two benefits. As a service provider, TfL can detect the problem and start to address it immediately. At the same time, some filtered information is passed to the public that will be important to plan their journey.

Similarly, auditing and monitoring are not only for engineers to find problems. They also should provide filtered, structured information to different parties that are important for their roles and responsibilities. As an example, the IT director would like to know the overall domain service availability for the last month. But it is not important for him to know each and every event that happened in the system in the last 30 days.

In auditing and monitoring, we also need to identify what to monitor and what is to be reported. Knowing each and every thing that happens in the system is good, but at the same time, unless it has been analyzed and prioritized, it will not allow engineers to detect the issues properly. Therefore, we need systems to audit and monitor the correct stuff and present it in a useful way.

In this chapter, we will look at the following:

- Monitoring Active Directory Domain Service-related events and logs
- Microsoft Advanced Threat Analytics to monitor identity infrastructure threats
- Active Directory monitoring with Microsoft **Operation Management Suite (OMS)**
- Advanced auditing for Active Directory Infrastructure

Auditing and monitoring Active Directory using inbuilt Windows tools and techniques

Microsoft does have inbuilt features and tools to monitor/audit Active Directory environments. In this section, we are going to review these features and tools and see how we can use them efficiently.

Windows Event Viewer

As an engineer, I am sure you are well aware of Windows Event Viewer. It is a built-in tool which can be used to view and filter event logs on a local or remote computer. Events in there are generated by the operating system, services, server roles, and applications. This is the most commonly used tool in Windows systems for auditing and troubleshooting purposes.

 We also can write custom events to event logs. This is useful if you plan to run a script or action based on a particular event ID. This can be done using the `Write-Eventlog` cmdlet.

As shown in the following screenshot, Windows **Event Viewer (Local)** has four different categories to group event logs:

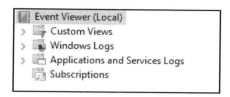

Custom views

Event Viewer allows creating **Custom Views** based on event level, time, log type, source type, event ID, task category, keywords, users, or computer. Event Viewer has thousands of different events. Using custom views, we can filter it and grab the information we are looking for. All these custom-made views will be listed under the **Custom Views** section. It also has predefined custom views.

These are based on the server roles. When **Active Directory Domain Services** roles are added, it also creates a custom view in the event log to group all the **Active Directory Domain Services**-related events:

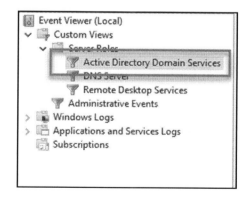

Windows logs

The Windows Logs section includes five Windows log files. These mostly contain OS-related events:

- **Application log**: This log contains the events collected from various applications running on the system. It can be from Microsoft or any other application.
- **Security log**: This log includes events such as successful and failed system login attempts, for example, a valid or failed user login for a particular system or its resources. Engineers can specify what security events need to be recorded using audit policies.
- **Setup log**: This includes events related to application setup and adding/removing server roles.
- **System log**: This log includes events related to Windows system components. As an example, an event related to automatic service start failure will be listed under this log.
- **Forwarded Events**: Using Event Viewer, we can connect to another remote computer and view the events. However, sometimes it may be required to watch for specific events from multiple sources. As an example, let's assume we need to collect events with ID 4321 from three computers. Using the *Subscriptions* event, we can collect only those events and forward them under the Forwarded Events log.

 Forwarded Events is the default location to push subscribed events. However, if needed, these events can also be forwarded to other log files.

Applications and Services logs

The Application and Services Logs category was introduced after Windows Server 2008. This stores the events related to applications and their components. Most of the events listed under here are more suited for application developers for debugging and application-level troubleshooting.

This category has four log types:

- **Admin**: Events listed in this log are understandable by end users and IT professionals. This information can be used for basic application troubleshooting. Most of these log entries will include instructions or links to knowledge-based articles from the application vendor.
- **Operational**: Operational events include information about configuration changes or status changes in an application/service. These events are useful for application diagnosis and analyzing.
- **Analytic**: This log is by default hidden and disabled. This is usually enabled during the application or service diagnosis process as it generates a high volume of events.
- **Debug**: This is purely used for troubleshooting purposes, by application developers and vendors. Similar to the *analytic* log, it is by default hidden and disabled.

Subscriptions

This category lists down the event subscriptions created with remote computers. Under this category, we can create/edit/disable event subscriptions, check the runtime status, and forcibly run subscription jobs.

When we open up an event, it gives different levels of information, such as:

- General description about the problem
- Log file name
- Event source to indicate where it came from
- Event ID number
- Level of the error (critical, information, or warning)
- Username of the error owner
- Links to TechNet, KB, or other sources to get more information about the event
- Time of the event
- Hostname of the source computer

Active Directory Domain Service event logs

Apart from the events under the Windows Log category, Active Directory Domain Service and related service events can be found under the following logs. These are located under the **Applications and Services Logs** category:

- Active Directory Web Services
- DFS Replication
- Directory Service
- DNS Server
- File Replication Service (only if using FRS)

Active Directory Domain Service log files

Apart from events, Active Directory Domain Service and related services have other system log files that record data about service install/uninstall, performance, service errors/failures, and so on. These log files can be used for audit, troubleshooting, or debugging purposes.

The default location for these log files is `%SystemRoot%\Debug`:

- `DCPromo.log`: This log file is created during the Active Directory promotion process. It will also record events during the demotion process. This log will contain events such as:
    - Active Directory Domain Service configuration settings
    - Information about schema preparation
    - Information about directory partition creation/modifications
    - Information about data replication
    - Service configuration status
    - Information about creating Active Directory databases and the `SYSVOL` directory

- `DCPromoUI.log`: This log file can be considered as a progress report for the Active Directory Domain Service promotion/demotion process. It starts the logging process as soon as the Active Directory Domain Service configuration wizard opens and ends when it completes the installation successfully (until reboot request accept) or when it is aborted due to errors. This includes result of each and every act of the system during the service installation and removal process. This log includes useful information such as:
    - Timestamp when the installation or removal process started
    - Detailed results of each validation test

- Name of the domain controller used for initial replication
- List of directory partitions that were replicated
- Number of the objects replicated in each and every partition
- Configuration summary
- Information about registry key changes related to configuration

- `DFSR.log`: This log file includes events related to DFS replication. This can be used for `SYSVOL` replication troubleshooting and the debugging process. (if `SYSVOL` uses DFS replication).

 After Windows Server 2008, Active Directory uses DFS replication by default, but if domain controllers have been introduced to a Windows Server 2003 environment, it will use FRS by default.

Active Directory audit

The only way to identify potential security threats and security breach in infrastructure is through continuous monitoring and auditing. When it comes to auditing, the Windows system itself provides advanced auditing capabilities to identify such security issues. In Windows, by default, only certain types of actions are audited. These auditing settings are handled by Windows audit policies.

 Here, we are only going to look at advanced security audit policies, which were first introduced with Windows Server 2008 R2.

There are 10 categories of events we can audit in a Windows system:

- System events
- Logon/logoff events
- Object Access events
- Privileged Use events
- Detailed Tracking events
- Policy Change events
- Account Management events

- DS Access events
- Account Logon events
- Global Object Access auditing

Each and every event category also has subcategories.

Legacy Windows auditing provides *nine* categories and each category also has subcategories. These are located under **Computer Configuration** | **Windows Settings** | **Security Settings** | **Local Policies** | **Audit Policy**. Also, categories and subcategories can be listed using `auditpol /get /category:\*`. Advanced security audit policies provides 53 options to tune up the auditing requirement, and you can collect more granular-level information about your infrastructure events than legacy auditing.

Auditing on these categories can be enabled using group policies. It is located under **Computer Configuration** | **Windows Settings** | **Security Settings** | **Advanced Audit Policy Configuration** | **Audit Policies**:

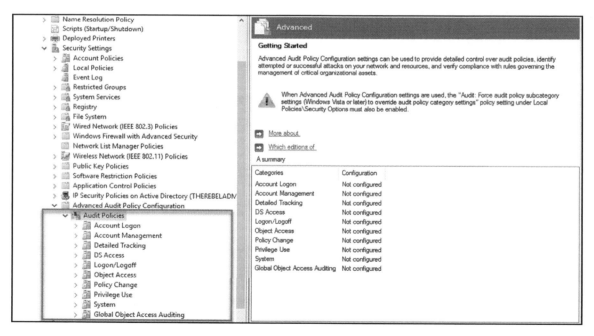

All these categories can collect a lot of system and service-related events relevant to Active Directory infrastructure activities, but in this section, we are only going to focus on **DS Access** events categories and its subcategories. it audits events related to AD objects access and AD object modification. Also, the settings under this category only apply to domain controllers.

DS Access events category includes four subcategories:

- Audit Directory Service Access
- Audit Directory Service Changes
- Audit Directory Service Replication
- Audit Detailed Directory Service Replication

Audit Directory Service Access

This category records events when an AD DS object is accessed. This will only work if the **system access control list (SACL)** is configured and relevant objects have been added. This is similar to directory service access in legacy auditing.

 SACL allows engineers to log access attempts to secured objects. SACL can generate audit records when an access attempt fails, when it succeeds, or both.

When auditing is enabled under this category, the following events can be found under security logs:

Event ID	Event message
4662	An operation was performed on an object

Audit Directory Service Changes

This category records events related to AD DS object changes such as:

- Create
- Delete
- Modify
- Move
- Undelete

When an object value is changed, it records the old value and the new value it was changed into. Again, the event will only be generated for the entries listed under SAC. Once auditing is enabled, the following events can be found under security logs:

Event ID	Event message
5136	A directory service object was modified
5137	A directory service object was created
5138	A directory service object was undeleted
5139	A directory service object was moved
5141	A directory service object was deleted

Audit Directory Service Replication

This category logs events when replication between two domain controllers begins and ends. When auditing is enabled, we will be able to find the following events in the logs:

Event ID	Event message
4932	Synchronization of a replica of an Active Directory naming context has begun
4933	Synchronization of a replica of an Active Directory naming context has ended

Audit Detailed Directory Service Replication

This category records detailed information about data replicated between domain controllers. Once auditing is enabled, it will generate a high volume of events and will be useful to troubleshoot replication issues. It will log the following types of events:

Event ID	Event message
4928	An Active Directory replica source naming context was established
4929	An Active Directory replica source naming context was removed
4930	An Active Directory replica source naming context was modified
4931	An Active Directory replica destination naming context was modified
4934	Attributes of an Active Directory object were replicated
4935	Replication failure start

| 4936 | Replication failure end |
| 4937 | A lingering object was removed from a replica |

Demonstration

In this section, let's see how we can use inbuilt Windows monitoring and audit capabilities in practice. In order to do these configurations, you need to have domain administrator or enterprise administrator privileges.

Reviewing events

Event Viewer can simply be open by running `eventvwr.msc`. The same MMC can also be used to connect to a remote computer using the **Connect to Another Computer...** option, as highlighted in the following screenshot:

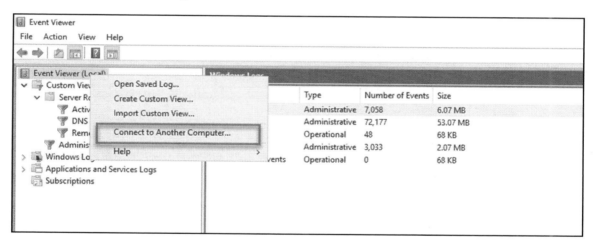

We can simplify this by creating server groups in **Server Manager**. Server groups allow us to group systems running similar server roles or acting as part of a distributed system.

Before we go ahead and create server groups, we need to take care of the following points:

1. We need an account that has administrator privileges for all the server group members to create server groups and use server groups.

2. We must enable **Windows Remote Management (WinRM)**; after Windows Server 2012, WinRM is enabled by default. Existing WinRM configuration can be reviewed using the PowerShell command `winrm get winrm/config`. If it's not enabled, we can enable it using the `winrm quickconfig` command.

3. Even if we are logged in as domain admin or enterprise admin, by default, it is not allowed to collect events from remote computers. In order to do that, we need to add a collector computer account (the server where the server group is created) to the Event Log Readers group. This is a built-in local group. Members of this group can read event logs from the local machine. We can add a computer account to the group using the following command:

```
Add-ADGroupMember -identity 'Event Log Readers'
-members REBELNET-PDC01$
```

REBELNET-PDC01 can be replaced with the collector computer account.

4. In order to create a server group, go to **Server Manager** from the dashboard and select **Create a server group**:

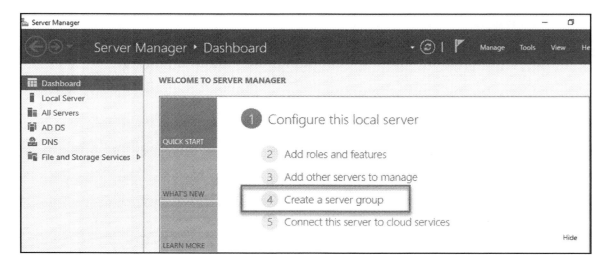

5. In the new window, we can provide a name for the group and add members to the group. It provides different methods to select from, in order to search for the members:

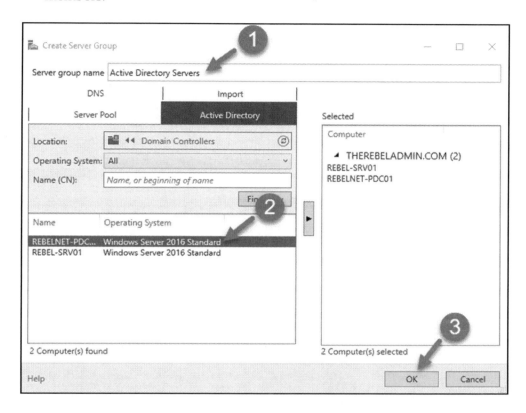

6. Once a group is created, you can access it using the left-hand panel in the **Server Manager**. Inside the group window, there is a separate section for events, labeled **EVENTS**. When we navigate through each member, it will show us events related to each in the events window:

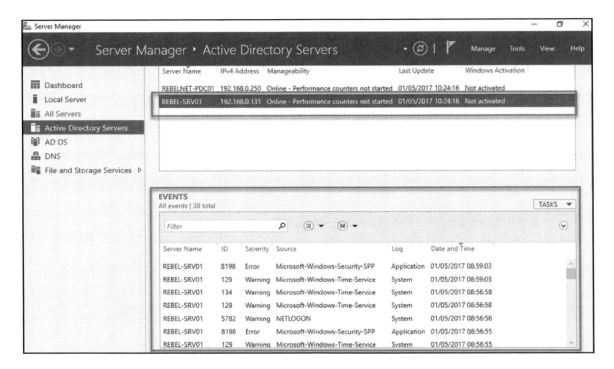

We can configure the event data and modify:

- Event severity levels
- Event time frames
- Event log files where the data will be gathered

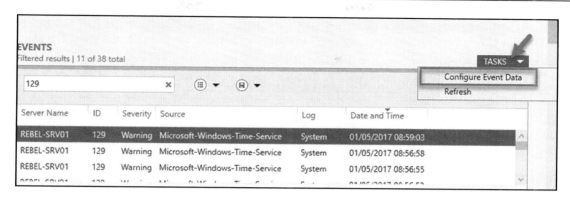

The following screenshot explains how we can configure event data using different options:

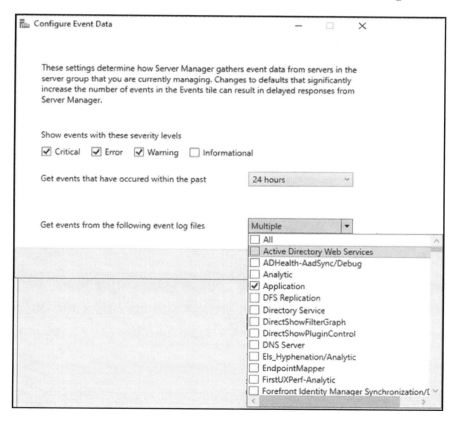

We also can filter events and save it as a query for future use. As an example, I need to list events with **ID** 129. I can just filter it out by typing 129 in the filter field. But at the same time, I can create a query for it and save it for future use. So, the next time, I can just run the query to filter out data:

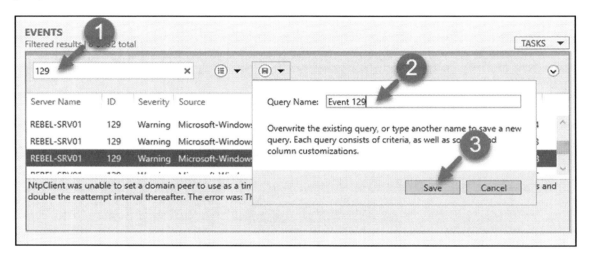

In the following screenshot, once the query is created, it can be accessed whenever needed:

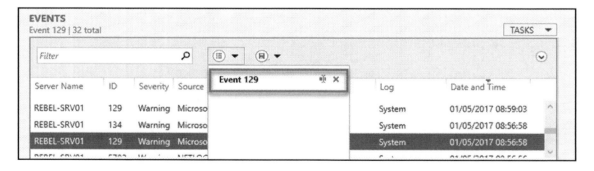

Setting up event subscriptions

Event Viewer contains lots of different event entries. It can be a few thousand events per day. Even if every event provides some useful information, we do not need to go through each and every one when we are troubleshooting a particular application or performing a service audit. There are specific events relevant to each server role, application, service, and system component. On some occasions, when we audit or troubleshoot, we need to review events on multiple computers. Event Viewer only allows us to connect to one computer at a given time. It can be a local computer or remote computer. Event subscriptions allow us to collect event logs from remote computers and review them on one console.

Before we configure event subscriptions, we need to perform the following steps:

1. Enable Windows Remote Management.
2. Add a Collector computer account to the Event Log Readers group.

Once the prerequisites are fulfilled, follow these steps:

1. Log in to the Collector server.
2. Open Event Viewer and go to **Actions** | **Create Subscription**.
3. In the new window, enter the following details:

   - **Subscription name**: Name of the subscription job.

- **Destination log**: Log file where collected events should appear. By default, it is the **Forwarded Events** log file. We can select any log file available in the drop-down menu:

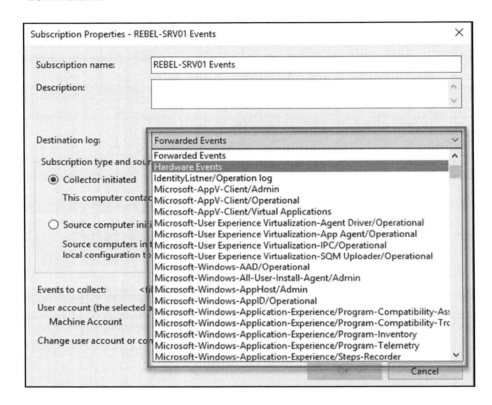

- **Collector initiated**: We can list the source computers here. It is not a one-to-one connection. It can be any number of computers:

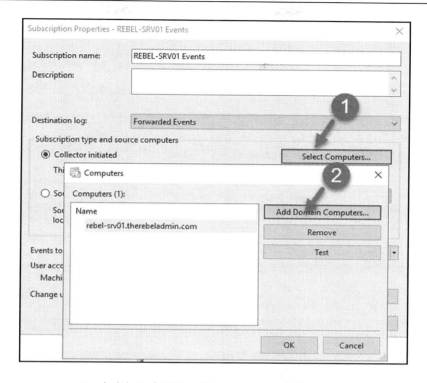

- **Source computer initiated**: This allows you to define a subscription without defining the event source computers. Then, the source computers will be defined using a Group Policy setting located at **Computer Configuration | Policies | Administrative Templates | Windows Components | Event Forwarding | Configure Target Subscription Manager**.
  In there, the collector should be added in the
  `Server=http://<eventcollector`
  `FQDN>:5985/wsman/SubscriptionManager/WEC,Refresh=10` format.

- **Event to collect**: Using this option, we can define what events are to be selected from the source computers. It is similar to a typical event filter window:

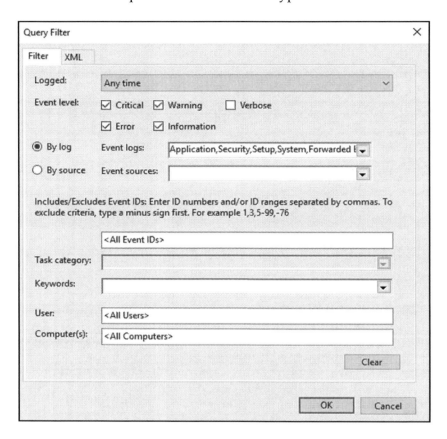

- **Change user account or configure advanced settings**: In this option, we can define separate account which can use by collector to extract events from source computers. It also gives options to optimize the event delivery settings. This is important if large number of events been collected:

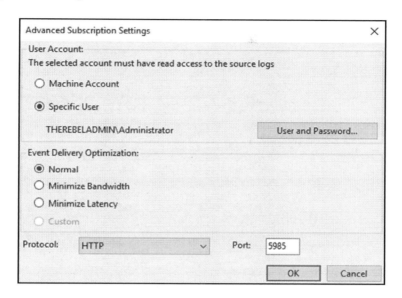

Security event log from domain controllers

In order to collect security logs from remote domain controllers, we need to add a network service account to the channel access permissions of the security event log. This is because the WinRM service is running under the network service account. This can be done by running:

```
wevtutil sl security
/ca:'O:BAG:SYD:(A;;0xf0005;;;SY)(A;;0x5;;;BA)(A;;0x1;;;S-1-5-32-573)(A;;0x1
;;;S-1-5-20)'
```

`O:BAG:SYD:(A;;0xf0005;;;SY)(A;;0x5;;;BA)(A;;0x1;;;S-1-5-32-573)(A;;0x1;` `;;S-1-5-20)` contains READ permission settings for network service account `(A;;0x1;;;)`. In the preceding SID value for network service account (`S-1-5-20`), and the channel access value `(O:BAG:SYD:(A;;0xf0005;;;SY)(A;;0x5;;;BA)(A;;0x1;;;S-1-5-32-573))`. Once all this is done, after a few minutes, we can see the **Forwarded Events**:

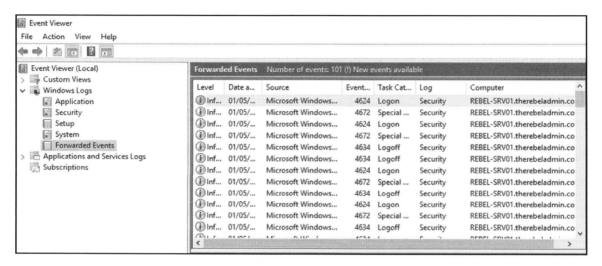

Enabling advanced security audit policies

As we have seen previously, for successful auditing, we need to have SACL configured for the relevant AD objects. If there is no SACL entry, no events will be generated against that object. In order to configure SACL, we need domain admin or enterprise admin privileges. To add an SACL entry, perform the following steps:

1. Open **Active Directory Users and Computers**.
2. Click on **View** | **Advanced Features**.
3. Right-click on the OU or the object that you'd like to enable auditing for. Then click on **Properties**. In my example, I am using the root container as I wish to enable it globally.
4. Click on the **Security** tab and then on **Advanced**.

5. Click on the **Auditing** tab and then click on the **Add** button to add a new security principle to the SACL. In our scenario, I am using **Everyone** as I'd like to edit all.

6. As the **Type**, I have selected the **Success** event type. Also, I've applied it to **This object and all descendant objects**:

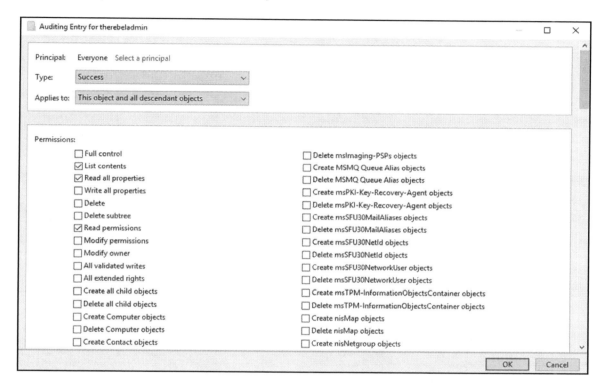

Once the SACL entries are in place, we can enable advanced audit policy configuration. In order to do that:

1. Go to **Group Policy Management**.
2. In the MMC, expand the **Domain Controllers** OU.
3. Right-click on **Default Domain Controller Policy** and select **Edit**.
4. Then navigate to **Computer Configuration** | **Policies** | **Windows Settings** | **Security Settings** | **Advanced Audit Policy Configuration** | **Audit Policies**.
5. In there, we can find all 10 audit categories. In this demo, we are only going to enable audit categories under **DS Access**.

6. Navigate to **DS Access** and double-click on the **Subcategory** entry. To enable auditing, select **Configure the following audit events** and then select the events you'd like to audit. It's recommended to audit both **Success** and **Failure**:

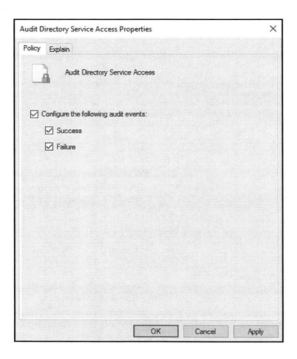

I have repeated the same configuration for the rest of the audit categories:

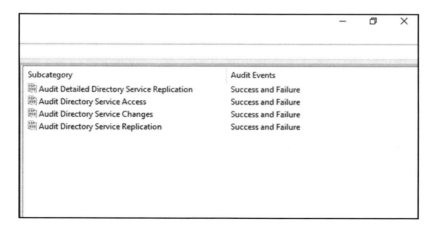

Once the group policy is applied successfully, it will start to log new events according to the audit policy.

Enforcing advanced auditing

Before Windows Server 2008, there were *nine* main auditing categories and subcategories. They still continue to appear under Windows Server 2016. It is recommended not to mix them up and only use advanced auditing. We can enforce the system to only accept advanced auditing policy settings if legacy audit policy settings are applied to the same category.

This can be done by enabling Group Policy setting under **Computer Configuration | Windows Settings | Security Settings | Local Policies | Security Options | Audit:Force audit policy subcategory settings (Windows Vista or later) to override audit policy category settings**.

Reviewing events with PowerShell

We also can use PowerShell commands to review event logs or filter events from local and remote computers without any additional service configurations. `Get-EventLog` is the primary cmdlet we can use for this task:

```
Get-EventLog -List
```

The previous command will list down the details about the log files in your local system, including the log file name, max log file size, and number of entries:

```
Get-EventLog -LogName 'Directory Service' | fl
```

The previous command will list down all the events under the log file `Directory Service`. We also can limit the number of events we need to list down. As an example, if we only need to list down the latest 5 events from the `Directory Service` log file, we can use:

```
Get-EventLog -Newest 5 -LogName 'Directory Service'
```

We can further filter it down by listing down events according to entry type:

```
Get-EventLog -Newest 5 -LogName 'Directory Service' -EntryType Error
```

The previous command will list down the first five errors in the `Directory Service` log file. We also can add a time limit to filter events more:

```
Get-EventLog -Newest 5 -LogName 'Directory Service' -EntryType Error -After
(Get-Date).AddDays(-1)
```

The previous command will list down the events with error type `Error` within the last 24 hours under the `Directory Service` log. We can also get the events from the remote computers:

```
Get-EventLog -Newest 5 -LogName 'Directory Service' -ComputerName 'REBEL-
SRV01' | fl -Property *
```

The previous command will list down the first five log entries in the `Directory Service` log file from the REBEL-SRV01 remote computer:

```
PS C:\Users\Administrator> Get-EventLog -Newest 5 -LogName 'Directory Service' -ComputerName 'REBEL-SRV01' | fl -Propert

EventID           : 1404
MachineName       : REBEL-SRV01.therebeladmin.com
Data              : {}
Index             : 79
Category          : Knowledge Consistency Checker
CategoryNumber    : 1
EntryType         : Information
Message           : This directory service is now the intersite topology generator and has assumed responsibility for
                    generating and maintaining intersite replication topologies for this site.
Source            : NTDS KCC
ReplacementStrings : {}
InstanceId        : 1073743228
TimeGenerated     : 02/05/2017 08:07:10
TimeWritten       : 02/05/2017 08:07:10
UserName          : NT AUTHORITY\ANONYMOUS LOGON
Site              :
Container         :

EventID           : 2405
MachineName       : REBEL-SRV01.therebeladmin.com
Data              : {}
Index             : 78
Category          : Internal Configuration
CategoryNumber    : 7
EntryType         : Information
Message           : This Active Directory Domain Services server does not support the "Recycle Bin Feature" optional
                    feature.
Source            : NTDS General
ReplacementStrings : {Recycle Bin Feature}
InstanceId        : 1073744229
TimeGenerated     : 02/05/2017 00:37:54
TimeWritten       : 02/05/2017 00:37:54
UserName          : NT AUTHORITY\ANONYMOUS LOGON
Site              :
Container         :
```

We can also extract events from several computers simultaneously:

```
Get-EventLog -Newest 5 -LogName 'Directory Service' -ComputerName
"localhost", "REBEL-SRV01"
```

The previous command will list down the log entries from the local computer and the `REBEL-SRV01` remote computer. When it comes to filtering, we can further filter events using the event source:

```
Get-EventLog -LogName 'Directory Service' -Source "NTDS KCC"
```

The previous command will list down the events with the source `NTDS KCC`. It also allows us to search for the specific event IDs:

```
Get-EventLog -LogName 'Directory Service' | where {$_.eventID -eq 1000}
```

The previous command will list the events with event ID `1000`.

> There is a recommended list of events which we need to audit periodically to identify potential issues in an Active Directory environment. The complete list is available for review at https://docs.microsoft.com/en-gb/windows-server/identity/ad-ds/plan/appendix-1--events-to-monitor.

Microsoft Advanced Threat Analytics

Latest Microsoft reports show that it can take an average of 146 days to identify an identity infrastructure security breach. There are certain reasons for this:

- We fight against human adversaries, and they keep changing their tactics for attacks, which cannot be detected by traditional perimeter defense solutions.
- Existing security solutions require time and knowledge to set up, fine-tune, and maintain.
- Going through a large number of logs and reports to identify risks and issues is not practical as engineers could miss important events.
- Most of the existing security solutions are for preventing attackers at the perimeter level. They do not have a way to detect the attackers once they have successfully logged in to the infrastructure.

I do not allow anyone to drive my car. Not even my lovely wife. I didn't make it, but from the day I bought the car, I've taken care to know everything about it. I am the one who brings it for **Ministry of Transport (MOT)** test, and I am the one who takes it to the garage. So I know the ins and outs of my car.

Microsoft built Active Directory and has maintained it for more than 20 years now. Many engineers are working on the product every day for further improvements. Every day, they are dealing with tickets regarding Active Directory infrastructure-related issues, including security. They also have a cloud version of Active Directory that people use via public internet. So, if someone knows the ins and outs of Active Directory infrastructure security threats, it will be Microsoft. Considering all these things, Microsoft released *Advanced Threats Analytics*, which provides a simple, fast, and accurate way to detect identity infrastructure threats at an early stage by identifying suspicious user and device activity with built-in intelligence. It also provides clear information in the form of email alert and timeline view in the web interface.

What is Microsoft Advanced Threat Analytics?

Microsoft **Advanced Threat Analytics (ATA)** is an on-premises platform to help us protect our identity infrastructure from advanced targeted attacks by automatically analyzing, learning, and identifying normal and abnormal entity (users, devices, and resources) behavior. It also uses deep packet analysis technology and data from additional data sources, such as Events to detect threats in real time.

ATA benefits

The following list explains why ATA is worth in the infrastructure:

- **Minimum configuration**: ATA has the required security intelligence built in. Therefore, there's no need for rule setup to detect security issues. The configuration itself is straightforward. Ongoing maintenance is also minimal.
- **Easy alerts**: With ATA, there are no more reports and logs to analyze. The system itself does all the data analysis and informs about critical alerts either as email alerts or in the form of an attack timeline in the web interface. If you've worked with products such as **System Center Operation Manager (SCOM)**, you may know how sensitive alerting can distract you from real issues. ATA minimizes false alarms and lets people know exactly what they want to know.
- **Equipped with knowledge to identify rising threats in the industry**: The Microsoft security graph is continually empowered by various data sources which allows it to identify rising security issues in identity infrastructures. These findings will be used by ATA, and it guarantees faster detection than traditional security tools.

- **Mobility support**: ATA does not care whether devices and users are connected from an internal or external network; if there is authentication and authorization involved, it treats all connections equally. There is no configuration change required to monitor connections from external networks.

What threats does ATA detect?

The following types of threats will be detected by ATA:

- Reconnaissance using account enumeration
- Net Session enumeration
- Reconnaissance using DNS
- Reconnaissance using directory services enumeration
- Brute-force attacks
- Sensitive accounts exposed in plaintext authentication
- Services exposing accounts in plaintext authentication
- Suspicious Honey Token account activities
- Unusual protocol implementation
- Malicious data protection through a private information request
- Abnormal behavior
- Pass-the-ticket attacks
- Pass-the-hash attacks
- Over-pass-the-hash attacks
- MS14-068 exploits
- MS11-013 exploits
- Skeleton key malware
- Golden tickets
- Remote execution
- Malicious replication requests

ATA components

There are three components involved in an ATA deployment:

- ATA center
- ATA gateway
- ATA Lightweight Gateway

ATA center

This is the main component of the ATA deployment. The ATA center does following:

- ATA gateway configuration
- Gathers parsed traffic from ATA gateways and ATA Lightweight Gateways
- Detects suspicious activities
- Runs ATA behavioral machine learning algorithms to detect abnormal behavior
- Runs various deterministic algorithms to detect advanced attacks based on the attack kill chain
- Web console to view the attack timeline, configuration settings, and notifications.
- Configures email notification settings

The ATA center is recommended to be installed on a separate server. One ATA center is recommended for one forest. Cross-forest configuration is not supported.

ATA gateway

The ATA gateway is a separate server which monitors domain controller traffic using port mirroring. Port mirroring settings depend on the virtualization solution you use. If it's physical, it requires network layer changes as well.

ATA Lightweight Gateway

The ATA Lightweight Gateway component can directly be installed on domain controllers to monitor Active Directory traffic without the need of port mirroring. This is the quickest way to get ATA up and running. However, it will increase the resource requirement of domain controllers.

Both gateways do the following:

- Capture and inspect domain controller network traffic
- Receive Windows events from different data sources such as SIEM, **Syslog** servers, and **Windows Event Forwarding**
- Retrieve data about users and computers from the Active Directory domain
- Perform resolution of network entities (users, groups, and computers)
- Transfer relevant data to the **ATA Center**

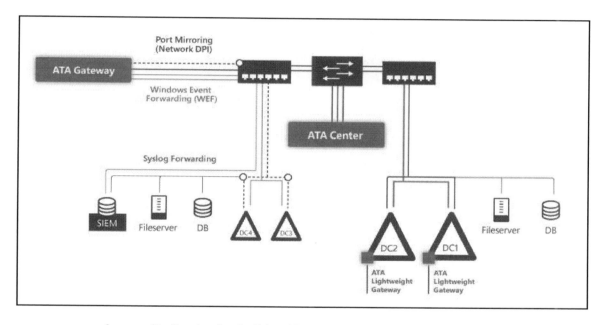

Image source: https://docs.microsoft.com/en-gb/advanced-threat-analytics/plan-design/media/ata-architecture-topology.jpg

ATA deployments

ATA deployments support three topologies:

- **ATA gateway only**: In this mode, Active Directory traffic is only captured by ATA gateway. All the domain controllers pass the traffic to the gateway via port mirroring.

- **ATA Lightweight Gateway only**: In this mode, it only uses Lightweight Gateways. This component needs to be installed on each and every domain controller.
- **ATA gateway and ATA Lightweight Gateway mixed mode**: In this mode, both gateway types will be used. But one domain controller should only use one gateway component.

ATA deployment prerequisites

The following prerequisites are needed before starting on an ATA deployment:

- Latest ATA installation files.
- Valid ATA licenses.
- Domain administrator or enterprise administrator account to install ATA center and ATA gateways.
- An account with read access to all the objects in Active Directory.
- ATA center needs a minimum of Windows Server 2012 R2 with latest updates. At least 4 GB RAM and 2 CPU cores are recommended.
- ATA center need to have additional IP address for Console.
- ATA Lightweight Gateway needs a minimum of Windows Server 2012 R2 with latest updates. At least 6 GB RAM and 2 CPU cores are recommended.
- SSL certificates to be used by gateway and ATA center. For easy installation, it is still allowed to use self-signed certificates that can be replaced later with public SSL or certificates issued by internal CA.

Demonstration

In this section, I am going to demonstrate how to install Microsoft ATA. In the demo environment:

- Domain and forest functional levels are set to Windows Server 2016.
- Only ATA Lightweight Gateway will be used. Every domain controller will have a gateway installed.
- ATA Center and ATA Lightweight Gateways will be installed on Windows Server 2016 systems.

Installing ATA center

ATA center can be deployed using the following steps:

1. Log in to the server as a domain and or enterprise administrator.
2. Run Microsoft ATA center `setup.exe`.
3. In the first window, select the relevant language and click on **Next**.
4. Accept the license terms and click on **Next** to continue.
5. Then it asks how we'd like to know about updates. It is recommended to use Microsoft Update for that. Choose the option **Use Microsoft Update when I check for updates** and then click on **Next**.
6. Then in the next window, we can define the application **Installation Path**, **Database Data Path** (ATA uses MongoDB), **Center Service IP Address: Port**, **Center Service SSL Certificate**, and **Console IP Address**. After these changes, click on **Install** to begin the installation:

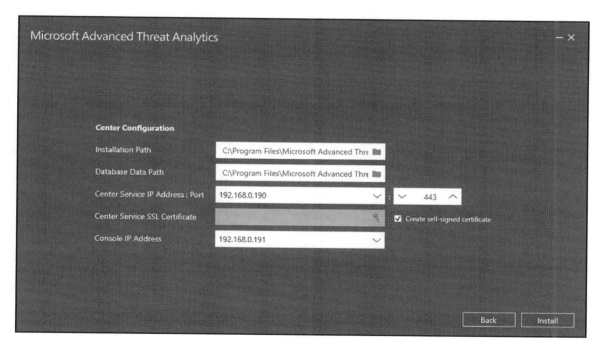

7. Once the installation has finished, it will give you the option to launch the ATA center.

8. After launching the ATA center, log in to it using the account used to install ATA center. It will be the default ATA admin account. In the system, you can later add additional administrator accounts.

9. As soon as you log in, it gives you a window to provide account and domain information to connect to Active Directory. This user account works as a typical service account. No additional permission is needed (except read permission for all AD objects). Once account details are entered, click on the **Test connection** option to verify the connection and then click on **Save**:

10. This completes the initial ATA center configuration and the next step is to get ATA Lightweight Gateways installed.

Installing ATA Lightweight Gateway

ATA Lightweight installation is straightforward. We can install it using the following steps:

1. Log in to the domain controller as domain admin or enterprise admin.
2. Launch IE and connect to the ATA center URL.
3. Log in to ATA center as `administrator`:

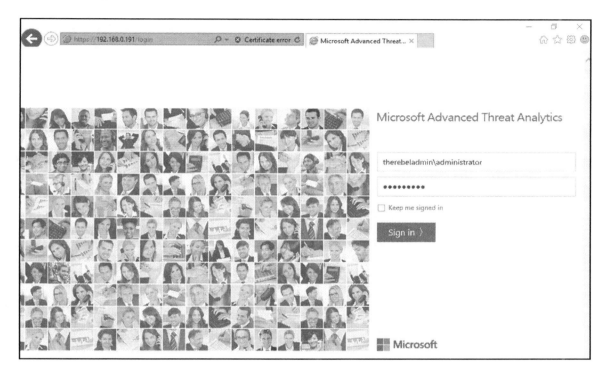

4. When you log in for the first time, it provides the following page. Click on **Download gateway setup and install the first Gateway,** as illustrated here:

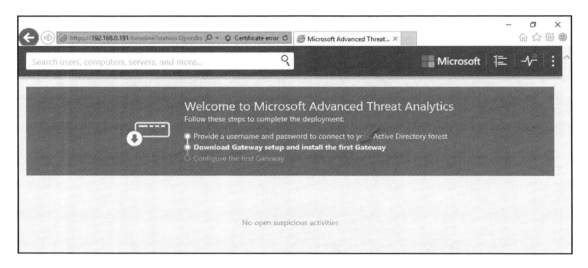

5. Then it gives you the option to **Download Gateway Setup** files. Click on the button to begin:

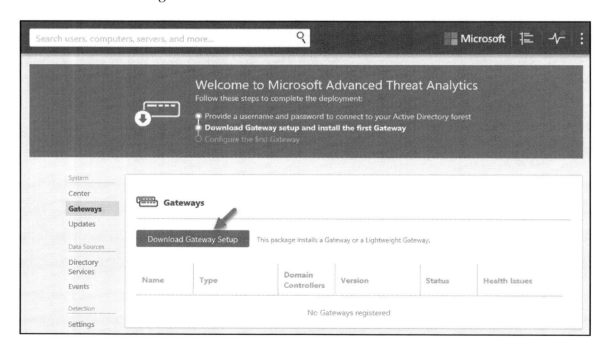

6. After the download completes, extract the ZIP file and run the Microsoft ATA gateway `Setup.exe`.

7. On the initial page, select the relevant language and click on **Next** to continue.

8. In the next window, it will give you a confirmation about **Gateway deployment type**. By default, it detects the type as **Lightweight Gateway**. Click on **Next** to proceed with the installation:

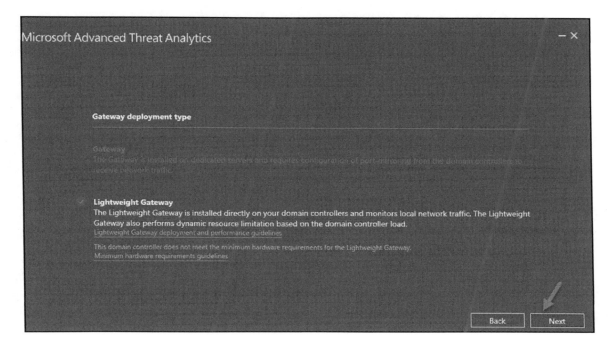

9. In the next window, we can specify the **Installation Path, Gateway Service SSL Certificate** information, and account details to register the gateway with the ATA center. This account should be a member of the ATA administrator group. After you type in the data, click on **Install** to begin the installation:

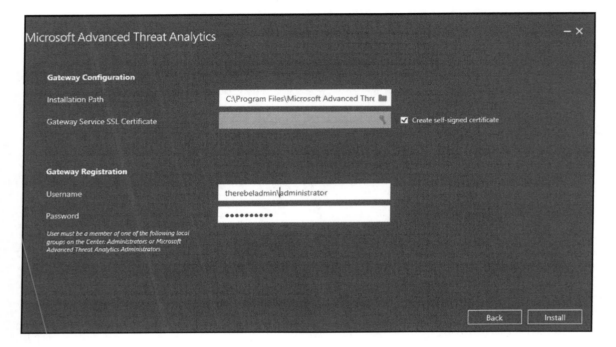

10. Once installation is completed, we can see the new gateway successfully connected with ATA center:

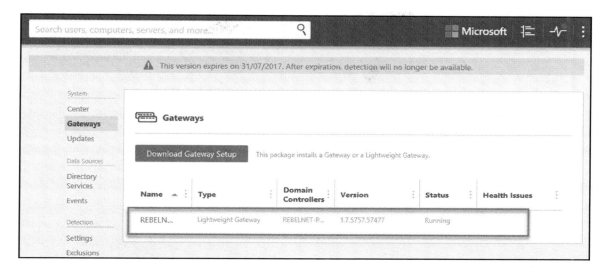

This completes the initial ATA deployment and it's ready to rock.

ATA testing

The easiest way to test the ATA functions is to simulate a DNS reconnaissance type attack:

1. Log in to a domain computer.
2. Open Command Prompt and type `nslookup – REBELNET-PDC01.therebeladmin.com` and press *Enter*. The server name can be replaced by any domain controller FQDN.
3. Then type `ls live.com`.

4. Then log in to ATA center and check the timeline. There, we can see the detected event:

5. It provides detailed explanation about the issue in a way that engineers can easily understand. These events also can be exported as a Microsoft Excel file.

6. ATA also allows us to send events as email alerts. This configuration can be done using **ATA Center | Configuration | Mail Server Settings and Notification Settings**:

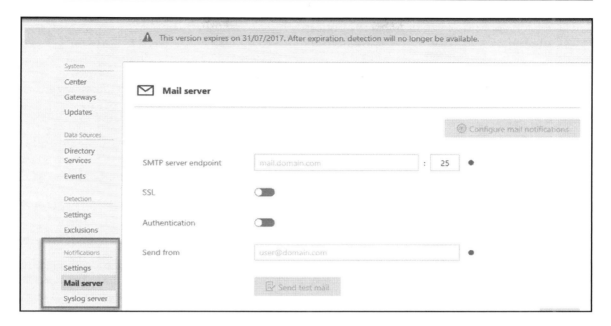

As we can see, the installation and configuration process of ATA is straightforward. But the benefits it provides are extraordinary. This product only reports about rising threats in Active Directory environment. Fixes to and prevention from these reported threats still depend on the engineer's response to it.

Microsoft Operations Management Suite (OMS)

Back in 2007, Microsoft released its system center product suite. It had four main components:

- **Configuration manager**: Allows organizations to manage device configuration centrally with software distribution
- **Operation manager**: SCOM provides advanced monitoring for systems and applications
- **Orchestrator**: Allows us to automate manual management tasks in the infrastructure using runbooks
- **Data protection manager**: Allows us to back up and restore systems and data in the infrastructure

This solution was purely to manage on-premises infrastructure. But in today's infrastructures, workloads are moving in to the public cloud completely or partially. Therefore, Microsoft started bringing this on-premises infrastructure management to Azure Cloud to provide a unified solution for cloud-only and hybrid infrastructures. As an example, the Microsoft OMS cloud-based solution is more aligned with System Center Operation Manager capabilities. Microsoft **Enterprise Mobility Suite (EMS)** is more aligned with System Center Configuration Manager capabilities. However, these cloud-based solutions still have more advanced features which we cannot use with corresponding on-premises products.

Benefits of OMS

OMS includes the following advantages that increase its values further:

- **Minimal configuration and maintenance**: If you've worked with SCOM before, you may know how many different components we need to configure, such as management servers, SQL servers, gateway servers, certificate authority, and so on. But with OMS, all we need is a subscription and initial configuration of monitoring agents or gateway--no more complex maintenance routings either.
- **Scalable**: Latest records from Microsoft show OMS is already being used by more than 50,000 customers. More than 20 PB of data has been collected and more than 188 million queries been run in a week. With cloud-based solutions, we no longer need to worry about resources when expanding. Subscription is based on the features and the amount of data you upload. You do not need to pay for compute power. I am sure Microsoft is nowhere near running out of resources!
- **Integration with SCOM**: OMS fully supports integration with SCOM. It allows engineers to specify which systems and data should be analyzed by OMS. It also allows us to perform smooth migration from SCOM to OMS in stages. In an integrated environment, SCOM works similarly to a gateway and OMS performs queries through SCOM. OMS and SCOM both use the same monitoring agent (Microsoft Monitoring Agent) and therefore, the client-side configuration is minimum.

Some OMS components such as *network performance monitoring*, WireData 2.0, and Service Map required additional agent files, system changes, and direct connection with OMS.

- **Frequent feature updates**: Microsoft releases a new System Center version every four years. But OMS updates and new services come more often. It allows Microsoft to address industry requirements quickly.

OMS services

OMS has four core services:

- **Log analytics**: In the infrastructure, we have different server roles and applications. Each of these components generate log files and events which we can use to monitor or audit their status. But all this comes from different sources in different forms, and it is not practical to go through each and every one of them. This large amount of data distracts engineers from real problems. OMS allows us to collect data from various sources and analyze it from a centralized system. In this section, we are only going to focus on this service.
- **Automation**: This automates manual management tasks using Azure automation. It works similarly to System Center Orchestrator.
- **Backup**: To back up and restore systems and data from physical and virtual machines.
- **Site recovery**: This provides high availability for critical workloads.

OMS in a hybrid environment

In a hybrid environment, we can integrate on-premises systems with OMS using three methods:

- **Microsoft monitoring agent**: Monitoring agent needs to be installed on each and every system, and it will directly connect to OMS to upload the data and run queries. Every system needs to connect to OMS via port 443.
- **SCOM**: If you already have SCOM installed and configured in your infrastructure, OMS can integrate with it. Data upload to OMS will be done from SCOM management servers. OMS runs the queries to the systems via SCOM. However, some OMS features still need a direct connection to the system to collect specific data.

- **OMS gateway**: Now OMS supports collecting data and running queries via its own gateway. This works similarly to SCOM gateways. All the systems do not need to have a direct connection to OMS, and the OMS gateway will collect and upload relevant data from its infrastructure.

What benefits will it have for Active Directory?

In an SCOM environment, we can monitor Active Directory components and services using relevant management packs. It collects a great amount of insight. However, to identify potential issues, engineers need to analyze this collected data. OMS provides two solution packs which collect data from an Active Directory environment and analyze it for you. After analyzing, it will visualize it in a user-friendly way. It also provides insight into how to fix the detected problems as well as providing guidelines to improve the environment's performance, security, and high availability:

- **AD Assessment**: This solution will analyze the risk and health of AD environments on a regular interval. It provides a list of recommendations to improve your existing AD infrastructure.
- **AD Replication Status**: This solution analyzes the replication status of your Active Directory environment.

Demonstration

In this section, we are going to learn how we can monitor an AD environment using OMS. Before we start, we need the following:

- **Valid OMS subscription**: OMS has different levels of subscription. It depends on the OMS services you use and amount of data uploaded daily. It does have a free version which provides 500 MB daily upload and 7-day data retention.
- **Direct connection to OMS**: In this demo, I am going to use direct OMS integration via Microsoft Monitoring Agent.
- **Domain administrator account**: In order to install the agent on the domain controllers, we need to have domain administrator privileges.

Enabling OMS AD solutions

The first step of the configuration is to enable AD modules in OMS. We can enable it using the following steps:

1. Log in to OMS at `https://login.mms.microsoft.com/signin.aspx?ref=ms_mm s` as OMS administrator.

2. Click on the **Solution Gallery**:

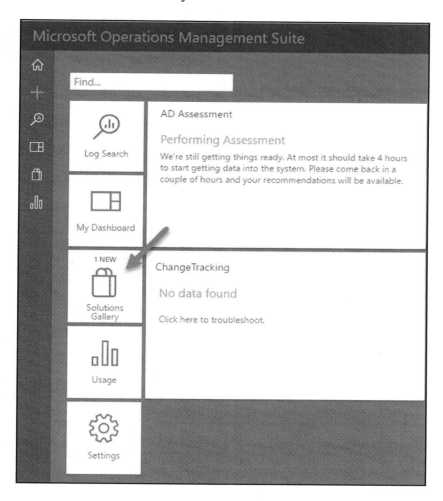

3. By default, the **AD Assessment** solution is enabled. In order to enable the **AD Replication Status** solution, click on the tile from the solutions list and then click on **Add**:

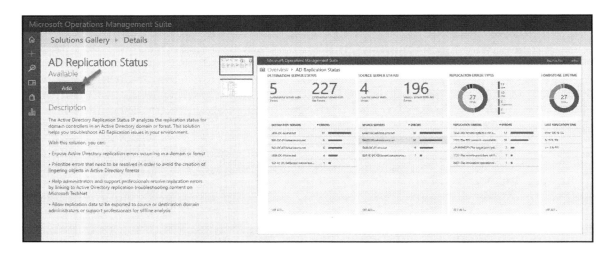

Installing OMS agents

The next step of the configuration is to install the monitoring agents on the domain controllers and getting them connected with OMS:

1. Log in to the domain controller as domain administrator.
2. Log in to the OMS portal.
3. Go to **Settings** | **Connected Sources** | **Windows Servers** then click on **Download Windows Agent (64bit)**. It will download the monitoring agent to the system:

4. Once it is downloaded, double-click on the setup file and start the installation process.

5. In the first window of the wizard, click on **Next** to begin the installation.

6. In the next window, read and accept the license terms.

7. In the next window, we can select where it should install. If there are no changes, click on **Next** to continue.

8. In the next window, it asks where it will connect to. In our scenario, it will connect to OMS directly:

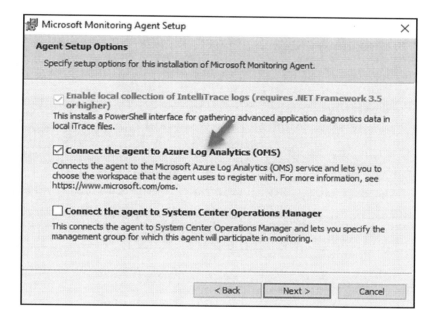

9. In the next window, it asks about the OMS **Workspace ID** and **Workspace Key**. These can be found in the OMS portal at **Settings** | **Connected Sources** | **Windows Servers**. If this server is behind a proxy server, we can also specify the proxy settings in this window. Once the relevant info has been provided, click on **Next** to continue:

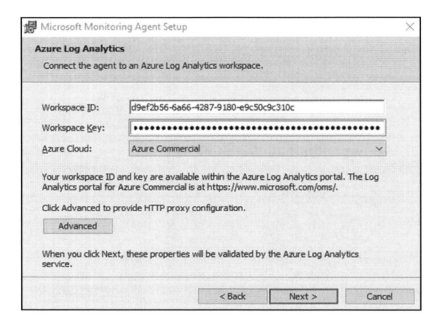

10. In the next window, it asks how I need to check agent updates. It is recommended that you use the Windows Update option. Once the selection has been made, click on the confirmation page, and click on **Install** to begin the installation.

11. Follow the same steps for other domain controllers.

12. After a few minutes, we can see that the newly added servers are connected as data sources under **Settings | Connected Sources | Windows Servers**:

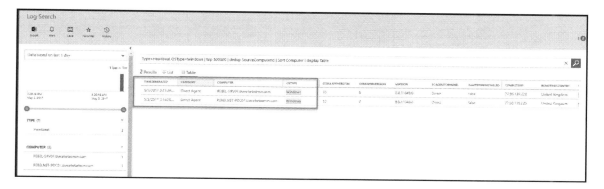

Viewing analyzed data

The following steps will help you analyze and view the data:

1. After a few minutes, OMS will start to collect data and virtualize the findings.

2. To view the data, log in to the OMS portal and click on the relevant solution tile on the home page:

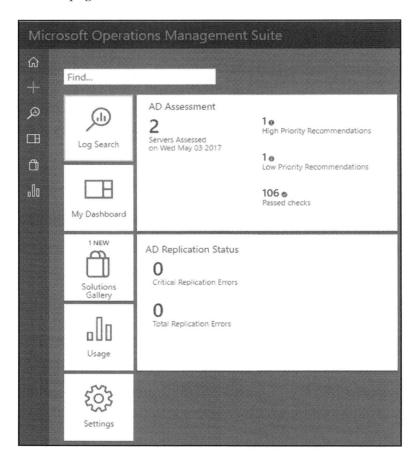

3. Once you click on the tile, it brings you to a page where it displays more details about its findings:

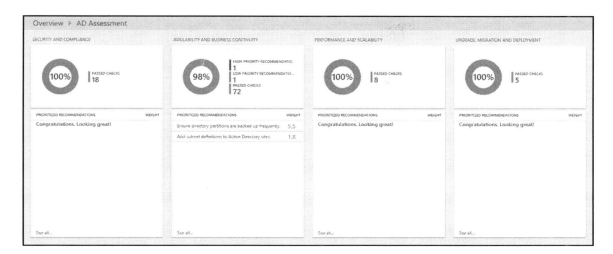

4. As I explained before, it doesn't just displays errors. It also provides a **RECOMMENDATION** on how to fix existing issues:

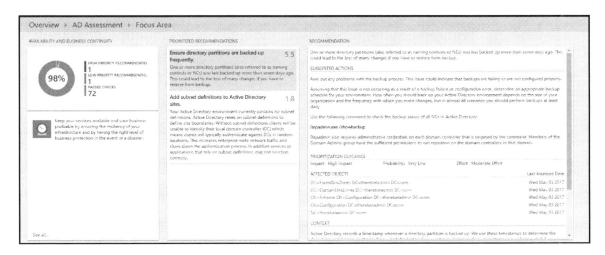

Collecting Windows logs for analysis

Using OMS, we also can collect Windows logs and use OMS analyzing capabilities to analyze those. When this is enabled, OMS space usage and bandwidth usage on the organization end will be higher. In order to collect logs, follow these steps:

1. Log in to the OMS portal.
2. Go to **Settings** | **Data** | **Windows Event Logs**.
3. In the box, you can search for the relevant log file name and add it to the list. We can also select the type of event to extract. Once the selection is made, click on **Save**:

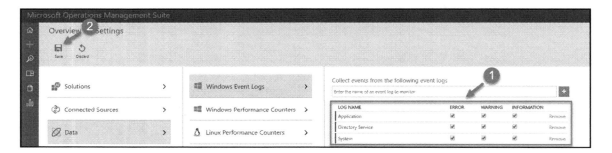

4. After a few minutes, you can start to see the events under the **Log Search** option. In there, using queries, we can filter out the data. Also, we can set up email alerts based on the events:

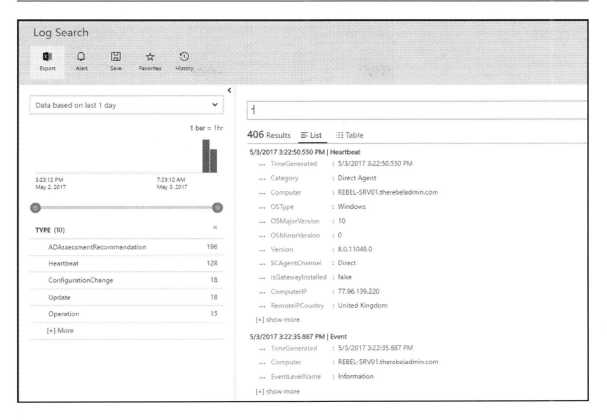

I believe now you have a basic knowledge of how to use OMS to monitor an AD environment. There are a lot of things we can do with OMS, and it's difficult to cover all those capabilities in a short chapter. There is a very good OMS community out there and I highly encourage you to go through the available documentation to get the best out of it.

Summary

Continuous monitoring and auditing is a must for an identity infrastructure to identify potential security threats and maintain a healthy environment. There are a lot of tools and methods out there to do this, but the success of these solutions depend on the accuracy of detection, the way it presents data, and how it helps identify the root cause.

In this chapter, we started with looking at Windows inbuilt tools and methods which we can use to monitor and audit Active Directory environments. First, we started with GUI tools and then moved to PowerShell-based auditing. Then we looked at Microsoft ATA and how it can help identify security threats in the infrastructure that cannot be detected using traditional tools and methods. Last but not least, we looked at the Microsoft cloud-based advanced monitoring and log analytics solution, OMS. Using a demo, I also explained how we can set it up and monitor an Active Directory environment.

After a long journey, we are now reaching the end of this book. In the last chapter, we will look at the most common Active Directory-related issues and how we can fix those.

19

Active Directory Troubleshooting

Like any other IT engineer, I also deal with the burden of broken systems from time to time. In the last 12 years of my career, I've spent long, sleepless nights fixing systems. I spent days in cold data centers. I missed long-awaited holidays. Worst of all, I dealt with the broken-system curse on Friday nights. Even if we do not like it, as engineers we spend most of our time *fixing* something. As with any other system, Active Directory environments also can have problems. Some of them have direct client impact and some don't. Not every system error has a direct solution. Most of the time, it's a part of a series of events.

In order to troubleshoot an issue and find a solution, we first need to have relevant knowledge about the application or the service. You do not need to be a master of everything but at least have enough knowledge to begin the troubleshooting process. Then we need to collect relevant data that can help us understand the situation. It can be in the form of logs, events, screenshots, or discussions. The next stage is to analyze collected data and try to find a solution.

I have been involved in many interviews over the past few years. As a part of the interviews, I always provide a description of an issue to the candidate and ask what he/she will do to fix it. But I always say that I do not need an exact answer. All I care about is the starting point of the troubleshooting process and the approach he/she will take to find a solution. To become a good troubleshooter, the starting point of the troubleshooting process is crucial. Otherwise, engineers can get distracted and take longer to find the root cause. In this chapter, we are going to look at the most common errors that can occur in an Active Directory environment and what steps we can take to troubleshoot/fix those. The issues will be categorized under the following topics:

- How to troubleshoot AD DS replication issues
- How to troubleshoot Group Policy issues
- How to troubleshoot network connectivity issues
- How to troubleshoot AD DS database issues

How to troubleshoot AD DS replication issues

An Active Directory environment with replication issues is a disaster. It can cause all sorts of problems. Active Directory uses a multi-master database. A change made on one domain controller should replicate on the other domain controllers to maintain consistency. There are two types of replication in an Active Directory environment:

- **Intra-site replication**: Replication between domain controllers in the same Active Directory site
- **Inter-site replication**: Replication between domain controllers in different Active Directory sites

In Chapter 11, *Active Directory Services*, I explained exactly how both types of replication happen. I encourage you to refer to it and refresh your memory before we proceed.

There is no smoke without fire. When there are replication issues, we can experience the following types of error:

- New user account holders are experiencing authentication issues to systems and applications
- Once the password is updated, user accounts get locked out frequently
- After a password reset, Active Directory integrated applications fail to authenticate users
- When an object attribute value is modified, not every domain controller can see it
- When a new Group Policy is created, it is only applying to a part of the target objects
- When there is a Group Policy change, it is not applying to the target object group or only applies to a part of the group
- When an Active Directory object is removed using one domain controller, it is still appearing on other domain controllers
- DNS name resolution issues

Identifying replication issues

In the preceding section, I have listed some common symptoms of replication issues. However, these symptoms are not only for replications issues. When we have a fever, it could be just a cold or part of another disease. If it does not go away with paracetamol, we need to go for further diagnosis to find the problem. When you walk into a GP's, they collect some reports and evidence before they come to a conclusion. Likewise, once we see the aforementioned symptoms, we need to find further evidence. There are a few tools and methods we can use for that.

Event Viewer

Event Viewer is the most commonly used tool to gather information about any application or service-related issue. Active Directory replication issues will also log certain events in Event Viewer. Some of those will help you identify the root cause directly and some will only provide insights we will need to follow with additional troubleshooting steps.

Event ID	Event description	Possible issue
2087, 2088	Active Directory could not resolve the following DNS hostname of the source domain controller to an IP address. This error prevents additions, deletions, and changes in Active Directory Domain Services from replicating between one or more domain controllers in the forest. Security groups, Group Policy, users and computers and their passwords will be inconsistent between domain controllers until this error is resolved, potentially affecting logon authentication and access to network resources.	• Source Domain Controller is in shutdown status or non-responsive status. • There is a network-layer communication issue between the source and destination domain controllers. • Due to a hardware or software failure, the source domain controller cannot be brought online. In such a situation, a metadata cleanup is required and we need to remove the relevant entries forcibly from AD. • There are DNS-related issues preventing name resolution.

1844	The local domain controller could not connect with the following domain controller hosting the following directory partition to resolve distinguished names.	• Source Domain Controller in shutdown status or non-responsive status. • Network-layer communication issue between the source and destination Domain Controllers. • Domain controller service (SRV) resource records not registered with DNS server. • It's recommended you test the DNS name resolution and see whether the domain controller name can be resolved properly. • It's recommended you try a forcible replication of the directory partition using **repadmin /replicate** to confirm whether it's a temporary issue or not.
4013	The DNS server is waiting for Active Directory Domain Services (AD DS) to signal that the initial synchronization of the directory has been completed. The DNS service cannot start until the initial synchronization is complete because critical DNS data might not yet be replicated onto this domain controller. If events in the AD DS event log indicate that there is a problem with DNS name resolution, consider adding the IP address of another DNS server for this domain to the DNS server list in the Internet Protocol properties of this computer. This event will be logged every two minutes until AD DS has signaled that the initial synchronization has successfully completed.	• Domain controller using wrong IP range or VLAN that prevents communication with the replication partner. • Network-layer communication issue between hosts. • DNS name-resolution issues.

1925	The attempt to establish a replication link for the following writable directory partition failed.	• Network-layer communication issue between hosts. • DNS name resolution issues. • Source domain controller is in shutdown status or non-responsive status • Check the maximum TCP packet size (can use the ping command with -f -l parameters) and verify compatibility with devices and network configuration.
1311	The Knowledge Consistency Checker (KCC) has detected problems with the following directory partition. Directory partition: %1 There is insufficient site connectivity information for the KCC to create a spanning tree replication topology. Or, one or more directory servers with this directory partition are unable to replicate the directory partition information. This is probably due to inaccessible directory servers.	• Network communication issues between Active Directory sites. • Verify that Domain Controllers that host the identified directory partition are accessible using **dcdiag /test:connectivity**.
8524	The DSA operation is unable to proceed because of a DNS lookup failure	• Due to hardware or software failure, the source Domain Controller cannot be brought online. In such a situation, metadata cleanup is required. • DNS name resolution issues. • Verify that the A, CNAME records exist for the source DC

8456, 8457	The operation failed because: Active Directory could not transfer the remaining data in directory partition <directory partition DN path> to domain controller <destination DC>. The source server is currently rejecting replication requests.	• The **directory system agent (DSA)** is not writable. Check the relevant registry keys in `HKLM\System\CurrentControlSet\Services\NTDS\Parameters`. • Insufficient disk space. • The Netlogon service has crashed or in paused status in source.
8453	Replication access was denied	• The `UserAccountControl` attribute on the destination domain controller computer account is missing either the `SERVER_TRUST_ACCOUNT` or `TRUSTED_FOR_DELEGATION` flags. • The default permissions of Active Directory partitions have been altered • Destination DC is RODC and ADPREP/RODCPREP wasn't executed. Or else, the enterprise RODC group does not have directory change replication permissions for the partition that is failing to replicate. • Trust relationships are no longer valid. • There is a time difference between the domain controllers that exceeds the maximum time skew allowed.
1722	The RPC server is unavailable	• System resource limitation. • IP stack issue. • DNS service issues. • Network routing issues. • Relevant TCP ports are blocked by firewall or application.
1127	Active Directory could not replicate the directory partition <DN path of failing partition> from the remote domain controller <fully qualified computer name of helper DC>. While accessing the hard disk, a disk operation failed even after retries.	• Application or corrupted system component preventing AD from writing data to hard disk. • Hard disk faults. • Firmware issues related to disk controllers.

1645	AD_TERM did not perform an authenticated remote procedure call (RPC) to another directory server because the desired service principal name (SPN) for the destination directory server is not registered on the Key Distribution Center (KDC) domain controller that resolves the SPN. Destination directory server: %1 SPN: %2	This can be due to a recent change to the domain controller such as domain promotion or demotion. Force replication using **repadmin /syncall** and check the registered SPN values.

System Center Operation Manager

SCOM can be used to proactively and reactively monitor the health of AD DS and related components. We need the relevant management packs to do it. The latest management packs for AD DS are available at https://www.microsoft.com/en-us/download/details.aspx?id=54525. If you're running SCOM 2016, you do not need to install this manually. Once domain controllers are added to the monitoring, the system will scan and recommend which management packs to install. Once the relevant management packs are in place, they can identify issues related to:

- Replication
- **Lightweight Directory Access Protocol (LDAP)**
- Domain controller locator
- Trusts
- Netlogon service
- **File Replication Service (FRS)**
- **Distributed File System (DFS)** replication
- Inter-site messaging service
- Windows Time Service
- **Active Directory Web Services (ADWS)**

- Active Directory Management Gateway Service
- **Key Distribution Center (KDC)**

Also, SCOM can:

- Monitor service availability
- Collect key performance data
- Provide reports

With the help of alerts, the relevant parties will be notified as soon as an error occurs. We also can automate some of the recovery tasks and run them in the form of runbooks with the use of System Center Orchestrator.

Microsoft Operation Management Suite (OMS)

In the previous chapter, I explained in detail how we can use OMS to monitor the health of an AD environment. OMS has a separate solution called **AD replication status**, which is capable of:

- Identifying AD replication errors between domains or forests
- Prioritizing errors that need to be fixed in order to avoid lingering objects
- Providing guidelines to fix replication issues
- Allowing replication data to be exported to source or destination domain controllers or even for offline analysis

Troubleshooting replication issues

There are certain Windows cmdlets and utilities which we can use for replication issue troubleshooting purposes. Among these, **Repadmin.exe** is the most commonly used Microsoft utility. It is available in servers which have the AD DS or AD LDS role installed. It is also part of the **Remote Server Administration Tools** (RSAT). This utility is recommended to be run as a Domain Admin or Enterprise Admin. However, it is also possible to delegate permissions only to review and manage replication.

 Microsoft had a great little utility called **Active Directory Replication Status Tool (ADREPLSTATUS),** which allowed us to review replication status and find any potential issues. It is no longer available for the public and has been replaced by the OMS AD replication status tool.

The following list contains the commands supported by repadmin:

Command	Description
repadmin /kcc	Forces the **Knowledge Consistency Checker (KCC)** on targeted domain controllers to immediately recalculate the inbound replication topology
repadmin /prp	This command allows an administrator to view or modify the password replication policy for **read-only domain controllers (RODC)**
repadmin /queue	Displays inbound replication requests that the domain controller must issue to become consistent with its source replication partners
repadmin /replicate	Triggers the immediate replication of the specified directory partition to a destination domain controller from the source domain controller
repadmin /replsingleobj	Replicates a single object between any two domain controllers that have common directory partitions
repadmin /replsummary	This will quickly and concisely summarize the replication state and relative health of a forest
repadmin /rodcpwdrepl	Triggers replication of passwords for the specified users from the source domain controller to one or more RODC
repadmin /showattr	Displays the attributes of an object
repadmin /showobjmeta	Displays the replication metadata for a specified object stored in AD, such as attribute ID, version number, originating and local **update sequence numbers (USNs)**, and the originating server's **globally unique identifier (GUID)** and date and time stamp
repadmin /showrepl	Displays the replication status when the specified domain controller last attempted inbound replication on AD partitions
repadmin /showutdvec	Displays the highest, committed USN that the targeted DC's copy of AD shows as committed for itself and its transitive partners
repadmin /syncall	Synchronizes a specified domain controller with all replication partners

Let's see some of these commands in action:

```
repadmin /replsummary /bydest
```

The preceding command summarizes the replication status for all domain controllers based on the replication destination. This parameter does not display the source domain controller.

```
repadmin /replsummary /bysrc
```

The preceding command summarizes the replication status for all domain controllers based on the replication source. This parameter does not display the destination domain controller.

```
repadmin /showrepl REBEL-SRV01.therebeladmin.com
```

The preceding command shows the replication partners for `REBEL-SRV01.therebeladmin.com` and the status of the last sync attempt.

```
repadmin /showrepl /errorsonly
```

The preceding command will list the replication partners that have replication errors (the last sync attempt failed).

We also can view results in CSV format:

```
repadmin /showrepl /csv
```

```
PS C:\Users\Administrator> repadmin /showrepl /csv
showrepl_COLUMNS,Destination DSA Site,Destination DSA,Naming Context,Source DSA Site,Source DSA,Transport Type,Number of Failures,Last Failure
Time,Last Success Time,Last Failure Status
showrepl_INFO,Default-First-Site-Name,REBELNET-PDC01,"DC=therebeladmin,DC=com",Default-First-Site-Name,REBEL-SRV01,RPC,0,0,2017-05-05 10:54:43
,0
showrepl_INFO,Default-First-Site-Name,REBELNET-PDC01,"CN=Configuration,DC=therebeladmin,DC=com",Default-First-Site-Name,REBEL-SRV01,RPC,0,0,20
17-05-05 10:54:43,0
showrepl_INFO,Default-First-Site-Name,REBELNET-PDC01,"CN=Schema,CN=Configuration,DC=therebeladmin,DC=com",Default-First-Site-Name,REBEL-SRV01,
RPC,0,0,2017-05-05 10:54:43,0
showrepl_INFO,Default-First-Site-Name,REBELNET-PDC01,"DC=DomainDnsZones,DC=therebeladmin,DC=com",Default-First-Site-Name,REBEL-SRV01,RPC,0,0,2
017-05-05 10:54:43,0
showrepl_INFO,Default-First-Site-Name,REBELNET-PDC01,"DC=ForestDnsZones,DC=therebeladmin,DC=com",Default-First-Site-Name,REBEL-SRV01,RPC,0,0,2
017-05-05 10:54:43,0
```

```
repadmin /syncall REBEL-SRV01 dc=therebeladmin,dc=com
```

The preceding command initiates domain directory partition synchronization with all replication partners of `REBEL-SRV01`.

It will also indicate whether there were any issues during sync:

```
PS C:\Users\Administrator> repadmin /syncall REBEL-SRV01 dc=therebeladmin,dc=com
Syncing partition: dc=therebeladmin,dc=com
CALLBACK MESSAGE: The following replication is in progress:
    From: e05aa0a0-dfdc-4964-9ae2-da7667fcce87._msdcs.therebeladmin.com
    To  : d3f89917-5fff-40a8-acc2-b148b60d9309._msdcs.therebeladmin.com
CALLBACK MESSAGE: The following replication completed successfully:
    From: e05aa0a0-dfdc-4964-9ae2-da7667fcce87._msdcs.therebeladmin.com
    To  : d3f89917-5fff-40a8-acc2-b148b60d9309._msdcs.therebeladmin.com
CALLBACK MESSAGE: SyncAll Finished.
SyncAll terminated with no errors.
```

```
repadmin /queue
```

The preceding command shows whether there are any unprocessed inbound replication requests. If the system keeps sending `queue` requests, it can be due to a high number of AD changes, system resource issues, or too many replication partners.

```
repadmin /showchanges REBELNET-PDC01 d3f89917-5fff-40a8-scc2-b148b60d9309
dc=therebeladmin,dc=com
```

The preceding command lists the changes that are not replicated between server REBELNET-PDC01 and REBEL-SRV01. In here, REBEL-SRV01 is the source server and it is listed with the object GUID:

```
PS C:\Users\Administrator> repadmin /showchanges REBELNET-PDC01 d3f89917-5fff-40a8-acc2-b148b60d9309 dc=therebeladmin,dc=com
Building starting position from destination server REBELNET-PDC01
Source Neighbor:
dc=therebeladmin,dc=com
pszDsa = d3f89917-5fff-40a8-acc2-b148b60d9309._msdcs.therebeladmin.com
==== INBOUND NEIGHBORS ======================================

dc=therebeladmin,dc=com
    Default-First-Site-Name\REBEL-SRV01 via RPC
        DSA object GUID: d3f89917-5fff-40a8-acc2-b148b60d9309
        Address: d3f89917-5fff-40a8-acc2-b148b60d9309._msdcs.therebeladmin.com
        DSA invocationID: 833e9bd7-4598-4acc-bf7b-6981b54e907e
        SYNC_ON_STARTUP DO_SCHEDULED_SYNCS WRITEABLE
        USNs: 30522/OU, 30522/PU
        Last attempt @ 2017-05-05 11:25:27 was successful.
Destination's up-to-date vector:
833e9bd7-4598-4acc-bf7b-6981b54e907e @ USN 30571
e05aa0a0-dfdc-4964-9ae2-da7667fcce87 @ USN 28944
==== SOURCE DSA: (null) ====
No Changes
```

```
repadmin /replicate REBEL-SRV01 REBELNET-PDC01 dc=therebeladmin,dc=com
```

The preceding command initiates immediate directory partition replication from REBELNET-PDC01 to REBEL-SRV01.

Apart from the repadmin, there are certain PowerShell cmdlets which we can use to troubleshoot replication issues. The `Get-ADReplicationFailure` cmdlet is one that can collect data about replication failures.

```
Get-ADReplicationFailure -Target REBEL-SRV01
```

The preceding command will collect information about replication failures associated with `REBEL-SRV01`.

This also can be done with multiple servers:

```
Get-ADReplicationFailure -Target REBEL-SRV01,REBELNET-PDC01
```

Further, we can target all the domain controllers in the domain:

```
Get-ADReplicationFailure -Target "therebeladmin.com" -Scope Domain
```

Or even the entire forest:

```
Get-ADReplicationFailure -Target " therebeladmin.com" -Scope Forest
```

The `Get-ADReplicationConnection` cmdlet can list down replication partner details for the given domain controller:

```
Get-ADReplicationConnection -Filter *
```

The preceding command will list all replication connections for the domain controller you logged in to:

```
PS C:\Users\Administrator> Get-ADReplicationConnection -Filter *

AutoGenerated                         : True
DistinguishedName                     : CN=1364adb7-76d4-46ec-83fa-21a4060d0538,CN=NTDS Settings,CN=REBELNET-PDC01,CN=Servers,CN=Default-First-Si
                                        te-Name,CN=Sites,CN=Configuration,DC=therebeladmin,DC=com
InterSiteTransportProtocol            :
Name                                  : 1364adb7-76d4-46ec-83fa-21a4060d0538
ObjectClass                           : nTDSConnection
ObjectGUID                            : c449cede-d8df-43f6-bf4d-c9d9e5d533da
PartiallyReplicatedNamingContexts     : {}
ReplicatedNamingContexts              : {DC=ForestDnsZones,DC=therebeladmin,DC=com, DC=DomainDnsZones,DC=therebeladmin,DC=com,
                                        CN=Schema,CN=Configuration,DC=therebeladmin,DC=com, CN=Configuration,DC=therebeladmin,DC=com...}
ReplicateFromDirectoryServer          : CN=NTDS Settings,CN=REBEL-SRV01,CN=Servers,CN=Default-First-Site-Name,CN=Sites,CN=Configuration,DC=thereb
                                        eladmin,DC=com
ReplicateToDirectoryServer            : CN=REBELNET-PDC01,CN=Servers,CN=Default-First-Site-Name,CN=Sites,CN=Configuration,DC=therebeladmin,DC=com
ReplicationSchedule                   : System.DirectoryServices.ActiveDirectory.ActiveDirectorySchedule

AutoGenerated                         : True
DistinguishedName                     : CN=ca959ad0-bf91-4c33-ade1-1182060474c2,CN=NTDS Settings,CN=REBEL-SRV01,CN=Servers,CN=Default-First-Site-
                                        Name,CN=Sites,CN=Configuration,DC=therebeladmin,DC=com
InterSiteTransportProtocol            :
Name                                  : ca959ad0-bf91-4c33-ade1-1182060474c2
ObjectClass                           : nTDSConnection
ObjectGUID                            : 0490d8a6-db8c-467e-8734-37a026346a40
PartiallyReplicatedNamingContexts     : {}
ReplicatedNamingContexts              : {DC=ForestDnsZones,DC=therebeladmin,DC=com, DC=DomainDnsZones,DC=therebeladmin,DC=com,
                                        CN=Schema,CN=Configuration,DC=therebeladmin,DC=com, CN=Configuration,DC=therebeladmin,DC=com...}
ReplicateFromDirectoryServer          : CN=NTDS Settings,CN=REBELNET-PDC01,CN=Servers,CN=Default-First-Site-Name,CN=Sites,CN=Configuration,DC=the
                                        rebeladmin,DC=com
ReplicateToDirectoryServer            : CN=REBEL-SRV01,CN=Servers,CN=Default-First-Site-Name,CN=Sites,CN=Configuration,DC=therebeladmin,DC=com
ReplicationSchedule                   : System.DirectoryServices.ActiveDirectory.ActiveDirectorySchedule
```

We also can filter replication connections based on attributes.

```
Get-ADReplicationConnection -Filter {ReplicateToDirectoryServer -eq "REBEL-
SRV01"}
```

The preceding command will list replication connections with the destination server as REBEL-SRV01.

We also can force-sync objects between domain controllers.

```
Sync-ADObject -object "adam" -source REBEL-SRV01 -destination REBELNET-
PDC01
```

The preceding command will sync the user object adam from REBEL-SRV01 to REBELNET-PDC01.

In Chapter 16, *Advanced AD Management with PowerShell*, I shared some scripts we can use with AD replication troubleshooting. I also explained some other PowerShell cmdlets we can use for troubleshooting and information gathering.

Lingering objects

Let's assume a domain controller has been disconnected from the AD environment and stayed offline for more that the value specified as the tombstone lifetime attribute. Then it was again reconnected to the replication topology. The objects that were deleted from AD during the time that particular domain controller stayed offline, will remain as lingering objects in it.

When the object was deleted using one domain controller, it was replicated to other domain controllers as a tombstone object. It contains a few attribute values but it cannot be used for active operations. It remains in the domain controllers until it reaches the time specified by the tombstone lifetime value. Then the tombstone object will be permanently deleted from the directory. The tombstone time value is a forest-wide setting and depends on the operating system running. For operating systems after Windows Server 2003, the default tombstone value is 180 days.

The problem occurs when the domain controller with a lingering object is involved with an outbound replication. In such a situation, one of the following can happen:

- If the destination domain controller has **strict replication consistency** enabled, it will halt the inbound replication from that particular domain controller
- If the destination domain controller has **strict replication consistency** disabled, it will request a full replica and will reintroduce it to the directory

Events 1388, 1988, and 2042 are clues for lingering objects in the Active Directory Infrastructure:

Event id	Event Description
1388	Another **domain controller** (DC) has attempted to replicate into this DC an object which is not present in the local AD DS database. The object may have been deleted and already garbage-collected (a tombstone lifetime or more has passed since the object was deleted) on this DC. The attribute set included in the update request is not sufficient to create the object. The object will be re-requested with a full attribute set and re-created on this DC. Source DC (Transport-specific network address): `xxxxxxxxxxxxxxxxx._msdcs.contoso.com Object: CN=xxxx,CN=xxx,DC=xxxx,DC=xxx Object GUID: xxxxxxxxxxxx Directory partition: DC=xxxx,DC=xx Destination highest property USN: xxxxxx`
1988	AD DS replication encountered the existence of objects in the following partition that have been deleted from the local **domain controllers** (DCs) AD DS database. Not all direct or transitive replication partners replicated in the deletion before the tombstone lifetime number of days passed. Objects that have been deleted and garbage collected from an AD DS partition but still exist in the writable partitions of other DCs in the same domain, or read-only partitions of global catalog servers in other domains in the forest are known as **lingering objects**. This event is being logged because the source DC contains a lingering object which does not exist on the local DCs AD DS database. This replication attempt has been blocked. The best solution to this problem is to identify and remove all lingering objects in the forest. Source DC (Transport-specific network address): `xxxxxxxxxxxxxx._msdcs.contoso.com Object: CN=xxxxxx,CN=xxxxx,DC=xxxxxx,DC=xxx Object GUID: xxxxxxxxxxxx`

2042	It has been too long since this machine last replicated with the named source machine. The time between replications with this source has exceeded the tombstone lifetime. Replication has been stopped with this source. The reason that replication is not allowed to continue is that the two machine's views of deleted objects may now be different. The source machine may still have copies of objects that have been deleted (and garbage collected) on this machine. If they were allowed to replicate, the source machines' might return objects which have already been deleted. `Time of last successful replication: <date> <time> Invocation ID of source: <Invocation ID> Name of source: <GUID>._msdcs.<domain> Tombstone lifetime (days): <TSL number in days> The replication operation has failed.`

Strict replication consistency

This setting is controlled by a registry key. After Windows Server 2003, by default, this setting is enabled. The key can be found under `HKEY_LOCAL_MACHINE\SYSTEM\CurrentControlSet\Services\NTDS\Parameters`:

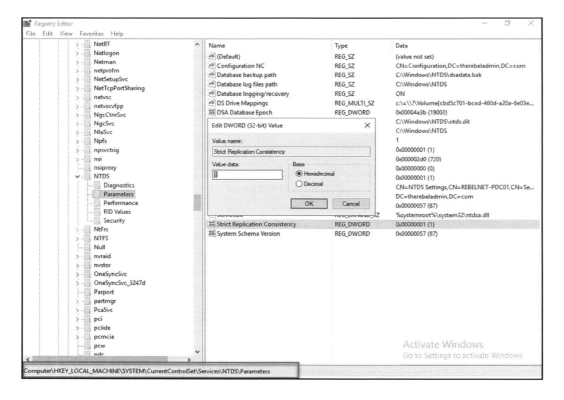

Removing lingering objects

Lingering objects can be removed using:

```
repadmin /removelingeringobjects <faulty DC name> <reference DC GUID>
<directory partition>
```

In the preceding command:

- `faulty DC name`: It represents the DC which contains lingering objects
- `reference DC GUID`: It is the GUID of a DC which contains an up-to-date database that can be used as a reference
- `directory partition` is the directory partition where lingering objects are contained

DFS replication issues

After Windows Server 2003, FRS is not used for SYSVOL replication. It is being replaced by DFS. But if you are upgrading AD DS from an older version, it will be still in use and migration from FRS to DFS is required. We have covered this in `Chapter 11`, *Active Directory Services*.

The `SYSVOL` folder in a DC includes the domain's public files such as Group Policy files, batch files, login scripts, and so on. Healthy replication of SYSVOL is required to maintain a functional AD environment. When there are SYSVOL replication issues, you may experience issues such as:

- Group Policies are applied partially or not applied at all
- Group Policies are being applied to part of the target object group
- Login scripts are not running

We also can see the following events in the event viewer under the `DFS Replication log` and `System log` files:

Event ID	Event description
4612	The DFS Replication service initialized SYSVOL at local path `C:\Windows\SYSVOL\domain` and is waiting to perform initial replication. The replicated folder will remain in the initial synchronization state until it has replicated with its partner <FQDN>. If the server was in the process of being promoted to a domain controller, the domain controller will not advertise and function as a domain controller until this issue is resolved. This can occur if the specified partner is also in the initial synchronization state, or if sharing violations are encountered on this server or the sync partner. If this event occurred during the migration of SYSVOL from FRS to DFS replication, changes will not replicate out until this issue is resolved. This can cause the `SYSVOL` folder on this server to become out of sync with other domain controllers.
2213	The DFS replication service stopped replication on volume `C:`. This occurs when a DFSR JET database is not shut down cleanly and **Auto Recovery** is disabled. To resolve this issue, back up the files in the affected replicated folders, and then use the `ResumeReplication` WMI method to resume replication. Recovery steps are as follows: 1. Back up the files in all replicated folders on the volume. Failure to do so may result in data loss due to unexpected conflict resolution during the recovery of the replicated folders. 2. To resume the replication for this volume, use the WMI method `ResumeReplication` of the `DfsrVolumeConfig` class. For example, from an elevated command prompt, type the following command: `wmic /namespace:\\root\microsoftdfs path dfsrVolumeConfig where volumeGuid="xxxxxxxx" call ResumeReplication.`
5002	The DFS replication service encountered an error communicating with partner <FQDN> for replication group Domain System Volume.
5008	The DFS replication service failed to communicate with partner <FQDN> for replication group Home-Replication. This error can occur if the host is unreachable, or if the DFS replication service is not running on the server.
5014	The DFS replication service is stopping communication with partner <FQDN> for replication group Domain System Volume due to an error. The service will retry the connection periodically.

1096	The processing of Group Policy failed. Windows could not apply the registry-based policy settings for the Group Policy object `<Object GUID>`. Group Policy settings will not be resolved until this event is resolved. View the event details for more information on the file name and path that caused the failure.
4012	The DFS replication service stopped replication on the replicated folder at local path `c:\xxx`. It has been disconnected from other partners for 70 days, which is longer than the `MaxOfflineTimeInDays` parameter. Because of this, DFS replication considers this data to be stale, and will replace it with data from other members of the replication group during the next replication. DFS replication will move the stale files to the local `Conflict` folder. No user action is required.

Troubleshooting

When there is a SYSVOL replication issue, we can carry out the following troubleshooting steps to rectify the issues.

Verifying the connection

Check whether the problematic SYSVOL holder can reach other domain controllers. A simple ping can verify the connectivity between nodes. Also try to access the replication partner shares using `\\domaincontroller` (network path). Verify that replication partners are also in a healthy state. DFS replication requires specific TCP and UDP ports. Make sure the following TCP and UDP ports are allowed via hardware/software firewalls:

Service name	TCP	UDP
NetBIOS Name Service	137	137
NetBIOS Datagram Service	-	138
NetBIOS Session Service	139	-
RPC	135	-
SMB	445	445
LDAP	389	389

In some organizations, engineers use antivirus and malware protection on DCs with settings made for desktop computers. I have seen on many occasions that the DFS process has been blocked by endpoint protection solutions. Therefore, if such a solution is in place, make sure you follow the guidelines provided by Microsoft and exclude the relevant files and processes. These guidelines can be found in `https://support.microsoft.com/en-us /help/822158/virus-scanning-recommendations-for-enterprise-computers-that-ar e-running-currently-supported-versions-of-windows`.

SYSVOL share status

We need to verify whether the SYSVOL share exists on the domain controllers. This can be done by running the following command on a domain controller:

```
For /f %s IN ('dsquery server -o rdn') do @echo %s && @(net view \\%s |
find "SYSVOL") & echo
```

This will list down the servers and the SYSVOL shares available:

```
C:\Windows\system32>For /f %s IN ('dsquery server -o rdn') do @echo %s && @(net view \\%s | find "SYSVOL") & echo
REBELNET-PDC01
SYSVOL       Disk            Logon server share
ECHO is on.
REBEL-SRV01
SYSVOL       Disk            Logon server share
ECHO is on.
```

DFS replication status

As part of the troubleshooting process, we need to verify the DFS replication status. The status of the DFS replication can be determined based on the status code.

Status codes for DFS are as follows:

- 0: Uninitialized
- 1: Initialized
- 2: Initial synchronization
- 3: Auto recovery

- 4: Normal
- 5: In error state
- 6: Disabled
- 7: Unknown

In order to review the status, we can use the following command:

```
For /f %r IN ('dsquery server -o rdn') do @echo %i && @wmic /node:"%r"
/namespace:\\root\microsoftdfs path dfsrreplicatedfolderinfo WHERE
replicatedfoldername='SYSVOL share' get replicatedfoldername,state
```

```
C:\Windows\system32>For /f %r IN ('dsquery server -o rdn') do @echo %i && @wmic /node:"%r" /namespace:\\root\microsoftdfs pat
h dfsrreplicatedfolderinfo WHERE replicatedfoldername='SYSVOL share' get replicatedfoldername,state
%i
ReplicatedFolderName    State
SYSVOL Share            4

%i
ReplicatedFolderName    State
SYSVOL Share            4
```

DFSR crash due to dirty shutdown of the domain controller (event ID 2213)

This is one of the common DFSR errors. This happens when a domain controller crashes. This can be fixed using the existing command listed for the event 2213. It will resume replication in the volume.

```
wmic /namespace:\\root\microsoftdfs path dfsrVolumeConfig where
volumeGuid="xxxxxxxx" call ResumeReplication
```

In the preceding command, the `volumeGuid` value needs to be replaced with the relevant value from your environment.

If this doesn't solve the issue, SYSVOL replication will need to be recovered, which will be explained later in this section.

Content freshness

With Windows Server 2008, Microsoft introduced a setting called **Content Freshness protection** to protect DFS shares from stale data. DFS also use a multi-master database similar to Active Directory. It also has a tombstone time limit similar to AD. It is 60 days by default. So, if there was no replication more than that time and a re-enabling replication in a DFS member, can create stale data. This is similar to lingering objects in AD. To protect from this, we can define a value for `MaxOfflineTimeInDays`. If the number of days from the last successful DFS replication is more than `MaxOfflineTimeInDays`, it will prevent the replication. In such a situation, you will be able to see event 4012. After Windows Server 2012, this feature is enabled by default and the initial value is set to 60 days.

We can check this value using:

```
For /f %m IN ('dsquery server -o rdn') do @echo %m && @wmic /node:"%m"
/namespace:\\root\microsoftdfs path DfsrMachineConfig get
MaxOfflineTimeInDays
```

```
C:\Windows\system32>For /f %m IN ('dsquery server -o rdn') do @echo %m && @wmic /node:"%m" /namespace:\\root\microsoftdfs pat
h DfsrMachineConfig get MaxOfflineTimeInDays
REBELNET-PDC01
MaxOfflineTimeInDays
60

REBEL-SRV01
MaxOfflineTimeInDays
60
```

The only way to recover from this is to use non-authoritative or authoritative recovery for DFS.

Non-authoritative DFS replication

In most situations, it's only one or a few domain controller (lower than 50%) which have replication issues at a given time. In such a situation, we can issue a non-authoritative replication request, so the system will replicate the SYSVOL from the PDC. In order to perform a non-authoritative replication, follow these steps:

1. **Back up the existing SYSVOL**: This can be done by copying the `SYSVOL` folder from the domain controller that has DFS replication issues to a secure location.
2. Log in to DC as Domain Admin/Enterprise Admin.
3. Launch the `ADSIEDIT.MSC` tool and connect to `Default naming context`:

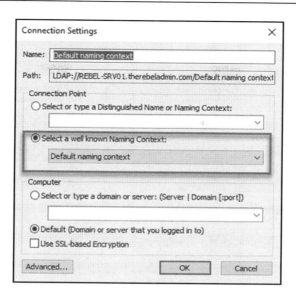

4. Browse to `DC=domain,DC=local | OU=Domain Controllers | CN=(DC NAME) | CN=DFSR-LocalSettings | Domain System Volume | SYSVOL Subscription`.

5. Change the value of the attribute **msDFSR-Enabled** to **FALSE**:

6. Force AD replication using:

```
repadmin /syncall /AdP
```

7. Run the following to install the DFS management tools (unless this is already installed):

```
Add-WindowsFeature RSAT-DFS-Mgmt-Con
```

8. Run the following command to update the DFRS global state:

```
dfsrdiag PollAD
```

9. Search for event 4114 to confirm that SYSVOL replication is disabled:

```
Get-EventLog -Log "DFS Replication" | where {$_.eventID -eq 4114} |
fl
```

10. Change the attribute value of **msDFSR-Enabled** back to **TRUE** (*step 5*).
11. Force AD replication as in *step 6*.
12. Update the DFRS global state by running the command in *step 8*.
13. Search for events 4614 and 4604 to confirm successful non-authoritative synchronization:

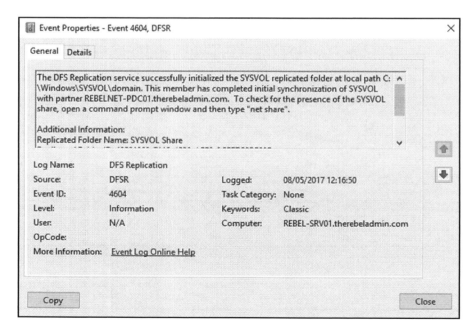

All the commands should be run from the domain controllers set as non-authoritative. It's only recommended you use this where lower than 50% of domain controllers have DFS replication issues.

Authoritative DFS replication

In the previous option, only a selected number of domain controllers are involved with forceful replication from PDC. But there are situations where we will need to recover SYSVOL from backup and then forcefully replicate it to all other domain controllers. This is also the recommended recovery option when more than 50% of domain controllers are experiencing DFS replication issues. In order to initiate an authoritative DFS replication, follow these steps:

1. Log in to the PDC FSMO role holder as domain administrator or enterprise administrator.

2. Stop **DFS Replication Service** (this is recommended on all the Domain Controllers).

3. Launch the `ADSIEDIT.MSC` tool and connect to `Default naming context`.

4. Browse to `DC=domain,DC=local` | `OU=Domain Controllers` | `CN=(DC NAME)` | `CN=DFSR-LocalSettings` | `Domain System Volume` | `SYSVOL Subscription`.

5. Update the given attributes values as follows:

- **msDFSR-Enabled** as **FALSE**
- **msDFSR-options** as 1

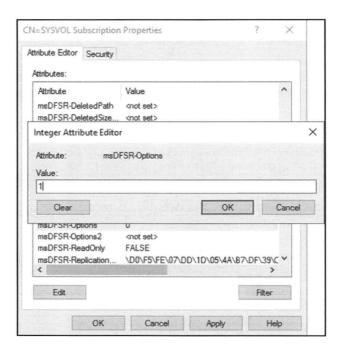

6. Modify the following attribute on all other domain controllers:
    - **msDFSR-Enabled** as **FALSE**

7. Force the AD replication using:

```
repadmin /syncall /AdP
```

8. Start the DFS replication service on the PDC.
9. Search for the event 4114 to verify that SYSVOL replication is disabled.
10. Change the following value, which was set in *step 5*:
    - **msDFSR-Enabled: TRUE**

11. Force the AD replication using:

```
repadmin /syncall /AdP
```

12. Run the following command to update the DFRS global state:

    ```
    dfsrdiag PollAD
    ```

13. Search for the event `4602` and verify the successful SYSVOL replication.
14. Start the DFS service on all other DCs.
15. Search for the event `4114` to verify SYSVOL replication is disabled.
16. Change the following value, which was set in *step 6*. This needs to be done on all domain controllers:
    - **msDFSR-Enabled: TRUE**

17. Run the following command to update the DFRS global state:

    ```
    dfsrdiag PollAD
    ```

18. Search for events `4614` and `4604` to confirm successful authoritative synchronization.

This completes the authoritative synchronization process. During this process, no one can use SYSVOL. But in a non-authoritative process, only DCs with DFS issues will be affected.

How to troubleshoot Group Policy issues

Group Policy troubleshooting is one of the most painful and time-consuming events for most IT engineers. The reason is that there are so many reasons for Group Policy issues. In the following table, I have listed some of most common reasons for Group Policy issues:

Reason	Description
Replication issues	AD and SYSVOL replication-related errors are the most common reason for Group Policy issues. In a previous section of this chapter, we looked into possible replication issues that can occur in an AD environment and how we can recover from those.
Poor design	Using group policies in the infrastructure is like eating curd with a two-edged sword. By design, it should be spot on, and continuous reviewing is also required to maintain it. In Chapter 10, *Managing Group Policies*, we learned how we can design a Group Policy infrastructure properly.

Connectivity issues	If users/devices do not have a stable connection with DCs, it also creates Group Policy-related issues. This is mostly not a problem for periodic disconnection as Group Policy refreshes every 90 minutes.
Loopback processing	Loopback processing settings can create a lot of hassles if you do not use the modes properly. My recommendation is to use *replace* mode whenever possible.
Group Policy permissions	If a user is having issues with applying certain group policies, always check whether the user has **Read** and **Apply Group Policy** permissions under Group Policy delegation.
Security filtering	GPO can target individual users, groups, or devices using security filtering. If a particular user or group is having issues with applying specific group policies, it's better to check whether the particular user or groups are targeted.
WMI filters	WMI filters are also used by group policies for granular-level targeting. These filters use system-specific settings such as operating system version, architecture, and so on. If WMI filtering is in place, make sure the rules get updated according to target changes.
Inheritance	Group policies by default allow inheritance, and it is important to control them wherever necessary. It prevents us applying unnecessary Group Policy settings, which can result in a longer Group Policy processing time and operation-related issues. We can review inheritance using the GPO inheritance tab. Based on the applying order, it will also decide which one is the winning Group Policy (if the same setting is used by multiple GPOs).

Troubleshooting

Apart from issue-specific troubleshooting steps, there are some common tools and methods we can use to troubleshoot Group Policy-related issues. In this section, we will look at some of those.

Forcing Group Policy processing

This is the most common starting point for any Group Policy-related troubleshooting. Once we log into a system, it refreshes group policies every 90 minutes. But if required, we can forcefully process the policies using:

```
gpupdate /force
```

If it's a user setting, we need to log off and log back in. If it's a computer setting, the system needs to reboot after running the command.

Resultant Set of Policy (RSoP)

In a system, RSoP can be used to extract details about the group policies that are already applied and also the policy settings that are planned to be applied. It also helps us determine which is the winning policy and in which order the policies have been applied.

RSoP has two modes. In planning mode, we can simulate the effect of policy settings that we like to apply to a computer and user. In logging mode, it reports existing policy settings for a computer and the user that is currently logged on.

RSoP and the command-line based tool GPRESULT both do the same work. However, after Vista, Microsoft recommended using GPRESULT instated of RSoP.msc as it doesn't show all the Group Policy settings. For example, Group Policy preferences are not shown.

GPRESULT

This is a command-line utility which can be used to display RSoP information for users and computers. It can be used either locally or remotely.

The following command will provide RSoP summary data for the currently logged-in user. This is similar to a `RSOP.msc` default run in logging mode:

Gpresult /r

```
PS C:\Users\Administrator> gpresult /r

Microsoft (R) Windows (R) Operating System Group Policy Result tool v2.0
© 2016 Microsoft Corporation. All rights reserved.

Created on 09/05/2017 at 09:49:13


RSOP data for THEREBELADMIN\Administrator on REBELNET-PDC01 : Logging Mode
-------------------------------------------------------------------------

OS Configuration:              Primary Domain Controller
OS Version:                    10.0.14393
Site Name:                     Default-First-Site-Name
Roaming Profile:               N/A
Local Profile:                 C:\Users\Administrator
Connected over a slow link?: No


COMPUTER SETTINGS
------------------
    CN=REBELNET-PDC01,OU=Domain Controllers,DC=therebeladmin,DC=com
    Last time Group Policy was applied: 09/05/2017 at 09:44:13
    Group Policy was applied from:     REBELNET-PDC01.therebeladmin.com
    Group Policy slow link threshold:  500 kbps
    Domain Name:                       THEREBELADMIN
    Domain Type:                       Windows 2008 or later

    Applied Group Policy Objects
    -----------------------------
        Default Domain Controllers Policy
        Default Domain Policy

    The following GPOs were not applied because they were filtered out
    ------------------------------------------------------------------
        Local Group Policy
            Filtering:  Not Applied (Empty)

    The computer is a part of the following security groups
    -------------------------------------------------------
        BUILTIN\Administrators
        Everyone
        BUILTIN\Pre-Windows 2000 Compatible Access
        BUILTIN\Users
        Windows Authorization Access Group
        NT AUTHORITY\NETWORK
        NT AUTHORITY\Authenticated Users
        This Organization
        REBELNET-PDC01$
        Domain Controllers
        NT AUTHORITY\ENTERPRISE DOMAIN CONTROLLERS
        Authentication authority asserted identity
        Denied RODC Password Replication Group
        System Mandatory Level
```

The preceding command will list the summary data for the user and computer configurations. We also can scope it out to user configurations using:

```
gpresult /r /scope:user
```

We also can scope it out to computer configurations using:

```
gpresult /r /scope:computer
```

We also can run this by targeting a remote system:

```
gpresult /s REBEL-SRV01 /r
```

In the preceding command, /s is to specify the remote computer name. It will use the same account details of the user who is running the command:

```
PS C:\Users\Administrator> gpresult /s REBEL-SRV01 /r

Microsoft (R) Windows (R) Operating System Group Policy Result tool v2.0
© 2016 Microsoft Corporation. All rights reserved.

Created on 09/05/2017 at 10:04:35

RSOP data for THEREBELADMIN\Administrator on REBEL-SRV01 : Logging Mode
---------------------------------------------------------------------

OS Configuration:        Additional/Backup Domain Controller
OS Version:              10.0.14393
Site Name:              Default-First-Site-Name
Roaming Profile:        N/A
Local Profile:          C:\Users\administrator.THEREBELADMIN
Connected over a slow link?: Yes


COMPUTER SETTINGS
------------------

    Last time Group Policy was applied: 09/05/2017 at 10:01:18
    Group Policy was applied from:      REBEL-SRV01.therebeladmin.com
    Group Policy slow link threshold:   500 kbps
    Domain Name:                        THEREBELADMIN
    Domain Type:                        Windows 2008 or later
```

We also run it by specifying user account details:

```
gpresult /s REBEL-SRV01 /u therebeladmin\R540328 /p 1Qaz2Wsx /r
```

The preceding command will use the therebeladmin\R540328 user account with its password specified with the /p parameter.

We also can export the result as an HTML report. This is really useful for troubleshooting:

```
gpresult /h r01.html
```

The preceding command will run RSoP summary data for the currently logged-in system and save it as an HTML report:

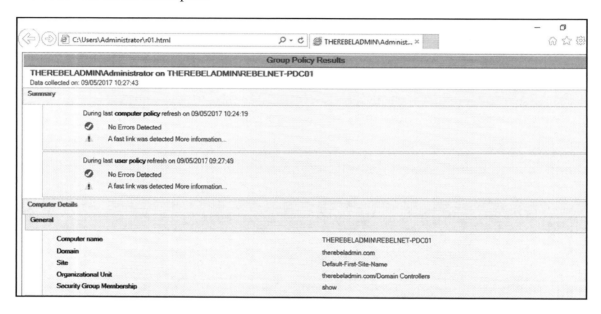

Group Policy Results Wizard

This is a tool we can use via **Group Policy Management MMC**. This does the same thing as GPRESULT but, instead of the command line, it uses a GUI. This allows us to access the results via the same console used to manage group policies. It is useful for troubleshooting as you do not need to move between different interfaces.

In order to access this, follow these steps:

1. Launch **Group Policy Management** (you can use the DC or any other system which has relevant management tools installed).

2. Right-click on the `Group Policy Results` container in the left-hand panel. Then click on **Group Policy Result Wizard...** from the list, as shown in the following figure:

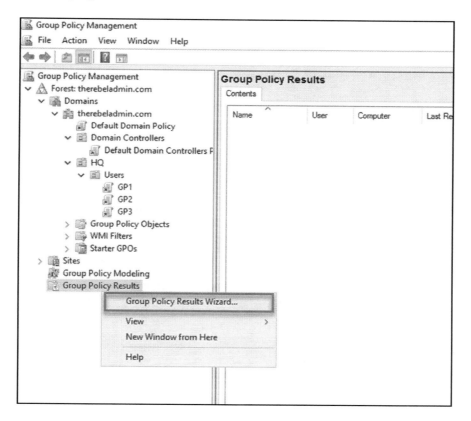

3. This will open up a new wizard. Click on **Next** to continue.

4. Then the wizard asks us to specify which system it should use as the target. It can be a local system or any remote system. Once the selection is done, click on **Next** to proceed:

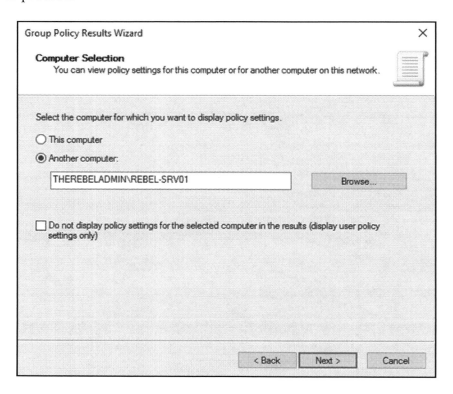

5. Then it asks us to specify the user to display policy settings for. The list only shows the users already logged in to the system and who have permissions to read Group Policy result data. If we only want to see the computer policy settings, we can select the option not to display user settings. Once the selection is made, click on **Next** to continue:

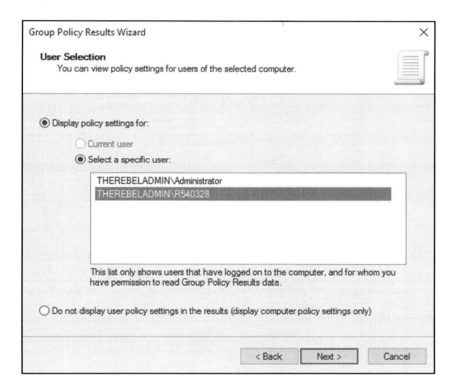

6. On the next window, it provides us with a summary for the selection. Click on **Next** to run the job.

7. Once it is completed, we can see the report in the MMC. If required, the same query can be run at any time.

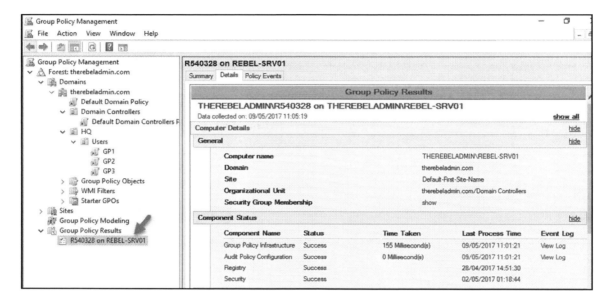

Group Policy Modeling Wizard

When we were looking at RSoP, I explained it has two modes. The planning mode allows us to simulate the Group Policy processing without really applying it. Engineers do not have to log in to different systems to see how they process the group policies. This is not only helpful for troubleshooting, but we can also use it for Group Policy designing.

In order to use the Group Policy Modeling Wizard, follow these steps:

1. Launch **Group Policy Management** (you can use the domain controller or any other system which has the relevant management tools installed).

2. Right-click on the **Group Policy Modeling** container in the left-hand panel. Then click on **Group Policy Modeling Wizard...** from the list:

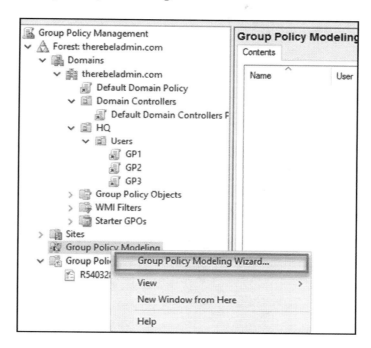

3. On the initial wizard page, click on **Next** to continue with the configuration.

4. In the new window, the wizard asks us to select the DC it should use for the simulation. It is recommended you use a DC in the same AD site. Once the selection is a mode, click on **Next** to continue.

5. On the user and computer selection page, we can select which user and device should be used in the simulation job. It can be based on an individual entry or be container-level. After the selection, click on **Next** to proceed:

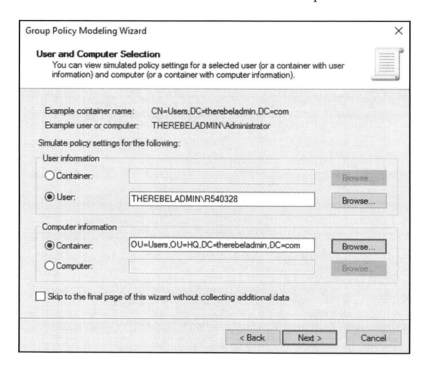

6. In **Advanced Simulation Options**, if required, we can select the **Slow network connection** and **Loopback processing** mode configuration options. We also can define the site which should be used for the simulation:

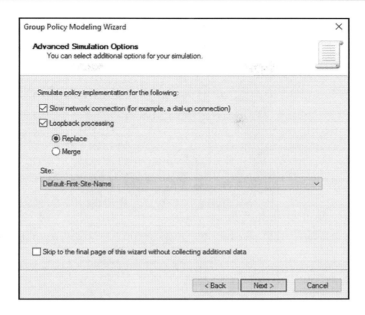

7. On the next window, if needed, we can select an alternative AD path to simulate changes to the network location of the selected user and computer. In this demo, I am using the defaults:

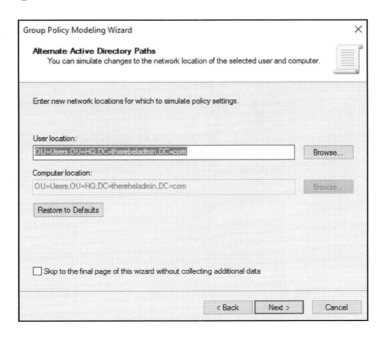

8. On the next window, if required we can select a user security group, to simulate. The default group will be **authenticated users**. When ready, click on **Next** to proceed.

9. Then it asks whether we need to define the computer security group for our simulation. You can add a group here or keep the default group, which is authenticated users.

10. On the next window, it asks whether WMI filtering for users is required. Once the necessary selections are made, click on **Next** to proceed.

11. On the next window, it asks whether WMI filtering for computers is required. Once the necessary selections are made, click on **Next** to proceed.

12. At the end, it gives us a summary window with the selected options. Click on **Next** to run the simulation job.

13. Once the process is completed, we can see the results in the console:

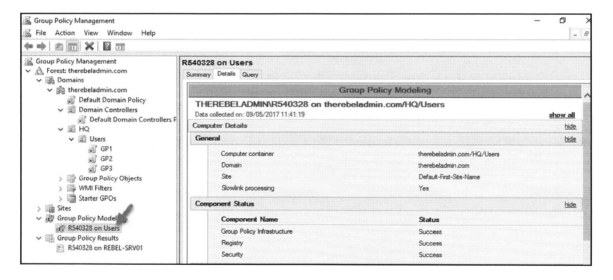

14. We also can rerun the simulation query at any time:

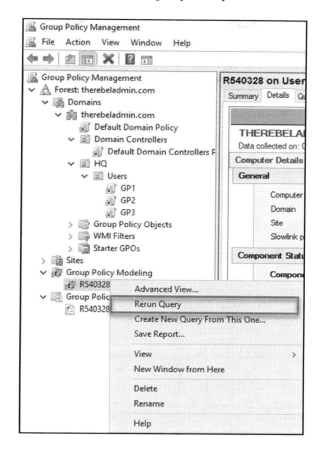

How to troubleshoot AD DS database-related issues

AD maintains a multi-master database. Like any other database, there can be data corruptions, crashes, data loss, and so on. In my entire career, I still haven't come across a situation where a full database recovery is required in a production environment. The reason is that an AD DS database keeps replicating to other available DCs and it is very rare that all the available DCs crash at the same time and lose data. Unlike other AD issues, there aren't many options for AD DS database troubleshooting.

In the following table, I have listed a few options that can cause AD DS database-related issues:

Issue	Description
Hardware failure	The AD database is located in `C:\Windows\NTDS`. This path can be changed, but it cannot be hosted on separate systems. If there is any hardware failure, we will lose the database along with the DC. If there are multiple DCs, it is not required to go for a recovery as we can simply introduce a new DC. If it's an FSMO role holder, it is still possible to seize roles from any working DC and make it the new FSMO role holder.
Software failures	AD runs on top of Windows. System software or any related service corruption can put the AD database in an unusable status. This also can be caused by virus or malware attacks.
Unexpected shutdown	Unexpected shutdowns can also corrupt an AD database.

In order to protect from AD DS database-related issues, we can take the following precautions:

Option	Description
Back up AD DS database	In `Chapter 11`, *Active Directory Services* we looked at AD backup options. There are many tools out there in the market which can be used to back up AD. The success of a backup or disaster recovery solution depends on the how fast and easily it can bring the system back to a working state.
Maintain additional DCs	It is not recommended you have just one domain controller, even if it's covered with a disaster-recovery solution. Each AD site should at least maintain two DCs. It is the fastest way to recover from any type of AD DS disaster. If any DC becomes unusable, the other available DCs can continue operations with minimal interruptions.
Change AD DS database and log path	The default location of the AD DS database file and the log files is `C:\Windows\NTDS`. It is recommended you change the path to a different drive. It can save database files from OS-level corruption. In `Chapter 11`, *Active Directory Services*, we learned how we can change the default path.

Defragmentation	Like any other database system, AD DS databases can also have data fragmentation. There are two type of data defragmentation. AD database uses online defragmentation, and it runs every 12 hours automatically. However, after a large number of object cleanups or a large configuration change, it is recommended you initiate offline defragmentation. The complete process is explained in `Chapter 11,` *Active Directory Services.*

Integrity checking to detect low-level database corruption

By running an integrity check, we can identify binary-level database corruption. This comes as part of the `Ntdsutil` tool which is used for AD database maintenance. This goes through every byte of the database file. The `integrity` command also checks whether the correct headers exist in the database itself and whether all of the tables are functioning and consistent. This process also runs as part of Active **Directory Service Restore Mode (DRSM)**.

This check needs to be run with the NTDS service off.

In order to run an integrity check, use the following steps:

1. Log in to DC as Domain/Enterprise Admin.
2. Open PowerShell as an administrator.
3. Stop the NTDS service using `net stop ntds`.

4. Type the following:

```
ntdsutil
activate instance ntds
files
integrity
```

```
file maintenance: integrity
Doing Integrity Check for db: C:\Windows\NTDS\ntds.dit.

Checking database integrity.

                  Scanning  Status (% complete)

          0    10   20   30   40   50   60   70   80   90  100
          |----|----|----|----|----|----|----|----|----|----|
          ...................................................

Integrity check successful.

It is recommended you run semantic database analysis
to ensure semantic database consistency as well.
```

5. In order to exit from the utility, type `quit`.

6. It is also recommended you run `semantic database analysis` to confirm the consistency of AD database contents.

7. In order to do it, enter the following:

```
ntdsutil
activate instance ntds
semantic database analysis
go
```

```
C:\Windows\system32\ntdsutil.exe: semantic database analysis
semantic checker: go
Fixup mode is turned off
......Done.

Writing summary into log file dsdit.dmp.0
SDs scanned:          117
Records scanned:      4456
Processing records..Done. Elapsed time 1 seconds.

semantic checker: _
```

8. If any integrity issues are detected, you can type `go fixup` to fix the errors.

9. After the process is completed, type `net start ntds` to start the NTDS service.

AD database recovery

If there is database corruption which cannot be soft-recovered (using the preceding method and the `ntdsutil` recovery command), you need to recover it from a backup.

In order to recover an AD database using a system-state-based backup, we need to use DSRM.

The relevant recovery steps using DSRM are explained on `Chapter 11`, *Active Directory Services*.

As I mentioned before, AD database issues are very rare in AD environments. If there are any, you most probably can recover from the situation using other options than restoring it from a backup. This should be the last resort in the troubleshooting process.

Summary

As with any other IT system, AD components also can face issues which can impact their operations. This can be due to many reasons such as poor design, the result of a management task, hardware or software issues, resources issues, and so on. No one is expected to know how to fix each and every AD-related issue. The most important thing is the starting point of the troubleshooting process and the engineer's approach to finding the solution. This chapter is meant to show you how to troubleshoot the most common AD infrastructure issues with the correct approach.

We started the chapter with AD replication issues. We looked into different scenarios which can cause replication issues and how we can recover from them. Then we looked into Group Policy-related issues and how to troubleshoot them using Windows' inbuilt utilities. Last but not least, we learned about AD DS database-related issues and the approach we can take to prevent such disasters.

After a long journey through 19 chapters, we've come to the end of this book. But this is not the end of learning AD. Learning never ends. As an IT engineers, continuous research and practice are a must to keep us on top of it. I heard about AD for the first time back in 2004. Yes, you are right; I am not that old! From day one, I fell in love with it. I read countless articles and books over the years. I spent countless hours testing things in my lab. I also learned from my mistakes. Identity management is a skill set that is always in high demand. The products and methods used with identity management can change, but core concepts about authentication and authorization will remain the same. With regards to the new things you learned from this book, put them into practice. Do not believe them just because they are in the book; try them yourself and understand them. Keep your eyes open for rising identity infrastructure threats around the globe and protect your infrastructure as it is the key to everything. Even though I've been writing articles on my blog and for Microsoft TechNet for years, this is my first IT book. Therefore, your feedback is really important for me as I too can learn from it. I also encourage you to follow me on my blog, `www.rebeladmin.com`, as I constantly keep updating it with AD-related posts. And on that note, it is time to say bye! Have a happy future with identity management!

Index

63738491R00404

Made in the USA
Middletown, DE
04 February 2018